A COMMENTARY
ON APOLLONIUS RHODIUS
ARGONAUTICA III 1-471

MNEMOSYNE
BIBLIOTHECA CLASSICA BATAVA

COLLEGERUNT

J.M. BREMER · L.F. JANSSEN · H. PINKSTER

H.W. PLEKET · C.J. RUIJGH · P.H. SCHRIJVERS

BIBLIOTHECAE FASCICULOS EDENDOS CURAVIT

C.J. RUIJGH, KLASSIEK SEMINARIUM, OUDE TURFMARKT 129, AMSTERDAM

SUPPLEMENTUM CENTESIMUM QUADRAGESIMUM PRIMUM

MALCOLM CAMPBELL

A COMMENTARY ON APOLLONIUS RHODIUS
ARGONAUTICA III 1–471

A COMMENTARY ON APOLLONIUS RHODIUS
ARGONAUTICA III 1–471

BY

MALCOLM CAMPBELL

E.J. BRILL
LEIDEN · NEW YORK · KÖLN
1994

The paper in this book meets the guidelines for permanence and durability of the Committee on Production Guidelines for Book Longevity of the Council on Library Resources.

Library of Congress Cataloging-in-Publication Data

Campbell, Malcolm, Ph. D.
  A commentary on Apollonius Rhodius Argonautica III 1-471 / by Malcolm Campbell.
      p.   cm. — (Mnemosyne, bibliotheca classica Batava. Supplementum, ISSN 0169-8958 ; 141)
  Includes bibliographical references and index.
  ISBN 9004101586 (cloth)
  1. Apollonius, Rhodius. Argonautica.   2. Epic poetry, Greek--History and criticism.   3. Argonauts (Greek mythology) in literature.   I. Title.   II. Series.
PA3872.Z4C348   1994
883'.01—dc20
                                                        94-29384
                                                        CIP

Die Deutsche Bibliothek – CIP-Einheitsaufnahme

[Mnemosyne / Supplementum]
Mnemosyne : bibliotheca classica Batava. Supplementum. –
Leiden ; New York ; Köln : Brill.
    Früher Schriftenreihe
141. Campbell, Malcolm: A commentary on Apollonius Rhodius
    Argonautica III, 1-471. – 1994
Campbell, Malcolm:
A commentary on Apollonius Rhodius Argonautica III, 1-471 /
by Malcolm Campbell. – Leiden ; New York ; Köln : Brill, 1994
    (Mnemosyne : Supplementum ; 141)
    ISBN 90–04–10158–6

ISSN   0169-8958
ISBN   90 04 10158 6

© *Copyright 1994 by E.J. Brill, Leiden, The Netherlands*

All rights reserved. No part of this publication may be reproduced, translated, stored in a retrieval system, or transmitted in any form or by any means, electronic, mechanical, photocopying, recording or otherwise, without prior written permission from the publisher.

*Authorization to photocopy items for internal or personal use is granted by E.J. Brill provided that the appropriate fees are paid directly to The Copyright Clearance Center, 222 Rosewood Drive, Suite 910 Danvers MA 01923, USA.
Fees are subject to change.*

PRINTED IN THE NETHERLANDS

CONTENTS

Preface	VII
Abbreviations and Bibliography	X
Commentary	1
Indexes	383
Prefatory Note	383
I Greek Words	385
IIA Greek Authors	396
IIB Latin Authors	411
IIIA Composition, Language & Style, Metre & Prosody	413
IIIB Text, Testimonia, Scholia	417
IV Mythology, Religion, Geography, Ethnography, Aetiology	419

PREFACE

If the third book of Apollonius' *Argonautica* was not an instant hit, it very soon became one, and its popularity has endured despite the chilly reception often accorded to the other three. It is surprising then that it still lacks a comprehensive and fully documented commentary. It is the aim of this and subsequent volumes to provide one. One of my main concerns has been systematic analysis of the Homeric subtext; I have not only put the material assembled in *Echoes* to work but have added considerably to it, chiefly by extending the range of its coverage (see Preface, p. VII). This I consider to be labour well spent: after all, no Greek poem presents us with a more sustained or more intricate manipulation of the two great epics of the archaic period; and recent attempts to throw light on the Homeric heritage have, with only a handful of exceptions, proved distressingly inadequate.

I have been conscious at every turn of my indebtedness to the writings of those scholars (F. Vian and H. Fränkel in particular) who spearheaded the Apollonian revival. There has been much less to get excited about in all the frantic repackaging of the past decade or so, but the few good things have been very good indeed, and I take the opportunity here to acknowledge an obligation to them, and to those earlier works which seem to me to have made outstanding contributions to the study of this poem. In a class apart are the three Budé volumes, F. Vian's commentary on iii (a finely crafted miniature: I have learned a tremendous amount from this) and his various papers, H. Fränkel's OCT (which really stirred things up) and his *Noten*, E. Livrea's commentary on iv and the rest of his writings. Others, in alphabetical order: Ardizzoni (1958 etc.) resolved a number of thorny problems of text and interpretation; Beye (1982) knows how to combine instruction with broad entertainment; Dräger (1993): some basic suppositions are flawed, but his monograph provides an invaluable new survey of *res Argonauticae*; Erbse (1953): a virtuoso (if partial) demonstration of Apollonius' incontrovertible dependence on Homeric annotation in its shortest and sweetest form (not suitable for those who suffer from tunnel vision); Faerber (1932): an exercise in severe compression, so heavy going in places, but full of penetrating insights in the best Wilamowitzian tradition, from a scholar with a sharp eye for detail and a sure command of Greek; Fantuzzi's book (1988) offers a wide-ranging and thought-provoking miscellany; Feeney (1991) provides an intelligent and often original appraisal of the divine apparatus; Fusillo (1985): narratology made easy (not as easy as it might have been: a work as dense as this cries out for multiple indexes), though others have followed with faltering steps; Haslam (1978) takes a searching look at the many quirks of Apollonian papyri; Herter's bibliographical survey (1944/1945) is beautifully organised, lucid, indispensable; Hoelzlin (1641) beat a lot of us to the post with his many shrewd observations; in an able paper Lennox (1980) did for a portion of Apollonius' text what Herter had done for one of the hymns of Callimachus; Platt (1914 etc.) was perhaps the first scholar to deal seriously with the question 'How much can textual critics and editors get away with?' in their treatment of the *Argonautica*; Rengakos' study of the *Homertext* (1993) is neither full nor ideally balanced, but it does raise issues which have barely been aired in the course of the present century; to van Krevelen (1949 etc.) we owe a number of fine textual and interpretive notes in the Wifstrand mould.

My obligations are not of course confined to the world of books. I had the pleasure of discussing at length with Professor C. J. Ruijgh in Amsterdam the idea of producing a detailed commentary on Apollonius iii; my thanks to him, and to Mr Julian Deahl, Senior Editor at E. J. Brill, for encouragement and advice. It was in the Netherlands too that I first met the late Dr D. A. van Krevelen; I still have vivid memories of his wide learning, his love of Hellenistic poetry and his infectious enthusiasm. Sir Hugh Lloyd-Jones had a hand in my first book: I greatly appreciate the interest he has shown since in my work, both published and projected, on Hellenistic and Imperial poets. A number of my early thoughts on the text and interpretation of the *Argonautica* were submitted to Professor F. Vian, and I am still learning from the rich collection of comments which he was kind enough to communicate to me. I am also most grateful to him, as to Professor M. Fantuzzi, for providing me in recent months with copies of papers which I would not otherwise have seen in time.

It remains to record a number of debts incurred closer to home. I am extremely grateful to Mrs Barbara Fleming, who with exemplary skill, patience and good humour typed page after page of closely handwritten commentary, and who was still nice to me after surfacing from the entry under Apollonius Rhodius in Index IIA. She also offered advice on and practical help with both word processing and printing, as did others in the School of Greek, Latin and Ancient History at St Andrews: Mrs Hilde Barrie, Mr Peter George,

Dr Adrian Gratwick, Dr Susanna Phillippo, Dr Christopher Smith. I am much indebted also to the Head of School, Professor Harry Hine, for providing word processing facilities, for looking favourably upon an application for a subsidy towards production costs, and, not least, for taking a keen interest in the whole project. Finally, I must thank my wife Dorothy and my sons Michael and Richard: I have had the great good fortune not only to enjoy their staunch support but also to draw upon their own considerable talents.

St Andrews, March 1994 M. C.

ABBREVIATIONS AND BIBLIOGRAPHY

A. *Ancient authors and texts*

I. In general, abbreviations do not differ markedly from those employed in LSJ, but some are more explicit: so 'Bacch.' rather than 'B.' Note as well:

1. i-iv refer to the four books of Ap.'s *Argonautica*; the lemmata usually reflect the text of VDB 2/2²: for the odd exception the reason will not be far to seek.
2. Homeric Hymns: the big ones are *HyDem*, *HyAp*, *HyHerm*, *HyAphr*, the rest *HyHom*; but *h.* 1-6 for Callimachus'.
3. Man. (i.e. 'Manethoniana'): cited by *single* book-number.
4. Gregory of Nazianzus: references to *Carmina* from Migne (*PG* vol. 37), cited *by page and line-number*.
5. Christod(orus) + line-number: i.e. from *AP* 2.

II. For the following collections of texts cited by editor(s) or editor(s)/title in abbreviated form continuous (line or fragment) numbering is employed where applicable. For *IG/SEG* and certain other epigraphical and papyrological publications see LSJ. Note that the fragments of Callimachus' *Hecale* are numbered according to Hollis' recent edition, other fragments coming from Pfeiffer and/or *SH*; Blem., Dion. Bass. and Pampr. are sourced from Livrea's editions, not from *GDK*.

CA	*Collectanea Alexandrina*, ed. J. U. Powell. Oxford 1925.
CAF	*Comicorum Atticorum Fragmenta*, ed. T. Kock. Leipzig 1880-8.
CEG	*Carmina Epigraphica Graeca*, ed. P. A. Hansen. Berlin and New York 1983/89.
Cougny	E. Cougny, ed. vol. 3 of Firmin Didot *Anthologia Palatina*. Paris 1890.
DK	*Die Fragmente der Vorsokratiker*, edd. H. Diels and W. Kranz. 6th ed., Berlin 1952.
EGF	*Epicorum Graecorum Fragmenta*, ed. M. Davies. Göttingen 1988.
EG Kaibel	*Epigrammata Graeca ex lapidibus conlecta*, ed. G. Kaibel. Berlin 1878.
FGE	*Further Greek Epigrams*, ed. D. L. Page. Cambridge 1981.
FGH	*Die Fragmente der griechischen Historiker*, ed. F. Jacoby. Berlin/Leiden 1923–.
GDK	*Die griechischen Dichterfragmente der römischen Kaizerzeit*, ed. E. Heitsch. Bd I 2 Aufl., Göttingen 1963; Bd II, Göttingen 1964.
GPh	*The Garland of Philip and Some Contemporary Epigrams*, edd. A. S. F. Gow and D. L. Page. Cambridge 1968.
GVI	*Griechische Vers-Inschriften*, Bd I: *Grab-Epigramme*, ed. W. Peek. Berlin 1955.
HE	*The Greek Anthology: Hellenistic Epigrams*, edd. A. S. F. Gow and D. L. Page. Cambridge 1965.
IEG	*Iambi et Elegi Graeci*, ed. M. L. West. 2nd ed., Oxford 1989/92.
IME	*Inscriptions métriques de l'Égypte gréco-romaine*, ed. E. Bernand (*Annales littéraires de l'Université de Besançon*, vol. 98). Paris 1969.

PCG	Poetae Comici Graeci, edd. R. Kassel and C. Austin. Berlin and New York 1983–.
PLF	Poetarum Lesbiorum Fragmenta, edd. E. Lobel and D. L. Page. Oxford 1955.
PMG	Poetae Melici Graeci, ed. D. L. Page. Oxford 1962.
PMGF	Poetarum Melicorum Graecorum Fragmenta, ed. M. Davies. (I) Oxford 1991.
PW	H. W. Parke and D. E. W. Wormell, *The Delphic Oracle*: II *The Oracular Responses*. Oxford 1956.
SH	Supplementum Hellenisticum, ed. H. Lloyd-Jones and P. Parsons. Berlin and New York 1983.
SLG	Supplementum Lyricis Graecis, ed. D. L. Page. Oxford 1974.
TGF	Tragicorum Graecorum Fragmenta, edd. B. Snell *et al.* Göttingen 1971–.

B. *Modern works*

I. Periodical abbreviations: as in *L'année philologique*.

II. Grammars, lexica and other basic works of reference cited by title, author(s), editor(s) in abbreviated form:

AH	Archaeologia Homerica, edd. F. Matz and H-G. Buchholz. Göttingen 1967–.
AHS	Allen, Halliday and Sikes.
ANRW	Aufstieg und Niedergang der römischen Welt, edd. H. Temporini and W. Haase. Berlin/New York 1972–.
BP	C. D. Buck and W. Petersen, *A Reverse Index of Greek Nouns and Adjectives*. Chicago 1945.
DGE	Diccionario Griego-Español, edd. F. R. Adrados *et al.* Madrid 1980–.
Echoes	M. Campbell, *Echoes and Imitations of Early Epic in Apollonius Rhodius*. Leiden 1981.
F-G	Fernández-Galiano.
FJW	Friis Johansen and Whittle.
GG	E. Schwyzer, *Griechische Grammatik*. Munich 1939-50.
GH	P. Chantraine, *Grammaire homérique*. Paris 1958-63.
GHD	D. B. Monro, *A Grammar of the Homeric Dialect*. 2nd ed., Oxford 1891.
GP	J. D. Denniston, *The Greek Particles*. 2nd ed., Oxford 1954.
Index	M. Campbell, *Index verborum in Apollonium Rhodium*. Hildesheim 1983.
KB	R. Kühner and F. Blass, *Ausführliche Grammatik der griechischen Sprache. Erster Teil: Elementar- und Formenlehre*. Hanover 1890-2.
KG	R. Kühner and B. Gerth, id. *Zweiter Teil: Satzlehre*. Hanover/ Leipzig 1898-1904.
LexCal	E. Fernández-Galiano, *Léxico de los Himnos de Calímaco*. Madrid 1976-80.
LexNonn	W. Peek (ed.), *Lexikon zu den Dionysiaka des Nonnos*. Berlin 1968-75.
LfgrE	Lexikon des frühgriechischen Epos, edd. B. Snell and H. Erbse. Göttingen 1955–.
LH	Ebeling (H., ed.), *Lexicon Homericum*. Leipzig 1880-5.

LIMC	*Lexicon iconographicum mythologiae classicae,* edd. H. C. Ackermann and J. R. Gisler. Zurich 1981–.
LSJ + Suppl.	H. G. Liddell, R. Scott and H. S. Jones, *A Greek-English Lexicon.* 9th ed., Oxford 1940; Supplement, Oxford 1968.
NH	Nisbet and Hubbard.
Noten	H. Fränkel, *Noten zu den Argonautika des Apollonios.* Munich 1968.
OCD	*The Oxford Classical Dictionary,* edd. N. G. L. Hammond and H. H. Scullard. 2nd ed., Oxford 1970.
PF	G. Paduano and M. Fusillo, ed. Ap. Milan 1986.
RE	*Paulys Real-Encyclopädie der classischen Altertumswissenschaft,* edd. G. Wissowa *et al.* Stuttgart/Munich 1893–.
RE Suppl.	Supplements to the above.
Studies	M. Campbell, *Studies in the Third Book of Apollonius Rhodius'* Argonautica. Hildesheim 1983.
Thesaurus	*Thesaurus linguae Graecae.*
VDB	F. Vian and É. Delage, Budé ed. of Ap. 3 vols, Paris 1974–: VDB 1: 2nd impression; VDB 2: 1980, VDB 2²: 2nd ed. 1993; VDB 3: 1981.

III. The following list embraces, with very few exceptions, other books and articles to which I refer more than once.

Allen	(A.) *The Fragments of Mimnermus.* Stuttgart 1993.
Ardizzoni	(A.) Ed. of Ap. iii. Bari 1958.
Ardizzoni 1956	(A.) 'Note critiche ed esegetiche sul testo di Apollonio Rodio,' *RFIC* 84.364-88.
Ardizzoni 1958	(A.) 'Su Apollonio Rodio,' *Orpheus* 5.45-7.
Ardizzoni 1970	(A.) 'Note sul testo di Apollonio Rodio e Callimaco,' *GIF* 22.40-6.
Arend	(W.) *Die typischen Scenen bei Homer.* Berlin 1933.
Armstrong and Ratchford	(D./E. A.) 'Iphigeneia's Veil: Aeschylus, *Agamemnon* 228-48,' *BICS* 32 (1985), 1-12.
Bechtel	(F.) *Lexilogus zu Homer.* Halle 1914.
Belloni	(L.) 'A proposito di alcuni Omerismi in Apollonio Rodio,' *Aevum* 53 (1979), 66-71.
Beye 1969	(C. R.) 'Jason as Love-hero in Apollonius' *Argonautika,*' *GRBS* 10.31-55.
Beye 1982	(C. R.) *Epic and Romance in the* Argonautica *of Apollonius.* Carbondale.
Beye 1993	(C. R.) *Ancient Epic Poetry: Homer, Apollonius, Virgil.* Ithaca and London.
Bissinger	(M.) *Das Adjectiv ΜΕΓΑΣ in der griechischen Dichtung.* Diss. Munich 1966.
Blumberg	(K.) *Untersuchungen zur epischen Technik des Apollonius von Rhodos.* Diss. Leipzig 1931.
Boesch	(G.) *De Apollonii Rhodii elocutione.* Diss. Berlin 1908.
Bowra	(C. M.) *Greek Lyric Poetry from Alcman to Simonides.* 2nd ed., Oxford 1961.
Brendel	(O. J.) *The Symbolism of the Sphere.* Leiden 1977.

Brunck	(R. F.) Ed. Ap. Strasbourg 1780/2nd ed. Leipzig 1810.
Buccholz	(A.) *Zur Darstellung des Pathos der Liebe in der hellenistischen Dichtung*. Diss. Freiburg 1954.
Bulloch 1977	(A. W.) 'Callimachus' *Erysichthon*, Homer and Apollonius Rhodius,' *AJPh* 98.97-123.
Bulloch 1985	(A. W.) 'Hellenistic Poetry,' *The Cambridge History of Classical Literature* I, 541-621. Cambridge.
Busch	(S.) 'Orpheus bei Apollonios Rhodios,' *Hermes* 121 (1993), 301-24.
Caggia	(G.) 'Due parole omeriche in Apollonio Rodio,' *RFIC* 100 (1972), 23-31.
Cairns	(F.) *Virgil's Augustan Epic*. Cambridge 1989.
Campbell *Echoes*	See BII above.
Campbell *Index*	See BII above.
Campbell *Studies*	See BII above.
Campbell 1969	(M.) 'Critical Notes on Apollonius Rhodius,' *CQ* n.s. 19.269-84.
Campbell 1971	(M.) 'Further Notes on Apollonius Rhodius,' *CQ* n.s. 21.402-23.
Campbell 1973	(M.) 'Notes on Apollonius Rhodius, *Argonautica* ii,' *RPh* 47.68-90.
Campbell 1974	(M.) 'Three Notes on Alexandrine Poetry,' *Hermes* 102.38-46.
Campbell 1976	(M.) Review of E. Livrea, ed. Ap. iv, *Gnomon* 48.336-40.
Campbell 1978	(M.) 'ΔΩΔΕΚΑ ΑΠΟΛΛΩΝΙΟΥ,' *Studi in onore di A. Ardizzoni*, 119-25. Rome.
Campbell 1982	(M.) Review of VDB 2, *CR* n.s. 32.14-6.
Campbell 1983	(M.) 'Apollonian and Homeric Book Division,' *Mnemosyne* 36.154-5.
Campbell 1990	(M.) Review of Hunter ed. Ap. iii, *Gnomon* 62.481-5.
Carspecken	(J.) 'Apollonius Rhodius and the Homeric Epic,' *YCS* 13 (1952), 35-143.
Casson	(L.) *Ships and Seamanship in the Ancient World*. Princeton 1971.
Chamoux	(F.) 'Une évocation littéraire d'un palais macédonien (*Argonautiques*, iii.215 sq.),' in *Ancient Macedonia: Fifth International Symposium*, 1989 (Thessalonica 1993), 1.337-43.
Chantraine *DE*	(P.) *Dictionnaire étymologique de la langue grecque*. Paris 1968-80.
Chantraine *EVG*	(P.) *Études sur le vocabulaire grec*. Paris 1956.
Chantraine *FN*	(P.) *La formation des noms en grec ancien*. Paris 1933.
Chantraine 1962	(P.) Review of Fränkel OCT, *RPh* 36.313-4.
Chuvin	(P.) Review of VDB 2, *RPh* 56 (1982), 331-2.
Ciani	(M. G.) 'Poesia come enigma,' in *Scritti in onore di Carlo Diano*, 77-111. Bologna 1975.
Clark	(R. J.) *Catabasis: Vergil and the Wisdom-Tradition*. Amsterdam 1979.
Clausen	(W.) *Virgil's Aeneid and the Tradition of Hellenistic Poetry*. Berkeley 1987.
Clauss	(J. J.) 'Hellenistic Imitations of Hesiod *Catalogue of Women* fr. 1.6-7 M-W,' *QUCC* n.s.36 (1990), 129-40.

Clay	(J. S.) *The Wrath of Athena: Gods and Men in the* Odyssey. Princeton 1983.
Coleridge	(E. P.) Transl. of Ap., London 1889.
Cook *Zeus*	(A. B.) *Zeus*. Cambridge 1914-40.
Couat	(A.) *Alexandrian Poetry under the First Three Ptolemies*. London 1931.
Crane 1987	(G.) 'The Laughter of Aphrodite in Theocritus, *Idyll* I,' *HSCP* 91.161-84.
Crane 1988	(G.) *Calypso. Backgrounds and Conventions of the* Odyssey. Frankfurt am Main.
Cunliffe *LHD*	(R. J.) *A Lexicon of the Homeric Dialect*. London 1924.
Damsté	(O.) *Adversaria ad Apollonii Rhodii* Argonautica. Diss. Utrecht-Rotterdam 1922.
De Jong	(I. J. F.) *Narrators and Focalizers: the Presentation of the Story in the* Iliad. Amsterdam 1987.
Delage	(É.) *La geographie dans les* Argonautiques *d'Apollonios de Rhodes*. Bordeaux 1930.
Del Corno	(D.) Review of *POxy* vol. 34, *Gnomon* 45 (1973), 542-5.
De Martino	(F.) 'Note apolloniane,' *AFLB* 27/28 (1984/85), 101-17.
De Mirmont	(H. de la Ville) Transl. of Ap., Bordeaux-Paris 1892.
Detienne and Vernant	(M. D./J.-P. V.) *Cunning Intelligence in Greek Culture and Society*. Hassocks 1978.
Dickie	(M.) 'Talos Bewitched,' *PLLS* 6 (1990), 267-96.
Diggle	(J.) *Studies on the Text of Euripides*. Cambridge 1981.
Doederlein	(J.) *Homerisches Glossarium*. Erlangen 1850-8.
Dräger	(P.) *Argo Pasimelousa: Der Argonautenmythos in der griechischen und römischen Literatur. Teil I*. Stuttgart 1993.
Drögemüller	(H.-P.) *Die Gleichnisse im hellenistischen Epos*. Diss. Hamburg 1956.
Duckworth	(G. E.) *Foreshadowing and Suspense in the Epics of Homer, Apollonius and Vergil*. Diss. Princeton 1933.
Duentzer	(H. D.) *De Zenodoti studiis Homericis*. Göttingen 1848.
Dyck	(A. R.) 'The Glossographoi,' *HSCP* 91 (1987), 119-60.
Edwards	(G. P.) *The Language of Hesiod in its Traditional Context*. Oxford 1971.
Elderkin	(G. W.) 'Repetitions in the *Argonautica* of Apollonius,' *AJPh* 34 (1913), 198-201.
Elliger	(W.) *Die Darstellung der Landschaft in der griechischen Dichtung*. Berlin 1975.
Erbse 1953	(H.) 'Homerscholien und hellenistische Glossare bei Apollonios Rhodios,' *Hermes* 81.163-96.
Erbse 1963	(H.) Review of Fränkel OCT, *Gnomon* 35.18-27.
Faerber	(H.) *Zur dichterischen Kunst in Apollonios Rhodios'* Argonautica. Berlin 1932.
Fantuzzi	(M.) *Richerche su Apollonio Rodio*. Rome 1988.
Feeney	(D. C.) *The Gods in Epic*. Oxford 1991.
Fehling	(D.) *Die Wiederholungsfiguren und ihr Gebrauch bei den Griechen vor Gorgias*. Berlin 1969.
Fernandelli	(M.) 'Il compito della Musa,' *QFC* 5 (1986), 85-104.

Fitch	(E.) Review of Mooney, ed. Ap., *AJPh* 34 (1913), 340-4.
Fowler 1989	(B. H.) *The Hellenistic Aesthetic*. Bristol.
Fowler 1990	(B. H.) *Hellenistic Poetry. An Anthology*. Wisconsin.
Fränkel *Einleitung*	(H.) *Einleitung zur kritischen Ausgabe des Apollonios Rhodios*. Göttingen 1964.
Fränkel *Noten*	See BII above.
Fränkel OCT	(H.) Ed. Ap. Oxford 1961.
Fränkel 1915	(H.) *De Simia Rhodio*. Diss. Göttingen.
Fränkel 1925	(H.) 'Zwei Stellen aus den *Argonautika* des Apollonios,' *Hermes* 60.489-92.
Fränkel 1928	(H.) Review of Gillies, ed. Ap. iii, *Gnomon* 4.563-70.
Fränkel 1936	(H.) Review of Marxer, *Gnomon* 12.470-6.
Fränkel 1950	(H.) 'Problems of Text and Interpretation in Apollonius' *Argonautica*,' *AJPh* 71.113-33.
Fränkel 1952	(H.) 'Apollonius Rhodius as a Narrator in *Argonautica* ii.1-140,' *TAPA* 83.144-55.
Fränkel 1963	(H.) Review of Vian ed. 1961, *Gnomon* 35.156-62.
Fraser	(P. M.) *Ptolemaic Alexandria*. Oxford 1972.
Frisk *GEW*	(H.) *Griechisches etymologisches Wörterbuch*. Heidelberg 1954-72.
Führer	(R.) *Formproblem: Untersuchungen zu den Reden in der frühgriechischen Lyrik*. Munich 1967.
Fusillo	(M.) *Il tempo delle Argonautiche*. Rome 1985.
Garson	(R. W.) 'Homeric Echoes in Apollonius Rhodius' *Argonautica*,' *CPh* 67 (1972), 1-9.
Giangrande 1973	(G.) *Zu Sprachgebrauch, Technik und Text des Apollonios Rhodios*. Amsterdam.
Giangrande 1976	(G.) 'Aspects of Apollonius Rhodius' Language,' *PLLS* 2.271-91.
Gillies	(M. M.) Ed. Ap. iii. Cambridge 1928.
Gillies 1924	(M. M.) 'The Ball of Eros,' *CR* 38.50-1.
Goodwin *MT*	(W. W.) *Syntax of the Moods and Tenses of the Greek Verb*. 2nd ed., London 1889.
Gould	(J. P.) 'Hiketeia,' *JHS* 93 (1973), 74-103.
Grajew	(F.) *Untersuchungen über die Bedeutung der Gebärden in der griechischen Epik*. Diss. Freiburg 1934.
Graz	(L.) *Le feu dans l'Iliade et l'Odyssée*. Paris 1965.
Griffin	(J.) *Homer on Life and Death*. Oxford 1980.
Griffiths	(A. H.) Review of Ardizzoni ed. Ap. i, *JHS* 88 (1968), 173-5.
Gualandri	(I.) 'Avieno e Dionisio il Periegeta,' *Studi in onore di A. Colonna*, 151-65. Perugia 1982.
Händel	(P.) *Beobachtungen zur epischen Technik des Apollonios Rhodios*. Munich 1954.
Haggett	(A. S.) *A Comparison of Apollonius Rhodius with Homeric Prepositional Usage*. Baltimore 1902.
Haslam	(M. W.) 'Apollonius Rhodius and the Papyri,' *ICS* 3 (1978), 47-73.
Headlam	(W.) 'Various Conjectures IV,' *JPh* 26 (1899), 110.
Henrichs	(A.) 'Scholia Minora zu Homer,' *ZPE* 7 (1971), 97-149, 229-60.

Herter *JAW*	(H.) 'Bericht über ... Ap. Rhod.,' *JAW* 285 (1944/45), 213-410.
Hoelzlin	(J.) Ed. Ap., Leiden 1641.
Huber	(G.) *Lebensschilderung und Kleinmalerei im hellenistischen Epos.* Diss. Basel 1926.
Hübscher	(A.) *Die Charakteristik der Personen in Apollonios' Argonautika.* Diss. Freiburg 1940.
Hunter	(R. L.) Ed. Ap. iii, Cambridge 1989.
Hunter 1988	(R. L.) '"Short on Heroics": Jason in the *Argonautica*,' *CQ* n.s. 38.436-53.
Hunter 1993	(R. L.) *The Argonautica of Apollonius: Literary Studies.* Cambridge.
Hurst	(A.) *Apollonios de Rhodes: manière et cohérence.* Rome 1967.
Hutchinson	(G.) *Hellenistic Poetry.* Oxford 1988.
Ibscher	(R.) *Gestalt der Szene und Form der Rede in den Argonautika des Apollonios Rhodios.* Diss. Munich 1939.
James	(A. W.) 'Apollonius Rhodius and his Sources: Interpretive Notes on the *Argonautica*,' *CL* 1 (1981), 59-86.
Janko	(R.) *Homer, Hesiod and the Hymns.* Cambridge 1982.
Kahn	(C. H.) *Anaximander and the Origins of Greek Cosmology.* New York 1960.
Kaimio	(M.) *Characterisation of Sound in Early Greek Literature.* Helsingfors 1977.
Kastner	(W.) *Die griechischen Adjective zweier Endungen auf -ΟΣ.* Heidelberg 1967.
Keydell	(R.) Review of Ardizzoni ed. Ap. iii, *Gnomon* 33 (1961), 35-6.
Kingston	(P.) Ed. material on Ap. in *POxy* vol. 34, 1968.
Klein	(L.) 'Die Göttertechnik in den *Argonautika* des Apollonios Rhodios,' *Philologus* 40 (1931), 18-51, 215-57.
Knox	(P. E.) 'A Note on *Aeneid* 1.613,' *CPh* 79 (1984), 304-5.
Köhnken	(A.) *Apollonios Rhodios und Theokrit.* Göttingen 1965.
Kurt	(C.) *Seemännische Fachausdrucke bei Homer.* Göttingen 1979.
La Roche *HTA*	(J.) *Die homerische Textkritik im Altertum.* Leipzig 1866.
La Roche *HU*	(J.) *Homerische Untersuchungen.* Leipzig 1869/1893.
La Roche 1899	(J.) 'Der Hexameter bei Apollonios, Aratos und Kallimachos,' *WS* 21.161-97.
Lasserre	(F.) *La figure d' Eros dans la poésie grecque.* Lausanne 1946.
Lawall	(G.) 'Apollonius' *Argonautica*: Jason as Anti-hero,' *YCS* 19 (1966), 119-69.
Lehrs	(K.) *De Aristarchi studiis Homericis.* 3rd ed., Leipzig 1882.
Lennox	(P. G.) 'Apollonius Rhodius, *Argonautica* iii.1f., and Homer,' *Hermes* 108 (1980), 45-73.
Lesky	(A.) 'Aia,' *WS* 63 (1948), 22-68.
Leumann	(M.) *Homerische Wörter.* Basel 1950.
Levin	(D. N.) *Apollonius Rhodius' Argonautica Re-examined*: I *The Neglected First and Second Books.* Leiden 1971.
Linsenbarth	(O.) *De Apollonii Rhodii casuum syntaxi comparato usu Homerico.* Diss. Leipzig 1887.
Livrea 1975	(E.) Review of Giangrande 1973, *Gnomon* 47.653-6.

Livrea 1977	(E.) Review of VDB 1, *Gnomon* 49.10-18.
Livrea 1982	(E.) Review of VDB 2, *Gnomon* 54.18-24.
Livrea 1983	(E.) Review of VDB 3, *Gnomon* 55.420-6.
Livrea 1992	(E.) 'The Tempest in Callimachus' *Hecale*,' *CQ* n.s. 42.147-51.
Lloyd-Jones 1963	(H.) Review of Vian ed. 1961, *CR* n.s. 13.156-8.
Lloyd-Jones 1990	(H.) *The Academic Papers of Sir Hugh Lloyd-Jones*. Oxford.
Lombardi	(M.) 'Aspetti del realismo nelle *Argonautiche* di Apollonio Rodio,' *Orpheus* 6 (1985), 250-69.
Lorimer	(H. L.) *Homer and the Monuments*. London 1950.
Ludwich	(A.) *Aristarchs homerische Textkritik*. Leipzig 1884-5.
Lührs	(D.) *Untersuchungen zu den Athetesen Aristarchs in der Ilias und zu ihrer Behandlung im Corpus der exegetischen Scholien*. Hildesheim 1992.
Maass	(E.) *Aratea*. Berlin 1892.
Manakidou	(F.) *Beschreibung von Kunstwerken in der hellenistischen Dichtung*. Stuttgart 1993.
Marxer	(G.) *Die Sprache der Apollonios Rhodios in ihren Beziehungen zu Homer*. Diss. Zurich 1935.
Matthews	(V. J.) '*Naupaktia* and *Argonautika*,' *Phoenix* 31 (1977), 189-207.
McLennan	(G. R.) 'The Employment of the Infinitive in Apollonius Rhodius,' *QUCC* n.s. 15 (1973), 44-72.
Meister	(K.) *Die homerische Kunstsprache*. Leipzig 1921.
Merkel (*Proleg.*)	(R.) Ed. Ap., Leipzig 1853-4; *Prolegomena* to this ed.
Meuli	(K.) *Odyssee und Argonautika*. Berlin 1921.
Mooney	(G. W.) Ed. of Ap., London-Dublin 1912.
Moorhouse	(A. C.) *The Syntax of Sophocles*. Leiden 1982.
Naber	(S. A.) 'Ad Apollonium Rhodium,' *Mnemosyne* 34 (1906), 1-39.
Natzel	(S. A.) ΚΛΕΑ ΓΥΝΑΙΚΩΝ: *Frauen in den* Argonautika *des Apollonios Rhodios*. Trier 1992.
Nelis	(D. P.) 'Demodocus and the Song of Orpheus,' *MH* 49 (1992), 153-70.
Neutsch	(B.) *ap.* R. Herbig, ed., *Ganymed*, pp. 119-24. Heidelberg 1949.
Newman	(J. K.) *The Classical Epic Tradition*. Madison 1986.
Nyberg	(L.) *Unity and Coherence: Studies in Apollonius Rhodius'* Argonautica *and the Alexandrian Epic Tradition*. Lund 1992.
Onians	(R. B.) *The Origins of European Thought*. 2nd ed., Cambridge 1954.
Oswald	(M. M. F.) *The Prepositions in Apollonius Rhodius*. Diss. Notre-Dame, Indiana 1904.
Otis 1963	(B.) *Virgil: A Study in Civilised Poetry*. Oxford.
Otis 1970	(B.) *Ovid as an Epic Poet*. 2nd ed., Cambridge.
Paduano and Fusillo	See IIB above.
Paduano	(G.) *Studi su Apollonio Rodio*. Rome 1972.
Page, *S&A*	(D. L.) *Sappho and Alcaeus*. Oxford 1955.
Palombi	(M. G.) 'Eracle e Ila nelle *Argonautiche* di Apollonio Rodio,' *SCO* 35 (1985), 71-92.
Parry	(H.) *Thelxis: Magic and Imagination in Greek Myth and Poetry*. Lanham, New York and London 1992.

Paul	(A.) *Die Barmherzigkeit der Götter im griechischen Epos*. Wien 1969.
Pavlock	(B.) *Eros, Imitation and the Epic Tradition*. Ithaca and London 1990.
Pendergraft	(M. L. B.) '*Eros Ludens*: Apollonius' *Argonautica* 3, 132-41,' *MD* 26 (1991), 95-102.
Perrotta	(G.) 'Studi di poesia ellenistica,' *SIFC* n.s. 4 (1925), 85-280.
Peschties	(E.) *Quaestiones philologicae et archaeologicae de Apollonii Rhodii Argonauticis*. Königsberg 1912.
Platt 1914	(A.) 'On Apollonius Rhodius,' *JPh* 33.1-53.
Platt 1918	(A.) 'Apollonius Again,' *JPh* 34.129-41.
Platt 1920	(A.) 'Apollonius III,' *JPh* 35.72-85.
Prescott	(H. W.) Review of Mooney, *CPh* 8 (1913), 369-72.
Pretagostini	(R.) 'Le metafore di Eros che gioca: da Anacreonte ad Apollonio Rodio e ai poeti dell' *Anthologia Palatina*,' *AION* (filol.) 12 (1990), 225-38.
Rank	(L. Ph.) *Etymologiseering en verwante verschijnselen bij Homerus*. Assen 1951.
Redard	(G.) *Recherches sur ΧΡΗ, ΧΡΗΣΘΑΙ*. Paris 1953.
Reinsch-Werner	(H.) *Callimachus Hesiodicus*. Berlin 1976.
Renehan 1975	(R.) *Greek Lexicographical Notes*. Göttingen.
Renehan 1980	(R.) Review of M. L. West, ed. Hes. *WD*, *CPh* 75.339-58.
Renehan 1982	(R.) *Greek Lexicographical Notes: Second Series*. Göttingen.
Rengakos 1992	(A.) 'Homerische Wörter bei Kallimachos,' *ZPE* 94.21-47.
Rengakos 1993	(A.) *Der Homertext und die hellenistischen Dichter*. Stuttgart.
Rieu	(E. V.) Transl. of Ap., London 1959.
Risch	(E.) *Wortbildung der homerischen Sprache*. 2nd ed., Berlin and New York 1974.
Robert	(C.) *Die griechische Heldensage*. Berlin 1921-6.
Robinson	(D. M.) Review of Mooney, *CW* 7 (1913), 172-6.
Ronconi	(A.) 'Arato, interprete di Omero,' *SIFC* n.s. 14 (1937), 167-202, 237-59.
Roscher	(W. H., ed.) *Ausführliches Lexikon der griechischen und römischen Mythologie*. Leipzig 1884-1937.
Rose 1984	(A. R.) 'Three Narrative Themes in Apollonios' Bebrykian Episode,' *WS* n.s.18. 115-35.
Rose 1985	(A. R.) 'Clothing Imagery in Apollonios' *Argonautika*,' *QUCC* n.s. 19.29-44.
Rosenmayer	(T. G.) 'Apollonius lyricus,' *SIFC* n.s.10 (1992), 177-98.
Roux	(G.) 'Sur Théocrite, Apollonios et quelques épigrammes de l'*Anthologie*,' *RPh* 37 (1963), 84-7.
Ruijgh 1957	(C. J.) *L'élément achéen dans la langue épique*. Assen.
Ruijgh 1971	(C. J.) *Autour de 'TE épique'*. Amsterdam.
Ruijgh 1991	(C. J.) *Scripta minora ad linguam graecam pertinentia*. Amsterdam.
Rzach	(A.) 'Grammatische Studien zu Apollonios Rhodios,' *Wiener SB* 89 (1878), 427-599.
Schmidt 1968	(V.) *Sprachliche Untersuchungen zu Herondas*. Berlin.
Schmidt 1976	(M.) *Die Erklärungen zum Weltbild Homers und zur Kultur der Heroenzeit in den bT-Scholien zur Ilias*. Munich.

Schmitt	(R.) *Die Nominalbildung in den Dichtungen des Kallimachos von Kyrene*. Wiesbaden 1970.
Schulze *KS*	(W. S.) *Kleine Schriften*. 2nd ed., Göttingen 1966.
Schulze *QE*	(W. S.) *Quaestiones epicae*. Gütersloh 1892.
Schwinge	(E.-R.) *Künstlichkeit von Kunst: zur Geschichtlichkeit der alexandrinischen Poesie*. Munich 1986.
Seaton	(R. C.) Trans. of Ap., London 1912.
Seaton 1891	(R. C.) 'On the Imitation of Homer by Apollonius Rhodius,' *JPh* 19.1-13.
Seaton 1905	(R. C.) Review of Oswald, *CR* 19.452-4.
Seaton 1908	(R. C.) 'Professor S. A. Naber on Apollonius Rhodius,' *CQ* 2.16-21.
Seaton 1915	(R. C.) 'On Apollonius Rhodius,' *CQ* 9.10-14.
Segal	(C.) *Pindar's Mythmaking: the Fourth Pythian Ode*. Princeton 1986.
Shipp	(G. P.) *Studies in the Language of Homer*. 2nd ed., Cambridge 1972.
Sideras	(A.) *Aeschylus Homericus*. Göttingen 1971.
Sittl	(C.) *Die Gebärden der Griechen und Römer*. Repr. Hildesheim and New York 1970.
Speake 1969	(G.) 'The Manuscript D of Apollonius Rhodius,' *PCPS* 195.86-94.
Speake 1974	(G.) 'The Scribal Habits of Demetrius Moschus,' *GRBS* 15.113-33.
Speake 1975	(G.) 'Some Fifteenth-Century Truths in Apollonius,' *GRBS* 16.103-13.
Stahl	(J. M.) *Kritisch-historische Syntax des griechischen Verbums der klassischen Zeit*. Heidelberg 1907.
Stinton	(T. C. W.) *Collected Papers on Greek Tragedy*. Oxford 1990.
Stückelberger	(A.) 'Sterngloben und Sternkarten,' *MH* 47 (1990), 70-81.
Svensson	(A.) *Der Gebrauch des bestimmten Artikels in der nachklassischen griechischen Epik*. Lund 1937.
Teufel	(M.) *Brauch und Ritus bei Apollonios Rhodios*. Diss. Tübingen 1956.
Thesleff	(H.) *Studies on Intensification in Early and Classical Greece*. Helsingfors 1954.
Thiel	(K.) *Erzählung und Beschreibung in den* Argonautika *des Apollonios Rhodios*. Stuttgart 1993.
Thomas	(R. F.) 'Catullus and the Polemics of Poetic Reference (Poem 64.1-18),' *AJP* 103 (1982), 144-64.
Troxler	(H.) *Sprache und Wortschatz Hesiods*. Diss. Zurich 1964.
van der Valk	(M.) *Researches on the Text and Scholia of the* Iliad. Leiden 1963.
van Herwerden	(H.) 'Ad Apollonii Rhodii *Argonautica*,' *Mnemosyne* 11 (1883), 107-21.
van Krevelen 1949	(D. A.) 'Kritische und exegetische Bemerkungen zu Apollonios Rhodios,' *Eranos* 47.138-47.
van Krevelen 1951	(D. A.) Title as for 1949, *SIFC* n.s. 25.95-103.
van Krevelen 1953	(D. A.) 'Zu Apollonios von Rhodos,' *Mnemosyne* 6.46-55.

van Krevelen 1961	(D. A.) Review of Ardizzoni ed. iii, *Mnemosyne* 14.157-8.
Van Nortwick	(T.) *Somewhere I have never travelled: the second self and the hero's journey in ancient epic*. New York/Oxford 1992.
Vian and Delage	See BII above.
Vian ed. 1961	(F.) Ed. of Ap. iii, Paris.
Vian 1962	(F.) 'Quelques remarques sur le livre iii des *Argonautiques* d'Apollonios de Rhodes,' *RPh* 26.36-45.
Vian 1963	(F.) 'Apollonios de Rhodes et le renouveau de la poésie épique,' *IL* 15.25-30.
Vian 1969	(F.) Review of Ardizzoni ed. Ap. i, *RPh* 43.137-40.
Vian 1970	(F.) 'Notes critiques au chant i des *Argonautiques* d'Apollonios de Rhodes,' *REA* 72.80-96.
Vian 1972	(F.) 'Florent Chrestien lecteur et traducteur d'Apollonios de Rhodes,' *BiblH&R* 34.471-82.
Vian 1973	(F.) 'Notes critiques au chant ii des *Argonautiques*,' *REA* 75.82-102.
Vian 1975	(F.) 'Quelques lecteurs d'Apollonios de Rhodes au XVIIe siècle,' *RHT* 5.87-95.
Vian 1978	(F.) 'ΙΗΣΩΝ ΑΜΗΧΑΝΕΩΝ,' *Studi ... A. Ardizzoni*, 1025-41. Rome.
Vian 1978b	(F.) 'L'isthme de Cyzique d'après Apollonios de Rhodes,' *REG* 91.96-106.
Vílchez	(M.) 'El epítheto en Apolonio de Rodas: tradicíon e innovacíon,' *Emerita* 54 (1986), 63-101.
Voigt	(C.) *Überlegung und Entscheidung: Studien zur Selbstauffassung des Menschen bei Homer*. Meisenheim am Glan 1972.
Wace and Stubbings	(A. J. B./F. H.) *A Companion to Homer*. London 1962.
Wackernagel *KS*	(J.) *Kleine Schriften*. Göttingen 1952.
Wackernagel *SU*	(J.) *Sprachliche Untersuchungen zu Homer*. Göttingen 1916.
Wackernagel *VS*	(J.) *Vorlesungen über Syntax*. Basel 1920-4.
Wåhlin	(L. P. O.) *De usu modorum apud Apollonium Rhodium*. Lund 1891.
Walther	(R.) *De Apollonii Rhodii Argonauticorum rebus geographicis*. Diss. Halle 1891.
Webster	(T. B. L.) *Hellenistic Poetry and Art*. London 1964.
Wellauer	(A.) Ed. Ap., Leipzig 1828.
Wendel *Schol.*	(K.) Ed. Schol. Ap., Berlin 1935.
Wendel 1932	(K.) *Die Überlieferung der Scholien zu Apollonios Rhodios*. Berlin.
West 1963	(M. L.) 'Critical Notes on Apollonius Rhodius,' *CR* n.s. 13.9-12.
West 1983	(M. L.) *The Orphic Poems*. Oxford.
West 1985	(M. L.) *The Hesiodic Catalogue of Women*. Oxford.
West 1990	(M. L.) *Studies in Aeschylus*. Stuttgart.
West *PP*	(S.) *The Ptolemaic Papyri of Homer*. Cologne and Opladen 1967.
Wifstrand 1928	(A.) Review of Gillies ed. Ap. iii, *DLZ* 52.2551-4.
Wifstrand 1929	(A.) *Kritische und exegetische Bemerkungen zu Apollonios Rhodios*. Lund.
Wifstrand 1933	(A.) *Von Kallimachos zu Nonnos*. Lund.

Wilamowitz *HD*	(U. von Wilamowitz-Moellendorf) *Hellenistische Dichtung in der Zeit des Kallimachos*. Berlin 1924.
Woodbury 1991	(L. E.) *Collected Writings*. Atlanta, Georgia.
Wyatt	(W. F., Jr) *Metrical Lengthening in Homer*. Rome 1969.
Zagagi	(N.) *Tradition and Originality in Plautus*. Göttingen 1980.
Zaganiaris	(N. J.) Review of VDB 1, *Platon* 31 (1979), 312-23.
Zanker 1979	(G.) 'The Love Theme in Apollonius Rhodius' *Argonautica*,' *WS* n.s. 13.52-75.
Zanker 1987	(G.) *Realism in Alexandrian Poetry*. London.
Zumbo 1975	(A.) Review of VDB 1, *GIF* 27.349-53.
Zumbo 1975/76	(A.) 'Contributi papiracei al testo di Apollonio Rodio: II,' *Helikon* 15/16.472-80.

C. Frequent reference is made in the commentary to the diction employed by 3rd century (pure, literary) hexameter poets, denoted by '3^H' – that is to say, Ap. himself and the relevant remains of Aratus, Callimachus, (genuine) Theocritus, and certain authors in *CA* and *SH*; I admit also *Megara*, and [Theocritus] 25.

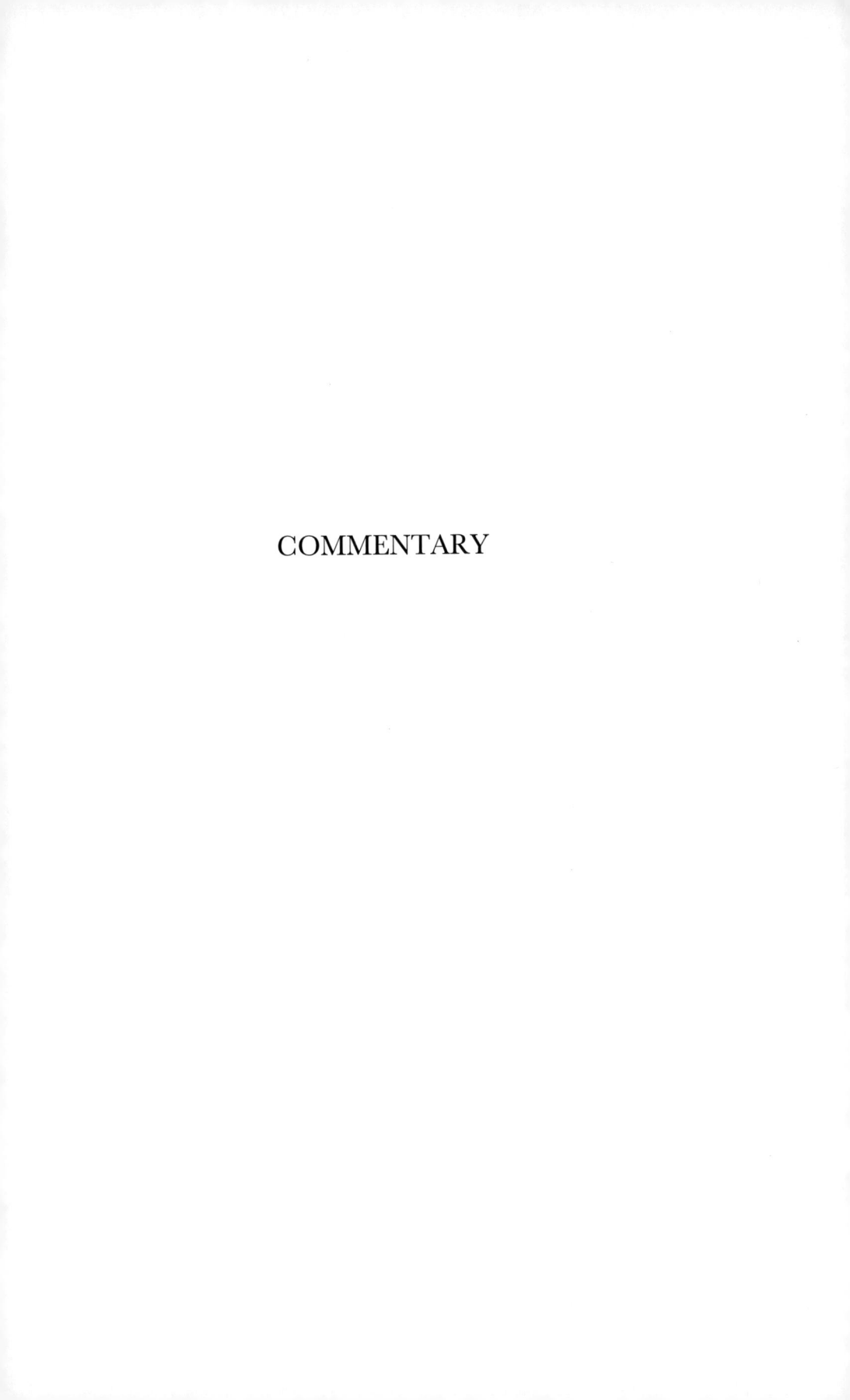

COMMENTARY

COMMENTARY

1-5 As Argonauts – and poet – reach their outward destination, the Muse is asked to give her stamp of authority to the ensuing story, an ancient epic story recounted with a new slant, and with a new emphasis; Erato, because here in the third book the theme of *eros*, hitherto occasionally but never extensively exploited (Nyberg 7, 51, 95 exaggerates), will really come into its own (cf. Lawall 150-1; De Martino 104, 107; Hutchinson 116 n.47) as a decisive element in the expedition's success, but also as a potent source of mental anguish (adumbrated in 4-5) and as an agent of ruin. The figure of Medea, victim of Erato's sphere of influence, fronts this crucial phase, and the next: she is central to the Argonauts' stay in Colchis; and the account of her flight (cf. iv.5) essentially sets the return-journey in motion. This highly worked proem is examined from various angles in *Studies* 1-7, to which the reader is referred for bibliogr. on Muse-invocations (Häussler is especially informative) and for discussion of certain peripheral matters.

In the first book the Muses, in the wake of a brief address to Apollo (*Studies* 128-9), had attracted an unceremonious though carefully followed through invitation to channel elements drawn from their comprehensive stock of information into the mouth of the poet (22, cf. Campbell 1990.481; astonishingly, some still cling to the absurdity of 'interpreters' here: most recent sighting: Beye 1993.195). The balance is redressed, for one of their number at least, right at the start of the third book, with an extremely elaborate fanfare closely matched by a similarly structured appeal to Erato (unnamed; differently De Martino 113) at the start of the fourth (see Campbell 1983.154-5); Muses, we know, were permitted to head Callimachus' *Aetia* 4, and there is a strong possibility (cf. lately Harder, *ZPE* 96 (1993), 11f., against Krevens, id. 89 (1991), 19f.) that they were brought in formally right after the preliminaries (cf. Ap.) in the first book: compare their delayed introduction in a number of Pindaric odes etc., where they could be used to effect a major transition (see the convenient summary in van der Weiden, ed. *Dithyrambs*, p. 47). In iii, as in i, the poet is dependent on his Muse for the telling of the story, which he will relay through her to his audience; in iv init., Beye's appraisal of which seems to me to be badly skewed (1993.195-6), he takes an explicitly aporetic stance (*Studies* 95 n.12, cf. below on 6), insisting that the 'goddess,' this time solemnly invoked as 'child of Zeus' (no poetic symbol this!), will have to devise *and* transmit the story herself: a variation perhaps on the Callimachean technique of framing direct responses to the questioning poet (where θυμός is involved, cf. Ap.'s νόος) from various named Muses; see below, and for discussion Harder, 'Callimachus and the Muses: Some Aspects of Narrative Technique in *Aetia* 1-2,' *Prometheus* 14 (1988), 1f.; cf. the ostentatious pose of 'judicial impotence' (Harries, *CQ* n.s. 39 (1989), 173) struck up by Ovid at the commencement of *Fasti* 5/6, and more generally hymnic ἀπορία about proper procedure (see on that Race, *GRBS* 23 (1982), 6f., id., *YCS* 29 (1992), 27).

That Ap. himself attached great significance to this phase of the story (the proem caught the attention of the roving Athenaeus, 555b: *Studies* 5) is indicated not only by the presence of a fresh invocation with its highlighting of the part played by *eros*, but also by the density and the range of the literary reminiscences incorporated within the space of five lines (the *Argonautica*'s opening quatrain, in illustration of which successive commentators have accumulated evocations of Homer(ica), Pindar and Euripides is not quite as richly textured). The poet will view Medea's condition dispassionately, clinically, but he will also penetrate her mind and scan her emotions; he will for the most part cultivate a determinedly epic style, but he will from time to time reflect the imagery and the intensity (occasionally too, the playfulness) of lyric/lyric-related genres and the sombre or animated tone of tragedy. In these opening lines there are more or less securely identifiable echoes, all of them worked into an appeal which in bare outline is essentially a standard epic routine ('Tell me, Muse, how it came about that ... because you ...') of Homer, Hesiod, *lyrici* including Pindar, Mimnermus, Empedocles, Euripides; Callimachus too perhaps, if we may set any store by the scenario in Ovid, *Fasti* 4.195f. (conversation with poet; etymologising, but no sure sign of this element in relation to named Muses in Call.: see e.g. Barchiesi, *PCPS* n.s. 37 (1992), 11) ~ *SH* 238.8 (*Studies* 4; on Ovid: Harries cited above, 171).

1 Homer is not the primary source for this line, but as so often in such cases we can detect the strong presence of multiple Homeric underpinnings:

(1) *Il.* 16.667 (+ vocat.) al. /εἰ δ' ἄγε νῦν in urgent appeal; seldom met with elsewhere: cf. Anon. parod., p. 103.26 Brandt, Q.S. 13.272,

Greg. Naz. 526.56, 1367.203, [Orph.] *A.* 255, and a further instance cited in note on ἄγε below.

(2a) *Il.* 17.179, *Od.* 22.233 (hence [Apolin.] 58.9) /ἀλλ' ἄγε δεῦρο .. παρ' ἔμ' ἵστασο καὶ ἴδε ... cf. *Il.* 11.314 (δὴ γὰρ ...); all in situations involving martial activity: not so here!

(2b) *Il.* 10.291 (Diomedes to goddess) νῦν ... παρίστασο καί με [ctr. Zen.] ... (ἀδμήτην 293); id. 5.809 (goddess/mortal) παρά θ' ἵσταμαι ἠδὲ ...

(3) *Od.* 12.112, 23.35 /εἰ δ' ἄγε .. μοι (vocat.) ... ἐνίσπες/; *Il.* 14.470 al. καί μοι .. ἐνίσπες (ἔνισπε)/.

(4) *Il.* 10.321 /ἀλλ' ἄγε ... -ο, καί μοι (ὄμοσσον/).

ἄγε For a review of this word as an ingredient of addresses to Muse(s) *et sim.* in lyric and elsewhere see *Studies* 6 (a note is promised by M. Davies, on Alcm. *PMGF* 14(a)1); a new one: /αἱ δ' ἄγε νῦν, then the Muses, Anon. hexam. (pap. 3rd/4th cent.) *POxy* 3537*v*8f. In Stesich. *PMGF* 240 it is coupled with 'cletic' δεῦρο (cf. Fraenkel, *Philologus* 86 (1931), 5f., West on Hes. *WD* 2, Renehan 1980.345) and a named Muse; in Alcm. id. 27 with a named Muse, then ἐρατῶν, cf. the *Rhadine* fragment referred to in 5n.

Empedocles too, almost certainly, played a part in the wider formulation of this proem: *Studies* loc. cit.; his *On Nature* may have opened with a hymn to *Aphrodite*, Sedley, *GRBS* 30 (1989), 290 [Lucr. 1.23 *amabile* after an ἐπήρατον??]. I do not know how I missed this one: DK31 B62.1-2 /νῦν δ' ἄγ', ὅπως .... ἀνήγαγε ... (αἶσαν 5; 4 fin. is imitated in iv.1423, with ὄρπηκες 1425 from 5; 10 init. is recalled iv.677 + 679). — Note also, in the realm of didactica, εἰ δ' ἄγε κτλ. in one (supposed) alternative proem to the *Phaenomena* of Aratus, *SH* 84.1.

νῦν νῦν (iv.1)/*nunc* are regularly employed in fresh invocations: West on [Hes.] *Theog.* 963, and pp. 48-9; Livrea on iv.1. See also on παρά .. ἵστασο below.

Ἐρατώ A name could reveal something essential about a person (Dodds on Eur. *Bacch.* 367), and this Muse's name is tailor-made for such probing: on the -ώ type see Gusmani, *RIL* 96 (1962), 405. Erato, whom Hesiod (*Theog.* 78~65, 70) no doubt thought of in a general way as imparting 'loveliness' to poetic composition, is here linked firmly with ἔρως/ἐρωτικά: 5n.

Detailed discussion of the form of the vocative in *Studies* 2-3. One might have expected Ἐρατοῖ given that there is no other vocative involved (Hunter calls in, in addition to Pind. *P.* 11.2, *PMG* 1018(b)1, but that – and it is not *absolutely* certain that actual vocatives are in question – occurs in a series, and so is subject to the rules of the game): but Ap. is of course pursuing an etymological point: ΕΡΑΤΩ (through ΕΡΩΤΙ) ~ ΗΡΑΤΟ (5), with only a gentle manipulation of pure vowel-sounds.

παρά .. ἴστασο In *Il.* 2.485 the Muses are thought of as being constantly 'present/at hand' as witnesses to deeds they may be called upon to recount (πάρεστε, καθολικῶς ἐπὶ πάντων schol. A, criticising a reading παρῆστε, scil. 'on that particular occasion'). The Muse here by contrast is asked to 'stand/take her stand by the side of' the poet, who is there with her as events unfold (see below), to render him assistance (Braswell on Pind. *P.* 4.1-2) at a time of special need, viz. here and now (νῦν).

Empedocles (either this, or a passage like it) may be the immediate model here (*Studies* 6): DK31 B131.3 (probably from *On Nature*, cf. for instance Woodbury, *Phoenix* 21 (1967), 171 = Woodbury 1991.182) εὐχομένῳ [a necessary correction: see, e.g., O'Brien, *Gnomon* 54 (1982), 226] νῦν αὖτε παρίστασο Καλλιόπεια (note μελέτας 2 cf. Ap. 4?). Such a borrowing does not of course rule out a passing reference to Pindar (*O.* 3.4 Μοῦσα ... παρέστα μοι, and esp. *P.* 4.1f., this ode being one of this book's primary models); indeed, the very expression 'stand by' the singer probably began life in ?Pindaric choral (yes, choral) performances: since the poet through his chorus can be said to 'take his stand' on arrival at a given locality (as *N.* 1.19 ἔσταν), it is natural that his Muse will occupy a standing position beside him in order to render support. Ap. himself has just arrived at Colchis (2n.), and now (cf. νῦν in conjunction with named Muse and indication of locality in Bacch. 6.10f., with Danielewicz, *QUCC* n.s. 34 (1990), 11) calls upon the services of a specialist from the troop accompanying him on his journey. (A less appealing option to my mind is the image of the poetic chariot, with the Muse as παραιβάτις I suppose: Verdenius on Pind. *O.* 3.4; I doubt whether Ap. is thinking specifically of a pose commonly depicted in Hellenistic-based artistic representations of Muse and poet, the former standing, the later sitting in the manner of the Homeric *aoidos*, see e.g. the illustration in Paduano, *ASNP* 39 (1970), 383.) Both parties then are on the scene in living presence, παρὰ τοῖς πράγμασιν as Plato put it with reference to the ψυχή of the rhapsode in *Ion* 535c (see on that Murray, *JHS* 101 (1981), 93). One may compare from Hellenistic poetry, for example, the sustained exercise in Call. *h.* 3: 'the narrator follows Artemis on her travels and knows what is going on ...,' Harder, *CQ* n.s. 42 (1992),392 – so much so that he can suddenly turn to her, rather than to his Muse, to elicit detailed responses to a series of queries relating to the goddess' personal preferences (186; hardly a dig at an Apollonian mannerism, as is suggested by Griffiths, *GRBS* 17 (1976), 366).

For an interesting echo preserved in a wooden schoolbook from Roman Egypt see *Studies* 7.

παρά θ' Confirmed by Π[19] – not that confirmation was really needed. παρ' ἔμ' was never an equipollent reading 'olim traditum' (Fränkel OCT): it is a Homerising error peculiar to Choeroboscus and to Choeroboscus alone (even so *cod*. C has παρά θ' in i.312.27 Hilgard). In fact, Ap. nowhere uses παρά with accus. pers. Note the jingle PAT PAΘ (the twang of the lyre, in which this Muse was εἰδήμων?!).

ἵστασο iv.370 ὑπερίστασο. In schol. *Il*. 10.291*b*[1-3] (Erbse ad loc.) the imperative *without* intervocalic sigma (see *GH* 1.474-5, and, among Homeric commentators, Hainsworth on *Il*. 10.291, Hoekstra on *Od*. 15.168, F-G on id. 22.233) is credited to Zen., Ar. and αἱ πλείους; among the seven remaining cases of ἵστασ(o) in *Il./Od*. there is a v.l. -αο at *Od*. 22.233. *Pace* Rengakos 1993.70-1, there is no real need to think in terms of deliberate rejection of a Zenodotean lection (see Erbse 1953.164), particularly given Emped. cited above; Merkel *Proleg*. 119 absurdly drags in Aristophanes.

μοι Our poet does not hesitate to speak in his own voice, but this is the only such first-person reference in the third book: cf. De Martino 107, 113.

ἔνισπε here and iv.1565, but ἐνίσπες i.487 (see VDB for L's reading), 832. 'As often, the use of the archaic ἐννέπω suggests that the matter is of importance or urgency to the speaker,' West on *Od*. 4.642, cf. *LfgrE* s.v. ἐν(ν)έπω, which notes 'may imply a certain solemnity,' giving examples of its use in Muse-invocations (cf. Ap. iv.2); Risch, *ZPE* 60 (1985), 2, draws a distinction between ἔννεπε ('erzähle mir') and the aorist, 'eine wichtige Mitteilung machen.'

On the two forms of this aorist cf. Wackernagel *KS* 149, 176; *GG* 1.800; F-G on *Od*. 22.166. Scholiastic observations, both lucid and garbled, are assembled in La Roche *HU* 255-6, cf. Erbse on schol. *Il*. 24.388*b*[1-2]. As claus. both ἐνίσπες and ἔνισπε have a firm hold in Homer's text (*Il*. 2×, *Od*. 9×; Allen on *Il*. 11.186, *Od*. 3.101; clausular ἔνισπε occurs in an eccentric papyrus of the 2nd cent. BC at *Il*. 10.426: Edwards, *ZPE* 56 (1984), 12), whereas ἔνισπε is metrically guaranteed in *Od*. 4.642 (the formulaic [μοι] νημερτὲς ἐ./ *Il*. 14.470 + *Od*. 6 × is rearranged and shifted to line-beginning; ἔνισπε was perhaps regarded as a present: *GH* 1.467), sim. *HyDem* 71.

Otherwise: ἔνισπε: Aesch. *Suppl*. 603 corr. and (probably) *fr*. 25d4

(Snell, *Gnomon* 25 (1953), 438), [Theoc.] 25.34 (˘⸺˘), Q.S. 14.209 claus. *codd. omnes*, a form also read by Parsons in Anon. hexam. *POxy* (pap. 3rd/4th cent.) 3537*r*11 (˘⸺˘); ἐνίσπες Anon. *PMG* 953.1 corr. (Muse); ἐνισπ̣ Call. *Hec. fr.* 20.2 (? cf. id. 17.1, Hollis ad loc.).

2 ἔνθεν Certainly 'from here' (and not 'from there': Feeney 91), Colchis, see *Studies* 95 n.2 and Campbell 1990.481; Fränkel *Noten* 328 n.5 deals pedantically with this detail. The poet travels with the Argonauts (see e.g. Carspecken 137, on the poem's close; Beye 1982.14, 18; cf. in general Braswell on Pind. *P.* 4.247-8, 247(b), 299(a)), taking the same path (recall the prominence accorded to πόροι in the proem, i.21, where note δολιχῆς!) – an image which of course has programmatic significance in Hellenistic poetry; indeed, since a sea-journey is in question, his song can be thought of as a πλόος from which he might be driven off course (i.1220; there are hints of the notion elsewhere in the poem): on this and allied concepts see the rich documentation in Helzle, *ICS* 13 (1988), 76-7. At ii.1090f. Ap. asks (scil. the Muses, rather than 'himself,' as e.g. Blumberg 48: cf. schol. P at 1090-4*a*, VDB 1.179 n.9): 'what was Phineus' purpose, that the heroes ἐνθάδε [cf. ἔνθεν here] κέλσαι …?' The immediacy of the adverb recalls that of 'performative' ἐνθάδε in *HyAp* 168, on which see W. G. Thalmann, *Conventions of Form and Thought in Early Greek Epic Poetry* (Baltimore 1984), 230 n.36; cf. too ἔνθεν in Call. *h.* 3.42 and esp. 98, the poet 'tracking' his subject (1n.). Note also, from a formal point of view, ἔνθεν in i.1108, ἐνθένδ' εἰς Ἰαωλκόν in iii.1114; and *Il.* 15.29-30 /τὸν … ἔνθεν … ἀνήγαγον ../ Ἄργος ἐς …

ὅπως 'how it was that' (perhaps there is a link here with Call. *fr.* 7.25-6 ἀρχμενος ὡς ἥρωες ἀπ' Αἰήταο Κυταίου/αὖτις ἐς ἀρχαίην ἔπλεον Αἱμονίην). The basic pattern is found in *Il.*: 16.112-3 /ἔσπετε νῦν μοι Μοῦσαι …,/ὅππως δὴ …, when events take a very different turn (cf. Duckworth 7). So *Il.* 1.1-2 *teste Aristox.* (Kirk, ed. 1-4, p. 52, cf. paraphr. in Plato, *Resp.* 545d, which draws also on 16.112f.), Hippon. *IEG* 128.3, Cratinus *PCG* (IV) 237.3 (presumably), Choer. Sam. *SH* 316.1 (where there would have been a Muse, I believe: contrast S. Koster, *Antike Epostheorien* (Wiesbaden 1970), 18-9), etc.; for an interesting reincarnation of Homer/Plato in Plotinus' *Enneads* cf. Ferwerda, *Hermes* 118 (1990), 206f. There is also a direct mode, in actual (iv.552, cf. Call. *fr.* 7.19, Theoc. 22.115) or implied (iv.450, note the tag γὰρ δή and ref. to the poet's song in 451) address to the Muse(s).

With 'how it came about that Jason brought back the Fleece

hence to Iolcus' we are incidentally presented with a programme for the rest of the work: *Studies* 2.

ἐς Ἰωλκόν i.e. right back home. Cf. [Hes.] *Theog.* 997 (ἀφίκετο ~ Eur. *Med.* 484 ἱκόμην), iii.89 ~ iv.1163; in other sedes: iii.1135 (ἵκηται/ cf. Theoc. 13.19 /ἵκετο .. ἐς .. -όν/); [Orph.] *A.* 835 (ἀφικέσθαι), 1369. Argo departed from (i.524f.) and landed at (iv.1781) Pagasae (cf. *Pagasae navalibus* in Prop. 1.20.17; Meyer *RE* 18.1, 2299; Pfeiffer on Call. *fr.* 18.12, 13). 'Iolcus' for Ap. means the inland city (e.g. 1091 infr.) and not the coastal district often said to be the starting-point of the voyage (Pind. *P.* 4.188, Theoc. 13.19 ~ 21, Diod. 4.42.1, Lucan 3.192f., etc.; Delage 74f., VDB 1.250, Dräger 107 n.311, 136 with n.395). Ovid impishly recasts the final line of our poem, ἀσπασίως ἀκτὰς Παγασηίδας εἰσαπέβητε, with *victor Iolciacos tetigit cum coniuge portus* (*Met.* 7.158). — Form: 1091n.

ἀνήγαγε κῶας Ἰήσων On the basis of Mimn., *IEG* 11.1, οὐδέ κοτ' ἂν μέγα κῶας ἀνήγαγεν αὐτὸς Ἰήσων Ap. has been represented as acknowledging a general debt to amatory elegy (cf. e.g. Zanker 1979.70 n.58) and also as aligning himself with contemporary admirers (see recently Allen 20f., 146f.) of a poet who was consumed by the flame of passion (De Martino 107 '... sotto l'ala del dolce Mimnermo'). Maybe so. In fact (see *Studies* 28) the main components of the line must have figured extensively in Argonautic poetry since (μέγα κῶας: cf. iv.171, 184, 439, Dräger 32 n.78, 34 n.85, Allen 89; ἀνήγαγεν: cf. iii.29, iv.1035, and Dräger 34f. with n.87; note too claus. κῶας Ἰήσων in ii.211, 871 ~ Theoc. 13.16), and there is nothing much in the rest of the fragment (or in *ffr.* 11a/12) to suggest that Ap. was specially taken with him. I suspect that the loss of a *later* elegiac work is a cause for greater regret: we are unable to gauge adequately, even at the level of basic phraseology relating to salient points of the story, the debt owed to Antimachus' *Lyde* by Ap., and, for that matter, by Call. in his (elegiac) account of *res Argonauticae* (see in general on the latter Knox, *HSCP* 89 (1985), 115; Cameron, *TAPA* 122 (1992), 309, pronounces with insufficient discrimination on what has survived, and with excessive confidence on the complexion of what has not).

2-3 ... Ἰήσων/Μηδείης ... Cf. *Studies* 1-2. We are brought sharply to a halt with ἔρωτι in 3, as Medea's 'love' forcefully signals the motive for recourse to Erato's expertise; but it is the name of Medea herself (as is often remarked, the poet has not taken the opportunity to raise the question of her crucial role hitherto: see e.g. Händel 10-

11, Levin 207) that arrests the dactylic sweep of the opening appeal and is emphatically placed, like *Turnus* at his first mention in Virgil, *A*. 7.56 (cf. the weighty *Gradivus* in the invocation of Statius, *Theb*. 4.36). The names of 'Jason' and 'Medea' are adjacent, yet separated by verse-division; 'Jason' is bonded more intimately to 'the Fleece,' the object of his enterprise, and the key to a safe return home.

Μηδείης ὑπ' ἔρωτι ~ [Orph.] *A*. 1030 /Μ. ὑπ' ἔρωτος. This preposition, 'supported by,' 'through the medium of,' causes Fränkel bother (*Noten* 329; Giangrande 1973.21 is not enlightening). Cf. *Il*. 6.171, or better (similar movement to ours) 16.698-9 Τροίην ἕλον υἷες Ἀχ-αιῶν/Πατρόκλου ὑπὸ χερσί, with *GH* 2.140. The expression is used again of the driving force of love in iv.567, Poseidon settled Corcyra there /ἁρπάξας ὑπ' ἔρωτι. In Call. ὑπ' ἔρωτι is accompanied by a passive participle: *h*. 2.49 (/ἠιθέου ὑπ'), 3.191, and so *GVI* 818.5 (Thebes, 3rd cent. AD), Anon. *AP* 11.52.1; contrast Nonn. *D*. 8.227 (/καὶ Σεμέλης ὑπ'), 13.555, 34.86, 47.245 (/'Ηριγόνης ὑπ'), Colluth. 192.

There can be little doubt that Ap. hereabouts means us to recall two very early lines in Euripides' *Medea*: 7-8 Μήδεια ... Ἰωλκίας/ἔρωτι ... Ἰάσονος (see in general Natzel 127).

ἔρωτι ΕΡΩΣ (but ἔρον i.613) first here in the poem, appropriately enough (not worked into the Hylas-episode, for example: ctr. Theoc. 13); often subsequently.

3 σὺ γὰρ καὶ ... Cf. *Studies* 95 n.4: γάρ explains why the Muse is qualified to make a contribution, as in iv.2, *Il*. 2.485, al. καί means not 'because *in fact*' but 'because *in addition*,' scil. to the other, normal activities of a Muse, compare σὺ γὰρ καί in iv.1199, with *Noten* 574, VDB 3.187, and see Campbell 1990.481: καὶ ... ἔμμορε ref. apportionment of spheres of influence at Hes. *Theog*. 414, a key theme in that poem (C. A. Sowa, *Traditional Themes and the Homeric Hymns* (Chicago 1984), 152f., Zanker, *BICS* 35 (1988), 73f.), clinches the matter (Ap.'s 'sharing' motif suggested by the sustained picture of a transfunctional Hecate, on which see Boedecker, *TAPA* 113 (1983), 81f.; cf. 3-4n.). Cf. Fernandelli 94 n.32.

3-4 Κύπριδος αἶσαν/ἔμμορες For the build of the clausula cf. *Il*. 18.327 al. (λάχοντα ..) ληίδος αἶσαν/.

αἶσα (*Studies* 95 nn.5-6) means 'allotted share/portion' (cf. *Il*. 15.209 with Janko's note, and gl. schol. bT μοίρᾳ μεμορισμένον; B. C. Dietrich, *Death, Fate and the Gods* (London 1965), 252), i.e. 'sphere of influence,' like μοῖρα (Adkins, *JHS* 92 (1972), 2, Lloyd-Jones (1990) 1.329;

cf. here Aesch. *Suppl.* 1041 δέδοται δ' 'Αρμονία μοῖρ' 'Αφροδίτας with FJW's note ad loc., and earlier λάχε μοῖραν in *HyHerm* 428), γέρας (see Richardson on *HyDem* 311f.), τιμή (West on Hes. *Theog.* 73-4, Pfeiffer on Call. *fr.* 119.2; note here *Theog.* 203f. Aphrodite ... τιμὴν ἔχει ἠδὲ λέλογχε/μοῖραν .../παρθενίους τ' ὀάρους κτλ., and also Prop. 3.3.33 corr. *diversae novem sortitae iura puellae*). For an early example of a goddess sharing in others' provinces expressed in similar terms cf. again (with Hoelzlin) *Theog.*, 421-2 (Hecate, see 3n.: τιμήν and αἶσαν). There is something of this flavour at the start of Menander's *Misoumenos*, Night possesses πλεῖστον μέρος of Aphrodite.

ἔμμορες is an aorist (see below) and should be translated accordingly. At the big share-out (ἔμμορες for ἔλαχες, a recurrent verb in this connexion: Mineur on Call. *h.* 4.74, cf. B. Borecký, *Survivals of some Tribal Ideas in Classical Greek* ... (Prague 1965), 44f.), Cypris received her due portion (as she was said to have done, comically, by the speaker in Ar. *Eccl.* 999! Cf. on that Sens, *CQ* n.s. 42 (1992), 529), but not as her exclusive property: there was another.

Κύπριδος We have seen that Cypris' special slot in the scheme of things is not all that special: Erato has a stake in it. We shall see in due course that Cypris, whose role in previous *Argonautica* cannot exactly have been a subordinate one (cf. 8n.), is destined to be upstaged, by her son Eros.

Cypris never rejoices in the name of Aphrodite in this poem: see Fantuzzi 155f., and earlier fitch, *TAPA* 33 (1902), lix, Faerber 69.

4 ἔμμορες An elevated equivalent of ἔλαχες, unusual in both form and construction. (1) Instances outside 3rd sing. are few: iv.62 -ες; Nic. *Ther.* 791 ἐξέμμορον (this forged from *Od.* 5.335: Leumann 95); *EtM* 335.24 ἔμμορον. ἔμμορε is a perfective (**sesmore*: Leumann 51, Dihle, *Glotta* 48 (1970), 4), but it was commonly glossed with an aorist: e.g. schol. D at *Il.* 1.278 (cf. Hesych. ε2386, and Henrichs 141) ἔλαχεν, ἔτυχεν, Hes. *Theog.* 414 gl. V ἔτυχε, M² ἐπέτυχε (Flach p. 190) ~ schol. Nic. *Ther.* 791 ἔμμορον· ἔλαχον, ἔτυχον. It was clearly regarded as such by Call. (below) and certain others; it is certainly inappropriate to talk of a 'mistake' on Ap.'s part, as does Gillies for instance. (2) With accus. αἶσαν here and infr. 208, as λαγχάνειν αἶσαν sim., and cf. Hes. *WD* 578 ἀπομείρεται αἶσαν/; more ambitiously iv.1749 σε .. -ε κῦδος/, as λέλογχεν in Pind. *O.* 1.53 (see in general KG 1.350; *Il.* 9.616, cited by Linsenbarth 37, Fränkel 1936.476, cf. too La Roche, *Homerische Studien* (Wien 1861), 157, even if ἥμισυ is accus., is an inept parallel; Hes. *Theog.* (426-)427: corrupt). Otherwise with gen. (but with accus.

+ ἐξ- Nic. loc. cit.): τιμῆς in archaic epic with the exception of Hes. *WD* 347 second instance (West on *Theog.* 414), and so Thgn. *IEG* 234, (Adesp. eleg. id. 12: v.l.), Adesp. *CAF* 51.52, *IME* 114:I 4 (cf. Peek, *ZPE* 10 (1973), 241), D.P. 239, Greg. Naz. 459.32, 533.137. Others: iv.62 ὁμοίης ἔμμορες ἄτης/ after Hom. ὁμοίης ἔμμορε τιμῆς/, Call. *h.* 3.208, Nic. *Alex.* 488 (not with accus.; βάρος = *in weight*), Antip. Thess. *GPh* 660, Cougny 3.74.11 (on this piece see Ludwich, *RhM* 34 (1879), 357f.) and 4.101.5; (Simon. *PMG* 519, *fr.* 79(a)4: context unknown).

4-5 It is a mystery to me how Zanker could have formed the impression that 'the gentler aspect of love is stressed' (1979.58, again 1987.199). On the contrary (*Studies* 2, cf. now Nyberg 88), Ap. hints broadly at its unpalatable aspects from the very start: 'unsubdued, unbroken virgins' are a primary target for Erato's own supply of '(gnawing) anxieties' with which she 'bewitches' her victims: see the ensuing notes, and more generally Buccholz 77-8.

ἀδμῆτας ... /παρθενικάς An uncommon collocation: i.671-2 -καὶ ... /-ῆτες (Beye has caught something of the effect of this word in the wider context, 1969.44; postposition of the type discussed by Wifstrand 1933.99f.; expanded by means of a participle phrase, as often, e.g. infr. 833, 840); Naumach. *GDK* 29.1-2 -ῆτα .../-κήν straight from Ap. (... μελεδήμασι); Nonn. *D.* 47.236 /-κὴν -ῆτα. But archaic epic already offered παρθένος ἀδμής/ *Od.* 6.109, 228 (with ref. to Nausicaa, one of Medea's role models in *Arg.*), *HyDem* 145, [Hes.] *fr.* 59.4 ~ Eudoc. *Hom.* 384, 387*c* (an echo of *Od.* 6.228), Greg. Naz. 1565.189, in reverse *GVI* 1980.1 (Thrace, 2nd/3rd cent.); and /παρθένῳ ἀδμήτῃ *HyAphr* 82 ~ [Orph.] *h.* 55.25 (nom. plur.).

The high profile here accorded to young unmarried girls *as a class* (see on this C. Calame, *Les choeurs de jeunes filles en Grèce archaïque* (Rome 1977), 1.65f.) may indicate a lyric model, specifically an Alcmanic 'Partheneion' (see the suggestive analysis of the portrayal of Lavinia in Cairns 159f.; more could be added from Ap. to n.74 on p. 174): cf. *PMGF* 1.76, 91 ἐρατ-, 45f. animal-imagery, 73f. a *venefica* almost certainly; our schol. in an informed note (1-5: from Theon beyond a doubt: *Studies* 4) relate Erato's invocation to her links with *dancing* and *marriage*.

ἀδμῆτας One such is Medea (δμηθεῖσ' ὑπ' Ἰήσονι [Hes.] *Theog.* 1000), whose emotions will become a prey to external forces, Erato here, as Cypris commonly (Campbell on Mosch. *Eur.* 75-6, Vetta, *SIFC* 44 (1972), 269f.) being a party to the process of 'taming': "δαμάζειν and cognate terms compare the effect of sexual drives to the external force that tames wild animals, rendering them helpless. The implicit metaphor is essentially that of enslavement" Hugh Parry, *Phoenix* 40 (1986), 255, cf. Parry (1992) 80 n.8, Campbell on Mosch. *Eur.* loc. cit.

δέ 'and as a consequence.'

τεοῖς μελεδήμασι θέλγεις Two late echoes: [Apolin.] 91.6 με τεοῖς .. ἔργμασι θέλγεις/, Paul. Sil. *Soph.* 1018 (cf. 471n.) μελεδήμασι θέλγων/.

τεοῖς 'your own.' Aphrodite got as her allotted portion 'the whisperings of girls; smiles; deceptions; sweet pleasure, intimacy and tenderness' (Hes. *Theog.* 205-6, transl. West; surely no meaningful distinction can be drawn here between goddess and victims). Add to the list μελεδήματα (cf. Hesiod again, *WD* 66): our Erato has her own stockpile. Ap. may also mean us to recall that the Muses at large make a practice of affording *respite from* 'cares' (as is underlined by Hes., *Theog.* 55, West ad loc.; Clay, *GRBS* 29 (1988), 331, takes too narrow a view of this sentiment): Erato does something different with hers (cf., in more general terms, the polemic in Eur. *Med.* 195f.).

μελεδήμασι Of special interest in the case of Medea: 452, 471, 752nn. Aphrodite inspires (or must dispel) μελεδῶναι Hes. *WD* 66, μέριμναι Sapph. *PLF* 1.26, id. + μέρμηραι Thgn. *IEG* 1323f.; *cura -ae* Catull. 64.72, 68.18 (Cupid 64.95); cf. too the splendid conceit in Theoc. 17.52. The term strikes a note of disquiet, and its force should not be diluted: e.g. Beye 1982.120, 'the affections you excite,' Fowler 1990 'your tender concern.' Ap., here in etymologising mood (5), may well have linked the element -εδ- with ἔδειν (see on that West and Verdenius on Hes. *WD* 66; ii.627 μελεδῶναι ~ 626 μελ-εϊστί!).

θέλγεις Cf. on 27, 27-8 (ref. love/Medea). Muses have the capacity θέλγειν their audience, like their ἀοιδοί from Homer on (cf. e.g. the vivid Pind. *N.* 4.2f.), though in this poem the power of this species of θέλξις is confined to personages inside the narrative: i.27 al. Orpheus son of a Muse (cf. Beye 1982.86), iv.894 Sirens daughters of a Muse; let us not forget Jason, whose story of adventures so far encountered (reported in dry outline by the singer, naturally!) had the desired effect on his royal listener (ii.772). When it comes to Ap.'s Muses, or rather single Muse, the force of θέλξις lies fairly and squarely in the realm of the erotic: Erato, like Cypris θελξίμβροτος, wields a deceptive sinister power that bewitches her victims, so that they (specifically females, especially young females) have no control over their actions: see schol. at iii.28, and Barrett on Eur. *Hipp.* 1274-6, Segal, *Arethusa* 7 (1974), 142f., Parry *passim*, esp. 24.

With θέλγεις παρθενικάς cf. infr. 86, 142-3; 27-8 ~ Mosch. *Eur.* 94.

5 παρθενικάς Type: Chantraine *EVG* 97f. Not that common in archaic epic; popular with Hellenistic poets: 3^H offers παρθ. as subst. Ap. 18 or (*CA* 12.11) 19 ×, Call. *h*. 4.298, 6.118, Theoc. 12.5, 18.2 (and [Theoc.] 8.59 if as early as this), Euphor. *SH* 416.2.

τῶ καί used in connexion with a point of nomenclature: cf. Call. *fr*. 75.58 (ἐφήμισαν), with Campbell 1990.481 [τῶ ῥα καί: Mineur on Call. *h*. 4.59], and for other formulations Rank 142.

καί Cf. *Studies* 95 n.8, and Campbell 1990.481. καί means 'you as well as Cypris.' The latter's name of course may be used metonymically: cf. the conceit in D.P. 508-9, Κύπρος .... ἐπήρατον ἄστυ .. Ἀφροδίτης.

τοι So now Π^19. The unsuitability of οἱ (which Wellauer espoused enthusiastically) was demonstrated long ago by Rzach, 536. It could only be upheld if we were prepared to tolerate a switch to 3rd pers. after σύ (3) and τεοῖς (4); the variant in *Il*. 4.129 is comparable. Ctr. the correction of Π^16 in iv.450 (see *Noten* 496), designed to 'tighten up' the apostrophe-sequence.

ἐπήρατον οὔνομ' Here only; but cf. *GVI* 1330.3 (Teos; 1st cent. AD?) ἐραστὸν .. οὔνο[μ', *Or. Sib*. 11.256 πολυήρατον οὔνομα –×; and ἐρατώνυμος. On οὔνομα + epithet relating to the import of a proper name see Whittle, *CQ* n.s. 14 (1964), 29, FJW on Aesch. *Suppl*. 320, and see *Studies* 3-4 for discussion of the significant name (with ref. to Hesiod, Plato *Phdr*. 259c, 'Stesich.' *Rhadine*, now *PMGF* 278) and of differentiation of functions/etymological awareness in previous literature.

Later formulations (Ovid etc.): *Studies* 5, cf. Fernandelli 88.

ἐπήρατον 'in which the element *eros* resides,' cf. ἐπαφρόδιτος, and see in general *GG* 1.465. In archaic verse both before subst. (Hes. *Theog*. 67 -ον ὅσσαν ἱεῖσαι/, where the text is probably sound; [Hes.] *fr*. , 3 ×) and after (Hom.; *HyAp*; Hes. *WD* 63 /παρθενικῆς καλ (⏑–⏑) ἐπήρατον ~ infr.1099 [similar in overall structure to *HyAp* 286]).

οὔνομ' ἀνῆπται Greg. Naz. 1520.198 σοι ... οὔνομ' ἀνάψω/. The clausula resembles the Homeric κήδε' (cf. ii.245) or πείρατ' ἐφῆπται. But the elision of metrically lengthened οὔνομα (ii.762, iii.1092, Call. *Hec. fr*. 90.1, *h*. 4.52, [Theoc.] 27.40, Parthen. *SH* 615, etc.) is not permitted in archaic epic: see *GH* 1.100, Mineur on Call. *h*. 4.52.

On οὔνομα/ὄνομα in the poem see Williams on Call. *h*. 2.70 (but something might have been said on, e.g., Arat., Theoc., and on the fragments of Hellenistic poets in general).

ἀνῆπται sounds technical: from Empedocles? Plato *Crat*. 410a προσάψαι scil. ὄνομα.

6-7 A fleeting glimpse of the Argonauts, to whom we shall return in 167f. They have reached Colchis under cover of night (ii.1260f.), disposed of sails and mast (1262f.), and rowed the low-lying (Fränkel *Noten* 72, cf. more generally Casson 44f., and see 198n.) Argo into a sequestered backwater close to the city (1266f. ~ 1283-4): Fränkel 1950.119-22 and *Noten* 323-4 pieces together a detailed picture of Argonautic movement from ii.1260 to iii.575.

Ap. habitually takes narrative compression to extremes. We have to deduce from ii.1271f. that Jason had intended to put in openly, a course of action implicitly accepted by the pilot Ancaeus when he proclaimed that the outward journey was over (ii.1277f.), until in ii.1281f. (the Phrixid) Argos recommended that the vessel be concealed: see Vian's analysis, 1973.101-2, and earlier Ibscher 46. But there is more: in following this through the Argonauts assume the posture of a squad of men ready to pounce – a sober version of the sort of activity envisaged by the overwrought Aeetes infr. 589f. And Ap. certainly goes out of his way to create an impression that the newcomers look set to move in a very positive direction (cf. also on ἀπονόσφι in 9):

(1) πυκινοῖσιν .. δονάκεσσι recalls *Od.* 14.473-4 κατὰ ῥωπήια πυκνά,/ ἂν δόνακας καὶ ἕλος ~ λόχον 469, while πυκινοῖσιν hints at cunning tactics: iv.464 πυκινοῦ .. λόχοιο 'son habile aguet' VDB, cf. Hutchinson 127 n.69; the context there rules out the interpretation 'massed,' πολυάνωρ (see *LH* 2.249.2-3 on Hom.'s πυκινὸς λόχος).

(2) ἀνωίστως in connexion with stealth, concealment: hapax ἀνωιστί *Od.* 4.92, where schol. MQ specify ἐνεδρευθῆναι in relation to this surprise attack.

(3) There are sharp echoes in 7 init. of *Od.* 16.368-9 ἐμίμνομεν .... λοχόωντες and 15.28 ἀριστῆες λοχόωσιν/. —

Thus the picture of a raiding party of ἀριστῆες (see Kirk on *Il.* 1.226-7) is presented so positively, so forcefully, that it must be meant, I believe, to imply *a complementary recommendation from Argos*, advanced in the absence of anything better. He and his brothers had reacted with horror to the idea of having anything to do with Aeetes in the attempt to acquire the Fleece (ii.1196f.), and Argos himself had been openly critical (1199): if a direct confrontation did not seem feasible (1202f.), he was no more happy about trying without Aeetes' consent given the insurmountable difficulties (1207f.). After Peleus' morale-boosting outburst, which accommodated both an open fight with (1220f.) and an approach to Aeetes, with a clear expectation that the latter course would be tried (1224, cf. i.245), Argos had evidently concluded that neither method could be contemplated.

Jason takes all this on board, because *timing* is all-important (note ὥρη in ii.1278). When he does put his foot down (iii.179f.), it is stated emphatically not just that everybody assented, but that nobody either offered a counter-proposal (iii.194-5). With 'nobody' Ap. is thinking particularly of Argos, who is unable on the spur of the moment to offer a viable alternative: there is still the problem of the inaccessibility of the Fleece after all (cf. ii.1208f.), a problem simply side-stepped by Peleus (Blumberg 52, Ibscher 44). As so often in this poem, expectations of some sort of full-blooded military venture evaporate (examples in *Noten* 468-72, 559f.; cf. also Blumberg 22, 32, Herter *JAW* 299-300, Fusillo 372): there will certainly be no 'heroic' λόχος of the kind carried out by Heracles in the course of his expedition to fetch Hippolyte's girdle (ii.967 /ἥρως .. ἐλοχήσατο, cf. Lawall 125).

6 ὣς οἱ μὲν ... The poet now, as the Muse's transmitter, carries the narrative forward with a resumptive formula: for the component μέν see West on Hes. *Theog.* 116. In the matching iv.6 (invocation then) ἤτοι ὁ μὲν ... the poet is physically and mentally incapable of performing this relaying function, and the Muse takes over herself, for a while at least: cf. *Noten* 454; VBD 3.147 (on 2); Campbell 1990.481; above, 1-5n.

Colluthus was to make his 'spectator-nymphs,' who masquerade as Muses, suggest an ὣς ὁ μὲν ... at the *opening* of the work (17: cf. W. Weinberger, *Studien zu spätgriechischen Epikern* (Iglau 1900), 122), led on by our passage (Keydell, *Gnomon* 47 (1975), 544).

On the resumptive formula itself: ὣς οἱ μὲν ... is discussed with reference to the standard Homeric book-division by Campbell 1983.154-5 (Hainsworth on *Il.* 9.1-3 underrates its evidential value: Ap. is not even mentioned! Rengakos 1993.94 just sidesteps the issue). Especially noteworthy are: *Il.* 8 fin. approach of dawn/9.1 (with shift of scene at the bucolic diaeresis: transition to an Olympian scene thus *Il.* 15.4, preceded by οἱ μὲν ... μένοντες, *Od.* 13.125; see in general Janko on *Il.* 16.124-5, Edwards on id. 18.314-5), 20.1f. ~ Olympian scene [cf. 4 init., *Od.* 5 init.]; also ὣς οἱ μὲν ... in *Il.* 12.1f. (2 ... -ημένον· οἱ δ' ἐμάχοντο/), *Od.* 6.1f. (2 'but Athena ...'). — *Oppositio*: *Od.* 4 fin. μένον λοχόωντες then 5.1f. dawn [Ap. ii.1285, cf. i fin., but also *Od.* 23 fin., not noted by Beye 1993.195, who talks of 'a kind of perversion of the notion of an ending'] + Olympian scene: for its sequel see 108f.n.
— A passage which does not conform is the switch to Olympus

towards the close of Il. 7: 442f. /ὣς οἱ μὲν πονέοντο .../οἱ δὲ θεοὶ ... But that was considered an interpolation by the Big Three: Kirk on 443-64, p. 289, cf. Rengakos 1993.77-8.

πυκινοῖσιν ... Shaped like *Il.* 11.576 πυκινοῖσι (βιαζόμενον) βελέεσσι/ (ἐνόησ' 575 ~ Ap. 7). Compare infr. 946(n.); Arat. 1112.

ἀνωίστως 6-7, 670nn. A slick transition to Olympus (cf. *Studies* 7/96 n.1). The Argonauts are out of sight, their presence detected by no one; but they do *not* escape the notice of Hera and Athena. ἀνωίστως 6, ἐνόησαν 7: cf. schol. bT at *Il.* 21.39 (Erbse ad loc.) ... νωίσασθαι γὰρ τὸ νοῆσαι and many other glosses associating ἀνώιστος with some element of νοεῖν (Livrea on iv.255), νόος being the vehicle of sensory perception: von Fritz, *CPh* 38 (1943), 79-93, esp. 87; Onians 83.

The adverb is peculiar to Ap. (Hom. ἀνωιστί; see 319n.): 'out of the blue,' of unexpected (and potentially aggressive) newcomers in i.680, of Medea about to launch a devastating attack on an unsuspecting Talos (cf. ἀπροφάτως i.1201, al.) in iv.1661. See above on 6-7.

... δονάκεσσι Cf. infr. 198, [Orph.] *A.* 800 ποταμοῦ δονακώδεος = Phasis, Philostr. Jun. *Imag.* 8 (cf. below on 123-4, 135-41), who pictures the river-god Phasis as lying ἐν βαθεῖ δόνακι, and the description of the Pontic coastline in Sen. *Med.* 212-3; one may recall also from an earlier stopping-place the account of the terrain at ii.818-26 (boar ambushing Idmon), with VDB 1.214 n.3. See further Vian 1963.28, VDB 2.17f. (esp. 17 n.2), Bömer on Ov. *Met.* 7.6. The present-day Kolkhiz Lowland possesses a humid subtropical climate and is predominantly fenland.

Ap. is certainly recalling here a verse from a poet telling of another exotic journey: Simias, *Apollo, CA* 1.7 (νήσους) ὑψικόμοισιν ἐπηρεφέας δονάκεσσιν (compare ἐνόησα in 9 with 7 infr.); Erbse (1953.186 n.2) detected an echo of this same verse in iv.144. For further points of contact with this 13-line fragment see 309, 749nn.; also *Apollo* 1 ~ ii.675; 2 claus. ~ iv.1513; 3b ~ iv.86b; 5-6 ~ ii.401; (Fränkel 1915.21) 9 ~ ii.394.

Livrea (1982.19) adduces Pind. *O.* 6.53-4, implying that Ap. is imitating; I see no reason to think this.

7a μίμνον ... bears some similarity to ii.528-9 ἀριστῆες .../μίμνον (ἐρυκ)όμενοι, .. δ' ...

ἀριστῆες = Argonauts 32 × in the poem: so Theoc. 13.17, 22.99, [Orph.] *A.*; cf. also perhaps ἀριστεῖς in par. schol. iii.515-21 with ref. to the *Naupactia* (*EGF fr.* 4). Employed in preference to ἄριστοι (Eur. *Med.* 5 ἀνδρῶν ἀρίστων, see Page ad loc. [but ἀριστέων Wakefield,

Diggle], [Apollod.] 1.9.16 etc.; on the equivalence see in general J.-L. Perpillou, *Les substantifs grecs en -ΕΥΣ* (Paris 1973), 268-70, and ctr. ἄριστοι in i.231, 548, iv.1307). — Cf. Val. Flacc.'s *duces* (+ Stat.), *proceres, reges* (+ Sen., Stat.).

λελοχημένοι Only here and infr. 168; on the analogy of δεδοκημένος etc. (see in general *GH* 1.435-6, and cf. Boesch 14). The pure middle (i.991, ii.967) is Odyssean.

7-166 *Events on Olympus*
'The epic machinery has to be heaved into position by a tiny Eros, bribed by a worldly Aphrodite' declares G. Anderson, *Eros Sophistes* (Chicago 1982), 3; others have fired similar shots. There is of course much more to the episode than this crude summary suggests.

Once the Argonauts are on *terra firma* (almost) the Olympians step in to influence events in a thoroughgoing way. The protagonists are Hera, Athena and Cypris (8n.), but the real moving force is Hera, one member of the *Iliad*'s dynamic duo, whose attitudes and behaviour are tellingly evoked on more than one occasion: if in the earlier poem both goddesses are consumed with hatred for Troy and her people (Hera more explicitly so, it must be said; cf. recently J. V. O'Brien, *The Transformation of Hera* (Lanham 1993), 81f.), here it is Hera and Hera alone who calls the shots, driven as she is by an inveterate loathing for a single individual, the hybristic Pelias, who must be punished at all costs. The formidable Queen of Heaven has not been much in evidence so far (see Herter *JAW* 276, *Studies* 115 n.17, VDB 3.233, right-hand column): she might easily have been worked into one or two of the main episodes, Phineus might have been nudged into elaborating on his pronouncement at ii.216-7, and so on. She has been held back deliberately, to create a big splash. If, *more Homerico* (see e.g. Janko, ed. *Il.* 13-16, p. 169; 10n. below), there is plenty to enjoy in the various confrontations, a dark and sombre note is struck by the vindictive goddess' aforementioned uncompromising lust for revenge, which spells suffering, humiliation, and, eventually, death for a succession of human beings. So it is with Eros, a *dämonisches Wesen* (cf. iv.448) brought to life with a vengeance: behind the picture of a dishonest, grasping child lurks an awesome and potent force; we catch a glimpse of that in the episode's dying moments as he makes his way to Colchis, enticed by the promise of an infant's toy.

In the *Iliad*, where passions run high, the gods habitually brawl. There is nothing to brawl about in the *Argonautica* (though there is that business of the mother and her boy ...). The Olympian scene is a study in manipulation. With admirable poise, her notorious bad temper nowhere in evidence, Hera makes Athena (in normal terms, easily her equal) look faintly ridiculous and Cypris (in the *Iliad*, a thorn in her side) downright laughable: the one thrust into an inimical environment (twice), the other exposed to the world as a hopelessly inept mother; not that her child has sapped her strength – this Cypris (81-2n.) has no strength in the first place.

The basic situations of which this episode is compounded are all familiar from archaic epic: goddesses in conclave, a house-call from a goddess in need of assistance, the antics of an outrageous child. But they are enlivened by sharply-etched pictorial detail (cf. Zanker 1979.70-1), by a wealth of gesture, both explicit and implied, and by the deployment of a remarkably wide range of tonal colour in the rapid succession of relatively brief speeches (for general analysis see Ibscher 51f.). In the opening exchange Hera is by turns mischievous and devious, resourceful and decisive, Athena evasive but confident on the surface, then uncharacteristically meek – entirely ready to oblige if she can melt into the background. At the start of the second interview Cypris is catty, then incredulous and conciliatory, then full of hopeless despair, and, finally, resigned; Hera for her part pulls out all the stops to convey her anxiety and alarm, and comes up with a nasty surprise for Cypris who, after receiving her instructions, is treated to a shamelessly dismissive and patronising parting-shot from the arch-plotter.

We are moving in high circles (cf. Cypris in 54, her 'big house' in 36). Or are we? While it is certainly not true that these goddesses 'could be Nausicaa's maidservants chatting over a load of laundry' (J. R. Harris, *Accidental Grandeur* (New York 1989), 58), it *is* hard to resist the suspicion that the whole episode was written with a view to evoking to some extent at least (or to rehousing in an epic setting??) the atmosphere of the 'mimetic' compositions familiar to us chiefly from Theocritus and Herodas, whose everyday characters, Theocritus' in particular, do not in any case exactly fight shy of heightened diction, high-flown imagery, extravagant metaphor and cunning literary reminiscence; *pace* Feeney 78, it is not *just* a case of the recreation of 'Homer's naturalism' (Feeney in fact takes a potshot at an extremely ill-defined target). While the opening scene smacks in general of bedroom-intrigue, the central action invites specific comparison with Herodas 1 (a young girl is visited by a wheedling old woman who is out for herself: cf. 8f., 'What a time it's been since I last saw you,' 19f. 'Go on, mock' ~ Ap. 56, see n.; a sexual target is envisaged) and Theocritus 15 (a domineering caller hustles a woman friend out of the house to see a show: cf. 1, 'What a time ...'); the last scene with Herodas 3 (a defiant schoolboy with a liking for gambling drives his mother to distraction), the pointed ἅτε κοῦροι ... in 118 relating life on Olympus to a world familiar to the audience.

Throughout the episode, however, the overriding concern is with the stunning effects produced by literary allusion. Ap. constantly plays off one scene or aspect of a scene against its Homeric counterpart. Pioneering work on this feature of the *Argonautica* was done by Lennox in his paper of 1980; see pp. 68-73 of that for a summary. The present commentary will scrutinise even more closely from this angle one of the most enterprising and spectacular passages in Hellenistic poetry. Its author must surely have realised that he had a winner on his hands here. There is a second extended Olympian episode in the fourth book. It all seems very staid in comparison, but there are strong undercurrents of humour (for instance, the picture of Hera Ζυγίη taking on the role of marriage guidance counsellor can hardly fail to raise a smile; there is priceless irony in 816-7, from Hera of all people!), with Thetis on the receiving end of a long disquisition (783f.) on Hera's favourites Jason and the Argonauts, on the dangers facing them, and related matters. Thetis is asked to help out, and she jumps to it, confident (836) in her abilities – not a shred of hesitation here! But it is this initial foray into the world of intrigue, with the goddess playing beautifully on the quirks of her two interlocutors as she skilfully engineers the efficient execution of the Ἥρης βουλή, that must carry off first prize.

7b αἱ δ' ἐνόησαν ... See above on 6, ἀνωίστως. Divine 'omniscience' in Homer operates selectively (West on *Od.* 4.379-81): these goddesses are on full alert (cf. Athena in ii.537f., Hera, with helper, iv.753f.), so they see what is going on. "The 'noticing' device is used for a change of scene or action" Kirk on *Il.* 5.711 (there there is a switch from earth to Olympus: ἐνόησε ... Ἥρη then 713 αὐτίκ' Ἀθηναίην ... προσηύδα, 714 Διὸς τέκος, 719 ὣς ἔφατ'; cf. 21.418f.). Regularly in the *Iliad* of course for focusing on individuals in difficulty or threatened on the field of battle (Kirk on 5.311-2): our Argonauts however are tucked away, and open combat is not in question at this moment, whatever Hera is to hint to the contrary (infr. 59).

8 ... Ἥρη Ἀθηναίη τε Cf. *Studies* 96 n.2. It is no coincidence that Hera is given priority, either here or in 91 infr.: she is pulling the strings (cf. Faerber 82). Ctr. *Il.* 4.20 (αἱ δ' -αν) al. Ἀθηναίη τε καὶ Ἥρη/, recycled by Antip. Sid. *HE* 474, D.P. 818. Ἀθηναίη τε at this point in the verse only *Il.* 7.58 – another 'watching' scene.

Hera and Athena are soon to be joined by Cypris and Eros. See G. Beckel, *Götterbeistand in der Bildüberlieferung griechischer Heldensagen* (Waldsassen/Bayern 1961), 77-9, 143-4; VDB 2.6f., 11f.; Braswell, ed. Pind. *P.* 4, pp. 6f. (extensive bibliography); *LIMC* 5.1.637. We know something of the part played by the three goddesses in earlier literary versions, but nothing of much substance: (1) Hera: protects Jason (*Od.* 12.72) and the Argonauts (Pind. *P.* 4.184f.), uses Medea to punish Pelias (Pherec. *FGH* 3 *fr.* 105); 'Thessalian' Hera's role in the saga: Dräger 136f. (2) Athena: associated with construction of Argo (Aesch., ?*Argo ffr.* 20-1 and often thereafter: VDB 1.74 n.4, id. 244, on i.112; infr. 340n.). (3) Cypris: took a hand (but probably not on the basis of any sort of developed Olympian scene) in the love-life of Aeetes in the *Naupactia* (see Matthews 198f., and also Braswell on Pind. *P.* 4.213-23, p. 296), *EGF fr.* 7[A] = schol. Ap. iv.86 (perhaps even used directly by Ap.: iv.11 after the ordeal φόβον ἔμ-βαλεν Ἥρη/: ctr. πόθον ἔμβαλε .. Ἀφροδίτη/ *EGF fr.* 7[A] 1?; iv.1473 cf. *fr.* 7[A] 3-4??), where the entire story is said to have been echoed by Herodorus, *FGH* 31*fr.* 53 (the doubts of Klein 22 are unwarranted); and fleetingly though vividly (see in general Buccholz 79f., Segal 62-3) in the Jason/Medea relationship, Pind. *P.* 4.213f. (πότνια ... βελέων): on this common pattern of intervention see the lit. cited by Brown, *Mnemosyne* 44 (1991), 333. Then Eur. *Med.* 526f., Jason to Medea (cf. Buccholz 85 n.3): 'I consider Cypris a saviouress.' — Id., 530f., 'Eros compelled you τόξοις ἀφύκτοις to save me,' provides the only pre-Apollonian literary evidence for the participation of Eros – from the lips of a point-scorer, not a story-teller. In Ap. Hera suggests that Eros (to his mother's deep dismay – the child evidently wears the trousers in this house) act as a go-between – something any respectable love-story cannot really do without (cf. Beye 1982.74, and also Segal 53 n.4)! Here, perhaps for the first time in the history of Greek poetry, is a sustained picture of two love-gods who really can be meaningfully differentiated (cf. note on 91f.), and who do not merely cause problems for others but are at loggerheads themselves.

8-9 Διός .... κιοῦσαι Abundant *Homerica* etc. are itemised in *Echoes* on 8-9 [correct *Il.* 18.524 to 5.524] and 9. One or two will be discussed below (ἀπόνοσφι ... in 9: 32n.).

Διός .. αὐτοῖο ... Conversely iii.920-1 αὐτοῖο Διός ... ἄλλων/ἀθανάτων ... — Call. *Hec. fr.* 70.10-11 (Campbell 1982.15) ... τε Διὸς δυοκαίδεκά τ' ἄλλων/ἀθανάτων is pretty close: note in the same fragment 8 ~ ii.384; 12 ~ i.177; 13 ~ iii.1162.

8-10 Cf *Studies* 7/96 n.3. The two goddesses detach themselves for their deliberations from 'Zeus himself and the rest of the immortal gods' on Olympus. In fact, Zeus is on the whole a pretty colourless figure in this poem (in Homer indeed he does not go out of his way to mix with the crowd: Kirk on *Il.* 5.753-4, Hainsworth on *Od.* 8.322-3), and none of the other Olympians shows any inclination to lay a finger on the Argonauts (Klein 247f., Herter *JAW* 278). As Feeney 64f. observes, it is Apollonian policy to have Hera and Zeus follow separate paths, but I do not believe that he is here positively 'highlighting his refusal to incorporate Zeus as a character' (66), or that he has 'domestic friction between Hera and Zeus' in mind (Zanker 1987.205), or that he is implying that the majestic Zeus would be averse to trickery (so VDB 2.12 n.2) so much as underlining the atmosphere of intrigue and deception (cf. 12n.) that characterises the Olympian episode as a whole (*Il.* 14.188f. Hera schemes 'without the knowledge of Zeus and the other gods' [*oppositio*: θαλαμόνδε not ἐκ θαλάμοιο; Athena not Aphrodite, who turns up later on; erotic deception, here oblique, there direct], 18.168 Hera acted 'without the knowledge of Zeus and the other gods' [I am not sure that her 'constant mistrust of her husband' is a factor here, as Edwards ad loc. alleges]); more immediately, we are looking ahead to the πεῖρα heralded in 10(n.): as schol. bT at *Il.* 14.189a remark, ἐν ἀπορρήτῳ τὰ τοιαῦτα πράττουσιν αἱ γυναῖκες. With regard to this aspect of the situation Vian's comment (ed. 1961 ad loc.) is entirely apt: 'Les déesses se mettent à l'abri des oreilles indiscrètes: détail familier'; cf. PF on 7-8 ad fin.

The retreat: see *Studies* 7/96 n.4. What sort of θάλαμος (for the word's range see *LfgrE* s.v., and cf. on 9 below)? θαλαμόνδε κιοῦσαι recalls *Il.* 3.423 Helen εἰς .. θάλαμον κίε, where she was to have intercourse (447f.). So our θάλαμος is definitely a bedroom. Whose? Certainly not Athena's: this is not the kind of environment she likes (cf. 32n.; for θάλαμος specifically cf. an oracle *ap.* Merkelbach, *ZPE* 8 (1971), 94.12 ἡ μὲν γὰρ θαλάμοιο καὶ ἔστ' ἀμύητος Ἔρωτος). It is Hera's bedroom (de Mirmont does not *quite* get there), a tightly-locked apartment which no intruder could penetrate, a perfect setting for some crafty scheming (*Il.* 14.166f., cf. Janko on 166-9 and 330-40). In ibid. 188f. Hera comes out of her bedroom (see above) to plot 'seduction'; here she gets Athena into her bedroom,and to set the ball rolling goes to work on her (see on πείραζε in 10!).

Schol. T at *Il.* 14.164*c* took things much more seriously: καλῶς δὲ ἐν τῇ ἀπάτῃ τῇ ἐρωτικῇ νῦν ἐκτοπίζει τῆς Ἥρας τὴν Ἀθηνᾶν, οὐ κατ' Ἀπολλώνιον, ὃς περὶ Μηδείας αὐτὴν εἰσάγει <συ>σκεπτομένην τῇ Ἀθηνᾷ cf. Eust. 975.43 (Wendel 1932.62).

9 ἀπονόσφι in connexion with the formulation of βουλαί: like νόσφιν in *Il.* 2.346-7; 10.415-6. — The intimate, clandestine atmosphere surrounding the preliminaries to the Argonauts' emergence from their place of hiding is sustained in 43f., Cypris on her own, 114f. Eros found by his mother ἀπάνευθεν in a secluded spot, not alone, but soon to lose touch with his companion, 167f. the Argonauts ἀπάνευθεν κτλ. Cf. Hurst 81.

θαλαμόνδε κιοῦσαι Contrast Antim. *fr. dub.* 151.6 ... θαλαμόνδε μο[λοῦσα/: the *Argonautica* has no example of trisyllabic participial forms of the simplex μολεῖν at verse-end: ctr. Hom., *Il.* 15.720, 24.492 v.l., *Od.* 3.44; 3[H]: Theoc. 2.96 [Theoc.] 20.38 is late], Euphor. *SH* 415 ii.19. — -δε κι-/: *Echoes* ad loc.

θαλαμόνδε θάλαμον δὲ L here, and similarly in other places: VDB I.LXXIII. Cf. schol. *Il.* 16.445*c*[1] with Erbse's note.

θαλαμόνδε 4 × in the *Odyssey*, always of a storeroom; 4 × in the *Argonautica*, always of a bedroom.

10 βούλευον 'they set about ...' The sentence extending from Διὸς δ' in verse 8 has gained momentum from the dactylic run in 9; βούλευον//, which brings it to an abrupt halt, throws the nature of the scene into sharp focus: a θεῶν βουλή (well, sort of) corresponding to the terrestrial ἀγορή of 167f. (ἀπάνευθεν, i.q. ἀπονόσφι). It is at this point, in fact, that *Hera's* βουλή (cf. iii.931, iv.241) embarks on its unstoppable course, as she steps in to influence events in a thoroughgoing way. The working-out of *Zeus'* βουλή on the other hand is presented more sporadically, in response to particular events pertaining either to the voyage or to the voyage's antecedents (βουλ- specifically: i.1315/1345/ii.154; iv.576f.). See in general Feeney 58f. (but one should not attach undue importance to the Διὸς νόος of [Hes.] *Theog.* 1002, for there the emphasis lies elsewhere: see West ad loc.).

πείραζε ... Ἥρη reminds one of the recurrent run ... πάρος (μεμαυῖαν: not applicable here!) Ἀθήνην/ *Il.* 4.73 (πειρᾶν 71), al.; compare also 2.156-7 and 8.426-7 Ἀθηναίην Ἥρη πρὸς μῦθον ἔειπεν/... Διὸς τέκος ..., and see on 25. Hera gets right down to business. The lead-in to direct speech is accordingly rapid, less than an entire verse (the norm in Homer); contrast *Il.* 4.5 ἐπειρᾶτο then a further verse containing a participial adjunct.

πείραζε has long caused problems: see *Studies* 97 n.14. The surface meaning is '(deviously) prodded her into saying something' (*Noten* 214f.), but given the 'bedroom-atmosphere' and the turn of the conversation (as manipulated by Hera) Ap. clearly had in mind a (verbal) *assault* on Athena's sexual innocence: cf., with *accus.*, πειρᾶν: LSJ s.v. A IV2, Renehan 1975.161, Neil on Ar. *Eq.* 517; πειρᾶσθαι: Pind. *P.* 2.34. There is certainly no need to appeal to 'koine' influence (so Boesch 33 and others), or to alter to Ἀθηναίης (West 1963.10). Cf. 16n. (on πεῖραν).

The πεῖρα of Hera which is being flagged at this early point will turn out to have wider implications, for it becomes progressively clearer that one of the primary sub-texts looted here is her escapade in *Il.* 14, a sparkling mini-comedy, but one which has repercussions for human beings who have no inkling of events outside the terrestrial sphere (cf. 7-166n., and on the ethos of *Il.* 14 also Golden, *HSCP* 93 (1990), 48f.; Pavlock cannot really mean what she says on p. 40).

Ἥρη Identification of speaker in the *immediate* run-up to direct speech. Iliadic practice is examined by de Jong 195f. *Nowhere* in *Arg.* does a named individual attract an epithet of any description (see conveniently for runs involving προσέειπε in Homer the table provided by Janko, *Mnemosyne* 34 (1981), 262) in such circumstances; iv.1260 ἰθυντὴρ Ἀγκαῖος, obviously a pertinent adjunct. A patronymic or equivalent is found occasionally instead (Αἰσονίδης, Αἴσονος υἱός, once elaborated ii.410; Ἀφαρήιος .. Ἴδας iii.556, Ἀμφιδάμας .. παῖς Ἀλεοῖο ii.1046 cf. *Od.* 1.399 al.). Otherwise: ὁ γεραιός Phineus ii.309, 419 (cf. de Jong 285 n.6), κούρη Medea iii.1025, iv.1011, δάμαρ Arete iv.1072, all of them context-related. Ap. is fonder than Hom. of the plain demonstrative ὁ etc.

10f. Clusters of speeches delivered in more or less close succession: the higher concentrations are naturally most frequent in the dramatically complexioned third book, viz. 2 ×/3 ×: the norm; 4 ×: iii.1122f., iii.10f.; 5 ×: i.656f.; 6 ×: iii.491f., 673f.; 7 ×: iii.51f., 302f., 974f.

10-11 The chiastic arrangement is striking: βουλεύον ~ βουλῆς, πείραζε ~ ἄρχεο, Ἀθηναίην ~ θύγατερ Διός, πάρος ~ προτέρη, Ἥρη ~ αὐτή (compare too 8 Ἥρη Ἀθηναίη matched by 10 Ἀθηναίην .. Ἥρη). Everything goes with machine-like precision, one might say.

11 Cf. *Studies* 8/Campbell 1990.481. Hera is in teasing mood, sharpening her wits for the imminent confrontation with Cypris. Ap. would have enunciated this line solemnly, but with a hint of gentle mockery. Hera is made to toy with the kind of language employed in appealing to a Muse for information (which is infallibly delivered). Although θύγατερ Διός is commonly applied to Athena (*Il.* 5.815 etc.; but the most famous Homeric example must be *Od.* 1.10 ~ Μοῦσα 1!), its conjunction with ἄρχεο brings to mind such runs as Alcm. *PMGF* 27.2-3 θύγατερ Διὸς ἄρχ᾽, *HyHom* 31.1 Διὸς τέκος ἄρχεο, Pind. *N.* 3.10 ἄρχε ... θύγατερ. Moreover, αὐτὴ νῦν heralds an address to a Muse in iv.1 (.... ἔννεπε .. Διὸς τέκος): cf. αὐταί in Anon. hex. *SH* 938.7 (pap. 3rd cent. AD), αὐτή in Anon. hex. *POxy* 3537r9 (pap. 3rd/4th cent.), αὐτὴ οὖν in the paraphrase of *Il.* 1.1 mentioned on 1 above (*Studies* 7), and, perhaps, Sappho *PLF* 124.

The joke of course is that it is not any old Muse-invocation still ringing in our ears, but an appeal to *Erato*: our Athena is an ignoramus in matters relating to her (32).

αὐτὴ νῦν See above; Hom. *Od.* 4.395, λόχον (cf. Ap.7) ibid. (note -λοχος in *Od.* 12.339 imitated later in this line).

προτέρη Hera has taken the initiative (πάρος 10), but she puts pressure on Athena right away. The latter does not meet the challenge: 24.

προτέρη ... ἄρχεο But *Il.* 4.67, 72 /ἄρξωσι πρότεροι, note the neighbouring Ἀθηναίην ... προσηύδα 69, πειρᾶν 71, and πάρος .. Ἀθήνην 73.

θύγατερ Διός will turn out to be making an extra special point: see on 32 (*Studies* 8).

ἄρχεο βουλῆς *Od.* 12.339 ἐξήρχετο βουλῆς/; in ?Tyrt. *IEG* 4.3 /ἄρχειν .. βουλῆς the meaning is different. — Surely a perfectly reasonable request of one who could match Zeus himself in βουλή (Hes. *Theog.* 896).

12 The veiled Muse-invocation (11n.) prompts questions (as often in Hellenistic poetry, following a time-honoured tradition: Braswell on Pind. *P.* 4.70-1(b)).

τί χρέος; 'What should be done?' They have an obligation (108,

131nn.): how is it to be met? τί χρέος; is an elevated expression from tragedy: Aesch. *Ag.* 85 ('What is the situation?' Note θύγατερ ...), cf. Fraenkel ad loc., Redard 76; Eur. *Hcld.* 95 ('What is their business?' Followed by ἦ [Blaydes: ἢ L] and a question), cf. Wilkins ad loc.

Given the pose struck in the previous line, perhaps Ap. is flirting with the Pindaric notion of the poet's 'obligation' (Braswell on Pind. *P.* 4.1(c)), here shunted unceremoniously in the direction of the 'Muse'!

ἦε δόλον ... Cf. *Od.* 10.380 /ἦ τινά .. δόλον .. ὀίεαι; (χρή ibid., ἐνόησεν 375, ... προσηύδα 377) and Aesch. *Cho.* 220. ἦε not ἠέ ἐρωτηματικός (129 etc.): La Roche *HTA* 265, Erbse on schol. *Il.* 16.12-3*b*. [Platt 1914.25 ventured ἠὲ ... τίνα (so E: cf. Vian 1962.36), misled by the false ἤ/ἦ of 14 init.]

δόλον .. μήσεαι Elsewhere apparently only [Opp.] *Cyn.* 2.28-9 δόλους .... ἐμήσατο; Hom. δόλον .. ἐπεμήδετο (*Od.* 4.437). μήσεαι 'are you going to ...?' She hasn't yet, as Hera well knows, though, so we are assured, she has made a start (18f.; E's μήδεαι, if it is a wilful alteration, presumably takes account of this point). Athena anyway is the one to ask (*Studies* 8): she prides herself after all on intelligence and cunning. Recall her boast in *Od.* 13.298-9, ἐγὼ δ' ἐν πᾶσι θεοῖσι/ μήτι τε κλέομαι καὶ κέρδεσιν, and see Richardson on *Il.* 22.214-47. The poet will go on to exploit further Athena's associations with ΜΗΤΙΣ: 30n. Hera however, in line with her Iliadic image (see notably book 14, and 19.96f.) proves to need no instruction in the art of deception; and she is following a familiar procedure: 'if your antagonist will not be persuaded, and his superior strength rules out force, then your only resort is cunning,' R. G. A. Buxton, *Persuasion in Greek Tragedy* (Cambridge 1982), 64.

Phineus' forecast of δολόεσσα ἀρωγή stemming specifically from the goddess Cypris (ii.423f.) was not pursued then (at his own insistence) and has not been pursued since. The Argonauts have had occasion to recall his advice (ii.617f., 646f., 1051, 1135), but not in terms of what would have been (and will later prove to be) a contentious issue; *pace* Zanker (1987.195f.), it is hardly possible to divine at this stage the overriding importance to be attached to the love theme in the account of the Fleece's acquisition (indeed the reader might well recall there events in the *Naupactia*, cf. Zanker 1979.69-70 and n. on 8 above: a perfunctory 'Cypris renders devious assistance'). δόλος resurfaces now, and Hera is at its source: her trickery (here and throughout the coming interviews) and that of Cypris (traditionally a weaver of wiles, she is not straight with visitors or son) and of Eros (a cheat, and a 'reincarnation' of the treacherous Pandarus) conspire to engage the services of δολόεσσα Medea (89); thereafter we are confronted with rampant deception and deceit on the terrestrial plane.

The distribution of the 25 examples of δόλος + cognates (Nyberg 109, 128 is inaccurate) is of some interest (see Campbell *Index*). In the first two books we have only (1)(a) i.52 a pair of Argonauts, experts in the field: their services are not called upon in the poem; (b) i.1295 Jason and certain others, falsely accused; (2) ii.423 above; (3) ii.948 erotic deception of Zeus by Sinope. In iii-iv (to the Circe-episode) δόλος abounds. In this scene: 12, 20; members of the Colchian royal family: Medea (girl and witch) iii.89, 687, 781, iv.59, (suggested by) Chalciope iii.720, Circe iv.687, Aeetes iii.578, iv.7, Apsyrtus iv.462 (cf. 438), Phrixids + iii.599; in iv Jason himself (who had deplored a stepmother's guile, iii.191) is dramatically caught up in duplicity, as a plan is devised to kill Apsyrtus: 404, 421, 456, 479 (so the false charges *are* fulfilled, in a different way: iii.373, 592, cf. iv.343).

See further Bulloch 1985.596 (esp. divine input); Zanker 1987.198- 9 (a skewed picture of an 'innocent' Medea; 'guile' needs closer definition); Hutchinson 117-20, 125-6; Nelis 163f.; Nyberg 108f., 126f.

12-3 ᾧ κεν ἑλόντες ... sounds, and is meant to sound, formal, imposing: note the context of iv.438-9 δόλον συμφράσσεται ᾧ (so Π[16]: ὥς, cf. *Noten* 493) κεν ἑλοῦσα/χρύσειον .. κῶας ... For ἑλεῖν cf. also iv.102 /κῶας ἑλόντες ἄγοιντο (*Il.* 3.72, 93 /κτήμαθ' ἑλὼν ... ἀγέσθω/), i.870-1, iv.366 -7, 1050 ~ [Orph.] *A*. 853; infr. 88n. On this type of relative clause cf. infr. 842 etc. (Wåhlin 52), and *GHD* 276-8; ᾧ κεν, but with subj., Hes. *WD* 57 (further lit. in Verdenius ad loc.).

13 χρύσεον Αἰήταο ... Note the order. Two important considerations (the Fleece is no ordinary one, cf. in general Wifstrand 1933.122f.; it belongs to Aeetes) need to be spelled out clearly. Athena is pretty clueless after all.

χρύσεον ... κῶας On the various permutations, and on Theoc. 13.16, see Fantuzzi 24 (but iv.341 is missing); later: [Orph.] *A*. 59, 765- 6, 834, 853. Cf. n. on δέρος χρύσειον in 88. It must of course go back a long way: see Dräger 33f.

Αἰήταο See above for the word-order; further notable examples of dislocation involving this genitive: ii.1207, iii.153, iv.684, 814.

μεθ' Ἑλλάδα .. ἄγοιντο The expression 'brought back the χρ. κῶας to Hellas' must have been a tag in Argonautic poetry, and Ap. must have worked hard to vary it. μεθ' Ἑλλάδα (iv.349, 369, both γαῖαν) is his exclusive property. On μετά = 'to' see Haggett 48f. or Oswald 185f. If Homer provides nothing that is strictly comparable (but *Il.* 6.511 = 15.268, and 20.33 come close), it seems unlikely that Ap. would have drawn a distinction between his μετὰ νῆα and the Iliadic μετὰ νῆας: μετά was commonly glossed with πρός or ἐπί, *LH* 1.1074.30f., Erbse on schol. *Il.* 1.423*b*; so schol. D often, e.g. at *Il.* 4.292, 5.165. (The variant at 23.230 has no evidential value.) — Ctr. *Il.* 1.478 -άγοντο μετά ...

For ... Ἑλλάδα κῶας ... cf. infr. 29 (ἀνάξειν), 339; ctr. ii.1192-3; iii.1060. As for the verbal element, see the patterns in iv.102; i.441 & ii.1193/1198; n. on ἀνήγαγε in 2; Dräger 34 n.87.

Ἑλλάδα 'Thessaly' is offered occasionally by our schol., influenced by Homeric usage (West on *Od.* 1.344)/exegesis (cf. Erbse on schol. *Il.* 2.684, 9.395*a*; Hope Simpson and Lazenby, *The Catalogue of Ships in Homer's Iliad* (Oxford 1970), 128f., Hainsworth on *Il.* 9.395). This is never essential, whereas in some places (notably i.1292, iii.391, 406, 1105, iv.204) 'Greece' is. Cf. Delage 22, *Noten* 562, VDB 3 on iv.[348*a*], 1000 (pp. 161-2/182). ii.209 Πανέλληνες (West on Hes. *WD* 527-8, Werner, *Philologus* 133 (1989), 172f.) = Argonauts: cf. 347n.

-οιντο See Wackernagel *SU* 89f. (but his survey is in need of an overhaul): 93 Hellenistic hexameters; 95-6 variants in Homer, cf *GH* 1.476-7 (with Kirk on *Il.* 1.343-4, Janko on 15.21-2, Edwards on 17.681 and 18.372-9), ἔλοιντο pap. at *Il.* 11.509*a*, West *PP* 104. Apollonian cases of -ντο -ατο in Gillies/Ardizzoni here.

14-5 Π¹⁹ provided a very welcome solution to the puzzles of 14 (οὐκ ἄρ: ἢ καὶ *codd.*) and 15 (ἤτοι μὲν: ἦ/ἢ/εἰ γὰρ ὁ μὲν or ἦ γὰρ ὅδ' *codd.*) The muddle in the manuscripts at 15 long drew attention away from the simple fact that ἢ καί in 14 cannot stand: 'Will you devise some stratagem to get the Fleece? Or could they persuade Aeetes?' puts a straight alternative which is not in fact suited to the answer Athena gives (18f.). Athena *agrees* that δόλος is necessary (20); but Hera, according to the manuscripts, has done nothing to refute the possibility of negotiation. Cf. Lennox 47 n.8. Evidently undeterred by such considerations, Rosenmayer misreads this passage totally (182f.).

For οὐκ ἄρ in 14 ('una variante deteriore' declares Del Corno 545) Lloyd-Jones (*ap.* Kingston 74) suggested οὐκ ἄν. But there is an exact parallel for this type of negative potential clause at *Od.* 14.122f. (cf. *GHD* 272-3, *GH* 2.217) οὔ τις .. ἀνὴρ .... πείσειε (!) γυναῖκα ... (preceded by 'Zeus and the other deathless gods' 119, cf. Ap. 8-9). Sense:

'They couldn't after all/when all is said and done ... Why, I can tell you ...' Cf. Campbell 1990.481-2.

ἦ καί is easily explained: somebody recalled Jason's speech about the relative merits of force and diplomacy at 179f. (Lennox loc.cit.; cf. too ii.1279-80). The corruptions in 15 admit of various explanations: a simple misreading (e.g. τοι with minute o can look very similar to abbreviated γάρ); or a desire to supply a specific subject: E's conjecture ἦ γὰρ ὅδ', founded on *Il.* 1.342 -οις· ἦ γὰρ ὅγ' [ὅγ' *cod.* F here: E is partial to ὅδε, see VDB *app. crit.* at iii.190, 721, 956; iv.546; ii.436, iii.723, iv.86; iii.775; i.709; iv.77; iii.48], though it cannot be seriously entertained (*pace* Giangrande 1976.276 and *JHS* 90 (1970), 214), does represent a pretty creditable attempt to sort out a sorry mess. The constant is γάρ, and perhaps the likeliest explanation lies in the realm of reinterpretation. Aeetes will not listen *because* he is ὑπερφίαλος provides a nice easy train of thought. One who is ὑπερφίαλος (cf. in part *Studies* 96 n.6) oversteps the bounds of μέτρον, 'due measure' in the field of human conduct: cf. the glosses in *LH* s.v., and schol. Ap. i.1333-5*a*, ii.54, iii.427-31*a*. So he will be impervious to normal civilised diplomacy. But the new coordination produces something much more Hera-like. The goddess, currently engaged in ensuring that the overbearing Pelias gets *his* just deserts, feigns alarm at the prospect of taking on his lookalike Aeetes with a comic echo of the nervy Argos' confession at ii.1202f. αἰνῶς ὀλοῇσιν ἀπηνείῃσιν [~ Hom. ὑπερφίαλος καὶ ἀπηνής] ἄρηρεν/Αἰήτης, τῷ καὶ περὶ δείδια [better περιδείδια] ναυτίλλεσθαι. Practice for going over the top with Cypris (56f.), no doubt. *But*: however formidable an adversary he may be, it is just not right to shrink from any πεῖρα — not even if it is an 'erotic' πεῖρα, so alien to Athena's nature.

τόνγ' With pronouns γε is often a 'dead' appendage, but here its full force can be felt: a contemptuous 'him of all people.' — τόνδ' S alone, cf. VDB *app. crit.* at i.15, 843, 1227, ii.457.

τόνγ' .../μειλιχίοις draws heavily on the resources of archaic epic: note *Il.* 24.771 τόνγ' (so *codd.*: cf. *Il.* 1.582; ii.54; τούσγ' in Eudoc. *Hom.* 47) ἐπέεσσι παραιφάμενος; Hes. *Theog.* 90, *HyDem* 336 μαλακοῖσι παραιφάμενοι (-ος, = [Orph.] *A.* 1093) ἐπέεσσιν/; *Il.* 9.112-3 μιν (the implacable Achilles: Lennox 47 n.8) ἀρεσσάμενοι πεπίθοιμεν (*GH* 2.296: -ωμεν Ar.; πεπίθοιεν sc. Achilles 9.181, cf. claus. 23.40) /... ἔπεσσι .. μειλιχίοισιν/.

Cf. [Orph.] *A.* 771 /μειλιχίοις ... παραιφάμενος ἐπέεσσιν/ viz. Jason/Aeetes, contextually similar.

παραιφάμενοι In iv.442 this verb is closely tied up with δόλος, here it is dissociated from it: ctr. *Od.* 16.286-7 = 19.5-6 (Stanford ad loc., F-G on 22.213, Miller, *GRBS* 23 (1982), 116f.) μαλακοῖς ἐπέεσσι/παρφάσθαι with Hes. *Theog.* 90, *HyDem* 336 cited in previous note. The milder sense 'say by way of encouragement, recommendation, consolation, mollification ...' is found in ii.287, 876, and also in παραιφασίῃσι infr. 554n. Cf. the range of glosses in *LH* s.v. παράφημι; schol. D's entries embrace παραινεῖν παραλογίζεσθαι παραμυθεῖσθαι παρειπεῖν πείθειν συμβουλεύειν. Not otherwise in 3^H.

15 μειλιχίοις Ancaeus' first alternative, μειλιχίη in approaching Aeetes (ii.1279), is swept aside, only to be revived by the human players (infr. 179f. /μειλιχίως 319, μειλιχίοισιν 385), who thus adopt 'an approach that Homeric society recognised as effective' (Hainsworth on *Il.* 9.113) – all to no avail.

The epithet, at the beginning of the verse and followed by a strong stop, unquestionably carries great emphasis: Hera spits it out. Cf. i.424 (μείλιχος is the operative word), infr. 898 (an urgent effort to 'sugar the pill' after the pronouncements of 891-5; reinforced by τερείνης in the same line), and in general Wifstrand 1933.113.

ἤτοι μέν See the fundamental discussion of Ruijgh, *Mnemosyne* 34 (1981), 276f. The same combination in ii.147, iii.523, 1221, iv.508, all followed up with an ἀλλά; the first two, as here, in animated direct speech (where ἤτοι surely carries *some* emphasis, see in general M. J. Apthorp, *The Manuscript Evidence for Interpolation in Homer* (Heidelberg 1980), 213). With a word interposed infr. 59, 171 and often.

ὑπερφίαλος Cf. above on 14-5, and also Forsmann, *MSS* 26 (1969), 27f., West on *Od.* 1.134. Aeetes is the classic tyrant: overbearing, violent both in deed and in comportment (cf. the sequel iii.367f. etc. and the association in iv.1083 πατρὸς ὑπερφιάλοιο βαρὺν χόλον).

αἰνῶς Like 695 infr. partly literal (cf. ii.1202 cited on 14-5 above), partly metaphorical, = ὑπερφυῶς, *exceptionally, in the extreme*; like δεινῶς, predominantly an Ionic usage: Thesleff 184-5, Kirk on *Il.* 3.158; glosses of the type ἐκπληκτικῶς etc./λίαν πάνυ in *LfgrE* s.v. αἰνός, 320.74f. In narrative only infr. 695; otherwise (3 ×) in speech: so almost invariably in Homer (Richardson on *Il.* 24.15).

16 Cf. Argos 476 infr.

ἔμπης δ' οὔ- Cf. *Echoes* at iv.799.

πεῖραν Hera's πεῖρα (10) will very soon resolve itself into an approach to the love-goddess (25f.): for the sexually innocent Athena

COMMENTARY 17

then a πεῖρα of a decidedly unnerving complexion. It is significant that the first πεῖρα of the book has a pronounced erotic colouring. Many more follow: testing of Jason and the Argonauts on a physical level (399, 405, 407, cf. also 68) goes hand in hand with extensive verbal soundings (105 Cypris/Eros, 179, 185 Jason/Aeetes, 476, 539 bis Argos/mother, 722 Chalciope/Medea, 642, 693 Medea/Chalciope, 1147 Jason and Medea). The poet of the *Odyssey* too had worked recurrent 'tests' into his tangled tale: see Russo/Rutherford on 19.215.

ἀποτρωπᾶσθαι Cf. *Od.* 21.112 ἀποτρωπᾶσθε ~ 113 πειρησαίμην. Only here with accus., but cf. ἀποτροπᾶσθαι in Numen. *SH* 583.2; ἀποτρέπεσθαι is commonly so used, e.g. Eur. *IA* 335f. μήτ' ... ἀποτρέπου τἀληθές, 'turn your back on the truth.' A grandiloquent word, and nicely suited to Hera's martial addressee, as the simplex is associated in *Il.* with turning tail on the field of battle.

ἔοικεν *it is becoming*, an appeal to Athena's sense of propriety: cf. for instance Hera's use of οὐ γὰρ ἔοικεν in *Il.* 21.379, and see in general F-G on *Od.* 21.319. Aeetes may not know how to behave (ὑπερφίαλος 15), goddesses do (*Studies* 8/96 n.5)!

17 *Variatio/oppositio*: (1) *Il.* 21.423 /ὣς φάτ', Ἀθηναίη δὲ [cf. *Od.* 22.224] ... (note also 418 ἐνόησε ... Ἥρη, 419 Ἀθηναίην ... προσηύδα, 420 Διὸς τέκος), *Il.* 8.357 (run-up similar to above) /τὴν δ' .. προσέειπε ... Ἀθήνη/. (2) *Il.* 1.511, 21.478 /ὣς φάτο, τὴν δ' [iii.106, iv.749] οὔτι προσέφη ... (3) *Od.* 4.375 al. ὣς ἔφατ', αὐτὰρ ἐγώ μιν ἀμειβόμενος προσέειπον, 4.471 al. ὣς ἐφάμην, ὁ δέ μ' αὐτίκ' ἀμειβόμενος προσέειπεν (~ ii.419 ὣς φάτο· τὸν δ' ὁ γεραιὸς ἀμειβόμενος προσέειπεν).

Batrach. 173 Ἀθηναίην προσέειπεν/ ~ 177 ὣς ἄρ' ἔφη Κρονίδης· τὸν δὲ προσέειπεν Ἀθήνη.

ὣς φάτο· τὴν δέ = iv.833. /ὣς φάτο 25 × in *Arg.*; nowhere else in 3^H.

παράσσον An instant response; if we expect an instant solution, we are soon disappointed.

On this adverb see Campbell 1978.123. It is an epicised παρεγγύς (cf. LSJ s.v., and παρασχεδόν, 440n.), peculiar to Ap.; always temporal in sense: i.383, ii.961, iii.125, 969 (see n.). — παρ-: *GG* 2.492-3. ἆσσον i.q. ἐγγύς: cf. most obviously in the poem i.702 (*Noten* 97-8; unconvincingly Henrichs, *ZPE* 6 (1970), 76-7), and see infr. 253n.; lexicographical material in Henrichs (1971) 145-6 and 233.

On the occasional division παρ' ἆσσον in the paradosis consult VDB i.LXXVI; παρ' ἆσσον Π19 here: cf. Kingston 75, West on Hes. *Theog.* 748, Naber 3.

Interpreters of the text may well have disagreed about the meaning early on. Schol. P at ii.955-61d takes ἆσσον (allocating παρ' to the following verb) locally; schol. iii.17 offers παραχρῆμα, εὐθέως, but gives as an alternative "supply 'sitting'" (from *Il.* 4.21??).

προσέειπε προσέειπ- figures in 23 of the 143 speech-introductions in the poem (μετέειπ- accounts for a further 4, the uncompounded verb, sometimes in association with μετά, for a further 20); there is much variation in the patterning, which would repay close investigation. (Riggsby, *TAPA* 122 (1992), 99f. offers bare tables, practically no statistics, and very little helpful discussion.)

18 Medea's πεῖρα (infr. 693) provokes a similarly worded claim in 697, with pointed 'role-reversal,' see n. ad loc.

καὶ δ'... (*Studies* 8) The exclamation 'And me myself too [cf. *GP* 199f.] ... you ask' amounts to 'Fancy that! *I* was myself ... and you ...' Athena is stuck, and plays for time.

μετὰ φρεσὶν ὁρμαίνουσαν Cf. *Il.* 18.419 al. (ii.950, iii.629, iv.56) μετὰ φρεσίν, *Od.* 4.843 ἐνὶ φρεσὶν ὁρμαίνοντες/. In early epic ὁρμαίνειν is accompanied by κατὰ φρένα, φρεσίν (so too [Apolin.] 139.9), ἐνὶ φρεσίν (cf. Opp. *Hal.* 4.360); later ὑπὸ φρεσίν Q.S. 9.238.

ὁρμαίνειν, which has much in common with the rarer πορφύρειν (23n.), denotes an intense, brooding, anxious mulling over of something which one finds problematic or perturbing: cf. in this poem iii.452, 697, iv.3, 724. See in general Voigt 13f.

19 Ἥρη .. ἐξείρεαι *Il.* 5.755-6 Ἥρη/... ἐξείρετο.

ἀπηλεγέως In archaic epic (Hainsworth on *Il.* 9.309) with ἀποειπεῖν (*Il.* loc.cit., *Od.* 1.373) and ἀγορεύειν (*HyHerm* 362), but of far wider application in Ap.: rich documentation, including lexicographical data, in Livrea on iv.689. It is otherwise extremely rare: Greg. Naz. 610.408 (ἀγορεύειν), 776.134 (πυρὶ θάψομαι); Cougny 4.48.12 (εἰπεῖν). — Athena uses strong language (on the adverb's Homeric resonances see Griffin, *JHS* 106 (1986), 52). Here (*Studies* 8-9) both 'straight out/ point blank' and 'unfeelingly' (cf. schol. here, ἀποτόμως, 'brusquely'): she means 'you come right out and ask'; but also, as we would say, 'you are cruel to come up with this!'

19-20 ἀλλά τοι ... A reminiscence of *Od.* 18.230, spoken by Τηλέμαχος πεπνυμένος to his mother: ἀλλά τοι οὐ δύναμαι πεπνυμένα πάντα νοῆσαι (*Studies* 9). Lennox (48) points to the similar phrasing in *Il.* 8.35-6 ἀλλ' ἤτοι then βουλὴν ... ἥ τις ὀνήσει: that a *confident* statement of intent from the ever-resourceful Athena of the earlier poem. See below.

οὔπω ... Cf. *Studies* 9. 'I do not think I have (I am aware that I have not) yet [she will eventually, of course!] devised this (particular) ruse (specified by you: KG 1.646).' A less charitable appraisal of Athena's potential will admit an alternative rendering of νοέω, 'have the wit *or* be resourceful enough' to (as e.g. *Il.* 5.665, *Od.* 11.62).

20 φράσσασθαι νοέω Ctr. *Od.* 5.188 νοέω καὶ φράσσομαι.

φράσσασθαι ... δόλον First here: Campbell on Q.S. 12.70.

20-1 ὅστις ὀνήσει/θυμὸν ... Cf. *Studies* 9/96 n.7: 'whatever it is that is going to help the Argonauts.' This, rather than 'be of service to the Argonauts' (cf. e.g. Gillies here) or 'further their purpose/gladden their hearts' (cf. Hoelzlin; 'raise their spirits' Rosenmayer 182) is probably all that this high-sounding expression means: schol. D on *Il.* 1.395 (cf. Henrichs 236-7): ὤνησας κραδίην Διός: ὠφέλησας τὸν Δία, περιφραστικῶς. Cf. further θυμόν in *Od.* 14.438 with Hoekstra's note, and for a related usage FJW on Aesch. *Suppl.* 515, p. 401.

For the diction cf. on the one hand *Il.* 7.173 ὃν θυμὸν ὀνήσεται (with Cheyns, *AC* 50 (1981), 146); and on the other *Il.* 8.36, 467 /βουλὴν ... ἥ τις ὀνήσει/ (the pause at line-end is not reflected here in Ap., see below on 26-8): the former line is from Athena, the latter from Hera; both occur in problematic surroundings (Kirk on 28-40 & 466-8), but there is no knowing whether Ap.'s *Athena* serves as a vehicle for implicit rejection of *Hera*'s pronouncement.

21 θυμὸν ἀριστήων Like /θυμὸν μνηστήρων *Od.* 18.161, a unique configuration in the Homeric poems.

ἀριστήων 7n. On the spelling ἀριστείων (Π[19]) see 853n.

πολέας ... bears a similarity to Call. *h.* 3.42 πολέας δ' ἐπελέξατο νύμφας/ [cf. *Il.* 3.126]. This particular feminine, normalised by E, not before the Hellenistic period (cf. in general Rzach 524-5, *GH* 1.252f., Kastner 17). πολέας: Nic. *fr.* 70.12 (Schneider ad loc., *Nicandrea* p. 83, citing Meineke, *An. Alex.* 208-9); πολέες: Call. *h.* 4.28 and *fr.* 80.22 (Pfeiffer, *Addenda* II.113). Cf. πολέων Call. *Hec. fr.* 69.7; ? iv.333; Anon. *APl* 35.1 (it is hard to see why πολέων in Bacch.5.100 must be so taken: so Jebb ad loc., *GG* 1.584). — 'Par goût du dactyle' Vian ed. 1961 ad loc. (a different view is taken by MacLennan on Call. *h.* 1.22, Mineur on id. 4.28).

... ἐπεδοίασα ... The assurance 'but I have (it isn't as if I haven't) wavered/dithered over *numerous* plans' ['balanced' Seaton, similarly some others, is too weak] harks back amusingly to the βουλή trumpeted in 11, which never gets off the ground as far as πολύβουλος Athena (Hoelzlin) is concerned. She has had no shortage of ideas (what ideas?): she just cannot put her finger on the right one.

The compound – cf. (LSJ s.) ἐπιδιστάζω – here only: see on 818-9 βουλάς/.. δοιάζεσκεν.

22-4 (*Studies* 9) invite comparison with the descriptive interlude in the Olympian scene of *Il.* 4, 20-4 (= 8.457-61). Our goddesses too are sitting down (cf. 36), but they contemplate in real earnest, with eyes fixed on the ground in an attitude of deep thought (see 22n.). Homer's Athena stays quiet because she is furious; our Athena, because she is outclassed.

22 ἦ καὶ ἐπ' *Il.* 1.219 and often. /ἦ thus 27 × in *Arg.* (Levet in *Mélanges* ... *J. Taillardat* (Paris 1988), 155f. makes the point that in Homer, Ap. and elsewhere this mode of speech-closure is normally associated with emphatic or solemn utterances). A breakdown (Homer etc.: *LfgrE* s.v. ἦ III; Hainsworth on *Il.* 9.620-3, F-G on *Od.* 22.8): (a) followed by same subject ἦ καί 14 × (including iv.1601 corr., see VDB 3.202), ἦ ῥα καί 5 ×, ἦ ῥ' ἄμα καί 1 ×; (b) by a change of subject ἦ καί iii.22, 36, iv.1461, ἦ ῥα καί i.1344, and with participial/adverbial adjunct then δέ, i.348, ii.19, iii.947. Close scrutiny will reveal a number of subtle manipulations of archaic models.

3[H]: (a) ἦ καί Call. *h.* 4.153, 228, ἦ ῥ' ... καί Theoc. 22.75; (b) ἦ ῥα καί [Theoc.] 25.84, ἦ ῥα + participle + οἱ δ' Theoc. 24.51.

ἐπ' οὔδεος .. ποδῶν πάρος ὄμματ' ἔπηξαν Similar in expression are: in Ap., infr. 422f. (the stunned Jason) ὣς ἄρ' ἔφη· ὁ δὲ σῖγα ποδῶν πάρος ὄμματα πήξας/ἧστ' then /βουλὴν ..., 1063 (Medea weeping, and unable to look Jason in the face [cf. 1066-8]) ὣς ἄρ' ἔφη, καὶ σῖγα ποδῶν πάρος ὄσσε βαλοῦσα, 1022 (M. and Jason, αἰδόμενοι) κατ' οὔδεος ὄμματ' ἔρειδον/, i.784 (Jason single-mindedly refusing to be distracted by the admiring womenfolk of Lemnos; cf. Herter *JAW* 347, Levin 74, and also Beye 1982.27, 90; simple coyness is surely not in question here!) ὁ δ' ἐπὶ χθονὸς ὄμματ' ἐρείσας/; in others, *Il.* 3.217 (πολύμητις Odysseus [μητιόωσα infr. 24, cf. Lennox 48; Zanker's suggestion, 1987.226 n.174, sounds far-fetched to me]: as if coy, but in reality concentrating his thoughts for the explosive oratorical display) κατὰ χθονὸς ὄμματα πήξας/, Theoc. 2.112-3 (the guilty Delphis, playing the part of the coy erastes) ἐπὶ χθονὸς ὄμματα πάξας [better probably πήξας here: Darms, *Glotta* 59 (1981), 173f., Ruijgh, *Mnemosyne* 37 (1984), 83] /ἔζετ' ..., Q.S. 5.328 (the stunned and heartbroken Ajax) ἐπὶ χθόνα δ' ὄμματα πήξας/. More florid turns of phrase in Kost's note on Musae. 160, where our attitude of deep thought, together with other attitudes associated with the lowering of the eyes, is lavishly illustrated. See further Grajew 49f., Muecke, *BICS* 31 (1984), 105f., and 422, 1008, 1022, 1063nn.; comparable gestures in Latin: Brown, *CQ* n.s. 33 (1983), 261, 262 n.49.

ἐπ' οὔδεος is extremely rare: Leon. Tar. *HE* 2084 (καὶ ...), Greg. Naz. 769.47, Nonn. *D*.3.229.

ποδῶν πάρος recurs in 422 and 1063, cited above; already in Eur. *Andr.* 1134. — πάρος + gen.: Hom., *Il.* 8.254; see LSJ s.v. B (tragedy). Elsewhere in *Arg.* only ii.101; 3ᴴ: Theoc. 24.58 πάρος .. ποδοῖιν/.

ὄμματ' ἔπηξαν Similar clausulae above: add *Or. Sib.* 7.162 ~ [Apolin.] 118.11.

23 ἄνδιχα πορφύρουσαι Ctr. διάνδιχα .... πορφύροντα in i.934-5 (with Fränkel 1925.490 and *Noten* 123). — διστάζειν occurs (uniquely) as a gloss on πορφύρειν in a papyrus fragment of Ap. Soph., ed. Renner, *HSCP* 83 (1979), 326, 330, but the interpretation of ἄνδιχα as 'in two minds' (Fränkel, *Noten* 330; cf. ἀνδιχάζειν, διάνδιχα [esp. Q.S. 3.94], διχθαδίην infr. 397, etc.) is plainly unsuitable here: VDB 2.111. The sense is lit. '(split) in(to) two (different bodies),' i.e. each separately/independently [cf. more explicitly iv.1291 after Emped. DK31 B20.5] following her own train of thought. The adverb no doubt points a contrast with *Il.* 4.21 (cf. above on 22-4, and see Kirk ad loc.). Our goddesses do not go into a 'huddle,' each is very much on her own; the concerted action (25) will be Hera's bright idea.

πορφύρουσαι The most informative perhaps of the many discussions of the literal (n.b. *Il.* 14.16f. ~ 20f.: Richardson on 21.551) and metaphorical uses of this verb are: Merkel *Proleg*. 185, Jebb on Soph. *Ant.* 20, Fränkel 1925.490, Viellefond, *REG* 51 (1938), 403f., Chantraine *DE* s.v. Of the two broad ancient explanations of the Homeric πολλὰ δέ οἱ (μοι) κραδίη πόρφυρε μένοντι (κιόντι) (*Il.* 21.551; *Od.* 4.427 = 572 = 10.309), ἐκινεῖτο ἐτινάσσετο, and κατὰ βάθος ἐμερίμνα (cf. *LH* s.v., Renner cited above, pp. 328, 330-1; schol. D on *Il.* 21.551, Erbse ad loc. ~ schol. Ap. i.461; par. ii.541-8*a*; iii.23), Ap. favours the latter while taking some account of the former: to engage in deep, brooding, agitated, troubled contemplation, a usage which reappears from time to time in later verse (usually with personal subject):

(1) + accus. rei i.461, iii.397 (θυμός): cf. Q.S. 1.369 corr., 706

(πολλά), 2.85, 4.77, 9.246 (πολλά), [Orph.] *fr.* 135.6 (id.); impersonal subj.: Greg. Naz. 441.32 πολλὰ δέ οἱ κραδίη ...

(2) Absol. ii.546, iii.23, 456.

(3) + dependent clause: iii.1161, 1406: cf. Q.S. 5.355f. (ἢ ὅγε .... ἢ cf. iii.397f. above); impersonal subj.: id. 6.32f. and 13.24f. (κῆρ); 14.41f. (ἦτορ).

(4) + prep.: Anon. hexam. *ap.* Suda σ2097 (Adesp. p. 217 in Crusius' ed. of Babrius). —

As Ardizzoni points out (ad loc. and on i.461), the Homeric πολλά leaves the way open for more than one interpretation: both were presumably current in Ap.'s own day.

ἐνὶ σφίσιν Cf. i.460-1 (Oswald 128).

23f. αὐτίκα ... *Studies* 13 n.1. The attitude of reflection adopted implies protracted deliberation (Natzel 146 interpolates: 'nach längerem Nachdenken ...'), but Hera in fact jumps in *at once* with a suggestion (no ὀψὲ δ' here!): see on 34-5. It is wrong to translate 'presently, in due course' or 'on a sudden' (for differing viewpoints about this word see Bühler, Mosch. *Eur.*, p. 202; Gow-Page on *HE* 1331f. and on *GPh* 1817; van Krevelen, *RhM* 117 (1974), 359f.).

Cf. *HyAp* 332-3 /αὐτίκ' ἤρατο ... Ἥρη/... καὶ φάτο μῦθον/, id. 353 /αὐτίκα ... Ἥρη/...

24 τοῖον *the following*, heralding direct speech, is first attested with certainty in the Hellenistic era: Campbell on Q.S. 12.7. Note in this book:

(1) μῦθον: 259, 974(n.) ~ *Batrach.* 77 /καὶ τοῖον φάτο μῦθον; 726(n.).

(2) ἔπος: 522(n.), 544; 1078(n.). Cf. Call. *h.* 4.265 ~ *Batrach.* 12 (sim. id. 92, 271); [Theoc.] 25.77.

(3) τοῖα: 51(n.); 687 ... δ' ἔειπε/τοῖα ~ Anon. epic. *CA* 2.54 εἶπε δὲ τοῖα/(τοῖον id. 66), *Batrach.*138 v.l. εἶπέ τε τοῖα/; 890(n.). Cf. Call. *h.* 4.108 ~ *h.* 6.97; Theoc. 7.91.

(4) (a) 303(n.) τοίοισι .. ἐπέεσσι/. (b) 55(n.) τοίοισιν ἀμειβομένη προσέειπεν/ (~ i.864) ~ Theoc. 24.72 corr. [1399n.] ἀνταμείβετο τοίοις/; 1025 τοίοισι .. προσπτύξατο.

See further Fantuzzi 69f.

μητιόωσα Cunningly chosen: *Athena*'s supply of μῆτις has run completely dry on this occasion (see on 34-5). μητιόωσα recurs in 210, where Hera assumes the role of the resourceful protectress of the *Odyssey*, cf. n. ad loc.

παροιτέρη ἔκφατο μῦθον But with a larger company παροίτατος ...

ii.1122, iv.494. [Hom. πρότερος (πρὸς) μῦθον (ἔειπε/); claus. φάτο μῦθον ~ infr. 259n.]

παροιτέρη In iv.982 used in a local sense, *fronting*, w. gen., as already in Arat. 306. The adjective (from a locatival *παροι [cf. πάροιθεν], like μυχοίτατος ~ Cypr. loc. μοχοῖ in Hesych., cf. *GG* 1.534, 549, F-G on *Od.* 21.146) is Homeric (*Il.* 23.459, 480, local), but rare: Greg. Naz. 403.18, 570.634, 624.587, Eudoc. *Cypr.* 2.325, Nonn. *D.* 37.391. Ap. has the adverbs παροίτερον (i.1146, iii.179: also Doroth. *Cat. Cod. Astr.* 6.89, p. 96, Greg. Naz. 540.238), παροιτέρω (ii.425 [see Campbell 1973.75], iii.686: exclusive to him); Euphor. -α (*CA* 34). Also παροίτατος Ap. alone, 5 ×.

... ἔκφατο μῦθον Cf. i.1255-6 αὐτίκα δ'../ἔκφατο, and for τοῖον ... ii.10 (same arrangement), 685. ἔκφατο μῦθον 9× in Ap. (claus. exc. ii.685), a unit shared only by Q.S. (Campbell on 12.24; μύθους/ [Apolin.] 143.19, 26, Paul. Sil. *Soph.* 247). Cf. also Fantuzzi 84 n.84.

25 δεῦρ' ἴομεν Aesch. *fr.* 47a, col. II7 (805) δεῦρ' ἐς παῖδας ἴωμεν ... Homer has /δεῦτ' ἴομεν (*Il.* 14.128) and ἴομεν μετὰ παῖδ' (*Od.* 23.83). Of the two, the former is the one to watch (*Studies* 96 n.9): the pattern of 25 reflects δεῦτ' ἴομεν πόλεμόνδε .. -άμενοι ... and prompts (or should prompt: Lawall and DeForrest, *CPh* 86 (1991), 342-3, misled I think by inadequate presentation, judge otherwise) a recollection of the wider context: Diomede there goes on to suggest that they get out of range of *missiles* in case they are wounded, contenting themselves with urging on (ὀτρύνοντες) others to battle. It is the very idea of 'missiles' that worries our Athena (32); she is not that taken either with the idea of 'urging on' (ὀτρύνομεν 26) Cypris, as she meekly (31) points out in 34-5. We should be beginning by now to latch onto another veiled allusion to the (for Athena) more straightforward world of the *Iliad* (cf. *Studies* 9-10). Meekness is not an attribute of Homer's Athena, who is only too ready to pitch in. There is an implied contrast here with this style of goddess. Much of the scene is based on *Il.* 7 init.: 17 ἐνόησε ... Ἀθήνη. She meets Apollo, who πρότερος προσέειπεν .... Διὸς θύγατερ, and makes a suggestion (23f.). Athena: τὰ .. φρονέουσα καὶ αὐτή/ἦλθον (34-5). Apollo: Ἕκτορος ὄρσωμεν κρατερὸν μένος (38). Then (43) ὣς ἔφατ', οὐδ' ἀπίθησε ... Ἀθήνη, (45) θεοῖσι ἐφήνδανε (βουλή) μητιόωσι. In an environment such as this Athena is a force to be reckoned with. But Hera here has different ideas.

ἴομεν But i.872 with initial longum, as *Il.* 2.440 al. (*GH* 1.457).

ἐπιπλόμεναι *approach, confront* a person as e.g. ἐπελθών in *Od.* 1.188, cf. infr. 127 of Cypris coming on the scene to tackle her son. In archaic epic ἐπιπέλομαι (like ἐπέρχομαι ἐπιγίγνομαι) denotes an oncoming period of time (cf. i.1080 al., Wifstrand 1929.79). Its scope had been widened (but note already *Od.* 13.60 and especially 15.408) by Sophocles, *OT* 1314 of the onset of Oedipus' blindness (νέφος ... ἐπιπλόμενον), and so i.465 of the onset of fear (τάρβος ἐπιπλόμενον, cf. VDB *app. crit.*). περιπλομένας infr. 1150 has a direct precedent in Homer (*Il.* 18.220, cf. ἀμφιπ- in *Od.* 1.352; used adventurously by Perses, *HE* 2864); περιέπλεο infr. 130 *circumvent, trick* (LSJ s.v. περιέρχομαι I3; cf. Merkel *Proleg.* 169) or rather *get the better of* (LSJ περιγίγνομαι I1). On ὑπερέπλετο in iv.1637, which has been variously interpreted, see VDB 3.204.

Such compounds were regularly glossed with -γίγνεσθαι/-ἔρχεσθαι: e.g. schol. D at *Il.* 18.220 (more in *LH* s. περιπέλομαι), schol. Ap. i.1080, iii.25*b*, (par.) 129-30, 1150. Cf. *Noten* 336, and below on 277. — Arat. 451 παρερχομένων ἐνιαυτῶν/ ~ Hom. περιπλομένων: see Ronconi 192.

δέ μιν ἄμφω Infr. 1296; Hom. claus. δέ οἱ ἄμφω *Il.* 16.348.

ἄμφω Hera spells it out clearly: she wants Athena there.

26 παιδὶ ἑῷ A rare hiatus (see on χεῖρα ἑήν in 591 for closer discussion) involving the recasting of the common genit. /παιδὸς ἑοῦ (so *GVI* 200.1, Rome 2nd/3rd cent., /μητρὶ ἐῇ ~ /μητρὸς ἐῆς); it recurs in Anon. *GDK* 64.147 and (2 ...) *Or. Sib.* 14.182. — Ctr. *Il.* 10.270 al. ᾧ παιδί.

Translations along the lines of 'suo bimbo' (Ardizzoni) are to be avoided (Marmorale, *GIF* 13 (1960), 82): we know nothing whatever yet about Eros.

εἰπεῖν ('have a word with') serves to highlight the importance Hera attaches to the *verbal* nature of the assistance she is after: see on 81-2. Cypris will not be very taken with the idea; but Athena too is quick to duck out of doing the talking (35) in such company. — *Il.* 17.654-5 /ὄτρυνον .../εἰπεῖν (οὐδ' ἀπίθησε 656).

ὀτρύνομεν Subjunctive, as *Il.* 9.165 ὀ. οἵ κε τάχιστα/, al. Cf. id. 10.55 ὀτρυνέω .. αἴ κ' ...

26-8 αἴ κε πίθηται ... *Il.* 11.791 εἴποις Ἀχιλῆι .. αἴ κε πίθηται/, cf. id. 1.419 (ἔπος) - 20. Hera knows that Eros, who is not a cooperative character, is going to have to be talked into doing what she wants, though she is not one to go on the off-chance that Eros will play: 'the αἴ κε locution does not ... necessarily imply any serious doubt about the outcome' Kirk on *Il.* 1.207, cf. id. on 2.72; infr. 113n.

Construction (Campbell 1971.403-4): 'be persuaded θέλξαι ὀιστεύσας'; like ii.1128f. αἴ κε πίθησθε/δοῦναι .... οἰκτείραντες (S: -τας cett.): Vian 1973.100 (Ardizzoni 1970.42-3 rightly championed -τες, but he misunderstood the passage). In Homer the expressions αἴ κε πίθηαι/ πίθηται (6 x) are invariably parenthetical/end-stopped. Ap. may have taken a different view of Il. 21.293f., 23.82f., but manipulations of this sort are common practice with him: cf. Campbell loc. cit., and on 20-1, 100-1. [No other explanation is feasible: Lennox 48, mistaking the whole tone of the projected interview, makes the extraordinary suggestion that Cypris is the subject of πίθηται; Livrea 1982.19 fares no better.]

Π19: I agree with Thomas (CR n.s. 20 (1970), 393) that the traces do not differ widely (if at all) from what the manuscripts offer: ωιπι itacism -ῶ(ι) εἰπεῖ-; then ικεπι rather than ινεπι or (Kingston 75) ηνειτ, in my opinion.

27 κούρην Αἰήταο Her designation in [Hes.] *Theog.* 992 /κούρην δ' Αἰήταο (a celebrity, not named: ctr. Solmsen ad loc., with Dräger 20 n.22), cf. iii.153 κούρη .. Αἰήταο/, iv.814-5 κούρης ... Αἰήταο/Μηδείης (solemn pronouncement from Hera) ~ [Orph.] *A.* 988-9 κούρη/Αἰήτεω Μήδεια, id. of Circe 1215 κούρη ὁμογνήτη μεγαλόφρονος Αἰήταο [cf. *Od.* 10.137]; the other way round in iv.731-2 βαρύφρονος Αἰήταο/κούρη, highlighting the grim father from whom Medea has fled.

πολυφάρμακον Cf. the πολλά/φάρμακα specified in 802-3 below. — So iv.1677 (Livrea ad loc.; cf. Belloni's discussion 'Medea ΠΟΛΥΦΑΡΜΑΚΟΣ,' *CCC* 2 (1981), 117-33, and also Parry 25, 27-8, 53) /Μηδείης .. πολυφαρμάκου ~ *Od.* 10.276 /Κίρκης .. π. — She is παμφάρμακος in Pind. *P.* 4.233. πολύθρονον Call. *Hec. fr.* 3 i.q. πολυφάρμακον i.e. ?Medea (θρόνα of Medea Lyc. 1313), cf. Hollis' note, and, more adventurously, in *ZPE* 95 (1993), 45f.

The Homeric association of the epithet with Circe (above) lends it a particular resonance in this context. Hera is again enjoying herself. Medea πολυφάρμακος is like Circe πολυφάρμακος, worker of θέλξις *par excellence* (cf. in this poem iv.667); Medea deals in θέλξις/θελκτήρια φάρμακα, yet is herself to be 'bewitched' (cf. lately Nyberg 8, 130), by Eros, a circumstance already hinted at in the proem (4), just as the τοξευτής Acontius was himself the victim of another's τόξον in the erotic sphere, Call. *fr.* 70, Pfeiffer ad loc., Rosen and Farrell, *TAPA* 116 (1986), 250 with n.34. This sort of talk does not do the inexpert Athena's nerves any good: she is unhappy about 'bewitchment' (cf. 33 ~ 28), as she is unhappy about '*his* missiles' (32 cf. 27).

Hoelzlin detected a streak of wry humour in the suggestion that such a high-powered pair should be prepared to resort to this type of aid to get them out of a pickle: 'ἦθος mulierum, quae rebus adversis recta contendere ad veneficas solent'!

27-8 οἷσι .... ὀιστεύσας 27 fin. harbours a sinister echo of *Il.* 1.42, σοῖσι [the wrathful and lethal Apollo's] βέλεσσιν/; cf., with reference to Eros, [Opp.] *Cyn.* 2.412 βελέεσσι .. σοῖσι, Musae. 149 (Kost ad loc.) ἑοῖς βελέεσσι, and see Barrett on Eur. *Hipp.* 530-4, along with id. *Med.* 530f. cited in 8n. above.

For ὀιστεύσας cf. Nonn. *D.* 1.261 βελέεσσιν ὀιστεύων, al.; Procl. *h.* 2.4 ὀιστεύουσι βελέμνοις/ scil. Ἔρωτες. Fränkel astonishingly labelled ὀιστεύσας 'neben οἷσι βέλεσσι θέλξαι ... leer und störend' (*Noten* 31): see the material assembled by Fehling (esp. p. 158); *Od.* 12.84 τόξῳ ὀιστεύσας, *Il.* 4.196 al. ὀιστεύειν + βάλλειν.

θέλξαι In association with Eros/eros: Kost on Musae.147; cf. on θέλγεις in 4 above. The verb possesses a particular bite here: see on πολυφάρμακον in 27.

ἐπ' Ἰήσονι Cf. the ὑπ' Ἰήσονι of archaic epic (*Il.* 7.469, [Hes.] *Theog.* 1000).

ἐπ' (θέλξαι) 'for' i.e. 'with love for' (cf. ... πόθῳ ... 86 below, and see Oswald 182). Hoelzlin compared Ar. *Eccl.* 966 Κύπρι, τί μ' ἐκμαίνεις ἐπὶ ταύτῃ; (Eros 967), whence (subject Eros) perhaps Ant. Lib. 34.1 (cf. Knox, *CPh* 78 (1983), 310 n.10). On related uses in erotic contexts see Page *S&A* 276, Gow on Theoc. 13.49; also Call. *fr.* 67.2, Ap. i.612, ?Ap. *CA* 12.6, Nonn. *D.* 42.23-4 Ἔρως ἐπὶ .. κούρῃ/δαίμονας ... βάλλεν ὀιστῷ/, al. (see *LexNonn* s.v. ἐπί, p. 549, 5a).

A reminiscence hereabouts maybe of Soph. *Trach.* 585 τὴν παῖδα .. θέλκτροισι .. ἐφ' Ἡρακλεῖ then 586 δοκῶ.

28 θέλξαι ὀιστεύσας ἐπ' Ἰήσονι Hera, in good Hellenistic fashion, varies her language when she instructs Cypris at 86. Cypris does likewise with Eros (142-3) – only, unbeknown to her, it's been said before.

28-9 τὸν δ' ἄν ὀίω ... Cf. ii.1166f. ὑπ' ἐννεσίῃσι δ' ὀίω/ἀθανάτων .../ἤ ῥα ... In early epic: *Od.* 22.159 τόν περ ὀίω/ [but strong stop]; *Il.* 5.894 σ' ὀίω κείνης [but this *of* Hera] τάδε πάσχειν ἐννεσίῃσιν/; *HyDem* 30 /τὴν δ' .. ἤγεν Διὸς ἐννεσίῃσι/.

ἄν With fut. infin. also ii.441-2 ἤ τ' ἄν ὀίω/γηθήσειν [basic model: *Il.* 5.350f.]. Literature on this construction in Verdenius on Pind. *O.* 1.110 (n.84). — In *Il.* 9.684 καὶ δ' ἄν τοῖς ἄλλοισιν ἔφη παραμυθήσασθαι (*GH* 2.311) there is a variant -σεσθαι.

ὀίω can cover anything from a strong impression or suspicion (Kirk on *Il*. 1.169-71, 552-9) to a firm belief/conviction: Hera has no real doubts on this score.

κείνης Emphatic third person pronoun, a usage apparently unfamiliar to Ap.'s translators. If *she* is brought in, success is assured.

ἐννεσίῃσιν For discussion of this word see *Noten* 283-4 (but the categories A and B are rather too rigorously opposed), Campbell on Q.S. 12.4, *LfgrE* s.v. ἐννεσίη. *Arg*.iii throws up 5 examples. Here 'with (specialist) prompting/directives from,' in the form of specific recommendations (cf. 1364); often of divine implantation of particular skills (cf. 478 Medea a practising witch schooled by Hecate), or of a heaven-inspired impulse to take a certain course of action (cf. 818, Medea changed course because Hera put it into her head to do so, 942 Jason will get a friendly reception from Medea because of 'input' from Cypris).

ἐς Ἑλλάδα κῶας ἀνάξειν 13n. A smug conclusion to the enunciation of a grand plan originally requested (indeed expected) from Athena: 29b echoes 13b, as μῆτις in 30 recalls μήσεαι in 12.

30 For the line as a whole cf. ii.1068 (and iii.912, iv.1380); also i.697-8 (*Echoes* ad loc.), 717 (id.).

ὣς ἄρ' ἔφη *Il*. 1.584 etc., 24 × in *Arg*.; 3[H]: Call. *h*. 4.99, [Mosch.] *Meg*. 56, Epic. adesp. *CA* 7.8 suppl.

πυκινὴ ... μῆτις A combination found in *HyDem* 414 and very commonly elsewhere: e.g. Pind. *P*. 4.58 (Medea's; from an epic *Arg*. perhaps), orac. *ap*. Hdt. 7.141.1 *et al*. (PW 95.2), Christod. 27. Cf. in general Detienne and Vernant 15.

συνεύαδε for συνήρεσε *met with her approval*; only here and [Phoc.] *Sent*. 191 -δον.

μῆτις Ἀθήνη (*Studies* 96 n.11) is a 'plant.' Ap. is toying with Hes. *Theog*. 886f. Μῆτιν/.... Ἀθήνην/τέξεσθαι .. ἔπειτα, but here ἔπειτ' .... πατὴρ τέκε (32) ... The echo vividly reminds us of Athena's intimate association with ΜΗΤΙΣ (cf. 12n. and Detienne and Vernant 179 *et circa*, L. Raphals, *Knowing Words* (Ithaca and London 1992), 271f., Janko on *Il*. 14.295-6), a quality she signally fails to exhibit here.

The clausula is like that of *Il*. 10.497, μῆτιν Ἀθήνης ('om. Zen. Aristoph., ath. Ar.' Allen ad loc.).

31 καί μιν ἔπειτ' Again in 78, also prefacing a speech; *Il*. 14.255 al. -τα.

ἐξαῦτις ἀμείβετο [Theoc.] 25.51 v.l.; *codd*. Hes. *Theog*. 654 /ὣς φάτο·

τὸν δ' ἐξαῦτις ἀμείβετο ... (read by Ap.? βουλάς 653 ~ μῆτις 30, ἀδάητα 655 ~ νήιδα 32). With ἐξαῦτις these two passages (along with iii.31, unless we are to interpolate a pause: 'this won her assent: and she *subsequently* <after bracing herself> came out with a<n actual> reply,' fingers crossed) infringe the Homeric practice (Lehrs 158) of having some sort of interlude before direct speech begins: *Il.* 1.223 and *Od.* 6 ×, and so Ap. ii.1159 (/ἐξαῦτις ... ἀμείψατο τοῖσδ' ἐπέεσσιν/ after *Od.* 16.193 al. and sim. ἐξαῦτις μιν ἔπεσσιν ἀμειβόμενος προσέειπεν), iii.1067.

The standard translation *denuo,* 'once again,' can of course stand here, though it is worth noting that schol. D at *Il.* 1.223 offers not only ἐκ δευτέρου but also εὐθέως, παραυτά: cf. παρᾶσσον 17, αὐτίκα 23??

ἀμείβετο μειλιχίοισιν A similar pattern in *HyHerm* 162 al. ἀ. κερδαλέοισι/; infr. 385(n.) ἀμείψατο μειλιχίοισιν/, cf. iv.1431 /μειλιχίοις ἐπέεσσιν ἀμειβομένη ([Hes.] *fr.* 280.25 ἀμ[ειβό]μενος .. μειλιχίοισι/). See also Fantuzzi 72, 83 n.83.

μειλιχίοισιν A delightful touch. Athena agrees to the plan, but definitely does not like one aspect of it. She adopts a meek, soothing tone, as she must with her notoriously irascible (χόλος Ἥρης and so on) interlocutor – who had given forth so sanctimoniously in 14-15! The description 'demi-refus poli' (VDB 1.206 n.2) does not quite do justice to the situation.

32-3 remind one of Anon. *HE* 3778-9 /οὐ γὰρ ... βολὰς (corr.) ἐδάημεν Ἔρωτος/... ἀλλὰ πόθων .., where Gow-Page adduce *Od.* 17.283 (cf. below on 32).

Fusillo (169), who contributes his fair share of improbable *prolepseis,* considers that our virginal Athena, and the rather backward Argonauts as well, are prefigured in ii.987f., the Amazons, 'populo di donne vergini e guerriere.'

32 Ἥρη ... The nervous Athena speaks earnestly and deferentially, while managing to blurt out what was for Hera a decidedly unpalatable chapter in the great god's reproductive career (see below on πατὴρ τέκε, ad fin.).

PF on 32-3 suggest that Athena's unwillingness to be associated directly with such a venture prefigures Jason's stance in 485f. This is true only in a very general way: there is no question of 'amore' in the latter instance; and the tone is very different.

νήιδα Homeric accus., *Il.* 7.198 (ἐμὲ νήιδα .... γενέσθαι), and so Bacch. *fr. dub.* 64.10, Opp. *Hal.* 1.760 (νήιδ' ἐόντα/: νῆιν? See below),

Q.S. 4.432, 5.506. Contrast infr. 130 νῆιν (ἐόντα/), as Bacch. 5.174, Call. *fr.* 178.33; on this form consult Rzach 504, Marxer 22, *GG* 1.464, 565.

The word has a special flavour (cf *Studies* 10, and infr. 130n.): 'νῆις of love/marriage' sim.: Bacch. 5.174, Call. *fr.* 75.49, Q.S. 4.432, 14.12, Nonn. *D.*, 10× see *LexNonn* s.v., with Vian on 2.108. Cf. *EtM* 604.11-2.

... πατὴρ τέκε ... Cf. *Studies* 10; 96 n.11. In *Od.* 16.118f. Telemachus outlines the male side of his lineage, and remarks /μοῦνον δ' αὐτ' Ὀδυσῆα πατὴρ τέκεν ... Athena has a different reason for specifying her πατήρ: not only is she a (or *the*) virgin, she does not even have a mother! (So Faerber 82 n.3.) Cf. πατὴρ τέκεν with a conceited point in Nonn. *D.* 9.218, and, e.g., *Od.* 13.324 (Odysseus to Athena: 'I beseech you by your *father* –'), *HyAphr* 8f. (dislikes ἔργα Ἀφροδίτης but likes ἔργον Ἄρηος and sim.), Aesch. *Eum.* 736f. (motherless; sides with males, πλὴν γάμου τυχεῖν), Call. *h.* 5.134-5 μάτηρ δ' οὔτις ἔτικτε θεάν, /ἀλλὰ Διὸς κορυφά (cf. below), Colluth. 180f. (motherless; ~ 185 φεύγεις φιλότητα).

The alert reader might have caught a whiff of the circumstances surrounding Athena's birth earlier on: iii.9 ἀπόνοσφι θεῶν .. κιοῦσαι echoes *HyAp* 331, Hera ἀπόνοσφι θεῶν κίε: because (id. 307f.) she took exception to the birth of Athena from Zeus' head, an event to which Ap. now smilingly alludes (see next n.).

... τοῖο βολάων *Od.* 17.283 ... ἀδάημων οὐδὲ βολάων/. Nicander no doubt had his eye on this line, and the next, when he penned /οἶδα .. μὴν ... τοῖο (scorpion's) βολάων/, *Ther.* 805 (Campbell 1982.15).

τοῖο (*Studies* 10): 'talk of the Devil, and he will appear'; but also, '*his* missiles,' as opposed to missiles of war. She emerged from Zeus' head fully armed (iv.1309f., Livrea ad loc., etc.).

On the technically interesting variants at the end of the line see Fränkel *Einleitung* 70-1, 81, 86.

33 The jittery πόθων ἀδίδακτος Ἀθήνη hurriedly moves on to the really worrying aspect of Hera's suggestion: 'nor am I acquainted with *any* object/thing [cf. Redard 69] that can generate *pothos* by bewitchment,' cf. θέλξαι πόθῳ infr. 86, 'bewitch with/by engendering *pothos*' in Medea. Recall the potent (and formidable) *range* of θελκτήρια (Athena is unschooled in the lot!) which adorn Aphrodite's magic love-charm in *Il.* 14 (215f.), and the contraption set up by the love-goddess for Jason's benefit in Pind. *P.* 4.214f. – and there was no shortage of other aids (cf. e.g. Faraone, *Phoenix* 44 (1990), 219f.)! We may well feel however that Ap. is exploiting the ambiguity of the genitive here (cf. the use of φάρμακον: Willink on Eur. *Or.* 1190), along the lines of 'any object [a φάρμακον most obviously, which θέλγει, cf. Hera in 27] that can charm *pothos* away <if I get hit>.' See Barrett on Eur. *Hipp.* 509-12 φίλτρα .. θελκτήρια ἔρωτος, with Parry 277; Braswell on Pind. *P.* 4.187(a). For the association of πόθος and θελκτ. cf. (86 infr. ~) Nonn. *D.* 16.133, and id. 16.236, 31.201; (Mooney, *Addenda* p. 455) Athen. 5.220f πόθων θέλγητρα.

θελκτ. + gen. again in the high-sounding (indeed tragic-sounding: after Soph??) θελκτ. φάρμακα ταύρων or βοῶν (iii.738, 766; iv.1080-1): perhaps Ap. left the reader to choose between a hazy 'exerting a spell over' (Aesch. *Suppl.* 447 corr.: 'exerting a soothing/healing influence on'; Greg. Naz. 906.303 'exerting charm over') and a more dynamic 'charming them away' (cf. Aesch. *Cho.* 670), i.e. i.q. *καταθελκτήρια (cf. in general KG 1.371), affording Jason an effective way of subduing them and removing the threat: cf. lately Giangrande 1973.24 (but there is no reason to label it a 'medical' metaphor), Belloni 68-9.

Some remarkable interpretations of this line are to be found in Gillies ad loc., Cataudella, *Misc. Rostagni* (1964), 356; Fränkel *Noten* 332 offers two, neither of them convincing.

θελκτήριον οἶδα recalls *Od.* 1.337 θελκτήρια οἶδας/ – an interesting echo, as Zenodotus read ᾔδεις or at any rate something quite different from what is offered by the paradosis (La Roche *HTA* 321; van der Valk, *Mnemosyne* 38 (1985), 378 n.7; West ad loc.).

πόθοιο (*Studies* 96 n.10). She avoids any mention of 'love' (Gillies p. 137 curiously states the opposite), though she comes close, as πόθος and ἔρως are often virtually indistinguishable (see *RE* 22.1179-80, H. Fliedner, *Amor und Cupido* (Meisenheim am Glan 1974), 48f.; cf. also Hardie, *LCM* 7 (1982), 50-1).

34 εἰ ... ἐφανδάνει Related runs in i.700, iii.485 (τοι αὐτῷ), 537 (αὐτοῖσιν ... ἦ τ' ἄν ...), iv.419, which should all be viewed against the background of *Il.* 9.42 /εἰ δέ τοι αὐτῷ θυμὸς ἐπέσσυται, *Od.* 16.387 /εἰ δ' ὑμῖν ὅδε μῦθος ἀφανδάνει, id. 13.16 al. ἐπιήνδανε μῦθος/.

μῦθος i.e. ὅδε μῦθος (cf. ἥδε/τόδε in i.700, iv.419), '<this> proposal' communicated by Hera (... μῦθον 24). The plain μῦθος, lit. 'spoken word,' 'speech,' amusingly paves the way for ... φαίης ἔπος in 35. (Del Corno 545 puts in a word for θυμός, Π¹⁹. Ap. would not be grateful for it. The confusion is common: see VDB, *app. crit.* at ii.478, 1219).

Hera is hardly going to change tack now. Athena accepts the

situation with resignation, and winds up the session with a formal expression of assent: 'you yourself' says it all.

34-5 ἦ τ' ἂν ... (*Studies* 10) 'I for my part [as my contribution] would certainly be prepared to accompany you [she is happy to keep out of it, until, finally, ἐφωμάρτησε 111] – but *you* in that event [κεν] could <if you don't mind> do the talking ...'

ἦ τ' ἂν ἔγωγε Iliadic clausula, *Il.* 19.205, again at iv.835. On the extensive use made of ἦ τε by Ap. see Ruijgh 1971.959-60.

ἑσποίμην Twice in Homer, *Od.* 19.579, 21.77, but accompanied by κεν not ἄν.

σὺ δέ κεν Cf. *Il.* 3.417, *Od.* 4.547; and not least Wellauer's certain correction in iv.381 (Fränkel *Einleitung* 115-6).

κεν φαίης On the optative 'pour donner ... un ordre poli' see *GH* 2.216, 221-2, KG 1.229-30. κεν seems very unusual (though here it certainly carries the heavy nuance 'in those circumstances,' 'in that eventuality'): normally plain optative, or negative + ἄν Hom.+, ἄν in positive clauses thereafter. Cf. (Wåhlin 23) Argos' tentative 'you may call me ...' in ii.1156.

φαίης ἔπος Cf. on 384.

ἀντιόωσα (*Studies* 97 n.12) Certainly 'when you make your request' (see on this sense of the verb Livrea's detailed note on iv.405, also *Noten* 577 n.263) and not 'when you confront her' (they are *both* going to do that: Athena is just not going to ask): cf. ἀντομένην in 77(n.), and, much later, Eudoc. *Cypr.* 1.223 ἀντιόων ... φάτο.

— Such then is Athena's contribution to the proceedings. Zanker (1987.205) asserts that both goddesses 'are presented as surprisingly bankrupt of ideas'; PF on 11-16 talk of Hera's uncertainty: similarly others. It is as plain as day though (cf. *Studies* 10) that Hera's reflectiveness is a pose. She has known all along what must be done, and she has been in firm control from beginning to end: πάρος 10/παροιτέρη 24, ctr. προτέρη in 11; μητιόωσα 24/μῆτις 30, ctr. μήσεαι in 12. It is all part of the Ἥρης βουλή (cf. 1on., and Feeney 63 on the general question of this goddess' foreknowledge). Athena, the resourceful, virginal, martial goddess, has been well and truly 'set up.' Hera has been playing with her, as she will soon be playing with Cypris. And the complication of a third speaking-part will not now arise.

36f. Cf. *Studies* 11, and Lennox 49f.

36-54 incorporate many elements of archaic 'Journey and Visit' routines, conveniently tabulated in Richardson, ed. *HyDem* p. 205; cf.

also Edwards, *TAPA* 105 (1975), 51f. We are reminded in particular of *Il.* 18.369f., Thetis' visit to Hephaestus' house. There are similarities, but also many points of contrast, notable amongst which are these:

(1) The requests of Thetis and Hera, both of pivotal importance for plot-development, are different, yet related: Thetis seeks divinely manufactured arms to enable her son to go into battle, Hera, fearful for the safety of her favourite, but also mindful that she has an old score to settle, aims to shield Jason from the perils of combat by asking that the god Eros discharge a missile against a girl: success for this hero will be assured by means of a weapon deployed on the battle-field of love (cf., in broader terms, Zanker 1987.226 n.176).

(2) Homer's Olympus may be associated with noisy wrangling, but not on this occasion. Hephaestus and Charis clearly live in close harmony, the husband working away in his forge (which appears to be the equivalent of the modern garage-workshop), the wife busying herself around the house. In Ap. there is no Hephaestus to be seen, while his Cypris cuts a pathetic, solitary, highly-strung figure, with a problem-child on her hands.

(3) Charis greets her visitor warmly (385f.): ctr. 51f.n.; and offers refreshments (387) and an ornate θρόνος (389-90): ctr. 47-50n.

(4) Hephaestus owes Thetis a favour (395f.), and will act accordingly (406f.). Cypris, who owes Hera and Athena nothing, goes out of her way to be objectionable and has to be manoeuvred into co-operating.

(5) The respective tales of woe (429f./56f.). Thetis offers a potted version of the story so far, whereas Hera, her egocentricity very much in evidence, does not bother. Thetis puts in a polite request, with talk of supplication (457f.), Hera mentions no such thing (ctr. the narrator in 77), but opts for the brutal approach (74-5).

(6) Hephaestus assents at once and gets on with the job; for Cypris life is not so simple.

36 ἦ, καὶ ἀναΐξασαι -σα in iv.842 (Thetis), the Homeric (*Il.* 24.440 v.l., 621) -ας in iv.1337. On the switch from sing. to plur. subject here see Ardizzoni. 'Spring to one's feet' from the sitting-position (explicit in *Il.* 24.597 ~ 621 [id. 440 s.v.l. is to be otherwise explained]; iv.782 ~ 842, 1332 ~1337) associated with βουλευταί. We may recall also that ἀΐσσειν is the *vox propria* for the spectacularly rapid darting or shooting movement of Homeric gods (Mineur on Call. *h.* 4.67; notable is *Il.* 4.73f.), who are in the habit of acting expeditiously whatever the circumstances (see e.g. Woodbury, *TAPA* 103 (1972), 566 = Woodbury

1991.237, S. West, *CQ* n.s. 34 (1984), 297): cf. in Ap. iii.286 (Eros) and especially ii.547 (Athena); there is a vivid adaptation of the notion in Emped. DK31 B134.4-5. Speed in fact is the order of the day (59, 109, 143-4, 156 etc.). The duo reach their destination by the end of the present verse; no leisurely sightseeing tour of the 'big' house, no accumulation of epithets such as we find in *Il.* 18.370-1 (37n.).

ἥ 22n.

ἐπὶ ... νέοντο This half-verse weaves its way around various Homeric components: *Il.* 5.213 al. μέγα δῶμα(/) (post-Homeric examples are not plentiful: Bissinger 134); 5.907-8 πρὸς δῶμα Διὸς μεγάλοιο νέοντο/"Ἥρη ... καὶ .. Ἀθήνη/; 14.335 al. πρὸς δῶμα νεοίμην (νέεσθαι)/.

ἐπὶ μέγα, with lengthened iota: *Od.* 19.58, Call. *h.* 3.55. Scribes often have problems with this sort of thing: even so, E's ἐπίπαρ is pretty startling.

37 Κύπριδος ... For a different relatival expansion after this genitive involving τε see i.803, *Echoes* ad loc. τε here: Ruijgh 1971.943.

ὅρρά ... δεῖμεν Cf. iv.251. On the variation ὅρρα/ὅ ῥα (etc) in the MSS see VDB i.lxxv (add to the list: *app. crit.* iii.37). We should adopt, with Rzach 483 (see his discussion: but on schol. here consult Wendell 1932.35), the original (Schulze *QE* 375 n.3, *GG* 1.407; *contra*: Janko on *Il.* 16.228-30) and pre-Aristarchean (Didymus at *Il.* 16.228; Merkel *Proleg.* 104f., La Roche *HTA* 389f.) form with gemination (cf. *GVI* 1964.3 = *CEG* (2) 693.3, Hansen ad loc., Rhodes 4th/3rd cent.); other poets: Rzach, *Wiener SB* 95 (1879), 694-756. Cf. Campbell 1982.15, also Chantraine 1962.314.

ὅρρα here means 'which as was to be expected,' 'as was expected of him'; iv.251 'the sanctuary which they built as a natural part/result' of this act of worship. See next note.

... δεῖμεν ... From *Il.*: 18.369-71 /'Ἡφαίστου δ' ἵκανε δόμον Θέτις .... [descriptive detail: 36n.] ὅν ῥ' αὐτὸς ποιήσατο κυλλοποδίων/ [for wife and self: cf. schol. D at *Il.* 2.701, ἔθος .. ἦν τοῖς γήμασι θάλαμον οἰκοδομεῖσθαι, cited by Hoelzlin here], 1.606-8 (λέχος 609) ἔβαν οἶκόνδε ../ἧχι ἑκάστῳ δῶμα ἀμφιγυήεις/"Ἥφαιστος ποίησεν, 14.239-40 "Ἥφαιστος δέ κ' .. παῖς ἀμφιγυήεις/τεύξει' ....; οἱ: cf. *Il.* 14.166, al., [Hes.] *fr.* 209.3.

For δῶμα + δέμειν compare perhaps Call. *fr.* 43.81, as read by Massimilla, *ZPE* 81 (1990), 19.

ΠΟΣΙς ἀμφιγυήεις Schol. D at *Il.* 1.607 ὁ ἀμφοτέροις τοῖς γυίοις, ὅ ἐστι τοῖς ΠΟΣΙ, χωλός; i.204 a relative of Hephaestus (see Platt 1914.5, van Krevelen 1953.52) πόδε [*cod.* E] σιφλός, cf. e.g. schol. *Od.* 8.300

ἀμφοτέρους εἶχε τοὺς πόδας χωλούς (more of the like in Henrichs 252; schol. D on κυλλοποδίων in *Il.* 18.371 cited above: χωλός; see further Chrétien on Nonn. *D.* 9.228-31). ἀμφιγ. (Kirk on *Il.* 1.607, Hainsworth on *Od.* 8.300, Verdenius on Hes. *WD* 70, Detienne and Vernant 270f. offer a range of interpretations) is rare outside Homer/Hesiod(ea): Panyas. *EGF fr.* 16.1, Q.S. 2.138, Nonn. *D.* 5 ×; Anon. *AP* 14.109.5; Call. (*fr.* 469) revitalises it.

On the pattern subst. (..) epithet at line-end (cf. infr. 627, 795, 853, 1031, 1128, 1228), its relative rarity in Ap. and in other Hellenistic poets, epithet-formation, general avoidance of strong end-stopping and of precise echoing of Homeric prototypes, see Wifstrand's excellent discussion, 1933.84f.

The representation of Hephaestus and Aphrodite as a married couple is exceedingly rare: *RE* 1.2747-8, Burkert, *RhM* 103 (1960), 133f., Vian on Nonn. *D.* 29.329-34. i.850-60 can hardly have prepared us for the present scenario; 37-8 however direct our thoughts right away to the song of Demodocus (41f.n.), its πρῶτος εὑρετής.

38 ὁππότε μιν//τὰ πρῶτα Two Homeric components (*Echoes* ad loc.) latched together. For the former cf. Nonn. *D.* 13.302-3 (ἤγαγε), 26.105, Max. 418; and for the whole (Svensson 86) Q.S. 1.14 /ὁππότε δὴ τὰ πρῶτα.

-α παραὶ Διός *Il.* 15.175, Call. *fr.* 75.36. On παραί see Campbell 1973.75.

... ἦγεν ἄκοιτιν '... to be his bed-mate' (cf. Kirk on *Il.* 3.447-8, 6.350, and see n. on 41f.). Similarly ii.239 Κλειοπάτρην ἕδνοισιν [to be understood here: cf. *Od.* 8.318f., infr. 41f.n.] ἐμὸν δόμον ἦγον ἄκοιτιν (~ Hes. *WD* 800), cf. *Il.* 18.87 ἀγαγέσθαι ἄκοιτιν/ and iv.194 (~ *Od.* 21.316), Rhian. *CA* 51 ~ Q.S. 3.102. See also, e.g., iv.798, and the material assembled by Barkhuizen in *Mnemosyne* 36 (1983), 151-2.

39 ἔρχεα 215n.

εἰσελθοῦσαι Suggested no doubt by εἰσελθοῦσα *Il.* 14.169 ~ 166f. 'θάλαμος which Hephaestus built.' Note also id. 24.477 εἰσελθών then στάς, 16.254-5, *Od.* 4.802-3 εἰσῆλθε then στῆ.

ὑπ' αἰθούσῃ θαλάμοιο For the prepositional phrase cf. *Od.* 3.399 al. A peristyle, perhaps; but if the subsequent description of Aeetes' palace is any guide, this open colonnade will run the length of the far wall opposite the main entrance (237n.) with a πρόδομος fronting not only the megaron but also adjacent bedrooms [see now VDB 2².112]. *Il.* 9.473 (*Studies* 11), a passage which provoked much puzzled comment (cf. schol. D/bT(*b*) with Erbse's notes; for detailed discussion see Hiller, *WS* n.s. 4 (1970), 16f.), may have been influential here: ἐνὶ προδόμῳ, πρόσθεν θαλάμοιο θυράων, interpreted as that area of the αἴθουσα fronting the θάλαμος? Our ὑπ' αἰθούσῃ θαλάμοιο, perhaps designedly, runs together *Il.* 9.472 ὑπ' αἰθούσῃ (but ἐν Ἀρ.) and 473 θαλάμοιο.

The visitors, who are not strangers (ctr. e.g. *Od.* 4.20f., and ἔσταν ... in 215, n. ad loc.), march right in and come to a halt before the open doors (44) of the bedchamber: it is here, rather than in the main hall, that one would expect the love-goddess to be – only there is no lover, indeed no husband even (41f.)! We hear nothing of the callers' reaction to the sight of her: it is Cypris who spots them standing there and whisks them in. For Athena, it is a case of moving from one bedroom into another.

40 ἐντύνεσκε θεὰ λέχος Both literally and figuratively, I think: 'was in the habit of making his bed [cf. Mosch. *Eur.* 164 λέχος ἔντυον and ἔντυον (-εν Nonn.) εὐνήν/ in *Od.* 23.289, iv.1130, Nonn. *D.* 20.32], goddess though she was' [nobody else could see to *that* job], and '... of sharing his bed' [cf. 840n.].

λέχος Ἡφαίστοιο Cf. 41f.n., and for the clausula *Od.* 8 again: 359 μένος Ἡφαίστοιο/ (~ 361 ὁ μὲν .. βεβήκει/, 362 /ἡ δ' ἄρα ... (Cypris)).

41f. We owe to Lennox (49-50) the acute observation that Ap. is playing with the celebrated song of Demodocus in *Od.* 8.266f.; its theme: Cypris, wife of χωλός Hephaestus (37n.), caught *in flagrante delicto* with Ares. The run-up to 43-4, where our expectations are dashed, possesses a strong Demodocean 'fingerprint': 8.268 τὰ πρῶτα ... δόμοισι ~ Ap. 36-8 δῶμα .... τὰ πρῶτα, 269-70 λέχος .../Ἡφαίστοιο ~ 40, 273-4 βῆ ῥ' ἴμεν ἐς χαλκεῶνα ... then ἄκμονα ~ 41, 277 θάλαμον ὅθι ... δέμνι' ... ~ 39-40 θαλάμοιο/.. ἵν' ... λέχος ..., 289-90 ἡ δὲ .... κατ' ἄρ' ἕζεθ' then εἴσω δώματος ~ 43-4 ἡ δ' ἄρα ../ἧστο δόμῳ, 325 ἔσταν δ' κτλ. ~ 40. For further oblique references to this episode see nn. on 62, 89, 102. The lead-in to the bridge-passage (41 '*but* he was well out of the way') is artfully orchestrated to create the impression that marital status and the marital bed are going to play an important part in the immediate sequel: 37 πόσις 'lawful husband' (ὁ κατὰ νόμον ἀνήρ Ap. Soph. 134.8 etc., see in general Shipp, *Antichthon* 11 (1977), 3f.; not always so in practice of course), 38 Cypris formally 'given away' by none other than πατὴρ Ζεύς ~ *Od.* 8.318f., 38 again 'bed-mate' (Chantraine, *REG* 59/60 (1946/47), 225; the word is often used ironically, see e.g. i.997 with Levin 100 n.3), 39 'bedchamber,' 40 'bed.' In the event, the dry ἄρα of 43 ('what else would you expect?') projects a picture of a goddess whose own life seems far removed from that suggested by her allotted sphere of activity; a pathetic character when the name of Eros crops up, but also before ...

Not that ἡ δ' ἄρα μούνη ... really brings down the curtain on the theme of seduction/seductiveness. Ironically, the image of a beckoning goddess is sustained in 45f.: the white shoulders, the loosened hair, the long locks (see on all of these McKeown on Ov. *Am.* 1.5.9-10 [10: *candida dividua colla tegente coma*] and 1.7.40); 'shoulders' and πλόκαμοι, inviting us to think back to Cypris' provocative pose sketched in i.742f., βαθυπλόκαμος Κυθέρεια ~ ὤμου ... 743f., linked with the person of *Ares* (on the literary and particularly the iconographical background to this much-discussed portrait see Fusillo 302-3 [bibliogr.: see esp. VDB, Shapiro], Hutchinson 142 n.100, Fowler 1989.112-3, Pavlock 36f., and also Hardie, op. cit. on 135-41 C, 19 with n.63); and, cruellest of all, 46-7 (see n. ad loc.) echoing *Il.* 14.175f., Hera about to seduce Zeus; our Cypris is not about to seduce anybody: she is a lonely, insecure character, and it shows.

On the face of it Cypris wants for nothing (cf. here *Studies* 11): her husband has furnished her with a big house (36), and also, we may suppose, with the elaborate throne (44) and golden comb (46); other δαίδαλα (42-3n.) are no doubt on the way. But Hephaestus puts work first, wife a poor second, for he is off early to a μυχός in an unspecified Πλαγκτὴ νῆσος. The picture of the 'bed' in 40 in conjunction with ἀλλ' ... in 41 suggests that Cypris is missing more than just a husband about the house and that Hephaestus has more to think about than a lovely wife (*Studies* 97 n.17, cf. Hollis cited by Lennox 50 n.13). So ... she sits at home all alone (cf. Aesch. *Ag.* 862 ἧσθαι δόμοις ἐρῆμον of a wife left at home by a husband who goes off on military service), magnificently enthroned and facing the door, just waiting for somebody to talk to, with nothing to do but dress her hair (46 κερκίδι: *aliae mulieres pectine discriminant telam: Venus crines* is Hoelzlin's perceptive remark), ready to forget her statuesque image in the interests of getting some company – regardless of quality.

41 Hephaestus is traditionally an energetic worker (*Studies* 97 n.17): *Il.* 1.600, 18.372f.; iv.76of.; Virg. *A.* 8.414-5 (where note *mollibus e stratis*); Stat. *Theb.* 3.277f. (Venus: Vulcan would work night and day for me); *Lydia* 70-1. — In Hor. *Carm.* 1.4.5f., where Venus is represented as dancing beneath the light of the moon, *dum gravis Cyclopum/*

Vulcanus ardens visit officinas, the implication of *ardens* (and, for that matter, of *gravis*) seems not to have attracted comment. (On the possible associations of Ap.'s ἦρι for Horace: Wilkinson, *CR* 50 (1936), 120-1, Stinton 370).

ἀλλ' There is no substance whatsoever in Moorhouse's claim that the particle here (see 41f.n.), and infr. 1000, bears no trace of adversation (*CQ* n.s. 2 (1952), 103).

ἀλλ' … βεβήκει Add to *Od.* 8.273 (above 41f.n.) id. 3.410, 6.11 /ἀλλ' ὁ μὲν … βεβήκει/, but of individuals dead and gone(!).

ἄκμονας The plural too in iv.761 ἄκμονες Ἡφαίστοιο/χάλκειοι ~ Call. *fr.* 115.17 χάλκευσαν ἐπ' ἄκμοσιν Ἡφ[αίστοιο/, id. *h.* 3.48.

ἦρι = (schol. D at *Il.* 9.360 and often elsewhere) ὄρθρου – *the* time to get started to work according to Hesiod, *WD* 577 [best treated as a loose 'first thing,' signalling the starting-point of an activity: for closer definition see Sommerstein, *CQ* n.s. 27 (1977), 269 n.5, Renehan 1980.356, Wallace, *TAPA* 119 (1989), 201f.; also Vian on [Orph.] *A.* 366].

42 νήσοιο Πλαγκτῆς Πλαγκτῆς rather than πλαγκτῆς Hoelzlin and subsequently Klein 23 n.10. On the Πλαγκταί in iv see VDB 1.269 (on ii.297) and esp. 3.43-6; also Heubeck on *Od.* 12.55-72 (lit.). Callimachus no doubt adverted to the genus in his collection of παράδοξα.

Cf. *Studies* 98 n.18. If we were to guess what 'island' (on the various choices see the bibliogr. in NH on Hor. *Carm.* 1.4.7) we should probably pick Ἱερὰ Ἡφαίστου (Therasia, Thermessa [cf. θερμήν iv.929?], mod. Volcano, *RE* 8.1397, Delage 242). There is a lack of precision in iv also, but for a different reason (VDB 3.174, on iv.764): here the seclusion and haziness attaching to Hephaestus' place of work makes him that much more remote from his wife on Olympus. — Allusive references: Virg. *A.* 8.416f. (Eden ad loc.), 'An island, close by Aeolian [*RE* 1.1032f.] Lipara …,' *Aetna* 440 *insula … a Vulcani nomine sacra*, Juv. 1.8-9 (*antrum*).

νήσοιο .. εὐρὺν μυχόν Cf. [Hes.] *Theog.* 1015 μυχῷ νήσων ἱεράων (! See above: a small world)/ sim. D.P. 128; Call. *h.* 4.160-1 νῆσον/…, ἱερὸν (n.b.) μυχὸν … Pind. *N.* 1.42 ἐς θαλάμου μυχὸν εὐρὺν ἔβαν, [Orph.] *A.* 747 μυχὸν εὐρέα.

μυχόν Call. *h.* 4.142 μυχά ~ 144 Ἡφαίστοιο. The 'recess(es)' <of a cavern> (cf. ii.737 ~ *Od.* 5.226 al.; Call. *h.* 4.65), hidden and undisturbed (see e.g. schol. D at *Il.* 21.23, Hesych. s.v. μυχοί). Cf. *Od.* 5.77 εὐρὺ σπέος; Virg. *A.* 8.424 *vasto Cyclopes in antro* …

42-3 ᾧ ἔνι πάντα/δαίδαλα ... Ctr. *Il.* 14.220 /ποικίλον [i.q. δαιδάλεον, cf. e.g. schol. D at *Il.* 5.60, δαίδαλα = ποικίλα], ᾧ ἔνι πάντα τετεύχαται, of an object owned by Cypris. E's ἧ (ἧ) presumably springs from ἧ immediately below, though this manuscript is often open to the charge of novelty for novelty's sake.

πάντα/δαίδαλα: cf. Hes. *Theog.* 581 /τῇ δ' ἐνὶ δαίδαλα πολλὰ τετεύχατο (ἀμφιγυήεις 579) picked up by πόλλ' at 583 beside *Il.* 18.400 (Hephaestus speaking) χάλκευον δαίδαλα πολλά/ (then 402 /ἐν σπῆι): δαίδαλα πάντα Zen. Aristoph. and a number of manuscripts (Duentzer 119, Ludwich 1.433, Rengakos 1993.63); with this reshuffle Ap. has tidied up a violation of Wernicke's Law (see Edwards ad loc., and below on 185). For πάντα cf. *Il.* 5.60 δ. πάντα/ (πολλά Ar. ed. alt., Ludwich 1.251), 19.13 id., = Q.S. 5.101; [Orph.] *fr.* 179.3 /δ. πάντ'; Nonn. *D.* 8.120 /τῇ ἔνι δ. πάντα. — δ. πολλά, represented in i.729 (2 ...) δ. π. ... ἐπέπαστο/ (corr.: ἐκέκαστο *codd.*; see Nonn. *D.* 28.6 /δ. π. πέπαστο *et circa*) is commoner; add to the above: (1) (2 ...) *Il.* 18.482 (Heph.) = Eudoc. *Hom.* 398; Mosch. *Eur.* 43 /ἐν τῷ δ. π. τετεύχατο (Hes. above); Q.S. 6.198; Nonn. *D.* 5.181 τῷ ἔνι δ. π. (Keydell: πάντα) τετεύχατο, τῷ ἔνι πάντα ... (cf. Hopkinson, ed. Call. *h.* 6, 151 n.3). (2) δ. π./: *Il.* 14.179 (ἐνὶ); [Opp.] *Cyn.* 1.355. (3) /δ. π.: Nonn. *D.* 3.134.

πάντα: emphatic, highlighting the god's preoccupation with his job: he has a whole range of objects to keep him busy. What are these δαίδαλα? Another set of finery for his wife? Cf. the sequel to *Il.* 18.400 (see above), with schol. bT, 400*c* Erbse (*Studies* 97 n.16).

43 ῥιπῇ πυρός i.1027, cf. Mooney ad loc.; Homeric, *Il.* 21.12 (ῥιπῆς π.: Graz 301f.), quite common elsewhere. An apt word here for the fierce blast of fire fanned by bellows, cf. ῥιπίς and cognates.

ἡ δ' ἄρα μούνη Q.S. 13.556.

43f. Venus and Cupid are transformed into respectable members of divine society in Claudian's imitation, *Nupt.* 102f.: Venus sits on a throne grooming her hair; one of the Graces *morsu numerosi dentis eburno/multifidum discrimen arat* ...; Cupid approaches, she snatches him to her bosom and kisses him (110, 116, cf. iii.138f.), accosts him with *quid tantum gavisus.../improbe* (111f., cf. iii.129), hastily binds up her hair (123) and promises her son a golden quiver. (See on the whole scene Roberts, *TAPA* 119 (1989), 328f.).

43-4 ἡ .... δόμῳ *Od.* 23.90-1 (πυρός 89) ὁ δ' ἄρα .../ἧστο (κάτ)ω; 13.424 /ἧσται ἐν .. δόμοις. For this 'sitting at home' cf. Aesch. *Ag.*

cited on 41f. But 'was sitting δόμῳ' also arouses the expectation that Cypris might be engaged in some useful household occupation while the bread-winner is out, most obviously spinning/weaving: cf. ἧστο in *Il.* 6.324, *Od.* 6.52, and e.g. θακοῦσιν in the account of inverted habits (men sit weaving indoors, women go out to work) in Soph. *OC* 339f., with Woodbury, *TAPA* 112 (1982), 250 n.17 = Woodbury 1991.401. Not a bit of it: the κερκίς turns out to be something decidedly exotic (46).

44 δινωτόν (*Studies* 97 n.15) As VDB note (2.112), δινωτός alludes to the elaborate craftsmanship of Hephaestus: i.q. πεποικιλμένος (schol. D on *Il.* 3.391, first entry); for other interpretations, ancient and modern, of this term see VDB loc. cit., Kirk on *Il.* 3.391, Erbse on schol. (*a/b*) there, *LfgrE* s.v. This is Cypris ποικιλόθρονος, an epithet elucidated (properly, in my estimation: cf. e.g. Stanley, *GRBS* 17 (1976), 309 n.26) by Page, *S&A* 5, on Sappho *PLF* 1.1, addressing 'the Olympian goddess seated at home in heaven.'

iv.222 σάκος δινωτόν + iii.1231 πολύρρινον ~ *Il.* 13.407 (ἀσπίδα) ῥινοῖσι .../δινωτήν, cf. Leaf/Janko ad loc., Jones, *Glotta* 37 (1958), 115, Erbse on schol. *Il.* 13.407*a*; Gow-Page on *HE* 2152 (add to their discussion Antip. Sid. *HE* 627; Arat. 462: Ludwig, *Hermes* 91 (1963), 445-6).

ἀνὰ θρόνον Both (δινωτῷ) ἐνὶ θρόνῳ (Fränkel OCT *app. crit.*) and my own ἀνὰ θρόνῳ (1971.414) produce an unacceptable double correption: Campbell 1973.86. ἀνά must mean 'up on,' 'perched on' the throne – the lonely goddess being afforded a good vantage-point. A variation, it would appear, on *Il.* 15.152-3 Κρονίδην ἀνὰ Γαργάρῳ ἄκρῳ/ἥμενον (150: /ἕζετο δ' εἰνὶ θρόνῳ!). [VDB 2.112 adduce iii.685, [Orph.] *A.* 958, neither a good parallel.]

ἄντα θυράων So, but with subst. πυλάων, [Apolin.] 126.14, Paul. Sil. *Soph.* 573. Homer has ἄγχι θυράων/, *Od.* 7.112.

45-7/50 Cypris' hair (cf. *Studies* 129). For hair-styles of the Hellenistic period see D. B. Thompson, *Troy*, Supplementary Monograph 3 (1963), 36f. Pictorialism: cf. Fowler 1989.55.

On Jason's cloak Cypris is pictured as βαθυπλόκαμος (i.742), i.e. she wears a 'melon-coiffure' characterised by braided locks set in deep waves over the whole scalp or concentrated to one side of it. She has here released (by removing the frontal stephane) over her shoulders and is unravelling the flowing/groomed hair (κόμαι), 'beating' it with the κερκίς prior to braiding. She is interrupted and so she ties up the uncombed free-flowing hair (χαῖται, cf. Ap. Soph. 166.13) in a knot with *both* hands (she is in a great hurry: ctr. χερσίν in 829) – very unstylishly, like a simple girl (cf. NH on Hor. *Carm.* 2.11.24). So she is not exactly looking her best when Ap. works in a barbed allusion to a beauty contest.

45 λευκοῖσιν ... ὤμοις i.223 does not quite match the elegant symmetry of '/white (... to either side ...) shoulders/': /κυάνεαι ... ἔθειραι/ tossed by the wind ἀμφὶ .. νώτοις/κράατος ἐξ ὑπάτοιο καὶ αὐχένος ἔνθα καὶ ἔνθα (221-2). For the trick of framing the verse with colour-adjective and accompanying noun cf. also ii.159, (iv.1710 ~ Triph. 88), Arat. 369, D.P. 1060, 1117, Q.S. 4.137 al., Triph. 66, 73, Colluth. 39 [hair, ἑκάτερθε], Wifstrand 1933.133f., and more generally McLennan on Call. *h.* 1.60.

λευκοῖσιν 'The traditional epithet for woman's flesh in Greek poetry,' Dodds on Eur. *Bacch.* 664-7, cf. Russo on *Od.* 18.196, though here, as infr. 875 (n.), it has a certain suggestiveness, see on 41f.; the combination here only, I think (Horace's *albo .. umero, Carm.* 2.5.18, specifies a particular degree of whiteness, cf. NH ad loc.). — *Il.* 5.314 πήχεε λευκώ of Aphrodite on the battlefield.

ἑκάτερθε Cf. ii.676 ~ Nonn. *D.* 13.92, Colluth. 39 cited above; and *Il.* 23.329 ... δὲ .. ἑκάτερθεν ... λευκώ/...

κόμας .. ὤμοις Cf. *HyDem* 279; and Nonn. *D.* 18.129 /ὤμῳ ἐπι- .. κόμην (ῥιπῇ ibid. ~ supr. 43).

ἐπιειμένη ὤμοις For the clausula cf. Thgn. *IEG* 649, and for ... ὤμοις Campbell on Q.S. 12.366. The verb (cf. *Studies* 130 n.1): καθιέναι is commonly used of letting hair grow long or simply flow freely (for example Eur. *Bacch.* 695 καθεῖσαν εἰς ὤμους κόμας, Xen. Ephes. 1.2.6, Nonn. *D.* 32.12-3), as at infr. 830 Medea's hair καταειμέναι ἠερέθοντο. So ἐπιειμένη here (middle: ... her *own* hair, cf. the middle ἀφίετο in *Od.* 23.240) is likely to be from ἐφιέναι rather than (see Lennox 50 n.14 for proponents of this view) ἐπιέννυναι (cf. Ov. *Met.* 6.168 *inmissos umerum per utrumque capillos*): so too iv.179 ἐπιειμένος ὤμῳ/ (ctr. *Il.* 15.308 /εἱμένος ὤμοιιν): cf. ποδηνεκές 180. καταειμ- at i.939 and διαειμ- at ii.372 must be from -ιέναι: Platt 1914.25, Ardizzoni on i.939; iv.604 ἀναειμέναι con. Campbell 1983.138. On ἐπι- rather than ἐφ- see 120n.

46 κόσμει Cf. Phil. *GPh* 2783 (*et circa*) κτένα κοσμοκόμην. Reposianus 73, Venus *ornans .. divino pectine crines*, may be an echo of our passage.

κόσμει χρυσείη ... *HyHom* 6.11 (to Aphrodite) ... χρυσέοισιν ἐκόσμεον ...

... διά See next note. διακοσμεῖν in tmesis (but not anastrophic tmesis) is Homeric: *Il.* 2.655 διὰ τρίχα κοσμηθέντες (cf. schol. D there τριχῶς διαταχθέντες; see further *LH* s.v. κοσμέω, 870.2f.).

χρυσείη .. κερκίδι So *Od.* 5.62 χρυσείη κερκίδ' ὕφαινεν, cf. above on 41f., 43-4. Lennox calls attention to the context (50-1): Ap. suggests 'a comparison between Aphrodite, serenely arranging her hair and soon to be interrupted [rather: 'to be given a nasty shock'], and the lovely Calypso, going about her womanly task in her cave and about to be upset by the message conveyed to her by Hermes.' The Calypso-scene yields rather more than this however: 108f.n.

The κερκίς (*Studies* 130 n.2) separates the strands of hair (διά: cf. schol. bT on *Il.* 14.176a, a passage in Ap.'s mind here: χαίτας πεξαμένη, glossed διακρίνασα καὶ διαχωρίσασα; but schol. D κτενισαμένη, cf. Ap. Soph. 129.30f., who relates the use to wool-carding, see H. Blümner, *Technologie* ... 1.2, 110f.). Literally, in all probability, the 'pin-beater,' a tool with a slight hook employed in weaving to separate the warp-threads as it is inserted between them: cf. Crowfoot, *ABSA* 37 (1936/37), 44f.; Antip. Sid. *HE* 194-5 κερκίδα .... ᾇ διέκρινε μίτους. See further *Noten* 332.

There could be a direct link here with the κτένα .. παγχρύσεον of Call. *h.* 5.31: he, like Ap. (see 46-7n.), goes on at once to use *Il.* 14.175f. (Bulloch on 31-2); note also χαίταν Call. 31 then πλόκαμον 32 but Ap. πλοκάμους 47 then χαίτας 50, and cf. below on 51f. (Beauty Contest).

The object sported by Cypris here, we may be sure, was from the stock of Ἡφαιστότευκτα (41f.n.; *Noten* 332). See also 118n.

46-7 μέλλε .... πλοκάμους Cf. *Studies* 130 n.3. Characteristic pruning of an Homeric model, *Il.* 14.175-7. For the curt μακρούς cf. *EtM* 677.7 πλόκαμοι· αἱ μακραὶ τρίχες, αἱ ἐπιτήδειαι οὖσαι πρὸς τὸ πλέκεσθαι, with S. Marinatos in *AH* B2, Hainsworth on *Od.* 5.58.

This sharply-etched description reproduces with variation some of the alliterative and rhyming effects of the Iliadic model: note here μ- μ-, πλ- πλ-, -ούς -ους at line-end/main caesura (and also κ- χ- κ- earlier in 46). The order of the key component, πλοκάμους ἔπλεξε, is inverted, with middle (hapax Hom., πλεξάμενος *Od.* 10.168, but not of hair) substituted for active.

μέλλε As Lennox remarks (51), 'was about to' makes us smile all the more when we recall how at *Il.* 14.175f. *Hera*, beautified to perfection, is about to meet *Aphrodite* and ask a favour: 'the goddess of love and beauty caught by her Iliadic rival with her face down!'

... δὲ μακρούς/ .. πλοκάμους Cf. iv.27-8 ... τε (read δὲ ??) μακρόν/ ῥηξαμένη [*codd., recte*] πλόκαμον, and *Cypria EGF fr.* 5.2 (Aphrodite, then) /πλεξάμεναι στεφάνους ...

πλέξασθαι See 26In. The aorist middle is an Homeric hapax, see above; πλέξεσθαι (conjectured by Naber 27) only Z[mg].

GVI 1163.10-11 (Megalopolis, 2nd/3rd. cent.) may be drawing on our passage: λουτρὸν (? λουτροῖς Henrichs, *ZPE* 3 (1968), 110) γὰρ φαίδρυνε καλὸν χρόα, πλεξαμένη δέ/τοὺς ἱεροὺς πλοκάμους ... (see on 300, 725, 832).

47-50 Much here is plundered from *Il.*: 10.476 /τὸν δ' .. προπάροιθεν ἰδών [cf. iv.482]; 11.645-6 (visitor θύρῃσιν ἐφίστατο 644) /τὸν δὲ ἰδὼν [cf. /τὴν δὲ ἴδε .. in 18.382] ... ἀπὸ θρόνου ὦρτο [see for this detail the examples in Richardson's note on 23.202-3] .... κατὰ δ' ἑδριάασθαι ἄνωγε/ [cf. 24.515; iii.439 ~ 5.13]; 9.200 (/στὰν ... 193, ἴδε 195) /εἷσεν δ' ἐν κλισμοῖσι [cf. i.788-9, *Echoes* ad loc.].

48f. present variations on the wily Circe's reception of visitors in *Od.* 10: 220 /ἔσταν ..., 230f. Circe opened doors, came out, 231 = 257 /καὶ κάλει, 233 /εἷσεν δ' .. κατὰ κλισμούς τε θρόνους τε/ cf. id. 310/313/314 (throne).

There is a comparable routine in iv.719-20 (Circe/Medea and Jason), Odyssean in texture: /εἷσεν ἐπὶ ... θρόνοισιν,/καὶ δ' αὐτὴ .. ἷζεν ~ 7.169-71 (cf. id. 162-3) + 5.198, cf. 1.130 ~ αὐτός 132. Cf. also Nonn. *D.* 4.22f. (αὐτή 23).

The choice of chair (*Studies* 98 n.20). In Ap. (i.788; iii.439, 455, iv.692, 719) visitors can be offered either a κλισμός or a θρόνος; occasionally the terms are interchangeable (cf. *LfgrE* s.v. κλισμός). But the κλισμοί here are plainly distinct from Cypris' own majestic θρόνος (44n.) – nobody is going to get that! Cf. Richardson on *HyDem* 191, West on *Od.* 1.130, F-G on id. 21.139, and contrast the imposing accumulation in *Il.* 18.389-90 (Charis sat Thetis down) ἐπὶ θρόνου ἀργυροήλου/καλοῦ δαιδαλέου.

48 ἔσχεθεν i.e. ἐπέσχεθεν, stopped what she was doing, cf. iv.1713 (Argonauts putting in for the night), LSJ ἔχω B I1 ad fin., ἐπέχω IV2. ἐσχεθέτην is intrans. in *Il.* 12.461 ('hold' ~ ἔσχεν 16.740), sim. ἔσχεθε ('held fast') in 13.608, 16.340.

ἔσχεθεν, εἴσω Ctr. *Il.* 16.340 εἴσω ..., ἔσχεθε ...

σφε κάλει On the question 'to augment or not to augment' see the lit. in Hopkinson on Call. *h.* 6.12, also Merkel *Proleg.* 107f. σφε κάλει here: La Roche 1899.180, 192; no mention of this instance in *Noten* 649-51.

Soph. *Aj.* 74 σφ' ('him') ἔξω κάλει (imperat.).

σφε On σφε in Homer see *GH* 1.267, Edwards on *Il.* 19.264-5. Here, and probably in ii.284 (a pair of Harpies, VDB 1.269, on ii.189), referring to two individuals, as 2 × *Il.*, 3 × *Od.*; the true plural 9 × (10 × if the Brunck/Platt conjecture is admitted in iv.1410; iv.556 presents us with σφ' then σφεὰς in close succession), as 1 × *Il.* — 3[H]: apart from Call. *h.* 3.197, 4.15 (Mineur ad loc., Rengakos 1993.119 n.1), where σφε = αὐτήν, always with a plural referent: Call. *h.* 1.80 v.l., 3.80, Theoc. 4.3 (ψε), 15.80 (neut.), [Mosch.] *Meg.* 48; the status of σφ' in Euphor. *CA* 60 is indeterminable.

E calls in its favourite pronoun (14-5n.) to obliterate the σφε altogether.

49 ἀτὰρ μετέπειτα Cf. i.302.

50 /ἵζανεν followed by a pause: cf. *Il.* 10.92; i.532, iv.694.

ἀψήκτους Ar. *Lys.* 658, ἀποψ- Soph. *Ichn.* 372 (*fr.* 314 Radt). Cf. *Studies* 130 n.4. It is easy to jump to the conclusion that this is a word associated with the lower genres (so e.g. Vian ed. 1961), but ψήχειν and compounds are quite at home in elevated surroundings (Ap. himself has ψήχειν and καταψήχειν).

Possibly 'ungroomed' (cf. Ardizzoni here) will do; but ψήχειν, *rub away at* or *scrape*, could hint at a back-combing movement designed to give the hair the fluffy appearance often in evidence in representations of the melon-coiffure (45-7/50n.) and other styles.

χεροῖν See 45-7/50n. On χερ- forms, by now prevalent in verse of every description, see Leumann 318f., and also Braswell on Pind. *P.* 4.271(c). Ap. has, besides χερσί: χερός (iv.852), χερί (3 ×), χεροῖν (6 ×), χέρες (iii.81), χέρας (iv.960). Certain scribes found them easy game: ii.243, iii.81, iv.44, 852.

ἀνεδήσατο χαίτας Cypris ties her hair up in a knot: cf. ἀνήψατο infr. 829, with VDB here (2.112). For the effect cf. 45-7/50n.; for the diction Antip. Sid. *HE* 510-11 οὔλας ἀνεδήσατο .../χαίτας, and earlier Pind. *I.* 1.28 (athletes).

Conceits involving Cypris' uncharacteristically disordered tresses (cf. *Studies* 129-30): Bion 1.20 (~ Prop. 2.13a.56), Stat. *Theb.* 5.62. 'Pinning' of her hair, sim.: Val. Flacc. 2.103, Claud. *rapt. Pros.* 2.15-6, id.

Gig. (2) 45 (corrected) ἀπλεκέας περόνῃ διεκρίνατο χαίτας/, Colluth. 82; in haste: Claud. *Nupt.* 123. See too the epigram *ap.* Marcovich, *ZPE* 56 (1984), 238 verse 4 (= *Studies in Greek Poetry* (Atlanta 1991), 219).

After Ap. (and cf. Claud. above): Nonn. *D.* 18.136 /ἀπλεκέας πλοκαμῖδας .. δήσατο ...

51f. Much of what follows is based on *Studies* 11-12. Hera's speech of 56f. focuses firmly on the fortunes of the Argonauts. But we are not finished with the Trojan saga quite yet. As we read 51 we should be beginning to latch on to an allusion to one of its more sensational episodes.

Cypris adopts a catty, low-key approach to the aggressive κερτομίη (cf. 56) beloved of certain Iliadic gods: 1.539 (Hera), 4.6 (Zeus), 5.419 (Hera and Athena). The speech-introduction here sets the tone: φιλομμειδὴς Ἀφροδίτη adopts a posture of feigned humility. ἠθεῖαι, with its suggestion that she is dealing with respected superiors, ironically anticipates the blunt ἐπεὶ περίεστε θεάων, while harbouring a veiled insult (52n.). Charis' address to her visitor in *Il.* 18.385-6 (36f.n.) τίπτε, Θέτι τανύπεπλε, ἱκάνεις ἡμέτερον δῶ/αἰδοίη τε φίλη τε; πάρος γε μὲν οὔτι θαμίζεις amounts to little more than 'I *am* honoured, and pleased to see you' (cf. ibid. 424-5, *Od.* 5.87-8). Cypris' approach is more direct: their call must mean that they are after something (the point is made more delicately in *Il.* 18.426-7, *Od.* 5.89-90). And why *have* they both come, these superior goddesses? She has rephrased her question to get in a dig about superiority.

Innocent sarcasm? Consider the ingredients: Hera, Athena, Cypris, cattiness about status. Callimachus (*h.* 5.21-2) and others (see Kannicht on Eur. *Hel.* 676-8 fin., Radt on Soph. *fr.* 361) represent Cypris as paying meticulous attention to her hair-style in preparation for the Beauty Competition on Mt Ida. The snide ἐπεὶ περίεστε θεάων, from a Cypris with *ungroomed* hair, now acquires a cutting edge. This suggestion receives some corroboration from what might appear at first sight to be a random echo of our passage. Ap.'s verse 51 finds a striking parallel in Colluthus, 158 (Cypris at the Competition) τοῖα δὲ μειδιόωσα προσέννεπε μηλοβοτῆρα. Compare too Colluth. 170 κερτομέουσα with infr. 56 κερτομέεις. (The malicious altercation in the later poet is of course prefigured in Eur. *Andr.* 287f.) Perhaps Colluth. saw what we see in Ap.; or perhaps he is using a (? Hellenistic) poem about the Competition which expressed itself in similar terms.

It may be indeed that 44f., with the allusion to an ornamented throne, the highlighting of colour/skin-tone, the creation of a 'still' effect with μέλλε …, the evoking of sharp contours through alliteration and rhyme, were written with an eye on a specific artistic representation of the Contest, though the more general theme of a preening Aphrodite was of course popular in the Hellenistic era. One element which is missing is the mirror: Cypris here cannot be allowed to be all that engrossed.

51 τοῖα … αἱμυλίοισιν Similarly iv.393-4 τοῖα δ' Ἰήσων/μειλιχίοις ἐπέεσσιν ὑποδδείσας προσέειπεν, τοῖα referring to the content, the dative to its tone. For τοῖα cf. i.350, ii.287, iv.1563, and see on 24.

μειδιόωσα φιλομμειδὴς Ἀφροδίτη does what we expect her to do. But the tables are turned by 100, and cf. 107. — Ctr. *Il.* 4.356 etc. ἐπιμειδήσας προσέφη …

προσέννεπεν Cf. i.792 μύθοισι προσέννεπεν αἱμυλίοισιν/; Colluth. 158 (Cypris) τοῖα δὲ μειδιόωσα προσέννεπε μηλοβοτῆρα (above, 51f.n.). Ap. is the only Hellenistic poet (with the possible exception of Lobon: *SH* 522.3) to use προσεννέπειν, exclusively in the run-up to direct speech: cf. also i.711; infr. 78, 433, 474, 710, and Fantuzzi 66-7. He was preceded in this by Stesich. *PMGF* S148i.2 ὧδε ποτήνεπε, and also by Pind. *P.* 4.97, 9.29, Bacch. 15.9 προσήνεπε(ν). The only later examples are in Colluth. (also 69 τοῖον, 126 & 376 τοῖα), the verb being otherwise uncommon in post-Hellenistic verse (Q.S. 2.93, 4.56, 9.230, 'formulaic'; Colluth. 189 τοῖα *after* a speech; Diosc. *GDK* 42.17.18). On its distribution in pre-Hellenistic verse see Führer 23-6, and on its flavour Risch, *ZPE* 60 (1985), 3.

αἱμυλίοισιν Cypris is as crafty a female (see West on *Od.* 1.56-7) as you will get; = calculated to deceive or create a false impression by fawning upon one (cf. *LfgrE* s. αἱμύλιος, αἱμύλος schol., Verdenius on Hes. *WD* 78). The wily goddess adopts a posture of feigned humility. In i.792 of the cool and calculated deception practised by the wheedling Hypsipyle, a tinge of which nuance is present in 1141 infr., the seductive talk of a cunning flatterer (see n. ad loc.).

52f. Cf. 7-166n.

52 ἠθεῖαι Cf. *Studies* 98 nn.21-2. ἠθεῖος in Homer seems to entail 'brotherly' affection or respect for a senior or one of superior status (Doederlein 2.344-5, Hainsworth on *Il.* 10.37, Richardson on id. 23.94, Wyss on Antim. *fr.* 52; for ancient pronouncements see the mass of material assembled by Erbse on schol. *Il.* 6.518, 10.37, 21.229, 23.94). In 54 Cypris, tongue-in-cheek, avers that Hera and Athena are her (respected) superiors: ἠθεῖαι ironically foreshadows that claim. That is not to say that the question of respective *ages*, which so worried schol. here (cf. e.g. Vian ed. 1961 ad loc., Lennox 51 n.16), is not also in Cypris' mind, particularly as δηναιός (53n.) can bear the sense *ancient*! In *Il.* 14 Hera had addressed Aphrodite with φίλον τέκος (190), to which the response was πρέσβα θεά (194); much more civilised.

In ii.1219 Peleus addresses Argos (son of Phrixus) with ἠθεῖε evidently in a tone of polite remonstrance (as δαιμόνιε): that is to say, ἠθεῖε is interpreted as θεῖε i.q. (schol. Ap. ii.1219-21a) θαυμάσιε, see in particular schol. bT at *Il.* 6.518b(2) (and Chamaeleon at 23.94!). Cypris' ἠθεῖαι also is uttered with a gasp of disbelief. Not otherwise in 3[H]. [The word is considered at length by Bettini, *RFIC* 116 (1988), 154-66. His treatment of iii.52 is superficial; I am not at all persuaded by his account of ii.1219.]

τίς ... After *Od.* 4.312 (cf. Redard 68) Menelaus visited by Telemachus /τίπτε δέ σε χρειὼ δεῦρ' ἤγαγε; (~ [Theoc.] 25.44, where see Gow). Nonn. *D.* 32.43 /τίς χρειώ σε κόμιζε; τί .. ἐνθάδε βαίνεις;/ draws on the present passage and on iv.555-6 τίς ἀπόπροθι τόσσον ἀνάγκη/ καὶ χρειὼ σφ' ἐκόμισσε;, where adverbial τόσσον is dissociated from χρειώ but perhaps close enough to suggest advocacy of a particular interpretation of τόσον in *Il.* 10.142 al. (see on the problem Redard 65-6, also West on *Od.* 1.225, 2.28): if so, it is at variance with that of schol. D at *Il.* 10.142, ὅ τι τοσαύτη χρεία κατέλαβεν.

For τίς .. νόος cf. ii.1090 ~ *Il.* 24.367; for δεῦρο, ii.146.

53 δηναιάς 'after a long time.' δηναιός in archaic epic once only, *Il.* 5.407 *long-lived*, of a person (cf. Bechtel 99, and Garson 2). In Ap.: (1) *lasting, of long duration* (γῆρας ii.183, χρόνος iv.1547) as Theoc. 16.54, Lyc. 876 and often later, e.g. *GVI* 1559.2 (Rome, 2nd/3rd cent.), Triph. 525, Greg. Naz. *AP* 8.33.6; (2) *after a long interval* here and iv.645, cf. Maiist. *CA* 8 (adj.!), Opp. *Hal.* 4.154; (3) adv. -όν = δήν i.334, iii.590 ~ Lyc.1139, Man. 3.143, 6.383, Q.S. 3.295 corr., Greg. Naz. 1325.2; ??Call. *Hec.*: Hollis ed. pp. 358-9. Otherwise in Hellenistic poetry: *ancient, primaeval* (first Aesch.): Call. *h.* 1.60, *fr.* 100.2, Lyc. 145, Leon. Tar.(?) *HE* 2574. In general δηναιός has the range of πολυχρόνιος (cf. gl. schol. D on *Il.* 5.407), χρόνιος (cf. in comparable scenes χρόνιος in Theoc. 14.2, χρόνῳ in 15.1, with Gow's notes).

αὔτως One of epic's trickier words; Ap. is greatly attached to it (13 × in the third book alone). See in general the excellent short note of Vian ed. 1961 here, and also Bechtel 77f., *LfgrE* s.v.; Cunliffe's entry in *LHD* is also useful. 'Just like that,' a caustic touch: here are visitors whom she has not clapped eyes on for ages simply arriving out of the blue. An intensive sense, 'after *such* a long time,' seems to be generally taken for granted by those who acknowledge the word's existence here. So, e.g., Vian loc. cit. (cf. the VDB translation), Giangrande, *CQ* n.s. 12 (1962), 212 n.3. I see no compelling reason to interpret the word thus in any passage of the *Arg.*; cf. 423n.

τί δ' ἱκάνετον ... The distinctive form ἱκάνετον (an Homeric, and an Apollonian hapax) is from *Il.* 9.197, where ἦ τι μάλα χρεώ follows: cf. ... χρειώ here in 52. In the mouth of the ungracious Cypris Achilles' rather rueful (and awkwardly expressed) parenthesis is turned into a blunt query.

... οὔτι πάρος γε ... An engaging adaptation of *Od.* 4.810-11 (Penelope, addressing the disguised Athena in a dream) τίπτε, κασιγνήτη, δεῦρ' ἤλυθες; οὔτι πάρος γε [this unit also in 18.164]/πώλεαι, ἐπεὶ μάλα πολλὸν ἀπόπροθι δώματα ναίεις. Cypris' 'because'-clause hinges on sarcasm; and her visitors live only a stone's throw (or two) away!

See also 250-1n.

53-4 οὔτι .../λίην Cf. *Od.* 15.405 /οὔτι .. λίην (and *Il.* 14.368); ctr. λίην .. πάρος γ' in *Il.* 1.553.

54 λίην φοιτίζουσαι Splendidly cutting: 'overmuch in the habit of coming a lot.' φοιτίζειν, founded on θαμίζειν (Ernst Fraenkel, *Nomina agentis* (Strassburg 1910/12), 2.38), a recurrent verb in greeting-scenes (Macleod ed. *Il.* 24, pp. 46-7), is very rare: *HyHom* 26.8 (see Càssola there), Call. *fr.* 500.1 (.. πολλάκις); cf. Boesch 55.

ἐπεὶ περίεστε θεάων After *Od.* 18.248 ἐπεὶ περίεσσι γυναικῶν/ (εἶδος 249: cf. 51f.n.) ~ 4.376 πέρ ἐσσι θεάων/, *Il.* 18.27 περί τ' εἰμὶ θεῶν (the all-powerful Zeus). For the element θεάων cf. *Il.* 18.364 (Hera) φημι θεάων ἔμμεν ἀρίστη/ (Lennox 51-2 works this passage too hard), Call. *h.* 4.218 (the same) πολὺ προὔχουσα θεάων/.

Thiel 196 goes right off the rails here.

55 For the line as a whole see *Il.* 3.437 τὴν δὲ Πάρις μύθοισιν ἀμειβόμενος προσέειπεν, for certain of its components *Od.* 4.234, 19.252 -οισιν ἀμειβομένη προσέειπεν/, *Il.* 14.263 /τὸν δ' .. προσέειπε ... Ἥρη/. Cf. also ii.419 (~ *Il.* 3.181 + *HyHerm* 201).

τοίοισιν ἀμειβομένη See 24n., and cf. Greg. Naz. 887.45.

56f. The artful Hera now proceeds to demolish the smiling Cypris, though τοίοισιν (55) gives nothing away. The speech has something in common with Athena's expression of anxiety for Odysseus' welfare in *Od.* 1.45f.: 48 is reflected in Ap. 56 (ἦτορ ~ κέαρ) and in 59-60, but the *Odyssey*'s sacrifice-theme (60f.) is turned on its head (Ap. 65). Now, at long last, the struggling leader of the Argonauts too will benefit with reasonable regularity from the attentions of a goddess determined to keep him alive at all costs.

56 See 7-166n. Hera begins with a flourish, treating the *love*-goddess Cypris to a high-sounding version of the sort of rueful comment associated with *lovers* in a real jam [cf. 66!]: Ar. *Plut.* 973 σκώπτεις, ἐγὼ δὲ κατακέκνισμαι δειλάκρα, Men. *Dysc.* 54 σκώπτεις, ἐγὼ δέ, Χαιρέα, κακῶς ἔχω (these are cited by Fränkel, *Noten* 332); cf. also Ar. *Ran.* 58, Theoc. 10.19, 14.8. — ὀρίνειν too can have an erotic connotation: cf. esp. *Il.* 3.395 Aphrodite/Helen τῇ δ' ἄρα θυμὸν ἐνὶ στήθεσσιν ὄρινε with schol. D: διετάραξε. τουτέστιν, εἰς ἔρωτα αὐτὴν ἤγαγε.

κερτομέεις (cf. *Studies* 13) Strong language: the word is rendered even more stinging (for its 'Trojan' resonances see 51f.n.) by the close proximity of κέαρ, reflecting the derivation from κέαρ and τέμνειν offered by schol. D at *Il.* 1.539 (cf. Erbse on schol. there, and Henrichs 257 nn.17-8), 4.6, cf. schol. Ap. i.486 and Troxler 119f.; Jones, *CQ* n.s. 39 (1989), 248 [?IE root **ker-t-*, 'to cut': Pârvulescu, *Emerita* 54 (1986), 299f.].

νῶιν δὲ κέαρ ... But *Od.* 24.313 θυμὸς δ' .. νῶιν ...

κέαρ then ἄτῃ: cf. i.274. κέαρ (cf. ἔαρ gen. ἤρος, Brugmann, *IF* 5 (1895), 341, Frisk *GEW* 1.787) 7× in Ap.; it was often used to gloss Homeric κῆρ, see e.g. FJW on Aesch. *Suppl.* 784-5. Prior to the Hellenistic era (wherein cf. Call. *fr.* 18.5 [Jason!] and id. (?) *HE* 1271 (v.l.), Cerc. *CA* 3.3, 7.4, *Batrach.* 209) in Pind., Bacch. (note 17.86-7 ἔνδοθεν κέαρ ~ i.274 κέαρ ἔνδοθεν, later in Q.S. 3.504, 5.568) and in tragedy (+ Ar. *Ach.* 5 paratr.). Rare in later epic: Q.S. , 16 ×, [Orph.] *A.* 1091; but common enough in other genres: e.g. *GVI* (1st–3rd centuries) 1237.3, 1763.3, 1903.13, Oppians 4 × (note *Cyn.* 2.545 ~ iii.760), orac. ap. Porph. *Plot.* 22 verse 46, Greg. Naz. (*Carm.* + *AP*) 13 ×.

κέαρ συνορίνεται The straight compound συνορίνεσθαι is an Homeric and Apollonian hapax: *Il.* 4.332 of battalions of fighting men (συνταρασσόμεναι schol. D, the sense here, cf. schol. Ap. 56*b*; Gillies is quite wrong), but cf. too *Il.* 24.467 οἱ σὺν θυμὸν ὀρίνῃς/; also *Od.* 17.216 ὄρινε δὲ κῆρ Ὀδυσσῆος/. Cf. 515n.

ἄτῃ (*Studies* 13) Often expanded into something like 'by <the fear of/a prospective> disaster/utter ruin' (so e.g. Vian ed. 1961, a translation taken over into VDB). Hera is being alarmist to gain her ends:

why spoil the fun? For ἄτη (primary sense 'damage' sim.? Cf. e.g. Dawe, *HSCP* 72 (1968), 95f.) in Ap. see *Noten* 149, 495, Vian 1978.1039 n.15. Much of the material assembled by J. Stallmach, *Ate...* (Meisenheim 1968), esp. 80f., will be of interest to students of this poem; see also Verdenius on Hes. *WD* 216, Edwards ed. *Il.* 17-20, p. 247, and the diachronic study of R. E. Doyle, *ATH: its Use and Meaning* (New York 1984).

57 ἤδη γάρ *Il.* 1.260 al., iv.191. 'It has come to the point where ... at this moment': ἤδη often signifies both 'by this time' and 'right now.'
ποταμῷ ἐνὶ Φάσιδι νῆα ... *Od.* 14.258, 17.427 /στῆσα .. ἐν Αἰγύπτῳ ποταμῷ νέας ... On the question of the accentuation of ΕΝΙ see Bühler, ed. Mosch. *Eur.*, 228 n.1.
νῆα κατίσχει Hera withholds the information that the Argonauts are in hiding and so secure for the time being: ctr. *Od.* 11.456 /νῆα κατισχέμεναι ~ 455 'secretly, not openly' [on the block 454-6: Heubeck ad loc., Rengakos 1993.106-7].

58 So, from Hera again in a similar situation, iv.785 Αἰσονίδης ἠδ' (οἱ δ' LG, cf. οἵδ' GD in this line: suitable in i.854 but not here; cf. Svensson 42-3) ἄλλοι ἀοσσητῆρες ἀέθλου. The Homeric precedents are *Od.* 2.209 /Εὐρύμαχ' ἠδὲ καὶ ἄλλοι ὅσοι ... (no verb expressed: ctr. Ap.) and *Il.* 12.61 al. ἠδ' ἄλλοι. Ctr. *Od.* 3.363 /οἱ δ' ἄλλοι ... ἕπονται/.
μετὰ ... 'follow <him> in the quest for the Fleece.' Cf. μετὰ κῶας in i.4, ii.211, 871 ~ Theoc. 13.16 (Pind. *P.* 4.68; id. *fr.* 172.5 Heracles went μετὰ ζωστῆρας ...), and infr. 365 [ὧλλοι .. ὅσοι] ~ Theoc. 13.17.

59-60 Jason has been singled out in 58. The last thing Hera wants to do (note ἤτοι) is give the impression that 'the rest of' the Argonauts are of no concern to her and her associate; still, the preoccupation with *Jason*'s welfare comes to the fore again. She is leading up to the unexpected twist of 64-5 (n.).
For the frame of this couplet cf. *Il.* 4.237 (οἵ περ ... 236) /τῶν ἤτοι αὐτῶν ... (πάντ-: cf. Opp. *Hal.* 1.646), Hes. *WD* 641-2 ἔργων μεμνημένος εἶναι/ὡραίων πάντων, περὶ ναυτιλίης δὲ μάλιστα. On ἤτοι .. μέν see 15n.

59 ἐπεὶ ... ὄρωρε Ctr. *Od.* 19.377 ἐπεί .. ὀρώρεται ... (Theodotus *SH* 764.3 ἐπεὶ ... ὀρώρει/).
πέλας ἔργον ὄρωρε Cf. Aesch. *Ag.* 1650 τοὖργον οὐχ ἑκὰς τόδε, *Il* 16.207 νῦν δὲ πέφανται/φυλόπιδος μέγα ἔργον, and for the clausula Q.S. 7.620 ἔργον ὀρώρει/.

πέλας i.e. imminent, 'unmittelbar vor' *Noten* 445 n.212.

ἔργον 'action,' with the suggestion of 'military confrontation'; cf. Hoelzlin here and see below on 81-2.

ὄρωρε 'has presented itself' in close proximity, i.e. immediately confronts them. Fränkel (*Noten* 344) rejects the commonly held view (e.g. Mooney on i.713, on whose note see Fitch 341; Ardizzoni on iii.203) that ὄρωρε in Ap. can mean simply *is*. It may be that in most if not in all cases rejection is justified (certainly in i.713: Marxer 56, van Krevelen 1949.139; after *Il.* 23.112, on which see Richardson ad loc., and Schmidt 1968.77-9; cf. further 203, 314, 457, 487nn.): but one is hard put to it to see it as anything else in Antip. Thess. *GPh* 627-8 ἄλλο λεόντων/ἄλλο γενειητῶν ἔργον ὄρωρε τράγων.

60 δείδιμεν ἐκπάγλως *Megara* 92-3 (the author of which was probably an early imitator of this poem) δειμαίνω .../ἐκπάγλως; ctr. *Od.* 10.448 ἔδεισεν ... ἔκπαγλον ἐνιπήν/. ἐκπάγλως (*ἐκ-πλαγ-λως, by dissimilation of λ-λ, Frisk *GEW* 1.477) is glossed ἐκπληκτικῶς in schol. D at *Il.* 1.268 and quite often elsewhere (cf. Henrichs 139, nn.8-9). Hera claims that they are frightened out of their wits. Cf. *Noten* 332, Kirk on *Il.* 3.415.

It may be remarked also that Hera uses a term to which Cypris can relate: ἔκπαγλος/adv. -α are associated with the latter's love for mortals in *Il.* 3.415, 5.423, *HyAphr* 57.

περὶ ... i.e. περὶ πάντων, περὶ δ' Αἰσονίδαο, a common economy: see e.g. i.1193, iii.757-8; Schneider, *Nicandrea*, on *fr.* 70.4, Pfeiffer on Call. *fr.* 714.3, Clausen 151 n.3. Following Gillies, Ardizzoni argues needlessly (and with a shaky parallel in the form of *Od.* 4.820) for δείδω + gen., a construction which, though perfectly possible in theory (cf. KG 1.365-7, *GG* 2.133-4) does not seem to occur in practice (Soph. *OT* 233-4 is to be construed otherwise). The present combination may have been regarded as Homeric by Ap.: cf. the articulation of (gen. +) ΠΕΡΙΔΕΙΔΙΑ advocated by some in *Il.* 10.93, 17.240 (with Erbse on schol. there). [In ii.1203 Ω and *test.* offer πέρι δείδια, E περιδείδια (cf. on this *Noten* 311); no gen. is involved there.]

61-3 Cf. *Studies* 13/98 n.27. Hera has been spokesperson up till now (νῶιν, δείδιμεν). Here she leaves her associate behind by proclaiming in the strongest possible terms that *she* will ensure Jason's safety, come what may: '... even if he takes it into his head to go on a voyage into Hades to free Ixion down below ...' Real shock-tactics for the delicate love-goddess: attempted rape may be regarded as insignificant in comparison with Pelias' maltreatment of her (65)!

The element of fantasy is intensified by the choice of Hades as the place of punishment, perhaps here explicitly for the first time (Dickie, *ICS* 8 (1983), 72 n.22 speculates on its origins). Ixion is located in the nether world (cf. schol. Eur. *Phoen.* 1185, Zeus ἐταρτάρωσεν him, and Cook, *Zeus* 1.198f., *LIMC* 5.1.857-8) in the Hellenistic tragic fragment *P. Osl. inv.* 1413, ed. Eitrem/Amundsen, *SO* 31 (1955), 7, 9, = *Trag. adesp. TGF* 680a9, and often later, particularly in Roman poetry: Roscher 2.766.43f., Bömer on Ov. *Met.* 4.461, Fedeli on Prop. 1.9.20. — There is definitely no mention of Ixion in Hades in the Hellenistic elegiac fragment *SH* 970i.7: Barns and Lloyd-Jones, *SIFC* 35 (1963), 214, = Lloyd-Jones 1990: 2.204, cf. Guys, op. cit. on 116 below, 62 n.70. There have been occasional suggestions that Pindar in *O.* 1 thought of him as being punished in the world below, but this seems exceedingly unlikely: see e.g. Drew Griffith, *GRBS* 27 (1986), 6 n.6.

The allusion to Hades sounds like a wry echo of Jason's own avowal in ii.642f. that he would not be afraid in future with such steadfast companions around him, not even if he were to attempt a journey διὲξ 'Αΐδαο βερέθρων: a hint *perhaps* of an actual infernal journey, or at any rate of an experience approximating to such a journey. Catabatic Argonauts have proved to be big business: see 216n., and the bibliographies [Meuli and others] in Davies, *CQ* n.s. 38 (1988), 282 n.29, Dräger 5 n.22, 204; a sample drawn from recent works: VDB 1.125f., Clark, *Phoenix* 24 (1970), 253f. (on iv.214f.) with the comments of Thaniel, id. 25 (1971), 237f., Clark (1979) 34f., al., Beye 1982.44-5, 113-4, E. Robbins in J. Warden, *Orpheus: the Metamorphosis of a Myth* (Toronto 1982), 7-8, Hunter 1993.184f. A balanced appraisal has yet to appear (a lot has been missed).

Maybe Hera is here distorting a sentiment resembling our 'I would go to the ends of the earth [cf. Hades in *Od.* 10/11] for you': cf. Theoc. 29.37f., 'For your sake I would even go and fetch Cerberus.'

61 τὸν μὲν ἐγών ... We are not accustomed to think of Hera as an unselfish and benign goddess, and we are soon to be disabused of any such notion (64-5). The Homeric echo called in here underlines the point by contrast: *Il.* 15.29, Zeus *to* Hera, vindictive persecutor of Heracles: /τὸν μὲν ἐγὼν .. ῥυσάμην ...

μέν emphasises τόν: 'now *he* is a man whom ...'

εἰ καί περ *even if actually*, a stronger form of the familiar εἴ περ (cf. West on *Od.* 1.166-8), and very unusual: see infr. 1190 and Campbell 1973.73. εἰ .. καὶ .. περ in *Il.* 7.204 is quite different (Kirk ad loc., ctr. *GP* 488), though Ap. may have thought otherwise. — περ is commonly appended to εἰ in Homeric conditional clauses of this type: *GH* 2.279.

ἐς ⁀Ἄιδα ναυτίλληται For voyaging associated with Hades (which has a 'harbour,' Bond on Eur. *HF* 770) cf. ii.642f. (above), iv.1699 and e.g. *Od.* 10.502, Eur. *HF* 427, Hermesian. *CA* 7.3; in epitaphs the deceased (particularly if he has been a sailor) is commonly said to have 'voyaged,' 'gone on his ship' to the nether regions (see e.g. Piejko, *ZPE* 51 (1983), 196).

⁀Ἄιδα The same accus. in iv.1510 (ἐς). This and related forms are discussed by Schmidt 1968.1-9 (esp. 6), other forms of the word in Ap. by Rzach 441, 516. ⁀Ἄιδ(α) –◡(◡): Arat. 299, Timo *SH* 779.8 corr., Nic. *Ther.* 181, Max. 187; also *GVI* 969.10 (Lydia, 1st cent. AD), 1483.5 (Cappadocia, 2nd/3rd cent.), 1684.17 (Chersonnese, 1st/2nd cent.).

... ναυτίλληται (*Studies* 98 n.25) For the conditional clause cf. *GHD* 266: 'this form [viz. εἰ + subj., principal verb a future, cf. KG 2.474-5] is naturally employed by a speaker who does not wish to imply that the occasion will actually arise.' ναυτίλληται = 'make to ...' [cf. Gillies, 'try to ...']: Jason never would really (cf. Stahl 149). The aorist (Naber 30, Platt 1920.80) is quite unwelcome, and altogether unworthy of inclusion in any future *app. crit.*

62 λυσόμενος ... δεσμῶν Cf. λύσατο δεσμῶν/ later in Greg. Naz. 489.13, 517.9, Nonn. *D.* 13.27; earlier with active verb, *PV* 1006, Eur. *fr.* 128.2: but cf. *Il.* 1.401 ὑπελύσαο δεσμῶν/ (with Livrea on Pampr. 1v15, and FJW on Aesch. *Suppl.* 1065), another passage involving Hera and Athena (*not*, in Zenodotus' opinion, according to schol. A at 400*a*, the latter, who has just vanished from view here); and the general use of λυσόμενος in *Od.* 10.284 (ctr. *Il.* 1.13 al.); Vian on Nonn. *D.* 26.140.

χαλκέων ... δεσμῶν A barbed descriptive detail. No talk of the would-be adulterer's 'wheel' (Pherecyd. *FGH* 3 *fr.* 51*b*, Pind. *P.* 2.22 etc): *Cypris*, we recall, had to do with such δεσμοί (*Od.* 8.273f.; the term figures in later *topoi*: NH on Hor. *Carm.* 1.13.18) as a result of adulterous conduct (cf. 41f.n. and Campbell 1990.482), not to mention Hera herself, trapped in and eventually set free from unbreakable δεσμοί in a scrape involving Hephaestus and probably Cypris as well (cf. Anon. hymn. *CA* 7, p. 80, with Janko on *Il.* 14.256-61, and M. Delcourt, *Héphaistos* (2nd ed., Paris 1982), 60f.)!

Ἰξίονα .. δεσμῶν Eur. *HF* 1298 Ἰξίον' ἐν δεσμοῖσιν.

Ἰξίονα νειόθι cohere (*Studies* 98 n.26): 'Ixion-down-under'; cf. ii.1030-1 (*Noten* 273), iv.1379 (id. 595 n.310), and (possibly) iv.330; further: Braswell on Pind. *P.* 4.258-9(b), Gow on [Theoc.] 9.4, Campbell on Mosch. *Eur.* 9.

νειόθι Twice in early epic, *Il.* 21.317, Hes. *Theog.* 567. Affected by Ap. (9 ×, also hapax ἐπι- iv.1615, on which see Campbell 1976.340), as by Arat. (7 ×: note 437 ~ Hom. ~ Ap. i.255; 534 δύνει ~ Ap. i.63), but apart from these in Hellenistic verse only in Nic. (*Ther.* 362, *Alex.* 137, 520). It made a reappearance much later: Greg. Naz. 1379.27; Nonn. *D.* 10.154, 11.380 (cf. ii.355), 25.400 (δυομένης); Jo. Gaz. 1.123, 2.246 (δύνει); Paul. Sil. *Soph.* 538, *Amb.* 110 (cf. i.990), 157, 278. The word is discussed, but inadequately documented, by M. Hofinger, *Études sur le vocabulaire du grec archaïque* (Leiden 1981), 47-8.

63 With σθένος Hera sets another trap for the unsuspecting Cypris, see 81-2n.

ὅσσον ... σθένος .. γυίοις Theoc. 1.42 (man fishing) γυίων .. ὅσον σθένος. In 716 infr. ὅσσον σθένος with ἐστίν, and so Opp. *Hal.* 2.444, Nonn. *D.* 31.227 (ἔην Eudoc. *Cypr.* 2.449); no verb: ii.589 ~ Opp. *Hal.* 4.91, cf. id. 3.101; *SEG* 30.1272.7 (Caria, late Hellenistic/early Roman). — Differently ii.1200; Leon. Tar. *HE* 2455, Nonn. *D.* 31.86, Anon. *AP* 9.457.2.

σθένος ἔπλετο Dion. Bass. 32.4 Livrea (suppl.); [Orph.] *L.* 410 (ἔπλετο equivalent to a present, as often in Homer: cf. ii.975, iii.1229, and *GH* 2.184, Stahl 129-30, Ruijgh 1991.620).

γυίοις Here 'limbs' (a notion which springs unbidden from mention of Ixion's fate, cf. γυιο- Pind. *P.* 2.41) making up one's entire 'body' (cf., e.g., schol. T at *Il.* 3.34 γυῖα πάντα τὰ μέλη, schol. D often μέλη) is preferable to just 'hands/arms' (e.g. Gillies, VDB). See 1262n. for wider discussion of the term.

64-5 Cf. *Studies* 13-4/98 n.28. We have heard of ἄτη in 56, of acute alarm in 60, of Hera's determination to preserve Jason in 61f. So we would expect 64f. to say something like 'to ensure that Jason escapes a horrible death.' Such, broadly speaking, is her approach in iv.783-832, the eloquent and reasoned appeal to Thetis. Here she is out to shock once again, hence the sudden twist. A simple profession of affection for Jason is not enough, for Hera needs to place a *real* burden on Cypris' shoulders. This is the kind of outrageous behaviour that she herself is bound to deplore ('shared experience' motif: cf. FJW on Aesch. *Suppl.* 215): she is a victim – and a terrible avenger – in this poem: i.614-5. That is why Hera returns to the point with such gusto at the close of her speech, where everything is made to depend on the hapless Cypris.

On the theme of failure to sacrifice and consequent punishment see Richardson on *HyDem* 311f. (the principle), VDB 2.112, Bömer on Ov. *Fast.* 2.548 (various stories), Dräger 142f. (lit.: 142 n.413), 299f. (with especial ref. to Hera-Pelias); neglect of 'Pelasgian' Hera: VDB 1 on i.14 (p.51 n.1), cf. Dräger 137 with n.399. Early epic may well have been the ultimate source for the motif of a grievously offended goddess who would stop at nothing (and certainly not show the slightest concern for the sufferings of any instruments she chose to use: K. J. Dover, *Greek Popular Morality ...* (Oxford 1974), 78) to bring a human miscreant to justice (surely a primitive element in this saga: cf. *RE* 19.321.43-4) and for that of repeated disregard for a particular deity; the account of a specific prior atrocity preserved by [Apollod.] 1.9.8 (Pelias killed Tyro's stepmother Sidero in the precinct of Hera, καὶ καθόλου διετέλει τὴν Ἥραν ἀτιμάζων) may have been based on one or both of Sophocles' *Tyro* plays (Pearson, *The Fragments of Soph.* 2.271, Radt ed. p. 463), though the playwright may have been drawing on an existing tradition. However that may be, as is so often the case with the expedition's antecedents, Ap. in good Iliadic style cultivates a single-minded eclecticism. Here the calculated slight is all that need concern Cypris; for us the passage serves as a reminder of a point made only in passing in the course of the rapid assembling of the chief divine backers (i.1 Apollo, 14 Hera, 19 Athena): Pelias was a deliberate, and persistent (Beye 1982.20 seems to think in terms of a one-off indiscretion rather than a policy or habit; see Dräger 299f.) offender: ctr. the blunt and unequivocal οὐκ ἀλέγιζεν in i.14 with *Il.* 9. (535 'the rest of the gods...') 537. It is now time for Hera to do something about it.

64 ἐγγελάσῃ Pelias is Hera's enemy and will if he has his way do what victorious enemies habitually do: laugh out loud. Supply of course μοι, comparing for the suppressed dative Soph. *El.* 807, Eur. *Med.* 1362: laugh at me/my discomfiture (cf. Barrett on ἐγγελαστής in Eur. *Hipp.* 1000), at having ... The verb not in early epic: this from Soph.?? Levin 16 n.4 sees a reflection of the aversion to ridicule in Eur. *Med.*, cf. more generally PF on 61-5, and also B. M. Knox, *The*

COMMENTARY 66-74

Heroic Temper (Berkeley and Los Angeles 1966), 30-1, bibliogr. in Bond on Eur. *HF* 285, Brown cited on 102 below, Pavlock 55 with n.78.

κακὸν οἶτον Homeric, also ii.172, iii.527 (see n.; nomin. ii.893), and later e.g. [Orph.] *A*. 1313 ref. Pelias, [Apolin.] 118.173, Max. 172. — The reader will naturally recall Pelias' gruesome fate at Medea's hands (cf. 429n.); Πελίης κακόν harbours a fleeting allusion to what may have been a commonplace in Ap.'s day, Medea a κακὸν Πελίῃ, see below on 1135.

οἶτον ἀλύξας Not Homeric (ctr. *Il.* 12.113 κακὰς ὑπὸ κῆρας ἀλύξας/); Nonn. *Par.* 12.47 (2 ...) οἶτον ἄλυξε.

65 Cf. *Studies* 14. Rancorous and eager for sympathy, Hera indulges in a literary reference to help her along: the framework of the verse recalls Priam's bitter outburst against the murderous Achilles, ὅς μ' υἱῶν πολλῶν τε καὶ ἐσθλῶν εὖνιν ἔθηκε (*Il.* 22.44).

ὑπερηνορέῃ A suitably imposing word, it recurs (in the plural, and not in a pejorative sense) in Cougny 6.264.28; Homer has partic. ὑπερηνορέ(ων) (ὑπεράνορεος [gen. -έων] is very doubtful indeed in Theoc. 29.19). Pelias is ὑπερήνωρ in [Hes.] *Theog.* 995, in connexion with his imposition of an ἄεθλος on Jason (cf. 39on.).

θυέων A wholly general term, Livrea on iv.247, J. Casabona, *Recherches sur le vocabulaire des sacrifices en grec* (Aix-en-Provence 1966), Index s.v.

ἀγέραστον ἔθηκε Hermesian. *CA* 7.15 (Campbell 1982.15). ἀγέραστος with gen. here only; like ἄτιμος etc. (KG 1.377): cf. i.615 (above on 64-5) μιν γεράων ... ἄτισσαν/ ~ *HyDem* 311-2 γεράων ... τιμήν/καὶ θυσιῶν ἤμερσεν ..., Hes. *Theog.* 395-6 ἄτιμος ... ἠδ' ἀγέραστος/ then γεράων. On γέρας in connexion with sacrifice see AHS on *HyHerm* 129.

ἀγέραστος is not particularly common before the Imperial epoch: *Il.* 1.119 (ὄφρα μή 118, cf. Ap. 64), Hes. *Theog.* 395; Eur. *Bacch.* 1378, *Hec.* 115; *GVI* 1689.2 (Athens, 4th cent.) = *CEG* (2) 595.4; Bion *fr.* 6.1, [Mosch.] 3.122.

ἔθηκε The aorist is used in the sense of a perfective, 'has rendered'; not 'rendered' on one particular occasion: cf. 64-5.

66-74 See in part *Studies* 14/99 n.29. The 'fairytale' atmosphere of this stunningly picturesque passage strongly suggests that we are dealing with a story of great antiquity (cf. Robert 35, 769), and it is difficult to resist the suspicion that the 'test' to which Hera refers in 68, so far from being an Apollonian invention (so e.g. Dräger 146, 303), originally involved both Jason and Pelias representing the courteous and discourteous types familiar from folktale (cf. Gillies on 65, and H. J. Rose, *A Handbook of Greek Mythology* 291): Jason obliged, Pelias rebuffed a goddess feigning helplessness. (Early *Argonautica* cannot have been as colourless and narrowly focused as the few surviving allusions suggest, an assumption that vitiates Dräger's monograph, a first-rate work in so many respects.)

Hera here though presses the point that her involvement with Jason preceded any offence: a chance encounter ensured her good will at a time of crisis. As we might expect of a tale directed at a gullible listener, some elements do not ring true. In particular, it is hard to dissociate Pelias from the proposition that Hera was roaming not randomly but in *his* home territory ἀνδρῶν εὐνομίης πειρωμένη: an adaptation perhaps of a story which told how the goddess came to earth with the express purpose of marking out as a future instrument of vengeance a hero whose εὐνομίη could be pitted against the hybristic Pelias; a hero currently being schooled, we may recall, by Cheiron δικαιότατος Κενταύρων (see below), cf. Jason's appeal to δίκη in Pind. *P.* 4.140, Ap. ii.1180, iii.427, and more generally (the Ὑποθῆκαι) Kurke, *TAPA* 120 (1990), 85f.

However that may be, Hera goes out of her way to make her solicitous concern for Jason hinge solely on the fact that a caring mortal had done her a favour (no small favour – conditions were extremely hazardous). She has seemed egocentric indeed (61 'I,' 63 'my,' 65 'me'); now she must redress the balance somewhat: her own desire for vengeance is complemented by a genuine 'love' for Jason, a love arising from recognition of the hero's virtue (cf., in lighter surroundings, Hera's praise of Thetis' sexual mores, iv.793f.!). Here, if you like, is Hera's response to an Homeric *aporia* (not to mention the unexplained *Od.* 12.72): 'It .. remains ambiguous .. how far the gods favour mortals for their virtue and how much they are swayed by personal motives and consideration of their own τιμή,' Rutherford, *JHS* 106 (1986), 148 n.19. Now Cypris of all goddesses must appreciate the significance of divine love for a mortal. Indeed, in assisting Hera out of pity (72), Jason had acted as gods commonly act when their favourites are in trouble (Cypris herself in this poem: iv.917f. μιν [Boutes] οἰκτείρασα ...).

The main cycles of myth generate 'doublets' almost as a matter of course. *Pace* e.g. Levin (18), there is no reason why the Argonaut story could not have accommodated, from an early date, two Anauros-crossings. In the episode recounted at i.8-11 (where we observe points of similarity in χειμερίοιο ... Ἀναύρου and προχοῇσιν but also of contrast in ποσσίν/ὤμοισι and in the employment of ἀντιβολεῖν) we find, as we do here, a chronological marker, but a more precise one: Pelias received an oracle about a man with one sandal (cf. on this detail VDB 1.239, on i.17, Braswell on Pind. *P.* 4.75(a), 184(e)); *soon after*, Jason crossed the Anauros, lost a sandal and met up with Pelias *right away*; *the moment* Pelias set eyes on him he proceeded to impose an ἄεθλος. In iii.66f. there is no sense of urgency, no breathless recital; instead, an unhurried description of a 'timeless' landscape, and little in the way of firm detail about the principal character or the activity in which he is engaged ('returning from the hunt,' scil. as a budding hero 'not yet securely placed in the community' [Segal 57] under Cheiron's tutelage: cf. Pind. *N.* 3.53 *et circa*, Xen. *Cyn.* init., with Kurke, op. cit. above, 97 n.50). In addition, Ap. relates the loss of the sandal to *Apollo*'s oracle. We do not know whether Hera had any *direct* role in this strand of the story (unless we count the afterthought in Pherecydes, *FGH* 3 *fr.* 105) in the pre-Imperial epoch (Hyginus *fab.* 13, Servius auct. at Virg. *Ecl.* 4.34).

The tales of Phaon/Aphrodite and Isis/Anti: is Ap. drawing on either or both? For various viewpoints see the bibliogr. in Herter *JAW* 371 (cf. also Dräger 302 n.31). Lennox (54f.) argues for Ap.'s close adherence to the former by positing a link between *Il.* 3.386f./4 init. and the mode of disguise adopted infr. 72 in the overall context of an Olympian scene. The link at this stage is not an especially strong one, and the echo of *Il.* 3.386 is effective enough in its own right. In fact, correspondences are not nearly as sharp as some have claimed: I am as unconvinced now as I was in 1983 (*Studies* 14). For other stories of disguised gods/goddesses roaming abroad among mankind see Pfisster, *RE* Suppl. 4.285.291-2, Richardson on *HyDem* 93, VDB 2.113 (on 73), Rutherford on *Od.* 19.215, Dräger 302 n.28; old woman (as one helpless, and deserving of respect; and who could move about unchaperoned: Henderson, *TAPA* 117 (1987), 108-9): Richardson on *HyDem* 101, Bömer on Ov. *Met.* 3.275, 278, Hopkinson on Call. *h.* 6.42.

66 καὶ δ' ἄλλως Lit. 'and even otherwise,' i.e. even in circumstances having no bearing on the question of my hatred of Pelias Jason became φίλος to me. The same unit in *Il.* 20.99 ('and even in a situation <quite> distinct <from that just described>'), and later Q.S. 4.107, 13.344, Greg. Naz. 1545.36; (2 ...) Antip. Thess. *GPh* 341.

μέγα φιλ- Not in early verse; examples in Bissinger 248, cf. next note.

φίλατ' φίλασθαι is common, especially of divine love for mortals: e.g. *Il.* 5.61, iii.1002, iv.990, Bulloch on Call. *h.* 5.58; Q.S. 1.234 μέγα φ. A passive sense (cf. the Homeric φιλήσομαι, Stahl 66-7, Hoekstra on *Od.* 15.281) appears to be confined elsewhere to the participle with the solitary exception of *SEG* 38.1102, undated epigram, verse 2 ἔξοχα .. φείλαθ' ἅπασι βροτοῖς: ('dearly loved Μούσαις,' cf. πεφιλημέν- e.g. Theoc. 11.6) *GVI* 1991.15-6 (Locris, 1st cent. AD?); (Rome?/Mysia, 1st/2nd centuries) 1546.2 and (μέγα) 1862.4. Cf. Wackernagel *SU* 91 n.2 (and id. *VS* 1.138, *KS* 674), and more generally Braswell on Pind. *P.* 4.243(d).

φίλατ' Ἰήσων *Od.* 12.72 (Hera preserved Argo) ἐπεὶ φίλος ἦεν Ἰήσων/; why, we are not told. Cf. above on 66-74, and also Dräger 302.

67 ἐξότ' ... owes something to *Il.* 17.263 /ὡς δ' ὅτ' ἐπὶ προχοῇσι and to id. 11.492-3 (cf. 5.87-8) /ὡς δ' ὁπότε πλήθων ποταμὸς .. κάτεισι/ χειμάρρους κατ' ὄρεσφιν ..., and also (Campbell 1982.15) bears some resemblance to Call. *h.* 2.47-8 ἐξέτι κείνου,/ἐξότ' ἐπ' Ἀμφρυσσῷ [cf. 47-8 ~ iv.430-1; 49 ~ iii.3]; later: Mosch. *Eur.* 31 /ἢ ὅτε ... προχοῇσιν ἀναύρων/, Colluth. 104 ἐπὶ προχοῇσιν ἀναύρου/.

ἐξότ' Not in Homer. 3[H]: the only sure instance (see *SH* Index s.v.) outside Ap. (4× in all) and Call. (loc.cit. above) is provided by Euphorion, *CA* 84.5.

προχοῇσιν (of Anauros also i.11) here as often means '(running, flowing) waters': see the bibliogr. in West's note on Hes. *WD* 757, and further VDB on iv.399 (3.96 n.3), FJW on Aesch. *Suppl.* 1024-5, Braswell on Pind. *P.* 4.20(d), Campbell on Mosch. *Eur.* 31. — Eur. *HF* 390 Ἀναύρου παρὰ παγάς (ref. Cycnus, cf. *Scutum* cited next).

... πλήθοντος Ἀναύρου *Scutum* 477-8 Ἄναυρος/ὄμβρῳ χειμερίῳ (~ i.9, cf. χειμ- in the glosses of ἄναυρος, Bühler on Mosch. *Eur.* 31, p. 81 with n.4) πλήθων. Cf. Kretschmer, *Glotta* 10 (1920), 52. It is hard to take at all seriously the speculations of Reinsch-Werner, 164f.

68 *Od.* 17.487 (Russo on 485-7) the gods in disguise visit cities ἀνθρώπων ὕβριν τε καὶ εὐνομίην ἐφορῶντες. The interest taken in ὕβρις (see 66-74n., init.) is not made explicit by Hera here, but we have just been alerted to Pelias' ὑπερηνορέη (65), and the Homeric line is spoken by one of the (doomed) ὑπερηνορεόντων suitors (Lennox 53-4); the Odyssean flavouring is sustained in 74-5, see the comment. For Ap. εὐνομίη clearly means εὐδικίη, 'righteous dealing' (ἡ δικαιοσύνη καὶ ἡ καλοπραγία schol. L[m]P here); it is interesting though that Hera's recent complaint about the distribution of sacrifices reflects the significance attached in the *Odyssey*-passage to 'fair dealing/fair distribution,' a notion which according to some lies behind the element -voμ- (see e.g. Erasmus, *AClass* 3 (1960), 54).

πειρωμένη On the importance of the motif of testing in this and related stories see Kearns, *CQ* n.s. 32 (1982), 14.

ἀντεβόλησε *w*'s incoherent -σα was perhaps generated by the verb's association with disguised gods (cf. 72) encountering humans (*Od.* 7.19, 10.277, iv.1551/1592/1754). Hera casually gives the impression that Jason just happened to 'bump into' her (see on this nuance F-G on *Od.* 22.360): *we* might feel inclined to think otherwise (66-74n.).

With ἀνδρῶν then ἀντ. contrast *Od.* 11.416 and 24.87.

69 θήρης ἐξανιών But *HyHom* 19.15 corr. (possibly 5th/4th cent.) /ἄγρης ἐξανιών (cf. AHS ad loc.) ~ ii.938 ἄγρηθεν ... εἰσαναβαίνῃ/, Anon. hex. *SH* 939.20 (pap. 2nd cent. AD) /ἐξ ἄγρης ἀνιοῦ[σ]αν. Cf. ii.278 /ὡς δ' ὅτ' ... κύνες δεδαημένοι ἄγρης/ [cf. Anon. *Blem.* 63 Livrea] from *Il.* 10.360 /ὡς δ' ὅτε ... κύνε, εἰδότε θήρης/; ii.698 /τοῖσι δὲ Λητοΐδης ἄγρην πόρεν but *Od.* 9.158 αἶψα δ' ἔδωκε θεὸς .. θήρην/ (Hes. *Theog.* 440-2 τοῖς .... ἄγρην .. θεὸς ὤπασε but there of fishing, as often). ἄγρη and θήρη are interchangeable in, e.g., Herodotus (Chantraine *EVG* 66; see id. 40f. on ἄγρη in general) and Callimachus (cf. Williams on *h.* 2.60 and Mineur on *h.* 4.229), *h.* 4.229 ἄγρης: *fr.* 75.24 θήρης (~ ἄγρηθεν ii.938 above).

νιφετῷ .. ἐπαλύνετο *were being powdered with* fine particles of *snow*, cf. schol. bT at *Il.* 10.6-7 with Erbse ad loc., and infr. 1247n. Hera means that it was actually snowing high up on the mountain-tops and ridges at the time, viz. νιφετῷ = (continuously) falling snow (ctr. infr. 1359 'snow *having* fallen'), as in the main model *Il.* 10.7, to be cited presently.

For the wording cf. Nonn. *D.* 8.275 νιφετοῖς ... παλύνεται (Alph. *GPh* 3548 νιφάδεσσι). Homer (*Il.* 10.7) has νιφετόν, ὅτε ... χιὼν ἐπάλυνεν ἀρούρας/, which was to find imitators in [Opp.] *Cyn.* 3.171 χιὼν .. ὅτε πάντα παλύνει/, Triph. 189-90 ὁπότε .... χιὼν ἐπάλυνεν ἀρούρας/; cf. the likely supplement in Pampr. 3.51, Livrea ad loc. The Iliadic 'Hera's husband' (10.5) naturally vanishes in Ap.'s description.

70 οὔρεα καὶ σκοπιαί Cf. (Campbell 1982.15) Posidipp. *HE* 3102 σκοπαὶ οὔρεά θ', but closer are Greg. Naz. *AP* 8.206.1, Nonn. *D.* 15.415 (~ 4.184) σκοπιαί τε καὶ οὔρεα (<τε> Greg. Naz.: *supplevi*).

Earlier Eur. *Phoen.* 233f. οὔρειαί τε σκοπιαὶ .. νιφόβολόν τ' ὄρος ... Ctr. *HyAp* 22-3 = 144-5 /πᾶσαι .. σκοπιαί ... καὶ πρώονες ἄκροι/.. ὀρέων ... (cf. *Il.* 12.282: snow).

σκοπιαὶ περιμήκεες The same combination in ii.1056 (gen. sing.); Ap. only (ctr. *Od.* 13.183 περίμηκες ὄρος), as iv.223 πεύκη; but iv.127 δειρή ~ *Od.* 12.90, later [Orph.] *L.* 429 (from Ap.), Anon. *APl* 90.1; iv.1632 ἱστός ~ *Od.* 13.107.

For the postp. adj. cf. *Od.* 12.90 (πάντες 89) -αὶ περιμήκεες, ἐν δὲ ⌣−×, id. 13.107 (λίθε)οι περιμήκεες, (ἔνθα) τε −×; Wifstrand 1933.100.

οἱ δὲ κατ' αὐτῶν Cf. *Il.* 12.469 οἱ δὲ κατ' αὐτάς/ [αὐτάς E here; to accommodate the pronoun to the nearer noun], *Scutum* 315 οἱ δὲ κατ' αὐτόν/; similar clausulae involving κατ' in other Hellenistic verse: Arat. 52, 523, Theoc. 1.30, [Mosch.] *Meg.* 23. On the anaphoric use of αὐτός see *Noten* 147-8. The pronominal article in such configurations is commonly accompanied by (δέ +): preposition + retrospective pronoun (e.g. infr. 221(n.), Theoc. 7.7), or prep. + new locality (e.g. infr. 744, 856), or prep./adv. alone (e.g. *Il.* 5.66, iv.1575). In the second category the new subject can be associated, directly or implicitly, with what precedes, but it is not always: Svensson 141f.

71 Pronounced alliteration (which no doubt attracted the attention of the compiler(s) of *EtM*: part of this line is cited at 488.51, elucidating καναχηδά) involving κ/χ in related descriptions: ii.569-70, 680, iv.215 (cf. ii.1189!).

χείμαρροι without accompanying ποταμοί sim. is post-Homeric (LSJ s.v. II), though with the appropriate articulation a purely substantival usage may have been envisaged by some in *Il.* 5.87-8 and 11.492-3. On the question of the word's accent see Erbse on schol. *Il.* 4.452a. There is presumably a link between our passage and Theoc. 22.49-50 κυλίνδων/χειμάρρους ... (preceded by ὦμον 48 ~ infr. 73, cf. Campbell 1982.15), cf. below on 222.

καναχηδά A clear echo (cit. Gillies) in Q.S. 14.5-6 /χειμάρροις ... φέρονται/ἐξ ὀρέων καναχηδόν. The adverb in Hellenistic verse only here and Call. *h.* 4.45 Εὐρίποιο .. κ. ῥέοντος/ after Hes. *Theog.* 367 ποταμοὶ κ. ῥέοντες/ (Reinsch-Werner 237 n.3; ~ D.P. 644 -ουσιν/: Rzach, *WS* 16 (1894), 231); it is not common: Pind. *N.* 8.15, Greg. Naz. 1507.20, Nonn. *D.* 2.486. -όν in verse first D.P. 145, then Q.S. 2.217 + 3, [Orph.] *A.* 1054, Nonn. *D.*, 5 ×.

The connexion with water (probably derived from descriptions of crashing torrents, or crashing rocks swept along by torrents, cf. below): Garvie on Aesch. *Cho.* 152-3.

καναχηδὰ κυλινδόμενοι For the association compare *Il.* 16.794 (~ Matro *SH* 534.19 ~ 20 κύματ' ...!). κυλ. of a heaving mass of water also ii.732, iv.152-3 ~ *Od.* 9.147, *Il.* 11.307 and sim.; but in connexion with rapid *descent* we may recall also (so Lennox 56) the picture of a (crashing) boulder swept along by a torrent in *Il.* 13.137f. (κυλίνδεται 142 cf. *Od.* 11.598, *Scutum* 378, 438).

κυλινδόμενοι φορέοντο So Opp. *Hal.* 5.66 -οι φορέονται/, Q.S. 14.494 -ας φορέεσκε/.

72 γρηὶ δέ μ' εἰσαμένην 'I *had* made myself look like ... and so ...' Only now does Hera divulge the disguise associated with the job (68n.). *Il.* 3.386 Aphrodite /γρηὶ δέ μιν εἰκυῖα ... ~ 389 /τῇ μιν ἐεισαμένη ...: she 'reminds' her listener of a disguise adopted by herself (Lennox 55) in dealing with a beloved (415) mortal; κακὸν οἶτον too is a shared element (417 ~ supr. 64). See further 66-74n.

ὀλοφύρατο ... Here only in the poem in the weakened sense (cf. Paul 16, 126; ctr. 806n.) with acc. pers. of 'take pity on,' as e.g. *Od.* 4.364 με .. ὀλοφύρατο καί μ' ἐλέησε/ (schol. here on ὀλ., ἠλέησεν: so schol. D at *Il.* 8.245, etc.).

72-3 μ' ἀναείρας/ ... φέρεν A number of like expressions in Nonnos, *D.* 16.88 /αὐτὸς ἐμοῖς ὤμοισιν ... ἀείρων/ sim. 6.315 (~ ἀνάειρε 319), 14.268, 45.196 ἑοῖς ὤμοισιν ἀείρειν(-ων)/; so in Greg. Naz. before him: 1488.114 ἑοῖς ὤμοισιν ἀείρας/, 1527.85 ὤμοισι τεοῖσιν ἀειρόμενός μ' .. οἴσεις/. For μ' ἀναείρας cf. *Il.* 23.724 (ἀνάειρ'), for /αὐτὸς .. ὤμοισι *Od.* 22.122.

73 Jason was reared by Cheiron, who included the withstanding of torrents in his programme of heroic training according to Stat. *Ach.* 2.143f. Carspecken's strictures on Jason's 'heroism' in connexion with this exploit (106) are misguided.

διέκ 'through and clear of,' 'right across.' On the use of διέκ with accus. (which LSJ acknowledges in Suppl. s.v.) see Campbell, *Index* s.v., supplementing Ardizzoni here/Livrea on iv.860, and Archil. *IEG* 32 (Renehan 1982.56). 'Tmesis' (Vian ed. 1961) is hardly in question: cf. particularly iv.963. See also 159n.

προαλές of a plummeting mass of turbulent water or rapids: '*hapax* hom. (*Il.* 21.262) qualifiant un terrain en pente sur lequel l'eau coule rapidement; A. R. a transféré l'épithète à l'eau elle-même' Vian ed. 1961 – a wry reminder of an episode with related subject-matter: the hero Achilles attempts unsuccessfully to withstand a river's assault: *Hera* had a hand in *his* rescue (328f.).

Etymology: see Campbell 1990.482. Schol. b at *Il.* 21.262 κατάντει, καθ' ὃν τὸ ὕδωρ ἔρχεται ἅλις: cf. supr. 67 ἅλις. Schol. D ibid. κατωφερεῖ, sim. schol. Ge καταφερές then καταφέρεσθαι, see Erbse on schol. 262a¹, *b, c* for comparable glosses (including those of schol. Ap. here): cf. supr. 70-1 κατ' …. φορέοντο (and φέρεν following προαλές in this line).

Other verse examples: of an animal (?) hurtling to the ground in Dion. Bass. *fr.* 35.8 (Livrea ad loc.) προπετής/πρηνής: π]ροαλὴς ἐπὶ οὔδει suppl. Lobel; *GVI* 785.3-4 (Africa, variously dated: Peek, *Ab. Sach. Akad. Leipzig* (1972), 63.4, p. 22, Helly, *ZPE* 14 (1974), 256) μόρος prob. *premature* (cf. van der Valk 1.285).

74 τῶ νύ 'That then is why …' τῶ νύ μοι = Q.S. 4.318, 14.440.

ἄλληκτον Adverbial in i.1148, ii.940, iii.805, as in *Il.* 2.452 al. (regarded alternatively as adjectival: *LfgrE* s.v. ἄληκτος, schol.), Call. *h.* 3.149; later: Man. 3.252, Q.S. 3.132 + 4, [Orph.] *L.* 36. Adj. once in *Arg.*, i.1299 (~ Q.S. 1.156). On the spelling see VDB 1.LXXII.

περιτίεται Here only (περιτιμήεσσα *HyAp* 65), but cf. *Il.* 4.46 μοι περὶ κῆρι τίεσκετο, id. 257, 8.161. An echo in [Orph.] *A.* 807 /"Ἥρη [-η Schneider] .. περὶ πάμπαν ἐτίετο, scil. Ἰήσονα. iv.784-5 (Hera asking help of Thetis) ἐμῇσιν ἐνὶ φρεσὶ τίεται ἥρως/Αἰσονίδης …

74-5 οὐδέ … The bombshell. Hera suddenly jumps back to the point made about Pelias in 64-5. She is anxious about Jason's safety, and she will make sure he survives, she has said (63), in order to bring the human miscreant to book. But that can only be done with Cypris' cooperation, for the fate of the Argonautic expedition is in *her* hands. Suddenly catapulted into the position of making a truly momentous contribution to the successful outcome of one of myth's great adventures, she clearly has no inkling whatever of the confident forecast delivered by Phineus to the Argonauts in ii.423-4 (~ iii.549-50 νόστον).

Lennox (54) drew attention to the Odyssean flavouring here, hard on the heels of the echo in (65~) 68. We recall that Odysseus needed divine backing to secure his νόστος, and we recall the λώβη of the suitors (cf. 18.347/20.285; 19.373; 20.169 θεοὶ τισαίατο λώβην/; 24.326), whose punishment was dependent on this safe return. Add to that (*Studies* 14) an unmistakable suggestion of an *Iliadic* crisis: 9.231, Odysseus pleads with Achilles to save the hard-pressed Greeks, … εἰ μὴ σύγε δύσεαι ἀλκήν/(δείδιμεν 230 ~ supr. 60). Some sort of set-to seems to be in the offing … (81-2n.).

λώβην/τίσειεν Cf. *Or. Sib.* 7.107, 12.18 /λώβην ἐκτίσεις ~ *Il.* 11.142 τίσετε λώβην/, orac. *ap.* schol. Pind. *P.* 4.313a (PW 376.1), Q.S. 1.326 ἀποτίσετε λώβην/.

75 νόστον ὀπάσσεις Cf. i.885 (and [Orph.] *A.* 617), and ctr. *Od.* 4.172 (Zeus) νόστον ἔδωκε/. For νόστον see 175n.

Pace Platt 1914.26 and Gillies p. 138, *w*'s ὀπάσσεις is preferable to *m*'s -ῃς: see Wellauer here, Wåhlin 82 and esp. VDB 2.53 n.2 (cf. id. 1.LXVI n.1 on the other variants). On the type εἰ μὴ βοηθήσετε in general see KG 2.466. The potential in the protasis has an Homeric precedent in *Il.* 24.56-7 (cf. *GH* 2.284).

76f. Cf. in part *Studies* 15/99 n.30. Cypris' immediate attack (aorist λάβε 76) of vocal paralysis is prompted by the substance of what she has *heard* (cf. ἀκούσας in *Il.* 17.694 cited in 76n., an element omitted, as here, in *Od.* 4.703f.): it is now all down to her. At the same time, a feeling of awe inspired by the *sight* (we can mentally supply the gestures) of the revered goddess (cf. 79) begging *her* (cf. below on 148-50) to intervene at a point of crisis (59f.) induced her to adopt a far different tone (ctr. 51) in her subsequent (ἔπειτα 78) reply. There seems no point in raising difficulties about the duration of her speechlessness (so Lennox 57-8) when its duration is not at issue (no δήν, ὀψέ).

76-80 *Il.* 5.416-22 /ἣ ῥα .... εἰσορόωσαι ... Ἥρη/.. ἐπέεσσι .... Κύπρις then (cf. infr. 81f.) a sermon about the proper ἔργα of Aphrodite, cf. 81-2n.

76 Clearly based on *Il.* 17.694-5, *Od.* 4.703-4 (concerning recipients of bad news) /ὣς ἔφατ' (φάτο) .../δὴν δέ μιν ἀμφασίη ἐπέων λάβε (οὐδέ τίς ἐστι χάρις *Od.* 4.695, ... κακὸν εἴη/ 697 cf. Ap. 82 and 79), but embellished with novel substitutions: (1) ὣς ηὔδα, occupying the slot filled by Homer's ὣς ἄρ' ἔφη, Ap. only, also infr. 564, 912, iv.99, 1380, 1562 (cf. Aesch. *Th.* 590-1 τοιαῦθ' .... ηὔδα, capping a speech). (2) A hapax ἐνεοστασίη, corr. Bigot (Vian 1975.91), Ruhnken (cf. the highly probable ἐνεό-φρων in Panyas. *EGF fr.* 12.11, where misdivision has likewise caused problems; Roth, *RhM* n.s. 134 (1991), 239f. argues unconvincingly for *codd.*'s reading): 'a (fixed) state, condition of ἐνεότης' Vian ed. 1961 (not 'a standing dumb' as LSJ and some others), mischievously implying that Cypris' speechlessness was to be a permanent condition; amplified by μύθων because ἐνεός *need* not mean 'dumb.'

(Ruhnken made the crude conjecture θυμόν, borrowing the clausula of infr. 284, where however more than mere 'speechlessness' is in question.) Given the paradosis there is nothing to be gained by insisting on δ' ἀνεοστασίη, preferred by Ruhnken and Ardizzoni, cl. Hesych. α4908 – indeed this is a most improbable concoction, drawing as it does on epic ἄνεω ἄνεῳ *ἄνεως.

77 ἅζετο of one god's respect for or awe of another: West on Hes. *Theog.* 532 (object Hera: *HyHom* 12.5). See on 76f. Cypris' whole manner is transformed by the sight of Hera's earnest supplication: after the sarcastic περίεστε θεάων (54), a genuinely deferential πότνα θεά in 79.

ἀντομένην In the sense *supplicate, implore* also ii.1123 (i.q. *SH* 1018?? See edd. ad loc. Cf. Eur. *Alc.* 1098), iii.149, 391, iv.1096 (Livrea ad loc.), 1555; first thus in Attic drama and (cf. Boesch 35) Emped. DK31 B3.4; cf. also *SEG* 17.502.12 (Miletus, 2nd cent. BC; Hermann, *Hermes* 86 (1958), 118). Occasionally thereafter: Luc. *Ocyp.* 155, [Orph.] *A.* 617, [Apolin.] 27.4. For the gen. pers. (here only) cf. the use of ἀντιόωσα in i.703. Cf. also 35n.

εἰσορόωσα A participle suggested no doubt by *Od.* 4.142 σέβας μ' ἔχει εἰσορόωσαν/ and the like.

78 καί μιν ἔπειτ' 3ın. *HyAp* 106, ii.462 ... ἔπειτ' ἐπέεσσιν ... (but not prefacing direct speech).

ἀγανοῖσι ... ἐπέεσσι Theoc. 13.54, cf. infr. 1146; closed up in Homer, *Il.* 2.164 al., and so Q.S. 14.443. ἀγανός applied to speech or to actions is broadly like μειλίχιος, 'mild,' 'gentle,' often 'winning,' 'soothing,' 'mollifying,' 'conciliatory,' 'propitiatory' and so on. See in general *LfgrE* s.v., and Scott, *ACD* 24 (1981), 1f. Cypris, previously brusque and sarcastic, now falls over herself to be pleasant and obliging: gods are not known for doing favours with no prospect of a solid return, but *she* will not insist on the principle of reciprocity (see on that e.g. Rutherford on *Od.* 19.365-8)!

προσέννεπεν .. ἐπέεσσι Similarly infr. 474 δὴ τότ' Ἰήσονα τοῖσδε προσέννεπεν Ἄργος ἔπεσσιν, cf. 433. On the verb: 3ın.

ἥγ' ἐπέεσσι *Od.* 4.136-7 codd. /ἕζετο δ' .../αὐτίκα δ' ἥγ' ἐπέεσσι κτλ. On ἥγ' here cf. Vian 1973.85.

79 *Homerica*: *Od.* 5.215 /πότνα θεά, μή μοι + *Il.* 22.358 al. μή τοι τι + id. 19.321 (οὐ ...) τι κακώτερον ἄλλο πάθοιμι/ (τι .. κακώτερον ἄλλο with gen. comparison: *Od.* 8.138).

COMMENTARY 81–2

Cypris invokes a curse on her own head (examples in KG 1.227, cf. infr. 728f., VDB 2.53 n.3): Hera is to feel free to regard Cypris as the most worthless/vilest thing in the world (hardly a novelty this, from many a miserable lover's point of view!) if ... For πότνα θεά in a similar outburst cf. *Od.* 20.61f., for τοι id. 17.513. Fränkel's οὐ (which gains no support whatever from *Il.* 19.321 cited above, *pace* Irigoin, *REG* 74 (1961), 515 and Chantraine 1962.314) is feeble (*Noten* 333-4); Brunck (ed. 1810) tried to cram in an ἄν!

πότνα θεά Although three times in *Il.* Zeus addresses his (quarrelsome/irritating) wife with the formal (and formulaic) βοῶπις πότνια Ἥρη/ (8.471, 15.49, 18.357), the Odyssean πότνα θεά is reserved for mortals respectfully/warily addressing deities whose power and superiority are of immediate concern: 5.215, 13.391, 20.61, cf. infr. 467; Bulloch on Call. *h.* 5.86.

πότνα is always vocatival in Ap. (infr. 467, iv.1026), as nearly always elsewhere: Schulze *KS* 325f., Richardson on *HyDem* 118, Pfeiffer on Call. *fr.* 63.8.

80 εἰ δὴ ... ἀθερίζω resembles i.123 Αἰσονίδαο λιλαιομένου ἀθερίξαι/, of Heracles (!) responding to Jason's ardent desire <put in the form of an urgent request> that he should participate in the expedition; so the accusatives here in 81, as the flow of 80-1 anyway indicates, must mean 'in respect of ...'; λιλ. 'absolutely' also i.350, iv.256, 802.

ἀθερίζω is generally taken to be a subjunctive (scil. κεν, 61n.), but it could well be a 'semi-prospective' pres. indic.: 'if it comes to this, that [cf. εἰ δή in *Il.* 1.61, 'if it is actually the case that,' with *GP* 223-4] I do <turn out to: cf. ἀθερίζειν infr. 548n.> ...' — On the verb in general see Hainsworth on *Od.* 8.212, Heubeck on id. 23.174-6, on its behaviour in Ap. Ardizzoni on i.123, Boesch 30; c. gen. pers./rei (as ἀλέγειν ἀλεγίζειν sim.) apparently in Ap. only. In Homer always accompanied by a negative: ctr. infr. 94, al., and Posidipp. *HE* 3076; often so later on, e.g. Man. 2.281, 6.217, [Orph.] *L.* 681, Nonn. *D.* 31.136, Colluth. 149. The verb not otherwise in 3[H].

81-2 Cf. *Studies* 14-5. When Hera confronts Cypris with a request for assistance in *Il.* 14, she mentions only ἔπος (190), and the latter picks up this element in her obliging and respectful (n.b. πρέσβα θεά 194) response at 195, cf. ἔπος 212. Our Cypris mentions ἔπος, but dwells on ἔργον. Hera has teasingly referred to an imminent ἔργον in 59(n.); her language in 63 has served to reinforce the image of strong-arm tactics (cf. *Noten* 333, on 76-82); underlying the climactic εἰ μὴ σύγε ... of 75 was Odysseus' plea that Achilles should enter the fray (74-5n.). Hera has indeed come to urge Cypris to use ἔπος (εἰπεῖν 26), but she has led her to suppose that what she is after is ἔργον.

However, Cypris' offer of help must be a qualified one: '... or any action that these two hands here could execute-with-effort, strengthless as they are.' This is not the familiar formidable overseer of the erotic sphere whose ἔργα are celebrated in *HyAphr*, and who possesses σθένος in good measure (Soph. *Trach*. 498, Eur. *fr*. 898.6, cf. on 91f.), but the ἄναλκις θεά of *Il*. 5.331, wounded by Diomede on her χεῖρα .../ἀβληχρήν (336f. cf. also 425), whose interference on the battlefield provoked caustic remarks from Hera and Athena (418f. cf. 76-80n.). Cypris of course is deadly serious, even if the poet is not. It is hard to see how she can be described as being 'confident in the strength of her right arm,' as Lennox asserts (59).

81 ἢ ἔπος ... Uses phraseology borrowed from Homer: *Od*. 3.99, 4.329 /ἢ ἔπος ἠέ τι ἔργον (both of Odysseus fighting at Troy, cf. above on 81-2); *Il*. 10.282 ἔργον, ὅ κε(ν); *Od*. 9.126 οἵ κε κάμοιεν/.

χέρες 50n. Ctr. *Il*. 5.735 κάμε χερσίν, id. 21.26 κάμε χεῖρας and sim.

αἵδε She holds them up. αἵδε, D only, is essential ('αἵγε seems here to trespass the bounds of belief' Platt 1918.135, who failed however to convince Gillies or Ardizzoni. See further Speake 1969.92 and 1975.109). S alone has the correct οἵδ' 326 infr., cf. Ω's false offerings at ii.848, iii.363, iv.1236.

Not αἶδε (Vian ed. 1961) as prescribed by Herodian (La Roche *HTA* 364, West on Hes. *WD* 80): cf. Irigoin, *REG* 76 (1963), 495.

82 ἠπεδαναί *infirm, feeble,* enunciated with telling emphasis (15n.). Cf. amongst the glosses notably schol. D at *Il*. 8.104, = ἀσθενής (ctr. σθένος... in 63), opp. ἔμπεδος. It is comical that Cypris uses a word associated with her husband Hephaestus (*Od*. 8.311, 'infirm,' Hephaestus there being the target of his wife's scorn; *HyAp* 316), particularly as κάμνειν is regularly employed in connexion with a craftsman the power of whose '*hands/arms*' was quite unaffected by his physical abnormality.

ἠπεδαναί then χάρις: these elements in reverse at ii.799-800.

καὶ μή τις ... In *Il*. 14.235/267/275 Hera wittily talks of χάρις/ Χάρις to Hypnos (cf. Lennox 58; Janko on 233-41); our Hera, unlike Cypris, does not have to bother resorting to bribes. On the contrary, Cypris, goddess though she may be (78n.), is quick to make the point that she wants no favour in return: if the service is free, the request may not be too extravagant! On top of that of course there is the question of just *who* Hephaestus' consort is (see Haslam, *HSCP* 94 (1992), 200 n.5)!

For ἀμοιβαίη χάρις cf. Leon. Tar. *HE* 2073, Nonn. *D.* 16.199-200, and earlier *Od.* 3.58 (+ dedicatory inscriptions) χαρίεσσαν ἀμοιβήν/; (cit. Gillies) Soph. *El.* 134. There is presumably some connexion with Call. *h.* 4.152 χάριτος δέ τοι ἔσσετ' ἀμοιβή/: κακόν 151, κάμεν 153, cf. Ap. 79, 81.

Clausula: sim. *Il.* 9.316, 17.147 (οὐκ .. τις) χάρις ἦεν/, scil. for *fighting*, see on 81-2; infr. 144.

On the variants in E see Fränkel *Einleitung* 46 n.1.

μή τις ... ἔστω Cf. *Od.* 2.230 = 5.8.

83 ὣς ἔφαθ' (*Il.* 2.807 etc.) also in iv.1363 (~ *Il.* 3.95 al.). Ctr. *Il.* 12.173 /ὣς ἔφατ' ... ἀγορεύων/, 20.379 /ὣς ἔφαθ', Ἕκτωρ δ' αὖτις ἐδύσετο ...

/ὣς ἔφατ' or ἔφαθ' 16 × in *Arg.*; nowhere else in 3ᴴ.

αὖτις .. ἀγόρευσεν But αὖτις .. ἀγόρευεν/ iv.756 Ω (cf. for this Ω at i.756, iii.567, in the latter case -ευσεν G only); see Vian 1962.39 and esp. 1970.86; infr. 544, 567nn. Not an Homeric combination.

ἐπιφραδέως Cf. *Studies* 15/99 n.32. Ap.'s own use of this adverb supports the interpretation 'in a considered fashion' (cf. Rieu, 'choosing her words with care'): i.1021 'no one had the presence of mind to realise,' i.1336/ii.1134 a considered reply/question. Hera has thought everything out: she is after all working to a prearranged plan. As expected, Cypris has got things wrong, and it is Hera's intention to get things right. Hera can assure her that no violence is envisaged, but rather a non-combative approach to her son: fine in theory, awkward in practice, as she artfully recognises. Cypris of course is not going to take kindly to the suggestion, but that is of no moment.

The adverb is rare outside Ap.: Parmen. DK28 B1.16 (skilfully, cunningly); Anon. hex. *PHamb* 123.4 (context not recoverable); [Orph.] *A.* 1362, heavy-handed, if the text is right: 'Hyperion was carefully angry,' i.e. 'jealously nursed his wrath' (?): Vian however emends to ἀριφραδέως; Max. 21, 498 (prudently, with presence of mind); Hesych. ε5395 ἐπιφραδέστερον· συνετώτερον.

84 We're not in the *Iliad* now! (Cf. Zanker, 1987.196, last full paragr.).

οὔτι ... ἱκάνομεν οὐδέ ... Cf. Jason infr. 386-8. Ctr. *Il.* 21.316 οὔτε [οὔτε E mistakenly here] βίην ... οὔτε τι ...

βίης ... χειρῶν In normal terms 'brute force' and 'violent measures' (cf. LSJ under χείρ IV fin.; also i.505 ~ *Il.* 3.431 + Hes. *Theog.* 490-1, cf. id. 677, and infr. 351n.), but Hera takes the opportunity to have a quiet dig at Cypris' pathetic pronouncement on 'hands' in 81. Marvellous stuff.

χατέουσαι Of being in urgent need of help in combat in *Il.* 9.518; no doubt χατίζει used in connexion with Thetis' (very different) approach to Hephaestus in *Il.* 18 (392) was also in Ap.'s mind here. Ctr. *Od.* 22.351-2 οὔτι ... οὐδὲ χατίζων/πωλεύμην ...

85 ἀλλ' αὔτως Cf. *Studies* 15/99 n.34. 'No, just...': αὔτως (here 'simply,' 'merely'; /ἀλλ' αὔτως *Il.* 18.198 vulg. al., infr. 769 al.) is immensely loaded. Hera will have heard of Eros and his ways: she lives on Olympus, he roams at large on Olympus – a κοῦρος who has been around long enough to have made his presence felt. Fränkel (*Noten* 334) curiously claims that Hera will know nothing of Cypris' problems. δηναιάς in 53 could imply that nobody goes near the mother unless it is absolutely necessary.

ἀκέουσα Cf. *Studies* 99 n.33; *Il.* 1.565 (+ imperative), *HyDem* 194 /ἀλλ' ἀκέουσα ... Here not 'without a word' (Gillies and some others) but 'peacably': no violent measures are called for, simply an instruction. ἀκέων is sometimes not σιγῶν but ἡσυχάζων (cf. schol. D at *Il.* 1.565 al., Henrichs 246 n.15, *LfgrE* s.v., schol. (a)): so e.g. *Od.* 2.311, 14.195 'in peace and quiet' (see West and Hoekstra on these passages for a contrary view), i.765 ἀκέοις of a bemused onlooker (~ ἠρεμέοντες i.514), ii.1086 ἀκήν (cf. par. schol. and van Krevelen 1949.143-4; Kirk on *Il.* 3.95), ἔκηλος (176, 969nn.)/ εὔκηλος (769, 1172nn.) often.

ἐπικέκλεο *call upon* to do, hence with dative as κέλεσθαι (e.g. infr. 838; but in iv.1343 φίλους not φίλοις should be read). Since imperat. 'instruct' may be expressed with either pres. or aor. (note e.g. *Od.* 17.345 /δὸς ... αὐτόν τε κέλευε/ as against 7.163 /εἷσον .. σὺ δὲ .. κέλευσον/), it is hard to say how Ap. envisaged either ἐπικέκλεο here or κέκλεο i.707 (the latter also [Orph.] *L.* 341, 623; Colluth. 74 [cf. ὄπαζε 73?]; Hesych. κ2058 κέκλεο· κάλεσον, 2069 κέκλου likewise). Unequivocally pres. formations (Boesch 13, Marxer 12; but κεκλόμενος had functioned as a pres. long before: *Il.* 8.346(-7!), Hes. *Theog.* 686, Aesch. [FJW on *Suppl.* 40], Soph. [Sideras 89, 109] etc.) are encountered for the first time in Ap.: ii.693, iii.908 κέκλομαι ([Orph.] *L.* 179; ἐπικέκλομαι [Orph.] *h. pr.* 17), i.716 κέκλεται (Opp. *Hal.* 3.311, 5.669); κεκλόμεθα occurs in *SEG* 15.853.14 (Alexandria, 2nd cent. AD).

(ἐ)κέκλετο and κεκλόμεν(ος) were commonly glossed with imperf./

pres.: *LH* s.v. κέλομαι, p. 757(a); schol. D Homer often, e.g. at 6.66, 8.346, 9.454, 11.91, 312. Cf. the comment on ἀγέρονται in 895.

86-9 Not so much a variation on as an artful elaboration of supr. 27-9, designed to appeal to a goddess who takes no pleasure in strong-arm tactics. Since Medea is, like Cypris herself (though that is not stated), δολόεσσα, the 'safe return' which must be secured by her (75) as a fellow-goddess who cannot condone Pelias' conduct will, Hera is convinced, be accomplished *with ease*, without incurring the dangers inherent in open conflict of the kind impishly hinted at in 56-75.

Hera is of course keeping her cards close to her chest. She here dissociates the question of Pelias' punishment (dependent on Jason's/ the expedition's return, 74-5) from Medea's projected involvement: in reality, the latter is being marked out as an instrument of terrible vengeance (iii.1134f./iv.241f.).

86 παρθένον *(young) daughter*, here plainly *unmarried* (echoing … παρθενικάς in the proem, cf. Buccholz 81) *daughter*. Cypris uses the same term infr. 142 for Eros' benefit, and only afterwards κούρη (153), which often denotes a young married girl. For παρθένος + gen. parent in the sense '(virgin/marriageable) daughter' see Pfeiffer on Call. *fr*. 2*a*25 (vol. 2, p. 103), id. in *SBAW* 1958.6.19, Bond on Eur. *HF* 834, Renehan, *HSCP* 87 (1983), 26, adding Lyc. 1175; iv.1743 Νηρῆος .. παρθενικῇσιν/. Cf. too Pearson on καλλιπάρθενοι in Eur. *Hel*. 1.

παρθένον .. θέλξον πόθῳ See on 4-5, 27-8, 33; Nonn. *D*. 16.133 πόθῳ φρένα θέλξον. Hera of course delicately avoids calling a spade a spade (Hutchinson 118, cf. 86-9n.): in fact, Cypris is being asked to set her δολόεσσα ἀρωγή in motion (~ δόλον 12).

πόθῳ Αἰσονίδαο The other way round infr. 752.

87 A recasting of *Od*. 6.313f., 7.75f. εἴ κέν τοι κείνη γε φίλα φρονέῃσ᾽ ἐνὶ θυμῷ κτλ., where a *woman*, Nausicaa's mother, will afford Odysseus hope of a return home. (*Od*. 6.313-5: 'plus-verses' Hainsworth ad loc.: not apparently for Ap., cf. νόστιμον ἦμαρ 311 ~ νοστήσειν 89?).

κείνη 28-9n.

συμφράσσεται Applied to Medea infr. 698, iv.438. Here, as infr. 918, 'act as counsellor, συμφράδμων' to. οἱ + σ.: *Il*. 1.537, 9.374, Hes. *Theog*. 900.

εὐμενέουσα A favourite with Ap. (12 ×); rare before the Imperial period: suppl. in *CEG* (1) 352, Corinth *c*. 650 (note that in *HyHom* 24.4, adduced by Boesch 41, εὐμενέουσα is not the transmitted reading), Pind. *P.* 4.127, Theoc. 17.62, Alcaeus *HE* 81, suppl. in Cercidas *CA* 5.5. On this type of clausula (cf. Hom. δυσμενής ~ -έοντες, and Marxer 36) see Leumann 116 n.83, Risch 308-9.

88 ῥηιδίως Ctr. Argos' gloomy – and realistic – οὐ μὰν οὐδ' ἀπάνευθεν ἑλεῖν δέρος Αἰήταο/ῥηίδιον at ii.1207f. I doubt if we are meant to think for one moment that Hera (who is bent on presenting a clinching argument, 86-9n.) *cannot* foresee the problems ahead (so Fränkel *Noten* 331).

ῥηιδίως .. ἑλόντα *Od.* 9.313 /ῥ. (ἀφ)ελὼν ...

ἑλόντα Cf. below, and ii.1207; 12-3n.

δέρος 12 × in the poem of the Golden Fleece, as Eur. *Hyps.*, I, II 23 τὸ χρυσεόμαλλον .. δέρος (cf. Bond, ed. p. 68) sim. Adesp. *TGF* 37a, *Med.* 5 τὸ πάγχρυσον -ος (v.l. -ας, Page ad loc.), 480 π. .. -ος (v.l. -ας), and later [Orph.] *A.* 890-1 δέρας (Ω: -ος) χρύσειον ἕλωμεν [cf. id. 939-40]/ῥᾷστα, 926-7 χρύσειον .... δέρας (v.l. -ος), 1019 δέρας (v.l. -ος). For various permutations involving the word see below on 180, 404 (v.l. -ας, cf. iv.1319), 620, and for 'golden δέρος' Wifstrand 1933.122-3, Fantuzzi 24 n.35; also 13n. on χρύσεον ... κῶας.

ὀίω 28-9n.

89 νοστήσειν ἐς Ἰωλκόν iv.1163 (-ήσας), see on 2. Cf. *Il.* 10.247 νοστήσαιμεν, ἐπεὶ (sim. 18.90) περίοιδε νοῆσαι/, *Od.* 20.328-9 ἐώλπει/ νοστήσειν.

ἐπεὶ δολόεσσα τέτυκται Odyssean models: 23.188 (/ῥεῖα ...) ἐπεὶ ... τέτυκται/, 17.102, 19.595 στονόεσσα τέτυκται/, 8.281 γὰρ δολόεντα τέτυκτο/. With this last (Lennox 59) Hera works in a further (41f.n.) snide reference to the entrapment of <the wily> Cypris by her <wilier> husband: indeed, all the other *Odyssey* passages cited above concern a *bed*.

There is a strong streak of irony in the epithet δολόεσσα. We think of the duplicitous Circe (for the parallelism see 27n.) who *stood in the way of* Odysseus' νόστος (*Od.* 9.32 ~ 34f.; Calypso too attracted the same label: 7.245, schol. T καὶ μὴν οὐκ ἦν φαρμακίς, ἀλλ' ὅτι αὐτὸν ἦγεν ἐξαπατῶσα καὶ ἀφῄρει τὸν νόστον, cf. Hainsworth ad loc.); but also of Cypris herself (cf. 86-9n.), whose δολόεσσα ἀρωγή unbeknown to her (74-5n.) was to *ensure the success of* the Argonautic expedition (ii.423-4, containing the only other example of δολόεις in the poem) – manipulated by Hera, who is now well on the way towards implementing the δόλος fielded in 12, where see comment.

δολόεσσα of Medea: Agath. *AP* 4.4.25 (παρθενική).

90 For the opening formula see 30n. (*HyHerm* 39 /ὣς ἄρ' ἔφη ... ἀμφοτέρῃσιν ...). — *Od.* 8.433 ὣς ἔφατ', Ἀρήτη δὲ μετὰ δμωῇσιν ἔειπεν (but not introducing direct speech), *Il.* 3.85 (/ὣς ἔφαθ' 84), 7.66 Ἕκτωρ δὲ μετ' ἀμφοτέροισιν ('both sides') ἔειπε/.

ἀμφοτέρῃσιν Cypris has been approached with an urgent request for assistance by two goddesses of stature (cf. 25 ἄμφω). She now tries somewhat weakly to suggest that the same procedure be adopted for Eros in the hope that he will not prove to be wholly devoid of shame. When that cuts no ice, Cypris' own sense of shame (102f.) leaves her with no option but to fall in with what both (ἀμφοτέρῃσι 104) want.

91f. Cf. *Studies* 15-6. As Hera well knows, there is a snag. The mother in this poem does not have βέλεα on tap, with the small armed Eros of the vase-painters in attendance to work her will (see on this Suter, *Glotta* 63 (1985), 148). Cypris is so taken aback that she blurts out her whole sorry story (cf. 102-3) – a concentrated package of themes attested here for the first time:

(1) Antagonism between mother and son: [Mosch.] 1 (an overblown epigram, in effect), Luc. *D. Deor.* 11 (passing reference).

Cypris is here represented comically (the more so, if we recall that in earlier literature Cypris and Eros are often to all intents and purposes indistinguishable, and the mother, like the son, can pack a mighty punch: see e.g. Davies, ed. Soph. *Trach.*, pp. 137-9) as falling foul of Eros in his capacity as a 'fighter': since he cannot be vanquished, she is fighting a losing battle anyway. And just as Eros can stir up animosity even amongst close relatives or friends, so he is bound to be at loggerheads with his own nearest and dearest. For these concepts cf., e.g., from tragedy, Soph. *Ant.* 781f. where Eros is responsible for νεῖκος amongst kinsmen (similarly ἔρις on a massive scale is generated by ἔρως in Eur. *IA* 585f., cf. Wilson, *G&R* 26 (1979), 16-7, Willink on id. *Or.* 1001-2), just as in iv.446 the Ares-like (136n.) figure of Ἔρως is said to be the source of ἔριδες when Medea is involved in her own brother's murder; id. *Trach.* 441-2 (and Deianeira in id. 492); Eur. *Hipp.* 525f., *ffr.* 430.3, 431.4-5.

(2) Her inability to control him once he is angered: Meleag. *HE* 4205, *Ciris* 133-4, Apul. *Met.* 5.30 al. The anger-motif is turned on its head by Hera, 109-10n.

(3) Threats to set fire to/break bow and arrows: from a (frustrated) lover Meleag. *HE* 4028f., Tib. 2.6.15f., Smith ad loc. See 96n. We may recall that Homer's *Hera* made an example of an obstreperous

goddess by turning her attention to her bow and arrows (*Il.* 21.489f.); but Hera was an expert in πόλεμος (487).

— There are of course general lessons to be learned from this tale of woe: cf. Beye 1982.17; *pace* e.g. Huber 39, this is not *pure* fun.

91 Ἥρη Ἀθηναίη τε 8n.

91-2 πίθοιτο .... ἐμοί Convincing pre-Apollonian examples of uncomplicated 'superlative for comparative' (whether followed up with ἤ or with gen. comparison) are hard to come by: KG 1.22-3 and *GG* 2.100 are both too accommodating. On the other hand, μάλιστα (though evidently not for the author of the tame Anon. encom. *GDK* 16.21) is in a special category, as the word often bears what is essentially a comparative nuance: 'more or less,' 'more than anything,' 'in comparison with others,' and so on. This is undoubtedly how one should explain Thgn. *IEG* 173-4, ἄνδρ' ἀγαθὸν πενίη πάντων δάμνησι μάλιστα (scil. 'more than anything': μάλιον Peppmüller, not an attractive suggestion),/καὶ γήρως .. καὶ ἠπιάλου; Eur. *IA* 1594, where an 'in preference to' is to be extracted from μάλιστα, also seems unimpeachable; cf. also E. Mayser, *Grammatik der griechischen Papyri aus der Ptolemäerzeit*, 2.1.54. So Cypris here switches from a heartfelt 'he would listen to you most of all/as to no other' [cf. *Il.* 10.57 /κείνῳ (-ου *vulg.*) .. κε μάλιστα πιθοίατο .. γὰρ ...] to an emphatic and rueful ἢ ἐμοί, '<sooner> than he would me.' For the liveliness of the expression cf. the use of *positive* for comparative in ii.225f. (the animated Phineus).

πίθοιτο We recall Hera's knowing ... πίθηται (26).

... ὔμμι μάλιστα *Il.* 6.77 /Αἰνεία τε καὶ Ἕκτωρ ... ὔμμι μάλιστα/. Cypris again (cf. *Il.* 10.57 cited above) borrows the language of men caught up in conflict – as she is herself (94f.).

ἢ ἐμοί 'sooner than to me': 'and I'm his mother' is left unsaid. Cypris' model is more explicit: *Il.* 8.190 '.../ἢ ἐμοί, and I'm her husband!,' another light-hearted (but for some, problematic) slice of life. The joke of course is that there is no reason why Eros *should* do what Hera and Athena tell him to do: but Cypris is anxious to pass the buck.

92 ὑμείων Emphatic: she points at them.

ἀναιδήτῳ ἀναίδητος for ἀναιδής again in iv.360 (ref. Medea's conduct: as often Eros' attribute is reflected in one of his victims); a useful-looking formation, but it does not seem to have caught on: Eudoc. *Cypr.* 1.302, Nonn. *D.* 48.342. See in general VDB 2.14.

93 τυτθή γ' Ap. is partial to this combination: ii.873, iii.603, 1250, iv.832. On -ή rather than -ός see LSJ s.v. *ad init.* and Kastner 24 (3^H: add Maiistas *CA* 29).

αἰδώς .. ἐν ὄμμασιν Not 'before your eyes, in your presence' (e.g. Ardizzoni) but 'of/towards you [cf. e.g. Pind. *P.* 4.218 τοκέων .. αἰδῶ] there will be at least a scrap of shame/respect in his eyes' – eyes, because αἰδώς is regularly said to be lodged in them: cf. [Longin.] *de subl.* 4.4 (citing *Il.* 1.225), infr. 1068, and the material assembled by Gillies here, Richardson on *HyDem* 214f., Bulloch, *CQ* n.s. 20 (1970), 270-1, Gould 88 n.74, Harder on Eur. *Cresph. fr.* 457. Cypris will be thinking of the defiant looks she is accustomed to receive from her impudent offspring. Castiglioni's ἐπ' ὄμμασιν (*ap.* Fränkel OCT), though it can muster plenty of support (*HyDem* 214f. ἐπί ... ὄμμασιν αἰδώς/, Thgn. *IEG* 85-6, Call. *SH* 239.7, Anon. *HE* 3788-9, Q.S. 14.39f.; also Theoc. 18.37) is almost certainly superfluous: cf. (on one interpretation) Call. *h.* 6.102 and, closer still (Campbell 1982.15, see now the commendation in VDB 2².150), Greg. Naz. 1576.318 /αἰδώς ... ἐν ὄμμασιν. As VDB say (2.113), it seems unwise to replace ἔσσετ' with ἕσσετ' (Fränkel *Noten* 334), familiar though the metaphor of 'sitting' is in expressions of this broad type (cf. Davies, *Maia* 36 (1984), 15-6, Hopkinson on Call. *h.* 6.102).

ὄμμασιν McKay (*Mnemosyne* Suppl. 6 (1962), 30 n.5) toys with the idea of reading ὄθμασιν here: far-fetched of course, though the possibility cannot be ruled out that with ὄμ(μασιν) .... ὄθ(εται) Ap. is glancing at what may have been perceived at the time as a distinctively Callimachean affectation (Pfeiffer on *fr.* 1.37, Schmitt 102 n.16) or even at a particular specimen of etymologising/word-play (ὄθμα associated with lack of shame: *fr.* 186.29, *SH* 239.(7~)10; ὄθεσθαι however is not so far known from Call., and there is no ancient evidence for associating the two words, as does, e.g., Doederlein 1.154).

αὐτὰρ ἐμεῖο An identical clausula in Call. *h.* 6.99 and orac. *ap.* Porph. *Plot.* 22 (PW 473.50); internally *Il.* 23.69 (in the course of a complaint).

94 οὐκ ὄθεται Cf. *Il.* 15.166 and 182 (4 ...; in a pentameter Androm. *GDK* 62.4); id. 107 /οὐδ' ὄθεται (split up in i.1267).

This rare verb evokes memories of wider contexts: (1) The bitter quarrel of Agamemnon and Achilles in *Il.* 1: 177 ἔρις, 181 ἀπειλήσω, 192 ἐρητύσειε .. θυμόν/: cf. Ap. 94, 97, 98. (2) Dione's outburst in *Il.* 5 to Aphrodite wounded by Diomede (cf. Lennox 60): Heracles was similarly violent, οὐκ ὄθετ' .../ὃς τόξοισιν (!) ἔκηδε θεούς (403f.), threat

(411f.). (3) *Il.* 15.107 Hera's complaint against the scornful Zeus, confident in his own superiority and physical power.

μάλα δ' αἰέν An elongated version of the Homeric μάλ' αἰεί from the whimpering mother: 'absolutely ... all of the time.' — ἐριδμαίνωσιν in *Il.* 16.260 (see below) is followed up with an αἰεί in 261 – a line athetesised by Aristophanes and Aristarchus (cf. Lührs 92f.).

ἐριδμαίνων Cf. *Studies* 99 n.36, and see above on 91f. Intrans. according to LSJ and some others. Eros is certainly a wrangler, but I see no reason (109 infr. tells us nothing) why the verb here cannot bear the significance it was generally held to possess, rightly or wrongly (Campbell on Mosch. *Eur.* 69), in *Il.* 16.260, an Homeric hapax (likewise in our poem) of boys irritating wasps, i.q. ἐρεθίζων (the phonetic make-up of the neighbouring ἀθερίζ- may not be coincidental), 'provoking': so schol. D *Il.* and others ad loc. Cf. Cypris' following words. Eros baits his mother all the time, whether in reality or in her bewildered imagination.

It may be worth dwelling on one detail thrown up by this striking Homeric wasp-simile: here the ἄναλκις θεός fights *with* her child; the wasps of *Il.* 16.259f., once disturbed (for interpretation of these vexed lines see the convincing analysis of J. Th. Kakridis, *Homer Revisited* (Lund 1971), 138f.), fight stoutly *for* their τέκεα (265) like seasoned warriors (266f.).

ἀθερίζει 80n.

95 The beginning of this verse echoes that of *Od.* 22.249, from an episode concerning an equally famous 'bow': (248 σχήσει ... χεῖρας ~ infr. 98-9) /καὶ δή οἱ Μέν(τωρ) ...; this same line houses the element κενὰ εὔγματα – in tune with Cypris' present endeavours. Cf. also *Od.* 13.30 δὴ γὰρ μενέαινε. Q.S. imitates: 12.567, Campbell ad loc.

μενέηνα With the animated καὶ δή (cf. *GP* 250f.) Cypris passes to a particular example of Eros' treatment of her: 'Just listen to what happened!' μενεαίνειν here embraces the two common connotations of passionate desire and <martial!> rage (cf. Doederlein 1.92, Adkins, *JHS* 89 (1969), 17f.), as in *Il.* 5.606 'be bent in your warlike fury on ...' and often. Fighting talk from Cypris, for a line or two at least: she was gripped by a furious desire to destroy Eros' weaponry; cf. Ardizzoni, 'mi venne una voglia matta di spezzargli ...'

If the interpretation of 97f. advocated below is correct, then Cypris here must be thought of as communicating her rage directly to Eros; so in a similar sequence iv.391f. (cf. on ἀμφαδίην in 97) Medea's desire to set fire to Argo and throw herself into the flames reads very weakly indeed as a mere intimation of her innermost thoughts (ctr. Herter *JAW* 386).

περισχομένη Cf. Campbell 1982.15. Cypris may be specifying an occasion when she was *particularly* oppressed, when Eros had gone too far: cf. schol. ὑπεραλγήσασα. Ardizzoni, who adopts this interpretation, prefers περὶ σχομένη (modified to πέρι σχομένη by VDB; cf. *Noten* 311). Better (so the majority, but often with little or no regard for the preverb) 'beset on all sides' by; cf. Sandbach on περιείχετο in Men. *Epitr.* 506.

περισχέσθαι is normally middle (in Ap. cf. infr. 706n., iv.82), but σχέσθαι and compounds can function as passives in Homer, Ap. (infr. 811n., iv.920) and elsewhere (Barrett on Eur. *Hipp.* 27, Wilkins on id. *Hcld.* 634, McLennan on Call. *h.* 1.28); pass. περισχόμενος: [Opp.] *Cyn.* 1.332, 3.188.

κακότητι ἔχομαι (-εται) κακότητι in *Od.* 8.182, 17.318 strongly suggest here 'by the sheer *misery* of my situation'; such is the usual meaning of the noun in our poem. At the same time, it is Eros who inflicts this κακότης, and it is open to us to think also in terms of his 'naughtiness,' 'bad behaviour' (cf. infr. 182; she calls him κακόν infr. 129).

96 αὐτοῖσιν τόξοισι In i.1194-5 Heracles 'put his quiver on the ground /αὐτοῖσιν τόξοισιν', τόξα there being *bow and arrows* (cf. 1205), here simply *bow*. This idiom (see *GG* 2.164-5) is naturally common in contexts where destruction (threatened or actual) of a person or thing is in question: cf. e.g. *Il.* 8.24, 9.542, Eur. *Med.* 164 with Page's note, i.1204 (cf. the tone of infr. 373), αὔτανδρον infr. 582; KG 1.433.

τόξοισι ... ὀιστούς Cf. *Il.* 5.171, *Od.* 11.607, but esp. *Il.* 23.871-2 /τόξον ... ὀιστὸν .... ἠπείλησεν ...

δυσηχέας Fränkel (*Noten* 334-5, q.v. for wider discussion of 95-9) thought of Eros' vague threat (98f.) in terms of a shameful passion to be inflicted on his mother. He noted her mortified reaction to having had sex with a mortal in *HyAphr* 247f., scil. through the agency of 'Eros': he might also have adduced id. 198-9, where she declares that the product of this union will be called Αἰνείας, because μ' αἰνόν/ἔσχεν ἄχος [cf. 243], ἕνεκα βροτοῦ ἀνέρος ἔμπεσον εὐνῇ. Before us now are laid -ηχής here (see below), ἀκηχεμένη 101, and a speech expressing embarrassment at what others think of her 102f. (cf. *HyAphr* 247f.); the name of Aeneas figures in the model for 91 supr., *Il.* 6.77 /Αἰνεία ... ὔμμι μάλιστα/. δυσ-: viz. inflicting δύσοιστα ἄχη; hinting at δυσέρως of course. Eros' arrow is πολύστονος infr. 279.

On the links of this Iliadic gloss (here only in *Arg.*) with either ἠχή or ἄχος (for the 'singers,' the latter probably: Hainsworth on 11.590) see *LfgrE* s.v., Erbse on schol. 18.307, Campbell on Q.S. 12.225. The alternative advocated by some for this passage (not that a *single* interpretation is mandatory given the word's background), 'whose sound has dire consequences' <for the victim> or more generally 'making an unpleasant racket' suits the complaining tone well enough: cf. Anon. hexam. (pap. 2nd cent. AD) *SH* 939.4 δυσκελάδου of an arrow, Anon. *FGE* 1256 βέλος ὀρφανὸν ἤχου/ of a sling, ? Q.S. 10.235 /ἰοῦ .. δυσηχέος (~ ἔβραχε 234).

ἄξαι The frustrated Pandarus threatens to break his own bow (important for the sequel in Ap.) in *Il.* 5.215-6, cf. Lennox 60-1; and see supr. 91f.n.

97 ἀμφαδίην Cf. *Studies* 16. A touch of pure bravado from δολοπλόκος Ἀφροδίτη: 'right before his eyes' (cf. my correction in iv.392: Campbell 1971.420), without resorting to guile. For a comparable sly dig at her habitual lack of openness in *Il.* cf. Paley/Willcock on 5.374, and for the word's emphatic function cf. *Od.* 5.120 (heavy sarcasm), the cutting ἀμφαδόν in *Il.* 9.370, and 15n. 3[H]: only Ap., 4 ×.

τοῖον γὰρ ... VDB (2.54 n.2) argue that it is Eros' threat that induces Cypris to think of breaking his bow and arrows. This implausible sequence of events, rendered more implausible still by the need to interpret τηλόθι in 98 as 'well away <from me/my person>' rather than '<my property>,' is precisely what Schneider's conjecture δ' ἄρ' was designed to eradicate. It is natural to take χαλεφθείς in 97 as marking the immediate reaction to μενέηνα ... in 95f. In truth (cf. *Studies* 16) we are dealing with the jerky thought-processes of a mother harried by a child devoted to her mental annihilation. The sense is '<but I didn't go through with it/it was no use> because this is what ...': cf. *GP* 61-2 for similarly compressed utterances.

τοῖον γὰρ ἐπηπείλησε: for *Homerica* see VDB 2.54 n.2 (*Il.* 8.415: n.b. ... ἄξειν, from ἄγνυμι, 417; subject: the all-powerful Zeus!).

χαλεφθείς A verb commonly applied (in poetry at least) to offended deities; clausular in its sole Homeric appearance, *Od.* 4.423: some more examples in Hopkinson on Call. *h.* 6.48. For the passive (see in general Boesch 17) not much need be added to LSJ s.v. II + Suppl.: Nic. *Ther.* 445, Q.S. 1.774 (but see below). In 109 infr. χαλέπτεο, a present form which perhaps gave rise to the Hellenistic middle (LSJ s.v. II again, but add Call. *fr.* 63.8, infr. 382; reclassify Q.S. 3.780 [~ id. 7.660]: note also Paul. Sil. *Soph.* 1023).

98-9 (*Studies* 16) The word-order reflects Eros' rage and conjures up a picture of his snatching the bow for which Cypris has made a lunge; as we might say, 'Hands – off!'

98 ἕως ἔτι ... Cf. Ardizzoni here. Hence Nonn. *D.* 23.233/233a ἕως ἔτι μῆνιν ἐρύκω/ (Wifstrand, *Gnomon* 33 (1961), 45) – perhaps: he has many such sequences, 21.266, 22.111, 34.328, 37.498, 48.619. — *Il.* 10.161 ... ἔτι χῶρος ἐρύκει/.

θυμὸν ἐρύκει Curb anger, cf. *Od.* 11.105 θυμὸν ἐρυκακέειν curb appetite or desire (failure to do which would have dire consequences). For the clausula cf. Hes. *WD* 28 and later [Apolin.] 68.38.

99 ἕξω rather than σχήσω (cf. 95n.): cf. *Il.* 1.97 Zen. *codd.* χεῖρας ἀφέξει/, and more generally Janko on *Il.* 13.47-51. For ἔχειν/-εσθαι in this connexion see Pfeiffer on Call. *fr.* 553.1, and for the fut. indic. in a threat ii.1224, iv.231-3, Goodwin *MT* 165-6.

μετέπειτα Cf. Homer's use of μετόπισθε (and ii.56 ἵνα μή μοι ἀτέμβηαι μετόπισθεν/); so ὕστερον sim. often. For the form of the threat Mooney and Gillies compare Hdt. 5.106.2. — μετέπειτά γ': i.302.

γ' ἀτεμβοίμην Echoes here of *Il.* 23.832 ἀπόπροθι, 833 /ἕξει, 834 ἀτεμβόμενός γε (n.b.), 836 /ὣς ἔφατ'. — Cf. *Studies* 16/99 n.37. γ' corresponds to our 'jolly well': cf. e.g. Ar. *Lys.* 656f. εἰ δὲ λυπήσεις τί με, τῷδέ γ' ἀψήκτῳ πατάξω τῷ κοθόρνῳ τὴν γνάθον, and *GP* 126. Eros does not say '(if you don't ...) you *shall*' but, menacingly, 'you *would* have <only> yourself to blame.' The optative reads naturally enough, however it is to be labelled: potential Wåhlin 21 and others; imperative optative Fitch 342, Gillies; wish = menace Vian 1962.36 n.3 (cf. *GH* 2.214). Anyway, Madvig's κ' can be safely ignored, as can Brunck's κε infr. 355(n.).

ἀτεμβοίμην In Ap. (also ii.56, 1199, iii.938), for whatever reason, the equivalent of μέμφεσθαι: cf. Marxer 55 (*Od.* 21.312 ἀτέμβειν equated with ἐνένιπεν 287, cf. Ap. iii.931 ~ 938); Vian ed. 1961 (*Il.* 11.705 misconstrued); Boesch 36-7, Erbse 1953.170 and at schol. *Il.* 23.445b, Fränkel *Noten* 310-11 ('glossographers,' cf. Dyck 128, 135); see also Bartelink and Gerhard in *LfgrE* s.v. ἀτέμβω ad fin., and F-G on *Od.* 21.312-3. Ap. is the only Hellenistic poet known to have used the verb (*SH* Anon. hexam. 912A ii.7 ἀτεμβ[, pap. 3rd cent. AD, cannot be dated). It recurs from time to time: (1) Q.S. 5.147, 173 (find fault with for being deprived); Nonn. *D.* 42.519 -όμενος περὶ νίκης/

fied about the victory (being deprived of it). (2) Homeric sense, 'be deprived of': *AP* 9: 597.2 (Comet.), 649.6 (Maced.), 765.4 (Paul. Sil.).

ἑοῖ αὐτῇ i.460 (~ *Il.* 13.495, *Od.* 4.38) ἑοῖ [Shipp 77] αὐτῷ/, third person; here i.q. ἐμοὶ αὐτῇ, ἐμαυτῇ, by now an entirely natural usage (ctr. Ardizzoni): see LSJ s.v. ἑαυτοῦ II (with Garvie on Aesch. *Cho.* 111, 221), *GG* 2.197-8, Marxer 61f., Erbse 1953.165f., and the more general remarks of Fränkel, 1963.161-2. Cf. on 186.

100-1 *Studies* 16. The smiles (no sign of a smile now from the φιλομμειδής goddess: 101 ἀκηχεμένη) and knowing looks (no sidelong glances!) make Cypris realise the futility of her suggestion (91-2) that *they* make the approach. Sheer embarrassment wins the day. Hera has manipulated Cypris, just as she has manipulated Athena.

ὣς φάτο .../ἀλλήλ- But *Od.* 18.320 ὣς ἔφαθ', αἱ δ' ἐγέλασσαν [~ infr. 102], ἐς ἀλλήλας δὲ ἴδοντο, of the handmaidens' scornful reaction to the 'wretched' (327) Odysseus.

For the opening of 100 cf. the Iliadic (also *Od.* 13.287) /ὣς φάτο, μείδησεν δὲ θεά: 1.595, Hera, after a tale of violence from Hephaestus; 21.434 [surely to be retained], Hera's reaction to Athena's rough treatment of Aphrodite on the battlefield: cf. Lennox 61, who also recalls 14.222, Hera craftily getting what she wants from Aphrodite in the plot to seduce Zeus, cf. 107n.

The close of 100 is an amusing adaptation of Priam's solemn utterance (ἄκουσα) θεοῦ καὶ ἐσέδρακον ἄντην/ at *Il.* 24.223 (~ Eudoc. *Hom.* 323; variations in Greg. Naz. 546.315, 1237.118, *Vis. Doroth.* 83, all end-stopped: 26-8n.).

ἀλλήλαις in 101 poses a problem: ἀλλήλας Ziegler, and so e.g. Linsenbarth 61, Gillies, Fränkel OCT. Vian ed. 1961 suggested that the dative can be explained by such Homeric constructions as *Il.* 9.372-3 οὐδ' ἂν ἔμοιγε/τετλαίη ... εἰς ὦπα ἰδέσθαι/: εἰς ὦπα is used in conjunction with ἐναντίον of looking one in the face at *Od.* 23.107, and one thinks of the association of εἰς ὦπα/ἄντ- with a dative in passages like *Il.* 3.158 θεῇς εἰς ὦπα ἔοικεν/ ~ 24.630 θεοῖσι .. ἄντα ἐῴκει/, *Od.* 2.5 al. θεῷ ἐναλίγκιος ἄντην/. Vian may be right, though (Campbell 1982.15) the similar dative immediately above arouses suspicion, and the differently configured clausula in Q.S. 4.300 ἐσέδρακον ἀλλήλοισιν cannot be held to 'guarantee' the dative here in Ap. Cf. also *Il.* 6.404 μείδησεν ἰδὼν ἐς παῖδα, *Od.* 10.453 ἀλλήλους εἶδον φράσσαντό τ' ἐσάντα/, 19.476 /ἦ, καὶ Πηνελόπειαν ἐσέδρακεν.

καὶ -δρακον ἄντην Cf. infr. 1010.

101 Ctr. *Il.* 22.449 /ἡ δ' αὖτις ... μετηύδα/, id. 5.363-4 (below) /ὣς φάτο ...,/ἡ δ' ... ἔβαινεν ἀκηχεμένη ... Q.S. remembers his Ap. in 7.66: /ὣς φάτο ... ἀκηχέμενον προσέειπεν/.

αὖτις On this detail see *Noten* 335. αὖτις with προσέειπεν: not (ctr. ἐξαῦτις) in archaic epic, *LfgrE* s.v., p. 1616.11f. The model for this interruption and resumption is in all probability *Il.* 15.100f., speech-capping then laugh then address νεμεσσηθεῖσα.

ἀκηχεμένη From *Il.* 5.364, part of another humiliating episode in Cypris' career (cf. Lennox 61); for the sequel see on 106. This participle in the run-up to direct speech also infr. 1104, 1156; in dat. plur. iv.1260 (Ω), though I am not convinced that the more recent editors have chosen wisely here: n.b. 1259 ἀμηχανίη rather than the expected participle (cf. ii.410, iii.423; ii.885, 1140) viz. to accommodate ἀκηχέμενος; the speech-content; δακρυόεις ... ἀσχαλόωντι/ 1277.

102f. A piquant contrast with 56f. Hera had disclosed her (and Athena's) private anxieties, and had won a sympathetic ear. Cypris has blurted out all *her own* troubles, with the predictable result (see on γέλως below)!

102 τἀμά in the Hellenistic era is especially common in epigram (e.g. *HE* 148, 255, 865, 1590); it occurs as early as Archil., *IEG* 109.1. I see no compelling need to follow Rzach (473), Svensson (36-7) and others in looking to Homer (or rather to conventions in Homeric orthography: J. van Leeuwen, *Enchiridium dictionis epicae* (Leiden 1918), 69-70) for justification of the crasis admitted here.

γέλως πέλει Nonn. *D.* 42.265 γέλως πέλε. The goddess' smiles are dolefully converted into *(food for) laughter*: cf. e.g. Soph. *OC* 902, and Crin. *GPh* 2068 τὰ θνητῶν δ' ἐστί σοι (Eros) γέλως ἄχη. Of the four examples of nominative γέλως in the Homeric poems, three are found in *Od.* 8: one cannot help but feel that the famous uproarious, derisive 'laughter' (cf. Hainsworth on 8.343, also Kirk on *Il.* 2.270, Brown, *Phoenix* 43 (1989), 283f.) provoked by the indiscretions of Aphrodite (326, 343) is made to haunt her here (cf. 41f.n.), even if she did shrug it off in Demodocus' lay (cf. Griffin 200-1). On a more general level of course it is Aphrodite who usually has the last laugh: see Crane 1987.167.

οὐδέ τί με χρή 'No/well, I should *not* ...,' see *GP* 191, citing *Il.* 16.721, and also Redard 51f. There should be a strong stop, or a dash, after πέλει. οὐδέ τι με χρή/ = *Il.* 19.67, *Od.* 19.118 (ὀδυνάων 117, -στονος 118). *Il.* 19.420-1 οὐδέ τί σε χρή./... οἶδα καὶ αὐτὸς ... strikes a more sombre note.

103 μυθεῖσθαι πάντεσσιν But *Od.* 8.497 πᾶσιν μυθήσομαι (ἀνθρώποισιν/).

μυθεῖσθαι In archaic epic this particular infinitive is known only from *HyAphr* 283, where the goddess is determined that one aspect of her private life *will* remain a secret.

πάντεσσιν A glum exaggeration, 'the whole world' (cf. e.g. Eur. *Andr.* 436), implying that anyone coming within earshot is treated, or liable to be treated, to a dose of the same.

ἅλις ... The familiar personal construction, <I am> enough = <it is> enough that ...; this particular usage is attested in tragedy, LSJ s.v. 5, Bowra, *Glotta* 38 (1960), 52; see too Verdenius, *Mnemosyne* 40 (1987), 17.

εἰδυῖα καὶ αὐτή καὶ αὐτή as a strengthened 'I myself' might have passed unremarked were it not for the fact that in comparable expressions καί denotes '*x* know(s) *as well* <as *y* = the speaker knows>' (cf. ii.1047 ἴστε καὶ αὐτοί/, based on the recurrent οἶδα or -ε καὶ αὐτός/); a slight illogicality then, quite in keeping with Cypris' state of mind.

104 Cf. *Il.* 9.344 /νῦν δ' ἐπεί (then ... εἰδότος· οὐδέ με πείσει 345), al., *Od.* 16.311-2 τόδε .../ἡμῖν ἀμφοτέροισι, *Il.* 19.56-7 τόδ' ἀμφοτέροισιν ἄρειον/ἔπλετο, id. 7.387 αἴ κε .. ὔμμι φίλον (~ iii.727) ... γένοιτο/, esp. 31-2 (προσέειπε 33) ἐπεὶ ὣς φίλον ἔπλετο ../ὑμῖν ἀθανάτῃσι, scil. whose wish was final: Zen. *vulg.* ἀθανάτοισι, but Aristophanes read here ἀμφοτέρῃσι· τῇ Ἀθηνᾷ καὶ τῇ Ἥρᾳ, οὐκ ἀπιθάνως schol. A, cf. Erbse ad loc., and also van der Valk 2.75, Rengakos 1993.69.

νῦν δ' 'But to turn to the situation in hand,' leaving aside the perennial problem.

τόδε δή She swallows.

πέλει Q.S. 1.442 τῇσι φίλον πέλει.

105 πειρήσω *et circa*. Traces hereabouts of *Od.* 2.310f. (speaker Telemachus, talking of his 'attempt' to deal with the formidable threat posed by the multitude of suitors): 311 ... ἀκέοντα (~ supr. 85), 312 ἅλις, 314/316 /νῦν δ', ὅτε δὴ ..../πειρήσω, 321 /ἦ ῥα καὶ ἐκ χειρὸς χεῖρα ...

Lennox (61) detects another (96n.) early echo of the action leading up to the Pandarus-episode in *Il.*: 4.66 = 71 πειρᾶν, cf. on 106 and 107. See also 16n.

μειλίξομαι Livrea on iv.416 (but 'pregare' is a trifle bland for some of the examples in his fourth category). Cypris means to render her son amenable by 'softening him up' not purely μειλιχίοις ἐπέεσσιν (cf. 148-9) but also with the promise of a μείλιον (cf. 135), as her listeners no doubt divine. At any rate, they are happy to depart in the sure knowledge that Eros 'will not say no.'

οὐδ' ἀπιθήσει Any more than did Athena Hera (*Il.* 2.166) or Zeus Hera (4.68) or Hera Zeus (5.767), and so on. This clausula *Il.* 10.129; cf. i.149, *Echoes* ad loc. It forms a ring with αἴ κε πίθηται/ in 26. Ctr. *Il.* 9.181 /πειρᾶν ὡς πεπίθοιεν.

106-7 Ctr. *Il.* 8.484 /ὣς φάτο, τὸν δ' οὔτι προσέφη .. Ἥρη/, and cf. supr. 55.

106 ῥαδινῆς ἐπεμάσσατο χειρός There is presumably (Gow is sceptical, Fraser 2.897 n.154 considers it probable that Ap. is the borrower) some point of contact with Theoc. 17.37 (Cypris) ῥαδινὰς ἐσεμάξατο χείρας/. For the epithet cf. Thgn. *IEG* 6 (v.l.), 1002, and later *SEG* 30.1272.12 (Caria, late Hellenistic/early Roman), *GVI* 681.8 (Athens, 1st cent. AD). Cypris is βραδίνα in Sapph. *PLF* 102.2, her feet ῥαδινοί in Hes. *Theog.* 195. 'Slender' (cf. Richardson on *HyDem* 183, along with the lexicographical material in Erbse on schol. *Il.* 23.583), here i.q. τρυφερή (schol.), *dainty, delicate*. There is a truly delicate Venus in Reposianus (arms, hands/palms, feet: 21-2, 32, 99, 110, 174). An amusing touch, ctr. Hera's χειρὶ παχείῃ/ (like Athena's in *Il.*), *HyAp* 340. Lennox (61) recalls the physical wounding of Cypris in *Il.* 5: cf. on 81-2, and see next note.

ἐπεμάσσατο ἀκηχεμένη put us in mind of the (literally) wounded Cypris in *Il.* 5 (101n.); in the sequel to that her mother Dione comforted her: /χειρί τέ μιν κατέρεξεν ἔπος τ' ἔφατ' ... (372). So ἐπιμαίεσθαι here may be the equivalent of ψηφαλᾶν, *stroked* her on the hand (cf. Vian ed. 1961, 'tâter, caresser, prendre doucement': for glosses in this vein cf. *LH* s.v. ἐπιμαίομαι, Radt on Soph. *fr.* 55). The alternative is *clutched* her by ... (cf. e.g. iv.18, Perses *HE* 2889, the latter wrongly classified in LSJ II2); perhaps Val. Flacc. took our line so (3.534). Whatever gesture Ap. envisaged (cf. in general Grajew 43f., Sittl 27f., Herter *JAW* 270, Richardson on *Il.* 24.360-3), it is plainly designed to console the grieving (101) goddess and to assure her that all will be well; this is what is done, after a fashion, in 110.

107 ἦκα δὲ μειδιόωσα Cf. in part *Studies* 16. So ii.61 (παραβλήδην 60) /ἦκα δὲ μειδήσας (= Paul. Sil. *Soph.* 246), and earlier Hes. *Theog.* 546-7 (cf. Wirshbo, *GRBS* 23 (1982), 107 n.19) προσέειπε .../ἦκ' ἐπιμειδήσας, both denoting the quiet smile of superiority and self-assurance, the former of Polydeuces, who relies on craft (72, 75) to combat the brutish Amycus, the latter of the wily (δολοφρονέων 550) Prometheus; here blended with satisfaction at having got one's own way (like Hera in *Il.* 14.222, δολοφρονέουσα 197, cf. Faerber 83 n.7, n. on 100-1, and below), and, of course, amusement. The tables are neatly turned, for at the beginning of the interview it was Cypris who μειδιόωσα προσέννεπεν αἱμυλίοισιν (51, cf. Ibscher 53).

μειδιόωσα .. προσέειπεν Ctr. *Il.* 23.786 /μειδιόων, καὶ ... ἔειπεν/.

παραβλήδην προσέειπεν Also i.835, ii.621, iv.1563; cf. in general Fantuzzi 78-9. What follows is a modified version of the discussion in *Studies* 16-7/100 nn.38-9, together with a postscript on the position now taken in VDB 2².

In *Il.* 4.6 π. ἀγορεύων/ (cf. Lennox 61), the only place in archaic epic in which this adverb occurs, ancient scholarly opinion was divided (Livrea on iv.1563, Erbse on schol. *Il.* 4.6a[1-2]), into two main camps: A *with intent to deceive*, B *in reply*. Ap. has it 8 ×:

(1) iv.1608 is best taken in a local sense: VDB 3.203; if not, in sense B.

(2) B suits the remaining seven: i.835, ii.60, 448, 621, iii.107, 1078, iv.1563:

ii.448 is a clear case: ἀλλήλοισι π. ἀγόρευον/ ~ ἀμειβομένων 449. So also ii.60 οὔτι π. ἐρίδηνεν/ in reply to a haughty challenge (Merkel *Proleg.* 167 compares Hesychius' ἐρεθιστικῶς). In i.835 and iv.1563 Ap. may be playing off B against A: in the former case Hypsipyle's manipulation of the truth is matched by a speech of signal candour from Jason; iv.1563 heralds a speech from Euphemus to a god claiming to be 'Eurypylus.'

It is open to us to insist that as παραβλήδην demonstrably denotes *in answer* in some passages it must do so universally: so e.g. Seaton 1891.11-12, Ardizzoni on i.835, Natzel 178 n.86, VDB (but see end of this note); likewise evidently the ancient commentators on the *Argonautica*, including Theon no doubt: cf. schol. iii.107 with *test.* in Wendel ad loc. One may suspect however that the choice of ambivalent glosses, particularly to characterise the tone of speeches, is deliberate and designed to tax the imagination: cf. the penultimate sentence of Vian, 1978.1038, and see 400n.

For our last three examples the context does not positively preclude A:

ii.621, Jason's πεῖρα: cf. van Krevelen, *Mnemosyne* 24 (1971), 416 (following de Mirmont) and more recently Hunter 1988.446-7; *contra*:

VDB 1.206 n.2. Perhaps. But the real point at issue here is not lack of openness but rather the tone adopted by Jason: in order to stamp his authority on the expedition he does not resort to strident self-justification but uses a 'softly softly,' caring approach *in response to* (cf. ii.60) Tiphys' forthright, if not high-handed instruction of 615f.; and it works.

iii.1078, in sense A according to Hunter loc. cit. and ed. on 106-7 and 1077-8 (with a switch from 'This may be the sense ...' to 'To the reader, at least, Jason speaks "deceitfully"'). Again, perhaps (the case is stronger here; n.b. οὖλος ἔρως earlier in the line – destructive *and* perverting/corrupting perhaps?). But one could not hope for a sharper 'response' to the three points raised in Medea's address: 1069f. ~ 1079f.; 1071f. ~ 1083f.; 1074f. ~ 1096f.

Lastly, the present line. Here, if anywhere, the possibility of a glance at A, keyed to a *specific* detail in the text of *Il.* 4 (of pervasive interest in our Olympian scene), deserves serious consideration:

In *Il.* 4.7f. we encounter the same cast: Hera and Athena, set against Aphrodite. The ἀπάτη practised by Zeus (cf. schol. at 6a[1]) relates to his raising the prospect that peace between Greeks and Trojans *might* be the preferred course <in which case steps would have to be taken to implement it>; in reality he wants the fight to go on. Hera here confidently assures the myopic Cypris that peace *will* one day obtain between mother and son; it won't, and Hera knows it. We may recall once again the story of how Hera pulled the wool over Aphrodite's eyes in *Il.* 14.197f.: she specified the resolving of νείκεα (205), talking of domestic χόλος (207) involving 'love.' The language of 110(n.) too leads us back once again to the world of the *Iliad*.

παραβλήδην is otherwise rare: add to Livrea on iv.1563: Q.S. 5.237 (probably 'by way of a retort,' cf. Vian and Battegay, *Lex. Q.S.*, 'en réponse'; but note the context); Greg. Naz. 1545.35 (παρβ-; 'maliciously'); Nonn. *Par.* 16.92 (ἀγορεύω; 'sideways,' 'not in a straightforward manner').

— VDB 2[2], pp. 151-2. Vian now detects in παραβλήδην across the board (with the exception of iv.1563, which will not yield) the sense '*à côté de* la vérité.' In some cases, it seems to me, such a sense can only be elicited by forcing the text (I point to the treatment of ii.60, 448 in particular); a firm line has to be drawn between (calculated) deception and disappointment (in a broad sense), and indeed between (gross) deception and (mild, harmless) disingenuousness.

108f. Cf. *Studies* 17-8. More fun for Homer enthusiasts. Lurking behind Hera's directions is the dire warning delivered by Hermes to δολόεσσα Καλυψώ in *Od*. 5. Our attention has been drawn towards this episode in 46 (see n.). In 5.28f. Zeus instructs Hermes to visit Calypso to secure Odysseus' release. Her abode is described (55f.), her lover is otherwise engaged (81f.). Calypso greets Hermes with τίπτε ... εἰλήλουθας κτλ. (87-8) and reluctantly agrees to do as he says. The god has a final word of advice (146-7): οὕτω νῦν ἀπόπεμπε, Διὸς δ' ἐποπίζεο μῆνιν,/μή πώς τοι μετόπισθε κοτεσσάμενος χαλεπήνῃ. The wrath-motif is delightfully refashioned. Cf. further 5.148-51 with infr. 110-3, and 159 ~ 127-8, 161 (πρόφρασσ') ~ 131, 181 + 184f. ~ 150 + 151f.

108 For the frame cf. *Il*. 10.192 (προσηύδα 191), al. /οὕτω νῦν + imperat., and id. 24.373 /οὕτω ... ὡς ἀγορεύεις/ (the same clausula, common in Homer, in ii.23, iv.1101); 'as you (publicly) declare you will' serves as a blunt reminder that Cypris has no room for manoeuvre.

Κυθέρεια Cf. *Studies* 17. High-sounding, exotic-sounding even (cf. Hainsworth on *Od*. 8.288, and also Càssola on *HyAphr* 6), spoken with gentle mockery; in i.742 (mentioned in association with Ares: cf. [Hes.] *Theog*. 934) the language is ornate, in iii.553 honorific (cf. its employment in, e.g., the major/minor Homeric Hymns in celebration of her).

Virg. *A*. 1.254-7 (~ Sil. It. 3.571-2) *subridens .... fatur:/parce metu, Cytherea* ... ~ 297 /*haec ait et* ... (~ infr. 111).

τόδε χρέος occurs in Aesch./Eur. in various senses. This, the χρέος specified at the start (12), is something Cypris is obliged to do; she duly passes on this obligation to her son: 131n.

109 ἔρξον ἄφαρ Q.S. 9.22. Hera does not add 'never mind your hair': she has no need to, as Cypris makes off at once. ἔρξον harbours another subtle deviation from Homeric usage: all five instances are followed up with a 'just as you like.' — ἔρξον (cf. La Roche *HTA* 258-9, B. Forssmann, *Untersuchungen zur Sprache Pindars* (Wiesbaden 1966), 28-32) *w*D, see VDB I.LXXIII.

109-10 Cypris' ill-humour, manifested so liberally in her dealings with many an offender (on the theme see Kost, ed. Musae. pp. 348f., Livrea 1977.13) extends to her domestic situation (cf. above on 91f., Eros). Hera wickedly transforms the language employed by the neurotic goddess to describe a fit of bad temper from her *son* (97) into a general prohibition directed at the *mother* herself: 'don't keep on getting riled ...' (the variants in LA/E at the end of 109 perhaps arose from the idea that Hera should now be warning against an imminent confrontation).

For the association of χωομένη with χαλέπτεο and ἐρίδαινε cf. *Il.* 18.107-8 ἔρις .../καὶ χόλος, ὅς τ' ἐφέηκε ... χαλεπῆναι/. Solmsen (*ap.* Fränkel OCT) suggested χωομένῳ, appealing to *Il.* 9.157 al. μεταλλήξαντι χόλοιο/ – and wrecking the flow of the wonderfully patronising comment (from a notoriously irascible goddess!) on the need to keep a bad temper in check. Of course the celebrated anger-motif of the *Iliad* is evoked here: if we stop to think about it, we will recall that Achilles did after all relent, eventually (cf. Lennox 62), though not by virtue of bribery! Then there is *Od.* 1.77-8, said with absolute confidence: Ποσειδάων .. μεθήσει/ὂν χόλον ~ 79 ἐριδαινέμεν. Hera however chooses not to be *too* specific: τάχ' αὔριον ἔσσετ' ἄμεινον, or perhaps a bit later than that. She has got what she wanted, and is unashamedly dismissive: Eros will stop <what he is doing: cf. infr. 951, μετελώφεον in i.1161, μεταπαυόμενοι in *Il.* 17.373> one day.

καὶ μή τι χαλέπτεο Q.S. 3.780. Cf. on 97.

μηδ' ἐρίδαινε is a truly exquisite borrowing from *Od.* 21.310, Antinous to the old beggar Odysseus: μηδ' ἐρίδαινε μετ' ἀνδράσι κουροτέροισι/ (who will sort you out!). On the corrupted verbal form in LA/E cf. above, and Wellauer here.

χωομένη σῷ παιδί For the pattern cf. iv.616 (~ *HyHerm* 236), and note *Od.* 24.33 σῷ παιδὶ ... ὀπίσσω/.

μεταλλήξει So Ω: on geminated forms see VDB i.lxxiv, and La Roche *HTA* 389f., Richardson on *HyDem* 339.

μεταστρέψει (G^g S^m, Wendel *Schol.* 220), 'he'll change his ways,' may represent somebody's idea of what a Homerising poet should have written (cf. *Il.* 15.203) rather than a straight 'gloss' on μεταλλήξει (μεταλλάξει Madvig, not a conjecture to treasure: cf. μεθήσει in *Od.* 1.77 cited above).

111-2 There is a leave-taking sequence at the close of the interview between the plotting goddesses in *Il.* 14.224f.: Aphrodite went to her house, whereas Hera left (λίπεν) Olympus, then σεύατ' κτλ. with the customary rapidity (36n.) of divine beings (cf. παλίσσυτοι here in 112).

111 is reminiscent of *Od.* 1.125, Telemachus dealing with Athena in disguise: ὣς εἰπὼν ἡγεῖθ', ἡ δ' ἕσπετο Παλλὰς Ἀθήνη (this closing tag avoided by Ap., 340n.).

111 ἦ ῥα καί An Homeric run (note especially *Il.* 20.438 /ἦ ῥα καὶ ... Ἀθήνην/), 5× in *Arg.* (and f.v.l. iv.1601); cf. *Echoes* at i.348. Elsewhere in 3^H only [Theoc.] 25.84. See 22n.

ἔλλιπε θῶκον *PV* 279 -συτον (~ infr. 112) θᾶκον προλιποῦσ', cf. Eur. *IA* 618.

ἔλλιπε So ii.1032, ἐνέλλιπε i.515. The geminated form (*GG* 1.310, 654) first in Antim., *SH* 69.4 ἔλλιπον, then in 3rd cent.: Call. *fr.* 75.69 and *fr.* 77, *GVI* 102.4 (Ithaca); next in ?Meleag. *HE* 4734, *GVI* 645.3 (origin unknown; 1st cent. AD). Later nearly always (Eudoc. *Cypr.* 1.32) the property of the epigram: Cougny 2.387.5 (~ Kramer, *Anec. Par.* 4.340.29), and in *AP*: Greg. Naz., 8.72.1; Agath., 7.589.3; Comet., 15.40.4 & 28; Ignat., 15.29.2; Anon., 1.49.1, 1.56.2.

θῶκον Hera has been provided with an easychair (49). In Homer (Hainsworth on *Od.* 5.3, Hoekstra on id. 15.468, cf. Fraenkel on Aesch. *Ag.* 519) a θῶκος is a formal 'session' or a seat used by gods or by an individual in a position of authority for engaging in debate (cf. i.667f., where Hypsipyle in assembly sits upon the stone θῶκος of her father), and it is not often used colourlessly in any period of Greek verse. The word here takes account of Hera's activity and of her dominant role: trans. 'the chair.' Cf. Gillies here.

ἐφωμάρτησε Three times in Homer. Also in i.201 κιόντι/ (cf. Hes. *Theog.* 201 ὡμάρτησε then ἰούσῃ/), = ἐπηκολούθησεν, the sense advocated by schol. D at *Il.* 8.191, 12.412 (but not at 23.414, ~ schol. T at 8.191); cf. on 111-2 (*Od.* 1.125). This verb was particularly affected by later poets, cf. e.g. Triph. 153, Nonn. *Par.* + *D.* 8 ×, Paul. Sil. *Soph.* 706.

'Ἀθήνη This is Athena's penultimate contribution to the action – if we count what is described at iv.959f. as 'action.' In iv the safekeeping of Argo is a matter for Hera rather: it is her show.

112 ἐκ δ' ἴσαν Cf. *Od.* 24.11 /πὰρ δ' ἴσαν and id. 501 ἐκ δ' ἤιον (scil. θύραζε); also *Il.* 24.247 /ἦ, καὶ ... οἱ δ' ἴσαν ἔξω/ and id. 643, 647 /ἦ ῥ' ..../αἱ δ' ἴσαν ἐκ μεγάροιο ...

ἄμφω ταίγε Neither has any reason to hang around: Hera has got what she came for, Athena has not been all that keen on the venture in the first place. So *both of them* make off with all speed, leaving the way open for Hera's directive to be carried out instantly (109).

παλίσσυτοι They now rush back (111-2n.) to the privacy of the θάλαμος (9) to watch events. This word 6 × in Ap.: for further discussion see Campbell 1990.482. Only found in Soph. *OT* 193, Eur. *Suppl.* 388 prior to the Hellenistic period: Lyc. 1461, [Theoc.] 25.231, Nic. *Ther.* 571, [Mosch.] 3.124. In later poetry (and prose) it was fairly popular: [Opp.] *Cyn.* 1.489, 4.102; Greg. Naz. 411.45 + 2; [Orph.] *L.*

121; Nonn. *Par.* + *D.*, 6 ×; [Apolin.] 29.4 + 2. — Ctr. *Il.* 9.656-7 /ὣς ἔφαθ', οἱ δὲ .... ἴσαν πάλιν .. δ' ...

ἡ δὲ καὶ αὐτή So 611 infr., and later [Mosch.] *Meg.* 52, Q.S. 2.665 (ἴσαν precedes); this unit heads the verse in Arat. 653, Kaibel *EG* 1046.38 (Rome, 2nd cent. AD). See in general Bühler on Mosch. *Eur.* 25.

113-5 Rich pickings from the Homeric epics:
(1a) *Il.* 5.167-9 Aeneas in search of the archer Pandarus, who is asked to mark out a victim: /βῆ δ' ἴμεν .... διζήμενος, εἴ που ἐφεύροι·/ εὗρε ... then (170) στῆ δὲ πρόσθ' αὐτοῖο ἔπος τέ μιν ἀντίον ηὔδα (~ infr. 127-8).

(1b) Closer still: *Il.* 4.88f. (cf. Lennox 62) Athena/Pandarus (/πειρᾶν ... 71, /βῆ .. κατ' Οὐλύμποιο ... 74) ... διζημένη, εἴ που ἐφεύροι· /εὗρε .../ἑσταότ' (~ infr. 121), where Ap. draws on the sequel, ἱσταμένη + address 92, δῶρα 97, ὀίστευσον 100, cf. infr. 127-8, 143, 152, and n. on 131f. — εὗρε δὲ τόνδε Zenodotus at 88 fin., leaving out (as does Π⁴¹, 3rd cent.) verse 89, cf. R. Pfeiffer, *History of Classical Scholarship from the Beginnings to the End of the Hellenistic Age* (Oxford 1968), 114, also Erbse on schol. *Il.* 4.88*a-b*, West *PP* 68-9, Rengakos 1993.58-9. Whatever one thinks of schol. A's comment on Zen.'s omission of the line, δοκῶν ἀνθρώπινον τὸ ζητεῖν εἶναι. καταλέλοιπε δὲ τὸ διζημένη, it is interesting that the 'searching' element is not reflected here (δίζομαι -ημαι in our poem 7 ×, subject always a human or humans), any more than it is in the adaptation of the Pandarus-episode in Virgil's *Aeneid* 12 (see R. R. Schlunk, *The Homeric Scholia and the Aeneid* (Michigan 1974), 134 n.8).

(1c) Ap. does not reproduce the 'marked asyndeton' (Kirk on *Il.* 4.89) of *Il.* 4/5; similarly Zen. (did he read τόνγε in fact?). One may compare here *Il.* 13.760-1 Hector in the thick of battle ... διζημένος, εἴ που ἐφεύροι·/τοὺς δ' εὗρ', and especially, again from the Pandarus-story, 5.794 /εὗρε δὲ τόνγε ἄνακτα ... (scil. Athena/Diomede, wounded by the archer).

(2) The elaborate πεῖρα practised by the devious Odysseus on his father in *Od.* 24 (see Heubeck on 226-31 for the 'insert' between discovery and confrontation, represented in Ap. by 115f.): 216 (Odysseus speaking) πατρὸς πειρήσομαι (cf. 221, 238, 240), 226 τὸν δ' οἶον πατέρ' εὗρεν ἐυκτιμένῃ ἐν ἀλωῇ (= πολυκάρπου ἀλωῆς 221, cf. below on 158), used for legitimate purposes. The son goes on to embrace and kiss his father (320), as Cypris embraces and kisses Eros (150), but whereas

Odysseus' deceitfulness has by then run its course, with Cypris it is only just surfacing (see on μειδιόωσα in that line). —

Nonnos (D. 33.61f.) made a thorough job of plundering: (Charis went) εἴ που ἐφεύροι/.. ἴχνος Ἔρωτος, 64 /εὗρε δέ μιν .. περὶ ῥίον ἄκρον Ὀλύμπου/κτλ., in the company of κοῦρος ἀθύρων with Ganymede acting as judge. His opponent is ἀχνύμενος (104). Cypris kisses her son (146), and promises a gift in return for his help (174f.), for which cf. id. 41.405f. ~ 422f.

113 βῆ ῥ' ἴμεν Homeric, also i.843, 1188 (*Echoes* ad loc.), iv.878 (id.).

Οὐλύμποιο κατὰ πτύχας *Oppositio*: *Il.* 11.77 κατὰ πτύχας Οὐλύμποιο/; where each god had his <own detached, private: on πτύχες etc. in general see Kannicht on Eur. *Hel.* 44-8, and cf. κατὰ πτύχας in ii.992> house. As Q.S. evidently inferred (114n.), Zeus' garden will have been in one of these πτύχες: gamblers like seclusion, but Eros is soon to be rudely interrupted.

More fanciful interpretations of Olympian πτύχες may have been in circulation in Ap.'s day: cf. on these Erbse on schol. *Il.* 20.5*b*, Schmidt 1976.81, 102, 104); the σφαῖρα of 135f., though rather a long way off, could be glancing at one of them.

εἴ μιν ἐφεύροι We can be pretty sure that Cypris had a good idea where her naughty son will have been hanging out (cf. Campbell 1990.482): not only is there no talk of 'searching' (see on 113-5), but the Homeric που, found in all the other echoes (*GDK* 32Cv60/ *Blem.* 60 Livrea διζήμενος, Nonn. *D.* 8.113 διζημένη, 16.374, 33.61) is dropped. On εἰ cf. Kirk on *Il.* 5.168-9 (and on 4.88); above, 26-8n.

114 ἀπάνευθε Cf. 9n. Scil. τῶν ἄλλων (θεῶν) (cf. *Il.* 1.498-9, 5.753-4), well away from/far removed from the bustle of life on Olympus – though he did have *one* companion (115). The status of the genitive Διός may have been a subject of debate early on: schol. 114-7*a* (led on by ἀπάνευθε Διός in Hes. *Theog.* 386??) expresses a preference for taking ἀπάνευθε as a preposition, without commenting on the general flow of the line or even explaining what 'well out of Zeus' way' might mean (because Eros was picking on his *eromenos* Ganymede??); '(in the garden) without Zeus' authorisation' can hardly have suggested itself as a feasible interpretation. Ctr. Q.S. cited below.

With ἀπάνευθε and its surroundings ctr. *Il.* 24.472-3 μιν ../εὗρ', (.. δ') ἀπάνευθε ... οἴω/, and for ἀπάνευθε then ἐν cf. *HyDem* 28 (ἐνί).

Διὸς ... ἀλωῇ Cf. *Studies* 22/100 nn.47, 48. See n. on 158f. concerning the question of Ap.'s dependence on Ibycus' account of the rape of Ganymede in the concluding part of this Olympian scene. Ibycus may well have mentioned Zeus' garden in this connexion. Such a spot (it was in similarly fecund surroundings that Zeus himself first lay with Hera, Janko on *Il.* 14.153-353, p. 171, Barrett on Eur. *Hipp.* 742-51, 748-9, founded on lyric? Cf. for a related image FJW on Aesch. *Suppl.* 592) is a suitable environment for an Ibycean μελέδημα: *PMGF* 288, cf. ? id. S257(a), col. i.7f. with West, *ZPE* 57 (1984), 23f.; θαλερῇ, though not applied to plants etc. in archaic poetry so far as we know, brings to mind θάλος in Ibyc. *PMGF* 288.1, θαλέθοισιν in id. 286.6. It is no doubt significant that the verb θάλλειν is applied to Eros' ruddy complexion in 122 (121-2n.), where χροιῆς .. ἔρευθος is reminiscent of the (lyric-based) flower imagery invoked in Plato *Symp.* 196b χρόας .. κάλλος κτλ. (cf. Dover ad loc. and see Calame on (his) Alcm. *fr.* 147, p. 555, Clarke, *AC* 43 (1974), 60f., *LIMC* 3.1.864f. for further illustration of Eros' association with 'Zeus' garden' and with flowers generally). πάγκαρπον in 158(n.) too may go back to a lyric source: it is a Pindaric word, and not particularly common (all the poetic examples save Meleag. *HE* 4408 in LSJ). Not that Eros' hold on the lush, sensual world of lyric fantasy is a strong one. We move on at once to the seamier side of life, as the grasping Eros does not even bother to deny that he is taking his companion for all he has got, though we catch glimpses of a lyric backdrop on the way: his association with knucklebones (Anacreon: 117f.n.; VDB 2.114 call attention to χρυσαστράγαλοι (φίαλαι) in Sappho, *PLF* 192), his μαργοσύνη (Alcman: 120n.) and his ball-playing (Anacreon again: 135-41n.).

This garden makes a reappearance in epic in Q.S. 10.335, Hera a spectator of human affairs ἑζομένη κατ' Ὄλυμπον, ὅπη Διὸς ἔπλετ' ἀλωή, a passage void of detail, presumably got straight from Ap. (the following line adapts i.671); Q.S. associates the πτύχας of 113(n.) with *Il.* 20.22-3 Zeus as spectator πτυχὶ Οὐλύμποιο/ἥμενος.

θαλερῇ .. ἀλωῇ The same combination in [Opp.] *Cyn.* 2.151, but there ἀλωή = 'threshing-floor'; *Od.* 6.293 πατρὸς ... τεθαλυῖα .. ἀλωή/.

θαλερός of course has strong sexual overtones. If the garden was the scene of Zeus' first encounter with Ganymede at Eros' prompting in Ibycus, then the union's sexual ripeness and potency may well have been matched by a sudden display of nature's generative powers: cf. -θηλέα in the course of the Διὸς ἀπάτη, *Il.* 14.346f.

115-7 Cf. *Studies* 22. The essentials of Ap.'s description of the snatching of Ganymede are to be found in *HyAphr* 202-3 (see on this passage van der Ben, *Mnemosyne* 39 (1986), 24) Γανυμήδεα .. Ζεύς/ἥρπασεν ὃν διὰ κάλλος ἵν' ἀθανάτοισι μετείη, with the important difference that Zeus' ἵμερος for the boy is here made quite explicit (cf. VDB 2.114, with Hainsworth on *Il.* 11.786). That ἵμερος was generated by Eros. His powers of subjugation thus extend far beyond the defeat of a gaming-opponent, for the highest of the gods is subject to his sway. This well-worn point (see e.g. Davies on Soph. *Trach.* 499-500), but an ominous one for the victim in the sequel, seems to have been made with reference to Ganymede by somebody, with none of the reserve in evidence here (Feeney 66, who does not discuss poetic motives, overreacts: 'salacious shock,' 'a scandal'), in Sophocles' *Colchian Women, fr.* 345, as Pearson ad loc. suggests; for a contemporary example cf. Call. *HE* 1069-70, with L. S. Tarán, *The Art of Variation in the Hellenistic Epigram* (Leiden 1979), 7f.

Verse 116 offers only a faint allusion to the blissful position of honour conventionally assigned to Ganymede by virtue of his good looks and high birth (cf. Bowra 176, along with K. J. Dover, *Greek Homosexuality* (2nd ed., Cambridge, Mass., 1989), 196-7, Erbse on schol. *Il.* 20.234d/Edwards on 233-5), that of cup-bearer to the gods: *HyAphr* 204f. installed by Zeus, cf. *Il.* 20.234f. snatched by the gods to take up this office /κάλλεος εἵνεκα οἷο (~ *Od.* 15.251 of Cleitus, a line rejected by Aristarchus: cf. ἀπενάσσατο 254 with Ap. 116 ἐγκατένασσεν, χολωθείς ibid. with Ap. 124 κεχόλωτο??). Here Zeus' favourite spends his time playing, and Eros, who was instrumental in getting him to Olympus in the first place, fearlessly humiliates him: if his family received handsome material recompense for his loss (AHS on *HyAphr* 211, Anon. *SH* 992.6-7), Ganymede himself was destined to be a loser. Another consequence of the rape is not spelled out as clearly as it might have been (116), the conferring by Zeus of immortality and agelessness (*HyAphr* 214): if Ganymede can be made to seem (despite χρυσείοις !) like an ordinary boy (cf. 118), we will appreciate the literary joke of infr. 124 (117/124n.) all the more.

Other elements in the description have a conventional ring to them: for ποτε, and for the uncompromisingly erotic slant which was present as far back as Ibycus (158f.n.) and also surely in the *Little Iliad* as well (cf. *EGF fr.* 6, with M. Davies, *The Epic Cycle* (Bristol 1989), 67, and also Griffin, *JHS* 97 (1977), 39f. on the 'sensationalism' of the Cycle in general; VDB 2.114), cf. Thgn. *IEG* 1345-6/καλοῦ 1350 (Vetta ad loc.), and note ποτε in the exemplum of Eur. *Hipp.* 454 (rape of Cephalus), ποτ' in Call. *HE* 1070 cited above; for ἱμερθείς cf. Pind. *O.* 1.41 ἱμέρῳ ~ 45 Γανυμήδης (Gerber ad loc.), and ἵμερον in Plato *Phdr.* 255c.

115 οὐκ οἶον, μετὰ καί On proclitic καί right before the main caesura, and on the concomitant caesurae in this verse, see Bulloch 1977.122, id. on Call. *h.* 5.103. Lit.: 'not alone, <but> Ganymede too with <him>': the ultimate model is the Homeric /οὐκ οἴην, ἅμα τῇγε καί ... (*Od.* 6.84) etc. For μετά cf. μετὰ δέ in *Il.* 2.446, al., Oswald 43 [E inserts a δέ here]; in *Or. Sib.* 12.20 μετά alone means 'with <them>,' 'as well.' Similarly σὺν καί i.74, al.: see Headlam on Hds 4.3, adding Nic. *Ther.* 8; suppl. in *GVI* 677.4, Ephesus 3rd/2nd cent. (needlessly challenged by Zucker, *Maia* 15 (1963), 395).

Γανυμήδεα If we are to think in terms of γάνυμαι and μήδεα (see on this Roscher 1.1597; Edwards on *Il.* 20.230-2), we have caught him at the wrong moment: cf. 123 κατηφιόων, 126 ἀμήχανος.

τόν ... Ζεύς *Il.* 21.35-6 (Achilles/Trojan prince) Λυκάονι, τόν ῥά ποτ' αὐτός/ἦγε λαβὼν ἐκ πατρὸς ἀλωῆς ..., cf. [Hes.] *fr.* 171.7]α, τόν ῥά ποτ' αὐτός/... (~ i.23); *Il.* 16.644 οὐδέ ποτε Ζεύς/... (Ζεύς at verse-end: Bühler ed. Mosch. *Eur.*, p. 103 n.5, Hoenigswald, *ICS* 16 (1991), 2f.). ῥα as often points to an individual who will be familiar to every reader: Ganymede is a true celebrity – but is not treated like one.

116 Cf. in general Kaibel *EG* 1046.90 (Rome, 2nd cent. AD) /νηῷ ἐνκατέθηκε συνέστιον.

οὐρανῷ ἐγκατένασσεν Gillies cited from the *Mnemosyne* of Moero (her son Homeros, a member of the tragic Pleiad, was doubtless known to Ap.) *CA* 1.7-8, Ζεύς/ἀθάνατον ποίησε καὶ οὐρανῷ ἐγκατένασσεν, scil. the eagle which brought nectar to nourish Zeus on Crete (on this: Knaack, *Hermes* 23 (1888), 311-12). If this is an adaptation (and there is no good reason to think otherwise; cf. from the same short fragment 1-2 τρέφετο .., οὐδ' .. τις ../ἠείδει μακάρων with Ap. ii.821-2 οὐδέ τις ἀνδρῶν/ἠείδει, οἷος δὲ ... βόσκετο ..., 3 ζαθέῳ .. ἄντρῳ/ with iv.1131 v.l. /ἄντρῳ .. ζαθέῳ), then we may be faced with the first known, if fleeting, allusion to Ganymede's own catasterism (material on this in Bömer's note on Ov. *Fast.* 2.145). Indeed, the evocation of the 'eagle' also tempts one to see in 'Zeus' an oblique reference to a version in which *Zeus himself* transported Ganymede to heaven *in eagle-form* – another 'first' ([Theoc.] 20 can hardly be 3rd cent.), for us at any rate (see the comprehensive notes of Bömer on Ov. *Met.* 10.155-61, Chrétien on Nonn. *D.* 10.259).

For the language cf. also /[οὐρανῷ ἐ]νκατένασσε (+ ἀστέρας) in the 3rd cent. AD hymn *ap.* Peek, *ZPE* 35 (1979), 168 (cf. too Luppe, id. 46 (1982), 165) = *SEG* 28.973.3, a line providing the only other example of this compound verb unless it is correctly restored in an oracle *ap.* schol. Lyc. 1378 (PW 301.2).

Ctr. Hes. *WD* 168 /Ζεὺς .. κατένασσε .. ἐν πείρασι (?) γαίης/.

ἐγκατένασσεν ἐφέστιον Cf. Dem. Bith. *CA* 6 /νάσσατο ... ἐφέστιος (*c. dat. loci*, as i.117).

ἐφέστιον ἀθανάτοισι only glances at his job of serving at the gods' table (115-7n.); in i.1319 Heracles is destined to enjoy a dignified and privileged existence: /ναίειν .. ἀθανάτοισι συνέστιον scil. as σύσσιτος, ὁμοτράπεζος (cf. *Od.* 11.603 [θαλίης = εὐωχίαις! Verdenius on Hes. *WD* 231] etc.). Cf. the use of ὁμέστιος, M. Huys, *P. Brux. Gr.* II 22 (1991), p. 62.

For ἐφ. + dat. pers. cf. iv.518.

117a κάλλεος ἱμερθείς This passive form (not in early epic) again at iv.1738 (overcome by sexual desire). The active appears in two late imitators, Greg. Naz. 500.19 /κάλλεος ἱμείρων (*Od.* 10.555 /ψύχεος ἱμείρων), Nonn. *D.* 42.242 -ουσι.

117f. For a description of games with knucklebones cf. VDB on 124 (2.114-5), and also Mau in *RE* 2.1793f., Lovett and others in *Folklore* 12 (1901), 280f., Gow-Page on *HE* 939 and Pref. to Antip. Sid. xxxii; bibliogr. in *LfgrE* s. ἀστράγαλος and in S. Laser, *AH* T: *Sport und Spiel* (1987), 118f.

VDB ibid. consider possible models in art; q.v. for bibliogr. (esp. Neutsch, on which see Sichtermann, *DLZ* 71 (1950), 413, Hampe; cf. also Webster 77-8). — Zanker's declaration (based on the supposition that 'the Alexandrian taste for *enargeia*' is somehow self-generating and non-interactive) 'There is no need to postulate direct influence from fine art on the passage' (1987.49; 105 n.56) is out of step with the reactions of successive generations of critics (cf. Herter *JAW* 370; see in general PF on 117-27), though it may be conceded that Ap. does not approach his task with the degree of self-consciousness exhibited by a number of Hellenistic epigrammatists (in Asclep. *HE* 906-7, for instance, we are surely looking at a painting, *pace* Gow-Page on ἐγράφη in 907), or, say, by Silius Italicus in his portrayal of Pan at 13.327f.

The scene is discussed, and related to Anacreon (*PMG* 398) and the epigram by Pretagostini, 225f.

117/124 ἀμφ' ἀστραγάλοισι .... κεχόλωτο plays with *Il.* 23.88 ἀμφ' ἀστραγάλοισι χολωθείς/ (the linking of the prepositional phrase with ἐψιόωντο in 118 may be going some way towards acknowledging the variant ἀμφ' ἀστραγάληισιν ἐρίσσας, on which see Richardson ad loc.): cf. ἀπάνευθε 83, ὁμοῦ 84, χρύσεος 92 [92 ath. Ar., Lührs 172f.], /τίπτε κτλ. 94. The context: Patroclus [somebody's *eromenos*?!] 'when he was little' killed a boy and had to migrate to a new home (Ganymede had already gone through the latter!). So vivid is the picture of κοῦροι at play that we *almost* forget that ἀνδροκτασίη is not a possible scenario here (cf. Lennox 63, and above on 115-7); ὀλέσσας in 125 no doubt harbours a jocular allusion to the suppressed murder-motif: Ganymede is a 'loser,' not a 'destroyer.' — Thiel, upon whose mind Jason's interest in the Golden Fleece exerts a powerful fascination, following T. M. Klein, pulls in here the eventual murder of Apsyrtus (198 n.2).

Schol. T at *Il.* 23.86a[1] is our source for the information that Alexander Aetolus dealt with this Iliadic theme ἐν Ἀστραγαλισταῖς (Meineke for ἀστρολογισταῖς): the murder was perpetrated παρὰ Ὀθρυονεῖ τῷ γραμματιστῇ (*CA* 10). Many have followed Shenkl's suggestion that this was a satyr-play (*WS* 10 (1888), 326-7). Snell however incorporated the scholion in *TGF* (1.101, *fr.* 1) somewhat reluctantly, and with good reason: one is hard put to it to dredge up any tragic remains from Alexander's pen (F. Schramm, *Tragicorum graecorum hellenisticae ... aetatis fragmenta* (Diss. Monast., 1929), 40-2), and I share Wilamowitz's suspicion (*HD* 1.167 n.1) that we are dealing with an epic – presumably a short-scale epic, transforming a passing detail in the master-poem into a full-blown episode focusing on the family history of one of its heroes (as Theoc. 24 deals with the domestic side of Heracles' career, bringing in a γραμματιστής in the person of Linus).

We are better informed about another recent predecessor's treatment of the knucklebones-motif, so vividly represented in lyric poetry by Anacreon, *PMG* 398 (cf. Pretagostini 226f.). Asclepiades *HE* 878f. (see McKay's ingenious discussion of the piece in *Mnemosyne* 21 (1968), 173f.) complains that the Erotes give him a hard time of it: 'If something happens to me, what will you do? ... ὡς τὸ πάρος παίξεσθ' [taken up by Meleag., *HE* 4076] ἄφρονες ἀστραγάλοις.' Once the pernicious Erotes have done their worst they will turn (as they have turned in the past, every time) to relaxation in the form of a frivolous game, with never a thought for their victims. So Eros here finishes his game and proceeds without scruple to implant the deadly fire of love in Medea's heart (*HE* 877 κακὸν ... φλέγετε ~ infr. 771 κακῶν, 773 φλέγει in the context of a cry of despair) before returning to his haunts on Olympus ...

Knucklebones are offered apparently as a bribe in Call. *fr.* 676, with the address φίλε κοῦρε. That the words (adduced by Huber 42, for instance) are spoken by Cypris to her son Eros is mere speculation. Cf. Pfeiffer ad loc.

117b ἀμφ' '(Play) with/at' is normally expressed by the simple dative (e.g. iv.950; Asclep. *HE* 879 παίξεσθ' .. ἀστραγάλοις/, Pherecr. *PCG* (VII) *fr.* 48 ἀντ' ἀστραγάλων κονδύλοισι παίζεται, LSJ s.v. παίζω I3), but as the game involves the capture of the opponent's pieces ἀμφί here does not differ essentially from ἀμφ' ἀργυρίδεσσιν in Pind. *O.* 9.90, 'over,' 'for the prize of'; cf. Seaton 1905.453. There is also *Il.* 23.88 (c.v.l.) to consider, cf. above on 117/124. Certainly not 'locative' (Haggett 39; Gillies, who, in a confused note, appeals to 623 infr., which is quite different, see ad loc.) or 'quasi-local' (Oswald 163).

118 χρυσείοις Not surprisingly, emphatically positioned epithets (15n.) denoting colour/substance are recurrent in ecphrastic and other descriptive passages (cf. infr. 140, and χρ. in *Il.* 18.418, 19.383, *Od.* 18.294, 296 etc.). Knucklebones could be inexpensive (Ar. *Vesp.* 295f., cf. the bumper bundle awarded as a schoolboy prize in *HE* 939), but we do hear of bronze, ivory and even gold ones (NH on Hor. *Carm.* 1.4.18): ours are naturally of premium quality, like, for instance, Cypris' comb (46), the κύκλα of Zeus' ball (137), Eros' baldric (156n.), Artemis' chariot (878n.), Apollo's bow (iv.1709), cf. Williams on Call. *h.* 2.32, Bornmann on 3.110-12, Mineur on 4.260f. for other examples of such divine accoutrements; made by Hephaestus, no doubt (see for the 'artistic' connexion Dodds on Eur. *Bacch.* 553-5, Lloyd-Jones, *CR* n.s. 32 (1982), 142/id. 1990, 2.227), they are as imperishable (Hainsworth on *Il.* 9.533, Verdenius on Pind. *I.* 2.2 & 26) as their owners.

For χρυσ. then κοῦροι compare *Od.* 7.100 (descriptive passage; Hephaestus is about). Hunter 1993.107 seems to me to exaggerate somewhat the effect of dissonance generated by the juxtaposition of the ensuing ἄτε κοῦροι ὁμήθεες to 'golden.'

ἄτε κοῦροι Nonn. *D.* 45.121 ἄτε κοῦρος. ἄτε (either *like* or *as one might expect from*, i.q. οἷα) is not Homeric but is common in Ap. and in Hellenistic verse generally.

κοῦροι ὁμήθεες Ctr. Hes. *Theog.* 60 κούρας ὁμόφρονας.

ὁμήθεες Also in ii.917. On the spread of this epithet in poetry (Call. +) see Campbell on Q.S. 12.216, and on its use here Chuvin on Nonn. *D.* 5.364. First attested in Plato in the form ὁμο- (on prevocalic ὁμο- ὁμ- cf. Wyatt 173-4). Schmitt 120 n.23 confidently labels the word 'alltagssprachlich'; but -ήθης compounds are quite at home in non-Attic verse: BP 716.

ἐψιόωντο *amuse oneself, play* here and infr. 950(n.); in i.459 /τερπνῶς ἐψιόωνται (/μυθεῦνθ' 458), ii.811 (n.b. 761 τέρποντο .. θυμὸν ἔπεσσιν/) of (pleasurable/pleasant) conversation at table. Caggìa 25f. discusses the ancient lexicographical material linking the verb with παιδιά/ἡ διὰ λόγων παιδιά/ἔπος together with examples from Homer on (Nonn. *D.* 11.399 and Paul. Sil. *AP* 5.288.1 have been overlooked); cf. also Rengakos 1982.40. On the unaspirated form (cf. ἔπος) offered by one or two witnesses in all four places (VDB I.LXXIII-IV) see Rzach 433-4, Hopkinson on Call. *h.* 6.38, Chrétien on Nonn. *D.* 10.326 (an echo of our line it would appear).

119-21 117-8 record an overall impression; this is followed up at once (καί ῥ' indicates an immediate/natural transition: cf. Braswell on Pind. *P.* 4.134(b)) with a breakdown of what is actually going on as we join the game. First, a snapshot of Eros, who by this time is keeping the palm of his left hand chock-full of knucklebones 'under his chest': he will be naked, and since he cannot stash them away, he presses his palm into the soft 'pocket' between chest and lower abdomen; for an artistic representation very close to what Ap. is describing see Neutsch 19-20. All the while he is standing upright, looming over his opponent (ἐφ- 121 cf. *Il.* 12.326) in predatory fashion.

How many does Eros have? It is a reasonable guess that he ends up with a score (four sets of five, five sets of four??) if we may set any store by the Homeric passage which inspired 146 /μείλια δ' ἔκβαλε πάντα, i.e. *Od.* 5.244 /εἴκοσι δ' ἔκβαλε πάντα. In epic terms, a fair number (Janko on *Il.* 13.260-1)!

119 καί ῥ' ὁ μέν On ῥα see above, on this particular run Campbell on Q.S. 12.169 (/ἀλλ' ὁ μὲν ἤδη Hom., *Od.* 3.410 al.).

ἤδη πάμπαν The other way round infr. 460-1 πάμπαν/ἤδη τεθνειῶτα (but *Il.* 19.334-5 /ἤδη ... πάμπαν/τεθνάμεν).

ἐνίπλεον First here, then [Orph.] *L.* 192 (-εον ἠύτε μαζόν/: Appel, *Gnomon* 57 (1985), 692), Nonn. *D.* 19.13. Of the two Homeric forms (on these see Risch 130), ἐνίπλειος introduced by *codd.* LAG here (also found in Antim. *fr.* 21.2, Leon. *HE* 2467 corr., Nic. *Ther.* 925, Q.S. 13.81, [Orph.] *L.* 276) and ἔμπλειος (also Antim. *ffr.* 23.2, 24.2, Arat. 1006, [Theoc.] 25.207, Q.S. 12.541, 13.5 corr.), Ap. has only the latter (infr. 1281, 1321). Call. (*fr.* 534) has ἔμπλεος, and this is the predominant form in the Hellenistic era.

119-20 Cf. Nonn. *D.* 3.397-8 μαζοῦ/... χειρὸς ἀγοστῷ/(ἀγοστῷ Ω in our line, from μαζῷ immediately above; for discussion see VDB 2.114; Chuvin on *D.* 3.398 cited our line as given by Ω without comment); iv.1734 ἐπιμάστιος (perhaps the source of D's ἐπὶ μαζῷ here; for a different explanation cf. Speake 1969.88/1974.119) ᾧ ἐν ἀγοστῷ/.

120 μάργος Ἔρως Obviously = *uncontrollably, irrepressibly greedy, grasping* if we are to harmonize the epithet with the immediate context, and that satisfies many (e.g. Pretagostini 234 n.31; the concept of (erotic) 'GIER (nach GOLD)' is overworked by Thiel 205, al.). But Eros also has to do with sexual μαργοσύνη (which he is to engender imminently in Medea's imagination: cf. iii.797, iv.375, 1019; Vian ed. 1961 here) and schol. in a sophisticated note recommends the interpretation ὁ μαργαίνειν ποιῶν (cf. 276n.). Perhaps we should say that as Eros inspires (a specific form of) lust in others, so he is (in a broader sense) 'lustful' himself, and projects this trait even when he is at play, where his immoderate urges are very much in evidence (cf. below on 121-2). For a different formulation see Buccholz 81; 'greedy, the poet calls him, a natural attribute of desire' Beye 1982.127 [see more generally id. 1993.209]: cf. the image in 1019 infr. Here (and not only here in this scene) one may detect an element of the 'sinister' which C. M. Bowra found so signally lacking when he took Ap. to task for indulging 'a frivolous prettiness' (*Landmarks in Greek Literature* (Harmondsworth 1966), 321); I am sure that J. B. Hainsworth was jesting when he told the world that 'no one takes these gods seriously' (*The Idea of Epic* (Berkeley/Los Angeles/Oxford 1991), 74).

Alcman had already spoken of μάργος.. Ἔρως in the context of παιδιά in the difficult fragment *PMGF* 58.1 (cf. Hafner, *MH* 8 (1951), 137f., Easterling, *PCPS* 20 (1974), 37f., Sutton, *ZPE* 51 (1983), 19f., Calame on (his) *fr.* 147); is the παῖς μάργος (whoever he is) of Aesch. *fr.* 281*a*31f., with his missiles and his 'mischievous behaviour' (Lloyd-Jones, *JHS* 76 (1956), 59 n.26) modelled on Eros?

(/)μάργος Ἔρως recurs in Nonnos: *D.* 10.337 ἵστατο in the context of 'competing'; 33.180 Eros and mother, shooting-scene etc., cf. esp. 180-1 ~ infr. 154-5; 48.277 Aura experiences a dream (in which μάργος Ἔρως figures), reckoned by her as μαχλάδος ... ἐπάξιος.

λαιῆς First in Parm. DK28 B17 (it is time that 'Tyrt.' [*PMG* 856.3] was removed from LSJ), but widespread by Ap.'s time; with χείρ also infr. 1160, iv.44.

ὑποΐσχανε Here only (recommended by Livrea 1983.425 in iv.1562, but Madvig's ὑπόεσχεθε is surely right); ὑποΐσχεται -το iv.169 (Livrea ad loc.), 473, cf. καταΐσχεται *Od.* 9.122 with *GH* 1.92, Wyatt, *Glotta* 70 (1992), 24f. Related 'open' forms in Rzach 466-7, Marxer 32-3; add from the Hellenistic era Maiist. *CA* 31 ἀναέγρετο, Anon. epic. id. 2.66 ἀναείρυεν (Wilamowitz *HD* 2.103), orac. in PW 381.2 ἐπιέξεται.

-ίσχανε does not deviate as much as Ardizzoni says it does from normal Homeric usage: Eros holds his palm tightly against his stomach as a *restraining* measure – he does not want his prize knucklebones to spill all over the ground.

χειρὸς ἀγοστόν See on 119-21 and 119-20. So in iv.1734 Euphemus in a dream has a small (1736) clod of earth in the palm of his hand, holding it to his nipple: to carry such a clod 'in bent arm' (on this sense see infr. 1394n., where ἀγοστός is discussed more fully) would be just too bizarre, even for a dream (Livrea ad loc. and VDB 3.208 consider that there is an ambiguity, but the transformation into a γυνή/κούρη occurs *after* the action described in 1734-5).

121 ὀρθὸς ἐφεστηώς So Nonn. *D.* 4.372 /ὄρθιον ἑστηῶτα (cf. *Il.* 18.246 /ὀρθῶν .. ἑσταότων, al.).

ἐφεστηώς See n. on 119-21 above. (-)εστηώς etc. (West on Hes. *Theog.* 519) 8 × in Ap. (including Mooney's certain correction at i.517). This form of the participle first in Hes. *Theog.* 519 = 747, then Antim. *fr.* 20.5 (corr.), but rare in Hellenistic verse outside *Arg.*: Call. *h.* 3.134, Nic. *Alex.* 334; widespread thereafter (ἐφ-: Man. 3.250 al., Triph. 575).

121-2 Note how the particular and the general merge, as with Eros' μαργοσύνη (120n.). Eros is flushed with victory, naturally (Köhnken 33-4); equally, he is often represented as rosy-skinned or rosy-cheeked (see Gow's note on Theoc. 7.117 μάλοισιν Ἔρωτες ἐρευθομένοισιν ὁμοῖοι/, noting also Antip. Sid. *HE* 632 ἐρεύθεται ἶσον Ἔρωτι/). The youthful beauty of his ruddy complexion ('the first roseate blush of post-pubescent sexual boyhood' writes Beye, 1982.127) is enhanced by the radiant flush that 'was blooming all over his cheeks' as we watch him play, just as at i.1230 the attractiveness of the πρωθήβης Hylas is heightened by the light of the <blushing: NH on Hor. *Carm.* 2.11.10> moon that suffuses his features (cf. Bremer, *CQ* n.s. 37 (1987), 424) κάλλεϊ καὶ γλυκερῇσιν ἐρευθόμενον χαρίτεσσιν: 'ἐρευθ. erotisch, vgl. Plato *Charmides* 158c (der Knabe errötete und das machte ihn noch schöner ...)' Faerber 63 n.6, cf. Palombi 76, and Stat. *Theb.* 4.274 of a physically attractive young warrior: *dulce rubens viridique genas spectabilis aevo*. Rather more contrived is the picture of the joyful Jason (compared to a young girl) as he picks up the Fleece in iv.170f., note παρηίσιν 172, ἔρευθος 173; cf. *Noten* 466-7, Livrea on iv.173, VDB 3.77 n.2; links with iii.120f.: Thiel 199f. (evocation of jubilant god, lure of golden prize; but taken a bit too far; sim. Nyberg 123-4).

γλυκερὸν ... Cf. in this sedes the Homeric unit γλυκερὸς δέ μοι ... (*Od.* 5.472); also Hes. *Theog.* 97, *HyHom* 25.5 γλυκερή οἱ ἀπὸ στόματος ...; *HyDem* 66 γλυκερὸν θάλος.

δέ οἱ ἀμφὶ παρειάς Repeated infr. 461, cf. iv.1279. Ctr. *Od.* 2.153 ... παρειὰς ἀμφί τε δειράς/...

χροιῆς χροιῇ Ω: this dative was no doubt taken over by Q.S., 9.471 /ἀχροιῇ γὰρ ἔρευθος ἐπήλυθεν, but neither *on the surface of the skin* nor (complexion, ruddy) *in respect of its colour* is credible. E put things right with the excellent conjecture χροιῆς, which reads very smoothly indeed: *a ruddiness of complexion*, cf. χροϊάν in Call. *h.* 5.28 ~ ἔρευθος 27, Plato *Symp.* 196b cited on 114 above, VDB 2.114 who aptly compare the expression χροιῆς ἄνθος.

θάλλεν See on 114. Of the condition of the skin in Archil. *IEG* 188.1; cf. Nonn. *D.* 16.73, a striking line.

ἔρευθος See above. For this word in general and for its association with παρειαί sim. in particular (cf. infr. 298, 963; iv.172-3) see Kost on Musae. 173 (note however that he misses Opp. *Hal.* 4.16, Paul. Sil. *Amb.* 84, as well as five further occurrences in Greg. Naz. and four in [Apolin.]); also Ardizzoni here, Bulloch on Call. *h.* 5.27 (with Arnott, *LCM* 10 (1985), 143), Drew Griffith, *TAPA* 119 (1989), 60; infr. 163, 298, 963nn.

122 ὁ δ' ... With this run Ap. brilliantly conjures up a quite different picture, *Il.* 22.141f. a hawk (~ conquering Achilles) aggressively and noisily swooping after a timid dove, ὁ δ' ἐγγύθεν ὀξὺ λεληκώς/..., cf. Campbell 1990.482.

ὀκλαδόν for ὀκλάξ (1308n.; ὀκλὰξ καθημένη Pherecr. *PCG* (VII) *fr.* 80, Kassel-Austin ad loc.) only here and in Nonn. *D.* (4 ×); but ὑποκλαδόν [Opp.] *Cyn.* 4.205. Derived presumably from what may be an old subst. (Frisk *GEW*, Chantraine *DE* s.v. ὀκλάζω) ὀκλάς preserved by Hipparchus in Arat. 517. Cf. in general Ardizzoni here, and *GG* 1.626, 734.

123 σῖγα Not in archaic poetry (it is read in a 3rd cent. papyrus at *Od.* 10.52, West *PP* 252-3; the f.v.l. at id. 15.440 is imperat. of σιγᾶν), but common enough in the Hellenistic epoch (10 × in *Arg.*). For σ. + ἧστο (122) cf. infr. 422-3 and earlier Ar. *Ach.* 59; for σ. + κατηφ- i.267, Nonn. referred to in next note; for σ. in conjunction with the next word and with ἀμήχανος in 126 cf. schol. on Pind. *P.* 9.92 (σιγαλὸν ἀμαχανίαν): ἀμήχανον δὲ τὴν σιγὴν εἶπεν ὅτι κατηφεῖς εἰσιν οἱ νικηθέντες.

κατηφιόων Eros, sensing imminent victory, is gleeful and noisy; Ganymede is silent, his head down, dejected and humiliated. For κατηφείη cf. schol. D at, on the one hand, *Il.* 3.51 αἰσχύνην, ὄνειδος, οἱ γὰρ αἰσχυνόμενοι κατηφεῖς εἰσι, and, on the other, 17.556 στυγνότης, λύπη· ἀπὸ τοῦ κάτω ἔχειν τὰ φάη, along with Erbse on schol. *Il.* 16.498, 17.556*a*, 24.253*d*. Blanc in *Mélanges ... J. Taillardat* (Paris 1988), 33f., although he may well be correct in analysing as *κατα-τηφής, related to τέθηπα etc. (clearly stupefaction *et sim.* are often in question), does not persuade me that the two nuances specified above were not felt *in actual usage* (for 'eyes' specifically cf. Eur. *Med.* 1012; 'disgrace, humiliation': e.g. iv.205, cf. Willink on Eur. *Or.* 881-3). The 'lowering of the eyes' (an element which may be excluded deliberately infr. 504: 503 'they kept looking at one another ...') is felt strongly here, as no doubt at i.267 σῖγα κατηφέες in the course of a scene replete with demonstrative displays of grief. See further 1402n., where further examples of κατηφείη sim. in the poem are examined.

This verb first in Ap. (also i.461); all the other verse examples are much later: *MAMA* 1.319 (Imperial); *GVI* 1732.11 (Isauria, 3rd/4th cent.); Q.S. 3.9; Greg. Naz. 548.342 + 4; Eudoc. *Cypr.* 1.178; Nonn. *D.* see *LexNonn* s.v. (note σιγήν and σιγῇ); [Apolin.] 34.29 + 2; Jo. Gaz. 1.354; Paul. Sil. *Soph.* 1000; Anon. *AP* 14.3.1.

On -ιᾶν in Ap. (and in Arat., cf. Gillies on 519) see Boesch 52-4, 56-7; but his argument, repeated by Wackernagel *SU* 184, that the presence of κατηφιᾶν in Plutarch and (perhaps, LSJ s.v.) Philo indicates koine influence could only be taken seriously if we were not dealing with one of the indispensable tools of hexameter poets from Homer onwards (cf. Marxer 36; Ardizzoni here and on i.461): Lobeck *Rhematikon* 175f., Meister 67f., *GH* 1.359, Shipp 97-8. The same goes for, e.g., μηνιᾶν in ii.247, on which see *GG* 1.732, ἐπιμειδιᾶν (earlier in Xen., but μειδιᾶν Hom. +) infr. 129.

123-4 δοιὼ .... ἐπιπροϊείς Vian's note (ed. 1961) runs: "δοιώ: s.e. ἀστραγάλω: comme l'indique l'emploi du part. prés., A.R. fait allusion ici aux deux derniers osselets que Ganymède se prépare à lancer et non à ceux qu' il a déjà lancés. ἔτ' αὔτως: 'encore une fois, comme il l'avait fait auparavant'; cf. *Il.* 23.268 λευκὸν ἔτ' αὔτως." Add to this VDB 2.114, on the game πλειστοβολίνδα: "C'est le jeu auquel se livrent Amour et Ganymède."

A few brief comments on an interpretation which seems to me to be right in the main: (1) ἐπιπροιέναι with dative again in iv.1617, of a destination (evidently after *Od.* 15.299, scil. νῆα), 'sent in a forward direction,' cf. 379n.; here 'on top of,' cf. ἐπί in the next line and iv.141 /ἄλλη ... ἑτέρῃ ἐπιτέλλεται. A reminiscence in Q.S.: 6.230-1 κεχολωμένος ἄλλον ἐπ' ἄλλῳ/ἰὸν ἐπιπροΐαλλε ... (2) The present participle marks the first sign of movement in what has been a static picture. As the mother comes (and we come) on the scene, Ganymede is in the act of throwing ... (3) ἔτ' αὔτως: see Campbell 1990.482. Cf. *Il.* 24.412-3 ἔτι .../αὔτως, and e.g. id. 22.484, schol. A ὡς καὶ πρότερον, *LfgrE* s.v. αὔτως 2. Here: 'still throwing as before' meaning 'still <as we join the game: given the ambience of the passage, analogous to ἔτι in descriptions of artistic representations, e.g. i.732, 736> at the stage of throwing two knucklebones one after the other/in succession as he did before,' i.e. finishing off the series of throws with the last two pieces remaining to him.

Vian later (cf. VDB 2.114, on 123) expressed a preference for 'en vain' (so Mooney), comparing the paraphrase in Philostr. Jun. *Imag.* 8. It is not entirely clear to me that Philostr. is reflecting αὔτως rather than the wider situation. But even if he is, it is only when we get to line 125 that we are told that he *lost* two pieces in addition to his previous ones: why anticipate the end result by importing a specific forecast when the general picture of Ganymede's downcast air, and Eros' own behaviour in 124, warn us of what is in prospect? In any case, this poem fails to throw up a single incontrovertible example of αὔτως (53n.) in the sense 'ineffectually,' 'to no purpose,' sim.; the echo of the Homeric configuration at *Il.* 23.268 nudges us in a definite direction.

δοιὼ δ' ἔχεν borrows language from yet another (122n.) picture of a warrior on a *winning* streak: *Il.* 12.464-5 δοιὰ δὲ χερσί/δοῦρ' ἔχεν ...

ἐπιπροϊείς This same participle occurs also in an oracle *ap.* Luc. *Alex.* 27; ἀπο- v.l. *Od.* 22.82. In view of the importance soon to be attached to the *Iliad*'s Pandarus-episode, ἐπιπροέμεν at 4.94 (ctr. Aristarchus: Rengakos 1993.163) may have been at the back of Ap.'s mind (cf. Lennox 63 n.39).

124 κεχόλωτο δὲ καγχαλόωντι *Il.* 16.585 κεχόλωσο δὲ –⏑⏑–×, *Od.* 23.1, 59 καγχαλόωσα/. Alliteration involving καγχ. is found in *Il.* 3.43 (Kirk ad loc.), the only case in Homer (ctr. Beck in *LfgrE* s.v.) where the verb carries the clear suggestion of raucous, derisive laughter (directed at a feeble foe), *cackle, guffaw* (cf. infr. 286 with the note, and ctr. iv.996 ~ γάνυσθαι 997, reflecting the more general sense of unrestrained joy, cf. schol. D at *Il.* 3.43, al.); Crane 1987.178 well compares Comatas' καχαξῶ in Theoc. 5.142.

Ap. seems to have in his head at this point Homer's account of the fight between Achilles and Asteropaeus: *Il.* 21.145 ἔχων δύο ..., 146 κεχόλωτο, 148 -σαν ἐπ' ἀλλήλοισιν ⌣–×, 149 προσέειπε. Here is another 'dead duck.'

125 καὶ μήν has none of the drabness that it possesses in introducing new personages in the Argonautic catalogue (i.69, 146, 161, 199): 'And just look!'

παρᾶσσον ἐπί 'right on top of': 17n.

ἐπὶ προτέροισιν Cf. *Od.* 22.264.

ὀλέσσας 117/124n.

126 κενεαῖς σὺν χερσίν Homer (*Od.* 10.42) has οἴκαδε νισόμεθα κενεὰς σὺν χεῖρας ἔχοντες (spoken by the comrades of Odysseus put out by their leader's acquisitiveness); closer in expression are *Rhesus* 792 (cf. Gow-Page on *HE* 1071) χειρὶ σὺν κενῇ, Rhian. *HE* 3228 (spoken by a lover defeated by his rivals) /σὺν κενεαῖς χείρεσσιν ἀπέρχομαι.

ἀμήχανος For discussion of this and related words, pervasive in the *Arg.*, see *Noten* 75 n.131, 430 n.182, Vian 1978.1031; n. on 422f. below. Stunned by his crushing defeat and so incapable of taking in what is going on around him Ganymede makes off, leaving the stage clear for mother and son. So Medea in more harrowing circumstances is ἀμήχανος in 1157f., compare 1150 τὰς δ' οὔτι περιπλομένας ἐνόησε/; similarly 951 of the preoccupied girl unable to concentrate on what she is doing. All this because of Eros, who, being an ἀμάχανον ὄρπετον himself (Sappho *PLF* 130.2, cf. *HyHerm* 434 ἔρος ... ἀμήχανος), inspires ἀμηχανίη in those with whom he has dealings (for the notion cf. e.g. Theoc. 1.85, where ἀμήχανος is linked with δυσέρως, and i.1232-3, where Cypris exerts the same paralyzing effect on the nymph who spots the stunningly attractive Hylas; Apollonian ἀμηχανίη afflicts a lover whose medical condition is hopeless in Maced. *AP* 5.225.3 ἐκ κακότητος ἀμήχανος ~ infr. 423n.).

οὐδ' ἐνόησε Homeric clausula, often elsewhere. Cf. 891(n.).

127 Κύπριν ἐπιπλομένην heralding a new confrontation forms a ring with ... Κύπριν· ἐπιπλόμεναι ... in 25, Hera's initial suggestion that Cypris be approached; for the verb see the note ad loc.

ἀντίη ἵστατο echoes the formula ἀντίος [see on this Rengakos

1993.76] ἵστασ' (ἐμεῖο/) *Il.* 17.31, 20.197, *Scutum* 449, all of confrontation on the field of battle; and sure enough Cypris *is* in bellicose mood – for a few moments: she ends up (see 128n.) ἀντομένη (149). Cf. later Paul. Sil. *AP* 6.54.3 ὁ δ' ἀντίος ἵστατο Πάρθις/, Musae. 100 ἀντίος (v.l.) ἵστατο κούρης/.

ἀντίη preceded by ἐνόησε/: ctr. *Od.* 19.478 ἀντίη then νοῆσαι/.

128 Cf. Q.S. 2.411 (note τίπτε 414) /καί μιν ἄφαρ προσέειπεν (*Il.* 1.441, 585 καί μιν προσέειπεν/).

ἄφαρ recalls Hera's directive at 109. Cypris launches an immediate frontal attack.

γναθμοῖο κατασχομένη Cf. *Studies* 18/100 n.40. κατα- is intensive: 'grip tightly' by ..., cf. Bond on Eur. *HF* 406 concerning the use of the active in this sense. In the pretty epigram of Jul. Aegypt. in *APl* 388 the poet is said to imbibe Eros τῶν πτερῶν κατασχών.

γναθμός can denote either 'one cheek plus that side of the upper and lower jaws' (Dover on Ar. *Nub.* 1109) or 'jaw,' more often than not 'lower jaw.' In reprimanding her child Cypris might be said to take hold of either, but in a face-to-face confrontation the latter is the more likely. Besides, she will then be automatically (and unwittingly) assuming the posture of a *suppliant* (cf. e.g. Headlam on Hds 3.72, G. Neumann, *Gesten und Gebärden in der griechischen Kunst* (Berlin 1965), 68f.), a posture well suited to the rapid swing from scolding (129-30) to appeal (131 [n.b. πρόφρων] -144)! Virgil's Venus is altogether more subservient from the very outset (*A.* 1.664f., cf. n. on 131f.) with a son who has more than his fair share of *gravitas*. For a different (and duller) interpretation see Giangrande, *GB* 1 (1973), 139.

Apuleius remembered this scene in *Met.* 6.22 (Jupiter) *prehensa Cupidinis buccula*... (cit. Prescott 371); in id. 4.31 Venus embraces and kisses her son long and hard *after* imploring him to shoot a girl: ctr. infr. 150f.

-σχομένη προσέειπε iv.82 (supplication).

129f. bring vividly to mind (*Studies* 18) Maia's rebuke in *HyHerm* 155 τίπτε σὺ ποικιλομῆτα ..., addressed to a shameless (156) god whose mischief-making likewise affected 'mortal men and immortal gods' (160-1). Maia at least made an effort; Cypris' attempts at child-discipline are pitiful. The echo of the *Hymn* arouses the expectation that the target of the reprimand will speak out: but the grabby Eros will not be allowed to do so (148n.), not publicly at any rate.

129 ἐπιμειδιάᾳς The compound here only in verse, I think (ἐπιμειδιόων cannot be right in Q.S. 5.88, cf. Vian ad loc. and Lloyd-Jones, *CR* n.s. 17 (1967), 275).

ἐπι-: cf. 124; 'over <him>' rather than 'après <ce mauvais coup>' Vian ed. 1961 (VDB: 'après ce que tu as fait'). In archaic epic ἐπιμειδᾶν can be used of a smile directed at an individual who is or is thought to be at a definite disadvantage (*Il.* 10.400, Hes. *Theog.* 547, cf. *HyAp* 531).

On -ιᾶν see 123n. -άᾳς (μειδιάᾳ Opp. *Hal.* 3.228, Q.S. 9.476; earlier -ιάων rather than -ιόων *HyHom* 7.14, ~ Bion *fr.* 13.11) like Homer's ὁράᾳς and ἐάᾳς (*GH* 1.75f.), but iv.383 κυδιάεις (~ Colluth. 179), cf. *HyDem* 170 κυδιάουσαι with the bibliogr. in Richardson's note. Ap. has invariably for the third person -ει, the norm in the Hellenistic era: Meister 68f. — Rzach (577) supports the poorly attested -εις here with the strange assertion that Ap.'s model is *HyHom* 10.3 μειδιάει. The double alpha is just too good to throw away.

ἄφατον κακόν Recycled by Nonnos, *Par.* 18.147, cf. Livrea ad loc. A representation in heightened epic diction (on ἄφατον cf. Bulloch on Call. *h.* 5.77, Hopkinson on id. *h.* 6.57; again infr. 1257, in an exceptionally 'heroic' environment) of the kind of thing an ordinary mother might say to an impossible child: cf. Headlam on ἀνώνυμος in Hds 6.14 (esp. Ulpian on sons). κακόν: cf. *Il.* 5.831 (Ares), *Od.* 12.118 (Scylla: id. 125, a πῆμα βροτοῖσιν/ ~ Ap. iv.445 Eros πῆμα ... ἀνθρώποισιν/, see on this Vetta, *RFIC* 100 (1972), 292), Hes. *Theog.* 570 (Pandora), etc., and for the use of the term in more down-to-earth contexts Gow on Theoc. 14.36. Naturally the label (like much else in this Eros-episode) has validity way outside the context in which it is uttered; 'in ἄφατον κακόν ... traluce già qualcosa dello σχετλιασμός di iv.445 sgg.' Livrea 1982.20, cf. also VDB 2.14.

αὔτως Cf. 53, 185nn.; 'just like that,' without the slightest conscience/without justification (matched by οὐδὲ δίκη ...) or 'as you are always doing' ('selon ta coutume' Vian ed. 1961, sim. VDB); the former is better. Schol.'s feeble ματαίως is not worth entertaining (cf. 123-4n. and Campbell 1990.482): there is no denying that the tricky Eros has effectively put one over on his green opponent, a fact which his mother positively deplores.

For the clausula cf. Arat. 65 ἀλλά μιν αὔτως/, Opp. *Hal.* 3.477 εἴτε ...

130 ἤπαφες Homer has the aorist of the simplex only in tmesis, *Od.* 14.488 παρά μ' ἤπαφε (Aristophanes is credited with ἤπαφεν for ἤγαγεν in *Il.* 10.391, cf. Ludwich 1.318); ἤπαφεν *Nosti EGF fr.* 7, ἤπα]φε f.v.l. *HyDem* 56. For ἀπαφίσκειν *dupe, fool, lead astray* sim. cf. *LfgrE* s.v., W. Luther, *Wahrheit und Lüge im ältesten Griechentum* (Leipzig 1935), 101f. It is part of the fun that the sanctimonious Cypris, who can herself 'smile' (cf. 129) or 'laugh' with the best of them over afflicted lovers (Sappho *PLF* 1.14, Theoc. 1.95 etc.), is made to use a term equally applicable to her own activities in the erotic sphere (cf. the connotations of νῆις later in the line, 32n.): *HyAphr* 38, cf. below on 152.

+ μιν: cf. *HyAp* 376.

οὐδὲ δίκῃ Cf. οὐδὲ δίκαιοι/ in ii.1180 (~ *Od.* 9.175) with VDB 1.233 n.1, Platt 1920.79, and more generally *GP* 190f., esp. 192, KG 2.293f.

There has been nothing in the text of course to indicate that Eros has actually been cheating. Yet we somehow feel that he must have been, since he is that sort (like his wily mother); and there is no denial. Cf. his affect on the minds of δίκαιοι, Soph. *Ant.* 791f., and on ἀδικία sim. related to the sphere of the erotic cf. Vetta on Thgn. 1283, Albiani, *QUCC* n.s. 5 (1980), 77f., Allen 73. Cypris' (rhetorical) question (she does more than 'wonder if...': Beye 1993.209) serves as a powerful 'symbol of love's untrustworthiness which Medea is to discover,' MacKendrick, *CJ* 49 (1953), 10 (cf. Medea's insistence on the upholding of δίκη specifically in iv.372). For an offbeat, and undisciplined, approach to this whole business of 'anticipation' cf. Klein, *CW* 74 (1980/81), 225-7 (taken up by Pavlock 43f.).

That 'love has also [scil. in addition to its unpalatable aspects] a sense of careless pleasure' (Beye 1969.49 on the κοῦροι at play) may be true, but if Ap. did mean to suggest such a notion he has made a good job of puncturing it with a minimum of delay.

περιέπλεο 25n.
νῆιν ἐόντα 32n.

131f. Two Iliadic scenes in particular underly Cypris' bribing of her son, 4.93f. (Lennox 63) and 14.232f. (*Echoes* 44).

(1) A disguised Athena prompted by Zeus in furtherance of the grand design confronts the archer Pandarus: for the various imprints of this episode see on 113-5. Cypris does not mimic Athena's carefully judged initial approach: instead of politely requesting obedience (4.93 ... πίθοιο), as we might have expected her to do (cf. supr. 26, 105, but ctr. 91f.!), she adopts Hera's suggestion that Eros be issued with a straight directive (85f. ~ 131, 142f.). But she is quick to back up the directive with a tasty bribe for the acquisitive god; the deceitful Athena does in due course get round to specifying 'gifts,' but only in ge-

neral terms (4.97): after all, Pandarus has the prospect of winning κῦδος as well (4.95).

A more sombre note is struck by the sharp parallelism of 4.98-100/Ap. 142-3: just as 'the warlike son of Atreus' is to be shot by an arrow (intended result: death), so 'the virgin daughter [and females are by convention 'unwarlike' and defenceless, infr. 563n.] of Aeetes' is to be shot by an arrow (result: bewitchment). Eros' missiles can be just as devastating as those of the archer on the battlefield as he targets his unsuspecting victims, as we shall presently come to realise.

(2) Hera's bribing of Hypnos in *Il.* 14: for the run-up to this scene see on 111-12. Hera is suitably subservient (like Virgil's Venus with Cupid in *A.* 1: above, 128n.): a deferential request for obedience (14.235) in the task of exerting θέλξις (cf. 14.252) on Zeus is backed up with a bribe, notably a golden throne which Hephaestus would manufacture (ctr. Ap. 135-6, the craftsman god does not enjoy a monopoly by any means); the δώσω of 14.238 is reflected in Ap., but not right away (142n.). The oath demanded by Hypnos to secure a further offer is met by Hera (14.271f.); Cypris on the other hand is amusingly made to *volunteer* an oath with the intention of keeping Eros sweet, and we strongly suspect her motives (150, 152nn.).

131 εἰ δ' ἄγε μοι Hom. *Il.* 6.376, *Od.* 4.832; often elsewhere.

μοι πρόφρων No doubt from *Il.* 1.77 (... ἀρήξειν/); cf. infr. 1071.

μοι .. τέλεσον But *Od.* 10.483 τέλεσόν μοι ...

πρόφρων τέλεσον So already Pind. *P.* 5.117 (οἱ ...) πρ. τελεῖ. Cf. Anon. hex. *SH* 900.4??

τέλεσον χρέος So (Campbell 1982.15) Maiist. *CA* 17 τελέσαι χρέος (= Jo. Gaz. 1.358).

Cf. *Studies* 18. χρέος = *obligation*, something he *ought* to do (cf. 108n.) for his mother, voluntarily and unselfishly (πρόφρων, often used of a god's beneficent aid). The reality is very different.

ὅττι κεν εἴπω On εἴπω cf. 81-2n. Cypris seems all business; but she follows up at once with a bribe. This is an Homeric clausula (note esp. *Od.* 19.378 ἀλλ' ἄγε ...); often elsewhere.

132f. Another rich crop from early epic:

(1) *Od.* 8.430-1 (Arete to Odysseus as ξεινήιον) /καί οἱ .. τόδ' ἄλεισον .. περικαλλὲς ὀπάσσω,/χρύσεον ...

(2) *HyHerm* 323 al. Διὸς περικαλλέα −× ~ id. 32 τόδε καλὸν ἄθυρμα/ (the property of another precocious divine child), *Od.* 18.300 περικαλλὲς ἄγαλμα/ (brought as a δῶρον).

(3) *Il.* 15.363 ποιήσῃ ἀθύρματα νηπιέῃσιν/ scil. παῖς cf. *HyHerm* 151-2 τέκνον/νήπιον then ἀθύρων/; *Od.* 5.452 (same sedes, different sense) οἱ ποίησε ~ *Cypria EGF fr.* 4.1-2 corr. τά οἱ .../ποίησαν (scil. goddesses for a goddess), *HyHerm* 52 τεῦξε ... ἄθυρμα/; esp. *Od.* 8.372-3 σφαῖραν καλὴν μετὰ χερσὶν (infr. 140) ἔλοντο,/πορφυρέην, τήν σφιν Πόλυβος ποίησε ... (as in 141-2 below the ball is tossed high into the air; Eust. on 8.376 mentions a game οὐρανία, cf. Hesych. 01830 and the simile-picture of iv.951-2).

132 κέν .. ὀπάσαιμι (Wåhlin 22) 'in that case I would be prepared to ...' Typical variation: in *Il.* 23.151, the only example of ὀπάσαιμι in the Homeric corpus, no modal particle is present (cf. *GH* 2.216).

132-3 περικαλλὲς ../κεῖνο Hence no doubt Leon. Alex. *FGE* 1870-1 περικαλλὲς ἄθυρμα/τοῦτο ... — For κεῖνο, τό ... cf. Nonn. *D.* 36.23.

132/135 ἄθυρμα .... σφαῖραν Cf. iv.950.

133 κεῖνο τό οἱ ποίησε ... Perrin *ap.* Stanford on *Od.* 8.373 (above, 132f.n.): 'The verse illustrates the Epic manner of enhancing the value of an implement by assigning it to some definite skilled artist of repute. This was no common ball'; see further Rutherford on *Od.* 19.56-8, 56-7. The present object, and its maker, are certainly out of the ordinary, to put it mildly. With κεῖνο, 'that well-known' [but also remote: it is not exactly to hand!] one feels that she is perhaps pushing her luck: is the ball a figment? Cf. on 150.

φίλη τροφὸς Ἀδρήστεια The echo of the formulaic φίλη τροφὸς Εὐρύκλεια (*Od.* 2.361 etc.) is designed to impart an exaggerated air of familiarity to 'dear nurse Adresteia.'

φίλη τροφός also i.668 (on the point of that see George, *Hermes* 100 (1972), 55 n.2), Call. *h.* 4.97, *Or. Sib.* 13.43, 14.284.

133-4 There is no doubt that we are on Crete. The cave in question (West on Hes. *Theog.* 477, id. 1983.132) is within easy recall: ii.1233-4 ὁ δὲ Κρηταῖον ὑπ' ἄντρον/Ζεὺς ἔτι Κουρήτεσσι μετετρέφετ' Ἰδαίοισι. So in Call. *h.* 1.47-8 Adresteia, sister of the Curetes (*h.* 1.52) according to schol. 47*c* ~ schol. Ap. 133, in the company of Δικταῖαι Μελίαι puts the infant Zeus to bed on Crete λίκνῳ ἐνὶ χρυσέῳ (there is a [wet-] 'nurse' in attendance, Amaltheia): cf. 'Idaean' 50 and κουρίζοντος/ 53; successive σπονδειάζοντες 46-7 ('Αδρ.) ~ Ap. 133 ('Αδρ.) -4 (cf. McLennan on *h.* 1.35). Behind all this (and behind Arat. below) may lurk an Orphic source: West 1983.127f., Pendergraft 101 n.25; note τρέφεται in [Orph.] *fr.* 162.

Earlier in the poem we heard, from the lips of Orpheus, of the 'Dictaean cave': i.508-9 (134n.) ὄφρα Ζεὺς ἔτι κοῦρος, ἔτι φρεσὶ νήπια εἰδώς [see on this detail Busch 314],/Δικταῖον ναίεσκεν ὑπὸ σπέος (cf. id. 1129 /Δάκτυλοι Ἰδαῖοι Κρηταέες then 1130 Δικταῖον ἀνὰ σπέος): on the alternation, which Ap. shares with Arat. and Call., see VDB on i.511 (1.253) and 1131 (1.265), Vian on Nonn. *D.* 1.322, Chuvin, *RPh* 51 (1977), 28-9, Martin on Arat. 33 (Idaean and Dict(aean) in connexion with Zeus κουρίζοντα/ 32, /ἄντρῳ ἐγ- and -τρεφ- 34, cf. Zumbo in *Scritti in onore di S. Pugliatti* (Milan 1978), 1039 n.15; Δ- must stand, *pace* Kidd, *CQ* n.s. 31 (1981), 357f.).

'Dictaean' is distinctively Cretan; 'Idaean' is not. Schol. 134 (no doubt preserving material from Theon's commentary, 134n.) has an interesting note: according to Demetrius of Scepsis Mt Ida *in the Troad* also claimed to be the god's birthplace (cf. VDB 2.115, and H. Verbruggen, *Le Zeus crétois* (Paris 1981), 37f., lit. in Kleywegt, *Mnemosyne* 44 (1991), 138). The absence of 'Cretan' here might indeed lead us to think of Adresteia in quite another setting (cf. i.1116 and Kirk on *Il.* 2.828-9, Lloyd-Jones and Parsons on *SH* 940.4, Hollis on Call. *Hec. fr.* 116) and, more pertinently, in a 'demiurgic' capacity: in *Phoronis EGF fr.* 2 ~ schol. Ap. i.1129, on the 'Idaean Dactyls' (see above) associated with the Phrygian 'Idaean Mother,' the 'Idaean men of Phrygia' are said to be θεράποντες ὀρείης Ἀδρηστείης/, and to have been the first to work iron, the province of the god Hephaestus: cf. Ap.136 and West on Hes. *WD* 150, Burkert, *RhM* 105 (1962), 39f.; Diod. 17.7 (Cleitarchus?) in a digression on Mt Ida in the Troad remarks that the (local) Idaean Dactyls learned their craft 'from the Mother of the Gods.' On the close association, in Ap. as elsewhere, of the Phrygian 'Mountain Mother' with the 'Idaean Mother' of the Troad see VDB on i.1116 and 1126 (1.263-4). Adresteia has come to Crete, and brought her metal-working skills with her. — A. in general: bibliogr. in Pendergraft 96 n.5.

134 ἄντρῳ ἐν Ἰδαίῳ Cf. for the *incipit HyHom* 26.6 /ἄντρῳ ἐν εὐώδει (where Dionysus grew up); similarly iv.1131 v.l. /ἄντρῳ ἐν ἠγαθέῳ (in connexion with Macris, who had to do with the infant Dionysus) ~ Hes. *Theog.* 483 /ἄντρῳ ἐν ἠλιβάτῳ (infant Zeus); also *HyHerm* 172, 359 /ἄντρῳ ἐν ἠερόεντι (Hermes ἐν λίκνῳ 358 cf. above on 133-4, Call.).

Ἰδαίῳ Pind. *O.* 5.20 Ἰδαῖον ... ἄντρον, another spot which attracted the attention of Demetrius of Scepsis (schol. 42a Dr., mentioning Theon; cf. above on 133-4).

ἔτι νήπια κουρίζοντι Cf. Q.S. 4.432 νηπιάχοισιν ὁμῶς ἔτι κουρίζοντα/.

κουρίζειν: this means 'be, behave like a κοῦρος' (Meerwaldt, *Mnemosyne* 56 (1928), 165f. made a real meal of this word); νήπια, 'with childlike ways' (cf. Zeus in i.508) pinpoints his stage of development. Zeus, the infant κοῦρος, νήπια φρονεῖ (cf. Suda κ2186 fin.), νηπιαχεύει: see Hans Herter *ap.* A. Skiadas, *Kallimachos* (Darmstadt 1975), 360 n.21, citing some later examples.

The verb occurs only twice in archaic epic (*Od.* 22.185, Hes. *Theog.* 347), is common in late verse, but relatively rare in the Hellenistic era: i.195 (of a young warrior, after *Od.*; /ὧδ' ἔτι κουρίζων ~ Anon. *APl* 372.5 /ἀλλ' ...), iii.666 (of a female); and Arat. 32 (Zeus, above on 133-4), Call. *h.* 1.54 (id.; cf. McLennan ad loc., but not an entirely fault-free discussion), 3.5 (Artemis: ἔτι), 4.324 (Apollo: παίγνια ibid. cf. ἄθυρμα and μείλιον Ap.132, 135).

There is a dash of irony in the description: Zeus was once upon a time 'still' at the stage of being entertained by a toy, Eros is at that stage now – and, in the conception of most, it is no more likely that he will mature than that Cypris will one day turn into a wrinkled crone: ctr. Hera in 110. —

Nelis 167f. sees in 134 a significant echo of a detail in Orpheus' song, i.508-9. However, the equation he seeks to establish, based as it is on multiple interpolations, is hard to swallow. In particular, 'Love' is *not* the real issue of the song ('intelligence and craft' still less), since Orpheus' aim is to warn against outrageous behaviour rather than to deliver a cloying sermon on the positive benefits of harmonious relationships (on the specifically admonitory elements see Lawall 141, and Fusillo 61-2, with bibliogr.): in fact, *pace* a number of critics (e.g. Beye 1969.53: 'its theme ... is the alternation of love and hate or strife as the two opposing and ruling forces in the universe,' construed as elaborating 'a motif which runs through the entire epic'; Thiel 126f., cf. Busch 308), there is no clear and positive indication of just how order was created in the physical world, and the effect is one of witty pastiche (for the various bits and pieces see Herter *JAW* 343, Pieri, *SIFC* n.s. 49 (1977), 98f., VDB 1.252-3, Dickie 278-9, Vian, *Prometheus* 19 (1993), 43 n.16), suggestive of the vast range of the singer's knowledge, presented in the grand didactic style (see on that Innes, *CQ* n.s. 29 (1979), 169f. [but 'anti-Callimachean' this is not!], Brown, *HSCP* 93 (1990), 318f.), in a summarising, oblique form as elsewhere with this son of a Muse – designed to avoid putting such incomparable talent on open display! (To call his poetry 'an unattainable ideal,' P. E. Knox, *Ovid's* Metamorphoses *and the Traditions of Augustan Poetry* (Cambridge 1986), 12, is to take things far too seriously.) Hunter's assertion (1993.149) that the reader has no idea who is singing the final six lines of the song is bizarre.

135-41 Eros, who plays the boy's game of knucklebones, can also be expected to be interested in the exotic plaything shortly to be described (cf. *LIMC* 3.1.914 & 987 for various artistic representations of a ball-playing Eros/Cupid), though uppermost in his *mother's* mind is a very different sort of βέλος, 143, 153: cf. Anacr. *PMG* 358 (with H. Fränkel, *Early Greek Poetry and Philosophy* (Oxford 1975), 292 n.5, and, among the host of articles devoted to this picture, Davidson, *Mnemosyne* 40 (1987), 133f., who lays proper stress on the ball *qua* missile) and Meleag. *HE* LIII (cf. Pretagostini 230f.).

A On the face of it what is on offer is a ball, comparable to a single star (141), representing the earth: see West 1983.33 (and id. 158 on a ball offered to Dionysus by the Titans, with Brendel 79f.); as Cook remarks (*Zeus* 2.1047) on the artistic motif of the earth as Eros' ball: 'we are meant to draw the moral *omnia vincit Amor*' (cf. Pendergraft 96 n.4, bibliogr. on *adult* Zeus' symbolic ball). Not that Eros' authority requires such concrete validation in our poem, since he is already master of all he surveys in 164f. (159-63n.).

Some examples of the concept of the earth/cosmos as ball(s) or sphere(s) are given in Hunter's note on 135 (see also D. R. Dicks, *The Geographical Fragments of Hipparchus* (London 1960), 23f.). Add to those a significant pre-Apollonian instance, Plato *Phaed.* 110bc, where the earth is likened to a coloured ball (William M. Calder III's interpretation, *Phronesis* 3 (1958), 123, is surely the only feasible one). Unlike Nelis 167 n.63, who has a particular point to prove, I would not place undue stress on the Empedoclean divine sphere, ordered by Love.

On a 'straightforward' reading of the passage, some sort of clarity can perhaps be extracted, along the following lines (for various attempts at elucidating what was in Ap.'s mind's eye, see in addition to the commentaries Peschties 33f., Gillies, *CR* 38 (1924), 50f., Herter *JAW* 368, Lendle, *Hermes* 107 (1979), 193f., VDB 2.115-6 along with Livrea 1982.19-20, Fowler 1989.15, Pendergraft 95f., Manakidou 144f.):

(1) Philostr. Jun. *Imag.* 8, in a very loose paraphrase of our passage, represents the *ball* as 'of gold.' Ap. says that *its* (οἱ) *circular pieces* are made of gold, viz. the ball must be *faced* with circular rings of gold

(like the ox-hide shield surely with its χάλκεοι κύκλοι *Il*. 11.33, see below for more in the way of shield-terminology). The nature of the ball's *interior* is not of interest (cf. further Livrea 1982.20), or at any rate not of immediate interest: the object does trail fire (141) <generated internally> (one may suppose).

(2) The 'circular pieces' look to be (an indeterminate number of) 'zones' encircling the sphere and so configured differently from the φύλλα or gores of the (run-of-the-mill) ball described in Anon. *AP* 14.62.1 (cf. Gow-Page on Leon. Tar. *HE* 2245).

(3) On the functions and possible configurations of ἀψῖδες see *LfgrE*. Around *each* of these κύκλα are wound *two* ἀψῖδες, = ἅμματα, 'fastenings.' Since these can be 'stitched' (139), perhaps we should think of a series of stepped pairs of thin semicircular metal strips drawn round (περιηγέες) each κύκλον to serve as clamps. For a different construction see notably Gillies 1924.51, who argues for just one *helix* to disguise the joins on each side of the ball (but he presses too hard the point that Ap. writes ἕλιξ, not ἕλικες; there is also the element 'two round each' to consider). — See 138n.

(4) But one cannot see the joins, as the 'stitches' are hidden from view: presumably strands of fine wire (cf. *Il*. 12.296-7 cited on 139 below) worked in to secure the outer plating.

(5) The 'stitches' are not visible, because [cf. in general Faerber 53 n.1] a *helix* runs/courses *over* every one of them − a winding, twisting, spiral decorative motif made of (an inlay of) dark-blue enamel. On the use of spiral motifs, wire and enamel see Fowler 1989.15.

B The ball, made on earth for a god on earth, might reasonably represent the earth. Closer scrutiny will reveal a different picture. 'The description in Arat. 401 of the Corona Australis, δινωτοὶ κύκλῳ περιηγέες εἰλίσσονται, may indicate that this ball is cosmic' Gillies ad loc.; Vian ed. 1961 suggested that ἕλιξ in 139 carried an astronomical connotation (cf. Plato *Tim*. 39ab). For the view that the ball 'symbolise l'univers' see VDB 2.115 (cit. Sittl; Cook: add id. 2.933); Livrea on Nonn. *Par*. 18.20. It is tempting to think specifically of a σφαῖρα οὐρανία: so Stückelberger 72 n.11, who elucidates the elements κύκλα 137, ἀψῖδες 138, ἕλιξ κυανέη 139-40 (cf. also Livrea 1982.19) on this basis, see nn. ad loc.; cf. too Pendergraft 95f., who stresses the links with various Aratean passages and argues for an armillary rather than a solid sphere. Stückelberger attributes the haziness and incompleteness of the description to a desire to avoid anachronism. That is one way of looking at it. The mother of course is in a hurry, and her job is to say just enough of the right things to make her son's mouth water. The presentation is exquisite! Here we have a work of a hallowed artist of old who anticipated contemporary interest in the miniature (cf. on that J. Onians, *Art and Thought in the Hellenistic Age* (London 1979), 119f.); the features contributing to its outstanding beauty (132) are presented in a rapid sketch in the style of *epici* with impeccable credentials (cf. the brief description, but in narrative form, in relation to the bribing of a goddess in *HyAp* 103-4; snappy digressions in Homer: Rutherford on *Od.* 19.226-31), a sketch capped by a succinct indication of the marvellous properties which will be in evidence when the toy is actually used. So: a baby ball for a baby Zeus: he has now graduated to a full-size one (see the artists), and has no further use for his 'plaything'!

C It is one of the ironies of the Olympian scene that as a result of the actions that unfold in one of the principal models, *Il.* 18, Achilles will be equipped with a shield as a prelude to a murderous onslaught. Eros, who will himself shortly 'take the field' (against a woman), has no need of new weapons: his deadly (278f.) bow and arrows are to hand (156-7). He does however emerge with a toy (or the promise of one at least), and it is natural to wonder whether the two objects enjoy a closer correlation. Shield-terminology does figure prominently in Ap.'s description (see under A above, and 137, 139, 139-40nn.; *Hephaestea* abound). It may be that 137f. display an early, if fleeting, awareness of allegorical interpretations of Agamemnon's shield in *Il.* 11 and Achilles' in *Il.* 18 (on these: Hardie, *JHS* 105 (1985), 15f., J. S. Romm, *The Edges of the Earth in Ancient Thought* (Princeton 1992), 14, Richardson, ed. *Il.* 21-24, p. 38): spherical earth *and* spherical cosmos (see above) formed part of later constructs, as did Hephaestus i.q. *demiurgic* (see on Adresteia, 133-4n.) fire as creator of the universe; Ap.'s miniature cannot accommodate the three world-divisions of earth, sky and sea, but these are all on view in 164f., a passage to be added to the 'views from space' listed in Hardie op. cit., 17 n.48 (earth including 'cities,' viz. centres of activity, sea, aether); or 'stars': but cf. 141 (on the shield in Aesch. *Theb.* 388: φλέγονθ᾽ ὑπ᾽ ἄστροις οὐρανὸν ...).

D When Eratosthenes made Hermes look out from his vantage-point upon the cosmos, and in particular upon our earth (*CA* 16, cf. Solmsen, *TAPA* 73 (1942), 207f.) he may well have been working with the sort of Hellenistic (? Aratean) didactic material that plainly underpins Ap's own delineation: note 2 σφαίρης, 3 (v.l.) the world's five ζῶναι περιηγέες, 4 κυάνοιο (/*caeruleae* in the richly wrought imitation of Virgil, *G.* 1.231f., cf. /κυανέη here in Ap., is more likely to have been inspired by some didactic model, rather than by *Il.* 4.282, as is suggested by Thomas, *HSCP* 90 (1986), 195f.).

135 σφαῖραν ἐυτρόχαλον Short noun first (here highlighting the prize: Eros has had to wait to be told what his present will be), longer epithet extending to the main caesura: many of the postp. epithets in Ap. follow this pattern, e.g. infr. 670 ~ 800, 847, 857; Wifstrand 1933.100.

ἐυτρόχαλον Cf. Livrea's note on iv.907, where the word is discussed at length (see too *LexNonn* s.v.). The sense 'perfectly rounded' is suggested by σφαίρῃ ἀθύρουσιν (cf. 132) περιηγέι in iv.950 (on this: VDB 3.111); cf. Hesych. ε7254 (one definition) εὔκυκλον ~ the Parmenidean εὐκύκλου σφαίρης DK28 B8.43, but also by 'like a star' in 141: σφαιροειδῆ τὰ ἄστρα, καθάπερ οἵ τ' ἄλλοι φασὶ καὶ ἡμῖν ὁμολογούμενον εἰπεῖν says Aristotle, *Cael.* 290a, cf. O. Gilbert, *Die meteorologischen Theorien des griechischen Altertums* (Leipzig 1907), 697f., and note τροχαλόν and τροχάλεια in Arat. 476, 530 (with Letoublou and de Lamberterie, *RPh* 54 (1980), 314 n.39, who also discuss the precise nuance of τροχόωσι in Arat. cited below).

But Ap. may be playing on the word's ambiguity. Cf. again 140-1: the ball 'runs' nicely when tossed, hurtling through the air at top speed (Hesych. loc. cit., another definition: ταχινόν) 'like a star': stars τροχόωσι rapidly Arat. 27, 227, 309, and the class of shooting-stars associated with atmospheric activity (cf. δι' ἠέρος in 141) are known as διαθέοντες (Arist. *Meteor.* 342b). See also West on τροχαλόν in Hes. *WD* 518. — 'Schön rund und infolgedessen gut rollend' Manakidou 148.

γε naturally latches itself on to the pronoun, but the real emphasis is on the negative, 'you certainly won't ...': *GP* 148.

μείλιον Cf. 146 infr. and also μείλιγμα in Nic. *fr.* 75.1 ('... young children'). If one were after a suitable gloss for the word here, one might well think in terms of an object ᾧ μειλίσσεται τὸν παῖδα (Cypris says μειλίξομαι, 105n., cf. Marxer 58): cf. schol. D at *Il.* 9.147 μείλια δέ εἰσιν, οἷς μειλίσσονται τοὺς ἄνδρας, and Erbse 1953.175-6/nn. on schol. *Il.* 9.147*a-b* with schol. Ap. here: τὰ παίγνια, δι' ὧν οἱ παῖδες μειλίσσονται (Wendel ad loc.). The word's range is examined by Livrea on iv.1190 (his epigram *BCH*... can now be *GVI* 1451; add Hesych. μ741 μέλκιον [μείλιον corr. Meineke] ...παίγνιον ~ schol. Ap. above, cf. Bühler, *Gnomon* 42 (1970), 348); he is wrong, I think, to brush schol. D aside (so too van der Valk 1.259-60). See further 594n.

136 χειρῶν From the skilful hands of a craftsman (a variation here perhaps on Arat. 529: Pendergraft 97); for the association of χεῖρες with artistic productions/productivity cf. LSJ s.v. χείρ IV init. and VIb, Headlam on Hds 4.72. The genitive marks the source, as with δέχεσθαι and the like: KG 1.394f.

Ἡφαίστοιο As Ap. has made the point that Hephaestus and Cypris are properly married (37-8), one might be tempted to infer that Eros is a product of this union. Wendel (*Überl. und Entsteh. d. Theokrit-Scholien* (Berlin 1920), 63-4; not Wilamowitz, as Page on *PMG* states) suggested such a grouping for Ibycus (*PMGF* 324); on it see the various Budé editors on Nonn. *D.* 5.138, 10.202, 29.329-34, and the amusing epigram of Palladas, *AP* 11.307. If so, it can hardly be a case of 'like father like son.' Our Eros looks, as he often looks elsewhere (e.g. Eros βροτολοιγός, Gow-Page on Diosc. *HE* 1511f., NH on Hor. *Carm.* 2.8.14; the Erotes in iii.764-5: Hutchinson 116), more like an Ares, whose sexual involvement with Cypris has been strongly hinted at already (41f.n.): 94f. ἐριδμαίνων, arrows etc. ~ iv.445f. στύγος, source of ἔριδες, asked to function as a κορυστής. (Here an important Homeric model has been missed: *Il.* 5.890-1, Zeus calls Ares ἔχθιστος of the gods, because to him ἔρις τε φίλη πόλεμοί τε μάχαι τε/, a passage which guarantees Ap.'s triple τε in iv.446).

Eros' parentage posed a well-known ἀπορία: see e.g. Plato *Symp.* 178b, Antag. *CA* 1 (surely turned on its head by Call. *h.* 1 init.), Theoc. 13.1-2 (with schol. and Gow ad loc.), Meleag. *HE* 4194f., Opp. *Hal.* 4.23f.; Meleag. entertainingly throws out the names of Aphrodite, Hephaestus *and* Ares in *HE* VIII. Cf. VDB 2.111 (on iii.26), *LIMC* 3.1.850f. (extensive bibliogr.), Livrea, *SIFC* n.s. 7 (1989), 26 n.8. Aphrodite was a natural choice for the mother. There is more variation in the case of the father: Simonides had plumped for Ares and Aphrodite (*PMG* 575; rejected by Simias *Wings* 8-9), in the context of a σχετλιασμός, interestingly enough (σχέτλιε παῖ ...): cf. Ap. iv.445f. referred to above.

καταχτεατίσσῃ A hapax, and a high-sounding one: cf. e.g. κτεατίζεται in Theoc.'s encomium, 17.105. Ap. shares with Theoc. loc. cit. the pure middle of the simplex, cf. ii.788, LSJ s.v. -ίζω, Boesch 21; the Homeric use of the active rather than middle provoked comment, (Erbse on) schol. A at *Il.* 16.57a. I am unable to work out what prompted Wåhlin to treat the verb as a subjunctive (49).

ἄρειον Hes. *WD* 157-8 ἄλλο .... ἄρειον/; note ἔτ' 157, Ζεύς 158, ποίησε ibid., cf. Ap. 132, 133,134.

137 χρύσεα ... Cf. Manakidou 146. The description of the ball, an object which can match anything that Hephaestus can produce, begins with an echo of *Il.* 18.375, the remarkable tripods made by him: χρύσεα δέ σφ' ὑπὸ κύκλα ἑκάστῳ πυθμένι θῆκεν, where schol. AT warn us against articulating as ὑπόκυκλα. Then (Lennox 63) there is *Il.* 13.22, Poseidon's house, /χρύσεα (μαρμαίροντ)α τετεύχαται, where schol. T remarks: Ἥφαιστος αὐτὰ ἐποίησεν. Cf. also *Il.* 18.573 Hephaestus ποίησε (Ap. 133) then 574 χρυσοῖο τετεύχατο, and *Od.* 19.563 μὲν ... τετεύχαται (/δοιαί 562).

κύκλα 135-41n. Stückelberger: '... finden in den von Arat. 480f. beschriebenen drei Parallelkreisen ihre Entsprechung.' For a variation on this see Pendergraft 100 (with 98 n.12).

ἀμφὶ δ' ἑκάστῳ A rare clausula: Paul. Sil. *Amb.* 257 (-ῃ).

138 ... διπλόαι ... *Il.* 4.133, 20.415 /χρύσειοι then καὶ διπλόος ..., *Od.* 19.226 /διπλῆν then χρυσοῖο τέτυκτο/.

ἀψῖδες On a 'normal' reading (135-41n.) semicircular fastenings; see in general Gillies 1924.50-1, Gow-Page on *GPh* 2708. Stückelberger: 'an die Kolurkreise (sich rechtwinklig schneidende Meridiane) zu denken liegt nahe'; cf. Pendergraft 100. In fact, it is hard to dissociate these from the type of crossed bands adorning the spherical cosmos illustrated in Brendel plate XVII (cf. id. 52f. for discussion).

There is an interesting echo (?: Campbell 1982.15) in Nicaen. *HE* 2700: a Hermes, moulded by ἀψῖδος κύκλος ἑλισσόμενος.

περιηγέες εἱλίσσονται After Arat. (above, 135-41n.), see in general Fraser 2.896 n.153/897 n.159. Rufinus (*AP* 5.60.3) shows us how to do something quite different with this hemistich.

περιηγέες Also i.559 ~ ii.994; infr. 1032, 1365; iv.950. First in Empedocles (DK31 B28.2; see also 814n.). Examples from Hellenistic verse in Hollis on Call. *Hec.* 81.2 (add Nic. *Ther.* 106); widespread thereafter, but no obvious *Apolloniana*.

139 κρυπταί Homeric hapax, *Il.* 14.168, another term associated with the craftsman god Hephaestus (see above).

ῥαφαί Another old hapax, this time from *Od.* (22.186), applied to a shield's layers of hide (shield-language: cf. *Il.* 11.33 cited in 135-41n.) ~ *Il.* 12.296-7 a shield which a χαλκεύς 'had *stitched* ... with *golden* strands of *wire* (?) ...' (cf. again 135-41n.). It is hard to see the relevance of the word's use as a t.t. for the suture of the cranium (Erbse 1953.187).

In the erotic epigram *AP* 12.44 a ῥαπτὴ σφαῖρα is one of the παίγνια which attract (or rather, once upon a time attracted) 'boys who like presents' (Glaucus *HE* 1811-2).

139-40 ἕλιξ ... See on 135-41. Stückelberger, q.v. for illustrations of κυάνεος and ἕλιξ: 'ein dunkelblaues gekrümmtes Band ... das die Ekliptik mit dem Zodiakos andeutet'; cf. Pendergraft 100-1. As a subst. yet another Homeric hapax to characterise a choice object (*Il.* 18.401, for ornament; Hephaestus once again), though there *may* also be some point of contact here with the decorative ἕλιξ which figures in the celebrated ecphrasis of Theocritus' first *Idyll* (31). Late echoes: Christod. 284 πλόκαμος .. ἕλιξ ἐπιδέδρομεν ὤμοις/; Paul. Sil. *Soph.* 419 ἕλιξ περιδέδρομεν ἄντυξ/; Jo. Gaz. 1.42 /κυανέαις ἑλίκεσσι.

ἐπιδέδρομε .... ἀτὰρ ... χερσί But Arat. 79-80 ἀτὰρ χέρες .... ἐπιδέδρομεν ...

κυανέη Often in ecphrastic passages, as *Il.* 11.26, 39, 18.564, *Scutum* 167 etc. (not however Mosch. *Eur.* 47: Campbell ad loc., q.v. for bibliogr. on the material denoted by κύανος, together with *LfgrE* s.v., Hainsworth on *Il.* 11.24, Edwards ed. *Il.* 17-20, p. 203). 'Darkblue [see Stückelberger above] enamel,' though Ap. may be *hinting at* 'black niello': ἕλιξ ... κυανέη could be a passing allusion to a linguistic controversy, viz. ἕλιξ = 'black' (Càssola on *HyHom* 6.19, Hainsworth on *Il.* 9.466-9, Gow on [Theoc.] 25.127, Hollis on Call. *Hec. fr.* 116.1, Rengakos 1992.26) ~ κυάνεος 'black' [cf. iv.1516] (e.g. Henrichs 241 n.22; *Il.* 11.24 μέλανος κυάνοιο/).

On the word's location see Wifstrand 1933.111; *Il.* 20.417-8 subst. + δέ then /κυανέη then χερσί, *Od.* 12.(74-)75 (topographical description); 118n.

140 ἑαῖς ἐνὶ χερσί Already in ii.332; on ἑαῖς *your* see lately Rengakos 1993.117. Ap. is echoing *Il.* 21.104 ... ἐμῆς ἐν χερσὶ βάλῃσι/ scil. a god/victims into Achilles' clutches (cf. also 15.571 /εἰ ... βάλοισθα/). ἐνί: i.e. 'if you were to [you don't have it yet, cf. Gillies here] have it in your hands and toss it' or, if you like, instrumentally (so Ardizzoni) 'toss it with ...'; not in my view 'so that it falls into your hands' (Fränkel OCT ad loc.). With ἵησι in the next line on the other hand she dangles a fact (? 'fact') before him.

It would be interesting to know if the species of shooting-star known as βολίς (*RE* 2.3.2440) was already familiar. In his discussion of such phenomena Aristotle (*Meteor.* 342a30) talks of ἡ φαινομένη αὐτῶν ταχυτὴς ὁμοία οὖσα τοῖς ὑφ' ἡμῶν ῥιπτουμένοις ('comparable to objects/projectiles thrown by people on earth').

141 ἀστὴρ ὥς But *Il.* 6.295, *Od.* 15.108 /ἀστὴρ δ' ὥς; *Il.* 19.381 ('golden' object made by Hephaestus) ἀστὴρ ὥς (4 ...); all short comparisons. As Ap.: Q.S. 5.131, Greg. Naz. 983.178. The initial syllable of this ὥς (*σϝώς, *vel sim.*!: see e.g. Szemerényi, *Glotta* 53 (1981), 116, Ruijgh, *Mnemosyne* 38 (1985), 179 & Ruijgh 1991.631-2, West, *JHS* 108 (1988), 157), which occurs 10 × in the poem (*Index* s.v.), is variously treated (so in Homer: cf. *GH* 1.126, F-G on *Od.* 22.299): 1 × producing hiatus (ii.267), 5 × preceded by a lengthened -ON (iii.1124, Homeric), -ΟΣ (i.1297 = iv.1145; ii.566), -ΕΣ (ii.1023, cf. *Od.* 11.413); otherwise: i.240, 546, iii.141, iv.1338.

On the vivid image employed here see Faerber 13, Newman 76f., Nyberg 35, and 135-41n. The key components of this brief comparison recur in the extended simile of 1377f., see n. ad loc. In Nonn. *D.* 7.198 Eros' βέλος enters Zeus' heart εἴκελος ἀστέρος ὁλκῷ/.

φλεγέθοντα Here only in the poem; suggested by Ibycus (more of him presently), *PMGF* 314 ('... like stars through ...')? Cf. also 135-41n. (Aesch.), and on the verb's spread FJW on Aesch. *Suppl.* 88 (but add Euphor. *CA* 160; and there are more Imperial examples).

ἠέρος One might mentally supply κυανέοιο (cf. 140!) in respect of the track of the 'star,' which stands out against a gloomy background (see on the notion FJW on Aesch. *Suppl.* 88-90): cf. e.g. i.777, iii.1379, iv.1287, and more generally Vian on Nonn. *D.* 2.193.

ὁλκόν 1378n.

ἵησι But *Od.* 9.499 βαλών then ἵησιν/.

142 ... ὀπάσω Ctr. ... ὀπάσαιμι in 132: as her son rises to the bait Cypris gives a positive assurance – and also a blunt order (ctr. 131).

A blend of *Il.* 10.294 /τήν τοι ἐγώ ... (situation: human's solemn promise to a goddess) and *Od.* 8.430-1 /καί οἱ ἐγώ τόδ' [ctr. 133] ἄλεισον .. περικαλλὲς [cf. 132] ὀπάσσω,/χρύσεον ...

142-3 παρθένον .... Ἰήσονι See nn. on 4-5, 27-8, 28, 33 and 86. Cypris delivers her instruction with chilling brevity and directness.

144 ... ἀμβολίη She remembers Hera's ἔρξον ἄφαρ. ἀμβολίη (also i.861, iv.396) for ἀμβολή, Hom. ἀνάβλησις first in Hellenistic poetry (Arat. 886, 1081, 1117; Ep. adesp. *CA* 2.74). I count 16 examples thereafter; note Q.S. 1.431-2 τῷ μή τις ἀμβολίη ../εἴη ... γὰρ ...

-βολίη formations are common enough in pre-Hellenistic poetry and prose (BP 139-40), but in Ap. otherwise only the absolute hapax συνηβολίη (ii.1157, cf. infr. 1145n.).

δὴ γάρ κεν ... εἴη A particularly clear example of κεν *in that case.* This run is found also in Doroth. *Cat. Cod. Astr.* 6.157 (p. 104).

ἀφαυροτέρη χάρις εἴη (cf. *Studies* 18-9) 'my feeling of gratitude would be weaker (fainter, slighter).' Cypris then is Cypris to the bitter end. She does not want to say 'You won't get the ball,' and resorts instead to a pompous circumlocution.

ἀφαυρός here is stripped of its purely physical associations (cf. schol. L^g P: ἐλάσσων) according to Fränkel *Noten* 190 n.94 (in similar vein: Garson 3). I would put it differently: with a humorous stroke of the pen Ap. makes this feeble goddess (81f.), now in 'macho' mode, lean heavily on the language of physical confrontation to press her point home: *Il.* 12.458 (ἵνα μή οἱ) ἀφαυρότερον βέλος εἴη/.

A late reflection of our passage: (Livrea on) Nonn. *Par.* 18.32. Clausula: supr. 82n.

145 The same line already in i.1103. This is the only case in the entire poem of a duplicated verse indicating speech-closure, with no attempt made to vary any of the components: ctr., e.g., i.717: ii.1068: iii.912: iv.1380. See Elderkin 200, Herter *JAW* 325, and for various later approaches to Apollonian self-repetition in general Fränkel *Einleitung* 34-7; Livrea, *Maia* 20 (1968), 18; Vian 1973.98-9 (particularly valuable, though there is inevitably room for disagreement from time to time); Ciani, *BIFG* 2 (1975), 191f. (esp. 198f.); Lombardi, *RCCM* 28 (1986), 91f. (esp. 110 n.7, 111 n.16).

Odyssean colouring: 8.295 /ὣς φάτο, τῇ δ' ἀσπαστὸν ... (δέμνια 296 cf. i.1104 εὐνῆς), the adulterer Ares propositioning the unfaithful Aphrodite. For the first hemistich cf. further iv.1450, and *Od.* 7.343, for the first four words *Echoes* at i.341 (cf. 17n.), for γένετ' *Od.* 19.569 ἀσπαστὸν ... γένοιτο/; with εἰσαΐοντι ctr. *Od.* 23.239 τῇ ἀσπαστὸς ἔην .. εἰσοροώσῃ/.

ἔπος γένετ' Q.S. 12.526.

εἰσαΐοντι Campbell on Q.S. 12.121. Read rather εἰσαΐόντι (352-3n.); the use of a *present* participle in *Od.* 23.239 cited above does not of course affect the issue (n.b. γένετ' here).

146f. (*Studies* 19) A switch to pure dactyls to describe Eros' feverish reaction; they are arrested by the insistent αὐτοσχεδόν in 148. Cf. in general Faerber 66-7.

146 μείλια δ' ἔκβαλε πάντα See note on 119-21 (*Od.* 5.244); μείλια:

135n. (Hephaestus no doubt makes the golden knucklebones which keep the boy amused, 118n.).

ἔκβαλε: scil. χειρός (120), cf. *Il.* 14.419; LSJ s.v.III.

146-7 recall two sombre, and finely-drawn, descriptions of the importunate child in *Il.*: 16.7f. (Achilles to Patroclus: why do you weep like a) κούρη/νηπίη, ἥ θ' ἅμα μητρὶ θέουσ' ἀνελέσθαι ἀνώγει,/ εἱανοῦ ἁπτομένη κτλ., 22.492f. [487-99 ath. Aristarchus] (Andromache, about an orphan's plight) ἄνεισι πάις ἐς πατρὸς ἑταίρους,/ἄλλον μὲν χλαίνης ἐρύων, ἄλλον δὲ χιτῶνος κτλ. Cf. also the three Eur. passages cited below, with Sifakis, *BICS* 26 (1979), 77-8.

Confronted with *codd.*'s χιτῶνος .... θεᾶς ἔχεν (where θεᾶς can hardly belong with ἀμφιμεμαρπώς, cf. Vian ed. 1961 ad loc. and note iv.1663 χειρὸς δέ ἑ χειρὶ μεμαρπώς/; or with ἔνθα καὶ ἔνθα), Brunck conjectured ἔχετ', Fränkel (OCT) θεάν, Erbse (1963.27) χιτῶνα. Despite Chantraine, 1962.314 (see also Merkel, *Proleg.* 91, with a crop of 'parallels'), something must be wrong somewhere. On the whole I incline towards the middle verb (see Eur. below), despite *Od.* 16.191 ἔχε νωλεμές ('held back,' 'kept in' <a tear>), where note 190 υἱὸν κύσε ... παρειῶν/, 193 ἀμειβόμενος; Gillies offered 'tried to hold her back' for ἔχεν, perhaps remembering this *Od.* passage, but ἔχετ' (cf. on the distinction *GH* 2.53), 'kept clinging *to* the goddess *by* her chiton' gives excellent sense and does not entail an unduly inelegant combination of genitives, particularly as χιτῶνος is some way off from θεᾶς. ἔχ-εν perhaps from the preceding ἔν- .. ἔν-. Compare *Od.* 9.434-5 χερσὶν ἀώτου ../νωλεμέως .. ἐχόμην, 12.437; 5.428 /ἀμφοτέρῃσι ... then 429 ἔχετο; i.269 ἔχετο ~ 270 ἀμφι-πεσοῦσα/. One can see how a sequence ΕΝ/ΘΑ/ΘΕ/ΑΣ might have ended up as ΕΝΘΑΘΕΑΝ; corruption to θεᾶς seems harder to explain. χιτῶνα is the least attractive of the three; cf. χιτῶνος in *Il.* 22.493 (above), and πέπλων in Eur. *Alc.* 189, *Held.* 49, *Tro.* 750 (+ ἀντέχῃ middle!).

ἀμφοτέρῃσι Bulloch on Call. *h.* 5.93.

χιτῶνος A garment always worn by females in Ap. (ctr. Hom.: schol. *Il.* 2.42c, Erbse ad loc.): i.744 (Cypris), iii.874 (873-5n.), iv.46. Cf. VDB 3.72, Gow on Theoc. 15.21. Cypris is out and about in her indoor dress, having been told by Hera that there was no time to lose (109). In Philostr. Jun. *Imag.* 8 she sprouts a peplos.

νωλεμές *de toutes ses forces*, holding on tightly with all the strength he could muster: VDB 1.274 (cf. Platt 1914.21), 3.85 n.4. See also on 346.

Cf. *Od.* 20.24 /νωλεμέως then ἑλίσσετο [ctr. our next line!] ἔνθα καὶ ἔνθα/.

ἔνθα καὶ ἔνθα is reinforced by ἀμφι-. Eros hops about from one side to another as a demanding child pulling at his mother's clothing does. If *hinc atque hinc* in Virg. *A.* 8.387 is an imitation, it is a pale one indeed.

ἀμφιμεμαρπώς Campbell on Q.S. 12.276.

148 λίσσετο ... Vian ed. 1961 ad loc. (cf. VDB 2.11) mistakenly claims that the incorporation of direct speech from a junior would have breached the conventions of epic (but cf. notably *HyHerm*, Call. *h.* 3) and of tragedy (but cf. Eur.: see Stevens on *Andr.* 504f., Collard on *Suppl.* 1114-64(A)). Ap. opts for the more economical indirect mode, and the effect is striking. If we have gained the impression from the record of Eros' threatening language in 98-9 that he is a miniature adult, we are given no opportunity to reinforce that impression from the present stream of urgent, insistent appeals (on the verb see below). Instead, we are treated to a rapidly executed sketch of a grabby, hyperactive child making a thorough nuisance of himself.

A novel – and nonsensical – appraisal of Eros' behaviour is fielded by Klein, *Eranos* 73 (1975), 24 n.18.

λίσσετο On the flavour of this verb see A. Corlu, *Recherches sur les mots relatifs à l'idée de prière* (Paris 1966), 293f.; does Eros in Sapphic mode use the cletic λίσσομαι (e.g. NH on Hor. *Carm.* 1.32.1) to the love-goddess?!

αἶψα .. αὐτοσχεδόν Greek can pair temporal (and of course other) adverbs to lend emphasis (a notable example is εὐθὺς παραχρῆμα); here 'with speed/right away [cf. *LfgrE* s. αἶψα VI] ... on the spot' vividly represents Eros' determination to reach an immediate settlement.

αὐτοσχεδόν *on the spot, there and then*. The word probably never (not even in iv.969) functions as a local adverb in Ap. (cf. VDB 1.78 n.1; *contra*: Livrea on iv.101, Zaganiaris 320-1); ctr. Homer and *Scutum* 190; Tyrt. *IEG* 11.29; Arat. 901 (+ gen.). (After Ap. the word vanishes from the scene.)

For this temporal significance cf. on παράσσον (17n.), παρασχεδόν (440n.) and ἐπισχεδόν (947n.), but note too schol. D on *Il.* 16.319 (αὐτοσχεδά) ἑτοίμως, παραχρῆμα (~ schol. Ap. i.35, par. i.1348-9*a*).

148-50 Cf. *Studies* 19/100 n.42. An economically presented sequence of events:

(1) Cypris responds to Eros' entreaties by imploring and coaxing him: he cannot have his reward there and then, but she cannot tell

him straight: she has learned that she cannot afford to be uncivil to him (cf. 95f.). What arguments or excuses she resorts to, we are left to imagine; only their tone (ἀγανοῖσιν ...) is specified. Cf. VDB 2.116 (on 150); ἀντομένην supr. 77 likewise refers to unreported entreaties carried over from the explicit request of 56-75: for related economies see e.g. *Il.* 24.141-2 ~ ii.1226f.; 24.632.

(2) In the course of these overtures she draws his cheeks towards her and kisses him (another attempt at mollification; we appreciate that a kiss from *her* should have a devastating effect!)

(3) having attached herself to him (ποτι-σχομένη rather than ποτ-ισχομένη, cf. schol. L^gP (περι)λαβοῦσα and the *Odyssey*'s κυνέω + περιφύς, ἑλών, λαβών -οῦσα) by getting hold <of his head>, which she continues to grasp (τόδε 151) as she swears. —

No emendation is necessary (see VDB *app. crit.* at 149 and 150, noting also ποτισχόμενον Damsté, *Museum* 37 (1930), 116); in Fränkel's analysis in *DLZ* 1930.874 the καί of 150 vanishes (cf. the amazing paraphrase offered by schol. at 148-50a). Participial strings: see e.g. Bond on Eur. *HF* 700; Κύπρις .. οὐ φορητόν, ἣν πολλὴ ῥυῇ one might say!

148-9 ἡ δ' ἀγανοῖσιν ... Cf. iv.994.

ἀγανοῖσιν .. μύθοισιν But in *Od.* 15.53 μύθοις -οῖσι (~ Stesich. *PMGF* 222(b)232); this way round: Anon. encom. *GDK* 31.31 ἀ]γα[νο]ῖς μειλίξατο μ[ύθοις/, Eudoc. *Cypr.* 1.241. For the epithet see on 78.

149 For the two halves of the line cf. *Od.* 23.99 /ἑζομένη μύθοισιν (then -είρ- ... -ᾶς/) and id. 18.172 (-αμένη ..) ἐπιχρίσασα παρειάς/.

ἀντομένη 77n. (an ironic throwback to that verse according to Lennox 64).

ἐπειρύσσασα παρειάς Christod. 199 ἐπ. προσώπῳ/, no doubt a direct borrowing. The verb only here in the poem, matching the Homeric hapax ἐπ-έρ-υσσε *Od.* 1.441 (ἐπεσπάσατο schol. EV). -ύσσ- for -ύσ- Brunck, as at iv.237 (ctr. Merkel ad loc.) and also at Theoc. 14.35 (ctr. Gow ad loc.; in [Mosch.] *Meg.* 116 he prints ἀνειρύσῃ rather than S's -ύσσῃ). Cf. *codd.* i.687, ii.1039, VDB *app. crit.* at iv.890 (and i.955), and in general *GH* 1.30.

150 κύσσε For the double sigma see VDB *app. crit.* here (read by Π[20] +) and at i.1238; a single sigma is offered by Ω at iv.26 (-σσ- Brunck). Cf. *LH* 1.945(a).

ποτισχομένη not περισχομένη: she does not throw her arms around him but takes a hold of his head, clamping him prior to making her final pronouncement on the matter of the 'present.' See 148-50n.

καὶ ἀμείβετο But in Homer (*Il*. 24.200 al.) καὶ ἀμείβετο −×.

μειδιόωσα 'μειδιόωσα is intriguing. Did Eros ever get his prize? And where did *she* acquire such a toy?' *Studies* 19; cf. 152n. Perhaps the well-known deceitfulness of Cypris should be taken even further. Is the ball a complete figment? It is not to hand after all (κεῖνο 133), and she feels it necessary to spell out what exactly the marvellous object, which has clearly never come to the attention of a boy who plays in Zeus' garden with Zeus' favourite, can do. (For Newman 76 n.11 the ball is somehow Eros' 'now.')

Whatever the truth of this, it is striking that Eros' devastating assault on Medea is prompted by a toy, or rather by the god's determination to get his hands on what looks to be a toy beyond compare. What defence can humans possibly have against such unbridled μαργοσύνη? See further Fusillo 297-8, PF on 132-41.

151 The basic building-blocks are these:

(1) *Il*. 15.36f. (goddess speaks; cf. PF here) /ἴστω νῦν [cf. i.466] τόδε ... then 39 ... σή θ' ἱερὴ κεφαλὴ καὶ νωΐτερον λέχος αὐτῶν ..., *Od*. 5.180 (Calypso δολόεσσα) μείδησεν then 184 /ἴστω νῦν τόδε ... Cypris, unlike Hera in *Il*. 15 above, offers no elaborate list: she puts everything into this single act of intimate physical contact (no bland synecdoche here!), staging an impressive display of maternal affection (see on head-holding in general Macleod on *Il*. 24.712).

(2) *Il*. 9.437, 444 (ἀπὸ) σεῖο, φίλον (τέκος). (For σεῖο *possessive* here cf. McLennan on Call. *h*. 1.8, Mineur on id. 4.119f.).

(3) *Il*. 6.446 ... ἠδ' ἐμὸν αὐτοῦ/ ~ *HyAp* 328 (σὸν ...) οὔτ' [ἢ Q.S. 14.292 corr.] ἐμὸν αὐτῆς/ (τοι 329).

φίλον κάρη φ. κάρα in tragedy, Aesch. *Ag*. 905 etc.; ctr. Hom. φίλη κεφαλή (cf. Janko on *Il*. 16.74-7). For φίλον cf. *dulce* in Virg. *A*. 4.493 (Pease ad loc.), *dilectum* in Sil. It. 8.107. Despite what is said above, φίλον is not *just* an expression of affection. As is well known, in Greek eyes φιλία entails reciprocal obligation: if you need help, it is the solemn duty of your φίλος to provide it.

κάρη Virg. *A*. 4.357 /*testor utrumque caput* 'by your head and mine,' see Pease ad loc. Cf. *Il*. 15.39 (above) and: 'swear by the head': *HyHerm* 274, Soph. *Trach*. 1185 (κάρα), Eur. *Hel*. 835 (id.), Call. *fr*. 110.40 (σήν .. κάρην), Pfeiffer ad loc.; 'swear ἁπτομένη the head': *HyAphr* 26f. On the practice see Sittl 139f.; R. Hirzel, *Der Eid* (Leipzig 1902), 33; Onians 96, 108.

152 Cf. *Studies* 19. The solemn oath brings to mind once again (cf. on 129f.) *HyHerm*: 462 (the nonplussed Apollo) δώσω τ' ἀγλαὰ δῶρα καὶ ἐς τέλος οὐκ ἀπατήσω – only our οὐδ' ἀπατήσω is nicely ironic on the lips of a notoriously treacherous goddess (cf. *Noten* 336 and above on 130, 150 ad fin.): Eros goes off to keep his part of the bargain with a promise from one who can 'deceive' people's minds (ἀπατῆσαι *HyAphr* 7 cf. id. 38) and who has allotted to her μειδήματα .. ἐξαπάτας τε (Hes. *Theog*. 205), just as her victims can practise deception by going back on their undertakings (e.g. φιλεξαπάτις Asclep. *HE* 867, φρεναπάτης Lyr. adesp. *CA* 1.18); after all, ἀφροδίσιον .. ὅρκον [cf. Bury on Plato *Symp*. 183b, Gow-Page on Call. *HE* 1093f., and NH on Hor. *Carm*. 2.1-8, p. 122] οὔ φασιν εἶναι! It is no wonder that Cypris is so much more obliging than either Athena or Hera in the bribing-scenes of *Il*. 4 and 14 (131f.n.).

ἦ μέν τοι *Od*. 14.160 (/ἴστω νῦν 158), al., cf. *GP* 389; note too *Od*. 19.235 al. /ἦ μὲν .. γ' ..., (lover) Theoc. 3.34 ~ δωσῶ 36.

τοι δῶρον Ctr. *Od*. 15.125.

δῶρον .. παρέξομαι Cf. *Il*. 19.140, 147 (and Zen. Aristoph. at *Il*. 18.466 perhaps, cf. Rengakos 1993.63-4); but more interesting is *Od*. 13.358 δῶρα διδώσομεν ~ 356 νύμφαι, where παρέξομεν Aristoph. (cf. Ludwich 1.602): iv.1420-1 δῶρα .... παρέξομεν ~ νύμφαι 1414 (*Echoes* ad loc., taken up by Rengakos 1993.91).

δῶρον The frequent association of this term with bribery should not of course pass unnoticed.

γε in the context of an oath: *GP* 128.

οὐδ' ἀπατήσω So *Od*. 4.348 al., but the clausulae of *HyAphr* 7 (above) and 33 are more pertinent here.

153 ἐνισκίμψῃς A choicer way of saying ἐμπήξῃς (cf. schol. D at *Il*. 16.612, schol. T at id. 17.437, Ap. Soph. 69.2, Hesych. ε3126 etc., Braswell on Pind. *P*. 4.224(e); πᾶξε in Theoc. 11.16), again infr. 765 (perfectly at home in a heavily physiological description, cf. e.g. Hp. *Morb*. 1.20); in iv.113 of the *impregnation* of light-beams. The verb is Homeric: cf. *Il*. 16.612 and 17.528 subject δόρυ and the splendidly expressive 17.437.

κούρῃ .. Αἰήταο 27n. Cypris ends with a curt reminder of Eros' target; the all-important 'missile' effectively disrupts the continuity of 'daughter of Aeetes.'

154 φῆ A very snappy 'She spoke' (see on 382) and Eros is off – after seeing to his possessions, naturally (cf. ἄρ'). For φῆ then verb

+ κόλπῳ cf. *HyDem* 231. There is no parallel for this particular hiatus (or for that in 718).

συναμήσατο Otherwise known only from *EtM* 83.3, συναμησάμενος· σωρεύσας, συνάξας, ἢ θερίσας. On the quantity of the initial alpha of the simplex see on 859. Cf. in Homer *Il*. 24.165 ... ῥα ... καταμήσατο –⏑⏑–× (treated as if it were the equivalent of συν- by ancient commentators: *LH* 1.675, Erbse on schol. ad loc.; συνῆξε Eust. 1344.4, cf. *EtM* above).

154-5 Cf. *Studies* 19. Eros dumps the astragali in a heap into his mother's κόλπος. This is the capacious pocket of the chiton (146), where he could be sure his property would be secure: cf. Gow on Theoc. 16.16, West on *Od*. 3.154. For the action envisaged here cf. (Campbell 1990.482) iv.24-5 ἀθρόα κόλπῳ [so Platt for κόλπων or (Speake 1974.131) -οις]/φάρμακα πάντ' ἄμυδις κατεχεύατο ..., '*inside* the fold forming the pocket' for purposes of transportation (as Fränkel saw, OCT ad loc./*Noten* 455-6, cf. further Platt 1914.37; κόλπων is unconvincingly defended by Livrea ed. ad loc. and 1983.421). Note also infr. 867 κάτθετο μίτρῃ, 'deposited <it> *inside* her breastband.'

φαεινῷ (*Studies* 19/100 n.45) implies a bright, clean appearance (*LH* s.v., 2.398; not just 'splendido,' 'bello,' Ciani, *AAPat* n.s. 85 (1972/73), 32). The astragali have been tossed on the ground, but Eros is not at all fussy about his mother's dress. Cf. in general *Il*. 5.315.

We have a long wait (even longer than in *HyDem* 169-70, /ὣς ἔφαθ', ἡ δὲ ... ταὶ δὲ φαεινά/... ἄγγεα –⏑⏑–×) for the noun, just as κάδ is left hanging for a while – all very unceremonious.

φαεινῷ then βάλε: ctr. *Il*. 16.399.

μητρὸς ἑῆς *Il*. 5.371 al. and often elsewhere. Note esp. the echo in Nonn. *D*. 33.180f. εἶπε θεά· καὶ μάργος Ἔρως ἀνεπάλλετο κόλπου/ μητρὸς ἑῆς καὶ τόξον ἐκούφισεν κτλ. Cf. in addition (Campbell 1982.15) Meleag. *HE* 4076-7 /ματρὸς .. ἐν κόλποισιν .../ἀστραγάλοις ... Ἔρως/.

εὖ πάντας ἀριθμήσας Not just because he has tossed them aside (146) and they require checking: he does not trust his mother any more than she trusts him. One more amusing detail with a serious side to it: cf. Beye 1982.27.

εὖ πάντας = *Od*. 10.452, 18.260. κὰδ then ἀριθμήσας: ctr. *Od*. 16.235 -ας ἀριθμήσας κατα-.

156-7 Eros now acts briskly and methodically, like Heracles in i.1194-5.

156 αὐτίκα ... -θετο μίτρῃ Cf. Parthen. *SH* 646.4-5 αὐτίκα μίτρην/ ... -εθήκατο.

ἰοδόκην -κη and -κος φαρέτρη (see below) often of Eros' quiver in Hellenistic and later poetry. For the subst. (Marxer 43) cf. ii.679 [~ Christod. 307-8], infr. 279, and Lobo *SH* 524.1 corr.; *HE* 125 (Alc.), 2273 (Leon. Tar.), 3073 (Posidipp.); Gem. *GPh* 2373; Leon. Alex. *FGE* 880 [ctr. Call. *h.* 2.33 φαρέτρη]; Q.S. 1.339, 3.33; Nonn. *D.*, 5 ×; Paul. Sil. *AP* 5.268.1. Homer in contrast has -κος with φαρέτρη, and so also Call. *h.* 3.212-3, Posidipp. *Ep. Gr.* 1723 Page [Asclep. *HE* 993], Meleag. *HE* 4029, etc. (Ω's ὀιστοδόκην ... φαρέτρην/ in i.1194 seems hard to uphold: -κον S, cf. Ardizzoni, *BCENC* 13 (1965), 7; conjectured by Headlam, 10).

χρυσέη Cf. Virg. *A.* 5.312-3; conj. in Melinno *SH* 541.2; 118n. (ref. bow/arrows of Eros/mother: Lyne on *Ciris* 160).

περικάτθετο First here: later Q.S. 6.196 (of donning armour), [Apolin.] 73.22. Sense: 'put on around himself/girded himself [cf. Heubeck on *Od.* 10.261-2] with ... by means of...' For -κάτθετο see Campbell on Q.S. 12.303, and id. 1969.279 n.4, 1990.482; κατεθήκατο in Asclep. *HE* 882 (subject Eros) as explained by G. Giangrande in *Fond. Hardt: Entretiens* 14 (1967), 129.

-κάτθετο μίτρῃ: infr. 867.

μίτρῃ = ζώνη *baldric* for a quiver, here only in this sense; cf. Gow on Theoc. 17.19.

157 πρέμνῳ κεκλιμένην Cf. *Il.* 21.18 (murderous warrior's spear) /κεκλιμένον μυρίκῃσιν, *Od.* 22.121 ἔκλιν' ref. a bow, and, for the form, *Il.* 21.549 /φηγῷ -ος *et sim.*; i.595 (~ *Il.* 15.740). The proximity of μίτρῃ may not be wholly fortuitous: Call. *h.* 4.209-10 ... ζώνην, ἀπὸ δ' ἐκλίθη .... ποτὶ πρέμνον.

A detail from a picture, no doubt. Rather differently Anon. *APl* 210.4, Eros' quiver and bow and arrows δένδρεσσιν ὑπ' εὐπετάλοισι κρέμαντο/, Claud. *carm. min.* 25.11-12.

ἀνὰ ... τόξον Cf. i.1205-6 ἀνὰ τόξα καὶ ἰούς/... ἑλών; *Il.* 5.209 [Pandarus, ... ἑλόμην 210: Lennox 64] al. ἀγκύλα τόξ(α)(/), ii.1043 ἀγκύλα τείνατο τόξα/ (cf. *Echoes* ad loc., and Nonn. *D.* 5.526 -α τόξα τιταίνει/); *Il.* 9.559 -αντίον εἵλετο τόξον/. On ἀγκύλος see e.g. F-G, introd. to *Od.* 21, p. 138.

158f. See in part *Studies* 22. Schol. iii.158 records that the ensuing description ('these verses') παραγράφει (cf. Lennox 64) the account by Ibycus of the rape of Ganymede (*PMGF* 289, Davies ad loc.).

See Richardson ed. *HyDem* pp. 279-81 for discussion of the possible relationships between *HyDem* 380f. (cited below on 159-63), Ibycus *PMGF* 289/?S223(a), Bacch. 5.16f. and the present passage. It is interesting that Ap.'s κορυφαὶ χθονός (162) resembles a detail in *Bacchylides'* depiction of the flight of Zeus' eagle (24 κορυφαὶ ... γαίας), a passage with which ours has nothing else in common: Bacchylides then must have got this from Ibycus (*Studies* 22; Barron, while making a similar point, carries speculation too far in his treatment of *PMGF* S223(a): *BICS* 31 (1984), 17f.; more cautiously: Jenner, id. 33 (1986), 64f.).

We do not know whether Ibycus described what Ganymede saw as he was carried aloft from Troy to Olympus (cf. Bowra 259) or what lay beneath *the eagle* as it soared earthwards (as our passage might suggest: cf. also the perspective of the bulk of Bacchylides' picture, cited above); Eros' exit, if it too belongs to the lyric model, could reflect the eagle's egress. In any event, there is some reason to suspect that there could have been an Olympian garden into the bargain: see above on 114. (There is no need of course to resort to the drastic expedient of relocating the scholion, as Wilamowitz suggested: 114-7*b* in Wendel.)

158 Eros' exit from the ἀλωή (114). The correct text must be βῆ δὲ διὲκ μεγάλοιο Διὸς ... Π[20] offers]ΗΔΕΔΙΟΣ (with ΕΚ above ΟΣ) ΜΕΓΑΛΟΙΟΘ[. μεγάροιο (*codd.*) is, *pace* Crönert, *APF* 1 (1900/01), 516 and some others, beyond question false, foisted in by someone influenced by the Odyssean formula διὲκ μεγάροιο βεβήκει/ or at least by the common association of διέκ with that substantive (cf. *HyDem* 281 /βῆ δὲ διὲκ μεγάρων, Anon. *SLG* 364.5]ε διὲκ μεγάρ[οιο]); we may even be dealing with a specific importation from *HyDem*: 379 διὲκ μεγάρων then 380f. ~ infr. 164f. (see n. ad loc.). The text of Π must originally have contained θεοῦ: that is to say, διὲκ was at some point supplanted by Διὸς, and θεοῦ inserted to eradicate an impossible repetition. See Platt 1914.27f. and esp. Wifstrand 1929.88-9 (with whom Keydell 35 concurred); and also now VDB 2².152.

θέων (/θέειν) (Reitzenstein, *Hermes* 35 (1900), 605f., Robinson 175, Seaton 1915.10f., Gillies p. 138, Thiel 197 n.4) is bad, θεοῦ (Levin, *CPh* 58 (1963), 107f., Haslam 68 n.50, Hunter) worse: on μεγάλοιο Διός see below. Worst of all: van der Valk 2.532-3: *codd.* are right, Ap. is being careless (in like vein already Wellauer, and, though not with any relish, Mooney).

The verse is thus akin to the type Μαριανδυνῶν ἀνδρῶν ἐριθηλέα γαῖαν/ (ii.723), on which see Bühler, ed. Mosch. *Eur.*, pp. 215-6, Campbell on id. 68. Cf. also infr. 337.

διέκ + accus., 'through and out of': cf. 73n.

μεγάλοιο Διός See in general Bissinger 67f., Hainsworth on *Od.* 8.82. This particular unit (*Il.* 12.241 etc.) also i.1315 (preceded by παρέκ), ii.289, both stressing the power and authority of the god. Perhaps there is a reflection here of Ibycus' eagle, which must be enjoying an unspoken presence in this passage (158f.n.) – the majestic bird of mighty Zeus (called εὐρυάνακτος ἄγγελος/Ζηνός Bacch. 5.19-20), a creature which homed in on its prescribed target with unswerving accuracy. The poet no doubt also signals Eros' place in the scheme of things as he leaves to exert a profound influence on the affairs of men: this is no sportive or frivolous frequenter of lush gardens on earth or in some indeterminate spot, but a dangerous, pernicious god who issues forth from the mighty Zeus' domain, a powerful being in his own right (cf. 164f.). His point of egress is further elaborated in 160-3. Sappho had him coming ἐξ ὀράνω πορφυρίαν περθέμενον χλάμυν (*PLF* 54, a tantalisingly short fragment; ~ Jason in i.722? Thiel 52): see 275n.

πάγκαρπον ἀλωήν But Homer (*Od.* 7.122, 24.221) πολύκαρπος (-ου) ἀλωή (-ῆς), which was to resurface in Christian poetry: Greg. Naz. 1369.219 ~ *AP* 8.18.1, 1550.109; Eudoc. *Hom.* 414. — πάγκαρπος: 114n. πάγ- may be designed to tell us what Ap. considered an ἀλωή to contain: for different notions about this see *LH* s.v., Erbse on schol. *Il.* 21.36a¹, and on the word's Homeric applications Ure, *CQ* n.s. 5 (1955), 225f., West on *Od.* 1.193, Hainsworth on id. 6.293. So in ii.138 ἀλωαί probably denotes 'areas under cultivation' generally rather than 'vineyards' (on this passage see Ardizzoni 1970.40-1). Cf. ἀλωεύς infr. 1401(n.).

ἀλ- (Chantraine *DE* s.v.) AE: see VDB I.LXXII; La Roche *HTA* 187; Erbse at schol. *Il.* 21.346.

159-63 Cf. the analysis in *Studies* 20-1, here expanded and modified in certain respects.

(1) 159 πύλας .. Οὐλύμποιο/. Iris confronts Hera and Athena /πρώτῃσι .. πύλῃσι ... Οὐλύμποιο/, *Il.* 8.411. These are described at 5.749f. (πύλαι .. οὐρανοῦ cf. infr. 161 init.), repeated at 8.393f. (exit-point). See Schmidt 1976.75f., esp. 76, 81f., Kirk on *Il.* 5.749-52. Ap. dispenses with the flights of fancy: no Horae, though -καρπον in the previous line may hint at one of them (Καρπώ: on her: West on [Hes.] *Theog.* 901); no creaking; and no 'cloud,' though αἰθερίας in 160 does not

positively preclude such a marvel (cf. *Il.* 15.20, 192; 16.364f. with the perplexities of the scholia, Lehrs 167f.). Rather, his description has a quasi-technical air, linguistically if not thematically reminiscent of the Parmenidean πύλαι Νυκτός [see 159n.] τε καὶ Ἤματός εἰσι κελεύθων/, followed up with /αὐταὶ δ' αἰθέριαι (DK28 B1.11, 13, cf. Pieri, *SIFC* n.s. 49 (1977), 84; see on this the sober and lucid analysis of Vos, *Mnemosyne* 16 (1963), 18f., esp. 29; various approaches are considered by Burkert, *Phronesis* 14 (1969), 1f.) and πάντων δὲ παλίντροπος ἐστὶ κέλευθος/ (DK28 B6.7). The studied parallelism of /αἰθερίας (160) and /οὐρανίη (161) serves to equate these zones (cf. in general Lehrs 163f., Leaf *Il. ed. maior* 2.599f.; Faerber 77-8 and Livrea on iv.443 are muddled, cf. Hopkinson ed. Call. *h*. 6, p. 114 n.1), with which Olympus may be identified (159; cf. 'gates of Olympus' *Il.* 8.411 ~ 'gates of οὐρανός' 5.749/8.393; Hainsworth on *Od.* 6.42-7). The point of all this?

(2) 160f. create the impression that Eros is going to descend from Mt Olympus and proceed thence over land and sea in the manner of Hera in *Il.* 14.225f. and Hermes in *Od.* 5.49f. (cf. Hainsworth on 50, and Campbell on Mosch. *Eur.* 113f.). In the event, with Eros about to take on the aspect of a cosmogonic force, the concretisation of Olympus as the mountain-home of the gods rapidly recedes: the viewfinder is directed past 'aetherial' gates and a path located 'in the sky' to the 'celestial vault' itself, supported by twin peaks at the known world's eastern extremities – and it is here, rather than in 'Pieria,' that Eros will eventually alight after his (? eagle-like) journey through the regions of 'aether' (166).

(3) πόλον corr. Platt (1914.26f.). The correction is unavoidable (cf. VDB 2.116, on 162), however much one sympathises with Ardizzoni's desire to add to the large stock of Aratean reminiscences in this poem (23 οὐρανόν, 24 δύω πόλοι ἀ- ..., cf. Man. 2.22 and Anon. *GDK* 24r41). The Aristotelian 'poles' adduced by Mooney are the wrong kind of poles (cf. VDB 2.116). A cosmological allusion (Warren, *CR* 25 (1911), 166 n.1) in the form of a 'polar path' from sphere to sphere may be safely discounted. Seaton (1915.11) made the desperate suggestion that Ap. refers to Pelion and Ossa, using πόλοι in the sense of 'peaks.' A 'pole' figures in the picture of Mercury's descent in Stat. *Theb.* 7.35f., but it does not help us here. On the other hand, *caelum* in Virg. *A.* 4.256 (cf. below) might be thought to offer some welcome external support for πόλον here: so Nelis, *REA* 92 (1990), 142-3.

πόλον ἀνέχουσι .... heaven is here conceived of as a plane parallel to the earth's surface (West on Hes. *Theog.* 127) and it therefore requires support. Platt suggested that the sun rises between the gigantic peaks of Caucasus and Parnassus (Paropamisus, the Hindu Kush, the Indian Caucasus, *RE* 18.2.1779) described by Aristotle in *Mete.* 1.350a18f. They would thus constitute the eastern equivalent of the Atlas range at the world's western limit (Barrett on Eur. *Hipp.* 3-6, West on *Od.* 1.52-4): perhaps Ap. has in mind two supporting mountains in either zone, cf. the 'four posts' in the ancient Egyptian system (Kahn 139). The obscure 'pillar' alluded to by Hesiod (*Theog.* 522, West ad loc.) in connexion with Prometheus' place of bondage (traditionally Caucasus in later accounts) could be relevant: note πόλον at *PV* 429, where it has been suggested that 'Prometheus (at the Caucasus) in the East performs a task parallel to that of Atlas in the West' (Worthen, *Glotta* 66 (1988), 12; but the whole passage bristles with unresolved difficulties), and perhaps also κορυφάς id. 722 (with West's vivid description, 1990.304 n.10). Dawn at her rising casts light 'over snowy Caucasus' (iii.1223-4). Aea itself of course has strong links with Helios; his 'rays': cf. Mimn. *IEG* 11a.2.

(4) A panoramic view of land and sea is implied in the simile of ii.541f. (Athena's journey from Olympus to the Thynian coast: *Noten* 200-1, Drögemüller 156f.) and in the account of Aeetes' fantastic journey in Helios' chariot (iii.309f., see the notes). Cf. also i.1110f., the spectacle that greets the Argonauts on Dindymum, and see Herter *RE* Suppl. 13.40.29f.; Phinney, *CJ* 62 (1967), 148; also Beye's fine analysis of i.547f., 1982.31 (cf. id. 1993.208). But the motif here has a special aptness, in that Eros majestically (cf. Beye 1969.49) surveys his own domain: cf. Eur. *Hipp.* 1272f. (Barrett on 1277-80, Bömer on Ov. *Met.* 1.464, R. Garner, *From Homer to Tragedy* (London and New York 1990), 82f.), where Eros is said to fly (cf. with ref. to Cypris ἀν' αἰθέρ' id. 447 ~ infr. 166) over land and sea and to exert his maddening influence on various categories of living creatures: note the presence of hills, sea, 'nurturing' land. See further 135-41n.

He sees by turns a flat landscape with areas supporting or harbouring life and the <lonely> mountain peaks which stand out in sharp relief (cf. the picture of the sea, rivers and ἄκριες confronting a chariot as it soars through the ἀήρ in *HyDem* 380f., and *apicem* in Virg. *A.* 4.246 considered below); and, all around, the 'sea,' particularly, we may suspect, the 'Black Sea' (Barrett on Eur. *Hipp.* 3-6; but one should not actually print Πόντος, as Fränkel suggested, OCT *app. crit.*), as he nears Colchis itself: cf. the 'homing-in' technique of iii.744f., πτόλιν 749.

See further on 158f. (Ibycus), and cf. as well the account of Aristeas' wandering soul, T19 Bolton: in aether, like bird, viewed γῆν καὶ θάλατταν καὶ ποταμοὺς καὶ πόλεις καὶ ἔθνη ἀνδρῶν ...

These lines were in Virgil's mind in *A.* 1.223-6 (Jupiter from aether views sea, lands, shores, peoples and finally Libya: ctr. the narrower range of *Il.* 8.51f., 11.81f., al.) and (cf. above) id. 4.246f. (Mercury in aerial flight to Libya descries Atlas, halts there, then soars over the waves like a low-flying bird [*Od.* 5.49f.], winging his way between earth and sky to his destination). But it is Statius (*Theb.* 7.34f.) who injects fresh life into the theme.

It may be that our Eros was one of the direct precursors of Eratosthenes' Hermes, a god who 'inspects the universe from the highest heavenly sphere' (Bulloch 1977.604).

159 αὐτὰρ ἔπειτα as *incipit Il.* 11.422 etc. On Ap.'s employment of this tag (Campbell on Q.S. 12.139) see Ruijgh 1957.53.

ἔπειτα .. -ήλυθεν Οὐλύμποιο *Il.* 8.25 ἔπειτα ... Οὐλύμποιο/, 20.125 Οὐλύμποιο .. -ήλθομεν.

πύλας .. Οὐλύμποιο 159-63(1)n. All subsequent poetic allusions to these gates are vague: Alph. *GPh* 3528 πύλας .. Ὀλύμπου/: 3529 αἰθέρος: 3531 οὐρανίη .. οἶμος, Q.S. 2.666 /αἰθερίας .. πύλας, Nonn. *D.* 47.699 πύλας ἐπέρησαν Ὀλύμπου/, al. (Vian on 2.177).

In iv.629f. we hear of 'the Gates of Night' [cf. Parmenides cited on 159-63] localised in the west (VDB 3.97 n.3), matching the gates of Olympus/heaven/ἀντολή of Sun here.

ἐξήλυθεν + accus. LSJ ἐξέρχομαι 1b, ἔξειμι (A) I3 (Athen. VIII 351d ἐξῄει τὰς πύλας), KG 1.300 (cf. ἐξέπλωμεν in ii.645, with Renehan 1982.64); Campbell 1990.482. I know of no other verse example, though Ap. himself uses (the Ionic/koine) διεκ(-) so (cf. 73n.).

160-1 Neither αἰθέριος nor οὐράνιος is to be found in the two Homeric poems, any more than is πόλος. Some sort of philosophical/ didactic source is probable, see above on 159-63(1) (Parm.); all these words occur in Aratus' *Phaenomena*, for instance. The same no doubt goes for καταιβάτις 160.

ἔνθεν ... κέλευθος ii.353 ἔνθα μὲν [Acheron, cf. καταιβάτην in Eur. *Bacch.* 1361 with Dodd's note and Nenci, *RFIC* 105 (1977), 165; and Lyc.90f. infr.] εἰς Ἀίδαο [cf. Lyc. 497] καταιβάτις ἐστὶ κέλευθος. For καταιβάτις + 'path' cf. Lyc. 90-1 Ἀχερουσία τρίβος/κατ.; Nonn. *Par.* 2.64, Paul. Sil. *Amb.* 219 (οἶμος).

Hom. καταιβαταί (*Od.* 13.110; θύραι 109 ctr. πύλας Ap. 159); -βάτις formations (i.754, Theoc. 3.32 παραι-) are not common: BP 428.

κέλευθος/οὐρανίη So *Or. Sib.* 6.9-10 κελεύθους/οὐρανίας, cf. too Nonn. *D.* 2.578. Ctr. the candescent *via* in Ov. *Met.* 1.168f., Bömer ad loc.

161-2 Ctr. *Od.* 6.123 ἔχουσ' ὀρέων .. κάρηνα/; *HyHom* 27.6-7 ... δὲ κάρηνα/ὑψηλῶν ὀρέων; *Od.* 9.113 ὑψηλῶν ὀρέων -ουσι κάρηνα/.

161 πόλον See 159-63n. Note *perhaps* this same accus. in Nonn. *D.* 1.364 (Vian there: 'Vague souvenir de Ap. Rh., iii.159-66').

ἀνέχουσι Cf. Paus. 5.11.5 (Atlas), with Maass 126 n.18; Hardie, *CQ* n.s. 33 (1983), 227.

Maass (133 n.32) noted the imitation in D.P. 150 δύω ἀνέχουσι κολῶναι/ (κέλευθοι/ 148; the passage is full of *Apolloniana*).

162 οὐρέων ἠλιβάτων rather than ἠλιβάτων ὀρέων: so (e.g.) infr. 1308 /ζεύγλῃ χαλκείῃ, not /χαλκείῃ ζεύγλῃ: see Wifstrand 1933.121 n.1 (and 107-8); cf. next note.

ἠλιβάτων First attested in Ap. with ὄρ(ος), but common enough after him. Cf *Or. Sib.* 1.262 and: (1) iii.162 /οὐρέων ἠλιβάτων(,) κορυφαί: (a) D.P. 389 /οὐρέων τ' -ων, conversely (/)-ων ὀρέων Q.S. 2.183, 8.198, Anon. encom. *GDK* 34iv39 (5th cent.); [Apolin.] 17.15. (b) Orac. in Porph. *ap.* Eus. *PE* 6.3 (PW 470.14) /-ων τ' ὀρέων κορυφαί [cf. *Or. Sib.* 3.680]. (2) i.739 /οὔρεος -οιο (κάρη): Q.S. 2.283, claus. 2.379. (3) iv.444 /ἄγριον -οιο κατ' οὔρεος (~ Paul. Sil. *Amb.* 77 /ἄγριον -ου κορυφῆς ...). (4) ii.169 -ῳ ἐναλίγκιον οὔρεϊ κῦμα/: ~ Q.S. 11.490 -οισι δ' ἐοικότα κύματ' ὄρεσσιν/ cf. id. 8.65 = D.P. 598 (sim. 691).

In Homer solely with πέτρ(η), as often later (so with the only other instance in 3ᴴ: Theoc. 26.10); not so in Ap., who seems to go his own way completely: cf. ii.361 ἄκρη (ἀκτή Nic. *fr.* 26.4), 729 κρημνοί, 1248 ἐρίπναι.

Speculation about the word's meaning and etymology was rife in antiquity. There can be little doubt that 163 adverts to the kind of explanation offered by Ap. Soph. 83.25, ἐφ' ὃ ἥλιος πρῶτον (n.b.) βάλλει (similar efforts in Merkel *Proleg.* 79-80, Erbse on schol. *Il.* 15.273b[1-2], id. 1953.173). That is not to say of course that Ap. would necessarily have insisted on a *translation* 'sun-beaten/-trodden' here. Another such foray is possibly mounted in ii.731, ἁλι- following hard on the heels of ἠλι- (? ἡλι-) 729: cf. Hesych. η352, *EtM* 427.48f.

For various viewpoints see Mooney and Ardizzoni on i.739, Faerber 78-9, Càssola on *HyAphr* 267, van der Valk 1.271-2, Livrea on iv.444.

κορυφαί *highest points*: cf. on 158f. (Bacch.: the eagle's flight not impeded by κορυφαί ... γαίης, earth's tallest peaks). I mention just for the record the presence of κορυφαί following on from a reference to the 'road of the immortals' (see van der Weiden, ed. pp. 157-8) in the extremely lacunose Pind. *Dith.*, 4.20.

Il. 8.83 ... κορυφήν, ὅθι τε πρῶται ..., in a radically different context.

ἠχί τ' First attested in Arat. 1009; also Nic. *Alex.* 7, 302; D.P. 67 (ἠλίβατος 68), 258; Q.S. 2.588, 8.421; Greg. Naz. 1304.55; [Orph.] *A.* 744; Max. 169. See in general Ruijgh 1971.476. Elsewhere in the poem Homer's ἵνα τε (ii.735, iii.1290, iv.630), ὅθι τε (iv.761), but not ἔνθα τε (cf. Ruijgh op. cit. 938).

ἧχι, the correct form (P. Monteil, *La phrase relative en grec ancien* (Paris 1963), 387; *GH* 1.249), was prescribed by Aristarchus, but ἧχι by Ap. Dysc. (see La Roche *HTA* 278-9; Erbse on schol. *Il.* 1.607a^{1-2}, together with Dyck, *RhM* n.s. 131 (1988), 192f./Theodoridis, id. 132 (1989), 409f.). What form, or forms, Ap. (the Budé offers ἧχι here, ἧχι in iv.925) and his contemporaries used, we do not know; there seems to be no 3rd cent. inscriptional evidence.

ἀερθείς See LSJ Suppl. s.v. ἀείρω I1, *DGE* s.v. αἴρω BII1, Renehan 1975.14; *Od.* 8.375 (ἀπὸ) χθονὸς (ὑψόσ') ἀερθείς/.

163 D.P. 1109-10 ἀνερχόμενος .../ἠέλιος πρώτῃσιν ἐπιφλέγει ἀκτίνεσσιν. Ap. for his part is thinking of *Od.* 11.16 Ἠέλιος φαέθων καταδέρκεται (?) ἀκτίνεσσιν (sim. Hes. *Theog.* 760). Cf. also iv.125-6 (~ Paul. Sil. *Amb.* 161-2) the Fleece (121-2n.) νεφέλῃ ἐναλίγκιον ἧτ' ἀνιόντος/ ἠελίου φλογερῇσιν ἐρεύθεται ἀκτίνεσσιν. For πρώτῃσιν cf. Eur. *Phaethon* 2-3 Diggle (245-6n.); for ἀκτίνεσσι 159-63(3)n. (Mimn.).

ἐρεύθεται *de ave phoenice* 35 *primum surgens Aurora rubescit.*

For the verb cf. iv.126 above, and on ἔρευθος, 'une lumière rougeoyante et éblouissante,' VDB 1.84 n.1; id. 2.116, 'ἐρεύθομαι qualifie la lumière de divers corps célestes dans certaines conditions (aurore, crépuscule, approche du vent, etc),' where they cite Arat. 797, 803 and (ἔρευθος/... νεφέων [iv.125 supr.] ἐρυθαίνεται) 834-5; i.778 (star; evoking a picture of the radiant beauty/complexion of loved ones; so in i.1230, Hylas, hit full on by *moon-beams*: 121-2n.).

As Eros is here setting out to shoot Medea and enlist her help in securing the Fleece, ἐρεύθεται can be said to be at least on the fringes of the recurrent (and much-discussed) erotic imagery of blushing/redness in association with heavenly bodies/youthful beauty incl. that of Eros himself/Fleece. See e.g. Lawall 158 n.10; Beye 1982.156; Rose 1985.38 n.30; Palombi 76; Newman 74f. (much is far-fetched); Pavlock 29f., 33f., 42, 66 (id.), sim. Nyberg 43.

I pass over a number of deplorable conjectures, engendered by the notion that the expression must mean 'is made red by its first rays.' Rather 'blushes red come/with its first rays.'

164 νειόθι 62n. Ctr. *Od.* 12.242 ὑπένερθε δὲ γαῖα φάνεσκε/...

γαῖα φερέσβιος Hes. *Theog.* 693, *HyAp* 341, also iv.1509; later: Q.S. 5.517, Nonn. *D.* 22.284; manipulations: Opp. *Hal.* 1.475; Q.S. 3.22 and (~ Ap. iv supr.) 8.466. On the epithet see Richardson at *HyDem* 450 (p. 298), and for the concept in relation to Eros 159-63(4)n.

ἄστεά τ' ἀνδρῶν As *Il.* 2.340 μήδεά τ' ἀνδρῶν/, cf. ii.155. It may be significant that lyric presents a parallel for the expression: Bacch. 13.188-9 ἄστεά τ' .. ἀνδρῶν (see above on 158f.); later on: *GVI* 627.2 (Thasos, 2nd/3rd cent.) ἀνδρῶν .. ἄστεα as a variation on *Od.* 1.3. Homer: *Od.* 15.82 /ἄστεα δ' ἀνθρώπων and sim. [but there can hardly be a pointer here to Odysseus' wanderings, as Lennox suggested: 66] cf. Euph.(?) *CA* 176.2; *Il.* 2.660 αἰζηῶν, *Od.* 15.492 al. βροτῶν (Theoc. 17.81). Others: φωτῶν Q.S. 4.150, orac. *ap.* Eunap. *VS* 27 (/ἄστεά τ' .. φ.); λαῶν Melinno *SH* 541.12.

165 φαίνετο After *Il.* 13.14 (... πόλις).

ποταμῶν ἱεροὶ ῥόοι An old, and a conventional, way of describing rivers (though Orpheus' song in i.501f. provides a sharp reminder of their numinous nature, cf. the 'rivers' heading the list in Simon. *PMG* 581.2, with Bond on Eur. *HF* 1232-4): cf. *Il.* 11.726 ἱερὸν ῥόον Ἀλφειοῖο/, and the similar configurations in Hes. *WD* 566, ii.515, [Opp.] *Cyn.* 2.143; also i.1208, iv.134, 1417; West on Hes. *Theog.* 788, NH on Hor. *Carm.* 1.1.22. Here perhaps the epithet makes a particular point: Eros is no mere abstraction, but a living force about to exert an unseen influence on a world where the divine plays an acknowledged part in the regulation of natural phenomena. See in general A. Pagliaro, *Saggi di critica semantica* (Messina 1962), 93f., 104f.

ῥόοι Ap. simply pluralises the familiar ἱερὸς ῥόος. The inevitable (and needless) task of normalising fell to Spitzner (cf. Hom. ῥοαί, and so ii.366 etc.; ῥοαί + ποταμῶν: Xenoph. DK21 B30.4, Q.S. 5.15, 8.465, *h. mag. GDK* 59.5.4); cf. Wellauer here.

ἄλλοτε δ' αὖτε *Il.* 18.159 (ἄλλοτε ...) al.; also iv.180, 1197, and often elsewhere. In 164 only E has ἄλλοτε; ἄλλοθι Ω, from the preceding νειόθι; hardly defensible as a variation on *Od.* 2.131 ἄλλοθι γαίης/. αὖτε then ἄκριες: cf. *Od.* 10.281.

166 ἄκριες 159-63(4)n. See *LfgrE* s.v. (an excellent entry) for early epic and for Ap. (4 × in all). This choice word (nowhere else in 3^H) usually occupies the fourth foot (the fifth in i.1273); here it effectively takes up a prominent position at the head of the verse, and it is then isolated by means of a strong pause. Such eminences are indeed attention-grabbing.

ἀμφὶ δὲ πόντος On this run see Campbell on Q.S. 12.175-6, and cf. the n. on 159-63(4).

ἀν' αἰθέρα πολλὸν ἰόντι αἰθέρι Ω, but despite Vian's vigorous defence (1962.37, cf. VDB 2.116), the dative termination seems to me to be a clear case of assimilation to the following ἰόντι. To object, as Platt did (1914.28f., with a fantastic conjecture thrown in), that Eros is actually descending, is pedantic indeed. We are not presented with a line harbouring κατ' αἰθέρος or ἐξ αἰθέρος because the journey is viewed through the eyes of the god himself, as he courses along on high, 'up along' aether (cf. ὕπερθεν in iv.958 of spectators up on the summit of Olympus, with Campbell on Mosch. *Eur.* 144), surveying what lies beneath (164 init.) him. We may think (if we wish to press the point) of the very gradual descent familiar in the era of the space-shuttle, or indeed from the flight-path of the eagle who lurks in this passage and frequents this zone (e.g. *Od.* 19.540, Bacch. 5.17, Maehler ad loc., ii.1254); cf. too the ἀν' αἰθέρ' of Eur. *Hipp.* 447 cited on 159-63(4).

There is nothing wrong in principle with construing πολλόν as an adverb (as VDB 2².152 insist: cf. iv.31 ἄνδιχα πολλὸν ἰούσῃ/, ? echoed by D.P. 539 with ἐπὶ πολλὸν ἰόντι/), but 'the great expanse of aether' is to be preferred: cf. Gillies comm. p. 138/Ardizzoni ad loc. and (Campbell 1982.15) *magnum* Virg. *A.* 1.300, *immensum* Ov. *Met.* 10.1, εὐρύν Q.S. 1.683 (κατ' οὐρανὸν εὐρὺν ἰόντι/), to which I can now add Eur. *fr.* 911.3 (von Arnim, *Suppl. Eur.*, p. 8) ἀν' αἰθέρα πουλύν (on this reading consult P. Maas, *Kleine Schriften* (Munich 1973), 46-7); id. *Or.* 321f. τὸν ταναὸν αἰθέρ' ἀμ-. It is just possible I suppose that the choice πουλύν has been replaced here.

167-8 We rejoin the Argonauts where we left them in 6-7, lines closely mirrored here; μίμνον .. λελοχημένοι· αἱ δ' ἐνόησαν .... βούλευον κτλ. gives way to λελοχημένοι ἠγορόωντο, marking the simultaneity of deliberations in heaven and on earth. With Eros' arrival in Colchis at 275f. the parallel strands of action converge, as the spotlight is trained on Jason and Medea (cf. 2-3). A combination of verbal exchanges, a wealth of description and an aethereal journey is matched by a single address from Jason followed by instant (198) action, a short (213) walk to the city (where the pace is slowed with an excursus), a lingering look at the palace-complex, a brief outburst from Chalciope heralding the immediate (270) commencement of preparations for a meal. Ap.'s intercutting of scenes has not won universal approval: the interruption of Eros' journey to earth by lines 167-274 is one example of his 'weaving two parallel paths in a ... sometimes cloyingly discontinuous way' in the estimation of Briggs, *ANRW* II 31.2.961.

167 A faint echo perhaps of *Il.* 7.419 (after ἀγορή) 'Ἀργεῖοι δ' ἑτέρωθεν ἐϋσσέλμων ἀπὸ νηῶν ...

ἥρωες δ' heads a resumption of the narrative also in i.1012, iv.522. One of the regular designations for the Argonauts in our poem, ἥρωες figured in the epicising *Fourth Pythian Ode* (58, 199; cf. Braswell on 12(b)); so, among Ap.'s contemporaries, Call. *fr.* 7.25, Theoc. 13.28, 73, 22.78, 92.

ἥρωες δ' ἀπάνευθεν An echo from one of the scenes on the shield in *Il.* 18: 558f. /κήρυκες δ' ἀπάνευθεν ... πένοντο /.. δ' ... αἱ δὲ ⌣—×; locality: a king's private property.

ἀπάνευθεν See on ἀπόνοσφι in 9.

ἑῆς ... But *Il.* 2.358 ἧς νηὸς ἐϋσσέλμοιο, *Od.* 12.358 al. ἐϋσσέλμου ἐπὶ νηός/.

ἐπὶ σέλμασι νηός Archil. *IEG* 4.6 θοῆς διὰ σέλματα νηός/, cf. Eur. *Cyc.* 144, *GVI* 1694.5 (Demetrias, 3rd/2nd cent.). Colluthus (322) has ἐπὶ σέλματα νηῶν/, with which cf. Aesch. *Pers.* 358-9, Eur. *Or.* 242, Opp. *Hal.* 5.175.

σέλματα also i.528 (cited below); alternatively ζυγά i.724 (cf. iv.913 and εὔζυγον in i.14, with Gow on Theoc. 13.21); or κληῖδες (1269n.). On these three much-discussed terms see Pollux 1.89, and cf. Casson 220f., Kurt 124f., Gerber, *ICS* 6 (1981), 3f., Hoekstra on *Od.* 13.101, Willink on Eur. *Or.* 241-2.

168 ἐν ποταμῷ ... λελοχημένοι Another reminder (167n.) of the ecphrasis in *Il.* 18: 520-1 λοχῆσαι/ἐν ποταμῷ, applied to the sort of activity envisaged by Aeetes infr. 592-3 (see on 6-7). The Argonauts in the event adopt a quite different approach.

καθ' ἕλος But *Il.* 20.221 ἕλος κάτα (βουκολέοντο/). *Od.* 14.474 members of a λόχος lay /ἂν δόνακας καὶ ἕλος, cf. above on 6-7 and on δονάκεσσι in 6; VDB 2.17. The Argonauts had been directed to this spot by Argos, ii.1283; it will be the focus of attention again in iii.489, 575.

λελοχημένοι 7n.

ἠγορόωντο In ii.1226 converse, here meet to talk in a formal assembly. In reflecting the form of *Il*. 4.1 (see below, and Kirk ad loc.), Ap. may or may not have been working from a note of the type found in schol. D ad loc. (cf. *EtM* 418.35, Hesych. α727, and see Erbse 1953.171, Merkel *Proleg*. 169): διελέγοντο, ἐκκλησιάζοντο, ἀπὸ τοῦ ἀγορεύειν, ἐξ οὗ ἠθροίζοντο (the order here has probably been disturbed). In any event, the use of the word in Hdt. 6.11.1 (Marxer 54, cf. Leumann 306) does not necessarily preclude reliance on Homeric exegesis. In labelling schol. D's note post-Aristarchean (cf. Porph. 1.67.27, who criticises Aristarchus for his interpretation of *Il*. 4.1: ἠθροίζοντο; Lehrs 360 thinks Ar. took *Il*. 8.230 in the same way) van der Valk (1.262-3) proceeds as often from the dubious premise that anything Aristarchean cannot ever be pre-Aristarchean.

168f. λελοχημένοι ἠγορόωντο ... See *Echoes* at 168 and 194; Hunter on 169-70; Campbell 1990.482. The clausula of 168 provides the first indication that Ap., as a *follow-up* to the sustained account of plotting in the divine sphere, is toying with Olympian scenes, mirroring as it does the form of *Il*. 4.1 (the gods by Zeus' side) καθήμενοι (cf. ἑδριόωντες infr. 170) ἠγορόωντο/(ἐν 2), where the great god goes on to practise a πεῖρα on Hera (ctr. πείραζε in the *previous* encounter, 10), who responds angrily. At the close of the scene (194) we are entertained by a rather arch reminder of Hes. *Theog*. 664, /ὣς φάτ', ἐπῄνησαν δὲ θεοί, scil. to a proposal to engage in fierce combat. Add to these the allusion to the imperious Zeus' ἀγορή at *Il*. 8.2f.: 4 αὐτὸς δέ σφ' ἀγόρευε, θεοὶ δ' ὑπὸ πάντες ἄκουον.

Ironic contrasts may be drawn: the leader of the expedition, in coming forward with a plan, is neither mocking nor domineering; he gets his own way by subtler means, and his crewmen, who sit quietly listening (ἠρέμα 170), make no waves when it is suggested that fighting is to be avoided.

Later: Q.S. 5.432 ἀκαχήμενοι ἠγορόωντο/ (433 ἀπάνευθε, ibid. rivername). Cf. also, in conjunction with infr. 170, Nonn. *D*. 27.242-3 /Ζηνὶ παρεδριόωντες .... ἠγορόωντο .. ἐπὶ θώκων/, id. 36.428-30 /ἑζόμενοι στοιχηδὸν .. ἐπὶ βάθρων/... ἀγορήσατο .... φίλοι ...

169 αὐτὸς δ' Αἰσονίδης No doubt an old Argonautic formula; also in ii.1271 (and [Orph.] *A*. 576), cf. i.494 (τ'). There is no lengthy run-up to the speech, culminating in a 'formulaic doublet' [174n.] ἀγορήσατο καὶ μετέειπεν. αὐτός says it all: Jason is in charge.

Αἰσονίδης μετεφώνεεν ii.1178, scil. as their leader. Cf. *Il.* 7.382 ἀγορῇ then 384 μετεφώνεεν, id. 9.11f. ἀγορήν, 52 μετεφώνεεν (the wise Nestor); *Od.* 22.69-70 /τοῖσιν δ' Εὐρύμαχος μετεφώνεε .../ὦ φίλοι ... The verb is not one of Ap.'s favourites for introducing direct speech: 3 × (143 speeches).

οἱ δ' ὑπάκουον Similarly *Od.* 14.484-5 (λόχος episode) προσηύδων .... ὁ δ' ἄρ' .. ὑπάκουσε/, but introducing a speech within a speech; Campbell 1990.482. On the flavour of the verb cf. schol. A at *Il.* 8.4a¹; ὑπακουός iv.1381.

170 [Orph.] *A.* 804 ἐξείης ἥρωας ὁμιλαδὸν ἑδριόωντας. The orderliness of the rowers is a constant theme in our poem, cf. most notably i.528f. cited below (εὐκόσμως in 530 picks up a detail from *Od.* , 13.77: Peschties 37). That passage marks the start of the voyage. The echo of it here suggests an important new phase: so in iv.199f. Jason urges the crew to sit at their oars in an organised way as they prepare to set out on the journey home. As far as the immediate context is concerned, Jason can be seen to be addressing not a restive mob, but a quiet and orderly band of men who are presently to be asked to act as one in the task confronting them.

ἠρέμα Again in iv.1314; not in archaic poetry: Campbell on Mosch. *Eur.* 50. LW's ἠρέμας (a form without parallel, though compare ἀτρέμα/-ας, with *GG* 1.405) is unlikely to be right. For hiatus after a terminal short alpha in this sedes cf. e.g. *Il.* 16.404; before ᾗ: *Od.* 10.61, 14.448. See also VDB 2.116. Perhaps an early hint that the audience, sitting there in a tranquil frame of mind, is going to succumb to Jason's powers of persuasion: cf. the use of ἠρεμέοντες in i.514.

ᾗ ἐνὶ χώρῃ Hom. (*Il.* 17.394 al.) -ῃ ἐνὶ χώρῃ/ (so iv.159 ~ *Od.* 21.366); cf. *Il.* 23.349-50 ἐνὶ χώρῃ/ἕζετ', and the common ἐν χώρᾳ *at one's post* (see FJW on Aesch. *Suppl.* 976); Mineur on Call. *h.* 4.192. In the matching passage i.528f. οἱ δ' ἀνὰ σέλματα βάντες ἐπισχερὼ ἀλλήλοισιν/... ᾧ ἐνὶ χώρῳ/... ἑδριόωντο/ the masc. is a little surprising, though J. H. H. Schmidt, *Synonymik der griechischen Sprache* (Leipzig 1876-86), 2.4f., seems to me to exaggerate the difference between χῶρος and χώρη in Homer and elsewhere (cf. *LH* under both, and note Zen. at *Il.* 12.423 [Duentzer 88, Hainsworth ad loc.] and the variant at *Od.* 21.366).

ἐπισχερώ (cf. ἑξῆς in *Od.* 4.580 al.; ἐνσχερώ in i.912) of Argo's crew also i.330 (ἑδριόωντο/, then speech from Jason), infr. 1269, and with dative similarly i.528 quoted above; in iv.451 (Livrea ad loc.) it is usually said to govern a genitive: this is difficult ('next in order in' instead of the expected 'next to,' cf. ἑξῆς etc.; A. Y. Campbell was clearly uneasy about this, *CR* n.s. 7 (1957), 4; De Martino offers an obscure analysis, *AC* 49 (1980), 236), so perhaps 'this (element) of song was coming (ἦεν?) next-in-succession for me.'

The word is rare outside Hom. and Ap.: 'Simon.' *FGE* 861, Arat. 243, Theoc. 14.69, Paul. Sil. *Soph.* 558. It *may* have started life as ἐπὶ σχερῷ, 'on the shore' (Doederlein 2.224f., Mooney on i.330, Janko, *Glotta* 57 (1979), 20f.): but see Ruijgh 1991.618. Cf. also Verdenius on ἐνσχερώ in Pind. *N.* 11.39.

ἑδριόωντες Intrans. in Hellenistic poetry only here, Theoc. 17.19, and (?: pap. 2nd cent. AD) Anon. eleg. *SH* 970i.3; in archaic epic ἑδριόωνται/-το, -άασθαι: on the alternation cf. Meister 74f. (Boesch 19, 57, compares intrans. compounds in -εδρεύειν), and see on -ιᾶν types 123n.

Thereafter: Cougny 6.214.24 & 31 (~ orac. *ap.* Phlegon *FGH* 257 *fr.* 37), [Orph.] *A.* 804 (above), [Apolin.] 100.14, Jo. Gaz. 1.70. παρ-ii.1039 and *IG* 10.2.1, 447.10 (2nd/3rd cent.), Nonn. *D.* 4.75, 27.242, Jo. Gaz. 2.262. ἐν-† Greg. Naz. 1228.7 θώκοισιν ἐνεδριόωντες, read ἐφ-: Colluth. 15 ἐφεδριόωντα θοώκοις/.

171-95 Jason's plan and its speedy acceptance. For the run-up to this address see n. on 6-7.

There is more to Jason than many would allow (see Beye 1982.130 for an entertaining character-assassination). He now makes a firm choice between the courses of action suggested by Ancaeus (ii.1279-80) by recalling, but also modifying, Peleus' words of encouragement at ii.1219-25.

(1) 171-5. Jason will express his preferred option, but it is proper that the crew should ratify his suggestion. Just as they have a shared goal in this expedition, so also are 'spoken words' (proposals, plans) shared, viz. policy decisions require nothing short of a consensus (πᾶσιν ὁμῶς). His strong insistence on collective decision-making (*Noten* 66f., VDB 3.127 n.2) is not misplaced: for the next move unanimity is crucial, the more so as Jason intends to leave most of the crew to their own devices for a while; it is important too, as Fränkel says (*Noten* 337), that when the expected breakdown occurs, there will be no room for recriminations. One *might* infer from 174-5 that Jason's accommodating stance as leader embraces a readiness to listen to other people's ideas. In fact, the lines are determinedly self-referent-

ial: the speaker himself by implication is treading the opposite path by coming forward with a plan for their salvation. Jason must realise that the course of action he is about to recommend *has* to be followed through if the path of least resistance, an amicable agreement carrying no risk, is to be tried, however remote the prospect of success. For him the safety of the crew is of paramount importance (cf. notably ii.634f., and see e.g. Levy, *Vergilius* 7 (1961), 28-9). So there is no direct exhortation to speak up, either here or by way of conclusion (ctr. i.664-6). The label 'democratic in council' (Zanker 1987.202; Beye 1969.38 talks of 'anti-heroic democracy') does not do proper justice to what Jason is about.

(2) 176-81. He proceeds to spell out, briskly and decisively, a clearcut plan of action, with himself as the leading figure (177, 179). If he is prepared to confront Aeetes personally in the company of a select few, he takes no chances with the ship (176, see n.). σὺν ἔντεσι in the same line rejigs Peleus' words in ii.1221: they will be under arms, but not actively so. Jason and his party must ascertain how the land lies: *might* Aeetes be willing to bestow the Fleece amicably, or *will* he 'dishonour' them (a prelude this to the point about the rights enjoyed by ξεῖνοι), relying on <the> βίη <which Argos has led them to expect in ii.1204f.>? Jason borrows the language used by Peleus in ii.1224 εἰ μὴ φιλότητι δέρος χρύσειον ὀπάσσει, but he goes further by suggesting an alternative route to fighting in the event of a rejection, viz.:

(3) 182-4. If Aeetes does misbehave (with κακότητα again a hint about Aeetes' likely attitude to the rights of ξεῖνοι), they must consider whether to take up arms or to think of some other scheme, if they are debarred from battle. Jason the diplomat omits to explore either avenue. The overwhelming numerical superiority of the Colchians, though brushed aside by Peleus in ii.1225 (ἔθνεα Κόλχων: cf. ii.1204-5) must make an open fight the least attractive proposition of all (cf. Rose 1984.132f.; Hera, and the martial Athena, who have no need to be tactful, do not even consider it: 11f.); Jason's policy is dictated by the needs of the moment: it is grossly misleading to aver that 'fighting is passé' *as a general principle*, Beye 1969.47, and similarly many others. As for the alternative (theft most obviously), there are practical difficulties, not to say insurmountable obstacles (ii.1207f.). Jason at this moment can have no more idea of how to proceed in such circumstances than do his listeners, but he must feel that in the end some sort of stratagem will be necessary (see 183-4n.); already emerging from the fertile brain of Hera (11f., μῆτις 30), it will be communicated to him for the first time in 475. (Schwinge 108-9 distorts

this particular aspect of Jason's tactics: but for Schwinge Jason is a loser from start to finish.)

(4) 185-7. As a sop to the fiery Peleus, no doubt, he abruptly reverts to the option of battle: but diplomacy should at least be attempted first (with ἔπεσσι .. πειρηθῆναι ctr. ii.1221). 186b-7 reiterate the need for the spoken word, while not excluding (πάροιθεν) eventual recourse to arms; astute indeed.

(5) 188-190 *init*. The series of recommendations that Aeetes be approached 'with words' (ἐπέεσσι 179, ἔπεσσι 185, with a switch to μύθῳ 187) is now resolved into a general principle: μῦθος, when properly deployed, can often achieve with ease what force of arms could achieve <only> with difficulty. On the sentiment, and the technique employed, see n. ad loc. Jason's manipulative approach recalls in spirit, if not in detail, the subtle ploy of Polydamas in *Il.* 13.725f. to induce the Trojans to retreat rather than fight: he stresses the need to pay due attention to '<words of> persuasion' (726), βουλή (727), and νόος (732). Jason can supply all three (174/187f.).

(6) 190b-3. The proof. Aeetes in fact must have responded to mollification when he took in Phrixus. Jason goes on what he has been told by Argos (ii.1146f.) and cannot know the truth (iii.584f.). Even so, he can be entertaining no illusions, given the description of Aeetes offered by Argos in ii.1202f., which must have put him in mind of the ἀτάσθαλος Pelias; and Amycus had already demonstrated the art of flouting the laws of hospitality (ii.1f., cf. Köhnken 96). In fact, Jason does not state that Aeetes harboured the refugee out of reverence for Zeus Xenios, but merely implies that he must have done so, because everybody shows such reverence. Not a solid argument then, it affords a fleeting glimpse of Jason's own lack of conviction on this score. See further on 176f. and 190. —

What Jason is after is the authorisation to give Aeetes a chance: they will talk to him rather than rob him, and if he cooperates, all will be well. If he does not, he will, in the terms outlined in 192-3, have put himself in the wrong (cf. *Noten* 338f.) and a different course of action will be necessary; the nature of that will have to be considered in due course. Put this way, the proposal could reasonably be expected to win a consensus (ctr. Rosenmayer 184). And so it proves. In the event of course Aeetes *will* prove to be hospitable – on *his* terms.

171f. are reminiscent in a general way (cf. *Echoes* ad loc.) of the tactful Nestor's words in *Il.* 9.100f. (note κρηῆναι 101): cf. infr. 175

ἀπούρας, 181 ἀτίσσει, 183 φρασσόμεθ', 185 ἔπεσσι, 187 μύθῳ .. ἀρέσσασθαι with 9.107, 111, 112 *bis*, 113 (this specifying 'gifts' also: here the boot is on the other foot: infr. 352!). 'Appeasement' did not work with Achilles, and it will not work with Aeetes.

171 *Il.* 7.191 and iii.523 both begin ὦ φίλοι, ἤτοι (the latter ἤτοι μέν), but relevant also are *Il.* 24.460 /ὦ γέρον, ἤτοι ἐγώ and 14.252 /ἤτοι ἐγὼ μέν. For the second part of the line cf. *Il.* 7.407 (ἤτοι 406) ἐμοὶ δ' (the commander Agamemnon) ἐπιανδάνει οὕτως/, *Od.* 2.114 ἀνδάνει αὐτῇ/, iv.395.

ὦ φίλοι Jason seeks to establish a close rapport at the very outset (cf. in particular iv.190; in i.332f./336 he begins on a businesslike note, then turns to his audience directly); he will start with the same mode of address when he gets back with the bad news (492). On this *Gruppenanrede* see Opelt, *Glotta* 56 (1978), 182-3, 189.

ἤτοι .. μέν 15n.

μοι ἐπιανδάνει αὐτῷ A wry echo surely of 34: what Jason 'personally' finds advisable will coincide with Hera's proposal – eventually.

172 ... ἐξερέω was perhaps suggested by *Od.* 9.364-5 ἐγώ τοι/ἐξερέω· σὺ δέ ... Details stemming from the Cyclops-episode will soon surface in abundance.

... τέλος κρηῆναι i.e. to ratify what I am about to propose by giving your formal consent: τέλος = 'Gültigkeit, Rechtskraft, Ratifikation,' κρηῆναι = 'beschliessen,' Fränkel 1928.569 and *Noten* 337, citing for elucidation of the latter Fraenkel's note on Aesch. *Ag.* 369; see further FJW on Aesch. *Suppl.* 601 and (κεκύρωται τέλος) 603. Comparable here is Aesch. *Suppl.* 624 (note the context) ἐπέκρανεν τέλος; on the association of these terms see the remarks of U. Fischer, *Der Telosgedanke in den Dramen des Aischylos* (Hildesheim 1965), 82 n.1, 142f. In the closest Homeric passage to ours, *Il.* 9.625-6 οὐ .. μοι δοκέει μύθοιο τελευτή/... κρανέεσθαι (but there the sense is its 'execution ... will be carried through,' see in general F. M. J. Waanders, *The History of ΤΕΛΟΣ and ΤΕΛΕΩ in Ancient Greek* (Amsterdam 1983), 53), schol. D gloss the infinitive with τέλος λήψεσθαι, τελειωθήσεσθαι.

As Hunter notes (on 171-2), Jason does not indulge in anything like the blunt ultimatum put by Zeus in the *Iliad*, 8.8-9: ἅμα πάντες/αἰνεῖτ' (scil. my ἔπος), ὄφρα τάχιστα τελευτήσω τάδε ἔργα. One is reminded too of the recurrent statement of intent ὧδε γὰρ ἐξερέω, τὸ δὲ καὶ τετελεσμένον ἔσται, *Il.* 1.212 etc. See further on 195.

173-4 ξυνὴ ... reflects Jason's eloquent deployment of paraenetic anaphora in the leadership-election, i.336-7 ἀλλὰ φίλοι, ξυνὸς γὰρ ἐς Ἑλλάδα νόστος ὀπίσσω,/ξυναὶ δ' ἄμμι πέλονται ἐς Αἰήταο κέλευθοι ... (cf. *Noten* 65-6). At this decisive moment, as at that, Jason will get his own way. Both passages are discussed, to little purpose, by Clauss 129f.

This anaphora first in [Hes.] *fr.* 1.6, ξυναὶ γὰρ τότε δαῖτες ἔσαν, ξυνοὶ δὲ θόωκοι (cf. Fehling 204), then Theoc. 7.35 ξυνὰ γὰρ ὁδὸς ξυνὰ δὲ καὶ ἀώς/, Theaet. *HE* 3365. There is a partial echo of i.336f. in [Orph.] *A.* 290, cf. id. 769.

Other examples, ξυν-:
(1) 2 ×: Greg. Naz. 507.8, 629.650 (⁓ δὲ κέλευθος/), 1479.21 (⁓ δέ τ').
(2) 3 ×: *GVI* 1726.2-3 (Pisidia, 'vor 212 n. Chr'; ⁓ δὲ κέλευθος/); [Opp.] *Cyn.* 4.(42 ξυνά enunciating theme +) 43-4 (⁓ δέ τ'); Agath. *AP* 7.551.2-4.
(3) 4 ×: Greg. Naz. 464.97-9 (⁓ δέ τε).
(4) 5 ×: Greg. Naz. 1235.96-8 (⁓ δέ τε, ⁓ ξυνοί τε θόωκοι/ leg. -οὶ δὲ ...).

173 γὰρ χρειώ ... μῦθοι ἔασι Ctr. *Il.* 10.118 al. χρειὼ γὰρ ..., id. 2.796 μῦθοι ... εἰσιν/.

χρειώ is like χρῆμα, the object of activity (cf. Redard 90), i.e. (object/purpose of) quest or assignment, mission, as infr. 332, iv.191 (/ἤδη γὰρ χρειώ, echoing the χρειώ specified here: third phase, moment of return), al. The interpretation 'need,' advocated by some, is intolerably feeble.

μῦθοι ἔασι Cf. i.479. On the point of μῦθοι see on 171-95(1). Jason is not talking here about the 'right' to speak in general terms (a common misconception). Cf. *Noten* 337 (on 171-5).

174 πᾶσιν ὁμῶς Campbell on Q.S. 12.211.
ὁ + partic.: 406n.
ὁ δὲ σῖγα Again in 422. On the adverb see 123n.
νόον βουλήν τε An inversion of the recurrent unit (*Od.* 2.281 al.) βουλήν τε νόον τε/, which belongs to the category of what O'Nolan terms 'formulaic doublets' (*CQ* n.s. 28 (1978), see on this specimen p. 31), a type of which Ap. is naturally not over-fond: note that whereas the Homeric expression rounds off the verse (O'Nolan 32f.), Ap.'s adaptation is integrated into the flow of the sentence; Hes. *Theog.* 122 νόον καὶ ἐπίφρονα βουλήν/.

τ' ἀπερύκων Cf. *Od.* 18.105 σύας τε κύνας τ' ἀπερύκων/. 'Withholding' could be expressed by the simple ἐρύκων (cf. Vian ed. 1961). Here however the clausular ἀπ-ερύκων, keeping *away from* <this company, scil. τοῦδε στόλου>, is to be matched by καὶ .. τόνδε στόλον .. ἀπούρας/, having *taken away from* this company ... into the bargain, the parallelism highlighting the inevitable consequence of such inconsiderate behaviour. Cf. *Noten* 337. The basic meaning of the compound (*Il.*+) is 'keep away from <other people>'; for a more adventurous use of the verb see on 327.

175 ἴστω 'had better know': cf. in Homer *Il.* 15.217.

νόστου A throwback to i.336 (above). A safe return home (*Noten* 66, Campbell *ap.* Vian 1973.92 n.8, Hutchinson 101 n.25, 110) is what they are all after: it cannot be thrown away. Jason really lays it on the line, as he must. Hutchinson 97f. rightly stresses the emotive force of the term in this poem, for Jason and for his crew; the 'return' is an overriding concern of Hera's too, as we have lately heard (75, a prophecy on its way to fulfilment: 74-5n.; 89).

τόνδε στόλον The noun is not found in archaic poetry; regularly applied by Ap. to the Argonauts (who make up a *manus heroum* sim. in Prop., Sen., Val. Flacc.); nowhere else in 3[H]. For τόνδε cf. ii.625 (Jason also), and earlier Soph. *Tr.* 226, Eur. *fr.* 105 (I am sure that tragic poets would have applied the term to the Argonautic 'expeditionary force,' but I know of no example).

... οἷος ... Shades of *the* returning hero: *Od.* 1.9 ἀφείλετο νόστιμον ..., 13 ... οἷον νόστου ..., 14 ἔρυκε.

οἷος ἀπούρας Shaped like αὐτὸς ἀπούρας/ in the strongly condemnatory *Il.* 1.356, al.; varied perhaps by Euphorion, *CA* 8 μοῦνος ἀπηύρα/ (Campbell 1982.15). The construction 'deprive *x* of' (iv.1433-4) is peculiar to Ap., though it is found occasionally with related verbs (KG 1.328-9). For its association with 'return' cf. iv.916 ~ *Od.* 13.132.

Jason makes his point forcefully: anyone who *is* <at this moment> keeping quiet can be sure he *has* robbed *single-handedly all* of his colleagues of a return home. I do not know why people translate ἀπούρας as if it were a present.

176f. *Echoes* ad loc. signals the first sharp correspondence in this stretch of the poem (there have been notable echoes before, particularly towards the close of the second book: some in Levin 203f.; cf. 193n.) with the celebrated Cyclops-episode in *Od.* 9 ('9' for the purposes of this note).

171f. ...... ἀγορὴν θέμενος μετὰ πᾶσιν ἔειπον·
ἄλλοι μὲν νῦν μίμνετ', ἐμοὶ ἐρίηρες ἑταῖροι·
αὐτὰρ ἐγὼ σὺν νηί τ' ἐμῇ καὶ ἐμοῖς ἑτάροισιν
ἐλθὼν τῶνδ' ἀνδρῶν πειρήσομαι, οἵ τινές εἰσιν,
ἤ ῥ' οἵγ' ὑβρισταί τε καὶ ἄγριοι οὐδὲ δίκαιοι,
ἦε φιλόξεινοι, καί σφιν νόος ἐστὶ θεουδής.

193f. δὴ τότε τοὺς ἄλλους κελόμην ἐρίηρας ἑταίρους
αὐτοῦ πὰρ νηί τε μένειν καὶ νῆα ἔρυσθαι·
αὐτὰρ ἐγὼ κρίνας ἑτάρων δυοκαίδεκ' ἀρίστους
βῆν . . . .

Since Jason is not working entirely in the dark (see on 171-95(6)), he formulates the object of his πεῖρα differently. If Aeetes comes unquestionably under the category of ὑβρισταί (ii.1202f.), he did take in Phrixus (ii.1146f.) – the mark of a φιλόξεινος. In his closing words Jason gives Aeetes the benefit of the doubt, but only after he has hinted at trouble ahead (181 and 182). His obvious mistrust is pointed up for us by the background presence of Polyphemus and his fellow Cyclopes, who most certainly give the lie to the universality of the principle enunciated in 193 (cf. 9.275, al.). If Aeetes rules over a nation conversant with seafaring and architecture, can convene ἀγοραί (iii.576, iv.214; ctr. 9.112) and is prepared to negotiate (if on his own terms) with foreigners (401f.), he is essentially, like Polyphemus, ἄθεμις (9.189 al.). He has no time really for strangers, contemptuously addressing the disadvantaged Jason as ξεῖνε (401 cf. 9.273); he *is* afraid of Zeus (scil. Zeus Xenios), but only because self-preservation was at stake (587f.; more uncompromisingly 9.275f.); and he is not the type to take kindly to a suggestion that a ξεινήιον be offered: indeed both Argos and Jason tread warily here (339, 349, 352 δωτίνη + offer of a deal; 389, 391 + repeated offer), whereas Odysseus is quite blatant, 9.267f. ἱκόμεθ', εἴ τι πόροις ξεινήιον ἠὲ καὶ ἄλλως [Aeetes is to 'borrow' this form of words in 402, but goes on to talk of 'other people's property']/ δοίης δωτίνην, ἥτε ξείνων θέμις ἐστίν, followed by an appeal and a reminder of the watchful Zeus Xenios (Argos tried that on the Argonauts, ii.1131f., but it was not to be tried on Aeetes).

The sequel presents further points of contact:

(1) 260f. Chalciope, in hurling bitter reproaches at her undutiful children, begins with ἔμπης οὐκ ἄρ' ἐμέλλετ' ... Cf. 9.475, Odysseus to the irreverent Cyclops. (Note in the run-up 256-7 ~ 9.294-5.)

(2) 268. A passing piece of fun with Aeetes, owner of the κριοῦ δέρος. The Cyclops' ram was, ominously, πανύστατος (9.452) θύραζε (9.444, 461). Cf. on 239.

(3) 315-6. Aeetes' apparently casual query about the whereabouts of the ship is, not surprisingly, simply ignored. When Polyphemus, by now downright aggressive, puts a similar question (9.279-80), Odysseus, who has already been evasive about his identity, resorts to a lie: Poseidon (Polyphemus' father) destroyed it. Aeetes is soon to hear of a *real-life* shipwreck, involving a *Colchian* vessel, brought about by *tempests* (320f.). — 'Guarding' of ship: ctr. 607 with 9.194.

An amusing detail in 316: Aeetes is made to apply an innocuous label to the ship (γλαφυρή); *not*, as in 9.279, 'well-constructed': see (Argos in) 340f.!

(4) 356-66. Odysseus' evasive reply to the Cyclops, embracing a boast about connexions with Agamemnon, who enjoyed μέγιστον κλέος (9.263f.), is matched on Argos' side by a comprehensive listing of the visitors' illustrious ancestors. We cannot think that the latter, despite the fact that he can actually point to blood-ties (359 and 362-3), has even a marginally better chance of impressing his 'host.'

(5) 372f. This outburst offers a foretaste of Aeetes' conviction that he is dealing with ληιστῆρες (589, see note): an immoderate reaction (as in 367 ἐπεχώσατο, ctr. 9.480, where Polyphemus ἐχώσατο, under far greater provocation), standing in pointed contrast to Polyphemus' (standard) query (9.253-4) μαψιδίως ἀλάλησθε,/οἷά τε ληιστῆρες …;

The alert reader will think back more than once to past barbarity: the vile ταμών in 378 recalls ταμών in 9.291, the cannibal preparing his gruesome meal; the clausula of 9.417 (the murderous Cyclops) is echoed in χεῖρε κεάσσας ibid. There is a touch of grim humour too in the prominence afforded to 'eyes' (372 cf. 371) given the significance attaching to ὀφθαλμός in the model (cf. 9.333 and *passim*).

(6) 382f.396f. Death (cf. ὀλοόν 384) induced by precipitate action; inner debate about whether to move in for the kill: cf. 9.299f. (κε … ἀπωλόμεθ' 303).

(7) 402f. A recasting in expository style of Polyphemus' impassioned plea at 9.529f. /εἰ ἐτεόν γε …/δὸς …

(8) 423. Jason ἀμηχανέων (cf. 432) as a result of Aeetes' fearsome imposition; comparable to the feeling of utter helplessness experienced by Odysseus and his companions (cf. iii.504) when confronted by the monstrous Cyclops (ἀμηχανίη 9.295). In both cases, the μῆχος/μῆτις required to set things right will materialize in due course. Jason will get the Fleece, just as Odysseus was to acquire the Cyclops' 'thick-fleeced' (9.425) sheep, and find salvation from an ἄωτον (9.434), despite the fact that both losers were forewarned (9.507f. ~ iii.597f.).

(9) Other correspondences: 198 ἀνὰ νηός (see n.) perhaps seeks to

do something different with 9.177; 199 ἐξαπέβησαν turns around 9.179 εἴσβαινον; the clausula of 200 recalls that of 9.183 (description); 215 τεθηπότες of sightseers cf. 9.153 and 218; 325-6 mirror the form of 9.216-7; 393 πρόφρονες from the visitors but 9.355 πρόφρων from the host. Cf. also 405n.

176 ΩΛΛΟΙ is written both with and without initial aspiration (the latter orthography is recommended by some, e.g. Erbse 1963.19) in our MSS: documentation in VDB i.lxxviif. For discussion of the form see the bibliogr. in Livrea's note on iv.253, adding to his examples i.1101, iii.992; also Erbse on schol. *Il.* 2.1*a*, Rengakos 1993.53-5. A form read by Zenodotus in two places that we know of, *Il.* 2.1 and 10.1 (Duentzer 75), arising no doubt 'auf Benutzung von Handschriften, die etwa aus ionischen Städten kamen' (Wackernagel *SU* 73), it will not be an independently conceived Ionic implant (so e.g. Erbse 1953.164) but a reflection of a Zenodotean line, to judge by the very close echo of both *Il.* 2.1f. and 10.1f. in i.1081f. (note also *Il.* 24.677f.). The only verse occurrences outside Zen. Hom. and Ap. appear to be Theoc. 18.17 ἀριστέες (cf. i.1081-2; 'sleep' Theoc. 9, 10, 12; 15 /κῆς ἔτος ἐξ ἔτεος ... 17 ἀριστέες ~ iv.1773 corr. ἀριστῆες ... 1774 /εἰς ἔτος ἐξ ἔτεος), 22.178 ὦλλοι πάντας [Ald.²: πάντες *codd.*] .. ἑταίρους/ (cf. iii.365 ὦλλοι πάντες ... ἑταῖροι/), unless one accepts ΩΛΛΟΙΣ in a late Hellenistic inscribed hexameter in *ZPE* 50 (1983), 1 (called into question by Peek, id. 60 (1985), 78).

ὦλλοι μὲν κατὰ νῆα: *Il.* 2.1 Zen. /ὦλλοι μέν, 10.1 Zen. /ὦλλοι μὲν παρὰ νηυσίν. — /ὦλλοι ... μίμνεθ᾽: but *Od.* 3.427 /οἱ δ᾽ ἄλλοι μένετ᾽ (cit. Svensson 45), id. 9.172 /ἄλλοι μὲν .. μίμνετ᾽ (see above on 176f.). — /ὦλλοι ... ἕκηλοι/: but *Il.* 11.75 /οἱ δ᾽ ἄλλοι then ἕκηλοι/.

κατὰ νῆα In other sedes ii.1035; *Od.* 8.232 al. The ship is thus kept out of the way, with good reason as it turns out. One may compare the precautions taken by Aeneas in an unknown environment, Virg. *A.* 1.310f. (the *secessu longo* of 159 and the *tuta* of 164 appear to have engendered the vague *longo .. tuta recessu/puppis* of Val. Flacc., 5.556-7).

σὺν ἔντεσι i.1059 (v.l.) al. ~ *Il.* 5.220 al. See the note on 171-95(2). They must be on full alert, but take no direct action themselves. — The noun's *nautical* associations (cf. κατὰ νῆα) suggest the possibility that there is a whiff of irony in the air.

μίμνεθ᾽ For the majority then it will still be a case of 'waiting' (cf. 7).

μίμνεθ᾽ ἕκηλοι Q.S. 12.348 μίμνον ἕκηλοι/, Campbell ad loc. ἕκηλος very commonly signifies 'inactive, at one's ease,' i.e. 'uninvolved' (Hainsworth on *Il.* 11.75-6), restraining oneself/keeping a low profile. Cf. e.g. *Il.* 15.194-5 (μενέτω), i.303 (μίμνε); Gow on [Theoc.] 25.100; 85n.

177 See on 176f. (*Od.* 9.173). Emped. DK31 B35.1 /αὐτὰρ ἐγὼ .. ἐλεύσομαι. Compare as well *Il.* 7.237 al. (infr. 788) /αὐτὰρ ἐγών; *Od.* 10.546 /αὐτὰρ ἐγὼ διὰ δώματ' ἰὼν .. ἑταίρους/ (infr. 178; ἐπέεσσι 547 cf. infr. 179); id. 2.259 al. ἐς δώματ' (ἴσαν sim.).

δώματ' .. Αἰήταο Cf. [Orph.] *A.* 860 (and id. 770, ξυνήν 769, ἐπέεσσιν 771); infr. 213-4.

178 υἷας .. Φρίξοιο The story of their encounter with the Argonauts: ii.1093f. For the designation cf. infr. 196 υἱῆας Φρίξου; otherwise the repeated /υἱῆες (-ας) -οιο (3 ×, 2 ×). Ctr. iv.81.

Although Argos is the oldest and the dominant figure, Jason will naturally want Aeetes to see all of them safe and sound (not that Aeetes will thank him for that); in any case, it will mean that there will be one less awkward question to deal with.

δύω ... ἑταίρους But *Od.* 10.208 δύω (καὶ εἴκοσ') ἑταῖροι/. One thinks of the two comrades + herald (here Jason himself, 197f.) dispatched by Odysseus, see *Od.* 9.90 (the Lotus-eaters), 10.102 (Laestrygonians). Jason does not name names at this point; he is quick to do so once he has full authorisation (196f.), without recourse to lots (ctr. Val. Flacc. 5.325f.).

τ' ἐπὶ τοῖσιν Given i.811 etc. (see VDB *app. crit.* here; add ii.953) it is hard to see how δ' could be justified. Passages such as *Il.* 24.231, *Od.* 24.277, ii.396 are clearly not comparable.

179 *Il.* 2.73, the miscalculating commander Agamemnon: /πρῶτα δ' .. ἔπεσιν πειρήσομαι (cf. on 185 below), note υἷας 72 ~ Ap. 178. Vian (1962.36) adduced this passage to establish the interpretation of παροίτερον as 'd'abord' rather than 'face to face' (Ardizzoni). In fact, the crucial question of who does what *first* is reformulated in 182 (πάρος) and reiterated in 185 (πρὶν ...) and 186 (πάροιθεν), just as 'with words' resurfaces in 185 and again in 187 (cf. also μετιόντας 181, 187).

πειρήσω See on 16 and (*Od.* 9) 176f., 405. ἐπέεσσι here recalls Hera's pronouncement in 14f.: a πεῖρα which places reliance on verbal persuasiveness will be quite ineffective. And Jason is not blind to this eventuality.

παροίτερον 24n. On E's περαίτερον (the copyist is thinking of περαιτέρω) see Campbell 1973.75.

-ερον ἀντιβολήσας Cf. the clausula of *Il.* 11.365 = 20.452 (followed by /εἰ ...).

ἀντιβολήσας In 193 Jason implies that Aeetes might be approached by the delegation as suppliants under the banner of Zeus Xenios. That is not to say that ἀντιβολήσας means 'entreat' (cf. 482n.) here, as Ardizzoni suggested. This verb is commonly applied to a direct encounter, a bold, no-holds-barred confrontation, and that suits the tone: 'I shall confront/square up to him and ...' Jason, conciliatory but none the less firm and self-assured, is the diplomatic counterpart of Achilles on the field of battle: *Il.* 19.70-1 ... Τρώων πειρήσομαι ἀντίον ἐλθών,/αἴ κ' ἐθέλωσ' ... If he has already dreamed up the idea of offering Aeetes a straight swop, he omits to spell it out here.

180 Cf. *Il.* 19.71 cited on 179, and: *Od.* 19.589 /εἴ κ' ἐθέλοις, *Il.* 6.165 /ὅς μ' ἔθελεν φιλότητι (different shade of meaning) ..., and, all from *Od.*: 4.619 = 15.119 ἐθέλω .. ὀπάσσαι/ scil. as a ξεινήιον, 4.131 /χρυσέην .. ἠλακάτην ... ὄπασσεν/ (id.), 8.430-1 ἄλεισον ... ὀπάσσω/ χρύσεον (id.).

εἴ κ' + optat., '<to see> if he *might* be willing ...': see for the construction Wåhlin 115, Boesch 26, *GH* 2.277f., 296. Cf. 479 'if we *could* win her over,' 535 'in the hope that she just might be able,' 693f. (πειρωμένη) 'to see if she just might ...' (sim. iv.459, πειρήσατο μύθοις/ 462) etc. For the sentiment cf. ἑκόντος in Pind. *P.* 8.14 (*Noten* 339).

φιλότητι ... ὀπάσσαι recalls Peleus at ii.1224: see on 171-95(2), and for δέρος χρύσειον 88n.

φιλότητι Scil. as an individual who has to do with ξεῖνοι could be expected to do. For the word's associations cf. i.961 (ἐυξείνως 963), 1179 (id.), ii.760; and *Il.* 3.354 (Erbse on schol. 3.207), *Od.* 15.196-7 etc., often thereafter. φιλότητι ... ὀπάσσαι: cf. Homer (+ διδόναι), *Od.* 10.43, 14.504-5.

181 ἠὲ καὶ οὔ iv.276. Ctr. *Il.* 2.238 al. (= Q.S. 13.561) ἠὲ καὶ οὐκί/; the model here: *Il.* 10.444-5 /ὄφρα ... πειρηθῆτον ἐμεῖο,/ἠὲ κατ' αἶσαν ἔειπον ἐν ὑμῖν, ἠὲ καὶ οὐκί.

The καί of ἢ καί very often (as in iv.276 above) indicates that the second alternative is the likelier one (no account is taken of this by Denniston *GP* 306, or by Verdenius, *Mnemosyne* 29 (1976), 181). For οὐ rather than μή in disjunctions see KG 2.191-2, 535. Here οὐ, following on from the extremely remote eventuality expressed by εἴ κ' ἐθέλοι, provides a broad hint (soon to be reinforced) of what Jason thinks is actually going to happen.

πίσυνος .. βίῃ .. ἀτίσσει A clever evocation of uncontrollable violence: cf. Ajax at *Il.* 9.237-9 Ἕκτωρ .. μέγα σθένεϊ βλεμεαίνων/μαίνεται ἐκπάγλως, πίσυνος Διί [but not our Aeetes!], οὐδέ τι τίει/ἀνέρας οὐδὲ θεούς ...

πίσυνος .. βίῃ: Hom. *Il.* 12.135 al. (furious fighting men) πεποιθότες .. βίηφι/ (adapted in iv.273-4, cf. *Echoes* ad loc.).

μετιόντας *approach* (with a request), as infr. 187, 1027, al.; not Homeric in this sense.

ἀτίσσει The sudden switch to the factual fut. indic. (cf. VDB 2.117) causes no surprise: Jason has been leading up to this. He is sure what will happen (surer still is the author of E's γε, unless that is a mere slip), and goes on to talk quite positively about the eventual need to take counsel (φρασσόμεθ', another fut. indic.) in the event of failure: but negotiation must at least (185) be attempted first.

With ἀτίσσει Jason has in mind Aeetes' likely failure to show them the 'honour' due to ξεῖνοι (in this case a transference of τιμή in the form of the Fleece just specified: see in general Adkins, *BICS* 7 (1960), 25f.): cf. ἄτισσε in ii.9 (Amycus), τίειν in *Od.* 15.543, 17.56, *Scutum* 85 etc., ἀτιμῆσαι in *Od.* 14.57, al. Aeetes' first words in 304-5 apparently hold out some reassurance: τὸν (Phrixus) περὶ πάντων/ξείνων ... ἔτισα/.

The future of this verb already in Aeschylus (single sigma); on -σσ- cf. Rzach 571 (and 567), Boesch 9, and 353n.

182 That is to say, if Aeetes plays the part of the aggressor and chooses to wrong us, we will get on with the job of deciding whether to take the offensive (as people who ἀδικηθέντες πόλεμον ἐγείρουσιν) or to think of something else.

ὧδε γὰρ ἐξ αὐτοῖο Cf. the clausula of ii.314; and infr. 920.

πάρος κακότητα ... A similar run (but syntactically different) in i.692.

... κακότητα δαέντες 'having experienced misconduct from ... in this fashion,' viz. by virtue of the act of ἀτιμίη envisaged in 181. So (Fränkel OCT) δαείς ii.57, i.q. γνούς, 'having learned by <bitter> experience,' cf. iv.234. Aeetes then will have 'started it': on this common theme see Rutherford on *Od.* 20.394.

κακότης = κακοεργίη. *Not* (a random choice) 'instruits ... de notre infortune' (VDB), 'sapremo ... la nostra disgrazia' (PF).

For the build of the clausula cf. (e.g.) κακότητα φέροντες/ *Il.* 12.332; (ἔργ)α δαέντες/ *HyHom* 20.5 (~ Theoc. 17.81), cf. i.916 ὄφρα δαέντες/.

183-4 *Od.* 10.192-3, Odysseus to his assembled (188) comrades (he feigns perplexity): ἀλλὰ φραζώμεθα θᾶσσον/εἴ τις ἔτ᾽ ἔσται μῆτις. Unlike Odysseus, Jason does not have a plan in the event of failure, but he has no need to say so outright: other options are firmly relegated to the future (φρασσόμεθ᾽ ...). See n. on 171-95(3).

εἴτε τις ἄλλη/μῆτις: cf. for this run iv.1023-4 (οὐδέ τις ~ *Od.* 19.157-8 accus.). εἴτε τις ἄλλη/ = Nonn. *D.* 41.358 (corr.).

Jason's language must engage our attention a little longer. In ii.383 Phineus had recommended recourse to μῆτις in combating birds, and this suggestion was taken up at ii.1049-50 (cf. 1058, 1068), ἀλλὰ τιν᾽ ἄλλην/μῆτιν πορσύνωμεν ἐπίρροθον, the basic cast of which Jason is made to recall here. Later, at iii.548, Mopsos echoes Phineus' appeal for μῆτις in ii.383, but in connexion with the scheme to enlist Medea's help (cf. Argos 475 ~ Hera 30). This nexus of ideas (discussed by Hutchinson 110-11) may suggest that embedded in Jason's mind is the notion that the eventual solution is somehow related to Phineus' pronouncements (the specific forecast of ii.423-4 has been set aside, 12n.).

183 φρασσόμεθ᾽ ... But *Il.* 9.619 /φρασσόμεθ᾽ ἤ κε νεώμεθ᾽ ... ἦ κε (v.l. ἠὲ) μένωμεν/. εἴτε/εἴτε in an indirect question (ii.1279-80, partially echoed here, iv.348-9, 1699) only once in Homer, *Il.* 2.349 (with variant ἠέ in the second member): *GH* 2.293.

ἄρηι συνοισόμεθ᾽ varies *Il.* 11.736 /συμφερόμεσθα μάχῃ, and id. 8.400 συνοισόμεθα πτόλεμόνδε/, taken up in *Scutum* 358 (cf. Edwards 81-2) συνοισόμεθα πτολεμίζειν/ (note 357 Ἄρης, 359 πειρηθῆναι/ cf. 185 infr.). In the two last the speaker strongly advises against such a course of action; Jason is more guarded (184).

ἄρηι For some account of the treatment of the initial alpha (long in thesis) see Rzach 441, and McLennan on Call. *h.* 1.77. Ἄρηι already in ii.991 (.. τέκε, ctr. *Il.* 2.513, 515 τέκεν ..../ Ἄρηι, [Hes.] *Theog.* 993-4 Ἄρηι/... ἔτικτε/). Ctr. *Il.* 2.385 κρινώμεθ᾽ ἄρηι/ (~ Theoc. 22.175).

184 ἐπίρροθος Cf. the uses of (ἐπ)αρωγός, ἐπίκουρος, sim. Either *a helper, defender*, esp. applied to one joining (the confused clamour of) battle (cf. 559n.), or, as adj., *affording succour* or *protection* in dangerous situations. With μῆτ(ις) also ii.225 (Phineus against Harpies), 1050 (ἀλλά τιν' ἄλλην/...) & 1068 (with an eye on the terrific *racket* designed to scare off the birds?); πύργον iv.1045. Not elsewhere in 3[H]. For discussion of the word see Brugmann, *BPhW* 39 (1919), 136f., Sideras 57-8, *LfgrE* s.v., Heubeck on *Od.* 24.182.

ἐεργομένοισιν Cf. Campbell 1978.122-3: 'supposing we are debarred from,' exactly like *Il.* 13.525 (preceded by "Ἄρης then ἄλλοι/... ἦσαν) ἐεργόμενοι πολέμοιο/ (κωλυόμενοι schol. D; cf. *Il.* 8.7f.). Merkel (*Proleg.* 139) saw fit to claim that Ap. is re-interpreting here ('a piece of Homeric criticism' Gillies): 'if we refrain from' – not the kind of sentiment we ought to be foisting (and that is the word for it) on the diplomatic Jason, who has clearly shown himself conscious of the fact that an uncompromisingly bellicose approach has been mooted (see Peleus at ii.1220f.). The mistake is regularly repeated.

ἀυτῆς 'fighting,' 'battle' (so e.g. schol. D at *Il.* 1.492; cf. Erbse on schol. *Il.* 11.802 and *LfgrE* s.v. Ic for the interpretation of ἀυτή as ἐπὶ τῆς φωνῆς [i.310 etc.] or ἐπὶ τῆς μάχης, and *DGE* s.v. II2), the blunt πόλεμος being totally avoided by Jason (ἄρηι 183, ἀλκῆ 185, ἠνορέη 189, ctr. Peleus in ii.1222). Cf. ἀυτή in iii.571 and (after *Od.* 11.383) iv.1005; a contemporary example appears in Theoc. 22.220.

185 An echo maybe in [Theoc.] 25.222 /πρὶν .. ἀλκῆς τε .. πειρηθῆναι/.

μηδ' αὔτως ... 'But we must not ... just like that – not at any rate before ...' Cf. 129n., and see *LfgrE* s.v. αὔτως 4 ('ohne weiteres' ...). Particularly close is Phineus' (sound) warning against precipitate action in ii.326 μηδ' αὔτως ... then 328f. /οἰωνῷ δὴ πρόσθε .. πειρήσασθαι/... ἐφίεμαι, there a confident δή, here a sober γε.

ἀλκῆ Jason again remembers Peleus' language: ii.1220; here *force of arms* or just *battle, combat*, as in iv.1156 and perhaps ii.64 as well. For the latter meaning see the entry in *LfgrE* (including the glosses: μάχη often), and also that in *DGE* s.v. III (Pind., trag.). Cf. on ἀυτῆς in 184.

πρὶν ἔπεσσί γε πειρηθῆναι See Campbell 1978.214. Ap. adapts and perhaps 'cleans up' the second half of *Od.* 24.240, from the notorious scene where Odysseus poses as a 'stranger' to make his approach, πρῶτον κερτομίοις ἐπέεσσιν πειρηθῆναι, with its violation of Wernicke's Law (see Stanford and esp. Heubeck ad loc. for discussion of the verse, and cf. on 42-3, 517 and 1084).

πρὶν ... πειρηθῆναι *Il.* 21.225 (οὐ ...) /πρὶν ... πειρηθῆναι/, but of *hostile* action, as in ii.6 (/μή τιν' ..) πρὶν πειρήσασθαι ...

COMMENTARY 186   165

ἔπεσσι .. πειρηθῆναι Cf. 179(n.) and infr. 1146-7 (verb second, as here). Most witnesses present us with ἐπέεσσι, very probably a reminiscence of *Od.* 24.240, but there is also ἐπέεσσι in 179 supr. to consider.

186 τόνδ' The pronoun lends a touch of immediacy: it is almost as if Aeetes is right there with them (note τόνδε 175) as a participant in the forensic process.

ἀπαμείρωμεν An elevated word. In the active here only (the simplex in verse only Pind. *P.* 6.27; pass. -όμενοι con. Schneider at i.749, but see van Krevelen 1949.139f., Livrea, *AC* 49 (1980), 149f.); passive: Hes. *Theog.* 801 (see West; f.v.l. ἀπομ-, which is the correct reading in *WD* 578, f.v.l. ἀπαμ-), Arat. 522 (see Martin; prob. f.v.l. ἀπομ-), infr. 785 (see note); middle: Nonn. *D.* 29.160 (but also Plato *Lg.* 777a in citing *Od.* 17.322, cf. J. Labarbe, *L'Homère de Platon* (Liège 1949), 252f., Russo on 319-23).

Solmsen's suggestion that ἀμείρειν evolved from ἀμέρσαι on the analogy of κέρσαι κείρειν (cf. Marxer 13-4, Leumann 162-3) is rightly questioned by Seiler in *LfgrE* s.v. (ἀπ)αμείρ(ομαι), q.v. for a collection of ancient lexicographical material.

σφέτερον Strongly put: 'what is his own ...' On Ap.'s use of this possessive adj. (its flexibility is too familiar to merit detailed listings here) see Erbse 1953.165 (alleged links with Zenodotus), Vian ed. 1961 on 99, Livrea on iv.1327, Rengakos 1993.118; cf. also 335n. (σφωίτερος). More general discussion: Verdenius on Hes. *WD* 2 (extensive bibliogr.), Braswell on Pind. *P.* 4.83(e), Mineur on Call. *h.* 4.233.

κτέρας Jason applies the same term to the Fleece in 389 ('other people's property': the target is widened by Aeetes in 591). In iv.1550 of the 'property' of Phoebus, 'Apollo's tripod' 1548, but the word is coloured there by its Homeric associations with 'gift' (*Il.* 10.216, 24.235: see *LfgrE* s.v.): the object was donated to Jason by Apollo and passed as an offering into Triton's hands.

κτέρας is uncommon (*SEG* 22.79.5 = *CEG* (1) 58.5, Attica *c.* 510-500; Anon. iamb. *ap.* Crönert *Gött. Nachtr.* 1922, p. 27 [pap. 1st/2nd cent.]) until the time of Nonnos and co.: *Dionysiaca* 5 ×, [Apolin.] 4 ×, Colluth. 3 ×, Jul. Aegypt. *AP* 9.445.5.

ἀλλὰ πάροιθεν Homeric clausula, *Il.* 4.185 (judged to be temporal rather than local? ἔμπροσθεν καὶ ἐπὶ τόπου καὶ ἐπὶ χρόνου Ap. S. 127.33), id. 14.427 (local prep.); also iv.339 (temp.), [Opp.] *Cyn.* 4.233, 264 (both temp.).

187 λωίτερον This neuter form occurs twice in archaic poetry: *Od.* 1.376-7 = 2.141-2 (Telemachus preaching) λωίτερον καὶ ἄμεινον [cf. on the 'doublet,' not picked up here, 174n.]/ἔμμεναι. Otherwise in *Arg.*: -ος, see 850n.

μύθῳ μιν ἀρέσσασθαι Cf. *Il.* 9.112-3 μιν (Achilles) ἀρεσσάμενοι .... ἔπεσι (171f.n.); and *Od.* 8.415 ~ ii.462.

μετιόντας 181n. He presses home the necessity of going to Aeetes direct.

188-90 In his speeches to date Jason has shown himself to be mainly interested in specifics: generalisations have been in short supply (i.298f., comforting his mother, ii.1179-80 on Zeus Xenios' watchful eye; ctr. the lyric treatment of Pindar, *P.* 4.139f., two gnomic reflections in the course of a single short speech), and the second half of the poem can throw up only one further example (infr. 429-30). If the low-key approach and the calculated argumentation are reminiscent on a general level of the oratory of the Odyssean (and Iliadic) Odysseus, and the formal, deliberative tone of the numerous policy-proposals and declarations of intent in Homer's Greek and Trojan assemblies, this neatly expressed combination of (a) eulogy of the power of the spoken word (b) affirmation of its applicability to the present case (c) concluding reflection seems to me to have a Euripidean feel: cf. Bond at *HF* 506-13, on the circular structure of γνώμη: παράδειγμα: γνώμη (not confined to him of course). Brunck indeed cited for the sentiment *Phoenissae* 515-7: χρῆν δ' αὐτὸν οὐχ ὅπλοισι τὰς διαλλαγάς,/μῆτερ, ποιεῖσθαι· πᾶν γὰρ ἐξαιρεῖ λόγος/ὃ καὶ σίδηρος πολεμίων δράσειεν ἄν.

188 πολλάκι τοι ῥέα ... πολλάκι(ς) is commonly employed with the aorist in general statements or appeals to experience (cf. Hes. *WD* 240, Thgn. *IEG* 137, 665-6; Stahl 132), as is τοι (cf. Soph. *El.* 415-6 πολλά τοι σμικροὶ λόγοι/ἔσφηλαν with *GP* 542f.); 'easily': *Il.* 17.177-8, Soph. *OC* 1535 etc.

ῥέα ... So an explicit acknowledgement of the difficulties inherent in a straight fight is cleverly side-stepped. Argos had been quite direct in pointing out how hard it would be to get the Fleece (ii.1207-8). For us, the question of the 'easy' method has in fact already been considered – and resolved: 88.

μόλις 634n.

ἐξανύσειεν The word is Homeric, but not in this clausular configuration (cf. i.897); perhaps borrowed by [Theoc.], 25.156 (not otherwise in 3ᴴ).

189 ἠνορέη (*brute*) *force*, as i.1198 and probably iii.1053 (like βίη καὶ χερσί, see n. ad loc.). The physical aspect of 'manliness' is quite often the dominant one, cf. ἠνορέη in (e.g.) Hes. *Theog.* 516, 619, ὑπερ-ήνωρ (associated with δύναμις), ἀνδρεία and related terms (e.g. *DGE* s.v. ἀνδρεία I2, s.v. ἀνδρεῖος *passim*), Lat. *virilitas virilis* etc.

τόδ' ἔρεξε *Od.* 4.242, 271, but there with true past reference (as later in Arces. Pitan. *SH* 122.5), and firmly in the context of military activity.

189-90 ... κατὰ χρέος, ᾗπερ ἐῴκει Punctuation after ἐῴκει (so Fränkel OCT) gives '... in line with what is required, exactly as is fitting, πρηΰνας,' i.e. μῦθος achieves the required result in a fitting and proper fashion (the reasonable, 'civilised' way of going about things). This articulation has the merit of isolating and giving added weight to the participle at the beginning of 190. Most prefer to associate ᾗπερ ἐῴκει with πρηΰνας. In that case, 'exactly as is appropriate' should perhaps be understood as 'in a manner exactly suited to the case in hand.' ἐοικέναι commonly means 'be suitable to one's (immediate) needs' (e.g. i.658); cf. *Od.* 4.239 ἐοικότα .. καταλέξω, 'words suited to the occasion.' — ἔικτο ('resembled' iv.1612; a related use in ii.39) can hardly be regarded as a credible alternative in this context, as Hackstein, *Glotta* 67 (1989), 54 n.18 seems to imply.

κατὰ χρέος In *Od.* 11.479 (whatever its exact sense) employed in connexion with the consultation of a seer; a reflection of that is to be seen in iv.530, Jason going to Delphi to consult the oracle. Elsewhere two broad categories may be discerned: (1) related to the above, 'in execution of a project, on business': ii.1127 corr.; Call. *fr.* 85.2 suppl. ~ id. *fr.* 178.7; Opp. *Hal.* 1.583. (2) 'duly, properly, appropriately, regularly,' sim.: *HyHerm* 138 ... τοι πάντα κατὰ χρέος ἤνυσε δαίμων/ (cf. τοι and ἐξανύσειεν here), and iv.888-9 πάντα/.. μηρύοντο κατὰ χρέος; Arat. 343; [Apolin.] 1.9 + 8; Anon. *AP* 9.804.1. Redard's treatment of the expression (75) is too sketchy.

πρηΰνας *by exercising a calming influence, mollifying*, a policy he attempts to implement in the subsequent interview (cf. 385, 396, with Vian 1963.26); aor. following on from ἔρεξε, hence ἐῴκει not ἔοικε. [Orph.] *L.* 774 μῦθοι .. ἐπρήυναν. — One can hardly fail to be reminded of Pind. *P.* 4.136f., Jason to Aeetes' counterpart Pelias: πραῢν δ' Ἰήσων μαλθακᾷ φωνᾷ κτλ., the first and fourth elements of which may be illustrated by two early examples of Jason's recurrent role of soother of distress or anxiety: i.265 (κατεπρήυνεν), 294 (μειλιχίοις ἐπέεσσιν παρηγορέων προσέειπεν); cf. on 385.

On the verb in early poetry (not Homer) see Braswell on Pind. P. 4.136(d). Of particular interest: Hes. *Theog.* 254, *HyHerm* 417 with ῥεῖα (cf. Ap. 188); personified subject: cf. Solon *IEG* 4.37 πραΰνει heading a pentameter.

190f. ὁ δὲ καί ... 187: an approach involving μῦθος must be used on Aeetes. 188: you must know that μῦθος can often be effective. 189 draws both considerations together by offering an illustration (indeed, καί ποτ' is reminiscent of the tag found in validating mythological *exempla*: lit. in Davies on Alcm. *PMGF* 80): 'And he [no name necessary] in fact on a past occasion *did* take in ...' <and so must have responded to the verbal 'softening-up' which customarily precedes formal recognition of the rights of ξεῖνοι>. ὁ δὲ (for the run δὲ καί ποτ' cf. iv.383) is superior to ὅδε (cf. 186): asyndeton, employed to great effect in 188, is quite out of place here. 'This' is one component in the curious confection (adopted by Brunck and by Fränkel, OCT) served up by E: ὅδε (scil. μῦθος) ... Φρίξον ἔπεισε followed up with δέχθαι in place of πάντες two lines on; plainly the work of someone who could not stomach (or who could not understand) the reversion to the unnamed man of the moment, but who was prepared to blot out the thrusting πάντες ἐπεὶ πάντῃ which heralds the speech's conclusion; 'Aeetes' anyway must still be understood, but this time as the suppressed object of ἔπεισε. Jason recalls Argos' report in ii.1147-8 μιν ἔδεκτο/Αἰήτης μεγάρῳ ... See further Wellauer here (a truly blistering attack on the reading adopted by Brunck, 'qua ineptius et languidius vix quidquam fingi potest'), Vian 1963.84 (with n.1), Campbell 1973.84.

190 ἀμύμονα The standard interpretation (West on *Od.* 1.29; Janko on *Il.* 13.641-2) of this much-discussed Homeric epithet (bibliogr. in Dräger, 69 n.204), which does not recur in our poem, 'blameless,' i.e. 'morally beyond reproach, flawless' (in the D-schol. regularly ἀγαθός, ἄψογος, ἄμωμος *et sim.*), is entirely apt here. For closer definition we need to look at a later passage, 585-6 περὶ πάντων/ξείνων μειλιχίῃ τε θεουδείῃ τ' ἐκέκαστο, also in connexion with Phrixus' reception by Aeetes; cf. the linking of ἀμύμων with θεουδής in *Od.* 19.109, along with A. A. Parry, *Blameless Aegisthus* (Leiden 1973), 81f., who includes among the qualities possessed by persons said to be ἀμύμονες 'gentleness' and 'fear of the gods' (p.113).

Implicit here is the suggestion that in some respects at least Phrixus and Jason are two of a kind, just as the predicaments of Jason and Argos and his brothers have much in common (see Nyberg 86-7). Jason at this moment is advocating μειλιχίη, and will practise what he preaches as a ξεῖνος in the presence of a foreign king (385). In ii.1179f. he had talked of θεουδέες (and he included not only Phrixus and Phrixids but also himself and his men in that category, cf. Fränkel's perceptive analysis, *Noten* 301-3) in relation to Zeus' watchful gaze and escape from the evil Ino (we may recall her ἀθέων βελέων, Pind. *P.* 4.162). In addition, just as Phrixus was effectively driven out of house and home by a wicked stepmother (one such is labelled ἀτάσθαλος in i.815), so Jason has been expelled (333f.) by the ἀτάσθαλος (390) Pelias; indeed, the θυηλαί to which he alludes in 191 are pertinent to his own plight (Jason echoes ii.1194).

If Jason does dangle before his listeners what looks like a reasonable precedent, he is not so incautious as to declare openly that Aeetes is therefore bound to extend the hand of friendship to him as well: he has already given a hint of his scepticism on that score (180f.). Nor is it to be thought that he is trying to convince himself. The final resounding flourish masks a suspicion that all is not as it seems. Cf. on 171-95(6).

ἀμύμονα Φρίξον ἀμύμονα followed by a proper name: deviation from Homeric usage is detectable on every level. In *Il./Od.* (and so [Hes.] *fr.* 43(a)82) the name extends to verse-end (cf. Vílchez 73-4), with a single exception, *Il.* 16.152, but configured – ⏑ ⏑; ctr. id. 20.484 ἀμύμονα Πείρεω υἱόν/.

On the distribution of the epithet in Hellenistic poetry at large see Campbell on Mosch. *Eur.* 93.

191 On the story see 336-9n.

μητρυιῆς 'the stepmother': so used allusively already by Jason in ii.1182, cf. earlier Pind. *P.* 4.162. A classic example of the type (cf. West on Hes. *WD* 825, Henderson, *TAPA* 117 (1987), 112, Dräger 86 n.254; also i.272, and the horrific i.815), she was variously named (Braswell on Pind. loc. cit.): Θεμιστώ according to Pherecydes (*FGH* 3 *fr.* 98). θέμιν in 193 seems a bit too remote to be taken as an allusion to this: but you never know.

φεύγοντα A (for us) wry reminder of ii.653f., Dipsacus/Phrixus according to the poet ἑοῖς ὑπέδεκτο δόμοισιν,/ὁππόθ' ἅμα κριῷ φεῦγεν πόλιν Ὀρχομενοῖο. The host on that occasion was a quiet individual who took no pleasure in ὕβρις. Jason (who had never met Dipsacus himself) is soon to be confronted with a 'host' possessed of a very different temperament.

-τα δόλον πατρός ... Ctr. *Od.* 4.437 -τα· δόλον ... πατρί/.

δόλον As is so often the case in his handling of the expedition's antecedents, Ap. practises a calculated economy: he does not concern himself with the fine details of the stepmother's machinations ([Apollod.] 1.9.1, Frazer ad loc.) which are directed towards Phrixus' 'murder' (ii.1181). We shall presently have reason to identify Jason still more closely with this refugee from an horrific injustice: Aeetes himself will prove to be signally δολόεις towards his visitors (iii.578, iv.7) – and will threaten to *burn* Argo αὔτανδρον (582) into the bargain; and Jason will have no option but to run away.

πατρός .. θυηλάς varies ii.1194 Φρίξοιο θυηλάς/, see on 336-9. On the term θυηλή in Ap. (10 ×, 'burnt sacrifice,' ctr. the solitary use in Homer, *Il.* 9.220, schol. D and others ἀπαρχαί) and elsewhere (Ap. was not the first to widen the word's application) see the richly documented discussion of Kost on Musae. 39; also Herter *JAW* 283, Livrea on iv.247.

192 πάντες ἐπεὶ πάντῃ ... With an allusion to (and variation of) Arat. 4 (Campbell 1982.15) πάντῃ δὲ Διὸς [Ap. ... Ζηνὸς ...] κεχρήμεθα πάντες/ Ap strikingly, and with some considerable irony, evokes an image of a world far removed from the harshness of heroic existence, a world presided over by a benevolent, protective god whom 'all of us everywhere' need.

For the jingle cf. too Call. *fr. incert.* 736 ἇ πάντῃ πάντα, and in epigram: 'Plato' *FGE* 597, Phil. *GPh* 3051; *AP*: 7.102.3 (D.L.), 11.155.1-2 (Ammian.?), 12.91.2 (Polystr.). Earlier examples in Fehling 182, 230 (in 'pre-Socratic' style: Timo Phl. *SH* 833.5-6).

ἐπεὶ ... κύντατος .... ἀλεγίζει Ctr. *Il.* 8.483 ἀλέγω, ἐπεὶ ... κύντερον ...

κύντατος On the imagery see 641n. The passage to recall here is *Il.* 13.623f. (αἴσχεος 622), Menelaus to the Trojans: κακαὶ κύνες, οὐδέ τι θυμῷ/Ζηνὸς .. χαλεπὴν ἐδείσατε μῆνιν/Ξεινίου ... In reality, benign human φιλοξενίη, unlike the Stoic Zeus (see note above), is emphatically not all-pervasive.

κύντατος applied to a person: cf. Timo Phl. *SH* 825.1, a usage no doubt influenced more by the appearance of the word under a variety of guises in comedy (cf. Kassel-Austin on Eubulus *PCG* (V) 83;

Aesch. *fr.* 432: 'e fabula satyrica?' Radt ad loc.) than of κύντερ- and κύντατ- in epic; cf. Suda δ1183 *ad fin.*, s. Διονυσίων σκώμματα, ὁ κυνῶν κύντερος. Perhaps ὁ κύντατος in iv.1433 (self-variation: ὅστις ...), in the course of a blistering attack on the thieving and murderous Heracles, would have struck a contemporary audience as an earthy expression, though it does keep elevated company. Here a solemn effect is achieved by the epic clausula -τατος ἀνδρῶν (*Il.* 15.111 etc.; varied: ii.4, 374) and also by the highly unusual (*Thesaurus* s.v. μάλα 533.38f.) intensifying μάλα + superlative in place of the normal μέγα (Thesleff 169; the familiar affirmative use is also felt to an extent here).

The reader might well recall this strongly-worded pronouncement when Jason is himself enmeshed in treachery involving the lure of 'gifts of guest-friendship' (iv.422), see Feeney 64.

193 Another allusion to the Cyclops episode, this time to Odysseus' appeal in the name of Zeus Xenios at *Od.* 9.269f. (*Echoes* at ii.1131-3, see 176f.n.), where note αἰδεῖο (269), αἰδοίοισιν (271), but also θέμις (268) and /οὐ .. Κύκλωπες Διὸς .. ἀλέγουσιν/ (275). This same passage served as a model for Ap. in ii.1131f. (note αἰδέσσασθε), Argos' (successful) plea to the Argonauts. If Jason ever did contemplate confronting Aeetes with the thought that ξεῖνοι are under the special protection of a watchful god, the explosive reaction of the latter to Argos' petition must have pointed to the clear need for a less emotional approach (391f.: ctr. 985f. appeal/990f. return of favour).

Ξεινίου .. Ζηνός After *Il.* 13.624-5 /Ζηνὸς .../Ξεινίου (cited above on 192); but ii.1131-2 Διὸς .../Ξεινίου, from *Od.* 14.283-4. On his role in the poem see Faerber 85-6.

αἰδεῖται See above, and cf. Aesch. *Ag.* 362 Δία .. Ξένιον .. αἰδοῦμαι (and id. *Suppl.* 478-9 Ζηνὸς αἰδεῖσθαι κότον/'Ικτῆρος), Alex. Aet. *CA* 3.14 Ζῆνα Ξείνιον αἰδόμενος/ (Call. *fr.* 64.4 /Ζῆν'] .. Ξείνι[ο]ν ἀζόμενοι/), [Hom.] *Epigr.* 8.3 /αἰδεῖσθε Ξενίοιο Διὸς σέβας, [Opp.] *Cyn.* 2.371 /αἰδόμενος μακάρων .. θέμιν, [Orph.] *A.* 549 /αἰδομένους Θέμιν .. ξενίην τε τράπεζαν/ (cf. id. 660 Amycus Ζηνὸς θέμιν οὐκ ἀλεγίζων/).

αἰδεῖται reflects the vulgate text of Homer (Kirk on *Il.* 5.528-32). Here the contracted form is located in the second thesis, as *Od.* 17.578 in the first; cf. iv.1048 /αἰδεῖσθε (~ [Hom.] *Epigr.* 1.1, 8.3, + Ξεν-) but ft 2 ... *Il.* 5.530, 15.562. See Rzach 582-3.

Singular verb, by attraction to the interposed relative clause carrying ὅστις in its common distributive function (West on *Od.* 3.355), cf. infr. 949-50. This and related idioms are amply illustrated by Vahlen, *Opusc. Academ.* 2.190f.; cf. *GH* 2.15, 21, KG 1.287.

Ζηνὸς θέμιν iv.700 Circe offered a purificatory sacrifice ὀπιζομένη Ζηνὸς θέμιν Ἱκεσίοιο/. On Ap.'s use of θέμις in the sense *divine ordinance* or *ruling* see VDB 3.162-3 (on iv.373), together with Hoekstra on *Od.* 14.56 (but the force of the word there should not be diluted) & 59, Gould 91 n.90. Ctr. *Od.* 16.403 Διὸς .. θέμιστες/, Eur. *Med.* 209 τὰν Ζηνὸς ὀρκίαν Θέμιν. The closest parallel for the wording here appears to be Pind. *N.* 11.8f. (see Verdenius ad loc. for discussion) Ξενίου Διὸς ἀσκεῖται θέμις (some print Θέμις, cf. id. *O.* 8.21f., with FJW on Aesch. *Suppl.* 360) ...

ἀλεγίζει Normally (as i.14, 813 ~ *HyHerm* 557 corr.) accompanied by a negative; for its absence add to the examples in LSJ: Nonn. *D.*, Peek *Lex.* s.v., + *Par.* 12.23; Musae. 248; [orac.] in PW 615. The verb not otherwise in 3[H].

The clausula resembles that of (e.g.) *Il.* 15.106 οὐκ ἀλεγίζει.

194f. The proposal meets with universal approval. On this recurrent theme and Ap.'s handling of it see *Noten* 66-7, and also above on 171-95. For the human players there is no grand plan, nor could there be in an undertaking so fraught with uncertainty: policy is shaped as each new situation presents itself by a succession of individuals who, with or without a struggle, command assent. (I cannot think that the sour and unsympathetic appraisal of Rosenmayer 192 is in tune with the author's intentions.) Jason has made the best use of the latest piece of 'luck,' the encounter with the Phrixids whose father reportedly met with a kindly reception from Aeetes, by minimising the risk without shutting off other avenues in the event of a setback.

194 ὣς ... νέοι The echo of Hes. *Theog.* 664 has already been noted (on 168f.). Similar are infr. 555 /ἴσκεν· ἐπήνησαν δὲ νέοι (with a pointedly different sequel); iv.503 ὣς ἔφατ'· ἤνησαν δὲ νέοι ἔπος Αἰακίδαο, also notable for its weighty clausular patronymic. For the speech-capping formula see 432n.

ἐπήνησαν ... ἔπος Ctr. infr. 907(n.). On the variants -νεσ(σ)αν (cf. infr. 555) see West on Hes. *Theog.* 664, and on the verb in the sense 'approve,' Hoekstra on *Od.* 13.47.

νέοι On this label see R. Roux, *Le problème des Argonautes* (Paris 1949), 137f. (ordeal originally imposed on κοῦροι ὁμήλικες [cf. Pind. *P.* 4.187]), F. Graf in J. Bremmer (ed.), *Interpretations of Greek Mythology* (London and Sydney 1987), 97f., and more generally Fränkel 1952.147 n.11, Lawall 124 n.9. If Ap.'s Argonauts embrace the extremes of adulthood (VDB 1.10, Vian, *BAGB* 3 (1982), 279f.), they can still be compared collectively to νέοι at a symposium (i.458); the term can of course cover a wide spectrum: Verdenius, *Mnemosyne* 22 (1969), 345-6, Leimach, *Hermes* 106 (1978), 269-70. It was no doubt at home in old *Argonautica*; it exhibits the recurrent sequence verb/adverb: δὲ νέοι (i.341, 1134, ii.194, 555, iv.184, 503), being used in an oblique case only once (i.382). For Beye (1982.130), who has it in for Jason (in a genial sort of way), it is fraught with meaning: an indication of 'just how silly the plan is'! Hunter's ragged selection of special cases (1993.16 n.34) indicates that the quest for ephebes and suchlike curiosities should not be pursued too diligently.

Cf. Val. Flacc.'s *iuvenes* (also Catull. 64.4)/ *iuventa* (1.113) and *pubes* (cf. Catull. ibid.).

195 πασσυδίῃ An adverb of variable meaning, but here beyond any doubt (cf. Wifstrand 1928.2553, against Gillies; van Krevelen 1953.53) *unanimously*, a stronger version of the standard πάντες in comparable routines (*Il.* 7.344 etc. and, e.g., [Orph.] *A.* 293, 301); cf. also i.323 πασσυδίῃ with iv.1363 πάντες (*Noten* 301 with n.391), and earlier Aesch. *Suppl.* 607 πανδημίᾳ (FJW ad loc.) ~ 608 κραινόντων (~ supr. 172). For discussion and extensive bibliography see Campbell on Q.S. 12.434, adding id. 1990.482 and Ronconi 243-4. In eight of the nine places in the poem where the word occurs, πασσ- is the universal reading or nearly so (cf. VDB 1.LXXVI); in iv.859 however LASG offer πανσ-, the form favoured by Aristarchus (Ludwich 1.202-3, Rengakos 1993.72; Zenodotus will have read πασσ-, La Roche *HTA* 394-5, Rzach 487) and the transmitted reading in *CA* 12.21 (cited by Parthenius), a piece often credited to Ap. A final flourish perhaps, the last of nine examples for once acknowledging an alternative orthography. Otherwise in 3[H]: πανσ- Arat. 649, 714 c.v.l.; πανσ- MSS but πασσ- papyri at Call. *h.* 4.159.

οὐδ' ... Cf. Campbell 1990.482, and above on 6-7. Everybody expressed (instant) assent, nor was there anybody (with the inclination) to issue a different directive. For the relative + optative cf. in particular *Il.* 2.687 οὐ γὰρ ἔην [ἔσκεν here: see *GH* 1.290, 320-1, Wathelet, *AC* 42 (1973), 401] ὅστις σφιν ἐπὶ στίχας ἡγήσαιτο, 'because there was nobody to lead them ...,' along with KG 2.428.

παρὲξ .. ἄλλο Lit. 'anything else deviating – from <what had already been recommended>.' On this combination, based on *Od.* 4.348 al., see Campbell on Q.S. 12.115. ἄλλ- usually comes first, as infr. 1051: 'and what is more (καὶ δὲ) I will suggest to you another ὄνειαρ, a different one' (not just 'in addition,' as Gillies and many others). An alternative suggestion, that παρέξ here belongs closely with ἔσκε, does not merit one moment's consideration. (Postponed ὅστις is common.)

Ctr. *Od.* 9.488 ... παρέξ .. δ' ... ἐκέλευσα/...

ὅτις G's intriguing ὅπις, with gloss ἐπιστροφή, is discussed by Fränkel, *Einleitung* 74. One might have expected it to crop up rather in 192, given the context of the following line. Could it be a vestige of a direction to refer ὅτις *back* to ἔσκε (ἐπιστρέφου i.e. 'n.b.')?

κελεύοι In ii.1282 Jason had issued an order (ἐκέλευσεν) about landing procedures on Argos' advice; otherwise the verb (recurrent in Odysseus' dealings with his companions) is not used with reference to him: (κελεύειν/κέ(κ)λεσθαι) i.348 (Heracles), 383 and proecdosis 519 (Tiphys), ii.693 and iv.1548 (Orpheus), iv.495 (Peleus; particularly robust).

196f. The fellow-ambassadors. Jason moves decisively and with great speed: not a single descriptive epithet to slow the pace, and no prayers and libations (ctr. ii.1271f.) in Homeric style prior to departure (see on those Hainsworth on *Il.* 9.174-7; Richardson on id. 24.281-321, p. 303). On the sons of Phrixus see 178n. It is always a good thing (in civilised dealings anyway) for ξεῖνοι to be able to point to an illustrious lineage. Augeias strikes close to home as the son of none other than Helios, the only Argonaut to be so favoured (362-3n.): he simply *had* to see his blood-relative Aeetes, leader of the Colchians (i.175), and 'see' (cf. 362-3n. again) would be all he would manage. Telamon has the advantage of being descended from the supreme god Zeus (infr. 363-4), who has just been in Jason's thoughts and by whom Aeetes had reportedly set some store. One or other of the sons of Leda could theoretically have served, but the question of their paternity is not entirely clear-cut (517n.), even if one of them could have exhibited the necessary fire (cf. Polydeuces' defiant reaction to the imperious Amycus at ii.20f.) to fuel a crisis that needs to be averted. As for the other Aeacid, the redoubtable Peleus is very much his own man: a reaffirmation of his readiness to take up arms against Aeetes in the event of a hostile reception is one eventuality which Jason cannot have wished to risk, however content Peleus was for the moment to keep quiet. So it is 'warlike' Telamon (iii.1174, cf. i.1043 and ii.121-2; also e.g. Pind. *N.* 4.25f., *I.* 6.27f., Anon. *SH* 1168 = *EGF* Adesp. 7, p. 161), an individual of fiery temperament (i.1289f. abuses Jason, pounces on Tiphys, has to be restrained with tough talking, is finally reconciled; cf. iii.515-6) who is chosen. He is to prove an effective foil to his level-headed leader in his quest for an amicable solution. The florid description of his blood coming to the boil impresses, the more so as it is rich in literary reminiscence (382-5n.); we must attribute his readiness to be restrained to the new bond of solidarity forged as a result of the above-mentioned altercation: his hot temper had been his undoing on a past occasion, when Jason had disciplined him politely but firmly (for comparison and contrast with Homer there see Faerber 100, Garson 6). Cf. further Hübscher 58, Lawall 137-9, *Noten* 153 n.352.

For this all-important mission Jason assumes the office of herald himself; there can be no question here of an heraldic approach in advance anyway. Aethalides son of Hermes (as it happens no friend of Aeetes, to judge by 588!), who had successfully practised Jasonian μειλιχίη on a previous occasion (i.650), gets another assignment later on, when he follows behind Telamon (πρό: the latter knows the way) to collect the teeth (1172f.). Those who do not like their poetry to convey more than is instantly discernible on the printed page will take no interest in the consideration that Jason, when he presented himself at the palace, will have been clutching an <imposing> σκῆπτρον, an object which is amongst other things a potent symbol of royal authority (cf. Griffin 9f. on the sceptre as an 'inherently significant object' in the Homeric poems): and Aeetes had a thing about σκῆπτρα (376, cf. 597).

196 καὶ τότ' ἄρ' ... See Campbell on Q.S. 12.122.

υἷας Φρίξου See below, and 178n.

υἷας 6 × in Ap., also Antip. Thess. *GPh* 435, Q.S. 13.216, Greg. Naz. 496.13 + 2, Nonn. *D*. 41.75, Max. 440; also 3 × υἷες (all these forms used by Ap. only of the Phrixids, see below), cf. *GVI* 221.3 = *FGE* 1626 (3rd cent. BC; Polemon *ap*. Athen. 436d, cf. Wilamowitz *HD* 1.133 n.3), D.P. 77, 560, Q.S. 2.539. Other case-endings appeared after Ap.: υἷα Nic. *fr*. 110, Greg. Naz. 1487.105, 1524.33, Nonn. *Par*. 13.131, *D*. 33.152. υἷος *Or. Sib*. 11.[251], Kaibel *EG* 862.1 (Eleusis, 'aet. Rom.'). υἷι Greg. Naz. *AP* 8.88.3, Kaibel *EG* 1034.1 (Thrace, Imperial). υἷων Greg. Naz. *AP* 8.118.5. υἱήεσσι(ν) Antip. Thess. *GPh* 467, Greg. Naz. 567.592, Nonn. *D*. 26. 256, Diosc. *GDK* 42.4.18, 42.6.25.

Debrunner, *IF* 53 (1935), 316, compared Hellenistic υἱέως (KB 1.508, LSJ s.v. υἱός 1847(a)7f.). In fact, the forms in Ap. look like straight variations on the familiar short-vowelled types (cf. Vian ed. 1961 ad loc.) υἱέες υἱέας; he uses them in the main to build a 'neo-formulaic' system (178n.). See in general *GG* 1.573-4, Marxer 22.

197 Αὐγείην iii.363, [Theoc.] 25.36, 43, Anon. *AP* 14.4.1, -είης i.172, iii.440, [Theoc.] 25.54, 108, [Orph.] *A*. 214, but Hom. -είας (*Il*. 11.701), though Zenodotus may well have chosen to read -είης (cf. La Roche *HTA* 301-2); however that may be, Ἑρμείης (588n.) could have provided an obvious model for a new 'hyper-Ionism.' On related forms in Ap. see Rzach 438 and more generally West ed. Hes. *Theog*., p. 80.

αὐτὸς .. ἕλεν But *Il*. 9.129 ἕλεν αὐτός/. Ap. recalls a σκηπτουχία of a very different sort: *Il*. 18.416f. Hephaestus ἕλε δὲ σκῆπτρον .. βῆ δὲ ../χωλεύων ...

197-8 Ἑρμείαο/σκῆπτρον Ctr. i.642 σκῆπτρον .. Ἑρμείαο/; but the weighty spondaic clausula is common to both. On father and son see VDB 1.80 n.3, 242, on the σκῆπτρον's various functions the detailed note of Kirk on *Il*. 2.109, along with that of West on *Od*. 2.37 (bibliogr.); of Hermes the θεῶν κῆρυξ specifically: F. J. M. de Waele, *The Magic Staff or Rod in Graeco-Roman Antiquity* (Gent 1927), 33f., Richardson on *Il*. 24.343-5.

198 ἀνὰ Ω ἄρα E. When set against the standards attained in the surrounding lines (viz. 190 ὅδε and ἔπεισε, 192 δέχθαι and ὅστις, 196 *ante corr*. υἷας, 199 χέρσον τ' ἀπεξέβησαν *et al*.) E's conjecture must be reckoned spectacularly good, and it is generally accepted (see outside the commentaries Platt 1914.20 and esp. Vian 1962.37). One might muster support from such runs as iv.661 ἐκ δ' ἄρα νηός/ (= [Orph.] *A*. 373), Q.S. 9.446-7 οἱ δ' ἄρα νηός/.. ἀπέβησαν. But ἀνὰ νηός is certainly what Ap. wrote; it is now adopted in VDB 2². I cite from Campbell 1990.482 (cf. Livrea 1982.20): "There is a studied progression, tersely expressed: 'up onto the ship ... over ... from and out of [scil. νηός cf. iv.246] to *terra firma*'". 'Up onto the ship' here means 'up onto the raised ἴκρια at the stern' drawn up close to the edge (cf. *AH* G99, Kurt 128f., and see in general West on *Od*. 4.785). In iv.78-80 ὁ δὲ κραιπνοὺς χέρσῳ (scil. riverside) πόδας ἧκεν Ἰήσων/ὑψοῦ ἀπ' ἰκριόφιν, disembarkation is described in more athletic terms (cf. iii.1280). Here they move up onto the ἴκρια and thence pass over reeds and water straight onto the raised bank (see on θρωσμοῦ in 199); for the rapid succession of prepositions cf. e.g. supr. 167-8. Fränkel 1950.121 curiously thought that the delegation 'waded ashore through reeds and water'; he was not the first to do so: Hoelzlin (de Mirmont rightly protested) pictured them getting to land *more heroico*.

Ap. gives a novel twist to the Odyssean ἀνὰ νηός, which would have struck him (cf. schol. H at *Od.* 9.177) as a prepositional phrase (cf. Heubeck on *Od.* loc. cit., *LfgrE* s. ἀνά III, p. 743; differently e.g. Haggett 40 n.1, West on *Od.* 2.416). Once again, the Homeric 'fingerprint' is in evidence: *Od.* 9.177 ἀνὰ νηὸς ἔβην coming after Odysseus' πεῖρα-speech (172f.) which Jason has just recalled; id. 2.413 ἕποντο then 415 ἐκέλευσεν then 416 ἂν δ' ... νηὸς βαῖν' ~ Ap. 196/195/198.

δόνακας 6n.

τε καὶ ὕδωρ is a clausula in *Od.* 3.300, al. (ref. ship(s)).

199 χέρσονδ' Homeric hapax, *Il.* 21.238 (ref. river-edge). See LSJ for further examples (note that χέρρονδε is not wholly secure in Alcm. *PMGF* 14(c)); it has been persuasively conjectured in Arat. 950: Ludwig, *Hermes* 91 (1963), 435 n.4, cf. id. 93 (1965), 132. After Ap. only Opp. *Hal.* 1.405 (ἐκβαίνειν, cf. ἐξῄει in *HyAp* 28; James' *Index* is inaccurate).

ἐξαπέβησαν Another Homeric hapax, *Od.* 12.306 ἐξαπέβησαν ../ νηός (cf. on the type Dihle, *Glotta* 63 (1985), 140f.) ~ infr. 326-7; without νηός iv.246. *EtG*^{B}/*EtM* s. χέρσονδε cite anonymously the words χέρσονδ' ἐξαποβάντες: somebody may have remembered infr. 326 as well, though jumbled terminations are rampant in such testimonia.

ἐπὶ θρωσμοῦ πεδίοιο Whatever the precise significance(s) of the expression ἐπὶ θρωσμῷ πεδίοιο/ in *Il.* (10.160, 11.56, 20.3; see Leaf on 11.56, Elliger 48, bibliogr. in *LfgrE* s. θρωσμός), for Ap. it means a raised river-bank on the edge of the plain, i.q. ὄχθη (cf. iv.67 ὄχθησιν ἐπηέρθη ποταμοῖο/, 'she got herself (up) onto the high banks'), πεδίοιο being amplified at once in 200f. The perspective is different in ii.823 ἀνὰ θρωσμοὺς ποταμοῖο/, where Idmon walks along an elevated river-edge and is spotted by a boar which jumps up at him from the screen of δόνακες beneath (against Stephanus' πεδίοιο there see Vian 1973.97; ἰλυόεντος ... ποταμοῖο forms a ring with ποταμοῖο 818/ἰλύι 819, just as ἐλειονόμοι 821 picks up εἰαμενῇ 818 and δονάκων 825 δονακώδεος 818). If Ap. meant to hint at the sort of explanation offered by schol. D at *Il.* 20.3, ὑψηλῷ τόπῳ, ὅθεν ἐστὶ καταθορεῖν, καὶ πηδῆσαι (cf. schol. Ap. ii.823*b* and more explicitly id. iii.199, where Wendel cites a string of similar lexicographical entries), then he has made his readers work hard: in ii.825 the boar jumps up at Idmon who is *on* the θρωσμοί, while here there is no mention at all of 'jumping to shore' (ctr. iii.1280, iv.79-80 cited on 198).

θρωσμός only Hom./Ap., for ΕΠΙΘΡΩΣΜΩΙ in Nonn. *D.* 37.531 must be written ἐπιθρωσμῷ, see Keydell ad loc.

νηός 198 then θρωσμοῦ: ctr. *Il.* 10.160 θρωσμῷ then 161 νεῶν.

200-9 Stranger than fiction? The narrative flow is suddenly arrested by a factual report in uncompromisingly ethnographic mode on the Colchian treatment of male and female corpses. We are projected into the present by means of an unbroken series of verbs that alternate (this is one poem that was not written in a hurry) between present and perfective; an aetiological tag (203) firmly distances us from the characters and the world in which they are moving. So, if the ambassadors can gaze in astonishment at the architecture of Aeetes' palace the moment they set eyes on it (215f.), the weird spectacle presented by Circe's Plain to all intents and purposes passes them by. In terms of level of detachment this passage (which appears to offend Bulloch, 1985.588) goes far beyond even the drily impersonal sequence in ii.964-1029, the θαύματα of which are thrown into the shade by the picture confronting us here (cf. Fusillo 167): while the Argonauts make no contact with a succession of peoples whose modes of behaviour are in various ways abnormal (Amazons, Chalybes, Tibareni, Mossynoeci), some details relating to all but one of them have been provided by Phineus (cf. Beye's analysis, 1982.107-8), and the travellers even come upon a place where certain Amazons with their strange sacrificial practices used to tread (ii.1169f. ~ 385f.). By diverting totally the picture of these extraordinary customs from the world as perceived by the characters in the narrative to the realm of verifiable fact – they persist up to this very moment – Ap. powerfully points up the cultural and behavioural gulf separating Colchian from Hellene. (The partial convergence represented by female interment does little to offset the impression of an alien world; ctr. Rose 1984.120, who considers that 'the mixed nature of their funeral customs ... might be said to anticipate the ambivalent attitude of Aeetes towards Greek conventions of hospitality.') No such gulf is discernible in basic religious outlook. If it is implied (cf. schol. 202-9a *ad fin.*; from Nymphodorus? See below) that Heaven and Earth rank high among Colchian deities (a pointer is provided by Chalciope and Medea in 699, 715-6, cf. Teufel 250 n.6, Fusillo 179 n.15; below on 207f.), it is also the case that Zeus has a firm footing in their scheme of things (to take but two examples, Jason can appeal as a matter of course to 'Olympian Zeus' and his consort in dealing with Medea at iv.95f., and an incensed Aeetes can invoke 'Helios and Zeus' at iv.229); Hermes, who had concerned himself with Phrixus and the ram, also (amongst others) had dealings with Aeetes (iii.587f.); and no action or attribute assigned to Athena, Ares, Hephaestus, Helios or

Hecate in relation to Colchis strikes a distinctively alien note. (See further VDB 2.19.)

The question of the unHellenic treatment accorded to the deceased male will resurface in iv (*Studies* 101 n.3). When the *Colchian* Apsyrtus is murdered, Jason (amongst other things) ἐν γαίη κρύψεν νέκυν (480); ἄγος (478) and θέμις (479) grimly recall key terms in the present passage (203, 205; note also 203 εἰσέτι νῦν ... ~ iv.480, and 204 ἐνὶ γαίῃ). On the general ambience see the suggestive remarks of Beye, 1982.135, with 61-3, 216nn.

The complementary processes of suspension and wrapping of male corpses and of female inhumation, in relation to the concepts of the four sacred elements as influences in the disposal of the dead and of a male Heaven and a female Earth, have been amply documented and discussed, notably by: Gillies on 209; Eitrem, *SO* 21 (1941), 57 with n.; Marconi, *RIL* 76 (1942/43), 309f.; Teufel 236f.; VDB 2.117-8 with Chuvin 331-2; Fusillo 178 n.14; cf. Dräger 206. For further literary treatments in similar vein see VDB loc. cit. Schol. 202-9a identify Nymphodorus (scil. in his Νόμιμα βαρβαρικά, see *RE* 17.1123f.) as the source, as they do also for the Tibareni (schol. ii.1010-4; the extra information could also stem from him) and for the Mossynoeci (schol. ii.1029). We may assume with some confidence that the preceding digression on the Chalybes (ii.1002f.) derived at least in part from him, since we know that his work included an account of Polyphemus' death among this people, a story touched upon by Ap. in iv.1472f., al. (schol. at iv.1472-7; tomb from N.? VDB 3.198, on 1477). The same no doubt goes for some of the Amazonian material (*via* Ephorus, cf. schol. ii.1029 for the connexion): this nation heads the concentration of *ethnographica* at ii.964f.; one may note the recurrent element 'not *x* but *y*,' ii.(987f.) 996/1002f.1006f./1023f., cf. iii.204f. with *Noten* 262-3. See further Walther 72f., Hoefer, *RhM* 39 (1904), 560f., Pearson, *AJPh* 59 (1938), 443f. (arguing for direct use of older sources, including Hecataeus), Fusillo 166f., 180 n.18, Dräger 206 n.178.

Dräger (205f., 315f.) argues implausibly that Phrixus' 'soul' in Pind. *P.* 4.159f. is in fact his mummified body, wrapped in hide, hence the report of Ap. 200f., and specifically in the Fleece itself, suspended as it was on an oak, πρόμαλοι in Ap. 201 being the equivalent of δρύες (p. 207); ii.1194f. ('Ich reise zum Opfer des Phrixos um Zeus' Zorn auf die Aioliden zu erleiden') ~ iii.336f. are to be interpreted on this basis (p.318).

200 Κίρχαιον On the accentuation see VDB *app. crit.* here, and for other references in ancient writers to the Circaean Plain id. 2.117 (on 201). Schol. ii.399-401*a* state that Timaeus referred to it (~ *FGH* 566 *fr.* 84); he may well have elaborated on Circe's links with Colchis in the course of his richly detailed treatment of Argonautic lore, but the surviving schol. cast no light on the matter in any of the numerous notes devoted to her.

The Plain has been mentioned by Phineus at ii.400 (used by D.P., 691f.), as one feature of the Colchian landscape. Only now do we learn that the Argonauts have put in right beside it, since it was not singled out in the arrival scene which partly echoed Phineus' description (ii.1266f.). The name here is tantalisingly pushed into a prominent position (as in i.216 al., see Vian 1962.38): we have to wait a while for elucidation. In the meantime, our expectation that something quite out of the ordinary is going to be presented is fully satisfied.

τόγε δή We now realise that the delegation is indeed about to travel across the very Plain mentioned by Phineus (see above). For the particle combination cf. *Il.* 7.281 τόγε δὴ καὶ ἴδμεν ἅπαντες/, 'that indeed is a fact we all do know,' with *GP* 245, Vian 1962.37; Eudoc. *Cypr.* 2.22 τό γε (τόγε) δὴ καλέουσιν/, in elevated surroundings, perhaps from here or from some other Hellenistic poem. A variation: infr. 1090 /Αἱμονίην δὴ τήνγε .. καλέουσιν/.

The sequence τόγε δή has been convincingly conjectured in Opp. *Hal.* 1.787 (West, *CQ* n.s. 13 (1963), 58); unconvincingly (by Fränkel, *Noten* 479) in iv.345, where Wellauer's supplement provides exactly what is required (cf. Campbell 1976.338, Livrea 1983.422; VDB adopt RQ's τόδε, another poor effort).

τόγε δή has the appropriate ring of authority; τόδε που (Ω, but τόγε δή schol. L *lemm.*, see VDB 1.XLIV for a possible explanation) is altogether too tentative. It would be rash to argue that τόδε που is an authorial variant presupposing a version of the poem in which the Circaean Plain is making its first appearance: if either the γε or the δή dropped out (likely enough), the 'impressionistic' που might well have seemed to somebody on the spur of the moment a reasonable stopgap.

... κιχλήσκεται· ἔνθα ... After *Od.* 15.403 ~ 412.

ἔνθα δὲ πολλαί A clausula in *Od.* 10.529 and in 12.127, in both cases Circe speaking of the weird and the wonderful. See also n. on 176f.(9). In D.P. 1009-10 ... πεδίον .. ἔνθα τε πολλοί/.. φοίνικες .. πεφύασιν/ read ἔνθα δὲ (cf. Tsavari's *app. crit. ad fin.*).

201 ἐξείης "Les arbres sont plantés à la file .... ils constituent une 'allée des tombeaux'" VDB 2.117.

πρόμαλοί ... To take this century's commentaries alone, on offer are: some variety of willow or osier (cf. Hesychius' second try, ἄγνος), or of wild oak (cf. *Et ap.* VDB TEST.; 200-9n.); or tamarisks (Hesychius' first entry); or elms. Gow-Page's note on Nicaen. *HE* 2706f. is to be commended: 'an unidentified tree, probably some kind of willow'; they remark that Theopompus of Colophon (*SH* 765.2) labels it οἰσύϊνον (corr. Kaibel; certain in my view; some doubts (?), Higgins and Winnington-Ingram, *JHS* 85 (1965), 67 n.35; flights of fancy, Giangrande, *MusPat* 4 (1986), 122), and that here in Ap. they are associated with ἰτέαι as in Nicaen. it is associated with λύγος (prob. the withy). So Teufel 252-3, "Keuschlammbäume und Weiden. Beides Weidenarten, sind sie 'unfruchtbare' Bäume, *arbores infelices*"; he provides lavish illustration of, and an extensive bibliography on, such trees in a funereal setting (cf. on ἰτέαι below) in Greek and in other cultures; cf. also H. Rahner, *Greek Myths and Christian Mystery* (London 1963), 286f. on the willow in Christian tradition.

... τε καὶ ἰτέαι *Il.* 21.350 *vulg.* (see Richardson) πτελέαι τε καὶ ἰτέαι ἠδὲ μυρῖκαι/ on river-bank (then πεφύκει/ 352; note πεδίον 348, νεκρούς ibid.), but *Od.* 10.510 (Circe speaking to Odysseus, who is to entreat νεκροί, about 'groves of Persephone') αἴγειροι καὶ ἰτέαι ὠλεσίκαρποι/, viz. ϝιτέαι (cf. Chantraine *DE* s.v.). τε is omitted here by *EtG* s.v. πρόμαλοι, see for discussion Campbell 1973.87; but as *test.* commonly leave out non-essentials and deal roughly with particles in particular, it is wise to stick to the consensus of Ω, even if it is otherwise flawed (πρόμαδοί, ἐκπεφ-). Cf. δ' ἰτείης in iv.1428 (on that: J. Murr, *Die Pflanzenwelt in der griechischen Mythologie* (Innsbruck 1890), 24, Teufel 253, VDB 3.197).

ἐμπεφύασι ἐκ- (Ω) is either the result of miscopying (mu and kappa can look much alike) or of koine influence (ἐκφ- = 'grow,' 'sprout,' cf. ἐκβλαστάνειν sim.). ἐμ- (*test.* but also D, cf. Speake 1969.92/ 1975.109, VDB 1.XLIV) draws on *Il.* 8.83-4 (83 was used recently, see 162n.) ὅθι .... ἐμπεφύασι (ἄκρην 83 ~ infr. 202), where schol. D glosses with a simple πεφύκασι (cf. *Od.* 7.128-9 /ἔνθα δὲ .. πρασιαὶ .../παντοῖαι πεφύασιν). From the most celebrated reporter of βαρβαρικά: trees ἐμπεφύκασι on the island of Chemmis, Hdt. 2.156.3.

202 τῶν καὶ ἐπ' should be preceded by a stop: 'now on the very top of these same trees ...' Cf. e.g. ii.362; and *GP* 294f., Verdenius, *Mnemosyne* 25 (1972), 251.

ἐπ' Against Naber's ἀπ' (which found a hesitant supporter in Seaton, 1908.19) see VDB 2.58 n.5. Yet another slice of self-variation is also relevant: with ἰτέαι ἐμπεφύασι .... ἐπ' ἀκροτάτων ctr. ii.733 πλατάνιστοι ἐπ' ἀκροτάτῃ πεφύασιν/ (after Il. 4.484).

ἀκροτάτων Corpses would normally *lie* on 'top' of a *pyre*, e.g. Sotad. CA 4(b)1 ἐπ' ἄκραισι πυραῖς νέκυες ...

νέκυες The nomin. plur. only once in Homer, Il. 21.302, of floating corpses 'suspended' in flood water.

202-3 σειρῇσι κρέμανται ... adapts and sets in a very different context Zeus' comical proposal to engage in a bizarre tug-of-war, to result in suspension in mid-air (Il. 8.19 /σειρὴν ... κρεμάσαντες/, note 20 ἐξάπτεσθε redeployed infr. 207), though σειραί may well have been specified by Nymphodorus.

δέσμιοι The notion, though not the actual word, derives from archaic verse: Il. 8 again, 26 /δησαίμην scil. the above mentioned σειρήν. '<Actually> fastened' might do justice to the prominent placement of the adjective (cf. 15n.).

203 εἰσέτι νῦν εἰσέτι first in Hellenistic verse, cf. Campbell on Mosch. *Eur.* 19, and also Wackernagel *VS* 2.226. With νῦν very often in aetiological contexts (see Griffiths, *BICS* 17 (1970), 34): cf. (1) εἰσέτι νῦν ii.717, 850, 1145, iv.1153 ~ Phanocl. CA 1.28, [Opp.] *Cyn.* 2.150, Nonn. *D.* 5.277 and *Par.* 5.63, Anon. encom. *GDK* 36.3.22 (5th cent.); (2) /τούνεκεν εἰσέτι νῦν i.1354, iv.534, = D.P. 950, 1029, [Opp.] *Cyn.* 3.80. Call. (*h.* 3.77) has the clausula εἰσέτι καὶ νῦν, for which cf. Antip. Thess. *GPh* 133, Greg. Naz. 1259.75 and *AP* 8.5.5, Anon. *AP* 9.532.1.

ἄγος Another unHomeric word; 'an act of sacrilege': 'To create *agos*, the offence must probably be directed against the gods or their rules' R. Parker, *Miasma* (Oxford 1983), 8; see also Fusillo 179 n.15. The term is complemented by οὐδ' .... θέμις in 204-5, θέμις being employed 'usually with reference to institutions and customs subject to some form of divine regulation,' Richardson on *HyDem* 207 (see 205n.).

The *agos*-theme in relation to disposal of the dead re-emerges in a more vivid and immediate form in iv.478, see n. on 200-9.

ὄρωρεν 59n. The suggestion probably is that cremation is still felt by Colchians to constitute (or presents itself to the enquirer as) an act of sacrilege ('macht sich geltend'? *Noten* 344). ii.312 seems broadly comparable: lit. 'all that has manifested/presented itself as being ...'

Cf. for the wording, from *Il.*: 13.122, 15.400 ... γὰρ .. (νεῖκ)ος ὄρωρεν/, 24.107 (νέκυι 108) (νεῖκ)ος (ἐν ἀθανάτ)οισιν ὄρωρεν/.

204 ἀνέρας οἰχομένους Cf. Triph. 593, Nonn. *D.* 40.130, with Livrea, *RFIC* 104 (1976), 448. Ardizzoni says that this use of the verb is primarily tragic, but the participle occurs thus quite often in the third cent. among the epigrammists, and also in Hermesian. *CA* 7.5, Call. *fr.* 228.73, cf. ii.840.

πυρὶ καιέμεν Q.S. 9.36 corr. (νέκυας). A diluted reading πυρὶ καέμεν (ref. cremation) is offered by a Ptolemaic papyrus at *Il.* 23.183 (West *PP* 182, Rengakos 1993.156; Richardson on 182-3); otherwise: *Il.* 21.361 πυρὶ καιόμενος, 24.38 /ἐν πυρὶ κήαιεν. — Hdt. 3.38.4 τελευτῶντας τοὺς πατέρας κατακαίειν πυρί.

οὐδ᾽ ἐνὶ γαίῃ A common clausula in later verse, e.g. [Orph.] *L.* 517; Hom. ἐνὶ γαίῃ/ (so ii.666, iii.856) and (*Od.* 19.200) οὐδ᾽ ἐπὶ γαίῃ/ (ὤρορε 201).

205 ἔστι θέμις An emphatic inversion (cf. Soph. *Phil.* 662) of the usual θέμις ἐστί, reflecting the reporter's wonderment. On θέμις see 203n. The term has been regularly used of Hellenic religious/funeral observances (Argonauts i.517, 960, 1061 ref. burial, ii.840 id.; Lemniades i.692 id.). Towards the close of the second book the perspective changes, and θέμις becomes a catchword for the inverted values of foreign peoples (ii.1019, 1174, cf. the plur. in 987 and, still earlier, in 17, Amycus: Rose 1984.118f.), an association recalled here right before the point where Jason is to confront a man who, he has asserted (in a roundabout way), will have regard for Ζηνὸς θέμιν (193).

Nymphodorus may well have talked in similar terms: οὐ θέμις is used of a divine sanction in relation to a non-Greek custom by Herodotus, 1.199.4.

The whole sequence is reminiscent in a general way of the account of Idmon's burial in ii: 836 νέκυος, 838 τάρχυον, 840 θέμις and οἰχομένοισι, 841f. κέχυται .. ἀνέρος ἐν χθονὶ ../τύμβος, σῆμα δ᾽ ...

στείλαντας for περιστείλαντας: cf., in connexion with νόμιμα βαρβαρικά, Hdt. 2.90.1 πᾶσα ἀνάγκη ἐστὶ ταριχεύσαντας αὐτὸν καὶ περιστείλαντας ὡς κάλλιστα θάψαι κτλ., and for the linking with cremation (cit. Ardizzoni) Call. *fr.* 194.40-1 χὤποτ᾽ ἂν νεκρόν/μέλλωσι καίειν ἢ [τά]φ[ῳ] περιστέλλει[ν; = *bury* (a corpse *dressed* in the usual fashion, as opposed to the outlandish procedure described in 206): *GVI* 114.4 (Chios, 3rd/2nd cent.), Apollonid. *GPh* 1180, 1199. In [Opp.] *Cyn.* 4.257, 557 στέλλειν rather = *convey* to burial.

ἐπὶ σῆμα χέεσθαι As Greeks (especially Greeks of the heroic age) might do, and as the Argonauts themselves had already done: cf. (these no doubt wholly or partially from Deïochus; Herodorus, Nymphis, Promathidas) i.1060f. burial, games, σῆμα (~ Hdt. 5.8, the well-to-do Thracians either cremate or bury their dead, and χῶμα .. χέαντες they engage in games for prizes), ii.836f. (above), 851f.

For the language ctr. *Il.* 10.466 ἐπὶ σῆμά (τ' ἔθηκε/) (different sense), id. 6.419 ἐπὶ σῆμ' ἔχεεν scil. a cremated body. The active is usual, but cf. Diot. *HE* 1737, *GVI* 1431.1-2 (Athens, 2nd cent. AD).

206 Ap. draws on: (1) *Od.* 20.141-2 (Odysseus refusing the normal comforts provided by a decent bed) /οὐκ .. ἐν .../ἀλλ' ἐν ἀδεψήτῳ βοέη ... (cf. id. 2 ... ἀδέψητον βοέην then ὕπερθε/ ~ Ap. 205); (2) *HyAp* 487 (as a prelude to a religious ceremony) /ἱστία ... κάθετον λύσαντε βοείας [see below]/, *Il.* 18.582 (two lions) -ἐν ἀναρρήξαντε ... βοείην/; (3) *Il.* 17.492 (a pair of fighting men) βοέης εἰλυμένω ὤμους/, id. 21.318-9 (of a grisly burial, where a warrior will never see a heaped-up σῆμα) κὰδ δέ μιν ../εἰλύσω ...

Nonnos possibly imitates our line at *D.* 14.129 /οἱ μὲν ἀδεψήτοισι .. κρύψαντο βοείαις/ (ἀδ. β. several times in the poem).

κατειλύσαντε A clear case of dual for plural, stemming directly from a particular archaic model, *HyAp* above, a modification of the entirely regular ... λῦσαν δὲ βοείας/ in id. 503 (Buttmann emended the subst., probably correctly: Janko 4-5). It is conceivable that the dual participle in i.384 (a certain reading, see VDB *app. crit.*; Ap. varies *Il.* 17.233 οἱ δ' ... βρίσαντες with τοὶ δὲ .... βρίσαντε) was prompted by the consideration that the Argonauts operate in two distinct groups (so Merkel *Proleg.* 104, cf. KG 1.71f., Thornton, *Glotta* 56 (1978), 1f., Rengakos 1993.77), but such an analysis is probably over-refined, here as elsewhere: plural participles follow in rapid succession. For discussion and further examples, real and alleged, see *GH* 2.28f., Livrea ed. Dion. Bass., p. 42, West on Hes. *WD* 186, Janko on *Il.* 13.626-7; (Arat.) Ronconi 201-2.

An amusing piece of rewriting: Naber 23 (different animal-skins, decidedly non-Greek).

207 δενδρέων ἐξάπτειν Shaped like *Il.* 24.51 /ἵππων ἐξάπτων (σῆμ' ibid. ~ Ap. 205). Note also id. 24.397 βοέους δ' ἐξῆπτεν ...

ἑκὰς ἄστεος Deviation from the (heroic) norm is now illustrated by an evocation of a particular case: *Od.* 3.256f., if Menelaus had found Aegisthus alive τῶ κέ οἱ οὐδὲ θανόντι χυτὴν ἐπὶ γαῖαν ἔχευαν,/ἀλλ' ἄρα

τόνγε κύνες τε καὶ οἰωνοὶ κατέδαψαν/κείμενον ἐν πεδίῳ ἑκὰς ἄστεος (v.l.)
... No such stigma could attach to the male dead among the Colchians, who have no tomb heaped over them, and who are located 'on a plain' well away from the confines of the city.

Outside Homer: Eur. *El.* 246 ἄστεως ἑκάς.

207f. ἠέρι δ' ἴσην ... Recalled in iv.1246 -ος ἠέρι ἶσα/ (where *codd.* deliver δ' ἶσα, a foolish attempt to plug an hiatus), with the expected variation: there just 'like sky,' here compendiously (cf. Linsenbarth 59; FJW on Aesch. *Suppl.* 497) 'equal to <that of> air/sky.'

ἠέρι δ' .... χθών But *Od.* 13.352 ... ἠέρα, .. δὲ χθών·/.

ἠέρι/χθών Ap. talks of corpses suspended <in *air*, before the open *sky*> (on ἀήρ see VDB 3.189, on iv.1247¹); but burial in *earth* is also practised. He does not spell out for us here a point made already no doubt by Nymphodorus, whose general approach seems to have been Herodotean (cf. from him e.g. 3.16.2 ἐκέλευσέ μιν (νεκρόν) ὁ Καμβύσης κατακαῦσαι, ἐντελλόμενος οὐκ ὅσια. Πέρσαι γὰρ θεὸν νομίζουσιν εἶναι τὸ πῦρ. Nymph. himself reported that the Sauromatae worshipped fire, *FGH fr.* 14), that Gaia and Ouranos are high-ranking Colchian deities; clarification comes infr. 699/715-6, see 200-9n. From a Greek standpoint Gaia mother of all might naturally be said to receive her due by reclaiming those born from her, viz. the whole of humankind. In this part of the world Gaia takes back only females, because she has to share with Ouranos, regarded by Greeks as 'a sort of pale complement of Ge' (West on Hes. *Theog.* 127), her 'equal' only in spatial terms (Hes. *Theog.* 126, cf. Soph. *El.* 87 γῆς ἰσόμοιρ' ἀήρ, 'having a domain in space, equal to that of the earth' Jebb ad loc.). For the Colchians Gaia and Ouranos enjoy equal status, and so can exercise equal claims by virtue of the kind of apportionment familiar from the Olympian system to each individual of a 'share/sphere of influence': indeed ἔμμορεν αἶσαν recalls supr. 3-4, where αἶσα related precisely to the province assigned to an Olympian goddess. So much at any rate is obvious with the benefit of hindsight. For the moment we might think rather in terms of the equality of status enjoyed by cosmological forces (see G. E. R. Lloyd, *Polarity and Analogy* (Cambridge 1966), 212f.) and in particular about the notion entertained by Empedocles (no stranger to this poem, cf. notably i.496f., iv.672f.; in.) that certain elements were equal, each presiding over a different τιμή (DK31 B17.27f.). There is nothing in any of the surviving fragments of Nymphodorus to indicate that his work possessed the philosophical/cosmological colouring commonly encountered in Hellenistic *ethno-*

graphica (see the survey of A. Dihle in *Fond. Hardt: Entretiens* 8 (1961), 207f.).

ἔμμορεν αἶσαν 3-4n. Hom. ἴση + μοῖρα.

208 ἐπεὶ χθονὶ ἐπὶ χθονὶ Ω: the easiest of errors, as Wellauer noted, but one can only marvel that nobody tried to sort out such an objectionable asyndeton sooner.

χθονὶ ταρχύουσι Ctr. iv.1500 (γαίη, middle). On the verb (not otherwise in 3^H), in Ap. just 'bury,' see Livrea on iv.1500, Kirk on *Il.* 7.85/ Janko on id. 16.456-7.

209 θηλυτέρας *females* as opposed to males (Bion *fr.* 15 provides an instructive example), the importance of *their* role being highlighted by the heavy stop after the word: cf. iv.368 (abbreviating *Od.* 11.434) /θηλυτέραις· *the female sex*, said with deep rancour. On this 'contrasting' comparative see *GH* 1.257, 2.150, and Wittwer, *Glotta* 47 (1970), 57-8. In early poetry it is linked with γυναῖκες; ctr. Ap. above and iv.1345, Matro *SH* 534.83, Call. *fr.* 80.8 (?), Theoc. 17.35 (Gow ad loc.: epigram), Phanocl. *CA* 1.10, Bion above, the Oppians *passim*, Nonn. *D.* often, etc.

Nymphodorus may have specified θήλειαι, cf. in an ethnographic passage Hdt. 4.23.2 ἔρσενες καὶ θήλεαι; and schol. paraphrase, 202-9a.

ἥ ... τέτυκται A high-sounding conclusion: elevated diction has been employed throughout this description of normal routine in Colchis. Lit. 'this is the way of ...' (cf. the examples below and more generally Hoekstra on *Od.* 14.59, H. Lloyd-Jones, *The Justice of Zeus* (2nd ed., Berkeley and Los Angeles 1983), 186-7), i.e. such is the method regularly adopted in executing the procedures prescribed for dealing with the dead. Similar language was used to *preface* an account of the Mossynoeci's unusual *life*-style, ii.1018 ἀλλοίη (an ethnographer's word: Hdt. 2.35.2) δὲ δίκη ('their way(s),' but with one eye no doubt on the 'style of judgement' indicated in 1026f.) καὶ θέσμια ('their established codes of behaviour and institutions'; the term was probably in vogue in Hellenistic poetry of this and related subject-matter, cf. Call.'s use of τεθμός, τέθμιον -ια with Bornmann on *h.* 3.173-4, Hollis ed. *Hecale*, p. 361) τοῖσι τέτυκται.

γάρ τε So Brunck for γάρ κε (cf. the variants at *Il.* 21.24, and West on Hes. *Theog.* 87): this is a *permanent* practice, unchanged to the present day (cf. Ruijgh 1971 *passim*, esp. 720f., 955 with n.8; Russo on *Od.* 18.263). Homeric borrowings: *Il.* 15.383 .../ἲς ἀνέμου· ἡ γάρ τε ... ὀφέλλει/; *Od.* 14.59 (*et sim.*) ἡ γὰρ δμώων δίκη ἐστίν/, 4.691 ἥ τ' ἐστὶ δίκη .. βασιλήων/ ~ 18.275 /μνηστήρων οὐχ ἥδε δίκη ... τέτυκτο/ (~ iv.694 ἥ τε δίκη .. ἱκέτῃσι τέτυκται/ after *Scutum* 85 + *Od.* 4.691 above + 8.546).

Fränkel's γάρ σφι (OCT) can be safely left out of the reckoning, *pace* Lloyd-Jones 1963.157 ('a reference to the women [*sic*] is needed': but Ap. is here summing up, 'of <their> θεσμός').

210-14 Hera in action. For full discussion of the difficulties presented by this interesting passage see Campbell 1974.42-4 (and also id. 1982.15); Rengakos 1993.65-6 offers merely a restatement of the indefensible. In sum, as the text stands, we must assume that as the men make their way over the <empty> plain a screen of mist prevents the vast city-population from 'seeing out,' from spotting them as they approach the confines of the city ('Hera covers Medea's hometown with a mist so that Jason and his henchmen can approach with impunity' Van Nortwick 101). In that case, it is natural to wonder why Ap. has expressed himself as he has in 210-2: the city-mist operates for the duration of the journey over the plain (νισομένοις) en route to Aeetes' palace (κιόντες), and only when the plain has been left behind (213 ἐκ πεδίοιο) is the mist dispersed. On any reasonable reading of the lines (and it is *not* reasonable to brush aside incoherence with an appeal to some peculiar, undisclosed property) the mist has been ousted from its proper place: it should be spread over the plain (δι' ἄργεος) and dispensed with once the men have reached their journey's end, viz. the built-up zone containing the palace complex. iv.645f. (drawing in part on *Od.* 7.14-5, see note on 211) are relevant here: ἀκτὰς .. εἰσαφίκοντο,/Ἥρης ἐννεσίῃσι δι' ἔθνεα μυρία Κελτῶν/καὶ Λιγύων περόωντες ἀδήιοι· ἀμφὶ γὰρ αἰνήν/ἠέρα χεῦε θεὰ πάντ' ἤματα νισομένοισι, they *reached their destination*, passing through *innumerable nations* unscathed, because *Hera* had shed *mist* about them *as they went.* Then there is ii.1204f. to consider: ἀμφὶ δὲ Κόλχων/ἔθνεα ναιετάουσιν ἀπείρονα, scil. around king Aeetes in his city. The delegation must get to the city unscathed, but also without being accosted by anyone (cf. for example *Od.* 7.16f. ~ Virg. *A.* 1.413f.). Hera's plans are well laid, and contribute powerfully to the drama of the situation. They are undetected until *Medea* spots them and reacts sharply – and she has been kept there in the house by none other than Hera herself (250).

Whatever Ap. is getting at, it is not unusual for beneficiaries of such divine assistance to be wholly unaware of it, cf. e.g. Scodel, *TAPA* 114 (1984), 52f.: and so it is here.

210 τοῖσι δὲ νισομένοις But i.53 /τοῖσι δ' ... νισομένοισιν/. The dative plural of this participle (a closed version of the Homeric ἐρχομένοις -οισι(ν)), not attested in early epic, is regularly applied to the seafaring Argonauts: i.556, 601, ii.726, 971, 1246, iv.648, 981. Cf. Nonn. *D.* 12.3 /τῇσι δὲ νισομένῃσι ..., al. It is the source of Virgil's *gradientis* in *A.* 1.411, cf. also *iter* in Val. Flacc. 5.400.

On the orthography (the paradosis strongly supports a single sigma: VDB I.LXXVI) see in general West on Hes. *Theog.* 71, Hainsworth on *Od.* 5.19 (with Ruijgh, *Mnemosyne* 38 (1985), 177), Heubeck on id. 9.58.

Ἥρη Hera's role as solicitous protectress of Jason and the Argonauts (59-60) was never in doubt, but now she is prepared to take an active part in the proceedings. Her interest is underscored by literary reminiscence: like Odysseus' Athena (*Od.* 7.14-5, the hero starting out for the polis), she intervenes to ensure that nobody interferes with her charges' progress as they go determinedly to put their case to the king. See further *Studies* 55. The difference is that, unlike Athena, Hera does not believe in the personal touch: she will certainly not, as she did on a previous occasion (iii.67f.), put herself in the path of her favourite, let alone hold a conversation with him. That does not make her contribution any less meaningful.

φίλα μητιόωσα Not an Homeric turn of phrase; *oppositio*: *Il.* 15.27 Ἥρη κακὰ μητιόωσα/. Later: Nonn. *D.* 31.104 /Ἥρη μητιόωσα, Greg. Naz. 1366.190 claus. pentam. φίλα μητιόων. In the *Odyssey*-model Athena is φίλα φρονέουσ(α) (7.15), as she was at ii.540 (Symplegades-episode); Hera here is appropriately invested with the μῆτις conventionally regarded as *the* attribute of Athena (cf. specifically ... μητιόωσα/ in *Od.* 6.14, 8.9), see above on 24, 30, 34-5.

211 ἠέρα On this haze or 'suspension,' employed by deities in epic, see Kahn 143f., and Renehan, *GRBS* 21 (1980), 108-9. To be compared, and contrasted, with the present passage and with iv.647-8 ἀμφὶ γὰρ αἰνήν/ἠέρα χεῦε θεά are: *Od.* 7.14-6 ἀμφὶ δ' (cf. *Il.* 17.268f., and Hainsworth on *Od.* 7.14-5) Ἀθήνη/πολλὴν ἠέρα χεῦε φίλα φρονέουσ' Ὀδυσῆι,/μή ..., then 18-9 /ἀλλ' ὅτε δὴ ... πόλιν .../ἔνθα ... Ἀθήνη/, 21 /στῆ δὲ ...; *Od.* 13.189-90 περὶ γὰρ θεὸς ἠέρα χεῦε/.. Ἀθηναίη ... ὄφρα..., then 197 /στῆ δ' ...; *Il.* 21.6-7 ἠέρα δ' Ἥρη/πίτνα .. βαθεῖαν ... See also 214n. (ἀπεσκέδασεν).

In the *Argonautica* protective ἀήρ is deployed exclusively by Hera (if we leave aside the self-screening of 275, see n.), as is fitting for one whose very name was associated with ἠήρ/ἀήρ (an element in evidence a moment ago, in a very different context!) both among allegorical interpreters of Homer (including schol. D at *Il.* 15.18; see Erbse on schol. *Il.* 21.6-7, Rank 47-8, F. Buffière, *Les mythes d'Homère et la pensée grecque* (Paris 1956), 106f.) and among philosophers (Scodel, *HSCP* 88 (1984), 19; including Empedocles, probably: see e.g. Longrigg, *CR* n.s. 24 (1974), 173). Ap., like Nonnos (Chuvin on *D.* 6.201, Vian on 29.175-8), nowhere makes the point explicitly. But Hera's tendency as the fourth book progresses to interfere with meteorological phenomena (241f. wind, 294f. meteor, 509f. lightning from aether, 576f. tempests, 640f. cry affecting aether, 753f. a grand weather-director) is in tune with the conception of her as a goddess who can influence atmospheric conditions in a variety of ways, exactly like her sky-god husband: cf. *RE* 8.397-8, and also Pease on Virg. *A.* 4.120, Richardson ed. *Il.* 21-24, p. 42, M. Murrin, *The Allegorical Epic* (Chicago and London 1980), 3f., Feeney, *CQ* n.s. 34 (1984), 184, on Virgil's Juno; the imagery of Aesch. *Suppl.* 165f. is of interest from this standpoint. Indeed, ἐφῆκε (211) has already been applied to Zeus in precisely this capacity (ii.1083, see below).

ἠέρα πουλύν Lifted from *Il.* (but later in the verse, cf. πουλύν in *Il.* 10.27/*Od.* 4.709): 5.776 ("Ἥρη 775), 8.50; Imperial poets also took this up (but only the last denotes divine mist): [Opp.] *Cyn.* 2.594, Man. 5.29, Q.S. 2.195, 11.291.

iv.647-8 αἰνήν/ἠέρα may indicate that Ap. regarded πουλύν in this combination as a feminine pure and simple (for ancient pronouncements see Erbse on schol. *Il.* 5.776*a-b*); cf. πολλὴν ἠέρα in the main model, *Od.* 7.15, and Hom. ἠέρα πολλήν *et sim.* πουλύν is masculine in ii.479, 944 (cf. πουλύς iv.276, and Call. 4 ×). On the form in Homer see *GH* 1.252f., West on *Od.* 4.709, Wyatt 195-6; also West on Hes. *Theog.* 9 (gender of ἀήρ) and 190 (πουλύς generally); Bühler ed. Mosch. *Eur.*, p. 184 with n.1 (gender of ἀήρ in Ap.; erroneous theorizing of Ap. Soph.).

ἐφῆκε δι' Together of course, cf. ii.1083-4 Κρονίδης .. ἐφέηκε χάλαζαν/... ἀνά τ' ἄστυ καὶ οἰκίας, and Campbell 1974.44.

ἄστεος† 210-4n. If ἄργεος is right, then Ap. will be neatly incorporating the variant ΑΡΓΕΟΣ of *Od.* 3.260 (: ΑΣΤΕΟΣ, imitated in 207 above). On the much-discussed ἄργος: Denniston on Eur. *El.* 1 (a controversial line), with e.g. Zuntz, *RhM* 113 (1970), 278f. (in like vein Donzelli, *RFIC* 108 (1980), 385f.); Stanford on *Od.* 24.37; Livrea ed. Dion. Bass., pp. 57-8; Hollis on Call. *Hec. fr.* 116.2; Campbell 1974.44.

ὄφρα λάθοιεν Cf. Antip. Thess. *GPh* 355 (-οιτε), Opp. *Hal.* 2.97 (-ωσι). Ctr. *Il.* 22.282 /ὄφρα ... λάθωμαι/.

212 Κόλχων μυρίον ἔθνος On ἔθνος *nation* linked with a particular people's name see Braswell on Pind. *P.* 4.252(b); a good example, from the late sixth century: *FGE* 694 = *CEG* (1) 179.3. Cf. here (1)(a) ii.1204-5 Κόλχων/ἔθνεα. (b) [Orph.] *A.* 857 /ἔθνος .. Κόλχων. (c) ii.1225, iii.1275, iv.5 ἔθνεα Κόλχων/ ~ Nonn. *D.* 13.248 ἔθνεα βάρβαρα Κόλχων/. (2)(a) *Od.* 11.632 ἔθνε' .. μυρία νεκρῶν/. (b) iv.646 and Simylus *SH* 724.5 ἔθνεα μυρία Κελτῶν/, Emped. DK31 B35.7 & 16 θνητῶν/, Theoc. 17.77 = [Opp.] *Cyn.* 1.166 φωτῶν/ (~ Q.S. 2.124-5 ἔ. φ./μ.), Dion. Bass. 19*r*37 ἔ]θνεα μυρία [Β]άκχων/. (c) Cougny 3.335.9 ἔ. μ. γαίης/.

If μυρίον ἔθνος sounds overstated, it is relevant to remember that one of the principal problems facing the Argonauts is their numerical inferiority: they are the outsiders, a mere handful of men who must survive encounters with whole nations − a point to bear in mind when reading, for instance, the highly elaborate description of the swarms of Colchians in iv.214f.238f. See in general Rose 1984.133. Further: there can be little doubt that the *funereal* atmosphere is being sustained here: the Colchians are past counting, like the dead, cf. *Od.* 11.632 cited above, and also the nn. on 61-3, 216!

ἐς Αἰήταο i.337 (κέλευθοι/).

213 ὦκα The journey has taken little time: VDB 2.17 n.5; ὦκα recurs at 489, the journey back to the ship. Ctr. *Il.* 2.785, 3.14 ... ἐρχομένων· μάλα δ' ὦκα διέπρησσον πεδίοιο.

δ' ἐκ πεδίοιο Cf. infr. 1365 with *Homerica* cited ad loc.; 473 claus. ἐκ πεδίοιο as *Il.* 21.541 (472 /οἱ δ' ... δήμου τε καὶ ἄστεος ἐκτὸς ... ~ 21.540 /οἱ δ' ἰθὺς πόλιος καὶ τείχεος ...).

πόλιν ... ἵκοντο draws on *Od.* 7.46-7 /ἀλλ' ὅτε δὴ βασιλῆος .. δώμαθ' ἵκοντο,/τοῖσι δὲ (apodotic, as δ' infr. 214) ... 'Αθήνη/, but note also id. 4.174 ... κε ... νάσσα πόλιν καὶ δώματ' ἔτευξα/, 10.13 τῶν ἱκόμεσθα πόλιν καὶ δώματα καλά/, *Il.* 3.421 /αἱ δ' ὅτ' .. δόμον .. ἵκοντο/ *et sim.*

213-4 δώμαθ' .. Αἰήτεω, τότε As Jason and his party reach the final destination of the outward voyage, Ap. recalls i.244-5 ... δόμους .../Αἰήτεω, ὅτε ..., words setting out a scenario that is far removed from the present reality.

214 τότε δ' αὖτις From *Il.* 11.63 (note .. νέφεα, πεδίοιο 56), where however δ' is a connective.

ἀπεσκέδασεν νέφος occurs in Triph. 37, but νέφος is there used metaphorically; note however the use of ἀποσκεδάσας νέφος in Nonn.

D. 2.662. The Homeric models are *Il.* 17.649 (Zeus) /αὐτίκα δ' ἠέρα .. σκέδασεν, *Od.* 13.352 (Athene) θεὰ σκέδασ' ἠέρα. There is a trace here of the notion that this goddess can influence weather conditions: see on 211, comparing infr. 1360 ἀπὸ .. νεφέλας ἐκέδασσαν ἄελλαι/ with Solon quoted there, *Il.* 5.525-6 ἀνέμων οἵτε νέφεα .... διασκιδνᾶσιν, σκίδναθ' in id. 16.375, διεσκέδασ' in *Od.* 5.370, 7.275, etc.

ἀπεσκέδασεν = *Il.* 19.309, but the context is quite different. Cf. the screening νέφος in *Il.* 23.188, drawn by Apollo πεδίονδε, νεφέλη in id. 5.345, al.

215f. The spectacle of the palace.

A After a rapid and uneventful journey from ship to palace, we look forward to the all-important encounter with Aeetes. We have to wait a while for that, but the poet is well-versed in the art of effective retardation. As we wait, we begin at last to build up a picture of this foreign king and his environment, with its blend of impressive regal splendour and weird, menacing other-worldliness. The newcomers, Phrixids included, are stunned by what they witness, as well they might be: to a considerable degree they are viewing, here ἐπὶ πείρασι γαίης, a world familiar to the narrator's audience. A truly tongue-in-cheek case of 'back to the future.' (See further on 216.) We are also made privy (as Jason evidently has not been) to a piece of information which indicates that Aeetes is indeed a man to be reckoned with, for he has at his disposal horrific agents of destruction (230f.), which Jason will have to encounter before he goes anywhere near the monstrosity reported by Argos in ii.1208f. In addition, there is a reminder (cf. Argos in ii.1204) of Aeetes' parentage, the father gaining a mention here against a backdrop of immense devastation and carnage, involving adversaries the like of whom have not yet been removed from the face of the earth; 'Phlegraean,' with its dire associations, reappears tellingly in the run-up to Jason's combat in 1227. 245-6 also evoke a picture of violent death (cf. the note). See further Fusillo 295-6.

The catalogue of Aeetes' family connexions (239f.) provides us for the first time with a composite picture of the royal household: Aeetes, wife, son, daughters are introduced to us through the medium of the narrative. Perhaps we are to imagine that Argos acts simultaneously as informant (like Athena in *Od.* 7.53f., see below) as they view the exteriors of the various rooms; 'you've heard about Medea from me before' says Argos to Jason at 477f., to the delight of narratologists (see n.).

B The palace description. Thiel 106f. needs to be approached cautiously, Manakidou 157f. is not very informative. Most helpful on particular aspects are Gillies, ed. pp. 135-6 (diagram; but wide of the mark in one or two respects), Vian ed. 1961 on 215f. and 235, VDB 2.118-9 (esp. on 217, 218, 235, 239), cf. now id. 2^2.152-5; the 'garden' etc.: Elliger 306-7; general approach: Fowler 1989.170-1.

(1) Perspective. We begin by viewing the scene through the eyes of the visitors (215f. cf. Elliger 307 with n.1; also Otis 1963.65, but his appraisal is coloured by his ill-disguised contempt for Ap.). They are still within our sights when they cross the threshold (219), but by the time the description of 219f. has run its course we have lost them, almost: Hephaestus created θέσκελα ἔργα (229; ~ τεθηπότες 215), for them as for us. After the 'appendix' of 230-4 they disappear totally, as the poet in severer style records the layout of the royal apartments and reports on family-history (no vocal goddess hereabouts, though see above). With οἵγε in 248 we suddenly rejoin the heroes, three of whom encounter Medea (fleetingly) for the first time.

(2) Discussion of individual details will follow in due course. A brief outline:

(a) The party stop before the palace, at its frontage or main entrance. From this vantage-point they observe:

(b) outside walls with main gates and an exterior colonnade (cf. 216-7n., and Gerbeau on Nonn. *D.* 18.81-4) encircling the whole palace-complex and surmounted by a stone θριγκός affixed to bronze γλυφίδες (on these terms see below).

(c) They cross the threshold and pass into the open courtyard; in the vicinity of the entrance are vines shading fountains.

(d) (235f.) As we pass through the entrance-gates we see directly ahead, but some distance away (cf. below) a central door of forged metal (? bronze) affording access to the megaron, and near it, to either side, a number of wooden double doors fronting (bed)chambers, with a decorated portico running the entire length of the wall.

(e) Located transversally, to right and to left, are (two) taller buildings housing the male royals, with Aeetes' towering above that of his son.

C The palace-area in the sequel.

(1) Little importance is attached in this poem to the nerve-centre of Homeric palace-life, the 'high-roofed' megaron where Eros shoots Medea (280f.). It is the place where guests are entertained; it is here (the passage of the assembled company into the room is simply assumed) that Jason and his party receive an increasingly chilly re-

ception. We nowhere gain the impression that Aeetes' megaron has that 'lived-in' look.

(2) The open courtyard (in which no altar to Ζεὺς Ἑρκεῖος may be seen) is witness to some of the action. Medea is there in 249f. (see below). Chalciope meets her sons there after she has run out <of her apartment: cf. 255/249> (her spinning δμωαί likewise: it looks as if they steer clear of the main hall). Aeetes and his queen first come across the visitors 'out of doors' (cf. 268) after emerging <? from the megaron; ? from their royal apartments>. It is spacious enough to accommodate a throng of servants who prepare a lavish meal (270f.).

(3) πρόδομος and οὐδός. A πρόδομος (not specified in the initial description) fronts (a) the megaron. Eros stands there ὑπὸ φλιήν scil. μεσσαύλου (278n.) then crosses the threshold (280) to shoot Medea, who is not such a recluse, today at any rate (cf. 250f.) as to absent herself from the main hall; (b) Medea's bedchamber, one of the θάλαμοι of 236 (cf. 247-8n.). In 647 she crosses ἕρκεος οὐδόν, scil. the threshold of her bedroom leading to the courtyard, but in 648 she stops in the πρόδομος, where her maidservants pass the night (839).

(4) The main centres of activity in the palace are of course the bedrooms (θάλαμος -οι, less often δόμος -οι) of the two sisters, with which the present account closes (249, with emphatic repetition, an early indication of intrigues to come: cf. esp.671; Natzel 46). To get from one bedroom to another it is necessary first to step out into the courtyard. This is where Medea spots the newcomers (253).

Medea's 'fragrant' (iii.839) chamber has double (iv.26 ~ iii.236) doors which may be bolted from the inside (iii.822); a glimpse of its furniture: in addition to the bed, a σφέλας κλιντῆρος ἔνερθεν (iii.1159); bed, doors, walls (~ iii.633): iv.26-7.

D Although Ap. shops around to produce a suggestive amalgam of Homeric scenes, the main point of reference must still be the opening episode of *Odyssey* 7. There Odysseus is on his way to Alcinous' palace, escorted by Athena, who shrouds him in mist (14f.). At 81f. he goes Ἀλκινόου πρὸς δώματ'. Like Jason and his men he pauses before crossing the threshold to take in the view. For Odysseus, who marvels (133,134), there is a true feast, as he 'stands' there (83). We are happy to sit back while he takes in more than can possibly lie within his range of vision: a gleam over the 'high-roofed' house, with lavish use made of bronze, enamel, gold, silver; miscellaneous noteworthy sights; then, 'outside the courtyard,' a cultivated area with trees, a wine-producing vineyard, vegetable-beds and finally a pair of fountains: the one irrigates the plants, the other supplies the townspeople (as well as the palace) with fresh water.

Jason and the rest are astounded by the sheer scale and symmetry of what they see: no flashes of light, no superabundance of precious metals, no variety of form. There is nobody at work on the vines: they are decorative, forming a canopy to shade the four fountains (Aeetes has an unfailing alternative source, 224 init.). In this strange (cf. Thiel 114 n.1) and cloistered world the marvellous fountains (which evoke memories of other Homeric *exotica*) are plainly for the benefit of the palace-élite: we are going to have to wait for our benign Alcinous, though *his* palace is not of course going to form part of the picture. The renewed description of 235f. reinforces the overall impression of vastness, but symmetry gives way to dissymmetry as we are confronted with taller, grander edifices for the heads of the royal family.

Lastly, there is Hephaestus. His contribution to the splendour of Alcinous' palace is no more surprising than Athena's interest in the activities of the womenfolk (110f.) – the Phaeacians are ἀγχίθεοι. Ap. has to offer an explanation for his presence here in Colchis: he acted not out of benevolence but to repay a debt (233-4). And while the bronze γλυφίδες of 218 sound innocuous enough (on the surface at any rate), the bronze creations of the χαλκεύς-god strike a sinister note: these bulls are creatures far more formidable and suggestive of brute violence than the watchdogs of Alcinous' palace, cf. Pavlock 52-3 (Elliger 307 n.4, putting the bulls in the wrong place, treats the passage as if it were a museum guide).

E Virgil's imitation (*A*. 1.411f.), which extends far beyond the arrival-episode (Ilioneus is a partial reincarnation of Argos, for example), is well-known; there, as in *Od*., a bustling scene greets the gaze: Aeetes' palace is as still as a graveyard.

Val. Flacc. 5.399f. reshapes the mist-accompanied journey: pictorialism runs riot, with remarkably instructive double doors (developing the god's efforts in Sol's palace, Ov. *Met*. 2.4f., on which consult Knox, *CQ* n.s. 38 (1988), 542-3) and a curiously prescient Mulciber.

Nonn. *D*. 3.124f. owes more to Homer than to Ap., though he too makes a point of harmonizing Odyssean *exotica* with the latest fashions (see the Budé ed., pp. 4-5, 139); cf. the blend in the more Apollonian *D*. 18.62f. (with Gerbeau, ed. p. 14).

215 Memories of *Od*. 7: 3-4 (but not the hero) ὅτε ... δώμαθ' ἵκανε,/στῆσεν ἄρ' ἐν προθύροισι, cf. 46-7 (213n.); 83 Odysseus ἰσταμένῳ,

133 στὰς θηεῖτο, 134 θηήσατο (at the *close* of the description; Ap. thrusts the onlookers' reaction to the forefront and in so doing expresses himself more economically, Elliger 306 n.1). The actual wording however owes more to *Od.* 8.325, 10.220 (Circe: cf. Thiel 112f.) /ἔσταν δ' ἐν προθύροισι, and to id. 24.392 (stunned reaction to appearance of Odysseus) /ἔσταν ἐνὶ μεγάροισι τεθηπότες (προμολοῦσα 388).

'They (etc.) took their stand' is a regular ingredient of archaic visiting-scenes: Arend 28f., cf. 39-40 above; Ovid redeploys it, *Met.* 2.22 (*consistit*). Their stopping ἐν προμολῇσι (see in general Hainsworth on *Od.* 7.50-1; for present purposes they are *all* represented as complete strangers) perhaps arouses the expectation that somebody will *emerge* and see them in (cf. προμολών in *Od.* 4.22 following right on from 20f. ἐν προθύροισι δόμων ..../στῆσαν, and see below). In the event, after taking in the sights they proceed unchallenged into the courtyard (219).

προμολῇσι The only known subst. in -μολή, first in Hellenistic verse (VDB 2.118 adduce Ar. *Ran.* 1333, but that is conjectural; in Archestr. Gel. *SH* 171.3 προχοαῖσι† Ribbeck's προβολαῖσι is preferable to Meineke's προμολαῖσι). Its origin is unknown. 'Possibly a v.l. (or Alexandrian emendation) at *Il.* 18.382' (scil. προμολοῦσα to greet a visitor), Griffiths 174. Perhaps the use of this actual verb both here and in *Od.* 4.22 in association with a house-front (see above) suggested a subst. προμολή -αί, 'exit-/entrance-point,' 'vestibule,' as a variation on πρόθυρον -α.

Distribution and applications. See in general Vian 1969.168-9 (range), 1970.83 (glosses of schol. Ap.; conj. in i.128), Livrea on iv.1160, *LexCal* s.v.

(1) In Ap. Here, as in i.1174, *entrance* to, *frontage* of a building. So iv.1160 grandiosely of a cave serving as a bedchamber ('devant le seuil nuptial' VDB). Similarly i.260 (cf. Seaton 1905.453, who stresses the concreteness of the word in this poem; Mooney ad loc. insists that 'a going forth' must be 'the primary sense'), 'at the palace-front, as <the heroes> were departing' (the subject of a genitive absolute containing a verb of motion is often not expressed: Bühler on Mosch. *Eur.* 115, Braswell on Pind. *P.* 4.232(a)), followed up with a look inside the palace itself; hardly 'at the issuing forth of them as they went.' i.320 (where Fränkel opted for ἐπιπρομολών in his OCT; obviously a conjecture) is more problematic. Perhaps 'le faubourg du port' (Vian 1969.139), cf. Chamoux 337 n.2, 'sur l'esplanade où ils [Argonauts] vont se rassembler autour de lui [Jason]'; perhaps (cf. de Mirmont) 'Jason took up position at the gangway' <of Argo, just specified>, to

which point the main company thronged, then (329f.) 'there on the ship they sat down for an assembly.' The former is on the whole preferable. Other interpretations in Mooney ad loc., Robinson 173, Gillies on iii.215.

(2) Elsewhere. (a) As above: Arat. 239 (v.l.) νότοιο see Martin's note; Call. *h.* 3.142 (reception-scene); Colluth. 310 (v.l.) πυλάων of Troy; similarly in all probability Antip. Sid. *HE* 334 v.l. (cf. Gow-Page ad loc., and Wifstrand 1928.2554), a town's *outskirts* or *approaches* (? i.q. προάστια). (b) *approaches* to, *foothills* of a mountain: Call. *h.* 3.99, Damag. *HE* 1379; (c) river-*mouth*: [Opp.] *Cyn.* 2.134 v.l. (other interpretations in Gualandri 162 n.49).

There are thus remarkably few post-Hellenistic examples of what is clearly a useful-looking word. In Imperial verse from time to time one encounters προβολ(ή) where a Hellenistic poet might have written προμολ(ή); occasionally no doubt the latter has been supplanted by the more familiar, prosaic-sounding form. Cf. Gualandri 162f. on the problems posed by D.P. 1013 (προβ-) and 1118 (προμ-, v.l. προβ-), προμ-Müller in both places (προβ- in the one, προμ- in the other now Tsavari).

τεθηπότες On the recurrent motif of astonishment at the sights see Gerbeau on Nonn. *D.* 18.91-2 (and id., p. 18 with n.4). Ap. employs a strong term (Heubeck on *Od.* 23.91-3, 105-7; Blanc, op. cit. on 123 above, 38f., 47f.), picked up by Virgil in *A.* 1.495, *stupet.* Cf., in addition to *Od.* 24.392 above, *Il.* 4.243, 246 (annoyed Agamemnon to slackers) ἔστητε τεθηπότες, 'dazed,' 'stupefied' like fawns (ἐκπεπληγμένοι schol. D, cf. schol. b at 243-5a[2] with Erbse ad loc.), and ctr., in arrival-scenes, *Il.* 11.776, *Od.* 16.12 /στῆσαν (ἔστη) ἐνὶ προθύροισι· ταφὼν δ' ...

τεθηπότες + accus.: 'Ap. insolenter obiectum addit' Linsenbarth 8; but *Od.* 6.168 σέ .. ἄγαμαί τε τέθηπά τε ... may have been so construed (Ardizzoni). For later examples see LSJ; quite often in Imperial verse, Q.S. 4.491 al., Nonn. *D.* several times (cf. Chrétien on 10.426), etc.

ἕρκε' ἄνακτος So Greg. Naz. 1493.182 ἄνακτος .. ἕρκεσι. — ἄνακτος: here is a picture of true regal splendour (see also 216n.).

ἕρκεα: hardly the courtyard enclosure (cf. VDB 2.118, on 217): they are the exterior walls of the enclosure, or rather (though only the front is viewed at this moment) the περίβολος of the entire palace-complex. Conversely, the plural is applied at iv.665, ἕρκεα πάντα δόμοιο/, to the interior walls of Circe's dwelling (ἑρκία needlessly Platt 1914.44; Fränkel's interpretation, *Noten* 521, is untenable): '<all> her apartments and every wall in the place ...' In a third case of the plural in the poem, the sense is 'courtyard area' (supr. 39).

216 εὐρείας .. πύλας Expected (Gerbeau on Nonn. *D.* 18.85-6), and imposing, but more than that: '*wide* gates' would have conjured up associations extending beyond mere dimensions and grandeur. The dwelling of *Hades* is 'wide-gated' (*Il.* 23.74, *Od.* 11.571), scil. to receive its multitudinous 'guests' (!), cf. e.g. Soph. *OC* 1570 corr., with FJW on Aesch. *Suppl.* 157; Diot. *HE* 1740 εὐρείας ... πύλας ('of Hades' to be supplied by the reader: Gow-Page ad loc.; see on these gates West on Hes. *Theog.* 741, Hainsworth on *Il.* 9.312, NH on Hor. *Carm.* 1.24.17, Clark Index s. 'Gate-entrance ...'); Virg. *A.* 6.552 *porta .. ingens* (+ pillars), etc. In fact, 215-6 look as if they are based on the onlooker's astounded reaction to the royal αὐλή (NH on Hor. *Carm.* 2.18.31) of the ἄναξ πολυδέγμων: there can be very little doubt that Ap. is refurbishing a scene from a *catabasis*-poem (? *Minyas* cf. i.101f., with Lloyd-Jones 1990, 1.186). See in general 61-3n., and J. Fontenrose, *Python* (Berkeley and Los Angeles 1959), 486: '(Aeetes) is plainly the infernal ruler'; Robert 760 n.2. [Crane 1988.37 made the interesting suggestion that by virtue of the description of Achilles' living quarters in *Il.* 24.448f. with its mention of a heavily bolted door (not gate, as Crane says; but see also the barrier at 446) the hero 'has come to resemble a lord of the dead.' For more in this vein see Van Nortwick 79.]

Aeetes' magnificent palace then possesses entrance 'gates,' with θύραι for internal apartments (ctr. πύλαι in Homer: Lehrs 124f., Williams on Call. *h.* 2.6): of Medea's bedroom infr. 645 θύρας (scil. δικλίδας: iv.26), 822; iv.41: the witch Medea is not kept under lock and key (cf. Dyck, *Hermes* 117 (1989), 456), but the by now deeply suspicious Aeetes (iv.9f.) will have bolted the bedroom door on the outside to keep his daughter in; cf., from an *Iliad*-episode lurking in the background hereabouts, 9.475f. the flight of Patroclus, who however had to resort to *brute force* to make good his escape *via* the θαλάμοιο θύραι. Some translate <palace-> 'gates'; they are mistaken. — In i.786 θύρας (Π⁸E) is now generally preferred (Zumbo 1975.351 wavers) to Ω's πύλας; Piñero (*StudPap* 14 (1975), 117) suggests contamination from -πύλης at the start of the line. Ap. is talking however about the gates of the splendid (785) palace through which Jason is conducted to Hypsipyle (-πύλης ... πύλας as he gains access to her, see on the imagery Beye 1969.44) *via* a *pastas* (on that: VDB 1.87 n.1); he draws on *Il.* 21.537 + (gate-leaves) 12.453-5/18.275 etc. (see *Echoes* on 786-7).

(-ας) τε πύλας καί An Iliadic run (5 ×), but always later in the verse.

216-7 καὶ .... ἄνεχον Pace Platt 1918.135-6 (an uncommon display of pedantry this), ἄνεχον is intrans. (as in ii.964 proecd., iii.851, 1383, iv.310): the model is *Od.* 19.38 ... τε .. καὶ κίονες ὑψόσ' ἔχοντες/... (θαῦμα 36, τοῖχοι 37); schol. V's entry at 37 should not pass unnoticed: ... τῶν κιόνων (!) .. οἵτινες (!) ἦσαν περὶ (!) τοὺς τοίχους (!) ...

We are to picture not an internal peristyle, but an external colonnade, 'tout autour de l'édifice, ou plutôt fait partie des propylées du palais' Vian ed. 1961 on 215f., cf. VDB 2².152, and see above on 215f., B(2)(b).

κίονας ... τοίχους But *Od.* 23.90 τοίχου then κίονα.

... περὶ τοίχους / ἑξείης -εχον .... ἀρήρει Ctr. *Od.* 2.341-2 (/ἔστασαν 341 init.) ... ἔχοντες,/ἑξείης ποτὶ τοῖχον ἀρηρότες, and *Il.* 18.374, *Od.* 7.95 περὶ τοῖχον. — ἑξείης last appeared in a very different context (201), and perhaps we are meant to recall that, given the resonances detected in 215-6.

217-8 θριγκὸς .... ἀρήρει adapts *Od.* 7.86-7 (Alcinous' megaron) /χάλκεοι ... τοῖχοι ἐληλέατ' ἔνθα καὶ ἔνθα,/ἐς μυχὸν ἐξ οὐδοῦ, περὶ δὲ θριγκὸς κυάνοιο: certain elements are scattered (χάλκεοι: 218; τοῖχοι: 216; ἐληλέατ', a variant, and ἔνθα καὶ ἔνθα/: 235-6 ἐλήλατο then ἔνθα καὶ ἔνθα/; οὐδοῦ: 219; περί: 216); cf. also Odysseus' αὐλή at *Od.* 17.266-7 and Eumaeus' at 14.10 ('stones'), along with *LfgrE* s.vv. θριγκός, θριγκόω, Gillies here. On θριγκός in this line see VDB 2.119 (on 218), now supplemented by id. 2².152 in the light of the paper by F. Chamoux; for γλυφίδες, generally taken to mean *capitals* (Corinthian capitals, either entirely of metal or with metal ornamentation, both features of contemporary palaces and other grand establishments: Roux 86-7) cf. now VDB 2² loc. cit.: Chamoux 338f. suggests rather 'une frise à triglyphes que couronnait la corniche.' Their new translation: 'au faîte du bâtiment, une corniche de pierre s'ajustait sur une frise ciselée de bronze.' (VDB adopt L's θριγχὸς, citing Diosc. 4.85 [v.l.]. Given the uncertainty attaching to the form in the post-Hellenistic era it is better to go for the standard spelling.)

θριγκὸς .../λαΐνεος Despite Eur. *El.* 1150-1 [see in general Manakidou 166] λάϊνοι .. θριγκοὶ δόμων, δόμοιο here is plainly governed by ἐφύπερθε (ctr. Gillies): cf. the translation above, and that of Roux loc. cit.: 'l'entablement [but see above] couronnant la bâtisse'; ἐφ. +

gen., post-Homeric: cf. in this poem ii.393, iv.1708; 3^H: [Mosch.] *Meg.* 74 (f.v.l. in Simias *CA* 1.10).

Livrea 1982.20 cites Archil. *IEG* 196a21 θρ]ιγκοῦ .. ἔνερθε καὶ πυλέων, but I doubt if this served as Ap.'s model.

λαΐνεος An Homeric hapax (*Il.* 22.154, preceded by εὐρέες, cf. Ap. 216), also in ii.386, where it is also postp. and first word in the verse: so λάϊνον in i.668 (... ὦρτο ~ *Il.* 12.178 ὀρώρει ..., cf. *Od.* 13.106). The use of the epithet here raises an interesting possibility. Hereabouts (in keeping with the general ambience of 215f., explained above) Ap. certainly has in his head Hes. *Theog.* 809f.: 809 /ἐξείης, 811 τε πύλαι καὶ χάλκεος οὐδός/, 812 -ῃσι -εσσιν ἀρηρώς/. In 811 there is a variant ('probably ... ancient' West ad loc.) λάϊνος. Perhaps the juxtaposition of 'stone' and 'brazen' indicates that Ap. is having a bite at both.

χαλκέῃσιν .. -εσσιν ἀρήρει Ctr. *Il.* 11.31 χρυσέοισιν -εσσιν ἀρηρός/.

χαλκέῃσιν In Alcinous' exceptionally metallic palace bronze is used in abundance: *Od.* 7.83, 86, 89, 13.4, cf. on its employment Wormell, *Hermathena* 58 (1941), 116f., Förstel, *RhM* n.s. 115 (1972), 116 nn.85-6, Hainsworth on *Od.* 7.83, 86, 8.321, West on Hes. *WD* 150. This metal is specified only here as an architectural feature, one that reflects (with cosmic overtones) contemporary practice. But bronze symbolism, lacking any suggestion of innocuous regal splendour and hinting at a dark and sinister world, will presently distance Aeetes more positively from his heroic environment: see the note on 230f.

γλυφίδεσσιν See above, first note on 217-8; for the standard interpretation *capitals* see the testimony of *EtM/EtG/*schol.: Vian ed. 1961 on 215f., Wendel ed. schol., entry on 218 with n. ad loc. Nonnos was to incorporate this term in his description of the κῆπος ἀνάκτων, *D.* 3.182 ('reliefs,' cf. Wifstrand 1929.90).

219 εὔκηλοι ... ἔβαν ἔσταν, followed up with '*then* ἔβαν': this deliberately expressed progression signals a departure from the main Homeric model: Odysseus stands outside looking at the view (or some of it), and only after playing the role of sightseer ὑπὲρ οὐδὸν ἐβήσετο (*Od.* 7.135).

Ap. here makes use of: (1) *HyHerm* 480 /εὔκηλος .. ἔπειτα ... (2) *Od.* 4.674, 16.407 ἔπειτ' .. ἔβαν δόμον εἰς ... (3) *HyHerm* 380 ὑπὲρ οὐδὸν ἔβην (= [Orph.] *A.* 988).

εὔκηλοι Hardly 'silent(ly)' (Gillies, so also e.g. Fowler 1990, 'quietly'; Thiel 113) or 'with peace of mind, unconcernedly' (so apparently

Fantuzzi 148) or 'recouvrant leur sang-froid' (Roux cited above) but (physically) 'unimpeded' ('unchallenged' Rieu, similarly some others). VDB (2.119) cite i.568; van Krevelen (1953.51 n.2) Q.S. 13.48, a wolf having escaped the notice of herdsmen and dogs βαίνει ποσσὶν ἔκηλος ὑπὲρ ποιμνήιον ἕρκος. So also, e.g., *Il.* 1.554 ('without interference on my part,' Cunliffe *LHD* s. εὔκηλος), id. 17.371 ('unbehindert' *LfgrE*), iv.61 ('undisturbed'), 1778 ('encountering no obstacles'), Theoc. 17.97 ('free of the distraction of enemy attack'). As nobody has emerged to meet them (215n.) they can proceed without let or hindrance.

ἄγχι δὲ τοῖο Ctr. *Il.* 17.10, *Od.* 21.433 ἄγχι δ' ἄρ' αὐτοῦ/; ii.94 = *Il.* 17.300 ὁ δ' ἄγχ' αὐτοῖο π-. The layout is compact: the vines, which are close to the courtyard entrance and inside it (cf. ἐνὶ μεγάροισι at 228), can be taken in at a glance. Ctr. *Od.* 7.112, the orchard is outside the αὐλή, and covers a wide area, scanned by the poet's roving eye. (Elliger 306 gets this wrong.)

220f. A new literary borrowing, this time from the description of Calypso's dwelling in *Od.* 5.68f., ἡ δ' αὐτοῦ τετάνυστο περὶ σπείους γλαφυροῖο/ἡμερὶς ἡβώωσα, τεθήλει δὲ σταφυλῇσι ... (Ap.'s ἐθήλεον is drawn from a later line, θήλεον 73); then, the κρῆναι: ἐξείης πίσυρες ῥέον ὕδατι λευκῷ,/πλησίαι ἀλλήλων τετραμμέναι ἄλλυδις ἄλλη. The episode from which these details are derived has already been signalled in 46 and 108f. (see nn.); a sharp echo of Hermes' address to the goddess will be put into Jason's mouth at 388f. For the present we might recall the (apparently) idyllic setting of Calypso's home, and perhaps also the wider context (Hermes is there on an errand, with a specific request): Jason is entering a positively menacing world, and he will not find his host compliant.

The vines, the four fountains. As so often in the poem, the old (in the form of literary reminiscence) and the modern (reflection of contemporary practices) are blended. Calypso's vine seems free-ranging, and to all appearances does not form a canopy over the close group of fountains specified in 70f.: our eyes are taken outwards, as they evidently irrigate all four corners of the island. Ap. may have thought differently (cf. on καταστεφέες in 220): the vines here are clearly associated with the fountains (221 fin.), which they overarch. We may discern in this picture Hellenistic interest in artificial bowers/caves of the broad type described by Webster, 161f.: vines/Dionysus, manmade fountains of milk/wine; from a grotto in the Procession of Ptolemy Philadelphus ἀνέβλυζον ... καὶ κρουνοὶ δύο, ὁ μὲν γάλακτος, ὁ δὲ οἴνου reports Athenaeus, 200c, cf. E. E. Rice, *The Grand Procession of*

Ptolemy Philadelphus (Oxford 1983), 82; various fragrant substances in other contexts: id. 46, 93. Here then, presented in a highly stylised fashion in keeping with Ap.'s strictly businesslike approach to botanical specimens (Köhnken 46 n.3), is an artificial bower overarching artificial fountains – but the last of these proves (so we are led to suppose, ποθι) even more miraculous than the fantastic products of modern artists and artisans.

220 On the *versus tetracolos* (a stylish bower this) see in general Hopkinson on Call. *h.* 6. 87, and Griffiths, *CQ* n.s. 22 (1972), 108.

Köhnken (11-12), using *Il. Parv. EGF fr.* 6.2 as a base, speculates on the relationship of this verse (and of i.1117/1121, iii.928) to Theoc. 7.(8-)9 (below), and concludes that Ap. must be drawing on Theoc., in all three cases. But (assuming that the five passages represent all the data necessary for an accurate evaluation) too much stress is placed on constituents which might have occurred to either poet independently (for instance, αἴγειρος/-οι in conjunction with κομόωσα/ -αι) and not enough stress on manipulation of the specific archaic model. Thus here ἡμερίδες (a hapax in the poem, matching the Homeric hapax ἡμερίς *Od.* 5.69) varies ἄμπελον of *Il. Parv.* verse 1, ἃς ../Ἥφαιστος echoes οὓς Ἥφαιστος of id. verse 3; into the mix go two commonplace elements (χλοερός and clausular πετάλοισιν are both frequent in Hellenistic verse) and one choice epithet (καταστεφής known only from here during this period, and serving to elucidate *Od.* 5.68-9, as is explained below).

χλοεροῖσι καταστεφέες πετάλοισιν Theoc. 7.9 (cf. above) χλωροῖσιν πετάλοισι [cf. in *HE*: Anyt. 735, Nic. 2770, Pamph. 2839, Simias 3277] κατηρεφέες [cf. [Orph.] *A.* 914] κομόωσαι ~ infr. 928, Nic. *fr.* 74.24 /χλωροῖς .. ἐπηρεφέες πετάλοισιν/, Nonn. *D.* 45.141 χλοεροῖς πετάλοισι κατάσκιος.

χλοεροῖσι In archaic poetry only *Scutum* 393; other epic: Anon. *CA* 9vi.6; *Batrach.* 162; Dion. Bass. 79′11 Livrea; Q.S. 8.208; Nonn. *D.*, 18 ×; Colluth. 119; widespread in Hellenistic verse generally. With πετ.: Eur. *Hel.* 244; [Opp.] *Cyn.* 4.394; Nonn. *D.* 26.188, 45.141. In i.546 with πεδίον (πέδον [Orph.] *L.* 160).

καταστεφέες First in tragedy: note here Eur. *Suppl.* 258-9 corr. χλόην ... φυλλάδος καταστεφῆ, and later Luc. *Trag.* 74 φύλλοις .. καταστεφεῖς. — 'Formant un berceau de ...' VDB; once again, Homeric exegesis may be operative: schol. PQ on *Od.* 5.68, τὴν ἄμπελον τετάσθαι περὶ τὸ σπήλαιόν φησιν ὥσπερ στέφανόν τινα. On the accompanying dative see Gillies.

221 ὑψοῦ ἀειρόμεναι *Il.* 21.307 al. /ὑψόσ' (but a third-cent. pap. has ὑψοῦ here, West *PP* 154) ἀειρόμενος (-οι -ων); in id. 10.465, 505 ὑψόσ' ἀείρας/ we are told that αἱ 'Αριστάρχου had ὑψόσε καὶ ὑψοῦ διχῶς (Erbse at schol. 465), and presumably this held good for other passages too (La Roche *HTA* 372).

For ὑψόσ' cf. the examples given by Bühler on Mosch. *Eur.* 144, adding *Or. Sib.* 5.252; for ὑψοῦ iv.154, Q.S. 6.288, [Apolin.] 67.43, 72.35.

Schol. censure the use of ὑψοῦ for ὑψόσε in iii.257, but it is so used from Homer on: cf. ii.587, al.

On ὑψόσε see 957n. (sole occurrence in the poem).

μέγ' Cf. i.1191, and Bissinger 252.

ἐθήλεον Hapax in Homer (*Od.* 5.73; based on the pluperf. τεθήλει, *GH* 1.347), hapax in Ap. Hence: Anon. *AP* 9.363.3-4 χλοερὴν ἐστέψατο .... θηλήσαντα ... πετήλοις/.

αἱ δ' ὑπὸ τῇσιν ... ii.1084f. τοὶ δ' ὑπὸ τοῖσιν/ἐνναέται ... See on 70.

222 Alcinous' two κρῆναι (*Od.* 7.129f.: 215n.) are replaced by four from Calypso (220f.n.): if we expect (as the prominence accorded to ἀέναοι might encourage us to expect; cf. in the model *Od.* 5.70 /κρῆναι ... πίσυρες ῥέον ὕδατι ...) the kind of general description of (shaded) springs with fresh running water associated with the *locus amoenus* (bibliogr. in Hopkinson on Call. *h.* 6.28), we are soon to be surprised.

ἀέναοι κρῆναι A cliché, but here the expression has point (see above): cf. e.g. Hes. *WD* 595, Antim. *fr.* 84.3 Wyss, *CEG* (2) 865.2, Theoc. 22.37, Kaibel *EG* 813.2. Ap. has this unHomeric epithet again at 860(n.), Homeric ἀενάων -οντος (Hopkinson on Call. *h.* 6.14) never; the latter is absent in 3[H], the former also in Simias *CA* 1.5, Call. *h.* 2.83, Theoc. 15.102, 22.37; in *SH* 924.4, which *could* be from an early piece, ἀεναο[could be supplemented with either form.

Perhaps Theoc. 22 preserves traces of this description: 37 ἀέναον κρήνην ... πέτρῃ/, 38 /ὕδατι ... αἱ δ' ὑπένερθε/, 39 κρυστάλλῳ ... ἰνδάλλοντο/, 40 πεφύκεσαν ἀγχόθι πεῦκαι/...

κρῆναι As we shall discover directly, these are τυκταὶ κρῆναι: see on this use of the term Wycherly, *CR* 51 (1937), 2-3, Renehan 1975.164-5.

πίσυρες The Homeric Aeolism -ες -ας (Janko on *Il.* 15.680) occurs also in i.671, ii.1110, iii.1367 (all nomin.). 3[H] offers only πίσυρες Arat. 722, πίσυρας Call. *h.* 3.105, πισύρων Arat. 478 (varied by Ap. at ii.1110).

222-3 ἃς ἐλάχηνεν/Ἥφαιστος Ctr. -ον, ἃς ⏑⏑−×/Ἥφαιστος ποίησεν, *Il.* 20.12. VDB point out (2.60 n.1) that Hephaestus is acting out of character – as an excavator (schol. at 222 try to play this down!) rather than a metalworker. True, but as we are already viewing a scene redolent at least partially of contemporary artistic productions (220f.n.), it is natural enough to infer that Hephaestus would have supplied the ornate metal spouts characteristic of Hellenistic artificial fountains (see e.g. Webster 163): bullhead (cf. Gow on Theoc. 7.6f., p. 134) rather than the usual lionhead, of course, if 230-1 are anything to go by: n.b. στόματα!

In any event, though Ap. has momentarily drawn us away from Alcinous' home to a different locality, he here returns to Phaeacia, following up his description of the fountains with a resumptive formula (228) recalling *Od.* 7.132. He may have inferred from id. 129f./132 that Alcinous' fountains were god-made rather than man-made – and maybe they were. As for the relative clause, *Od.* 7.92 is in the poet's mind (/οὓς Ἥφαιστος ἔτευξεν, at a much earlier stage; the banal verb gives way to something really choice).

On the association of Hephaestus with Helios/Aeetes see on 230f.

ἐλάχηνεν = ἐξελ-, 'excavated' from the rock (227). ἀμφιλ- at *Od.* 24.242 is an absolute hapax (f.v.l. in i.374, cf. VDB 1.251, also Zumbo 1975.350, Haslam 56f.). *Hoe around* to loosen the soil seems appropriate there, but the word's etymology has not been satisfactorily explained: Frisk *GEW* s.v. λαχαίνω, *LfgrE* s.v. (ἀμφι)λαχαίνω; de Lamberterie, *RPh* 49 (1975), 237, unconvincingly relates it to an assumed λαχύς (clear away vegetation which might render a plant 'velu,' 'en le recourrant,' ἀμφι-). Later poets use it in the sense *dig, excavate*. The simple verb occurs in Call. *fr.* 701, Lyc. 624, [Mosch.] *Meg.* 96, ἐκ- in i.374 (see above), iv.1532. Subsequently λαχ- Opp. *Hal.* 3.121, 5.597, D.P. 1115, Nonn. *D.* 12.331, Paul. Sil. *AP* 7.609.2 and *Amb.* 115, [Orph.] *fr.* 280.6 ~ Max. 461; δια- (tmes.) Opp. *Hal.* 5.264, ἐκ- Triph. 208.

/Ἥφαιστος· Emphatic: 'Hephaestus no less' (*Il.* 14.167, 339 do not carry the same stress). There is certainly a strong element of surprise detectable here: it has not been looking as if the favours enjoyed by Alcinous will be mirrored here in the land of Aeetes (the mention of 'bronze' at 218 had failed to draw the poet out).

223-7 Confronted with the grouping milk, wine, fragrant oil/perfume, critics have naturally thought from time to time of an adynaton (Theoc. 5.124f. rivers of milk, wine, honey) or of actual miracles (e.g. Eur. *Bacch.* 142f. streams of milk, wine and μελισσᾶν νέκταρ, cf. infr. 831-2, [applied by Medea] ἀλοιφῇ/νεκταρέῃ, and see further Dodds on *Bacch.* 704-11, NH on Hor. *Carm.* 2.19.10). To the contemporary reader, however, these creations might not have seemed especially marvellous, see 220f.n.; it is interesting that in the run-up to the description of the χλωραὶ σκιάδες in Theoc. 15.119 (cf. Gow ad loc.) mention is made of fruit-bearing trees (112: these include the vine), perfume (114: cf. the πηγαὶ μύρου of Luc. *VH* 2.13, cited by Gillies), honey and oil (117). In fact, *the* τεθαυματουργημένον of the passage is the wholly extraordinary *water* of spring number four (225f.); you can forget your πηγαὶ Σκαμάνδρου after this – if you are prepared to swallow the story.

223 καί ῥ' ἡ μέν 119n. ῥ': you would expect something out of the ordinary (in theory at least! Cf. above); so again ἄρ' 225.

... μὲν -εσκε γάλακτι ... Ctr. *Od.* 10.304 (used infr. 854-5, iv.977-8; all θαύματα) ... μὲν .. ἔσκε, γάλακτι δὲ ...

ἀναβλύεσκε The frequentative follows on naturally from ἀέναοι, and so again 225; but the second and fourth slots are occupied by straight imperfectives, 224/227 (on the alternation cf. 200-9n.).

(-)βλύ(ζ)ειν 5 × in the poem (Livrea on iv.788); Homer only ἀποβλύζειν, *Il.* 9.491. Both in simple and compound form the verb was widespread in Hellenistic poetry (especially in connexion with springs/fountains) and worked to death later on (in the koine as well). No doubt prevalent long before in Ionic-speaking areas (cf. Boesch 44), it was probably in general circulation by the later fourth century (in Aristotle often).

Intrans.: so ἀναβλύζειν iv.923 and (e.g.) Theoc. 17.80; Diosc. *HE* 1579 κρῆναι ἀναβλύζοιεν ἀκρήτου/ (Jacobs: -ον, a necessary correction); Nonn. *D.* 48.878 οἶνος ἀνέβλυε from spring. Cf. LSJ s.vv. ἀναβλύζω -βλύω. For the accompanying dative cf. [Orph.] *A.* 1130, Nonn. *D.* 2.71, [Apolin.] 113.16.

Quantity of upsilon: short iv.1238 and (ἔβλυσεν) 1446, long iv.778, 1417; other Hellenistic verse: long in Nic. *Ther.* 497 βλύοντι, otherwise short: ἔβλυσε (sim.) often and βλύουσαι Lyc. 301.

224 ἡ δ' οἴνῳ So i.473 δ' οἴνῳ/, 1185 /οἱ δ' οἶνον, and occasionally in Homer: *Il.* 9.224 δ' οἴνοιο, *Od.* 3.40 + 2 ἐν δ' οἶνον (id. 15.334 ἠδ' οἴνου).

τριτάτη Properly 'third and last,' here rounding off a somewhat jejune list; the fourth provokes extended comment, leading off this time with a transitive verb.

Od. 10.352 (κρηνέων 350, προρέουσι/ 351) ἡ μὲν ..., 354 /ἡ δ' ..., 356 /ἡ δὲ τρίτη ... οἶνον ..., 358 /ἡ δὲ τετάρτη ὕδωρ ... For the more numerically minded: iv.773f. /πρώτην ..../δεύτερα δ' .... ἀτὰρ τρίτον ~ Call. *h.* 2.72f. πρώτιστον ../δεύτερον αὖ .., τρίτατόν γε μὲν ...

θυώδεϊ .. ἀλοιφῇ See on 223-7. This combination nowhere else: ctr. *Od.* 2.339 εὐῶδες ἔλαιον, Archestr. Gel. *SH* 176.6 εὐώδη ... ἀλοιφήν/. Oil was used in making perfume, by introducing an additive. This ἀλοιφή comes ready-scented.

ναεν *Od.* 6.292 ἐν δὲ κρήνη νάει. Ap. constantly strives for variety of form: (καλὰ) νάοντος iv.1300 (Livrea ad loc.), ναεν here (picking up ἀέναοι 222), but ὕδατι ναῖε/ almost certainly in i.1146 (Ω: ναε con. E, taken up by Fränkel [cf. *Einleitung* 86]; Ardizzoni, q.v.; VDB): see Merkel *Proleg.* 122-3. On the form ναῖε (Ar. ναῖον at *Od.* 9.222, Ludwich 1.574, Rengakos 1993.101-2; Matro *SH* 534.77 ἔναιεν ἐν ἅλμῃ, "simul 'habitabat in mari,' 'natabat in muria'" Meineke) see *GH* 1.167, Frisk *GEW* and LSJ s.v. νάω, Heubeck on *Od.* 9.222-3; *GVI* 1945.3 (Phrygia, 2nd/3rd cent.?) 'as long as ποταμοὶ ναίουσιν.'

The only other secure examples of the verb in 3[H] are: Call. *h.* 3.224 ναεν (φόνῳ), Euphor. *CA* 23.3 (καλὰ) νάουσαν.

On the accompanying dative see Ardizzoni here.

225-7 Last, but not least, a water-fountain, with echoes this time from *Il.* 22.147f. (the vividness of which seems to me to be underestimated by Elliger 59):

κρουνὼ . . . . ἔνθα δὲ πηγαί
δοιαὶ ἀναΐσσουσι Σκαμάνδρου δινήεντος.
ἡ μὲν γάρ θ' ὕδατι λιαρῷ ῥέει, ἀμφὶ δὲ καπνός
γίγνεται ἐξ αὐτῆς ὡς εἰ πυρὸς αἰθομένοιο·
ἡ δ' ἑτέρη θέρεϊ προρέει ἐϊκυῖα χαλάζῃ,
ἢ χιόνι ψυχρῇ, ἢ ἐξ ὕδατος κρυστάλλῳ.

Yet again, there is more than a suspicion that Homeric exegesis plays a part (see Erbse's ed. of schol., with the relevant notes): Ap. specifies (obliquely) both winter and summer, in that order ('Supply χειμῶνι in 149') and he closes with an ἀνα- compound + gen., = 'from' ('In 148 supply ἀπό or ἐκ with ἀναΐσσουσι'); we may note too νάοντες schol. 147a[1-2], ἀναβλύζειν id. b[1], and perhaps also (an entry has probably dropped out: Erbse on 149) λιαρῷ = θερμῷ (Ap. θέρμετο).

For Hellenistic interest in springs exhibiting variations in temperature we need look no further than the *thauma* in Call. *fr.* 407 (XVI) τῶν δ' ἐν "Ἄμμωνι κρηνῶν λέγειν Ἀριστοτέλη [*fr.* 531 R²], ὅτι τὴν μὲν Ἡλίου γε νομιζομένην μέσων μὲν νυκτῶν καὶ μεσημβρίας γίγνεσθαι θερμήν, ἕωθεν δὲ καὶ δείλης καθαπερεὶ κρύσταλλον, ἡ δ' ἄλλη διότι ἀναβαίνοντος μὲν ἡλίου πιδεύει, ἐπὶ δυσμαῖς δ' ἰόντος ἵσταται (see Pfeiffer ad loc., and Bömer on Ov. *Met.* 15.309-10). Hunter indeed (n. on 221-7) states: "By recalling this famous natural wonder [scil. 'the spring of Helios' described by Herodotus, 4.181], Ap. can keep his description within the bounds of traditional geography and ethnography, as he had in describing the Plain of Circe." A curious misreading of the passage: that is precisely what Ap. is *not* doing. He is not prepared to endorse it (ποθι, 225n.); indeed, he locates it firmly in the past, beyond the scrutiny of the scientific enquirer. One need only contrast the treatment of the Plain of Circe (200-9n.), and, *inter multa alia*, ii.734f., the chilly exhalation which is melted by the midday sun (735: 'there *is* a cave ...'), iv.599f., '*to this day* the lake exhales a vapour ...' So too Sil. It. 3.669f., 'there *stands* close by the temple a marvellous spring, whose water ...' Like Calypso's four springs then (*Od.* 5.70), they are locked into the world of the story (ctr. Alcinous', *Od.* 7.129f. with Elliger 307; Scamander's, *Il.* 22.147f.).

What we *may* be dealing with here is an elaborate reflection of interest in temperature-regulation in domestic environments (see Stat. *Silv.* 1.2.155-7 for a notable later example). That Ap., working as he did in Ptolemaic Egypt (the palace will have had numerous cisterns fed by a system of underground channels from the Nile), is adverting to the management of water-supplies is scarcely capable of proof; still, this would give some point (and a tinge of humour) to his scepticism about the level of sophistication attained in *heroic* palaces, and Aeetes' residence must in other respects have looked oddly familiar to a contemporary reader.

225 ἡ δ' ἄρ' ὕδωρ *Il.* 18.347-8 = *Od.* 8.436-7 /ἐν δ' ἄρ' ὕδωρ ἔχεαν .... θέρμετο δ' ὕδωρ/; here in Colchis however we are dealing with no run-of-the-mill heating process.

προρέεσκε The error in *codd.* LSE προέεσκε (προρέεσκε L²AG) might be thought to favour the conjecture προΐεσκε (Fränkel OCT and Vian independently: see Vian 1962.38 for discussion, also id. *REG* 100 (1987), 173); -ίεσκ- also infr. 274, iv.622, 799 ~ Hes. *Theog.* 157, cf. Rzach 595. But there is much to be said for retaining the element 'flow': -ναοι ... ῥέον neatly picked up by ναεν .... -ρέεσκε, with ἀναβλύεσκε and ἀνεκήκιε on either side. Then there is the *Iliad*-model (above), 22.149 ὕδατι .. ῥέει + 151 /ἡ δ' ... προρέει. All in all, it seems best to regard ὕδωρ προρέεσκε as a variation on this (cf. Campbell 1982.15), utilising *HyAp* 380 (AHS ad loc.) προρέειν .. ὕδωρ/ of a κρήνη, this perhaps founded on an idiosyncratic interpretation of *Il.* 21.366 προρέειν scil. ὕδωρ from 365, 'let his water flow in a forward direction.' See further LSJ s.v. ῥέω II, Gow on Theoc. 5.124; Boesch (31) discusses the trans. use of a number of related verbs in the *Argonautica*. It looks as if [Orph.] read προρέεσκε here: *A.* 1132 ὕδωρ προρέων (ἀμβλύζων 1130 ~ Ap. 223). On variants further down the line see VDB *app. crit.*, Speake 1974.126. [προρέεσκε now the Budé: see VDB 2².155.]

προρέειν, then πέτρης (227): Hes. *Theog.* 792 ἐκ πέτρης προρέει (785-6 ὕδωρ/ψυχρόν).

ποθι Not 'at some point, approximately' (cf. Vian ed. 1961, 'vers le moment de,' McLennan on Call. *h.* 1.38) – the temperature variation is absolutely regular and predictable, the datives marking a fixed point in time, Linsenbarth 64 – but 'reportedly': the poet cannot vouch for the accuracy of his story (so που often). For Homeric ποθι in Hellenistic poetry cf. (I leave aside Merkel's conjecture at iv.1228, cf. VDB 3.122 n.6; παρὰ Campbell):

(1) ii.881 (οἱ μὲν .. ποθι), 'it would appear/one has to assume that they have met their destined end' <we must think now of those who are still with us> (Fränkel well compares *Il.* 24.209: *Noten* 240); iv.275 (τὰ μὲν ἤ ποθι [~ *Il.* 10.8 ἠέ ποθι] ~ [Opp.] *Cyn.* 3.519 τὸ μὲν ἄρ ποθι), the 'reporter' here being a personage in the story, 'these are inhabited, allegedly – or (as is more likely) they are not' [*not* 'some are ... some are not']; iv.319 'they had not up till now, it would seem (rather than temporal, 'ever'), set eyes on ships' ('... eine Vermutung des Dichters selbst' *Noten* 124); Arat. 730 (εἰ .. ποθι, Homeric) 'if perchance' (rather than 'if ever'); Anon. epic. *CA* 4.21 (ὧδέ ποθι = που; Hom. ὥς ποθι *Il.* 24.209).

(2) In iii.1061 (τηλοῦ ποθι, i.444 /τηλόθι που) and iv.1443 (οὔ ποθι, Homeric), it is used locally. So in Call. *h.* 1.38 (-ε τὸ μέν ποθι, of a χεῦμα), 'somewhere (viz. not immediately) by the actual city,' id. *Hec. fr.* 18.3 'anywhere' (οὐδέ ποθι, Homeric). [Theodotus *SH* 757.3 οὐδέ ποθι con. Ludwich.]

The word is uncommon in later verse: add to [Opp.] above Opp. *Hal.* 2.489, 3.165, Q.S. 10.40.

225-6 δυομένῃσι/.. Πληιάδεσσιν ... ἀνιούσαις Hes. *WD* 383-4 /Πληιάδων .. ἐπιτελλομενάων/... δὲ δυσομενάων (v.l. δυο-)/ (cf. Anon. *PMG* 976.1-2, Mnasalces *HE* 2600 Πλειάδα δυομέναν/, and Nonn. *D.*

42.288); *Od.* 1.24 οἱ μὲν δυσομένου Ὑπερίονος, οἱ δ' ἀνιόντος. The genitive is usual in expressions of this kind (for example Call. *HE* 1224 Ἐρίφων .. δυομένων/, Anon. *AP* 11.336.2 δυομένων Ἐρίφων/), but cf. Pancrat. *HE* 2856 Ὑάσι δυομέναις/; also e.g. iv.979, with Linsenbarth 64-5, KG 1.445.

'The matutinal rising of the Pleiads marks the beginning of summer, as their setting ... marks the beginning of winter' Gow on Theoc. 13.25f. So Aeetes has hot water in winter (from some time in November, let us say, for a sixth-month period) and ice-cold water in summer. Cf. in general Gow on Theoc. loc. cit.; West on Hes. *WD* 383-4; VDB 2.59 n.4 ('winter and summer': cf. schol. 225-7a ~ *EtG* s. Πλειάδες).

δυομένῃσι Cases in Ap. of the initial longum in present and imperfective (non-Homeric) are collected by Ardizzoni on i.581, who rashly toys with the possibility of inserting a sigma in some of them (this one included). He makes no mention of earlier examples in the hexameter (*HyHerm* 197, cf. Schulze *QE* 316: -δυσο- Voss; Emped. DK31 B54) or in other Hellenistic poets: Arat. 309, 627, 724, 840/880 ἢ ἀνιόντος ἢ .. δυομένοιο/ (cf. Ronconi 245), 853; *HE* above and 843 (Asclep.), 1194, 1224 (Call.); *Batrach.* 302; to this period perhaps belongs also Anon. eleg. *SH* 962.13. Very common subsequently in all genres.

θέρμετο 225n. On the correpted -o, which Hermann did not like (cf. Wellauer here), see Fantuzzi 159; ctr. the *incipit* θέρμετ' *Il.* 23.381. In id. 22.151 θέρεϊ and ἐϊκυῖα (ctr. ἴκελον in Ap. 227) are housed in the same clause.

ἀμοιβηδίς *Od.* 18.310 ἀμοιβηδὶς δ' ἀνέφαινον/; this adverb otherwise only *Il.* 18.506 (ἀμοιβηδόν Ar.; cf. Livrea on iv.199-200, adding Anon. eleg. *SH* 964.42), *HyDem* 326.

227 κρυστάλλῳ/ἴκελον Q.S. 6.476-7 ὕδωρ/κρυστάλλῳ ἀτάλαντον. Homer's more leisurely comparison (he deliberately slows the pace here) presents a studied progression in terms of coldness (cf. schol. bT at 152): *Il.* 22.151-2 'But the flowing stream of the other emerges in summer like [as low in temperature as] hail, or snow, or ice formed from water' (on this last element, trimmed by Ap., see Bollack, *Empédocle III: Les origines*, Comm. vol. 1 (Paris 1969), 247 n.1; perhaps we should think of the glassy surface of, e.g., a frozen pool, which presents a colder aspect than snow turned to ice [*Od.* 14.477]).

κοίλης .. πέτρης Naturally very common at all times: e.g. *Il.* 21.494 (κοίλην εἰσέπτατο πέτρην/), Aesch. *Eum.* 22-3, Lyc. 494, [Phoc.] *Sent.* 172.

ἀνεκήκιε *kept oozing up* (for all the world like a natural spring) from the hollow(ed) rock, scil. *via* tunnels or pipes (cf. in general Dunkley, *ABSA* 36 (1935/36), 188f.).
On the verb see Livrea on iv.600. (ἀνα)κηκίειν of sea-water *Od.* 5.455-6 θάλασσα δὲ κῆκιε πολλή/ἂν στόμα ..., i.542 /ἀφρῷ δ' ... κελαινὴ κήκιεν ἅλμη/, Call. *fr. incert.* 763 πολιὴ δ' ἀνεκήκιεν ἅλμη/, Euphor. *SH* 442.6 νοτερὴ δ' ἀνεκήκιεν ἅλμη/. In iv.600 ἀνακηκίειν (like κηκίειν in iv.929) denotes the *exhalation* of vapour from the surface of water (cf. Campbell on Q.S. 12.505 for the association with smoke sim.): perhaps Ap. was influenced in his choice of verb here by the vivid picture in *Il.* 22.149-50.

228-9 Recalled by Val. Flacc., 5.451-2 *haec tum miracula Colchis/ struxerat* (~ ἐμήσατο, see n.) *ignipotens* ...
Cf. *Studies* 23. Given *Od.* 7.132 /τοῖ᾽ ἄρ᾽ ἐν Ἀλκινόοιο (scil. δόμῳ) ... (cf. i.768 and the examples in Bühler ed. Mosch. *Eur.*, p. 108 with n.3, adding Stat. *Theb.* 7.61 *talem .. Mulciber* ...), we might have expected an immediate resumption of the narrative (*Od.* 7.133 'There he stood and marvelled,' i.769 'He then took a hold of his spear,' and so on), leaving Hephaestus' input unexplained. In fact, clarification comes at once, though not entirely straightforwardly. In *Od.* 7.112f. we gather that we are moving to a point 'outside' the palace-complex. Here we must also be; but the connexion between the 'bulls' and the 'Plain of Ares' (passed by the Argonauts in ii.1268) has yet to be made. We must wonder for a moment whether Ap. is tacking on a note about bulls as palace φύλακες, like the remarkable '*gold* and *silver* dogs which *Hephaestus manufactured*' in *Od.* 7.91f., cf. the apotropaic bronze bulls on Mt Atabyrius that bellowed warnings to the Rhodians (Timaeus *FGH* 566*fr.* 39).

ἐνὶ μεγάροισι *Il.* 11.76 etc., and cf. infr. 528 μεγάροισιν ἐνι- Αἰήταο/; for .... ἐμήσατο Haggett (61) compared iv.7-9 μητιάασκεν/οἷσιν ἐνὶ μεγάροις .../Αἰήτης ~ *Od.* 3.213 (cf. id. 16.93-4) /ἐν μεγάροις ... μηχανάασθαι/ (variants: μητιάασθαι, μητίσασθαι).

μέγαρον -α can sometimes refer primarily to an area outside the main hall but within the overall complex, viz. the αὐλή (e.g. *Od.* 19.552; so *HyDem* 379, perhaps); here however the sense is 'in, inside the palace' generally as opposed to the area outside (cf. above): Elliger 306.

Κυταιέος Αἰήταο On Cyta/Cytaea (the town, a Hellenistic invention?) and 'Cytaean,' a grandiloquent term for 'Colchian,' see Robert 762 n.2, Delage 186-7, VDB 1.196 n.1, and P. Chuvin, *Mythologie et géographie dionysiaques* (Clermont-Ferrand 1991), 56. First (of six occurrences in all) in the mouth of the knowledgeable Phineus (ii.399, in a passage which must reflect the manner of a typical Hellenistic *periplous*), it was evidently a name to be conjured with (cf. the at times unfathomable Lycophron, 174, 1312; the showy Euphorion, *CA* 14.3), and was to live again in lesser *Argonautica* (Val. Flacc., [Orph.]); see further Fedeli on Prop. 1.1.24. Here it serves to highlight the fact that Hephaestus, who actually sired one of the Argonauts (i.202f.), has been at work in a remote and exotic environment.

Κυταιέος Αἰήταο/ also ii.403 (Phineus, speaking of the eventual arrival at their destination: cf. ii.1267); but ii.1093-4 (which reads like the start of the narrative portion of an 'epyllion') /υἶηες .... ἐνέοντο παρ' Αἰήταο Κυταίου/ matched by Call. *fr.* 7.25-6 ἥρωες ἀπ' Αἰήταο Κυταίου/... ἔπλεον.

229 τεχνήεις Ἥφαιστος In plainer language (flights of fancy in Thiel 116-7), Hephaestus is a τεχνίτης, a constructor of artificial (τεχνικαί) κρῆναι. — τεχνήεις: possibly an epithet of Hephaestus in Epic. adesp. *CA* 7.11. Not so in Homer: ctr. *Od.* 8.297 (δεσμοί) /τεχνήεντες ... Ἡφαίστοιο/ (~ Q.S. 5.97 corr.); maybe there was a variant τεχνήεντος. Nonn. *D.* 27.71 has Ἡφαίστου τεχνήμονος; also found are κλυτοτέχνης Hom. +, πολυ- Sol. *IEG* 13.49, χαλκεο- Q.S. 2.440; τεχνοδίαιτος [Orph.] *h.* 66.3.

τεχνήεις applied to persons in poetry: *Od.* 7.110 (/ἔργα 111); Damag. *HE* 1429; Boeth. *GPh* 1769; Q.S. 8.296; Greg. Naz. 1370.239-40 .... ἐμήσατο; Anon. *AP* 9.209.4.

ἐμήσατο θέσκελα ἔργα So *Scutum* 34 (subject Zeus), [Hes.] *fr.* 204.96 (id.) μήδετο θέσκελα ἔργα/. Cf. from Homer *Od.* 3.194, 303 (οἴκοθι) Αἴγισθος ἐμήσατο –⏑⏑–×, and *Od.* 11.429 ἐμήσατο ἔργον ἀεικές/; also id. 11.374 ἐν μεγάρῳ then θέσκελα ἔργα/.

On the type of line-ending exemplified by θέσκελα ἔργα in Ap. see Harrison, *CQ* n.s. 41 (1991), 140 n.7 (but all but one of the Ap. passages for which H. provides no parallels from archaic epic have close analogues in the Homeric poems).

ἐμήσατο Of skilful/artful manufacture, as in Simon. *PMG* 593, infr. 780(n.).

θέσκελα 'miraculous' (schol. D at *Il.* 3.130 θεῖα, θαυμαστά, sim. at id. 23.107; cf. Erbse at schol. 3.130*b*), like the awe-inspiring relics of the ἡμίθεοι in iv.657; of art-work in *Od.* 11.610 (belonging to the deified Heracles; product of Hephaestus?? τεχνησάμενος, τεχνήσαιτο, τέχνῃ 613-4). On the word see Heubeck at *Od.* 11.373-6, and on Hephaestus the worker of marvels Schrade, *Gymnasium* 57 (1950), 49f. θέσκελος, and also the unit θέσκελα ἔργα, were much affected by later poets, but the adj. itself does not occur elsewhere in 3^H (*SH* 1153 does not look particularly Hellenistic).

230f. Cf. *Studies* 23/101 nn.4-6. The detail that Hephaestus made the bulls is known to have been Antimachean: schol. 409-10, schol. Pind. *P.* 4.398*d* (2.152.2 Dr.) ~ *Lyde fr.* 62 Wyss, *fr.* 6 Gentili-Prato, who attempt to put schol. Pind. into verse (if it is indeed the case that Ἡφαιστοτεύκτους – the word is popular with summarizers, see for instance under Proclus in *EGF* p. 47, line 14; under Stesich. *PMGF* 234 – metrically intractable as it stands, represents an imposing Antimachean epithet, then the source may have been tragedy: Sophocles? Cf. *Phil.* 987, and also Aesch. *fr.* 69 of the Sun's cup [below] Ἡφαιστοτευχὲς [*vel sim.*: Radt ad loc.] δέπας. See further Radt on Soph. (?) *fr.* 1135, though the gap in schol. Pind. may have contained some other detail illustrating the Pindaric lemma). The motif is likely in fact to have been much older: Hephaestus is credited with the manufacture of animate metallic figures as early as *Il.* 18.417f. (Edwards on 417-20); and the accompanying plough was labelled by Pindar ἀδαμάντινον (*P.* 4.224, Ap. ἀδάμαντος), a term strongly implying divine provenance (cf. Troxler 19f., and 232n.). On the bulls in earlier accounts see also Pherecydes *FGH* 3 *fr.* 112, Eur. *Med.* 478.

For Hephaestus at work in Aeetes' palace cf. Val. Flacc. 5.433-4, 451-2, and much later Nonn. *D.* 29.202-3 Αἰήτῃ .../χαλκοπόδων μόρφωσε συνωρίδα δίζυγα ταύρων (ἀδάμαντος 197, Ἥφαιστος .. κάμε τέχνῃ/ 200). Surprisingly, there are few occasions on which he is represented as working on Helios' (infr. 233) behalf: Mimn. *IEG* 12.6 etc. his bed/cup (see e.g. D. A. Campbell, *Greek Lyric Poetry*, pp. 228-9); Ov. *Met.* 2.5f. his palace, 106 his chariot (story of Phaethon: cf. note on 245-6). We do not know whether Antimachus supplied a reason for the association (none is provided by Val. Flacc., 6.433f.). It could go back to tragedy: both τίνειν χάριν (233, also ii.799, iii.990) and Φλεγραῖος (234, also iii.1227) are first attested in this genre (Aesch. *Ag.* 821-2, and *PV* 985, cf. Lyc. 1092; Aesch. *Eum.* 295, Eur. *HF* 1194, cf. Lyc. 115). Thiel 116 compares the broad situation in *Il.* 18, grateful Hephaestus provided Achilles with weapons.

Whether this is original Ap. or not, the atmosphere he evokes is striking:

(1) If Aeetes, like the Argonauts, belongs to the age of heroes/ ἡμίθεοι, the creatures he controls, like Talos later on (iv.1641f.), takes us back to the grim violence of the Hesiodic Bronze Race. Here

χαλκό- ... χάλκεα sharply recalls the anaphora of *WD* 150 χάλκεα ... χάλκεοι; key terms are reproduced in the description: δεινόν (231: *WD* 145), στιβαροῦ (232: *WD* 149), ἀδάμαντος (232: *WD* 147).

(2) Jason will soon be involved with these bulls. A sinister note is struck by the recollection of *Il*. 6.182/?Hes. *Theog*. 324 in 231 (*Echoes* 46): the Aeolid hero Bellerophon, whose career resembled that of Jason in a number of respects (Crane 1988.159 n.26, Hunter on 231), had imposed upon him the task of confronting the fire-breathing Chimaera.

(3) Jason's future fight with the Earthborn (an element absent in some accounts) is not mentioned directly, but there is a broad hint of things to come: the (bull-drawn) plough owed its very existence to the combat with *Giants* born from Gaia. See further on 215f.(D).

230 χαλκόποδας ταύρους In reverse order, once specified by the poet: infr. 410 /ταύρω χαλκόποδε, repeated in 496 (on the pattern see 135n.). There was debate about the exact significance of χαλκόπους in Homer: i.q. στερεό- schol. D, ctr. schol. T at *Il*. 13.23, Erbse ad loc.; here there can be absolutely no room for argument.

On χαλκό- then χάλκεα see above on 230f.; Ovid imitates, *Heroid.* 12.43 *aere pedes solidi* (ref. to στερεό- debate?) *praetentaque naribus aera* (*terribilis* ... 42 ~ δεινόν 231).

κάμε Recurrently of Hephaestus from Homer (*LfgrE* s.v. κάμνω 4a) onwards; for οἱ ... cf. *Il*. 19.368 οἱ Ἥφαιστος κάμε, al.

231 ἧν στόματ' Ctr. *Il*. 2.489 στόματ' εἶεν/ (χάλκεον 490).

ἐκ Scil. ἐκ στομάτων, cf. 1304, and see on 280.

ἐκ ... ἀμπνείεσκον Cf. above, note on 230f.: *Il*. 6.182, ? Hes. *Theog.* 324 (... ἧν ... 321 ~ Ap. 231?) δεινὸν ἀποπνείουσα πυρὸς μένος αἰθομένοιο (Chimaera, see the note of Braswell on Pind. *P*. 4.225(a) for like descriptions); *Il*. 19.17 /δεινὸν ... ὡς εἰ σέλας (scil. πυρός) ἐξ-. Similar phraseology is employed infr. 1292, 1327; cf. 411n.

πυρὸς .. σέλας Cf. 1292, 1327 mentioned above, and iv.68: πυρὸς σέλας ~ *Il*. 19.366 etc. (common in all periods).

σέλας = ἔκλαμψις, *éclat* (Graz 311), a dazzling effulgence: fire does not emerge from their mouths in a steady, continuous stream, but is exhaled in sudden and brilliant bursts, like flames responding to the bellows' blasts (infr. 1300; σέλας is quite often associated with the emissions of the fire-god himself: some examples in LSJ s.v., cf. also Theoc. 2.134).

ἀμπνείεσκον A weighty σπονδειάζων (cf. lately Thiel 112; so infr.

1292), the frequentative emphasising the constancy and regularity of this breathing-process: the bursts of fire are not turned on and off at will but are part of the bulls' physiology. These animated metallic creatures arc ἔμπνοοι (see Farraone, *GRBS* 28 (1987), 260) with a vengeance!

Not with accus. in early verse: cf. LSJ s.v. ἀναπνέω III [on the text of iv.472, see VDB 3.166], *DGE* s.v. IIIB; note here Pind. *Dith*. 2.15 κεραυνὸς ἀμπνέων πῦρ.

232 πρὸς δὲ καί occurs some twenty times in Hdt.; again in 1046, but there πρός is a preposition.

αὐτόγυον στιβαροῦ ἀδάμαντος ἄροτρον So 1285 [see 410n. on the repetition] αὐτόγυόν τ' ἐπὶ τοῖς στιβαροῦ ἀδάμαντος ἄροτρον. On αὐτόγυον cf. Hes. *WD* 433 with West's note (and the illustration on p. 266); VDB 2.60 n.3 (*EtG*: Wendel 1932.71; Erbse 1953.182). Whereas in Hesiod the share will have been iron (probably), here the key parts of the contraption are metal as well: the ἔλυμα and γύης, in one piece for rigidity (the ground, we shall discover, is exceptionally hard), are made of unbreakable adamant, like the ἐχέτλη (1325) which is securely attached or welded (εὖ ἀραρυῖαν) <to the blade in this single block>; the ἱστοβοεύς (1318) is made of bronze, and joined firmly to the bronze (1284, 1308) yoke. So not even best-quality Boeotian can match this.

στιβαροῦ Cf. στερεοῖο in Theoc. 17.21 (this no doubt a reflection of contemporary exegesis: cf. *LfgrE* s.v. ἀδάμας, schol.: στερρός *et sim.*). στιβαρός, much favoured by Ap., can be applied to extremely hard substances capable of resisting enormous force or pressure; ii.598 πέτρη held on to by Athena as she shoves Argo through the Rocks, iv.762 Hephaestus' τυπίδες, 1439 ὄζος = Heracles' stout club, and so on.

ἀδάμαντος Pindar's ἀδαμάντινον ... ἄροτρον (*P.* 4.224), see on 230f., and also West on Hes. *Theog*. 161, Braswell on Pind. *P.* 4.71(c), Campbell on Q.S. 12.195.

233 ἤλασεν Cf. the forceful image used by Phineus in ii.231 (no βροτός could tolerate close contact ...) οὐδ' εἴ οἱ ἐληλάμενον κέαρ εἴη, scil. even if possessed of a heart forged [so definitely metal, rather than stone] of <your proverbially hard> adamant <not normally associated with ordinary mortals>.

ἐλαύνειν is a t.t. for bronze-working in *Il*. (and often thereafter): *Il*. 12.296 /ἤλασεν, pause (but ἐξέλασ' Zenodotus: Duentzer 36, 115),

20.270 (Hephaestus; a much-vexed passage), al. Cf. 235n., and also Edwards, ed. *Il.* 17-20, p. 201.

233-4 Ἡελίῳ ... On the participation of Helios and Hephaestus in the Gigantomachy see VDB 2.119 (on 234).
 Ἡελίῳ τίνων ... [Orph.] *L.* 153 /τίνων Ἡελίῳ ζωάγρια ...
 τίνων χάριν Gods expect favours to be repaid. For the expression τίνειν χάριν see 230f.n. Other examples: Leon. *HE* 2064-5, Honestus *GPh* 2443, Babr. 27.3 and 107.8, Triph. 658 (suppl.), Nonn. *Par.* 7.92, *D.* 8.185, 36.123 (/πατροκασιγνήτῳ τίνων χάριν: τίνων F², τινύων L, τανύων Graefe); verse inscriptions: (3rd/2nd cent.) *GVI* 1214.5, 1550.6, Kaibel *EG* 787.2; (1st cent. AD) *SEG* 23.220(b) 6-7 (iamb.).
 ὅς ῥά μιν ... ῥα commonly implies familiarity (while not necessarily excluding poetic invention!) on the part of the listener/reader. Cf. /ὅς ῥά μιν ... in *Il.* 5.650 (but there *failure* to repay is in question), 'who, as you well know ...'
 Il. 6.483 ἡ δ᾽ ἄρα .. δέξατο ..., cf. *HyDem* 231.
 ἵπποις i.e. horse-drawn chariot (as often, 'only the animate motive power is expressed,' *LfgrE* s.v.). Helios' chariot plays a strictly functional role throughout the poem: iii.309f. (implied in the simile of 1230, it is vividly concretised in the ensuing action by means of its earthly counterpart: *Noten* 437), iv.598 (and 219f., the replica here on earth). Night's chariot is mentioned in connexion with nightfall infr. 1193, but even there pure decoration is not in question (cf. comment ad loc.).
 Φλεγραίῃ κεκμηότα δηιοτῆτι Recalled by Nonnos, *D.* 46.93 γυναικείῃ κεκαφηότα δηιοτῆτι/.
 Φλεγραίῃ Again infr. 1227 (producing another link between Aeetes and the violent past), applied to the Giant Mimas vanquished by Ares in the battle on the plain of Phlegra, usually localised at Pallene in Chalcidice (κλείτεα Παλλήναια i.599: "on voit ... qu'Apollonios ne cherche pas à donner à son itinéraire un aspect mythique: lorsqu'il rappelle une légende, il emploie le terme ancien de Phlégra, mais il préfère celui de Palléné en décrivant le voyage des Argonautes" Delage 82); cf. Braswell on Pind. *N.* 1.67. For the epithet see above on 230f. (tragedy), and Anon. *PMG* 985.12 (reconstructed: Alcyoneus the Giant), Lyc. 115, [Orph.] *h.* 32.12 (Giants). Roman poets were addicted to 'Phlegraean battle' and the like (*castra, militia, proelia, pugnae, tumultus*); only here so far in Greek.
 κεκμηότα Cf. *Studies* 23-4. Possibly 'hard-pressed' (cf. e.g. Eur. *Suppl.* 709), but more likely 'fatigued,' 'worn out.' Schol., who find the

whole story implausible and appeal to Hephaestus' powerful display in *Il.* 21.342f., impute to Ap. the suggestion that the god's condition was due to his χωλότης; modern critics follow suit. Ap. of course says nothing about any disability, and the criticism is in my view misplaced. Hephaestus was not trounced, as schol. imply, but was taking a breather. Helios is a charioteer in attendance at a series of single combats, on hand in Iliadic fashion to convey from the battlefield anyone in need of ἀνάπνευσις (we may recall that this is a luxury unknown to himself! Cf. Mimn. *IEG* 12, with Allen 100; horses ~ κάματος: Aesch. *fr.* 192.6): cf. κάματος in *Il.* 4.230, and the variation here on id. 11.802/16.44 κεκμηότας ἄνδρας αὐτῇ/. The Gigantomachy was notoriously a most strenuous engagement for all concerned (Jupiter himself is represented as *fessus* in Stat. *Theb.* 11.7-8, cf. earlier Heracles πολύπονος in Eur. *HF* 1190f.); gods are as likely as anybody to beat a hasty retreat when the going gets tough (e.g. Ares in *Il.* 5.864f.); in the Typhonomachy Zeus himself had to 'recover his strength' and be helped by gods ([Apollod.] 1.6.3), and he got into trouble and had to be 'rescued' by another god (Opp. *Hal.* 3.16), cf. the remarks of Mondi, *TAPA* 116 (1986), 30 with n.18.

In any event, κεκμηότα suggests a rather whimsical action, of sorts: the κάματος experienced on that occasion was the ultimate reason for the κάματος expended in manufacturing the bulls (κάμε 230), who are themselves instrumental in producing another batch of Giants, both destined to come under the category of κάματοι (iv.364-5).

δηιοτῆτι Ap. has eight examples of δηιοτής, one of archaic epic's staple words for 'battle,' 'combat,' sim. (cf. H. Trümpy, *Kriegerische Fachausdrücke im griechischen Epos* (Basel 1950), 138f.), but no sharp echoes are discernible in any of them; nowhere else in 3[H] (Anon. *SH* 928.2 looks Imperial).

235f. A rather dry description which makes some use of the account of part of Priam's palace in *Il.* 6.242f. (compared in *Echoes* 46, and also by James 65) but divests it of its 'fanciful and romantic' elements (Wace and Stubbings 489); a prelude to Hector's meeting with his mother, 251f.: ~ infr. 253f. (the latter much more animated). The interest here lies primarily in the occupants, both individually and collectively: the unity of the family whose members are now paraded before us systematically is soon to be shattered.

235 ἔνθα δὲ καί = *Il.* 18.230; ii.743 (~ Antim. *fr.* 34). ἔνθα i.e. ἐνὶ μεγάροισι (228). One might have expected the narrative to start up again now (*Od.* 7.132 'such then' followed up with 133 'ἔνθα Odysseus ...'); mention of the μέσσαυλος makes it immediately clear that we are dealing with descriptive ἔνθα δέ (cf. in the main models *Od.* 7.98, 114, 122, 127, and *Il.* 6.245, 249: ἔνθα 251, narrative resumed).

μέσσαυλος i.e. ἡ μέσαυλος/μέταυλος, 'the door between the court and the megaron' (Gillies ed., cf. id. *CR* 41 (1927), 9-10, and Gardiner, *JHS* 21 (1901), 300f., B. C. Rider, *The Greek House* (Cambridge 1916), 236f.). Ap. takes into epic a non-Homeric employment of the term often remarked on in ancient commentaries (e.g. schol. A at *Il.* 17.112a οἱ .. Ἀττικοὶ τὴν μέσην θύραν τῆς αὐλῆς, see *test.* in Erbse ad loc.). Cf. VDB 2².153f.

μέσ(σ)αβος *w*: 'υ and β confused' Herter *JAW* 372, cf. Gillies *CR* cited above; talk of ploughs cannot have helped (μέσσαβα schol. 232*a*).

ἐλήλατο Gillies again: '"had been forged.' The entrance to the megaron was a wrought metal of such significance as to attract the notice of strangers in the courtyard, and to call for comment by the narrator." Cf. Roux 87.

ἐλήλατο, following on from ἤλασεν (233), may imply that Hephaestus, as well as producing true miracles (229), also had a hand in the palace architecture. In any event, to be compared here is v.l. *Od.* 7.86 (217-8n.), interpreted 'forged,' 'beaten' (scil. having bronze plating?); χάλκεοι there suggests that we should mentally supply χαλκοῦ here. Cf. also Mimn. *IEG* 12.6-7 (ref. Helios' 'bed') ... Ἡφαίστου χερσὶν ἐληλαμένη(,)/χρυσοῦ ..., and VDB 2².154.

235-6 τῇ δ᾽ ἐπὶ ... By/close to the central door, to either side, numerous doors giving access to apartments. Presumably these are all bedrooms (θάλαμοι .. ἔσαν ~ *Il.* 6.248 ἔσαν ... θάλαμοι), two of which are occupied by the sisters (247n.), the others by the large staff (F-G on *Od.* 22.421-2) of palace maidservants (247 ἀμφίπολοι, not those of both sisters: Medea's own ἀμφίπολοι do not occupy a θάλαμος, 838f.). The apartments of the *female* royals are not so grand, naturally: that does not mean that they should be sidelined (so, in effect, Natzel 44: sisters 'nur als Anhängsel der Familie ...').

δικλίδες Adjectival in Homer: with θύραι (cf. Arat. 192-3), πύλαι (cf. i.786-7: 216n.), σανίδες; with σταθμοί iv.26 (Medea's bedroom; s.v.l.). Elsewhere subst.: Theoc. 14.42 (see Gow); *HE*: 860 (Asclep.), 3240 (Rhian.), 4682 (Meleag.); Eratosth. *AP* 5.242.4; Paul. Sil. id. 5.256.1 and *Soph.* 579, *Amb.* 242.

εὐπηγεῖς i.e. constructed from solid boards or leaves, cf. εὐτύκτοισιν ἀρηρεμένας σανίδεσσιν/ in i.787, with Edwards' note on *Il.* 18.274-6.

COMMENTARY 238 217

For the adjective cf. ii.381A (πύργοι), infr. 1235 (δίφρος), and, from 3^H, [Theoc.] 25.207-8 Heracles' βάκτρον/εὐπαγές. Homer would have said εὔπηκτοι (εὐπηγής Od. 21.334 [F-G ad loc.] of human physique).

ἔνθα καὶ ἔνθα Homeric clausula (in descriptive passages: Od. 7.86 etc.), often elsewhere.

237 A στοὰ ποικίλη (so par. schol. 237-8, rejected by Chamoux 340f.) runs the length of (παρ-) the series of θάλαμοι which open behind it (as was often the case with stoas) away from (-ἐξ) the main door, to either side (ἑκάτερθε scil. θύρης: Od. 7.91). θάλαμοι appear to be fronted by, or built into, αἴθουσαι in Priam's palace, but the overall picture is hazy (Kirk on Il. 6.242-50); cf. further 39n. above, and West on Od. 3.399.

Again, the workmanship of Hephaestus may extend to elements in the palace-complex (cf. δαίδαλα 43, etc.). Mercifully, Ap. does not do a Valerius Flaccus and regale us with all the pictorial detail ὑπ' Ἠελίῳ.

δαιδαλέη Regularly glossed with ποικίλος (see above). Cf. in general Braswell on Pind. P. 4.296(b).

δ' ... -ερθε τέτυκτο Cf. Od. 17.210 (artificial fountain 205-6, trees 208, cold water flowing from rock 209-10).

238 λέχρις Glossed with πλαγίως (schol. i.1234-9a), ἐκ πλαγίου (par. schol. iii.237-8), i.e. *transversally*, cf. VDB 2².153-4. λέχρις (orthography: VDB 1.LXXIV) only in Ap. (i.1235, infr. 1160) in the wake of Antimachus, *fr*. 44.1 corr. (see Wyss ed. pp. XLVIIIf., Boesch 5); λέχριος Soph. Eur.+ (3^H: Call. *h*. 4.236), λικριφίς Hom. (Chantraine *DE* s.v., cf. *GG* 1.551,620).

αἰπύτεροι δόμοι 'more elevated buildings.' On the lack of symmetry, which has a realistic ring (ctr. the fanciful sets of θάλαμοι ἐναντίοι in *Il*. 6.244f.), see the lit. cited by Vian ed. 1961 on 235, VDB 2.119 (on 239), and more generally VDB 2².154-5. Ap. may have had in mind *Od*. 1.425-6 (not an entirely clear picture), Telemachus had a θάλαμος built in the courtyard which was /ὑψηλός (i.q. αἰπύς, cf. ὑψηλότεραι par. schol. here) ..., περισκέπτῳ ἐνὶ χώρῳ/.

Nonn. *D*. 4.13 δόμον αἰπύδμητον, sim. Colluth. 235-6.

ἔστασαν ἀμφοτέρωθεν heads the verse in *Il*. 12.55; cf. also *Od*. 7.89 + 101; 113, with Thiel 118. ἀμφοτέρωθεν: on both sides of the courtyard, one δόμος occupying one side (239), one the other (241). τοὺς δ' ... in 247 are quite distinct from both of these (see note there).

ἔστασαν (Ω) may be due to a muddled recollection of Homer: *codd*.

at *Il.* 12.56 (cf. id. 55 above) offer ἔστασαν (see schol. at 55-6, 56a[1-2], Erbse ad loc.; ἵστασαν is now generally accepted).

239/241 ἀλλ- ἀλλ- *Pace* Wellauer, -ον should be read in both cases (so S alone; 239 E also, 241 GD also): Ap. has ναίειν with accus. 10 ×, with dat. never. At the root of the confusion lies the wholly predictable error -ων in 239 (whence -ῳ *m* at 241), following on from τῶν ἤτοι (cf. e.g. supr. 59); perhaps the famous καὶ ὑπείροχον ἔμμεναι ἄλλων played a part too.

239 τῶν ... ὅτις καὶ ... Cf. ii.453 /τοῖς ... ὅτις καὶ ... (but an optative follows); id. 465 ὅτις ἔξοχος scil. ἦεν (~ *Il.* 12.269, scil. ἐστί).

Of interest here is the reading of a Ptolemaic papyrus (2nd half of 3rd cent.) at *Od.* 9.432: ὃς ὑπείροχος εἶεν viz. ἦεν, μήλων ὄχ' ἄριστος *vulg.* (West *PP* 240): shades of the ram (see the note on 176f.(2))?!

ὑπείροχος For the literal employment of the word cf. ii.369; also the architectural terms ὑπεροχή ὑπερέχειν, and -οχος in ἔξοχος. In Anon. *AP* 9.656.2 (οἶκος) πανυπείροχος has both a literal and a metaphorical meaning; and this is how Thiel 118 views ὑπείροχος here.

240 κρείων Αἰήτης Again in 1177; perhaps an old Argonautic 'formula.' κρείων is used sparingly in the poem: /κρείων Ἀλκίνοος iv.1009 and (along with his ἄλοχος, cf. the present line) 1069 (Hom. *Od.* 8.382+ /Ἀλκίνοε κρεῖον).

For Ap., a straight βασιλεύς fits the bill: cf. Rhian. *CA* 1.21 corr. /Ζηνὶ θεῶν κρείοντι = βασιλῆι, Call. *h.* 4.271 κρείοντι = ἄνακτι, and, after [Hes.] *fr.* 26.7 & 31a, Call. *h.* 3.268 (but with μέγα he perhaps leaves some room for manoeuvre), 4.219 (ἄνασσα 221), Theoc. 17.132 (βασιλῆας ibid.), iv.574, all κρείουσα. So glossed by schol. D *et al.* Alternatively, κρατῶν, ἄρχων, sim. were ventured (even when no genitive accompanied the word: e.g. schol. D at *Il.* 2.576 κρείων Ἀγαμέμνων/, cf. *LH/LfgrE* s.v., with Erbse on schol. *Il.* 22.48b): cf. Call. *h.* 6.138 μέγα κρείοισα θεάων/, + gen. = κρατοῦσα, κρατιστεύουσα; [Mosch.] *Meg.* 31 μέγα κρείουσα γυναιξί/, + dat., a sophistication for which LSJ find no space.

There is no precise parallel for this particular configuration in Homer (Vílchez 75) or in archaic epic at large; the same goes for '/King Alc.'

... ναίεσκε ... So *Il.* 5.708 ναίεσκε then (cf. Ap. 241) 710 /ναῖον. iv.574-5 ἵνα κρείουσα Καλυψώ/ Ἀτλαντὶς ναίεσκε.

ναίεσκε δάμαρτι But *Od.* 4.126 Πολύβοιο δάμαρ, ὃς ἔναι' ...

241 Cf. [Orph.] *A.* 797 Ἄψυρτος δ᾽ ἀπάνευθε δόμους ναίεσκε πό-
ληος, where Ruhnken conjectured τοκῆος on the basis of our line.
  πάις Αἰήταο Like πάις Ἀγχίσαο/, *Il.* 2.819 al.; cf. iv.697 Αἰήταο πάιν.
Ap. has πάις (F-G on *Od.* 21.415) 12 × (La Roche 1899.194 wished to
reduce this count), παῖς only 2 ×; the former in 3^H: Maiist. *CA* 18,
Anon. epic. id. 7.26.

242-3 Apsyrtus' parents. The forceful πρίν περ ('though it was
before ...,' or 'n.b., *before* ...': cf. i.999, 'before actually ...') underlines
the point that Apsyrtus was the product of a pre-marital liaison, and
therefore older (VDB 2.81 n.4, Hutchinson 125), not younger, than
Medea and her sister: contrast πρίν ποτ᾽ in the corrupt Soph. *fr.* 546.4,
with Pearson ad loc. and Roscher 1.3-4. There may also be an im-
plicit rejection of a claim that Eiduia was his as well as Medea's
mother, if we may set any store by the generally discredited Tzetzes
on Lyc. 798 (in Dion. Scyt. *fr.* 20 Rusten Medea has a *brother*, Aigia-
leus; the natural use of the plain 'brother' for Apsyrtus, Eur. *Med.*
167, 1334 etc., may have confused the issue). For Ap. the mother was
a local Orestiad, a Caucasian nymph by the name of Asterodeia,
rather than a 'Nereid' (Soph. *fr.* 546), an apt mate for an individual
boasting an Oceanid mother (243n.). The source for her name (vari-
able: Robert 762 n.3, Roscher 1.3) and provenance is uncertain: *per-
haps* Diophantus alias Diophanes [Schwartz *RE* 5.1051], who in his
Ποντικαὶ ἱστορίαι alluded to the parentage of Aeetes (so schol. at 240,
FGH 805). It may be however that the name Asterodeia was origin-
ally the property of *Phaethon*'s mother (for the connexion see 245-6n.)
and has been transferred by Ap. himself – a 'stellar' equivalent of
Ῥόδη, Helios' wife and nymph-mother of Phaethon, Lampetie, Aigle
and Phaethousa (so schol. HQV at *Od.* 17.208: Aesch. ? Diggle, ed.
Eur. *Phaethon*, pp. 31-2). It is perhaps worth noting that Ἀστεροδία
(leg. -όδεια) is mother of (a different) Μήδη (but Μέδη Asius *EGF fr.* 10)
according to schol. HPQ at *Od.* 4.797 (?Pherecydes; see on all this
M. Broadbent, *Studies in Greek Genealogy* (Leiden 1968), 308f.); some-
times adduced here is the sequence Ῥόδεια .... Ἰδυῖα in the catalogue
of Oceanids at Hes. *Theog.* 351-2: although Asterodeia is definitely no
Oceanid (schol. 242-4 foolishly say otherwise), I suppose that in the
tangled world of genealogy anything is possible.

242 A little-known, or invented detail (242-3n.)? There is no at-
tempt made at any rate to work in an ἄρα/ῥα pointing to a fact with
which the learned reader *might* be expected to be acquainted (cf. 233-

4n.): ctr. i.625-6 (with VDB 1.256 for possible sources) Σικίνου .. τόν ῥα Θόαντι/νηιὰς Οἰνοίη νύμφη τέκεν ~ *Il.* 14.443f. Σάτνιον .... ὃν ἄρα (imparting an air of familiarity in the context of an 'obituary') νύμφη τέκε νηὶς ../"Ηνοπι ... — For νύμφη τέκεν cf. also *Il.* 20.384, varied by Q.S. 6.465.

243 Ap. is no doubt toying with both *Il.* 23.263 /θῆκε γυναῖκα ... ἰδυῖαν/ and *HyAp* 313/*HyAphr* 44 ἄλοχον ποιήσατο κέδν' εἰδυῖαν/.

Similar phraseology will be applied by Arete to Jason's prospective union with Medea: κουριδίην θήσεσθαι ἐνὶ μεγάροισιν ἄκοιτιν iv.1085 [cf. iv.96f.], this an ironic (cf. iv.814-5!) adaptation of *Il.* 19.297-8 'Αχιλῆος ../κουριδίην ἄλοχον θήσειν (note too *Od.* 21.316 ... ἐὴν θήσεσθαι ἄκοιτιν/; θέσθαι: cf. id. 21.72).

κουριδίην ... ἄκοιτιν Hom. κουρ. + ἄλοχ(ος); *Od.* 13.44-5 γυναῖκας/-ίας cf. i.611, 804-5 and in later verse Greg. Naz. 900.215-6, Nonn. *D.* 13.410, Agath. *AP* 5.302.5. For ἄκοιτις cf. iv.97 /-ίην ... -ιν/, 194-5 -ιν/-ίην, 1085 (above); *GVI* 293.1-2 (Paphlagonia, 2nd/3rd cent.) κατεθήκατ' -ιν/-ίην; also iii.623 /-ίην παράκοιτιν echoed in Q.S. 13.410, nomin. Nonn. *D.* 4.162.

κουρ. with ref. to legal marriage often in the poem: cf. Kirk on *Il.* 1.114-5, and the lit. in *LfgrE* s.v.

θέσθαι See above, and cf. Bacch. 5.169; ctr. the active in Q.S. 3.568, 5.547.

Εἰδυῖαν Aeetes may have enjoyed a casual affair, but his status and family connexions demand that for a permanent consort he acquire somebody with the best of backgrounds. He marries a blood-relative, θεῶν βουλῇσιν according to [Hes.] *Theog.* 960 (cf. Dräger 28): Aeetes and his sister Circe were children of Helios and the Oceanid Perse/Perseis (*Od.* 10.138-9, [Hes.] *Theog.* 956-7 etc. ~ iv.590-1 'Circe, daughter of Perse and Helios'). 'Her name made her a suitable mother for Μήδεια' West on [Hes.] *Theog.* 960, cf. Waser in *RE* 5.2098, who cited εἰδυίῃσι/ ἰδυίῃσι πραπίδεσσι, *Nosti EGF fr.* 6.2.

For ΕΙΔ- rather than ΙΔ- (*Theog.* 352, 960, see West's notes and Richardson on *HyDem* 195; ΙΔ- LA here and at 269) cf. not only Soph. *fr.* 546.4 (but ΙΔ- has been conjectured there from time to time), Lyc. 1024 (Aeetes = Εἰδυίας πόσις) etc., but also the rhyming ΕΙΚΥΙΑΝ ΑΚΟΙΤΙΝ in *Il.* 9.399. Accent: VDB Test. + *app. crit.* here and at 269.

244 Τηθύος Ὠκεανοῦ τε Q.S. 2.117; cf. from early epic Hes. *Theog.* 362-3 Ὠκεανοῦ καὶ Τηθύος ἐξεγένοντο/πρεσβύταται, id. 841 (*Od.* 24.11) Ὠκεανοῦ τε in the same sedes.

Gillies: 'Her descent from Oceanos dates from the earliest legend, when Aea was supposed to lie on the border of Ocean.' *Locus classicus*: Mimn. *IEG* 11a the city of Aeetes, where the rays of Helios are stored 'Ὠκεανοῦ [cf. iii.1230] παρὰ χεῖλος – Jason's destination; Tethys and Oceanus produced rivers, including Phasis, Hes. *Theog.* 337/340.

πανοπλοτάτην Here only. There were 3000 Oceanids according to Hesiod (*Theog.* 364, West ad loc.; cf. *PV* 137 etc.): so Eiduia was something special. For the element 'oldest' in such contexts cf. [Hes.] *Theog.* 945-6 /'Αγλαΐην δ' Ἥφαιστος .../ὁπλοτάτην Χαρίτων .. ποιήσατ' ἄκοιτιν/ (ctr. *Il.* 14.267: Hypnos can't actually have *the youngest*!), *Od.* 11.281-3, Theod. *SH* 759.7-8.

-οπλοτάτην γεγαυῖαν *HyDem* 116 ὁπλότεραι γεγάασιν/. Similar units head the hexameter in Theoc. 22.176, [Orph.] *A.* 410 (cf. *Il.* 4.325).

245-6 Apsyrtus, also known as Phaethon (so Timonax, *FGH* 842 *fr.* 3, according to schol. iii.1236; his *Scythica* must have been replete with Argonautic lore, to judge by the report of schol. iv.1217-9a ~ *FGH* 842 *fr.* 2). The latter designation (see in general Huyck, *HSCP* 91 (1987), 218 with n.5) suggests Ἥλιος Φαέθων: he outshone all his peers, just as Helios may be thought of as surpassing in brilliance the stars in the heavens. But, as has often been noted (see e.g. Fusillo 42-3, Newman 79), our thoughts must also turn to Phaethon son of Helios, who met an untimely end in his father's chariot (iv.597f.) – another prince who, in Euripides' play, lived with his 'parents' in the extreme East (Aethiopia), beside Oceanus (*Phaethon*, prologue, 2f. Diggle, cf. πρώτην there with πρώτῃσιν in iii.163): for the immediate significance of this see on 215f.(A). The association is strengthened in iii.1235f., where 'Phaethon' handles the chariot of his father Aeetes son of Helios (cf. 1229-30), a passage matched by iv.224f., 'Apsyrtus' with this same chariot, whose horses were donated to Aeetes by Helios (219f.). I suspect that another *Phaethonteum* lurks in the simile of iv.460f. ἀταλὸς πάις οἷα..., where Apsyrtus' tender years in other versions (242-3n.) are no doubt alluded to (Faerber 43 n.1): [Hes.] *Theog.* 989 describes Phaethon (son of Eos) as παῖδ' ἀταλὰ φρονέοντα.

Literary reminiscence (like so much else in the poem, better appreciated at the re-reading stage) cleverly deepens the atmosphere of foreboding. The basic model is *Il.* 6.402f., with a contribution from id. 22.506f. (both signalled in *Echoes* 46). Homer tells of Astyanax, so called by everybody but his father because ...; a 'star-like' individual (on the image cf. Kost on Musae. 22, *Exkurs* pp. 164f., NH on Hor. *Carm.* 1.12.47, 48), illustrious, preeminent, like Apsyrtus (the element 'star,' suppressed here but hinted at in 'Ἀστερό- 242, comes out into the open in what appears to be an imaginative borrowing by [Theoc.], 25.139: cf. Gow on 139 and 129f., and also *Il.* 2.480f.!). Now Astyanax is a child of tender years (cf. *Il.* 6.400 /παῖδ' ... ἀταλάφρονα, νήπιον ..., see above), like Apsyrtus in the usual version; and Astyanax, like Apsyrtus, will in the not too distant future meet with an untimely death at the hands of a ruthless enemy.

245 καί μιν ... Cf. ii.361 καί μιν καλέουσι ...

Κόλχων υἷες The younger set, we might say (cf. in general Richardson on *HyDem* 266), rather than periphrastically for 'Colchians' (see on that idiom West on Hes. *Theog.* 240, Hoekstra on *Od.* 13.315, Renehan 1975.156-7). In D.P. 489 Κόλχων υἷες denotes Colchians of military age.

ἐπωνυμίην Not in archaic poetry (ἐπίκλησιν καλέουσιν/ in the model, *Il.* 22.506), but common by the Hellenistic era (see Rank 137f., *LexCal* s.v.), cf. ii.910 (καλέουσιν/ ~ Call. *h.* 3.205 etc.), iv.658.

246 ἔκλεον οὕνεκα Imperfect: Fraenkel on Aesch. *Ag.* 681, Wilkins on Eur. *Hcld.* 86-7. For the sequence 'call *x* by (another) name because ...' cf. *Il.* 6.402f., 22.506f. above, id. 9.562 καλέεσκον ἐπώνυμον, οὕνεκ' (sim. *HyAp* 373, cf. West on Hes. *Theog.* 144-5), 'Orph.' DK1 B13.2-3 ἐπίκλησιν καλέουσιν,/οὕνεκα κτλ., and see Rank 136, 142. — Ctr. *Od.* 7.10 ἔξελον, οὕνεκα πᾶσι/...

ἔκλεον in the sense *call by name* (cf. ἐπικλείειν, Campbell on Q.S. 12.453; Schulze *QE* 285 *et circa*; Marxer 53 is wide of the mark) here only in the active; but κλεί- i.217, ii.687, iii.277 ὅν τε ... -ουσι, 357, 1003 τόν τε -ουσ', iv.829 τήν τε -ουσι Κράταιιν/, 987 (not *celebrate*: cf. καλεῖν in Pind. *O.* 9.63), and so Call. *h.* 1.51 τά τε κλείουσι Πάνακρα/, ? Dem. Bith. *CA* 14, Nic. *Alex.* 22,36 /τὴν .. τε -ουσι, 539, D.P. 151 τήν τε -ουσι Κάραμβιν/ [+ Ap. ii.361], Opp. *Hal.* 5.536 /τήν τ' .. -ουσι, [Orph.] *L.* 195 (κλεῖον, the only past tense), id. *fr.* 315.4.

In i.238, ii.977 the passive κλείονται -εσθαι, cf. Opp. *Hal.* 1.379 -ονται, *GVI* 1904.18 (Amorgos, 3rd cent. or later) κλείετ' imperf.; but Call. *h.* 4.40 ἔκλεο, Nic. *fr.* 71.5 corr. κλέεται, *GVI* 946.7 (Calymnos, 2nd/1st cent.) κλεόμαν, id. 1904.16 (see above) ἐκλεόμην. [Soph. *Trach.* 639 corr. κλέονται need not, and probably does not, mean 'be called.']

Middle (?): Nic. *Ther.* 104 corr. Gow (ἥν τε .... κλέονται. Some correction is certainly required).

οὕνεκα .. μετέπρεπεν Phal. *HE* 2937 /οὕνεκα συμποσίοισι μετέπρεπεν.
πᾶσι μετέπρεπεν -οισι Cf. *Il.* 2.579 *vulg.* ὅτι πᾶσι [cf. suppl. in Anon.

Blem. 40, Livrea ad loc.] μετέπρεπεν ἡρώεσσιν/ [~ i.100, [Orph.] *A.* 169]. Related runs in Ap. are: (1) ii.784 ὃς πάντεσσι μετέπρεπεν ἠιθέοισιν/: cf. *Il.* 16.194 [sim. *SEG* 30.1540.6; undated] ὃς πᾶσι -ε Μυρμιδόνεσσιν/, *Od.* 17.213 and 20.174 αἳ πᾶσι -ον αἰπολίοισι/. (2) iii.334-5 οὕνεκεν .... πάντεσσι -εν Αἰολίδῃσι/. (3) iii.443 ... δ' ἐν πᾶσι -εν Αἴσονος υἱός/ ~ [Orph.] *A.* 806 ... δ' .. ἐν πάντεσσι -ε δῖος ᾽Ιήσων/, cf. Q.S. 1.41 (*Il.* 2.579 *vulg.*, Hes. *Theog.* 377 πᾶσι -εν ~ *Od.* 2.194 ... δ' ἐν πᾶσιν ...). — Various other mutations may be found in [Theoc.] 25.131, Q.S. 1.169, 4.129, 187, Greg. Naz. 1503.318.

πᾶσι μετ- ἠιθέοισι Theoc. 2.125 πάντεσσι μετ' ἠιθέοισι καλεῦμαι/.

μετέπρεπεν ἠιθέοισι Cf. ii.784 cited above. So *SEG* 20.85.2 (Cilicia, 2nd cent. AD) μετέπρεπον ἠιθέοισι/, cf. *GVI* 1519.5 (Moesia, 1st cent. BC) ἠιθέοις .. μεταπρεφθείς ~ Opp. *Hal.* 5.466 ἠιθέοισι μετέπρεπεν.

μετέπρεπεν Scil. like a star (see on 245-6): cf. e.g. Sappho *PLF* 96.6f., Aesch. *Ag.* 6 (with Fraenkel on id. 242), i.239-40. Note too πρέποντα in schol. T at *Il.* 6.402-3a.

ἠιθέοισι i.e. young batchelors, like Apsyrtus still living in the parental home (241): cf. *LfgrE* s.v.

247 τοὺς δ' ἔχον Hom. /οἳ δ' ἔχον. τούς harks back to the θάλαμοι of 236 (Vian ed. 1961, on 247; VDB 2.120, on 248), and has nothing to do with the δόμοι (*two* in number) of 238f. (ctr. Mooney, and Gillies pp. 135-6). Ap. has started with the central door and moved to its immediate vicinity, but he puts off mention of Medea because she (τῇ μὲν ἄρ' ... 248) will get the narrative going again. The remaining royal apartments are therefore dealt with first.

It has often been remarked that the sisters do not occupy the upstairs γυναικωνῖτις we expect to find in the heroic period (cf. Hopkinson on Call. *h.* 6.4; there are some uncertainties however, see e.g. Russo on *Od.* 17.492-506). In this palace there is free and immediate access to (and movement from) θάλαμοι as the sisters, and the Phrixids, hatch their plans; we are able to enjoy a clear view of Medea as she struggles to step out of her apartment into the open courtyard to join Chalciope (645f.); and she is before us right now, in the path of Jason and the others, as she moves ἐκ θαλάμου θαλαμόνδε. To some degree then the open courtyard serves as a stage.

ἀμφίπολοί τε καὶ Αἰήταο θύγατρες On ἀμφίπολοι see 235-6n. With the wording ctr. (a) *Od.* 6.320 /ἀμφίπολοι τ' ...; (b) *Il.* 22.155 (sim. *HyAp* 446) ... ἄλοχοι καλαί τε θύγατρες/, *HyDem* 105 ᾽Ελευσινίδαο θύγατρες/. Medea is called Αἰήταο .. θυγατρί/ iv.1297, cf. D.P. 1022 /Αἰήταο θυγατρός.

248 ... ἄμφω ... Contrast *Il.* 5.152-3 ... Ξάνθον τε Θόωνά τε, Φαίνοπος υἷε,/ἄμφω ... ἄμφω: not 'the two daughters' but 'the daughters, both of them'; their bedrooms are located in this same sector of the palace: that is important.

Χαλκιόπη Μήδειά τε now appear on the scene, in reverse order (248f.253f.). Ap. will presently bring together the principal actors in the drama: the sisters, Aeetes, Jason, Argos (cf. *Noten* 341). Chalciope will be the one to take centre-stage first; briefly, but long enough to fix firmly in our minds the theme of maternal protectiveness.

Chalciope mother of the Phrixids: VDB 1.170 with n.5, Matthews 203.

248-9 Had Ω presented us with τὴν .... μετιοῦσαν, we might have entertained the possibility at least of an anacoluthon: so for instance Mooney, scil. ἐνόησαν or the like; he compared iv.852, but Fränkel's στῆ is exactly what is required there. *Lw*'s τῇ however (which must be Μηδείη, not 'there,' as Platt suggested, 1918.136-7: 'there <was> Medea, on her way to join [μετιοῦσα] Chalciope'; so Gillies) indicates that a line (or two) expressing the newcomers' encounter with the priestess has dropped out: ὁπλοτέρη ξύμβληντο, τάφον δέ μιν εἰσορόωντες *exempli gratia* Fränkel 1950.125 n.28 and OCT.

No amount of tinkering will enable us to dispose cleanly of οἵγε, as Wellauer stressed: on the long wait for the pronoun, to which Gillies took exception (p.138), see Vian 1973.100. That is one reason why Gerhard's βῆ μὲν ἄρ' ἥγε .... μετιοῦσα (in Erbse's estimation 'a masterpiece,' 1963.24) is just not acceptable: it is based in any case on a run ἡ μὲν (.. ἤει ....) μετιοῦσα, all conjectures of E. For even more hair-raising emendations see the *nefanda seges* in Merkel's *app. crit.*/id. *RhM* n.s. 1 (1842), 614-6, and Damsté 43-4.

249 ἐκ θαλάμου θαλαμόνδε = 671 infr., cf. n. on 215f.C(4); combines *Il.* 24.275/*Od.* 22.140 + *Od.* 21.81/22.161 (2.348 θαλαμόνδε κα- later in verse).

κασιγνήτην μετιοῦσαν Cf. iv.389.

250-2 We have not been permitted to wonder, let alone be in suspense about (*pace* Klein 228) how Eros/Jason will come across Medea in the palace. We are now informed that she was there, and why she was regularly elsewhere, as a prelude to her imminent appeal to Hecate (467f.), and to her eventual departure for the day (cf. VDB 2.61 n.2).

This is the second (cf. 210f.) in a series of succinctly presented explicit interventions in the wake of the Olympian scene (*Studies* 55-6). We are to imagine Hera as an ever-present spectator, keeping an interested eye on proceedings, not as a goddess who simply pops up out of the blue at odd moments; so here it is not said that she *had* arranged Medea's stay, but that she was *in the process of* doing so, as the newcomers arrive on the scene.

Like many Iliadic gods who control events decisively (and often without prior warning), Hera exercises a restraining or curbing influence. One may compare the use of ἐρύκειν in such passages as *Il.* 21.6-7 Hera spread a mist ἐρυκέμεν the fleeing Trojans, 384 Ἥρη γὰρ ἐρύκακε, scil. with a blunt warning to combatants (note also *HyAp* 99 /Ἥρης ... ἥ μιν ἔρυκε/); similarly in *Arg.*, iv.509-10 ἀλλ' ἀπέρυκεν/ Ἥρη, scil. the pursuing Colchians by discharging lightning (so too ii.287 κατέρυκεν/432 ἐρύκακε Iris/the Boreads, whom she accosted as they chased the Harpies). Here there is no actual confrontation (Buccholz 82 n.2), whether by means of a dream (as in the case of Nausicaa) or by divine messenger or by direct contact in fully or partially materialized form: Hera, like Eros, and like the Iliadic gods on some occasions, works λάθρῃ. It is open to us to say that Ap. really means that Hera has imposed her will upon Medea to keep her there (a variation on the often unceremonious ἐπὶ φρεσὶ θῆκε routine, e.g. *Il.* 1.55, cf. iv.1199). In fact, his chosen mode of presentation is far more vivid and suggestive than that: Medea is a captive, confined to the house by an unseen divine warder. There is no room here, any more than there is in Homer (see amongst recent commentators Hainsworth on *Il.* 10.515-22, Janko on id. 15.461-70), for chance (Val. Flacc. 5.329 *forte* ...), still less for 'Tyche ... an instrument of divine will' (Fränkel 1952.152). See further Lawall 160-2 for discussion of 'divinely ordained coincidence' in the poem. (Nyberg, 18, 46f., is muddled.)

For a different (but not, alas, unique) view of things see lately Natzel 44.

250-1 πρὶν δ' ... But *Il.* 18.386 al. πάρος γε μὲν οὔτι θαμίζεις/ (cf. the variation on this in 54-5 above, followed up with ἐπεί), ii.451 πρόσθεν ... κεῖσε θάμιζον/.

For πρὶν δ' οὔτι cf. ii.336 πρὶν δ' οὔτι (θ- .. ἐρύκω/; πονέεσθαι/ 335) ~ *Il.* 9.523 (λίσσεσθαι 520 ~ Ap. 336), *Od.* 22.59; for οὔτι θάμιζεν/ *Od.* 8.451 οὔτι ... θάμιζεν/ (different sense; ἐπεί 452 'ever since' ctr. ἐπεί Ap. iii.252).

θάμιζεν/έν Nic. *Alex.* 578 ἐν δονάκεσσι θαμίζων/, 'that frequents the reeds' Gow-Scholfield.

ἐν μεγάροις *Od.* 3.213 etc. Not μεγάρῳ (*EtG, EtM*); from δόμῳ above. The singular can denote the entire palace (so as early as Homer, *pace* Braswell on Pind. *P.* 4.134(c): cf. some at least of the examples in *LH* 1.1027.10f., and in our poem e.g. iv.1121), but Ap. has only the plural with ἐν/ἐνί: i.285, 909, ii.304, 776, iii.228, 305, 585, 1117, iv.8, 1085, 1162.

251 Ἑκάτης The figure of Colchian Hecate will be discussed at length in a succeeding volume.

πανήμερος 'all day long' (cf. infr. 819f.828f./1138f.1143f.), but we can take it that 'every day' also applies (cf. 895, and also the highly sarcastic πανημέριον in i.873; πανήμεροι in ii.1191): σαίρω δάπεδον θεοῦ/ παναμέριος .../λατρεύων τὸ κατ' ἦμαρ says Ion in Euripides' play (121f.).

πανήμερος (also i.873, 1015, ii.811, 1191) in pre-Hellenistic literature: Hdt. 7.183.3, [Aesch.] *PV* 1024, Ar. *Ran.* 387 (prob. f.v.l. in Soph. *Trach.* 660, cf. Davies ad loc.), *Certamen* 119 (δαίνυντο: cf. ii.811); it is not common subsequently: Call. *h.* 4.261, 6.87, Strat. *AP* 12.247.5, Opp. *Hal.* 3.360, Max.107.

Given Homer's πάννυχος παννύχιος and the like (also ἐτερήμερος) the word may have occurred in archaic verse (Schulze *KS* 834). For the alternation cf. e.g. ἐφήμερος ἐφημέριος (*BP* 100 ~ 320) and more generally Chantraine *FN* 37, Williams on Call. *h.* 2.79, Hopkinson on id. 6.87.

πανήμερος -πονεῖτο Cf. ii.667 (oxen) πανημέριοι πονέονται/. ἀμφεπονεῖτο for ἀμφεπόλευε (e.g. *CEG* (1) 93.2, Attica *c.* 410-400?: the daughter of Callimachus /ἡ .. Νίκης ἀμφεπόλευε νεών/) only here.

252 ... νηόν 842 and 915 Ἑκάτης ... νηόν; but 737-8 (where the 'temple' is uppermost in Medea's mind) νηόν/... Ἑκάτης.

'.../temple' (pause) forces itself on the attention: it is to prove an important focal point in the evolution of the Jason-Medea relationship.

ἐπεί ῥα From *Il.* 5: 511 ἡ γάρ ῥα πέλεν .. ἀρηγών/ (ἐπεὶ ἴδε 510 cf. Ap. 253); 77-8 ὅς ῥα Σκαμάνδρου/ἀρητὴρ ἐτέτυκτο, θεὸς δ' ὣς τίετο δήμῳ. Cf. also *HyAp* 304 ἐπεὶ πέλε ...

ῥα *bekanntlich*: you know the story (cf. 233-4n.).

θεῆς This form is amply documented by Campbell on Q.S. 12.112. Add θεῆς from Call. *SH* 253(b)14, and θεῇ from *CEG* (1) 422/ suppl. 423, Samos 6th cent.

ἀρήτειρα A high-sounding word, building an imposing σπονδειάζων; based on Homer's ἀρητήρ (cf. *LfgrE* s.v., and Bulloch 1977.102f.). The earliest known examples are to be found in Ap. (also i.312 Iphias Ἀρτέμιδος πολιηόχου ἀρήτειρα/; Nelis, *CQ* n.s. 41 (1991), 96f., suggests links between this priestess and Medea, cf. earlier C. S. Broeniman, *Thematic Patterns in the* Argonautica *of Apollonius Rhodius: A Study in the Imagery of Similes* (Diss. Univ. Illinois, 1989), 75f.) and in Call. (*h*. 6.42 ... Νικίππᾳ, τάν οἱ πόλις ἀράτειραν/δαμοσίαν ἔστασαν). Medea too will owe her appointment to the *polis* whose womenfolk she serves: observe the 'spokesperson' approach of 893-5.

Other examples of the word: [Orph.] *A*. 905 (Medea), Musae. 68, Christod. 139, epigr. in *SEG* 30.1272.9 (Caria, late Hellenistic/early Roman), Kaibel *EG* 872.1 (not dated), epigr. *ap*. Peek, *ZPE* 7 (1971), 206 verse 1, orac. *ap*. Merkelbach, id. 8 (1971), 94 verse 15. On its formation see Kost on Musae. 68, Hopkinson on Call. *h*. 6.42.

253-6 Our first view of life within the palace. The atmosphere is highly charged from the very outset, as Medea's loud cry triggers alarm and commotion. We will automatically recall two powerful Iliadic scenes where individuals react sharply to a tragic loss (*Echoes* 46); (1) to the death of Achilles' close companion Patroclus in 18.28f.: /δμωαὶ δ' .... μεγάλ' ἴαχον, ἐκ δὲ θύραζε/ἔδραμον ἀμφ' ..., χερσὶ δὲ πᾶσαι/ κτλ. (35 ... ὤμωξεν, ἄκουσε δὲ ...); (2) to the death of Hector, whose wife in 22.447f. (Huber 49) /κωκυτοῦ .. ἤκουσε ...·. χαμαὶ δέ οἱ ἔκπεσε κερκίς (δμωῇσιν 449, μεγάροιο διέσσυτο 460).

We need not concern ourselves with differences of detail and emphasis. The point here is that this loud cry or shriek (of astonishment, and of alarm: strangers are present) is interpreted by the mother and by the servants as a κώκυμα (cf. *Il*. 18.28 ~ 22.447). There is no 'trivialisation' of *Il*. 22 (Zanker 1987.226 n.183, paraphrasing 'Chalciope's handmaids drop their sewing' (!)). Chalciope and her immediate circle have been living in dread of bad news about the sons, who took themselves off so inconsiderately: now it seems to have arrived. Medea's sharp cry and the consequent stampede thus constitute an effective substitute for the standard Homeric reaction of (silent) amazement at an unexpected arrival (examples in Richardson on *Il*. 24.482-4).

Time and again critics have thought fit to make ἀνίαχεν work harder still. So, for instance, VDB 2.39, in analysing this fine scene, remark: "Le cri involuntaire poussé à la simple vue de Jason et de ses compagnons ... marque la naissance de l'amour en même temps qu'il met en marche toute l' action en provoquant l' entrée en scène des protagonistes. Le 'coup de foudre' exprimé par le seul verbe ἀνίαχεν [it is unelaborated, effectively isolated within the verse: Hurst 84] précède et justifie l'intervention d'Amour qui n'aura lieu que vingt-deux vers plus loin." Similarly Knox (304): "Medea's sudden, involuntary cry, caused by the sight of Jason, is the first sign of her passion." Virg. *A.* 1.613, which Knox cites in support, is different however; by then Dido has been confronted directly by Aeneas: *obstipuit* recalls Ap. 284, while *aspectu* and *casu* recall 453f./459f. (cf. Val. Flacc. 5.373f., where Jason has been beautified by Juno).

I have not taken the trouble to track down the πρῶτος εὑρετής. He may go back a long way, for Brunck thought it necessary to incorporate in his generally austere linguistic commentary this note (pretty bland, admittedly): "(σφεας) refertur maxime ad Phrixi filios, quos in Graeciam profectos, quum Medea reduces inopinato videret, prae admiratione et gaudio exclamavit." No matter. ἀνίαχεν has nothing whatever to do with the awakening of passion (or even a mild flutter), which starts when Eros has shot Medea: then, stunned, she responds to his charms, 287f.

Homer and/or Ap. are imitated by Virgil (*A.* 9.476f.), Ovid (*Met.* 4.229), Nonnos (*D.* 41.305f. cf. 45.49); cf. also Q.S. 1.445-6.

253 ὡς ἴδεν = *HyHom* 19.39; in Hom./Hes. ὡς ἴδε(v) occupies the first foot (thereafter pretty mobile). iv.1720-1 σφεας ὁππότε .... ἴδοντο/.

ἆσσον It matters little whether ἆσσον is construed as <drawing> 'closer' (VDB 3.178, on iv.853; fully expressed in ii.107) or just 'in the vicinity,' as for example i.702 'she addressed *x* ἆσσον ἐοῦσαν' = Homeric ἐγγύς (see *Echoes* ad loc. and 17n.); cf. for the latter (e.g.) *Od.* 17.301 ὡς ἐνόησεν Ὀδυσσέα ἐγγὺς ἐόντα/.

ἀνίαχεν 253-6n. The verb before Ap. (also ii.270, οἱ δ' ἐσιδόντες/ ... -ον) only in Eur. *Or.* 1465 ('formed like ἀναβοάω' Willink ad loc.); later: Antip. Thess. *GPh* 477, *Or. Sib.* 1.173, Triph. 375, Q.S. 14.31, Greg. Naz. 507.3 (~ *AP* 1.92), Nonn. *Par.* + *D.* 15 × in all (*Par.* 18.79 δερκομένη ...). [I doubt if Ap.'s ἀνιάχω 'is based on the old variant ἀνίαχοι' (Janko, taken up by Rengakos, 1993.135) at *Il.* 13.41.]

ὀξὺ δ' ἄκουσε She hears 'sharply' because she takes in a sharp piercing cry (cf. Kaimio 38f.), exactly like Ajax in the model, *Il.* 17.256 ὀξὺ δ' ἄκουσεν (Menelaus /ἤυσεν .. διαπρύσιον 247). For ὀξύ cf. further Aesch. *Suppl.* 910 corr. (Sideras 146-7, FJW ad loc.; but Eur. *Or.* 1530 is different), Pl. *Lg.* 927b; also Nonn. *Par.* 19.150 ὀξὺς ἀκούσας/.

254 ... Χαλκιόπη· She is thrust into the limelight. Ctr. the model, *Il.* 17.256 (above), where the name closes the verse.

<ποδῶν> προπάροιθε Triph. 262 ποδῶν -εν ἐλυσθείς/ (ctr. *Il.* 24.510); earlier in the verse *Od.* 17.357, Mosch. *Eur.* 93, [Apolin.] 49.6. ποδῶν was restored by Chrestien (Vian 1972.478) and later by Hoelzlin, with justified confidence (Fränkel *Einleitung* 26): 'sic certe scripsisse Apollonium non opinor, sed scio.'

... προπάροιθε βαλοῦσαι Ctr. *Il.* 21.104 (.../'Ἰλίου) προπάροιθε (ἐμῆς ἐν) χερσὶ βάλῃσι/, as well as *Od.* 9.482, 10.172 /κὰδ δ' ἔβαλε (-ον) προπάροιθε ... The violent verb puts one in mind of ἔρριψε at *Il.* 22.406 (contextually similar to id. 447f., see 253-6n.).

255 νήματα καὶ κλωστῆρας The translation 'yarn and thread(s)' (e.g., Seaton; Fowler 1990) seems singularly pointless (hardly explicable as a 'display' combination of Homeric and unHomeric elements), and the distinction, such as it is, is hard to uphold in the face of such expressions as Antip. Sid. *HE* 193 εὐκλώστου νήματος (sim. Anon. id. 3824-5), Triph. 345-6 νήματα ~ κλωστοῖσι ... Better would be 'yarn [in the process of being spun] and skeins [spun yarn now ready for the loom],' but iv.1062 points to a more satisfactory explanation. There κλωστήρ clearly means 'spindle': Livrea ad loc. cites schol. τὴν ἄτρακτον, Suda κ1837. Note also Antip. Sid. *HE* 184-5 ... ἄτρακτον,/κλωστῆρα ... (i.e. the *instrument* [-ήρ] that ...); Nonn. *D.* 24.263 (νήματα 264) with Chuvin on id. 3.330 (κλωστήρ = ἄτρακτος Μοιρῶν; add 40.2); Ov. *Met.* 4.229 (above 253-6n.) *fusus*. This is not the place to discuss Theoc. 24.70, opinions about which differ markedly: see e.g. Gow/Dover ad loc., and Gow, *CR* 57 (1943), 109; White, *Eranos* 74 (1976), 24f. and her ed. ('spindle,' as a number of older critics).

Whatever the precise meaning is, the point is that the everyday palace routine (including that of Chalciope, who, unlike Medea, lives a domesticated life: Natzel 45) is disrupted, violently disrupted, by this intrusion.

ἀολλέες .. πᾶσαι *Od.* 22.446 (wailing δμωαί) αἱ δὲ γυναῖκες ἀολλέες ἦλθον ἅπασαι/ ~ iv.1182-3 ... δὲ γυναῖκες ἀολλέες ἔκτοθι πύργων/βαῖνον .., σὺν δ' ...

ἔκτοθι Schol.: 'for ἐκτός [L]/ἔκτοσε [P].' See further examples in Campbell *Index* s.v. (the word nowhere else in 3[H]), and for -θι Vian ed. 1961 ad loc., Schneider/McLennan on Call. *h.* 1.30; but n.b. Antim. cited in 373n.! Cf. e.g. τηλόθι for τηλόσε infr. 261 al., ὑψόθι iv.1709 (~ ὑψόσ' *Il.* 10.461) al. (3^H: Arat. 558, 992, Call. *h.* 1.30, Theoc. 24.57, Euphor. *SH* 413.8).

ἔκτοθι is a variant for ἔκτοσε in *Od.* 14.277.

256 ... **ἔδραμον** After *HyDem* 187-8 αἱ δὲ .../ἔδραμον, ἡ δ' ἄρ' ..., another fast-moving narrative. Ctr. *Il.* 18.30 cited in n. on 253-6: /ἔδραμον then πᾶσαι/.

ἡ δ' ἅμα τῇσιν See for this run Campbell on Q.S. 12.182. Scil. ἐκδραμοῦσα, cf. i.637 (*Echoes* ad loc.), Fränkel OCT here. Ardizzoni (1956.368f./1958.45) deals very effectively with the once popular τοῖσιν (AD only).

ἑοὺς υἱῆας ~ 712 τεοὺς υἱῆας. See on 196.

257 ὑψοῦ .. **χεῖρας ἀνέσχεθεν** adapts *Od.* 9.294-5 κλαίοντες ἀνεσχέθομεν Διὶ χεῖρας [cf. Theoc. 22.129-30]/... ὁρόωντες (~ iv.593 χεῖρας ἀνέσχεθον ἀθανάτοισιν/), cf. note on 176f.(1); and *Il.* 10.460 (cf. Vian ed. 1961) τάγ' .../ὑψόσ' ἀνέσχεθε χειρί (~ iv.1709 /δεξιτερῇ .. ἀνέσχεθε ὑψόθι τόξον/).

ὑψοῦ 221n.

χάρματι .. **ἀνέ-** But infr. 724 ἀνέ- χάρματι.

ἀνέσχεθεν· ὣς ... Ctr. *Il.* 7.412 /ὣς then ἀνέσχεθε.

ὣς δὲ καὶ αὐτοί The same run in iv.991 (in iv.1482 Ω's οἱ should certainly be read, cf. Campbell 1976.340); earlier in the verse Q.S. 7.164.

258 *HyHom* 6.15-16 (gods ~ Aphrodite) οἱ δ' ἠσπάζοντο ἰδόντες/ χερσί τ' ἐδεξιόωντο (v.l. τε δεξ-).

δεξιόωντο i.e. δεξιῇ ἠσπάζοντο (*Il.* 10.542, cf. *HyHom* above, Càssola ad loc.). In ii.756 a more general 'welcome,' 'greet' (LSJ s.v., numerous glosses in *LH*) is meant: ὥστε θεὸν .. δεξιόωντο/ ~ *Il.* 22.434-5 θεὸν ὥς/δειδέχατ', the latter verb regularly glossed by schol. D and others with δεξιοῦσθαι.

ἀμφαγάπαζον denotes actual physical embrace in *HyDem* 290, 436 (/γηθοσύνας 437 corr.), cf. id. 439, and later e.g. Opp. *Hal.* 5.482. Such probably is the force of the verb infr. 1167 (see n.), /οἱ δέ μιν ἀμφαγάπαζον ὅπως ἴδον, and not just 'welcome warmly' (as in *Od.* 14.381 ἐγὼ δέ μιν -ον/, *Il.* 16.192, cf. Hoekstra on *Od.* 16.17-9). ἀμφαγαπῶντες in Hes. *WD* 58 finely combines the literal and the metaphorical, Verdenius ad loc.

259 /γηθόσυνοι· pulls the sentence up sharply (more so than in i.350 .../γηθόσυνος, καὶ τοῖα .. ἀγόρευσεν/, with no change of subject) and catches our attention. We are all the more surprised by the tone of what follows.

γηθόσυνος occurs a round dozen times in *Arg.*; very common in later verse. See Campbell on Mosch. *Eur.* 117.

τοῖον δὲ .. φάτο μῦθον New (24n.) + old: φ. μ./ Homer etc. (*Od.* 2.384 al. -αμένη φ. μ./), in Ap. only here and infr. 974(n.) καὶ τοῖον ὑποσσαίνων φ. μ./; not popular in 3[H], it would seem: Theoc. 2.113 /ἕζετ' ... καὶ ἑζόμενος φ. μ./ after *Il.* 24.597-8 /ἕζετο δ' .... δὲ .. φ. μ./. For an elaboration on this clausula see 24n.

κινυρομένη The panic is over: the sons are safe and sound. But we still get the 'lament' we have been led to expect (253f.) as Chalciope in the company of her 'chorus' of maidservants confronts her errant offspring (cf. Beye 1982.123 on the 'staging' here). The initial display of mutual joy, thrown into sharp relief by the parallel strands υἷας ἰδοῦσα, χάρματι: μητέρα ἰδόντες, γηθόσυνοι, gives way at once to tearful recrimination as the mother indulges in an orgy of self-pity, lamenting the agonies to which she has been subjected by her late husband and neglectful sons (262 δειλή, 264 ἀνίας, 267 ἀχέουσαν). After this her obsessive determination to shield her sons from danger is wholly believable. (Händel 98-9 displays an astonishing insensitivity in his handling of this entire scene.) Faerber (98) contrasts this passage with the description of Penelope's reunion with her son in *Od.* 17: conscious of the grief his absence will have caused (7f.) he goes to find her; he is accosted by nurse then by δμωαί, who κύνεον ἀγαπαζόμεναι ...; Penelope tearfully embraces her son, kisses him and (40f.) ὀλοφυρομένη ἔπεα πτερόεντα προσηύδα·/ἦλθες, Τηλέμαχε, γλυκερὸν φάος κτλ.: "aber wie erquickend liest sich deren kurze Rede gegen die der Chalkiope, die bis zum Rand mit Rührseligkeit angefüllt ist."

We also catch in this scene echoes of the mournful address (κινύρετο i.292, cf. Herter *JAW* 342) of Alcimede to her son as he leaves home for distant shores (notably: i.279 δειλή, ibid. ... ἐφετμήν, 280 κηδέων, 285 λελείψομαι, cf. 295 ἀνίας). There are differences though. Jason's mother was grief-stricken, but resigned; Chalciope clearly put up a fight, as she will later on to shield her sons from harm. And no room is found here for a soothing reply to match Jason's speech of consolation in i.295f.: sentimentality has no place subsequently, either before Jason's ordeal, when Argos plays the part of the calculating plotter, or after it, when he and his brothers *do* leave home for good (differently Herter *JAW* 373).

The verb: mothers in particular κινύρονται, see Campbell on Q.S. 12.486 for discussion (also, briefly, Bulloch on Call. *h.* 5.119). This expressive word had been applied to Alcimede, overwhelmed with sorrow at the prospect of her son's departure (i.292, see above), and to the Lemniades as they were about to lose their sexual partners (i.883). It recurs in two further harrowing pictures, infr. 664 ('loss' of 'husband'), iv.1063 (poor orphaned children). Cf. κινυρὸν .. γόον of the mourning Heliades in iv.605.

260-7 Assonance (see in general *Noten* 637) and terminal rhyme play a large part in Chalciope's outburst: -όθ- 261 is picked up by πόθ- .. -ποθ- 262; 262 -ον -ον, 262-3 -ης/-ης, 264 -ὰς .. -ας, 265 -η -η; 265-6 'Ορχ./'Ορχ. As the speech draws to a close the internal pauses come progressively later (264 πατρός, 265 ἡμετέρῃ κραδίῃ, 266 ὅστις ὅδ' 'Ορχομενός); its climax is expressed in a single unstopped line at 267, ἀποπρολιπόντες forming a ring with and intensifying λιπόντες at the close of 260.

260 Chalciope exercises no self-restraint: 'In spite of everything [rather than 'actually,' 'assuredly' or the like] it turns out that you were not after all going to [cf. Campbell on Mosch. *Eur.* 73] ...' Cf. οὐκ ἄρ' ἔμελλες *Od.* 9.475 (176f.(1)n.) and sim.; this particular run is uncommon subsequently, it would appear: *GVI* 2022.9 (Bithynia, 1st/2nd cent.), Q.S. 13.368.

ἀκηδείῃ ii.219 (Phineus to the Argonauts) μηδέ μ' ἀκηδείῃσιν ἀφορμηθῆτε λιπόντες may be taken as representative of the kind of appeal Chalciope will have directed at her sons when they took it into their heads to wander off. On ἀκηδείη see 298n. The Phrixids' 'lack of care,' 'indifference' is to take on a positively sinister aspect in 597 below (see n.) when their grandfather feels threatened.

261 τηλόθι πλάγξεσθαι Similarly /τηλόθι μοι πλάζοιτο in Meleag. *HE* 4456, cf. τηλοῦ in i.1220; earlier Parm. DK28 B8.28 /τῆλε .. ἐπλάχθησαν. For -εσθαι (not well-attested: -ασθαι Ω) see Vian ed. 1961, VDB 3.182 (on iv.1000²); the run οὐκ ἄρ' ἔμελλ- in Homer nearly always involves the future infinitive: *GH* 2.309. It is impossible to be wholly sure however: πλάγξασθαι is hardly barbarous (not that Naber 27, who himself conjectured -εσθαι, concerned himself with any such niceties), and we could be dealing with a case of *variatio* in 1066:

-εσθαι (so Ω). Lloyd-Jones 1963.157 regarded the aorist here as *lectio difficilior*.

τηλόθι 255n. τηλόθι is a variant for τηλόσε in *Od*. 5.59: see Campbell on Mosch. *Eur*. 92.

πλάγξεσθαι Sarcastic of course; and even more cutting in the light of 'literary' models. The mission prescribed by Phrixus (263) truly necessitated πλαγκτοσύνη, as endured by the Argonauts at the behest of Pelias (i.22, iv.1321 cf. i.81 cited below), by Odysseus (*Od*. 1.2 etc.; ctr. here 16.64 ... πλαζόμενος· ὡς γάρ οἱ ἐπέκλωσεν τά γε δαίμων) and by, e.g., Heracles (*HyHom* 15.5 [v.l.] πλαζόμενος πομπῇ ὑπ' Εὐρυσθῆος ἄνακτος). The difference here is that the Phrixids were *not allowed* by 'Destiny' to 'wander' any great distance.

μετὰ δ' .. ἔτραπεν The splitting of μετατρέπειν makes the point forcefully: 'back you were turned ...' Not an Homeric tmesis with the active verb: ctr. 649n. (*Od*. 10.469, Hes. *Theog*. 58 περὶ δ' ἔτραπον – ×, i.400 ἐπὶ δ' ἔτρεπον).

Ctr. Pind. *fr*. 177 μοῖραν μετατραπεῖν ('change the course of ...').

Αἶσα gives substance to οὐκ ἄρ' ἐμέλλετ'. The idea that αἶσα or μοῖρα can influence specific events in an individual's life (usually to his detriment) is known to Homer, e.g. *Od*. 5.206-7, see Hainsworth on 7.196-8 and also U. Bianchi, *Dios Aisa* (Rome 1953); cf. in Ap. esp. iv.36 (... ἀπενόσφισεν αἶσα/); τις αἶσα infr. 328 is not essentially different, cf. n. ad loc.

For the whole sequence compare and contrast i.78 οὐ μὲν ἔμελλε/, 79 αἶσα, 81 /πλαγχθέντας (scil. a very long distance).

262 One is reminded of the movement of *Il*. 24.253f., a couplet addressed by the tetchy Priam to his bad children, then /ὤμοι ἐγὼ πανάποτμος, followed by some thoughts on the good ones. Chalciope on the other hand can only concern herself with bad.

δειλὴ ἐγών So S. Editors of late have consistently got it wrong here. Brunck in 1780 actually conjectured ἐγών; Wellauer disagreed, saying of the hiatus (ἐγώ Ω) 'nullus est.' But Ap. never admits hiatus after ἐγώ, whether it is followed by a strong stop or not: ctr. iii.636 (/δειλὴ ἐγών, οἷον, ἐγώ GD)/976 (οὔ τοι ἐγὼν οἷοι, ἐγώ G) with i.279/ iii.771, id. 674.

For /δειλὴ ἐ. cf. [Opp.] *Cyn*. 3.229, 231, Nonn. *D*. 8.316 (δ. δ' ἐγώ Leon. Tar. *HE* 2403); Hom. ἐγὼ δειλή: *Il*. 18.54/22.431, sorrowing mothers. οἷον following an exclamation of this sort: Davies on Soph. *Trach*. 1206.

πόθον Ἑλλάδος must be an echo of ποθεινὰ .. Ἑλλάς in the highly coloured Pind. *P.* 4.218 (cf. Braswell on 184(b) and 218(b); n.b. τοκέων (!) .. αἰδῶ, and φρασί ~ Ap. κραδίη 265, ὀδυνᾶν ~ Ap. ἀνίας 264), there a longing instilled by Cypris in Medea (present now, soon to be a victim herself of a πόθος she cannot understand, one which embraces the allure of a distant Hellas), here a longing generated by an inexplicable infatuation externally imposed, causing them to act as they would not normally have acted.

Ἑλλάδος 13n.

ἔκποθεν ἄτης Shaped like i.1037 (-ος) ἔκποθεν ἄτης/ (= Nonn. *Par.* 17.34).

ἔκποθεν reinforces the uncomprehending οἷον. The word is attested first in Ap., but note Plato *Phdr.* 244d ἐκ μηνιμάτων ποθέν, 'as a result of acts incurring blood-guilt of one kind or another,' al., and see Wackernagel *VS* 1.299, Ardizzoni here. Distribution: Campbell on Q.S. 12.509.

Platt (see on 263) asserted that in Ap. the genitive depending on ἔκποθεν is not qualified. There is a world of difference of course between the expressions ἔκποθεν ἄτης λευγαλέης and ἔκποθεν ἀφράστοιο κευθμῶνος χθονίου, however that is to be explained (infr. 1289-90, see n.).

ἄτης 56n.

263 λευγαλέης Against Platt's λευγαλέῃ (1914.29, conjectured independently by Haslam, 58 n.28; thinking of *Od.* 12.226 Κίρκης .. ἐφημοσύνης ἀλεγεινῆς/ ?) may be set i.1255-6 ἄτην/.. λευγαλέην, ii.438-9 (σέθεν) ἄτης/.. λευγαλέης (καὶ δ' ἡμέας .../τηλόθεν ...) – not that λευγαλέης requires justification: it sounds just right.

On the position of the adjective (Homeric practice differs) see Wifstrand 1933.112 (and id. 104, on ἀργαλέος). Livrea on iv.338 surveys Apollonian usage; no *specific* borrowings from Homer, but note here *Il.* 9.119 ἀασάμην φρεσὶ λευγαλέῃσι πιθήσας/; also i.1218-9 πρόφασιν πολέμου .../λευγαλέην ~ *Il.* 13.97 πολέμοιο .. λευγαλέοιο/; iv.338 λευγαλέῃ ... δηιοτῆτι/ ~ *Il.* 14.387 δαῒ λευγαλέῃ.

Sense: *woeful, dire, grievous, grim* ... Take your pick. My own choice for this example is *pernicious*, which suits the overwrought tone, and which is in accord with interpreters of *Il.* 9.119 cited above: schol. D there (and elsewhere) ὀλεθρίαις, schol. A (119*a*) τὸ ὀλέθριον παρὰ τὸν λοιγόν, schol. b (119*b*[2]) ὀλεθρεύειν ... τὰς φρένας, Erbse ad loc. So e.g. iii.598 ('doom-laden'), iv.338 ('fatal,' 'catastrophic'), 1671 ('deadly').

-οιο ἐφ- Cf. for the hiatus e.g. *Il.* 2.625, 7.63, 14.154; ii.955.

263-4 ἐφημοσύνῃσιν ../πατρός 602n. πατρός carries a bitter emphasis: they forsook their *mother* ([260 ~] 267), cf. *Noten* 341. Initial πατρός has stress in *Od.* 3.16 ('your father, no less'), id. 5.395 (pathos: 'their <beloved> father': ἄλγεα 395, στυγερός 396); in ii.1096 (cited on 264-5) the point is: 'immense wealth, wealth that actually belonged to their father: for it was he who on his death-bed ...' Ctr. the dispassionate ... πατρὸς ἐφετμάων ... from Argos in ii.1152.

ἕλεσθε Haslam 58 n.29, on Π²¹: 'I have seen a photograph, on which λ looks better than ν ... Not θ ...' ἔθεσθε (Fränkel, *Noten* 341) is in any case hopelessly flat, and given the mass confusion in *codd*. we can look elsewhere with a clear conscience. ἕλεσθε, conjectured by Huet (Vian 1975.95) then by Brunck, has real bite. πόθος can be said to 'take hold of' (αἱρεῖν) one (iv.619 ~ *Od.* 4.596); πόθον ἑλέσθαι means 'to find oneself conceiving [under the influence of ἄτη] a longing,' much like ἀείρεσθαι. Cf. κῆδος ἑλέσθαι in ii.858, iii.692, and Campbell 1982.15, Vian 1962.38 n.5, VDB (who opt for ἔθεσθε) 2.120. See in general Davies on Soph. *Trach.* 673. [ἕλεσθε is now read by the Budé: see VDB 2².120.]

Cf. further Haslam 58f. (reflections on the comic/pathetic ἔεσθε); Zumbo 1975/76.476f. fights long and hard for the unpromising ἔνεσθε, which also appeals to Livrea (1982.20).

264-5 ὁ μέν The particle is emphatic ('He, to be sure,' she says reproachfully), but also anticipatory: 'But how could you have carried out his instructions, leaving your mother to her grief [ἀχέουσαν 267 ~ ἀνίας 264]?'

θνῄσκων *Il.* 2.106; 24.743 (/οὐ γὰρ .. θνῄσκων ctr. ii.1096 below).

στυγερὰς .... κραδίῃ At ii.1093f. we read 'The sons of Phrixus were on their way to the city of Orchomenos ἵν' ἄσπετον ὄλβον ἄρωνται/ πατρός· ὁ γὰρ θνῄσκων [compare Argos at ii.1150f.] ἐπετείλατο τήνδε κέλευθον/.' The fraught mother is here made to indulge in a strained recasting of ii.1096 (Faerber 98 n.3). She cannot say (e.g.) 'στυγεροὺς ἐπετέλλετ' ἀέθλους upon you': they wanted to go. Rather, the father with his death-bed commands (ἐπιτέλλειν -εσθαι is the *vox propria* for the sort of 'heroic' instruction the mother cannot appreciate: Kirk on *Il.* 6.207-8) 'enjoined' pains/sufferings on *her* (ἡμετέρῃ emphatic) heart.

Perhaps a tragic model underlies this utterance: cf. in a general way Soph. *Aj.* 972-3 ἐμοί/λιπὼν ἀνίας ... διοίχεται, id. *Trach.* 41-2.

στυγερὰς ἐπετέλλετ' ⏑–× *Il.* 9.454 (πατήρ 453), used differently infr.

712. Q.S. 6.576 στυγεράς ὑπεδύσετ' ἀνίας/, cf. id. 3.763 al., Greg. Naz. 1497.243. Further: Livrea on iv.8.

ἐπετέλλετ' For the narrative aorist in ii.1096 (above) cf. *Od.* 1.327 (Zumbo 1975.352). Here we expect the imperfect, to denote the 'insistent charge' (Gillies; cf. e.g. *Od.* 11.622, the weeping Heracles speaking, ὁ δέ μοι χαλεπούς ἐπετέλλετ' ἀέθλους/, sim. *Scutum* 94), and this is what Π²¹ offers; so too *codd*. RQ, probably by mere accident (Speake 1975.109; D has -τέλλετο at ii.1096).

265 ἡμετέρη κραδίη In genit. Greg. Naz. 516.15, [Apolin.] 48.6 (cf. id. 31.11), in accus. Eudoc. *Cypr.* 2.424 (later in verse). Homer: *Od.* 10.79 /ἡμετέρη ματίη (in context of long hard voyage).

265-7 τί .... ἴκοισθε; "ἴκοισθε: potentiel du passé: 'comment avez-vous pu aller ...?'" Vian ed. 1961 (on 267), cf. Wåhlin 29, Speake 1974.127, and more generally Hulton, *CQ* n.s. 8 (1958), 139f. For Chalciope the whole sorry affair is over and done with (260-1), but she cannot resist a robust complaint: 'but why in that case (κεν: once you had seen the effect all this was having on me) would you have gone?' means 'but how *could* you have found it in you to go all the way to [cf. 261] ...?'

We have to wait a while for the main verb, for the sons' indifference to their mother's agonies, prefaced by a disparaging remark about 'Orchomenos,' is made to form an incisive climax to Chalciope's outburst. Both μητέρ' ἐήν (cf. above on πατρός 264) and the imposing ἀποπρολιπόντες carry great emphasis: how could you have gone when it meant the total abandonment of your own mother?

265-6 On Orchomenos, and the associations of the term 'Minyan' (cf. below) with both Boeotia and Thessaly, see VDB 1.10-12. Chalciope, married to an individual who fled from 'the city of Orchomenos' (ii.654), and the mother of sons who had lately set off for the same destination (ii.1093, 1153, cf. 1186), professes not to know (or to care) who 'Orchomenos' is. Medea on the other hand can call the city 'opulent' (iii.1073 ἀφνειοῦ, see comment), this complementing Jason's reference (ii.1186) to 'the opulent city of θεῖος Ὀρχομενός' – plainly an allusion to the city's eponymous founder (cf. e.g. i.186 πτολίεθρον ἀγαυοῦ Μιλήτοιο/). iii.1093f. confront Medea – and us – with a statement from Jason that *Minyas* reportedly founded 'the city of Orchomenos' from Iolcus; the relationship of M. to O., that 'vague genealogical figure' (Rose in *OCD*), which was evidently fluid

(Roscher s. *Orchomenos* 5, pp. 939-40), is simply not specified. As if to hammer home the close association of the two cities, Argos talks of Orchomenos as the journey's end (iv.257, a much-vexed passage, but this much at least seems to me to be incontrovertible).

What is clear in all this is that the haze surrounding Boeotia's links with Argonautic saga and Orchomenos' place *qua* hero in the Aeolid stemma is quite deliberate. The city, from which Phrixus departed on the ram whose fleece was to be brought back to Hellas by the Argonauts, can from one standpoint supplant Iolcus, itself an opulent city, though hardly a match for Orchomenos (is ἀφνειόν in Theoc. 13.19 provocative?), as the voyage's ultimate τέλος (both must have come under the same broad sphere of influence in the Mycenean era: Vian ed. 1961, p. 17). The hero likewise can in one context be thought of as eponymous founder (the standard story), in another as having given his name to a city founded by one with whom the Argonauts – or most of them – had blood-ties (i.229f.; cf. 578n.).

πόλιν Ὀρχομενοῖο = ii.1186, πτόλιν ii.1093, πόλιν with v.l. πτόλιν ii.654. Cf. Pind. *fr. dub.* 333a8 πόλιν ἐς Ὀρχομενῷ.

266 ὅστις ὅδ' Ctr., from *Il.*, 3.167 (tell me) /ὅστις ὅδ' (this person before your eyes) ἐστὶν Ἀχαιὸς ἀνὴρ..., 5.175/16.424 (shoot at this man/so that I can learn) /ὅστις ὅδε (here in front of us) κρατέει...; and the softer and subtler *quicumque est* of Virg. *A.* 5.83.

There is irony here of course, as many have noted (265-6n.: just who Orchomenos is is not a question to which there is a clear-cut answer); Crane, *ZPE* 66 (1986), 271 n.14 detects irony of a different kind.

κτεάνων Ἀθάμαντος ἕκητι Chalciope throws back at her sons the very words they will have used to justify their trip: the same half-line from Argos in ii.1153 (νεύμεθ' ἐς Ὀρχομενὸν ...).

κτεάνων UnHomeric, but cf. Hes. *WD* 315, and Braswell on Pind. *P.* 2.290(e). Again infr. 334; 3[H]: [Theoc.] 25.109 κτεάνων; Call. *fr.* 81.1]κτεαν[(unless compound adj.).

The word was no doubt suggested to Ap. by [Hes.] *fr.* 257.5 (ἀπο-προλιπών 3, Ὀρχομενόν 4).

ἕκητι Again, a departure from Homeric usage (Vian ed. 1961, LSJ s.v. I and II); so often in *Arg.* (see *Index*), but in 3[H] otherwise only Euphor. *SH* 413.12.

267 μητέρ' ἑήν Once in Homer, *Od.* 2.195 (*his*, cf. infr. 609, later in the verse); also [Mosch.] *Meg.* 20 (*their*); Anon. *AP* 3.16.2 (pentam.; = ὑμετέρην, as here, cf. Rengakos 1993.117-8).

ἀχέουσαν Medea is to apply this word to Chalciope in 643 below.

ἀποπρολιπόντες The verb often denotes total, wilful abandonment: cf. Giangrande 1973.15, on i.1285. -έλειπον in i.1230 is the only non-participial example: cf. i.1285 -λιπόντες ἔβησαν/, and [Hes.] *fr.* 257.3 (/ἵξεν δ'), *GVI* 1251.4 = *CEG* (2) 597.4 (Rhamnus, 4th cent.), Antim. *fr. dub.* (pap. 3rd cent., ~ *CA* p. 249) 151.3, Hermesian. *CA* 7.21 (.... ἐσικέσθαι), 44 (ἦλθεν), Nicias (?) *HE* 2784, Mosch. *Eur.* 147 (Campbell ad loc.), *GVI* 986.3 (Sparta, 2nd/3rd cent.), 590.3 (Rome, 3rd cent.), [Orph.] *A.* 263 corr. (ἔβαινον/..), [Apolin.] 64.3 *pref.* -οντες ἔβησαν/.

-οντες ἵκοισθε ends the line at *Od.* 11.104 (κε ...), al.

268-70 Fränkel (*Noten* 341, cf. *Einleitung* 19) rewrote these lines in order to get the queen out first, Aeetes 'last.' The text as it stands is not incoherent, but it is rather awkwardly expressed: Aeetes stirred himself out of doors last of all; *but* [cf. VDB 2.61 n.5] Eiduia herself emerged <as well>, because she heard Chalciope (her penetrating 'lament') <and had to investigate>. In normal circumstances the husband (with or without retainers) would be expected to deal with the matter. σὺν δ' αὐτή would produce tighter coordination (scil. θύραζε from the previous line; cf. i.131 /ὡρμήθη· σὺν καί οἱ .. κίεν, ii.813-4 κατήισαν .../καὶ δ' αὐτὸς σὺν τοῖσι Λύκος κίε, iii.517-8 /ὦρτο .../σὺν δὲ ...). Π[21] indeed carried a marginal variant, now lost (cf. Haslam 64, and see 270n.), and some fresh evidence would be very welcome. For the fulness of expression cf. iv.1069-70, 'king Alcinous and Alcinous' .. wife Arete.'

For Faerber (99) the late entrance was a sign of *stolze Gelassenheit* (cf. Hoelzlin here). He certainly bides his time: he does not march out and confront the newcomers directly, but stays silently in the background (clearly no words are exchanged before 304f.) until the necessary preliminaries have been attended to. One may contrast Pelias' approach in Pindar, *P.* 4.134f.: Jason and his men came to the palace and went inside, τῶν δ' ἀκούσαις αὐτὸς ὑπαντίασεν Τυροῦς .. γενεά κτλ. In any event, with 'last of all' (see on the literary backdrop 176f.(2)n.) Ap. squeezes the last drop of suspense out of the situation (Hübscher 49): we have heard about this dreadful character, and now, finally, he is here before us.

268 ὣς ἔφατ' ... But iv.236 /ὣς ἔφατ' Αἰήτης .. δ' ... Cf. *Il.* 8.409 al. /ὣς ἔφατ', ὦρτο δ(έ) then name, *Od.* 9.444 /ὕστατος ... ἔστειχε θύραζε/ (see on 176f.(2)). Cf. on 83.

ὦρτο θύραζε But *Il.* 24.572, *Od.* 21.388 (-ος) ἆλτο θύραζε/, describing a brisk exit. Aeetes is not so quick off the mark.

269 ἐκ δ'... See on 268-70. Cf. *Il.* 2.588 /ἐν δ' αὐτὸς κίεν, *Od.* 24.492 /ὣς ἔφατ', ἐκ δ' υἱὸς Δολίου κίεν (~ infr. 650, cf. 869; for /ἐκ δ' ... cf. i.207).
Εἴδυια δάμαρ .. Αἰήταο Cf. 240; 243(n.). For the formal-sounding δάμαρ (probably, like ὄαρ, a pre-Hellenic word: Ruijgh 1991.490; usage: see in general Stevens on Eur. *Andr.* 4) + husband's name (so invariably in the Homeric poems: Chantraine, *REG* 59/60 (1946/47), 224) cf. iii.922(n.)/iv.959, and, e.g., Alex. Aet. *CA* 3.26, Call. *Hec. fr.* 100. She is in fact a remote figure in this poem: see PF here.

270 Χαλκιόπης ἀίουσα Π[21]'s marginal]πην μ[ετιοῦσα ? (*ex* 249?) is interesting, and indicates some instability in or dissatisfaction with the text hereabouts (cf. 268-70n.). Ap. seems however to be remoulding *Od.* 24.47-8 /μήτηρ δ' ἐξ .. ἦλθε σὺν .../ἀγγελίης ἀίουσα· βοὴ δ' ... ὀρώρει/... (re-accent there, and here, ἀιοῦσα: 352-3n.).

270-4 αὐτίκα: as an immediate consequence of the household-head's entry. No direct instructions from Aeetes are reported (VDB 2.120, on 274): ctr. i.266-7, Jason and his δμῶες, echoing the start of the Hesiodic *Days* (766). The king thus remains a remote figure right up to the point at which he questions his grandsons (302f.).
As for the cast of this sequence (cf. *Studies* 24), the 'typical scene' resembles two in particular in *Od.* (1.109f., 10.352f. ~ i.1182f., see Arend 71; cf. also *Od.* 14.418f.), but only superficially. There is no reason to credit Ap. with the invention of the more ambitious procedures of a large palace environment of the kind found in Roman epic (Odysseus' residence in fact seems to be well-staffed, F-G on 22.421-2, but we hear nothing of bustle on this scale): Virg. *A.* 1.703f. (large number of servants; Homeric ingredients in G. Knauer, *Die Aeneis und Homer* (Göttingen 1964), 377-8; differences Arend 129f.); in Cyzicus' palace: Val. Flacc. 2.651f. (id.; *pars/pars*; on the scene cf. F. Mehmel, *Valerius Flaccus* (Diss. Hamburg 1933), 69f.); in Adrastus' palace: Stat. *Theb.* 1.515f. (*Homerica*: H. Juhnke, *Homerisches in römischer Epik flavischer Zeit* (Munich 1972), 62, 319; *tumultu* 516, cf. ὁμάδοιο; *pars* etc.; note also *turba* of servants in id. *Ach.* 1.741); at a magnificent feast in Hannibal's honour: Sil. It. 11.274f. (*turba*; *his/his* etc.; *strepitu* .../*murmurat* .. *domus*).
One may recall too the host of amazingly energetic δμῶες in Nonn. *D.* 18.93f. (ἄναξ 93, bulls 94+, δρηστῆρες 98), with Gerbeau on 93-9.

270-1 τὸ δ' .... ἐπεπλήθει Aratean in flavour, like so much in this poem: 774 αὐτίκα πεπληθυῖα/, 346 ὅρμον ἐσερχόμενοι· τὴν δ' αὐτίκα πᾶς ἀνακόπτει (compare from later didactic poetry Opp. *Hal.* 3.296 ἧκ' ἀναδινεύων· οἱ δ' αὐτίκα πάντες ἕπονται).

ὁμάδοιο Not just 'throng' or the like: the reference is to the characteristic 'murmur of a mass' of servants setting about their various tasks: the courtyard was 'buzzing.' Cf. e.g. Ap. Soph. 120.18 θόρυβος, παρὰ τὸ ὁμοῦ αὐδᾶν, Erbse on schol. *Il.* 2.96a (*disertim*), Henrichs 258 n.7, and see on 564 infr. Elsewhere in the poem: '(noisy, confused) throng/company': i.347 (in the mouth of a sarcastic Heracles!), 1051 ('in a confused mass'), ii.1077 (n.b. κλαγγή in the same line), iv.198 (n.b. κλαγγῇ 219).

ἕρκος ἐπεπλήθει compresses the memorable scene in the hospitable Alcinous' palace at *Od.* 8.57f. πλῆντο δ' ἄρ' αἴθουσαί τε καὶ ἕρκεα καὶ δόμοι ἀνδρῶν/ἀγρομένων (... preparations for a feast).

ἐπεπλήθει 'had been filled' = 'was filled in an instant.' For the reinforcing αὐτίκα (in prose often εὐθύς, ταχύ) cf. e.g. i.1329 ἐσσυμένως ἐβεβήκει/, infr. 450 /καρπαλίμως ... βεβήκει/, and see on the idiom *GH* 2.199f., *KG* 1.153.

271-2 A regal banquet (*Studies* 24): cf. on the Shield (βασιλεύς 556, a reward for his deserving workers? Cf. Edwards on 560) /κήρυκες δ' ... δαῖτα πένοντο,/βοῦν δ' ἱερεύσαντες μέγαν ἄμφεπον, *Il.* 18.558-9. No talk of any 'sacrifice' here however.

τοὶ μὲν μέγαν ἀμφεπένοντο *Il.* 4.220 τοὶ ἀμφεπένοντο (/τόφρα δ' 221 ~ Ap. 275); id. 13.656 /τὸν μὲν .. μεγαλ(ήτορες) ἀμφεπένοντο/.

μέγαν ../ταῦρον iv.468 μέγαν .. ταῦρον/. Hom. (*Il.* 17.389) ταύροιο .. μεγάλοιο, but note Call. *h.* 3.150 /ταῦρον ... μέγαν, as well as Kaibel *EG* 1082*b*7 (*aet. Rom.*) ταῦρον μέγαν.

ἀμφεπένοντο/ταῦρον Dion. Bass. *fr.* 20*v*4 Livrea τ]ράγον ἀμφεπ[ένοντο/, cf. iv.883 (δόρπον), and also Call. *h.* 3.158 (Bornmann ad loc., F-G on *Od.* 22.199) μέγαν περὶ θῆρα πονεῖτο/.

ἅλις *a swarm of*..., closely with the subst. as infr. 329 etc.; cf. the δμῶες .. πολεῖς ... at Iolcus, i.261. Ctr. Nic. *fr.* 72.3-4 δμῶες ἅλις περιχανδέα χύτρον/πλήσαντες κτλ.

272-3 ξύλα κάγκανα The adj. was often glossed with *dry/dried* (e.g. schol. D at *Il.* 21.364, schol. Ap. i.1182-3*a*), viz. ξ. κ. = firewood; for detailed discussion of the word see Athanassakis, *TAPA* 106 (1976), 1f., and also Moutsos, *Glotta* 61 (1983), 96. δὲ ξύλα κάγκανα = *Il.* 21.364, scil. to boil water (362 cauldron ζεῖ ... πυρί, 365 ζέε δ' ὕδωρ/), *Od.*

18.308, for λαμπτῆρες (309 κεκεασμένα χαλκῷ/; 311 δμωαί), *HyHerm* 136 (κάγκαν'). Ctr. i.1182 οἱ μὲν ξύλα κάγκανα, τοὶ δὲ ⏑–×, Theoc. 24.89 /κάγκανα δ' .. ξύλ'.

ξύλα .../κόπτον The only parallel known to me is *Or. Sib.* 3.651 ξύλα κόψεται. ξυλοκοπία and ξυλοκοπικός are attested in 3rd cent. inscriptions: LSJ + Suppl. (cf. under -κοπέω -κόπος); Kindstrand, *AC* 52 (1983), 97f.

Od. 20.161 κέασαν ξύλα scil. δρηστῆρες (cf. Ap.274).

273 λοετρὰ πυρὶ ζέον On bathing see 300n. Call. (*Aet.*) *fr.* 43.48-9 ζείον]τα λοετ[ρά/χεῦαν (ref. 'hospitality'); Pind. *O.* 1.48 ὕδατος ... πυρὶ ζέοισαν ... ἀκμάν (46 ἄφαντος, 49 τάμον, cf. Ap. 275/273).

The transitive use of the uncompounded verb (see Boesch 31) is first in Ap.: he may have interpreted *Od.* 10.360 ζέσσεν ὕδωρ [χαλκῷ ibid.] thus ('she ...' 358 *bis* then 361, 364 and so on); *Il.* 18.349 however is not so accommodating.

Other examples: Phil. *GPh* 2859 (metaph.), Anon. didact. *GDK* 64.34. To these I would add i.734 ζείουσαν ἀυτμήν/ (Ω: -μῇ K²D, 'fort. recte' VDB). The accusative, which I take with Wellauer to be governed by the verb (i.q. ἀναζ-) rather than as loosely in apposition to <ἀκτῖνα> (so Mooney and others), is supported by Marianus *AP* 9.626.5 ἀναζείουσιν ἀυτμήν/, the dative by Q.S. 13.150 Ἡφαίστου μαλεροῖο [μαλ. πυρός Ap. here] περιζείοντος ἀυτμῇ/ (-ή Ω: impossible). If we recall that Marianus turned our *Argonautica* into iambics, and add to that the weight of Ω, the accusative seems hard to resist, even if Q.S. did have the dative in his copy (or one of his copies) of the poem.

οὐδέ τις ἦεν ... A clausula in *Il.* 24.610; also iv.976, Q.S. 2.529, 11.437, followed by ὅς id. 13.130; cf. also Musae. 69-70 with Kost.

274 καμάτου μεθίεσκεν redeploys *Od.* 5.471-2 με μεθείη/... κάματος. When Eros arrives on the scene he engenders in Medea κάματος of a very different kind (289).

ὑποδρήσσων βασιλῆι Cf. Paul. Sil. *Soph.* 270 /εὐκαμάτων .. ὑποδρήσσων βασιλήων/, [Apolin.] 77.27 ὑποδρήσσειν βασιλῆος/. For the spread of this verb see Campbell on Q.S. 12.134; first here in Ap. Homer has a clutch of related words: ὑποδράω, (ὑπο)δρηστήρ (cf. Hoekstra on *Od.* 15.330), δρήστειρα (700n.), δρηστοσύνη, and also ὑποδμώς (West on *Od.* 4.385-6). -δρήσσω i.q. -δράω may have been suggested by simple association (πρήσσω: cf. e.g. schol. Q on δρήστειραι at *Od.* 10.349: ... ἀπὸ τοῦ δρῶ τὸ πράττω). Marxer (49f.) compared Apollonian πρήσσω (iv.819, 1537, both solidly attested) beside πρηστήρ. For further discussion see Boesch 61; Debrunner, *IF* 21 (1907), 229, 255-6; Ardizzoni here.

275 Cf. 167-8n. A positive indication of simultaneity of action is provided here, as by τόφρα δ(έ) i.1207, ii.301, iii.609, 1246, τόφρα answering ὄφρα in the snappy sequence iv.778-80, τείως δ' αὖτ' i.640, all discussed by Köhnken 122-4. Köhnken overlooks a particularly elaborate example at i.354f., an early pointer to the sophisticated handling of concurrent events in this poem. The newly-elected leader organises his schedule: ὄφρα they go and fetch oxen, τόφρα we can launch the ship ...; (359f.) τείως δ' αὖ we can also build an altar; then (362f.) launching, (402f.) altar, (406f.) τείως δ' αὖτ' they had brought oxen.

The narrative now flows in a single stream as Ap. focuses on the crucial meeting with Aeetes (cf. Fusillo 191, 197, 261): we hear nothing of the waiting Argonauts, and once Eros has done his job divine machinery in its fully developed form is rested. But when the time comes for the delegation's departure, we must sense that straightforward sequential handling of the roles of the various personages (Argonauts, Argos/the other three Phrixids, Chalciope, Medea, Aeetes, Olympians) will be impracticable.

πολιοῖο δι' ἠέρος We last saw Eros as he left Olympus, travelling up along the clear, translucent aether (166n.). Now, unseen, he reaches his destination δι' ἠέρος, i.e. through a self-manufactured blanket of the stuff of invisibility; the manner of his arrival at the palace thus parallels that of Jason and his men, who are similarly screened by Hera (210f.). Eros cannot be seen by anybody either now or later on: just as he is invisible in personalised form at 275-86a (since in Ap. at any rate he is not a member of the Magic Circle, he must have taken the necessary precautions as he alights and strides over to Jason), so when he has gone 'eros' is there 'deep down in the heart' (287), undetected now as before: 296 λάθρη ~ 280 λαθών cf. λάθοιεν 211 ἠέρα ibid.

The accompanying epithet: effective obfuscation was provided by schol. 's διαφανοῦς, a vapid suggestion taken up by a string of modern interpreters. πολιός could signify (or was taken to signify) 'bright' or 'clear': cf. e.g. West on Hes. *WD* 477, Willink on Eur. *Or.* 1375-6 (αἰθέρ'! See Diggle, *SIFC* n.s. 7 (1989), 203), Gow on Theoc. 18.26f., Hopkinson on Call. *h.* 6.122, G. Reiter, *Die griechischen Bezeichnungen der Farben Weiss, Grau und Braun* (Innsbruck 1962), 61, E. Irwin, *Colour Terms in Greek Poetry* (Toronto 1974), 167-8; Diosc. *HE* 1623, cited by Prescott 371 and again by Gillies, is not a helpful parallel. But it is hard to believe that Ap. is expressing in condensed form the kind of situation presented by Val. Flacc. at 2.115, a goddess hurls herself to earth *piceo per sudum turbida nimbo*: Eros arrived through the ἀήρ invisibly <because shrouded in ἀήρ>. In any case, *bright* ἀήρ is *not* part of Apollonius' world-picture: see the other 25 examples in the *Index* (αἰθέρος con. D, perhaps to get round this difficulty).

There have been occasional dissenters: Seaton; Pfeiffer, *Philologus* n.s. 41 (1932), 201 (one would expect 'undurchsichtig'); Vian ed. 1961 (sim. VDB transl.) 'à travers une vapeur blafarde,' citing from later epic Q.S. 2.554, 6.229, to which may be added (*Studies* 103 n.13) Anon. epic. *GDK* 24v5 (pap. 4th cent.) Hermes πολιοῖο δι' ἠέρος ἐστιχεν (it is dark: 3f.); Fowler 1990.

In fact, ancient definitions of πολιός could stretch to both λαμπρός and μέλας: see e.g. (Erbse on) schol. *Il.* 9.366b, and cf. Leumann 148 on the similarly flexible treatment of γλαυκός. I suspect however that the ultimate source for the association found here is Homeric: *Il.* 1.359 Thetis ἀνέδυ πολιῆς ἁλὸς ἠΰτ' ὀμίχλη [= ἀήρ, schol. D]/, i.e. in the form of a mist rising from the πολιὴ ἅλς (cf. Kirk ad loc., West on Hes. *WD* 550-3)?

A related picture in lyric, perhaps (I am not here raising the question of whether πορφ. is to be interpreted chromatically or not; see among the various discussions notably Schrier, *Mnemosyne* 32 (1979), 322): could Sappho *PLF* 54 (cited on 158 above) πορφυρίαν περθέμενον χλάμυν be a vivid adaptation (cf. for example *Il.* 14.282 /ἠέρα ἐσσαμένω *et sim.*, Virgil's *amictu* in *A.* 1.412; see NH on Hor. *Carm.* 1.2.31) of Athena's entry into the conflict at *Il.* 17.551 (πορφυρέῃ νεφέλῃ ...) as she comes to inflict sufferings on men (547f. rainbow: cf. Alcaeus *PLF* 327?)? Cf. also perhaps (ctr. Skutsch ad loc.) Enn. *Ann.* 18 (probably Venus descending from Olympus) *transnavit .. per .. caliginis auras*.

For the possible relevance of πολλόν 166 and esp. πουλύν 287 see Campbell 1990.482 ((Erbse on) schol. *Il.* 15.190).

-οῖο δι' ἠέρος Cf. for the pattern i.777 (with VDB *app.crit.*), infr. 1379. ΕΡΩΣ ... -ΕΡΟΣ: the assonance cannot be accidental: cf. 210-11 (with 211n.). So Hera is not the only deity whose name can be associated with ἀήρ.

... ἷξεν But *Il.* 14.288 δι' ἠέρος .. ἵκανεν/, iv.968 δι' ἠέρος ἵκετο, cf. *Echoes* at 1.777. ἷξεν (form: C. P. Roth, *HSCP* 77 (1973), 184f. and *Mixed Aorists in Homeric Greek* (New York and London 1990), 77f.; Ruijgh, *Mnemosyne* 38 (1985), 178) rather than ἵκετ'/ -εθ' in this sedes: *Il.* 22.462.

ἦξεν (Hoelzlin) will not do: apart from the fact that 'arrived on the scene' is entirely apt, this aorist form is not Apollonian. wE's ἧξεν/ ἦξεν is to be explained as a normalisation of epic ἵκω (on ἵκω/ἥκω cf. La Roche *HTA* 287-9): see e.g. the long list of variants in *LfgrE* s.v. ἥκω, and also Ruijgh, *Mnemosyne* 21 (1968), 121.

ἄφαντος Livrea on iv.536 (3[H]: add Rhianus *CA* 1.18). Elevated diction is a key ingredient in this highly-wrought description of the archer-god's momentous intervention.

276-7 The first developed simile for some time (Carspecken 62, cf. Herter *JAW* 268), a memorable prelude to Eros' onslaught, taking us way beyond the fast-approaching 'strike' (cf. in part *Studies* 25-6 and 102 n.3). The comparison heralded by the arresting τετρηχώς is not open-ended: the gadfly attacks 'young grazers,' but no provision is made for an apodosis harbouring κούρη or the like; indeed, there is *no* 'attack' at this point: in situations where such imagery is evoked (see on οἶστρος below), there is an expectation that the victim will charge about (noisily) – this will not, cannot, happen here. The 'turmoil' trumpeted by the poet looks ahead to the disorientation and torment which will follow on imminently and in the succeeding hours, culminating in ἄλγεα which ἀπείρονα τετρήχασι (iv.447) as Medea is induced by Eros (who resurfaces in something approaching anthropomorphic guise only here after the present episode) to engineer Apsyrtus' death. Another, fainter, throwback to this scene may be discerned at iv.449, where ἔμβαλες ἄτην (under which the affliction of erotic frenzy may be subsumed) recalls the βέλος with which the god set in motion the whole sorry train of events. (I can make no sense of Feeney's appraisal of the shooting-scene: 81.)

Echoes of Homer's account of Pandarus' bow-shot will soon make themselves felt. The fly-simile of *Il.* 4.130-1 may, as Lennox suggested (67), have provided the spur for Ap.'s own succinct yet powerfully suggestive image. Here though is a species of fly which cannot be scared away (cf. schol. T at *Il.* 4.130-1) just like that: indeed, you cannot even see it coming (cf. ἀπροιδής in Nonn. *D.* 42.188); and Medea has nobody to shield her: she is hit full on.

276 τετρηχώς See for extended discussion and examples of this word Gow-Page on Leon. Tar. *HE* 2351, Livrea on iv.447 (citing Wilamowitz, Marxer, van der Valk, Erbse). The underlying image is that of a turbulent, choppy sea (see in general Lehnus, *BICS* 31 (1984), 87 n.17). The association with Eros specifically (cf iv.447 in particular) is a natural one, as his sea-born mother had strong links with that element (lit. in Kost on Musae. 249-50), rendering the 'sea of love' motif an enduringly popular one: NH on Hor. *Carm.* 1.5.16, Zagagi 81f., Favilene, *QUCC* n.s. 13 (1983), 135f., Barsby, *LCM* 14 (1989), 9-10. Many have detected here a link with metaphorical τρηχύς/τετραχυμμένος [cf. schol. L^gP here]: 'aufgeregt, leidenschaftlich erregt' Erbse 1953.174, invoking schol. D at *Il.* 7.346; VDB 2.120 cite τρηχὺν ἔρον in i.613, sim. [Opp.] *Cyn.* 2.187; Mynors on *asper* in Virg. *G.* 3.149: 'the τετρηχώς of Ap. Rhod., a Homeric word which Hellenistic poets seem to have connected with τραχύς rather than ταράσσω.' Such a colouring does not rule out the more fundamental association with the notion of ταραχή (cf. 1393n.; ταρασσόμενος in Theoc. 13.55 may have been suggested by Ap. i.1265f. + τετρηχώς here): Eros is (lit. 'in disturbed motion,' Kirk on *Il.* 7.344-6) 'full of turmoil,' 'tumultuous' (Mooney); but it is also implied (cf. on μάργος in 120, and, e.g., the use of μαινάς 'mad/maddening,' Braswell on Pind. *P.* 4.216(a)) that he may instil panic and disorder, like a gadfly stampeding grazing animals (Platt 1914.29 offers pedantic objections); or, if you prefer, 'Le poète attribue à Eros les désordres de la passion, qu'il suscite chez les autres' Vian ed. 1961 (cf. Ellis on Catull. 64.95). One may recall Anacreon's μανίαι and κυδοιμοί (= ταραχαί, sim.) in connexion with Eros: *PMG* 398 ~ Hermesian. *CA* 2.83-4 ἔρωτος .. κυδοιμόν/μαινομένου (φαινόμενον *cod. Athen.*: μαινόμενον?); and Eur. *Hipp.* 969 ὅταν ταράξῃ Κύπρις ἡβῶσαν φρένα, with Davies, ed. Soph. *Trach.*, p. 137.

The view that τετρηχώς here represents τετριγώς (Wifstrand 1929.91, Marxer 19f./Debrunner, *IF* 53 (1935), 315 n.1; Brunck actually offered this as a conjecture) is effectively dealt with by Erbse 1953.173-4. See also Lloyd-Jones, *SIFC* 77 (1984), 69-70/1990: 2.247.

Future lexicographers may wish to take account of these later examples: Euphor. *SH* 415 i.20, Opp. *Hal.* 5.244, D.P. 599, Triph. 250, Greg. Naz. 506.2 (~ *AP* 1.92), Eudoc. *Hom.* 393.

οἷόν τε with finite verb (cf. *Studies* 102 n.4) is Aratean: 962, an elegant line. It is used very sparingly in *Arg.*: infr. 1020 (οἷόν τε .../τήκεται) and probably (ctr. Ruijgh 1971.946) 1229; see Ruijgh again, 947, 964; Carspecken 66.

Also οἶον δέ iv.1280 and (Campbell 1973.78; *lectio difficilior*, by a large margin) ii.662 v.l.

I would not call D's οἷός here 'intelligent' exactly (Speake 1969.88/1974.126).

νέαις .. φορβάσιν 'young grazers,' unschooled and so an easy prey; out in the open and so exposed to a merciless attack (the effect of ἄγραυλος is similar, Homer etc., iv.551, F-G on *Od.* 22.403, cf. Gow on [Theoc.] 25.135; on grazing cattle so bothered see Pocock, *CR* n.s. 8 (1958), 109, and Beavis cited on 277 below, p. 228). Medea is of a tender age: *Noten* 278, 369 n.54; VDB 2.81 n.4. For the image cf. notably δάμαλις, μόσχος, πόρις, πόρτις, all at one time or another designations of *the* victim of an οἶστρος, the κόρη Io (cf. Campbell on Mosch. *Eur.* 45), a figure recalled by numerous critics here (see esp. Lennox 67; Natzel 49 offers pedantic objections).

The subst. is applied to a heifer in iv.1449, later in Anon. *Blem.* 61, Livrea ad loc. (λέων .. ἐπὶ φορβάδι); ἐπὶ φορβάσιν: cf. [Opp.] *Cyn.* 1.386. Ap. may be using a tragic source here (cf. Eur. cited below on οἶστρος); but φορβάς is quite at home in technical writings too (LSJ s.v.): see 277n. (identification of μύωψ).

οἶστρος is often used figuratively of the frenzy-inducing 'sting' of Eros/eros and sim.: see Headlam on Hds 1.57, Kost on Musae. 134 (p.325), VDB 2.120 (on 277), Chalk, *JHS* 80 (1960), 39, and many further examples in LSJ in the cluster οἰστράω [Gow on Theoc. 6.28] -οἰστρώδης; on the image in general: FJW on Aesch. *Suppl.* 110, MacLachlan, *Phoenix* 43 (1989), 97-8. Here the οἶστρος comes to life in a developed simile, in the wake of *Od.* 22.299f. (panic-stricken suitors likened to βόες, τὰς μέν τ' αἰόλος οἶστρος ἐφορμηθεὶς ἐδόνησεν κτλ.), but with an erotic colouring possibly inspired (Faerber 31 n.1) by Eur. *IA* 547f. or something in similar vein (cf. more generally Buccholz 84 n.1): ... μανιάδων οἴστρων, ὅθι δὴ δίδυμ' Ἔρως ὁ χρυσοκόμας τόξ' ἐντείνεται (!) χαρίτων, τὸ μὲν ἐπ' εὐαίωνι πότμῳ, τὸ δ' ἐπὶ συγχύσει (!) βιοτᾶς. So earlier in our poem Heracles, shattered by the loss of Hylas, charges around and bellows like a bull stung μύωπι i.1265f. ~ οἴστρῳ 1269: the sheer ferocity of his reaction, together with certain other features of the Hylas-episode (though not those advanced by J. F. Collins, *Studies in Book One of the* Argonautica *of Apollonius Rhodius*, Diss. Columbia 1967, 97), should alert us to the fact that Ap., though never absolutely explicit, means us to think in terms of a relationship which goes deeper than the mere 'virile affection' suggested by VDB 1.41; cf. for detailed discussion and a record of various viewpoints Palombi 78f., and earlier esp. Faerber 30-1, Livrea 1977.18, Beye 1982.94.

Later epic similes involving a μύωψ (ctr. οἶστρος Q.S. 11.209): Triph. 358f., see Gerlaud ad loc. (a sustained picture of an extremely loud and violent Cassandra, compared to a πόρτις stung by a μύωψ), Nonn. *D.* 42.185f. ox οἰστρηθείς by βουτύπος .. μύωψ [cf. *LexNonn* s.v.], Colluth. 41f. (πόρτις/μύωψ). Oppian, *Hal.* 2.521-31, offers an extended description of the behaviour of cattle attacked by the βουτύπος οἶστρος.

Anacreontea 33.27f. (Eros) με τύπτει/... ὥσπερ οἶστρος·/ἀνὰ δ' ἄλλεται καχάζων: lifted from Ap. (~ infr. 286 καγχαλόων). For a θαῦμα based on inversion consult Couat 325 n.1.

277 τέλλεται See *Studies* 102 n.8. ἐπὶ ... τέλλεται = ἐπιπέλεται (cf. περιτέλλομαι for -πέλομαι), = ἐπέρχεται, ἐπιγίγνεται (cf. the glosses on -πέλεσθαι cited in 25n., and Merkel *Proleg.* 169); ~ ἐφορμηθείς *Od.* 22.300. Hesych. ε5310 ἐπιτέλλει ... ἐπέρχεται, id. s. τέλλεται ... γίνεται (cf. the variant in Arat. 543, with Kramer, *ZPE* 49 (1982), 70). So probably ἐπιτέλλεται in Call. *fr.* 492, Pfeiffer ad loc., cf. from Ap. himself ὑποτ- in ii.83 βρυχὴ δ' ὑπετέλλετ' ὀδόντων/: *Il.* 11.417-8 ὑπαὶ δέ τε κόμπος ὀδόντων/γίγνεται (an amusing adaptation, matched by a number of others, still hidden, in this not-so-serious boxing-match). Cf. in addition Aesch. *Ag.* 1133 τέλλεται, par. schol. γίνεται, Arat. 723 v.l. ὑποτέλλεται i.q. -πέλεται (Keydell, *Gnomon* 30 (1958), 584); Ronconi 192, on Arat. 451 (25n.); Gamberale, *SIFC* 101 (1973), 421f.

The ὡραῖος καὶ Ἔρως ἐπιτέλλεται of the Theognidean corpus (*IEG* 1275) adduced by Vian ed. 1961 and by VDB 2.120 is quite different: it is akin to the examples cited in LSJ s.v. ἐπιτέλλω (B)1.

On schol. 's στέλλεται cf. Maehler on Bacch. *fr.* 61.1, and note Alcaeus *fr.* 347V v.l., Aesch. *Ag.* 1133 codd.

ὄν τε ... νομῆες Thomas, *HSCP* 86 (1982), 83 (cf. earlier Lennox 67) argues that the *Alexandrian* Callimachus' <οἶστρον: surely> βουσόον [cf. perhaps ἔσσυτο ταῦρος/ in i.1265: Schechter, *TAPA* 105 (1975), 362 n.36], ὄν τε μύωπα βοῶν καλέουσιν ἀμορβοί (*Hec. fr.* 117) deliberately inverts the order of the Aeschylean description of 'the μύωψ, called οἶστρος by οἱ Νείλου πέλας' (*Suppl.* 307-8: *Aeschylea* in Call.: (a mixed bag in) Capovilla, *SIFC* 42 (1970), 94f.), and in so doing demotes μύωψ 'to the functional sphere,' οἶστρος being 'pushed' as the more poetical of the two (due to its close associations with Io); Ap. takes his cue from this. Ingenious as this is, it must be said that Ap. did not adhere to any such principle in i.1265f., where the two terms are synonymous. The comment on nomenclature here is to be explained on just this basis. If no pre-Hellenistic poetic source draws distinctions, the two *were* broadly differentiated in the technical tradition (Wellmann, *Hermes* 26 (1891), 344f., M. Davies and J. Kathirithamby, *Greek Insects* (London 1986), 161, I. C. Beavis, *Insects and other Invertebrates in Classical Antiquity* (Exeter 1988), 226). Our poets are saying (or one of them for sure is saying) that the μύωψ and the οἶστρος are indeed one and the same: herdsmen (generally) treat them as such, and they are in a position to know. For an appeal to professionals in the realm of nomenclature cf. in Ap. iv.175 (ἥν τ' ... καλέουσι/, in a simile; more esoterically ii.671, iv.1695), and outside Ap., with respect to this particular line of business (*Studies* 102 n.7) Nic. *Ther.* 554 (two different names for horehound) /τὴν ... ἐπικλείουσι βοτῆρες/, *Alex.* 346 (*buprestis* = *cow-inflater*) τὴν .. ἐπικλείουσι νομῆες/ (later: Anon. encom. *GDK* 16.7 κλήζουσι βοτῆρες/); see further Hollis on *Hec.* loc. cit. (under ἀμορβοί); in similar vein, but in the realm of narrative, is Euphor. *CA* 96.3 (name Βοιωτός; βοῶν 4) τὸ .. καλέσαντο νομῆες/ (c.v.l.). Not all that different (given the need for technical exegesis!) in general complexion is the memorable simile of *Il.* 14.290-1 ... ὄρνιθι λιγυρῇ ἐναλίγκιος, ἥν τ' ἐν ὄρεσσι/χαλκίδα κικλήσκουσι θεοί, ἄνδρες δὲ κύμινδιν (ref. Sleep, involved in Zeus' seduction, in concealment).

ὅν τε ... κλείουσι 246n.

μύωπα // βοῶν Colluth. 43 ... μύωπι, βοῶν ...

βοῶν .. νομῆες (*Studies* 102 n.5) is not strictly comparable to the type βοῶν ἐπιβουκόλος (Fehling 159, West on *Od.* 3.422; cf. i.627), since a νομεύς can tend a variety of animals: *LH*/LSJ (I) s.v.; compounds αἰγι- αἰγο- ἱππο- μηλο-. Poets do often use it without amplification in the sense of 'cowherd,' but exactitude is called for here in the context of an appeal to the relevant 'experts.'

κλείουσι νομῆες adapts the clausula of *Od.* 17.246 φθείρουσι νομῆες; *oppositio* with βοῶν here: in the Homer passage there is anything but (ἀρνῶν, ἐρίφων, μῆλα, αἰγῶν).

Faerber (31 n.2) asserted that Ap.'s clausula 'simplifies' the corresponding ἀμορβοί (Hollis on *Hec. fr.* 76; infr. 881n.) of *Hec. fr.* 117: he avoids learned glosses in close succession. I am not sure that μύωψ comes squarely under this category! In any case speculation on interrelationships seems unwise given our ignorance of the context of Call.'s line (Knaack *RE* 2.128 even talks of 'Polemik'; malicious recasting by Call.: Perrotta 131).

Fränkel (*Einleitung* 43 n.1) toys with the idea of writing -ουσιν ἀμορβοί in Ap. – if you can't beat them, join them?

278f. On Eros the archer (for Natzel 49 a comic archer, believe it or not) see VDB 2.121, on 279 (Euripides: Barrett on *Hipp.* 530-4, cf. above on 276, *IA*), and the extensive bibliographies in Bömer, ed. Ov. *Met.* 4-5, p. 324, *LIMC* 3.1, 852 & 878-81: especially useful: A. Greifenhagen, *Griechische Eroten* (Berlin 1957).

The shooting of Medea. Cf. *Studies* 26-7. Although Ap., like the epicising Bacchylides (5.74f.), clearly borrows details from the account of Pandarus' treacherous attack on Menelaus at *Il.* 4.116f. (Lennox

67-8, Ciani 96f.), we must also bear in mind the possibility that fully developed scenes involving the archer Eros and his unsuspecting victims of the kind found not only in the much-discussed Ov. *Met.* 1.466f./5.379f. (choice arrow selected by Cupid; cf. notably Otis 1970.383f.) ~ *Ciris* 158f. but also in Nonn. *D.* 7.192f. (a nest of conceits) were commonplace in Hellenistic poetry: something of the sort may lie at the back of the elaborate shooting sequence in Anon. hexam. *SH* 939.1-5. The role of archers/archery in our poem is surveyed by Peschties 68f.; the plainer lines ii.1042-5 present some points of correspondence with the present passage.

The Pandarus-episode, imprints of which strikingly point up the materiality of the βέλος which is soon to burn deep inside, 'like flame' (287), is reworked with the expected quest for variety and shifts of emphasis. *Il.* 4.105-15 keep us in suspense (so Ovid above, though to a lesser degree; also Sil. It. 14.397f., Nonn. *D.* 29.70f.); Ap. comes straight to the point: the actions of bow-stringing and arrow-selection (4.112 τανυσσάμενος κτλ. then 116-8, αὐτὰρ ὁ σύλα πῶμα φαρέτρης, ἐκ δ' ἕλετ' ἰόν/ἀβλῆτα πτερόεντα, μελαινέων ἕρμ' ὀδυνάων) are presented here in close succession, the arrow attracting by way of descriptive detail only the key elements of 'newness' and 'pains' (not surprisingly, the problematic ἕρμ' is left well alone). Again, there is drastic trimming in 282-4, corresponding to 4.118 αἶψα δ' ἐπὶ νευρῇ κατεκόσμει πικρὸν ὀιστόν and 122(-6) ἕλκε δ' ὁμοῦ γλυφίδας τε λαβὼν καὶ νεῦρα βόεια [cf. *Od.* 21.419 ~ 420 ἧκε δ' ὀιστόν/] κτλ.: the operation is noiseless (but 4.125 /λίγξε βιός, νευρὴ δὲ μέγ' ἴαχεν ...), though the archer is not (286); no 'the arrow struck home,' only a curt reference to its instantaneous stunning effect (284); it burns 'deep down in the heart' (but 4.139 /ἀκροτάτην ... ἐπέγραψε χρόα ...); the victim's πυκιναὶ φρένες are blasted from her στήθεα, 288-9 (contrast 4.152 ἄψορρόν οἱ θυμὸς ἐνὶ στήθεσσιν ἀγέρθη, Lennox 67).

The whole scene is remarkably vivid – too vivid for comfort perhaps (cf. *Studies* 26). As Eros' movements are mapped out for us a strong impression is created that, invisible as he was, he would have been spotted had he not acted with extreme caution in making himself ready, like a Homeric warrior, to strike his target (cf. e.g. VDB 2.121, on 279, 'bien qu' il soit invisible!'). He can of course be expected to act furtively whatever the circumstances (compare Buccholz 89 n.2). Even so, it is tempting to see at work here yet another display of the poet's love of pictorial description: Eros *is* being watched, in a very real sense.

278 ὦκα Eros works quickly (cf. 280), like Pandarus (cf. *Il.* 4.105 αὐτίκ', 118 αἶψα); this is a feature of later incursions into the field: McKeown on Ov. *Am.* 1.1.21-2. With /ὦκα then τόξα τανύσσας/ ctr. *Il.* 5.97 /αἶψ' ... ἐτιταίνετο .. τόξα/, with /ὦκα δ' then τανύσσας/ *Od.* 5.373 /αὐτίκα δὲ ... τάνυσσεν/, and finally with /ὦκα δ' then /ἰοδόκης *Il.* 15.444 .../ἰοδόκον· .. δ' ὦκα ...

ὑπό '<moving> to the foot of' (cf. Vian ed. 1961), the terseness reflecting Eros' fast pace.

φλιήν 'door-post' (the sense in *Od.* 17.221, hapax Hom., hapax Ap.) rather than 'lintel' (Mooney and others): he stands to one side, not right in the centre, as he strings his bow and selects a suitable shaft (*Studies* 26). An apt port of call, as the φλιή 'intervient souvent dans la littérature érotique' (VDB 2.121, on 279; cf. Vian on Nonn. *D.* 26.263). For discussion of the term (παραστάς and ὑπέρθυρον are not the only possibilities) see Gow on Theoc. 2.59-62 and on [id.] 23.16f. (cf. with that ... σταθμούς in iv.26-7), Gow-Page on Call. *HE* 1080.

προδόμῳ ... Of the megaron (285) proper, as in *Od.* 20.1 etc.: see Lorimer 415f., Fantuzzi 105, and cf. n. on 215f.C(3).

προδόμου (D and *EtG* interestingly coincide: on this see Speake 1969.92/1975.109-10, Fränkel *Einleitung* 90, VDB 1.XLIV) – hence προδόμου ἐνὶ Brunck, then *dub.* Fränkel OCT – is best forgotten: φλιή and πρόδομος are easily drawn together. προδόμῳ ἔνι: Hom. ἐνὶ προδόμῳ ~ infr. 648n.

τόξα τανύσσας So Nonn. *D.* 46.85 τόξα τανύσσης/, cf. i.993-4 (αἶψα) τανύσσας/τόξον ~ *Od.* 21.254-5 (-α) τανύσσαι/τόξον. An enormously popular picture in later poetry, see the rich note of Kost on Musae. 17 Ἔρως ... τόξα τιταίνων/.

279 ἰοδόκης Cf. on 156. The verse is neatly framed by 'arrow-container ... arrow': see below for the Odyssean version. Homer is compressed, as expected: 'he took the lid off his φαρέτρη and picked out an arrow ...,' *Il.* 4.116.

ἀβλῆτα 'unshot,' 'never fired before': see *LfgrE* s.v.; Chuvin on Nonn. *D.* 7.129-35. Eros chooses a prime specimen, really sharp (cf. Ov. *Met.* 5.381): his reward depends on it. A different explanation was advanced for the word by Ap. Soph., 2.28: ... ἢ πολυβλῆτα, οἷον πολλοὺς βεβληκότα: it may not be a coincidence that πολυ- follows on directly here in Ap. — ἀβλής elsewhere only Greg. Naz. 677.123.

πολύστονον calls on, and gives wider application to, the isolated Homeric *iunctura* (*Il.* 15.451) πολύστονος –⏑⏑ ἰός/ as an instrument of physical pain (schol. D: πολλῶν στεναγμῶν αἴτιος), but note as well

Od. 21.12, 60 ... ἰοδόκος (-ον), πολλοὶ δ' ἔνεσαν στονόεντες ὀιστοί (cf. F-G on 21.12). This same adjective is used to characterise the love-smitten Medea's suffering in iv.65 (cf. Livrea ad loc.; not dissimilar, *pace* VDB 3.162, is στονόεντα id. 354, recalling ... ἀνῖαι in 351); and from Eros himself issue στοναχαί (iv.446).

One is also reminded in a general way of the frequent epigrammatic outbursts against the miseries caused by Eros' weaponry etc.

Hence perhaps [Theoc.] 25.213 ἰὸν ἐχέστονον, then (cf. Ap. 281 init.) /πάντῃ δ' ὄσσε φέρων κτλ.

ἐξέλετ' ἰόν Cf., in addition to *Il.* 4.116, id. 8.323-4 φαρέτρης ἐξείλετο πικρὸν ὀιστόν,/θῆκε δ' ἐπὶ νευρῇ, and Bacch. 5.74f. ... δ' .. ἔξ/είλετο ἰὸν ἀναπτύ-/ξας φαρέτρας πῶμα.

280 Eros crosses the threshold and so enters the main room (cf. Richardson on *HyDem* 188, and see n. on 215f.C(3)), like Delphis in Theoc. 2.104 θύρας ὑπὲρ οὐδὸν ἀμειβόμενον ποδὶ κούφῳ/ then 106f. love-symptoms of girl; perhaps this already constituted a 'significant act' (Richardson) in erotic writing: see in general Brenk, *QUCC* n.s. 26 (1987), 121f., and also Segal, *ClAnt* 4 (1985), 103f. Cf. the fresco recalled by VDB 2.121 (on 279). Ap. no doubt remembered also the strong association of the threshold with the lethal archer Odysseus in *Od.* (refs in Russo on 18.33).

ἐκ δ' See *Studies* 103 n.16. ἔνθ' ὅγε (*vel sim.*) is commonly used to mark a temporal progression. Ap. chooses instead to conduct us, as viewers of a succession of separate scenes, from Eros' present stopping-place to the next: he leaves the *vestibule* behind and crosses over the *threshold* (into the *megaron* and) over to *Jason* (the company has by now left the courtyard and is waiting for the throng of servants to complete their preparations). ἐκ then is adverbial, or rather, the genitive is unexpressed, as in *Il.* 18.480 (cf. 231n.). Not with ἄμειψεν (e.g. Vian ed. 1961): the verb requires no amplification, see below; nor with the nearer verb (e.g. Gillies): ἐκλανθάνειν *escape detection altogether* does not occur [cf. Kamerbeek, *Mnemosyne* 20 (1967), 390].

ὅγε ... οὐδὸν ... Cf. *Od.* 16.41. This strengthened pronoun habitually serves to pinpoint a subject.

καρπαλίμοισι *Od.* 7.135 (the Alcinous-episode) καρπαλίμως ὑπὲρ οὐδὸν ἐβήσετο δώματος εἴσω.

καρπαλίμοισι .. ποσίν [Theoc.] 25.156; different configurations in archaic epic (all in *LH/LfgrE* s. καρπάλιμος, cf. Janko on *Il.* 16.342-4), *Galeomyomachia* 11 (text in *ZPE* 53 (1983), 15) and Q.S. 4.556 ~ 7.126 (after Homer), id. 10.442, Greg. Naz. 1464.181 (~ *Il.* 22.166), Max.

322, 405. The adj. here only in the poem, the adv. 7 ×; neither anywhere else in 3^H. See next note.

λαθών As if he were a warrior about to strike: cf. λαθών in *Il.* 11.251, 15.541, and see on 278f. 'With καρπ. feet' too has associations with an armed warrior moving in for the kill, in two of the three Iliadic examples, and also in *Nosti* ('Ατρειδῶν Κάθοδος) *EGF fr.* 8.1.

ποσὶν οὐδὸν ἄμειψεν Cf. (1) *HyDem* 188 ἐπ' οὐδὸν ἔβη ποσί, Bacch. 18.16-7 ἀμείψας .. ποσὶν .. κέλευθον. (2)(a) Hes. *Theog.* 749 ἀμειβόμεναι .. οὐδόν/; infr. 647 οὐδὸν ἄμειψεν/; Nonn. *D.* 4.15 οὐδὸν ἄμειψε. (b) Theoc. 2.104 cited above; Opp. *Hal.* 1.201, [Orph.] *A.* 908 ὑπὲρ οὐδὸν ἀμείψῃ (-ψας)/.

281 ὀξέα δενδίλλων Meleag. *HE* 4204 Eros (of a rather different kind: Slater, *BICS* 21 (1974), 135) ὀξὺ δεδορκός/ (after Mosch. 1.7-8).

δενδίλλων Cf. *Studies* 103 n.12. *Il.* 9.180 δενδίλλων: either περιβλέπων, one explanation offered by schol. D (for the other cf. Nonn. *D.* 22.120 /νεύμασι δενδίλλων), or διαστρέφων τοὺς ὀφθαλμούς, as suggested by schol. bT (for more see *LH* s.v., Wendel on schol. Ap. 281*a*, also Radt on Soph. *fr.* 1039) may serve as a reasonable approximation to the sense required here, viz. παπταίνων (glosses on that: cf. e.g. *EtM* 651.11 βλέπειν καὶ περισκοπεῖν, schol. D at *Il.* 4.200 περιβλέπων, ἐρευνῶν), like the armed warrior (above 278f., 280nn.) looking around searchingly for his victim: so for instance *Il.* 8.269 Teucer τόξα τιταίνων; see also 279n. As for the accompanying adverb, cf. ὀξύ at *Il.* 11.343, al.; *HyHom* 19.14 /ὀξέα δερκόμενος of the efficient huntergod Pan. Eros needs to locate both Jason and Medea, who one presumes will be some distance apart at this moment.

αὐτῷ δ' ... iv.73 /αὐτῷ τ' Αἰσονίδῃ. Here however the name is postponed, coming in imposingly at the start of the next line.

ὑπό A striking picture, no doubt inspired by art (cf. Webster 78): 'Éros se blottit aux pieds de Jason, si bien que le trait d' amour paraît partir de Jason lui-même' Vian ed. 1961.

βαιός There is an early example of this word (also ii.86, iv.1711) in Hes., *WD* 418, and perhaps another in Sappho, *PLF* 99 i.1; surprisingly, 3^H offers otherwise only Arat. 358, with no showing of Homeric οὐδ' ἠβαιόν outside this poem (3 ×) unless Phylarchus *SH* 694A3 belongs here (ἠβαιήν Call. *fr.* 625 ~ *SH* 238.14; Numenius *SH* 570.1 ἠβαιῇ corrected from ἢ βαιῇ).

βαιός is used attributively in the unit βαιὸς Ἔρως several times in Nonn. *D.* and in epigram (Anon. *AP* 9.616.2, 784.2, *APl* 202.3), where the theme of his diminutive stature, done to death in Moschus 1, is recurrent (cf. also [Theoc.] 19.8 τυτθός, and, e.g., *pauxillus* in Naev. *com.* 55, *parvus* in Ov. *Fast.* 2.463, with Lyne on *Ciris* 138). βαιός here is very different: 'de manière à se faire tout petit' Vian ed. 1961 (cf. Platt 1914.29). If we gain the impression in the Olympian scene that Eros is a youngster (cf. κοῦροι in 118), he is nowhere in the poem represented as the tiny δόλιον βρέφος who hounds his desperate mother in Moschus 1. The 'smallness' here looks forward to the image of 294-5: cf. Nonn. *D.* 7.271 /βαιὸς Ἔρως then 274 ὀλίγῳ πυρί. On the motif and its effects in art see Fowler 1989.150-3.

ἐλυσθείς A brilliant blend of literal and metaphorical. ἐλυσθείς (cf. 1313 below, where the verb will be examined in detail) is like the Homeric ἀλείς, 'having drawn oneself together, contracted one's body,' with the purpose of escaping detection or taking evasive action (*Il.* 13.408 al.) or of making a strike (id. 21.571 al., cf. Gow on [Theoc.] 25.246). Schol.'s excellent συστρέψας ἑαυτὸν καὶ ὑποκαλύψας (281*b*) may be compared with, e.g., schol. b at *Il.* 13.408 ἑάλη· συνειλήθη καὶ συνεκρύβη, and Eustath. 1362.2 on *Il.* 24.510 ἐλυσθείς· συστραφείς (cf. *LH* s.v. εἴλω for much more in this vein, and see Ronconi 182-3).

Luckily, we are also in a position to take an Archilochean image into account (cf. on 296-7): *IEG* 191.1, a clearly devastating φιλότητος ἔρως ὑπὸ καρδίην ἐλυσθείς, 'having curled itself up/concentrated itself at a point deep down in the heart,' well out of sight (cf. M. S. Silk, *Interaction in Poetic Imagery* (Cambridge 1974), 131f., who relates this passage to the celebrated Odyssean ὑπὸ γαστέρ᾽ ἐλυσθείς/, 9.433; A. Carson, *Eros the Bittersweet* (Princeton 1986), 47). The god Eros is already on his way to becoming the 'eros' (though see the comment there) which will burn inside Medea's body: εἰλυμένος at 296 describes the condition, i.e. concentrated there, συνεστραμμένος.

282 γλυφίδας ... νευρῇ For Homeric models see on 278f. and 279, and cf. *Studies* 103 n.18. These two nouns are combined in *Il.* 21.419, Greg. Naz. 1310.40, Nonn. *D.* 15.332-3. γλυφίς -ίδες with ref. to Eros/Erotes: Arch. *GPh* 3589, Nonn. *D.* 7.201.

For definitions of γλυφίδες see schol. at *Il.* 4.122 [where note ἐντίθεται] with the material assembled there by Erbse, and *LH* s.v. The Homeric plural probably denotes two nocks at right angles: so McLeod, *CR* n.s. 14 (1964), 140-1 (further lit./discussion: *LfgrE* s. γλυφίς, Kirk on *Il.* 4.122, F-G Introd. to *Od.* 21, p. 140). Ap. though will no doubt have treated it as ἀντὶ ἑνικοῦ (schol. bT at *Il.* 4.122-3).

ἐνικάτθετο Cf. on the one hand *Il.* 10.265 μέσσῃ δ᾽ ἐνὶ –⏑⏑–×, and on the other *Od.* 11.614 -ῇ (hiatus) ἐγκάτθετο τέχνῃ/. ἐνικάτθεο is the transmitted reading in Hes. *WD* 27: but ἐγκάτθεο -ετο *Il.* 14.219, 223 (both with variant ἐνι-), *Od.* 11.614, 23.223, *HyDem* 286, Hes. *WD* 627 (v.l. ἐνι-) and (ἐγ- or ἐσ-) *Theog.* 487, 890, 899, [Hes.] *fr. dub.* 343.7. Later: ἐγ- Anyt. *HE* 702, Call. *h.* 3.229, Agathyllus *SH* 15.1, Q.S. 7.338; ἐνι- Nic. *Alex.* 616 (v.l. ἐγ-), [Opp.] *Cyn.* 3.11, Anon. epic. *ap.* Schubart, *Gr. Lit. Pap.* (1950), 15v36 (pap. 3rd cent. AD), Nonn. *D.* 9.61, Musae. 271 v.l. (Kost ad loc.), Cougny 347*b*2 (p.590), Anon. *AP* 9.207.1.

283 Brunck compared Virg. *A.* 9.622-4. Ap. here, as so often elsewhere, writes with extreme economy: no τόξον/-α, no ἰόν (the latter for ἰθὺς δ' *EtG*^A).

ἰθύς *Il.* 20.99 the all-conquering Achilles' unerring spear ἰθὺ βέλος πέτετ', *Od.* 22.8 Odysseus ἐπ' Ἀντινόῳ ἰθύνετο πικρὸν ὀιστόν/.

διασχόμενος There does not appear to be a parallel for the middle (but -σχόμενος is widespread in epic, and cf. in a similar context *Od.* 22.15 ἐπισχόμενος βάλεν ᾧ/) or for the sense, i.q. διατεινάμενος (cf. LSJ s.v. II2, ii.1043f. ἀγκύλα τείνατο τόξα/ἧκε δ' (?) ἐπ' οἰωνὸν (?) ταχινὸν βέλος ...).

... παλάμῃσιν Ctr. *Od.* 19.577 = 21.75 ... ἐντανύσῃ βιὸν ἐν παλάμῃσι/.

284 ἧκ' ἐπί Cf. on 283 (ii.1044), ii.1036 quoted below, and (Ardizzoni; Ciani 97-8) *Il.* 1.382, the lethal Apollo; also id. 7.269, *Od.* 9.538, al. /ἧκ' ἐπι-.

τὴν ... θυμόν We might have expected a reference to the missile's progress to follow on at once, as in ii.1036 ἧκ' ἐπὶ οἷ πτερὸν ὀξύ, τὸ δ' ἐν λαιῷ πέσεν ὤμῳ κτλ. This is put off till 286, by which time Eros has departed, leaving Medea to occupy centre-stage. Instead, we hear, briefly, of the immediate paralyzing effect on 'her ... her θυμός' (cf. Köhnken 59 n.1 & 65 n.1, and earlier Buccholz 87-8). This arrow does not tear through flesh on entry, but it is no less stunning for that. Ap. echoes *Il.* 17.695 (Antilochus, devastated by bad news), *Od.* 4.704 (Penelope, likewise) /δὴν δέ μιν ἀμφασίη ἐπέων λάβε, divesting his models of the qualifying complement 'of words'; together with *Il.* 14.475 (ἄχος), 23.468 (μένος) ἔλλαβε θυμόν/. Cf. later [Orph.] *L.* 573 /ἀμφασίη δ' ἥρωα λάβε.

On ἀμφασίη (Wyatt 80-1, Risch 215) see *Noten* 390-1, Ciani 98-9, pointing to links with the pervasive ἀμηχανίη, and with ἀφασία [cf. *DGE* s.v.]. It was variously defined: ἀφωνία, ἔκπληξις [cf. Eur. *Hel.*

549 ἔκπληξιν .. ἀφασίαν τε], ἀπορία: see schol. D at *Il.* 17.695, schol. H/Eust. at *Od.* 4.704, schol. Ap. ii.409, par. iv.1-5, Ap. Soph. 29.8, *EtM* 88.39, *EtG* s. ἀμφασίαν, Hesych. α3922, 8572, Suda α1691. In practice, one or more of these aspects of profound mental shock or stupefaction may be operative in any given case: ii.409 (followed not only by 'he spoke ὀψέ' but also by ἀμηχανέων), the present passage (she is stunned, but equally there is no vocal reaction to the strike; Knox 305 suggests that ἀμφασίη here prompted Virgil's *obstipuit* at *A.* 1.613), iii.811 (Medea, paralyzed by fear), id. 1372 ('dumb amazement': ctr. ἴαχον at 1370), iv.3 ('an inability to find voice, out of sheer perplexity'). In the erotic sphere one may recall Bion *fr.* 1.1, ref. Apollo shattered and bewildered by Hyacinth's death. I mention finally the flabbergasted latecomer Menophilus because of the exalted company he keeps: *SH* 558.6 (the word is quite common in Imperial verse).

The motif of (temporary) φωνῆς ἐπίσχεσις specifically may have been a conventional component by now in catalogues of symptoms: cf. Sappho *PLF* 31.7f. (below 286b-98n.), Theoc. 2.108-9, and a number of passages collected by NH on Hor. *Carm.* 1.13.5. It is variously deployed later on: 683f. (Medea with Chalciope; erotic overtones), 967f. (Medea and Jason when they first meet), 1011-12 (the smitten Medea, overjoyed), 1063 (Medea, falling silent and bursting into tears at the prospect of losing Jason). In 1157f. Medea's ἀμηχανίη robs her of the *will* to speak.

285 αὐτὸς ... Eros in his *personal* manifestation departed, leaving *eros* behind: 286 βέλος ἐνεδαίετο [cf. ὀιστοί and αὐτοῦ in the memorable picture of *Il.* 1.46-7, with Vivante, *Eranos* 81 (1983), 3]: 296-7 αἴθετο ἔρως. See however 296n.

αὐτὸς ... μεγάροιο ... A sophisticated echo of *Od.* 22.239-40, Athena, like a <winged> bird: /αὐτὴ δ' .. ἀνὰ μεγάροιο μέλαθρον/ ἕζετ' ἀναΐξασα ... Eros on the other hand makes himself scarce.

ὑψορόφοιο ... μεγάροιο A novel combination, as far as we can tell; Nonn. *Par.* 19.61 /ἔκτοθεν ὑψορόφων μεγάρων. Different configurations in Homer: *Il.* 24.317 ὑψορόφοιο .. θαλάμοιο ⏑–× (ἀΐξας 320; ref. winged bird, cf. above), *Od.* 4.121 θαλάμοιο .. ὑψορόφοιο/.

We will recall the palace's 'high-roofed megaron' in 293; we may also imagine that Eros while still indoors soars triumphantly into the air as he starts to wing his way back to Olympus to collect his reward (cf. *Studies* 27 & 103 n.22).

παλιμπετές Cf. *Studies* 103 n.21. Here applied to the winged Eros, as to an eagle at ii.1250 (παλ. ἀίσσοντα/; cf. Campbell 1971.416); the association with πέτεσθαι is clear also in Arat. 1032. Schol. D at *Il.* 16.395, Ap. Soph. 126.34 and others (Erbse on schol. *Il.* loc. cit.) relate the word to πίπτειν (both 'falling' and 'flying' were on offer for δυ-πετής: West on *Od.* 4.477, Janko on *Il.* 16.173-5, E. Heitsch, *Aphroditehymnos, Aeneas und Homer* (Göttingen 1965), 26-7): cf. iv.1315 (schol. and Livrea ad loc.), and *Il.* 16.395, *Od.* 5.27, Call. *h.* 3.256 (Bornmann ad loc.), 4.294, Nonn. *Par.* 21.17, *D.* 3.30 (where there is no good reason for labelling it adjectival; see further *LexCall* s.v.).

This is the closest Ap. comes to treating Eros as a πτερόεις god (Lasserre 220f. provides illustration), equipped with the wings which would come to have real curiosity-value among *litterati*, Ovid in particular): not even his arrow is so described (279: ctr. *Il.* 4.117; and ii.1038(!)). There is no room for a Muppet-like figure in this poem.

ἐκ μεγάροιο Homeric clausula, also infr. 442, iv.1121, 1222 (cf. *Od.* 19.60).

286a καγχαλόων 124n. Eros there had no difficulty in getting the better of his gaming-partner. Now he has picked off another sitting target, and he cannot suppress his glee once he has implanted the πολύστονος ἰός. Cf. Buccholz 88-9, who refers to the laughing Eros of Meleager, see the material adduced by Crane 1987.167-8. A general point made by Sir Hugh Lloyd-Jones may be recalled here: "the frivolous irresponsibility of the agent stands in inverse proportion to the formidable consequences of the action," 1990: 2.247. (Imit. *Anacreontea*: 276n.)

ἤϊξε 36n., cf. also on 285 (*Od.* 22.240). Eros acts like the human archer: he rapidly makes himself scarce once he has discharged his missile.

286b-98 A pathological catalogue which is neither exhaustive (notable omissions: the ἀχλύς shrouding the eyes, only hinted at in the echoes of Archil. *IEG* 191 in 281 and 296: cf. later 962-3, and also 725-6; immobility: 964-5) nor systematic (the familiar fire heads the list, but is quickly dropped, only to be revitalised in a developed simile at 291-7; internal and external symptoms are intermingled: burning, unseating of reasoning powers, flood of mixed emotions, with shooting glances, alternating paleness and blushing).

'Such lists of symptoms depend ultimately on Sappho's celebrated catalogue' NH on Hor. *Carm.* 1.13.5, cf. the brief analysis of Privitera, *QUCC* 8 (1969), 71f. Other probable or possible Sapphic echoes out-with *PLF* 31 will be signposted in the commentary on the ensuing lines. We have moved some distance away from the studied directness of that famous fragment, and the recipe is quite different: although fire (obligatory) and pallor are in evidence, there is no obscuring of the vision (see above), no humming in the ears (ctr. iv.17), no sweating or (ctr. iv.53) trembling; the symptom of speechlessness is curtailed and moderated, the 'heart in the breast' is radically recast. Whether Ap.'s simile of 291f. owes anything to the closing line(s) (?πένητα) we cannot say; for an attempt to divine the content on the basis of Ap./Theoc. [see below] cf. Nannini, *QUCC* n.s. 5 (1980), 38. L. Rissman, *Love as War: Homeric Allusion in the Poetry of Sappho* (Meisenheim 1983), 81-2, comparing this Sappho-fragment, relates Medea's symptoms both here and infr. 962f. to the pathology of fear, expressed in descriptive terms ultimately traceable to the language of war in Homer. It is certainly true that Medea will prove to be anxiety-ridden, but this aspect of her condition is not under scrutiny in either passage.

286bf. On love's fire/Eros' fiery missiles see the lit. assembled by Williams on Call. *h.* 2.49 (esp. Pease on Virg. *A.* 4.1 & 2), and by Kost on Musae. 19. It is noteworthy that fire (a thoroughly familiar image by now) plays little part in the subsequent case-study: 'smouldering …' 446, 762; an outburst prompted by ἀμηχανίη that her πῆμα φλέγει ἔμπεδον (n.b. βελέεσσι 774!); ἡδεῖαν .. φλόγα oxymoronic at 1018; obliquely in a cutting remark by Mene at iv.58 (περιδαίομαι). When (warlike) Eros is regenerated at iv.445f. there is no sign of ἔμπυρα τόξα.

The notion of a fire-carrying missile is *implied* in Theoc. 2.82 (*Sapphica* follow) πυρί (pap.: περὶ *codd.*) θυμὸς ἰάφθη/, 3.17 (~ iii.762-3). Bonanno, *RFIC* 115 (1987), 196f. (see now also the same scholar's somewhat prolix *L'allusione necessaria* (Rome 1990), 162 *et circa*), in discussing πυρί in the former passage, suggests that Theoc. was influenced by 286-7: 'in Teocrito il fuoco, senza neppure dichiararsi come dardo, può colpire *tout court* il cuore di Simeta.' This could be so: there are clear correspondences, among them 110 ~ infr. 964-5, see n. there.

Commentators quote Catull. 64.91-3, where eyes and internal fire are specified, in that order (then an apostrophe to Cupid), i.e. the flame emanating from Theseus [cf. iii.1017f.] is absorbed through Ariadne's eyes into the depths of her body. Ap. (who has no truck with 'marrow' – or 'bones') arranges things rather differently.

286b-7 βέλος ... κούρῃ recalls 153: Eros' job is now done.

The missile started to 'burn' inside her (cf. Faerber 18). The verb is rare enough (Diggle sought to produce a further example with his correction of the desperately corrupt Eur. *Hcld.* 892: *PCPS* n.s. 15 (1969), 40-1) to provoke the suspicion that Ap. is blending one of his primary epic sources with an important lyric model, viz. *Od.* 6.131-2 ἐν δέ οἱ ὄσσε/δαίεται scil. πυρί construed as *in tmesi* + Pind. *P.* 4.184 (γλυκὺν ἡμιθέοισιν πόθον) ἔνδαιεν (echoed recently: 262); later in the poem: iv.1147 /δαῖε δ' ἐν ὀφθαλμοῖς [cf. Hom. again] γλυκερὸν πόθον, 1726 (corr. Vian) γλυκερὴ δ' ἐνεδαίετο τοῖσι/κτλ. Cf. Ciani 99, who cites from earlier literature for the notion of the καυστικὸν βέλος (initially literal, soon to be equated with ἔρως) *PV* 649-50 Ζεὺς .. ἱμέρου βέλει/.. τέθαλπται scil. for Io [276n.]. It is also pertinent to note that Ap. persists in pulling in words and images from the Iliadic battlefield before he leaves this Pandarus-like figure behind: the second half of 286 is shaped like that of 14.439; ... νέρθεν ὑπό ..., like 16.346f. .../νύξε· τὸ δ' .. δόρυ .../νέρθεν ὑπ' ...; κραδίη/wound: 13.442; φλογὶ εἴκελ(ον) *passim* in war situations (see below); then ἀντία .../βάλλεν, cf. ἀντίοι (v.l.: Edwards on 17.661-3, Rengakos 1993.76) of ἄκοντες at 11.553, 17.662, and ἀντίον at 5.569, ἄντην at 12.152 (Meleag. *HE* 4718 ἀντωπὸν .. βέλος); αἰεί: cf. e.g. 16.105 βάλλετο δ' αἰεί/. (More in like vein will follow, notably at 761f. and 962f.) The striking ἀμαρύγματα serves as a very effective brake.

287 νέρθεν ὑπό (286b-7n.) = Theod. *SH* 757.8, Opp. *Hal.* 2.492, [Orph.] *L.* 450, pentam. Agath. *AP* 5.294.12, the second and third of these with ref. to wounding.

With this and the sequel ctr. *Il.* 10.9f. πυκίν' .../νειόθεν ἐκ κραδίης, .. δέ οἱ φρένες ...

ὑπὸ κραδίῃ Picked up at 296; cf. Q.S. 5.597 al. After Archil.'s ὑπὸ καρδίην (281n., cf. too Alcm. *PMGF* 59(a)2, Sapph. *PLF* 31.6, Eur. *Hipp.* 1274, al.); Virgil *sub pectore*, *A.* 4.67, Pease ad loc. (add Ov. *Met.* 11.225). Theoc. 11.15-6 could be a jocular allusion to our poem: 'having ὑποκάρδιον ἕλκος <in the form of> a missile which, prompted by mighty (!) Cypris [cf. iii.142f., 153] he [Eros, who else?] had planted [cf. iii.153, 765] in his liver.'

φλογὶ εἴκελον An Iliadic expression, applied to warrior(s) about to launch or in the act of launching a ferocious attack on the field of battle (cf. on 286b-7); 'like flame' here points up the devastating effect (cf. οὖλος in 297) of Eros' missile (φλόξ: 'c'est une puissance, une action ou une transformation matérielle violente' Graz 206). Ap. no doubt has in his head *Scutum* 451 (~ i.544) φλογὶ εἴκελα of the weapons wielded by οὔλιος Ἄρης, -βαλε 453. φλογὶ εἴκελον in this sedes *Il.* 13.688, iv.173 (see Livrea's note), and very probably Antim. *fr.* 46.1 corr. (Wyss ad loc.).

εἴκελον, spelling: VDB 1.LXXIII.

287-8 ἀντία .../βάλλεν ... '... if ... Medea had closed her eyes or turned them elsewhere ...' mused Boccaccio (see Stone, *ICS* 9 (1984), 224). Medea's 'missiles' are fired *full on* or *directly* (ctr. λοξά in 445, VDB 2.62 n.3; cf. Chuvin on Nonn. *D.* 4.9), but there is also fire *in the opposite direction*, as a βέλος has been discharged from a point close to Jason himself (281f., cf. *Noten* 413 n.145). For the idea cf. Soph. *fr.* 474.4 (lover's direct and reciprocated glances: Pearson and Radt ad loc., Walker, *PCPS* n.s. 38 (1992), 138f.), Eur. *IA* 584f. (Paris/Helen) ἐν ('with') ἀντωποῖς βλεφάροισιν ἔρωτά τ' ἔδωκας (Blomfield: δέδωκας; δέδορκας Jaya Suriya, *CR* n.s. 24 (1974), 175, but do we really want a perfect?) ἔρωτι δ' αὐτὸς ἐπτοάθης. There is a difference here though: despite the language employed, there is not *true* reciprocity at this stage, and in this regard Ap. is in fact following convention: interest on the part of the beloved is either played down or excluded altogether (see e.g. Giacomelli, *TAPA* 110 (1980), 138-9). Medea's constant stream of βέλεα, the shafts of light that are commonly said to transmit or kindle desire (see the passages collected by Pearson in *CR* 23 (1909), 256-7, id. on Soph. *ffr.* 157, 474, and more generally West on [Hes.] *Theog.* 910, Thomson on Aesch. *Ag.* 418-9, Griffiths, *BICS* 37 (1990), 133) are for the moment ineffectual, on a conscious level at least: see 1077-8. It is as if this respectable virgin princess, whose αἰδώς is nowhere in evidence here, is looking her bridegroom straight in the eye at her actual wedding (see on the practice Oakley, *AA* 8 (1982), 113f., Armstrong and Ratchford 9-10).

The human body can put up defences against most disorders, including love, temporarily if not permanently: by 444-5 Medea has gained enough self-control to indulge her fascination less obtrusively. The theme of eye-contact, in conjunction with that of αἰδώς or the lack of it, is to be important in the subsequent meeting: 1008-10, 1018- (... βάλλον ...) 1023, 1068, cf. VDB 2.39.

Cf. and ctr. the description of Ariadne eyeing Theseus in Catull. 64.86f.

ἐπ' There is no hope for the once popular ὑπ' offered by *m* (cf. Platt 1918.137; Ardizzoni 1956.371f./1958.45; Wellauer turned black into white in an effort to accommodate it); it must have come from ὑπό immediately above. For ἐπ' (which Naber 28 actually conjectured here) cf. 444f.

ἀμαρύγματα Scil. (ἀπ') ὀμμάτων, flashing, darting glances, emanating in rapid succession (cf. n. on 1018-9; iv.857 ὠκυτέρη ἀμαρύγματος, 'faster than a brilliant burst of <reflected> light') – not as obtrusive as a single starry-eyed stare, but obtrusive enough: Eros' initial onset is overwhelming, and αἰδώς melts away.

Sappho's ἀμάρυχμα λάμπρον .. προσώπω (*PLF* 16.18) is sometimes taken to refer partly, primarily or exclusively to the eyes: see e.g. Gow on [Theoc.] 23.7, Page *S&A* 54. But it could equally well denote the playing of bright flashes of light (i.q. φάος ἔρωτος Koniaris, *Hermes* 95 (1967), 260 n.2: too feeble) on the complexion ('bright sparkle of the face' D. A. Campbell; cf. Nonn. *D.* 10.316 ἀμάρυγμα προσώπου/, Paul. Sil. *AP* 5.259.3; and Triph. 71. See further *LfgrE* s.v.; there is much that is unsatisfactory about Brown's discussion of the word in *QUCC* n.s. 32 (1989), 7f.). Unequivocal examples involving 'eyes' outside our passage are all late: Nonn. *D.* 5.342 ὀφθαλμῶν, id. 7.249 ~ Paul. Sil. *Soph.* 998 βλεφάρων. — Infr. 1018-9 Jason/Medea τῆς δ' ἀμαρυγάς/ὀφθαλμῶν ἥρπαζεν (~ Jo. Gaz. 1.208 /μαρμαρυγὴν ἥρπαξεν): cf. *HyHerm* 45 ἀπ' ὀφθαλμῶν ἀμαρυγαί/ = [Opp.] *Cyn.* 3.32, 90; [Apolin.] 31.[18] /ὀφθ. -άς. — iv.728 βλεφάρων .. μαρμαρυγῇσιν/: see LSJ s.v. μαρμ. 1, and: [Opp.] *Cyn.* 3.348-9; Nonn. *Par.* 9.46, 20.54, and *LexNonn* s.v.; [Apolin.] 103.69; Musae. 56; Christod. 281-2.

288-9 καί .... φρένες *Il.* 14.294 μιν ἔρως πυκινὰς φρένας ἀμφεκάλυψεν/, *HyAphr* 38, and iv.1018 (Medea reviewing her conduct) ἐμοὶ ἐκ πυκιναὶ ἔπεσον φρένες point firmly to 'her shrewd wits/powers of reasoning were blown/blasted (clean) out of her chest' (Wifstrand 1929.91-2, VDB 2.40 n.1, *Studies* 104 n.26). This is the regular denotation of πυκ(ι)ναὶ φρένες: *HyAphr* 243, Alc. *PLF* 39.9, Stesich. *PMGF* 588 i.19, Bacch. *fr.* 1.1 (love of gain masters even ...), Eur. *IA* 67, Thgn. *IEG* 1388 (Cypris masters man's ...; Vetta ad loc.), Man. 2.58, Greg. Naz. 1539.247; cf. πυκινόφρων. φρένες: the seat of sense and reason, J. Bremmer, *The Early Greek Concept of the Soul* (Princeton 1983), 61-2; the epithet highlights 'the intellectual function of φρένες which love overcomes' Sullivan, *SO* 58 (1983), 17 with a review of lyric usage/id., *Glotta* 57 (1979), 169. Cf. also *Il.* 14.217 ... ἥτ' ἔκλεψε νόον πύκα περ φρονεόντων/, and Hes. *Theog.* 122 Eros δάμναται ἐν στήθεσσι (n.b.) νόον καὶ ἐπίφρονα βουλήν, with 298 below. Its referent lends the expression an added piquancy, in that Medea (whose very name is significant) is a clever and cunning witch: so Wifstrand loc. cit., who referred to Mene's stinging πινυτή fired at the love-smitten practitioner of magic in iv.65; recall also πυκινὰν ... in Pind. *P.* 4.58.

For a comparable if less forceful expression cf. Catull. 66.24-5 (*Lock of Berenice*) *toto pectore ../sensibus ereptis mens excidit*; and, from contemporary poetry, Call. *fr.* 80.9 πυκι[νοῦ γ]νώματος ἐξ[έ]βαλ[ο]ν, Theoc. 13.48 ἔρως ἁπαλὰς φρένας ἐξεφόβησεν/ i.e. ἐκ στηθέων (~ Archil. *IEG* 191.3), id. 2.19/11.72.

Wind, blowing from within (ctr. e.g. Eur. *Hipp.* 563 Cypris δεινὰ ... τὰ πάντ' ἐπιπνεῖ), combines with the inner fire to wreak havoc. On the wind of love see the discussion and documentation in 967f.n. This most fleeting of images may have been inspired by Ibycus *PMGF* 286.8f./12-3 πεδόθεν φυλάσσει† (λαφύσσει West: see Borthwick's important paper, *Eranos* 77 (1979), 79f.) /ἡμετέρας φρένας, subject a never-resting [cf. καμάτῳ here] love, like Boreas; or by something in Sappho very like it (cf. in her *PLF* 47 Ἔρος δ' ἐτίναξέ μοι/φρένας κτλ. and see below on καμάτῳ). Note in lyric also the highly expressive Bacch. *fr.* 20B.8 Κύπριδός τ' ἐλπὶς <δι>αιθύσση φρένας.

The view that Ap. refers rather to the effect of passion on the respiratory system, though reasonable enough in principle, can only be upheld by recourse to loose paraphrase (as Fowler 1990: 'her breath came in panting gasps,' thinking perhaps of Call. *HE* 1103f. and of καματηρὸν αὐτμένα in ii.87?) or by assigning to στηθέων ἐκ a role to which it is by nature unsuited (as Seaton: 'within her breast her heart panted fast'; similarly Bulloch 1985.588: 'in her breast her heart ...'). Equally inadmissible is the notion that palpitations are in question: so Ardizzoni, followed by Ciani (100-1) and by Lombardi (265). Here too πυκιναὶ φρένες takes on an unfamiliar aspect, and again στηθέων ἐκ causes real problems: Ardizzoni just leaves this element out of the translation accompanying his text. In fact, 755, to which he appeals, is different on all fronts: πυκνὰ [adv.] δέ οἱ κραδίη [ctr. 287/296] στηθέων ἔντοσθεν [n.b.] ἔθυιεν. The same goes for 962 (κάματον 961; cf. 954), which Platt (1918.137) no doubt had in mind when he proposed 'her heart jumped into her mouth.' This is one organ that cannot possibly be displaced at the moment: the missile/*eros* is burning deep down in her heart right before (287) and right after (296) the present development.

The theme of the lover's inability to control the φρένες/νόος recurs briefly in 298, rounding off the episode with a clear warning of things to come, and in 446-7, 471 (resumptive again), cf. the ψυχή in 1151. So it is not overplayed: it is for us to observe Medea's behaviour, and to listen to her monologues, in one of which she is made to exclaim πάντῃ μοι φρένες εἰσὶν ἀμήχανοι (772). Cf. VDB 2.39f. & 47 with n.2.

ἄηντο See above, and 688n., *Studies* 104 n.23; *Il.* 21.386 δίχα δέ σφιν ἐνὶ φρεσὶ θυμὸς ἄητο/. The Hesychian definition (see α1521, i.q. φέρεσθαι, cf. *EtG*[B] s. ὑληουργοί, schol. here and at iv.1673), recalled by Platt (1918.137) and by Vian (ed. 1961), is too colourless: the glosses in schol. *Il.* 21.386a-c Erbse and in *EtM* 23.15 are better.

στηθέων ἐκ adapts the *incipit* of *Il.* 10.95 (κραδίη δέ μοι ἔξω) /στηθέων ἐκθρῴσκει.

καμάτῳ Ap.'s description of the Erotes who implant searing pain as ἀ-κάματοι (765) might be thought to impart some light relief to a harrowing picture. It is the lover's lot to endure κάματος, and from the outset Medea experiences the debilitating effects of a disorder which entails intense physical discomfort and emotional stress and disorientation. γλυκερῇ in 290 provides only a momentary glimpse of a contrary sensation, before we are confronted with a bleak illustration of unremitting toil.

The term is applied to Medea again in 961 (physical distress in the short term, emotional distress in the longer term: cf. *Studies* 62); iv.1 (the physical and emotional traumas to which she has been and will presently be subjected); and, obliquely and strikingly, in iv.37: as she leaves home she is compared, despite the κάματος she has endured to date, with a girl from a rich background who has never experienced μογερὸς κάματος, but goes in fear of δύην καὶ δούλια ἔργα, i.e. of all the hardship and degradation (not just 'emotional perils,' Hunter *CQ* n.s. 37 (1987), 137) that the grind of slavery will inevitably bring – Medea feels that insecure (νοσφισάμην 362 is an ironic echo of ἀπενόσφισεν 36).

For other examples of κάματος in the erotic sphere see Nonn. *D.* 42.200 (δυσέρωτα δυσίμερος 202, cf. iii.961), al. (Peek, *LexNonn* s.v.).

The word may have been borrowed from lyric, like much else in the present description: cf. the run κάματος φρένα in Sappho *PLF* 43.6, though there κάματος appears to denote 'fatigue' due to lack of sleep (see e.g. Meerwaldt, *Mnemosyne* 13 (1960), 110); κλόνει appears in the line before (? wind-imagery).

289-90 i.e. she had a mental 'block' about everything except Jason. Cf. on the theme G. Serrao, *Problemi di poesia alessandrina I: Studi su Teocrito* (Rome 1971), 97f., 147 n.66. Her fixation is to be put in positive form at 453f.

οὐδέ *Od.* 21.70-1 οὐδέ τιν' ἄλλην/μ-; the substantive is an Homeric hapax, *Od.* 13.279-81 ... οὐδέ τις ἡμῖν/δόρπου μνῆστις ἔην ...,/ἀλλ' ... (cause: physical *exhaustion*).

μνῆστιν ἔχεν -οις Nic. *Ther.* 958, *Alex.* 630; common in later verse:

GVI 587.4 (Rome, 2nd/3rd cent.), 1547.10 (ibid., 2nd cent.), Greg. Naz. 414.77 (τινα), 1472.286, Nonn. *D.* 3.158 al.; *AP.* 5.287.4 (Agath.), 9.384.22 (Anon.); *APl* 367.6 (Anon.). Before Ap. μν. ἴσχειν (Soph. *Aj.* 520, 1269).

290 γλυκερῇ ... ἀνίη On the 'bitter-sweet' motif see the material assembled by Kost on Musae. 166 (pp. 362 & 363), along with Voigt on Sappho 130, NH on Hor. *Carm.* 1.27.11, Renehan 1980.346, VDB 2.62 n.5. One would very much like to know if this particular combination is yet another borrowing from the poetess who wrote ... μηδ' ὀνίαισι δάμνα/.. θῦμον. The Medea of tragedy will have experienced and may even have discussed conflicting emotions (cf. Phaedra and the nurse in Eur. *Hipp.* 347-8).

ἀνί(η) is one of the key elements in her future ordeal: 764, 777, 1103, iv.19, 351, cf. Mawet, *AC* 50 (1981), 513-4, and 446n. below. And for Medea, as for most, it is the pain that predominates. γλυκερός is deployed to negative effect in 751 (contrast however 815, and 1018), and lends more than a touch of irony to the reflections on Medea's imminent marriage to Jason at iv.1166f.: πικρὴ ἀνίη is an invariable concomitant of εὐφροσύναι, as in the present case fear gripped the pair γλυκερῇ περ ἰαινομένους φιλότητι.

Anon. *HE* IX had this memorable scene in mind (lover caught by Eros): ὑπὸ κραδίας (: ὑπὸ κραδίη), βλέμμα (: ἀμαρύγματα), τηκέσθω (see below on κατείβετο), πόνος (: καμάτῳ), and finally (verses 3688-9) ἐν πυρὶ γὰρ νοῦς/βέβληται γλυκερῆς ἄχθος ἔχων ὀδύνης.

Val. Flacc. 6.663 *saevae .. dulcedine flammae* perhaps combines this line and infr. 1018.

... κατείβετο ... Built like *Il.* 24.794. Fire, wind, now liquid in an epic-lyric blend: *Od.* 5.152 κατείβετο δὲ γλυκὺς αἰών/, 'was pouring away' <like the flood of tears pouring down his cheeks> (cf. the glosses in *LH* s. κατείβω; metaph. (κατα)λείβω, καταρέω, *defluo;* imitation in *SH* 1031), Alcm. *PMGF* 59A Ἔρως .../γλυκὺς κατείβων καρδίαν ἰαίνει, 'flowing down <into the heart> and flooding <it>.' So here 'was flooded, inundated,' compare 1131 κατείβετο θυμὸς ἀκουῇ/, 'overflowed <with joy> at what she heard,' and 695f. (see n.) ἐπέκλυσε θυμὸν ἀνίῃ/δείματι, τοῖ' ἐσάκουσεν. For copious illustration of love as a liquefying process see Davies, *Hermes* 111 (1983), 496-7, Vox, id. 120 (1992), 375-6, and for related imagery cf. 1009-10, 1019-21, with the comments thereon.

κατετήκετο A, κατήγετο G: see on these Fränkel *Einleitung* 65. (-)τήκεσθαι (commonly conjoined with λείβειν *et sim.*: e.g. Plato *Resp.* 411b,

Plut. *Mor.* 136b) serves as a gloss in S^m here, in par. L^m/P at 1131, and in schol. V at *Od.* 5.152, al. Nothing in the immediate context of [Apolin.] 106.53 (cited below) suggests 'Apollonian' influence.

θυμόν Fitch's θυμός deserves serious consideration, and not just because of 1131 cited above. LAG*d* have nomin. γλυκερὴ ... ἀνίη, which could have prompted an alteration to provide some sort of coherence: for such a clausula cf. [Apolin.] 106.53 κατετήκετο θυμὸς ἀνίη/, Q.S. 10.282 καταίθετο θυμὸς ἀνίη/. On the other hand, we encounter θυμὸν ἀνίη/ in a variety of contexts: Q.S. 1.243, 14.202, Greg. Naz. 1362.125, Nonn. *D.* 11.484 (and *Par.* 16.79 -ίαις), and the accus. could be regarded as a case of *variatio* (so Linsenbarth 22); cf. Eur. *Andr.* 532 λείβομαι δάκρυσιν κόρας. We thus have a match for μετετρωπᾶτο παρειάς closing the description after the intervening simile; otherwise the studied alternation of impersonal with personal subject – ἐνεδαίετο, βάλλεν, ἅντο, ἔχεν – might have been held to indicate the need for 'her θυμός ...' rather than 'she ... in respect of ...'

291f. In the wake of the κάματος which besets Medea (289n.), the first in a series of 'domestic' (PF on 291-8) similes illustrating her affliction, though we have to wait some time for the next (Carspecken 90). *Pace* Clack, *CJ* 68 (1973), 311, it presents a thoroughly bleak picture of a closed-in existence (the melancholy scene of private grief involving characters of privileged status in i.261f. achieves a broadly comparable effect, not least through the simile of 269f.: cf. on that Beye 1982.81f.). Its subject is a poor woman ἀπὸ τῶν ἔργων τῶν ἰδίων χειρῶν ζῶσα (thus schol. D on χερνῆτις at *Il.* 12.433), who operates not in the surroundings of a high-roofed palace (cf. 285) but in a lowly abode (cf. 293), working in the hours of darkness (ibid.) to make ends meet. An Iliadic simile arising from martial activity (grim and bloody wounding and killing) provides the primary reference-point. The occasion that triggers 291f. is not so dissimilar: Medea has just been shot by the archer Eros, whose missile burns in her heart 'like flame' (cf. 287n. for the resonances of this comparison, and note 'destructive eros' in 297). Homer's essential framework is retained, but each and every component is varied: 12.433f. ἔχον ὥς τε .. γυνὴ χερνῆτις ../ἥ τε .... ἵνα ... /ὥς ... ~ Ap. /ὡς δὲ γυνὴ .../χερνῆτις, τῇ περ .../ὥς κεν .... τοῖος ... Homer's woman must be widowed (Faerber 20): in the complementary simile of iv.1062f. (cf. Livrea there), where the pathetic element in Homer 'has become the very essence of the matter' (Garson 9), that point will be put across tellingly (1064) as Medea is about to *acquire* a husband (so e.g. Beye 1982.154; Hutchinson 133 takes a hardline approach). The '<orphan> children' of the model are dropped here, only to surface, portentously, in iv.1063 (cf. e.g. Hurst 122-3, Fusillo 338; not everyone sees deep significance in this detail). Now the spotlight is on a single resourceless woman who has to struggle to stay alive (cf. Zanker 1987.77; Beye 1982.137 [cf. id. 1993.207] talks of 'a life of dependency and bondage') – a situation with which Medea will presently be confronted. Homer gives no indication of working-hours: we are entitled to assume that the woman pursues her task 'all day,' to quote Paley ad loc. In Ap. the woman is said to need light not because (or not just because) she lives in a humble abode (in the ill-lit megaron of the *Odyssey* spinning takes place ἐν πυρὸς αὐγῇ, 6.305) but because she works in the night-hours. This aspect of a cheerless and disadvantaged existence is vividly represented for the Hellenistic era by 'the poor man's poet,' Leonidas of Tarentum *HE* LXXII (cf. Huber 49, VDB 2.121, Livrea 1992.148 n.4; Faerber 19 was moved to speculate about its applicability to 'the proletariat of Alexandria'); it is related to Medea's own tormented insomnia in iv.(1058-)1063, with characteristic deviousness: Νύξ put to rest *human activity*, but sleep did not put to rest *Medea*, who suffered the distress of a *woman working* ἐννυχίη (iii.744f., which in certain respects serve as a bridge between the present simile and the picture of iv.1058f. [cf. Fantuzzi 143-5], present an astonishingly elaborate variation on the familiar theme 'Everybody else slept but not our wretched lover').

Eros' missile started to burn (286) deep down in Medea's heart, 'like flame': its intensity is not specified, but we can be in no doubt about its potency, even at this juncture: 287n. Initially, this process is related (though not straightforwardly: see on μαλερῷ in 291) to an early stage where love is like a burning brand, a stage at which the flame can arguably be extinguished (cf. the graphic imagery of Call. *fr.* 195.23f.) – if you know about it. Medea, whose body and mind are feeding the flame (cf. *Noten* 342), does not know what is happening to her (cf. 296, and 288-9, 298), and is in no position to control it, any more than the working-woman who fuels a brand to keep herself going can anticipate that a modest flame will result in a conflagration that wipes out precious resources, all in one fell swoop (cf. on this aspect of the simile, underplayed or simply ignored by many, *Studies* 27f., and more briefly Buccholz 90, Händel 100).

The simile-apodosis (296 ὑπὸ κραδίῃ …) conjures up unmistakably the familiar image of love as πῦρ ὑπὸ τῇ σποδιῇ, dormant under the ashes but ready to blaze up when fuelled or fanned (cf. Call. *HE*

1081-6 with Gow-Page on 1081f., Headlam on Hds 1.38, McKeown on Ov. *Am.* 1.2.11-12, Call. *fr.* 195.23f. mentioned above, and also the heavily ironic Theoc. 11.51 [a 'Cyclopean' δαλός: ?Anon. *PMG* 966]). So the picture of the ferocious blaze and wholesale destruction in the body of the simile itself (cf., in lighter vein, Meleag. *HE* 4080-1) has taken us far beyond Medea's present predicament. The nature of what lies in store for her is indicated by the emphatic 'destructive eros' which caps the sequence in 297: here is a positive affirmation at the very outset that eros, like elemental fire, may have small beginnings (cf. ὀλίγοιο 294, with βαιός of Eros in 281), but none the less has the power to destroy comprehensively and without warning. On the passage's prospective complexion (in the estimation of the unsympathetic Otis, 1963.72, Ap. never sees further than his nose) cf. notably Faerber 19-20 (like him, I see nothing to suggest that the *short duration of passion* is in question – an occasional aberration; cf. Natzel 50), Drögemüller 183f., VDB 2.14 & 48 (they point to the apostrophe of iv.445f./οὐλόμεναι 446), *Studies* 27f., and more generally Beye 1982.26.

The Homeric simile, and Ap.'s imitations, were reworked by Virgil in *A.* 8.407f. (echoed, in pure narrative, by Valerius Flaccus, 2.136f.): see the commentaries, and also, with ref. to Ap., e.g. Schmidt, *Mnemosyne* 26 (1973), 360f., Briggs, *ANRW* 2.31.2. 973, Rieks id. 1047, R. O. A. M. Lyne, *Further Voices in Vergil's* Aeneid (Oxford 1987), 42f. (not every shred of λεπτότης has been scooped up). Ovid likened the destructive burning endured by a lover to the effect of fire, whether spontaneous or induced, on combustible material in three engaging similes: *Met.* 1.492f. (a beautiful blend of accident and design), 3.373f., 6.456f.; a fourth, illustrating the transformation of smouldering love into a bright blaze with the example of a small spark hidden under the ashes and fanned by wind, occurs in his diverting account of Medea's involvement with Jason: 7.79f. This same poem provides more than just a glimpse of a poor woman bringing the fire back to life with dry material after raking away the ashes: 8.641f. (Bömer on 641-2), cf. [Virg.] *Mor.* 8f.; Hollis on Call. *Hec. fr.* 114 and *CR* n.s. 15 (1965), 259.

291 ὡς δὲ γυνή heads a simile in *Od.* 8.523 (verb: subjunctive; apodosis: /ὣς ..., ctr. /τοῖοι ... *Il.* 4.146 following on from /ὡς δ' ὅτε ... γυνὴ ... 141; iv.1062f. /οἷον ὅτε .. γυνὴ ..../ὣς ...); subject: a widow doomed to a life of πόνος. On introductory ὡς δέ see Carspecken 64.

μαλερῷ For Ap. the Homeric μαλερὸν πῦρ (not elsewhere in 3[H]) means 'fiercely blazing *or* devouring, ravening fire' (i.734, 1297, iv.393, 834), and this is the epithet's usual signification: Graz 126-7, Garvie on Aesch. *Cho.* 324-6 (Silk's 'iconymic freedom,' *CQ* n.s. 33 (1983), 322, seems unsubstantiated to me). Here something different is called for. Since the brand cannot be described as blazing with a violent intensity at the moment it is being fuelled, we must translate 'capable of burning/soon to burn fiercely' (not very satisfactory) or admit a weakened sense 'burning' or 'glowing' (see e.g. schol. b at *Il.* 21.375, *EtM* 574.36, schol. L + P at i.734) or even (cf. Merkel *Proleg.* 181, Gillies here; i.q. μαλακῷ [LSJ s.v. I1; Archestr. Gel. *SH* 192.4 πυρὸς μαλακὴν (con. μαλερὴν!) .. τέφρην/]) 'softly-/slow-burning,' 'smouldering' (cf. Lloyd-Jones and Parsons at *SH* 1087). Whatever one decides, it is plain that the word hints at the impending ferocious combustion (*Studies* 104 n.25).

περί πυρὶ Ω, not surprisingly: μαλ. πυρί *Il.* 2 ×, iv.393; for the confusion see West on Hes. *Theog.* 694, id. 1990.150. Virg. *A.* 1.175-6 *arida circum/nutrimenta dedit* …, cf. Bömer on Ov. *Met.* 8.642-3 (and 644-5).

κάρφεα Not in archaic poetry (Hom. καρφαλέος: v.l. iv.1442, but W only; κάρφω: iv.1094) or elsewhere in 3[H] aside from infr. 295 (κάρφω Call. *fr.* 44, Euphor. 3 ×).

χεύετο rather than -ατο: cf. the aorist χεύοντο (Ω at) ii.926, and i.565, Ardizzoni comm. and OCT/VDB *app. crit.* ad loc. (with West on Hes. *Theog.* 83, *WD* 583), Marxer 14. περὶ .. χεύετο is presumably a variation, both in form and in application, of ἐπεχεύατο in *Od.* 5.487 (see below).

δαλῷ A δαλός is a key feature of the simile at *Od.* 5.488f. (compared by our schol.), where Odysseus, a prey to κάματος (493), is 'keeping alive the spark of life' (Hainsworth ad loc.). The subject of the simile is described as using the brand to preserve σπέρμα πυρός (490, Gow on Theoc. 24.88): schol. B etc. καὶ τὸ σπέρμα γὰρ ἐξ ἐλαχίστου αὔξεται: cf. Ap. 294-5.

292 The postponement, positioning and amplification of χερνῆτις (ctr. *Il.* 12.433) lays maximum stress on the woman's laborious lifestyle (*Studies* 27), itself emphasised by the element ταλα- (cf. below): see 291f.n. *ad init.*

χερνῆτις This Homeric hapax (above) in verse also Eratosth. [Erbse 1953.182 n.2] *CA* 10.1 (ἔριθος), Crin. *GPh* 2043, 'Phil.' (Lacon) id. 3134, Nonn. *D.* 33.270 (γυνή ~ 275 γυνὴ ταλαεργός, id. 3.86 /οἷα γυνὴ ταλαεργός ~ iv.1062 /οἷον ὅτε .. γυνὴ ταλαεργός).

τῇ ... μέμηλεν The pattern is familiar from Homer: cf. here

Od. 5.66-7 ... κορῶναι/εινάλιαι, τῇσίν τε [LA insert τε after περ here in 292] θαλάσσια ἔργα μέμηλεν, and 12.116 τοι πολεμήια ἔργα μέμηλε/ ~ infr. 562 ὕμμιν π. ἔργα μέλοιτο/ ~ *Or. Sib.* 3.428 ὁπόσοις π. ἔργα μέμηλεν/. Others in Ap.: ii.376 -ι σιδήρεα ἔργα μέλονται/ like *Il.* 2.614 -ι θαλάσσια ἔργα μεμήλει/ cf. *Od.* 5.67 above; iv.794 κείνῳ γὰρ ἀεὶ τάδε ἔργα μέμηλεν/ ~ *Il.* 6.348 al. τάδε ἔργα, plus id. 5.876 τ' αἰὲν ἀήσυλα ἔργα μέμηλεν/. Similar runs occur frequently in later poetry.

ταλασήια An epicised version of ταλάσια: Xen. *Oec.* 7.6 ἔργα ταλάσια. It is rare: [Orph.] *fr.* 178.2 (Renehan 1982.131; Athena) ἱστὸν ἐποίχεσθαι ταλασήιά τ' ἔργα πινύσσειν, Nonn. *D.* 6.142 (ἱδρώς); Suda 4.498.25 ταλασήιον ἔργον· ἡ ἐριουργία, which Hollis is inclined to claim for *Hecale* (ed. pp. 360-1; Livrea 1992.148 suggests its insertion in *fr.* 18.5; Lehnus, *ZPE* 95 (1993), 6, agrees, thinking it may have been used of the poor Hecale herself). In the matching simile of iv.1062 the woman is ταλαεργός – an obvious wink in the direction of ταλασία, even if we do not join Livrea (ed. ad loc. and op. cit. above, 148 n.5) in actually translating *wool-worker*; Homeric exegesis may have played a part in all this: schol. AT at *Il.* 12.433-5 τάλαντον [cf. *Il.* 12.433] δὲ παρὰ τὸ ταλαὸν καὶ ὑπομενητικὸν τοῦ βάρους.

293 κεν: περ E. The same impulse to obliterate κεν when used in conjunction with an optative was at work in i.159 (περ *d*) and in iv.1719 (περ *m*).

ὑπωρόφιον Hers is a humble abode, ctr. ὑψορόφοιο in 285 (*Studies* 103 n.22, cf. above on 291f.). Another Homeric hapax, *Il.* 9.640; also in iv.168 (ὑπωροφίου θαλάμοιο/ corr. Bigot, Merkel, cf. Mosch. *Eur.* 6 δόμοισι, Bühler ad loc., Nonn. *Par.* 11.138 μελάθρου with Livrea on id. 18.75) and in other Hellenistic poets: Campbell on Mosch. *Eur.* loc. cit.

νύκτωρ See on 294. This adverb again in iv.101, 495; in archaic poetry only Hes. *WD* 177, Archil. *IEG* 49.7 (v.l. *Od.* 2.105: *ex gloss.*). 3[H]: no further examples.

σέλας Scil. πυρός (as *Il.* 17.739, al.): she wants a blazing fire to illuminate her labours and to provide warmth (on this dual function of σέλας see Graz 310f.); but it gets out of hand (294-5).

ἐντύναιτο Commonly (in epic particularly) of providing oneself with one's basic needs. Quadrisyllabic forms of this verb do not build σπονδειάζοντες in early epic: ctr. in 3[H] i.1189, iii.510, iv.1191, Call. *h.* 2.8, suppl. Euphor. *SH* 416.2 (*SH* 923.12: not from a new piece of Rhianus, for sure; Imperial in my view).

294 ἄγχι μάλ' †ἐγρομένη The following is a restatement, with some changes of emphasis, of the arguments presented in favour of ἑζομένη in *Studies* 28-9.

(1) VDB 2.121-2 offer a robust defence of the transmitted text (see now also VDB 2².155). But it is hard to believe in a 'double awakening' serving to reinforce the theme of love's awakening. (I can make nothing of Drögemüller's 'das Feuer wacht wieder auf – noch zeitiger als die ärmliche Spinnerin,' *Gymnasium* 72 (1965), 471). The sequence ἐγρομένη ἀνεγρόμενον looks downright awkward: the relative position of these participles provokes the suspicion that a very straightforward process of corruption has occurred.

(2) The same editors also, quite reasonably, relate the use of the brand here to the celebrated description of the early morning in Call. *Hec. fr.* 74.22f. (ἑωθινὰ λύχνα, people asking for a light, cf. Hollis' commentary for the details). But I doubt whether the *precise* period indicated by 'in the hours of night' is actually an issue, any more than it is in iv.1063, where the wholly general ἐννυχίη, if we were moved to press the point, could be referred to the *early* stage of the night specified in 1058f. In fact, there is a dismal lack of orientation and clarity (ctr. such expressions as τοῦ ἄγχιστα ἀποθανόντος, 'the one who had died at a point in time closest <to the present>, most recently,' Hdt. 2.143.3) in the proposed progression 'in the <late> hours of night, having got up at a point very close <to those <late> hours>' — ἄγχι is not ἄγχαυρος.

(3) ἀνεγρόμενον looks just right: certainly none of the emendations I have seen inspires confidence: 'Brunck ... proposed ἀνερχόμενον, perhaps to show his contempt for the poet' Platt 1914.30, coming up himself with ἀναιθόμενον (which mars Gillies' text) or περθόμενον or (never!) περθομένου; Damsté 44-5 ἄγχι μάλ', ἐργομένη [G], truly preposterous ...

Hemsterhuis' neat correction ἑζομένη ([Opp.] *Cyn.* 3.200 /ἄγχι μάλ' ἑζόμενος) was recommended by, among others, Wilamowitz (*HD* 2.209 n.1), Faerber (19 n.2: 'Eine Emendation von seltener Schönheit') and Keydell (35). The woman lacks the hearth of wealthy establishments and so huddles up close to the source of the heat (cf. *Od.* 17.572 /ἀσσοτέρω καθίσασα παραὶ πυρί), sitting as she works (cf. *Od.* 6.305, 7.106, *Il.* 18.601; Ap. will be thinking of the wool-worker as rubbing the yarn smooth on her knee: Theoc. 24.76, Gow ad loc.; when she weaves of course she moves to and fro, *Od.* 5.62, al., Pind.

P. 9.33 etc.). A sharply visualised detail I think rather than a superfluous one (cf. VDB 2².155).

ἄγχι μάλ' Many editors appeal to *Od.* 19.300f. ἐλεύσεται ἤδη/ἄγχι μάλ', οὐδ' ἔτι τῆλε .../δηρὸν ἀπεσσεῖται to explain the adverb here: Eust. records the interpretation *soon, in the near future* (but note τῆλε). I suppose that a superficial reading of *Il.* 23.759f., where this same *incipit* occurs, might have provoked a similar response: 758 ὦκα then .../ἄγχι μάλ', ὡς ὅτε τίς τε γυναικὸς (weaver) κτλ. (but note ἀγχόθι in 762 and ἐγγύθεν in 763). In fact, 'temporal' ἄγχι is in itself unexceptionable: cf. Sappho *PLF* 43.9 ἄγχι γὰρ ἀμέρα, and more generally VDB 2.121-2. The problems come from other directions.

Huet, an intelligent critic, would clearly have none of this: he suggested ἦρι μάλ' (Vian 1962.38, 1975.95).

ἐγρομένη† iv.671 (670 'when dawn arrived') on the other hand is quite straightforward. One can see why Merkel (*Proleg.* 114) sought to treat the participle as if it were ἐγειρομένη (*pervigilans*): that does not make his πάγχυ μάλ' any easier to take.

294-5 τό Scil. σέλας <πυρός>, the 'blaze' of the fire being the agent of destruction: cf. Nonn. *D. bis* cited under ἀμαθύνει below. Fränkel (OCT) tentatively suggested replacing σὺν in 295 with πῦρ, but the former makes a point, the latter we can do without (and it jars on the ear).

ἀθέσφατον A strong word, H. Fränkel, *ANTIΔΩPON* (*Festschr. Wackernagel*, 1923), 281f.: of indescribable extent, volume, ferocity, intensity etc., going far beyond what may be considered normal. The meaning is the same whether the α- is regarded as privative or as intensive: cf. the test. in *LfgrE* s.v., Chantraine *DE* s. θέσφατος. Also in ii.1115 (after *Il.* 10.6), iv.636 (adv., West on Hes. *Theog.* 829-30), 1140 (~ [Theoc.] 25.24); 3[H]: also [Mosch.] *Meg.* 104 (φλόξ).

ἐξ ὀλίγοιο In conjunction with μέγα Sol. *IEG* 13.59, Q.S. 10.59 (ctr. Theoc. 22.112-3, a nice reversal!). A close parallel is to be found in [Phocyl.] *Sent.* 144 ἐξ ὀλίγου σπινθῆρος ἀθέσφατος αἴθεται ὕλη (Nonn. *D.* 5.591-2 μείζονι πυρσῷ/ἐξ ὀλίγου σπινθῆρος). Cf. also Sol. *IEG* 13.14 ἀρχῆς δ' ἐξ ὀλίγης (corr. West) γίγνεται ὥστε πυρός.

ἀνεγρόμενον Cf. ἤγειρεν in Aesch. *Ag.* 299; metaph. ἀν- (not Hom.): *DEG* s.v. II2.

σύν Injudiciously filed under συναμαθύνειν (so the majority) in the *Index* (one user wrote to say that ἀμαθύνειν at iii.295 appeared to be missing). To my ear, despite e.g. *Il.* 12.384-5 ~ 23.673, it belongs rather with the nearer πάντ', 'all together,' 'in one fell swoop,' whether as an 'adverb' or 'in tmesi.' So in *Il.* 10.224 /σύν τε δύ' ἐρχομένω, *Od.* 9.289 /σὺν δὲ δύω μάρψας, 429 /σύντρεις or σὺν τρεῖς αἰνύμενος, σύν is most naturally taken in conjunction with the numeral (cf. *Od.* 14.98); but opinions differ, see e.g. schol. B/H at *Od.* 9.429, Leumann 75, Janko 156.

πάντ' ἀμαθύνει Opp. *Hal.* 2.611, -ναι Q.S. 14.645. The word is used of the effect of fire in *Il.* 9.593 (object: an <entire> city, here the woman's precious resources), Theoc. 2.26 (below), Q.S. 8.8, 13.437, Eudoc. *Cypr.* 1.239, Nonn. *D.* 23.263; subject σέλας: id. 2.513, 9.63. Something along the lines of a colourless 'consume, devastate, obliterate' will cover all the known examples (for a fair number see Hester, *LCM* 11 (1986), 53-4), including in all probability *HyHerm* 140 (see *LfgrE* s.v.). That is not to say that an association with ἄμαθος was never felt: 'reduce to σποδός' (schol. bT at *Il.* 9.593*b* σποδὸν καὶ κόνιν ἐργάζεται, cf. Erbse ad loc.) suits here, as in the contemporary Theoc. 2.26 (a lover: 'may he turn his flesh into τέφρα': σποδόν 25, ἀνίασεν 23, αἴθω 24, φλογί 26 ~ Ap. 290, 296, 287).

296-7 EROS operates in two modes: as a fully anthropomorphised god, or as an impersonal force (cf. in part *Studies* 130). The moment Eros leaves for Olympus there is a switch to the latter (cf. on αὐτός in 285), for no subsequent passage in the third book confronts us with an unambiguously personalised being (297/1078; 972; 1018; ctr. the 'Erotes,' 452n.). None the less, the tight parallelism of 296 with the earlier description of the god in action (λαθών 280, ἐλυσθείς 281; note too ὑπὸ κραδίῃ echoing 287, the home of the 'missile') suggests that the one cannot easily be divorced entirely from the other; certainly Lennox's 'the dart has been transformed into an abstract οὖλος ἔρως' (68) goes too far. In iv.445f. (cf. Buccholz 88) Eros is presented in a guise far removed from that of the wicked boy we encounter in the Olympian scene: he is an agent of pure destruction – like the EROS here (οὖλος 297n.). A modern printer though will *have* to plump for ἔρως here and later on in iii (sooner that than weird manipulation of the font), *pace* Vian 1963.28 and some others. Cf. also K. Quinn, *Latin Explorations* (London 1963), 172f.

296 ὑπὸ κραδίῃ 287n.

εἰλυμένος 281n. Ap.'s use of the Archilochus fragment is scrutinised by VDB, 2.121 (on 282).

αἴθετο A cliché, e.g. Call. *fr.* 67.2, Theoc. 2.40, 7.56, *HE* 3040

(Polystr.), 4343 (Meleag.); it will not be put to further use (earlier, but obliquely, i.1245: see e.g. Köhnken 73 n.2).

-ετο λάθρῃ Cf. (*Od.* 15.430), infr. 1369, Q.S. 10.434, al. On λάθρῃ cf. 280n. (and λανθάνειν in Pl. *Symp.* 196a, ἐλάνθανεν in Call. *HE* 1103); Virgil's *caeco .. igne, A.* 4.2, *tacitum sub pectore volnus*, id. 67, see Pease's notes, and Kost on Musae. 85, McKeown on Ov. *Am.* 1.2.5-6 (Prop. 2.12: he believes in the 'boy' all right, but he has done a disappearing trick!). For an exceptionally λαθραῖος Cupid see Val. Flacc. 6.657f., with Hudson-Williams, *Mnemosyne* 26 (1973), 27f.

297 οὖλος ἔρως (cf. 1078) invites comparison with οὖλος Ἄρης *Il.* 5.461; it is implied that EROS is not purely an externalisation of human feeling (cf. 296-7n.) but a potent living force (for Ciani 100 'οὖλος ... impedisce l' interiorizzazione dell' imagine'). The comparison is an apt one: this οὖλος (etymology: see conveniently Koch, *Glotta* 54 (1976), 216, 220-1; for different ones see the commentators on the relevant places in Call. *h.*, with Rengakos 1992.24, and *LexCal* s.v.; also Edwards on *Il.* 17.756, Greppin, *TAPA* 106 (1976), 177f.), harking back to the picture of total annihilation at the close of the simile (295), means ὀλέθριος, ὀλέθρου αἴτιος (see e.g. schol. D at *Il.* 5.461, Erbse on schol. *Il.* 2.6c; infr. 618 ὀλοοὶ .. ὄνειροι ~ Homer's οὖλος Ὄνειρος), and Eros is in effect a death-dealing war-god in iv.445f.: see on 136 and 296-7. For more on this piece of sinister foreshadowing see VDB 2.14, 48, and on οὖλος itself van Krevelen 1949.144-5, Ardizzoni ed. 1956.374 n.3, Vian ed. 1961 ad loc., Nyberg 32 n.107. Fränkel's interpretation 'mit voller Macht' (espoused by Schwinge 133), founded on an astonishingly blinkered view of 1077-8 (*Noten* 418-9), though acceptable in principle (see the passages adduced by NH on Hor. *Carm.* 1.19.9), is unappealing, and not only because ?Mosch. *HE* 2684 (ref. Eros *the archer*, in *threatening* mood) does not support it.

Here is a selection from a very different set of responses: '*oulos Eros* ... lacking in resonance,' 'the wound he inflicts is wholly psychological,' 'the simplicities of the narrative ...,' 'Apollonius in the full brazen courage of his frivolity ...': W. R. Johnson, *Darkness Visible: A Study of Vergil's Aeneid* (Berkeley 1976), 42f.

297-8 A vivid conclusion. Medea's mind is the victim of 'acedia': it is so benumbed (cf. 284) that she can make no effort to conceal or to control the outward manifestations of the sensations she is experiencing. Horace, *Carm.* 1.13.5-6 (lover consumed by 'fires' burning within) is more matter-of-fact: *tunc nec mens mihi nec color/ certa sede ma-*

net. For alternating states cf. Ov. *Met.* 7.78 (Medea), Stat. *Theb.* 1.536f., *Ach.* 1.309f. (Prop. 1.15.39, cited by Mooney and others, refers to different shades of *pallor,* cf. Fedeli's note).

ἁπαλὰς ... παρειάς The epithet, which was suggested by Archil. *IEG* 191.3 (cf. 281, 296-7nn.), is apt, since in the erotic sphere, as in others, 'softness is vulnerability' (so Dover on Theoc. 13.48). For female cheeks so characterised compare *Il.* 18.123 (women, shedding tears) παρειάων ἁπαλάων/, Aesch. *Suppl.* 70-1 (maidens, grieving; FJW ad loc.) δάπτω τὰν ἁπαλὰν .. παρειάν, and later [Opp.] *Cyn.* 3.214 (lamenting mother) /δρυπτομένην ἁπαλήν .. παρηίδα (Q.S. 13.324 [ἀταλὸς πάις, weeping] ἁπαλῇσι παρηίσιν).

Hence: [Orph.] *A.* 795 ἁπαλὴν Μήδειαν.

μετετρωπᾶτο For (μετα)τρέπεσθαι referring to a change of complexion consult West on Hes. *WD* 416, LSJ s.v. τρέπω II3. μετατρωπᾶ-σθαι is very uncommon: Nonn. *D.* 10.26, right after an echo of Ap. iii.1340.

χλόον Cf. χλωροτέρα in Sapph. *PLF* 31.14 (the image is softened here: ctr. Longus 1.17.4): Medea has the same sallow complexion which (*pace* e.g. FGW on Aesch. *Suppl.* 566-7, F-G on *Od.* 22.42, Edgeworth, *ACD* 27 (1984), 121f.) takes on the tint of χλωρότης under the influence of emotion or fear: cf. the description of the fevered Simaetha's χρώς in Theoc. 2.88, with Thomson on Aesch. *Ag.* 1122-3, Smith on Tibull. 1.8.52, and Brown, *CQ* n.s. 34 (1984), 38 with n.8, and ctr. λευκὴν .. παρηίδα in Eur. *Med.* 923, with Braswell on Pind. *P.* 4.212.

χλόος is associated with the cheeks (cf. Call. *h.* 4.80 ὑπόχλοον ἔσχε παρειήν/ with Mineur's note, and also χλοᾶν in Nonn. *D.*) in ii.1216 πολέεσσι δ' ἐπὶ χλόος εἷλε παρειάς/ (~ Call. *fr.* 75.12 τὴν δ' εἷλε .. χλόος), iv.1279 χύτο δὲ χλόος ἀμφὶ παρειάς/. Elsewhere in verse only Nic. *Alex.* 474 (ἐπὶ χλόος ἔδραμε), 570, 579 (κατεχεύατο), Nonn. *D.* 8.200, 11.245 (ἀμφεχύθη), 21.342 (χλόον ἀμφὶ προσώπῳ/), 33.23 (.. παρηίδος).

Given Hippocr. *ap.* Gal. 19.155 (see Erbse 1953.189) and the context of Call. *fr.* 75.12 (above), it seems unlikely that χλόος was an independent poetic creation, though it could have been readily elicited from adjectival -χλόος (> χλόη: already εὔ- Soph., ἁ- δονακό- Eur.; note the force of -χλοος in Call. *h.* 4.80). Marxer (38) regarded it as a back-formation from χλοερός on the analogy of γόος/γοερός sim. ('Apollonian' according to her, and now 'Callimachean' according to Schmitt 54-5).

ἄλλοτ' For the suppression of ἄλλοτε in the first member cf. in tragic dialogue Soph. *El.* 752, *Tr.* 11, Eur. *Hec.* 28, but note also, in archaic poetry, *Il.* 24.511 (schol. T: λείπει τὸ ἄλλοτε μέν, similarly schol. b), al. (*LfgrE* s.v. ἄλλοτε, 566.35f.).

ἔρευθος 122n. The terms 'flush' (cf. 963 ~ cheeks), 'pallor' and 'torpor' impart a clinical air to this record of symptoms: cf. ἔρευθος, χλοῦς and ἀκηδία (the first two certainly, the last almost certainly pre-Hellenistic) in the *Index Hippocraticus*, along with Ardizzoni 1956.375 n.1. Ciani 103 and Lombardi 267 both point to the characteristic Homeric underpinning embedded in the unHomeric description: *Il.* 18.123 (see above); -τρωπᾶσθαι; pallor ~ παρειαί *Il.* 3.35; patterning of 298 claus. as *Od.* 11.272 al. (cf. T. Jahn, *Zum Wortfeld 'Seele-Geist' in der Sprache Homers* (Munich 1987), 70).

ἀκηδείῃσι νόοιο ἀκηδείη means 'indifference' (cf. ii.219, iii.260, 'lack of care,' 'inconsiderateness'), νόος is the reasoning faculty. The reason, which governs self-control, is in a state of torpor: it does not care about, and so does not resist, this onslaught on the bodily functions. (In the event of course Medea does recover enough to put up a fight.) This is the explanation of Ardizzoni (1956.372f., cf. his ed.), who cites this same clausula from Empedocles [*Studies* 129], DK31 B136.2, and exposes the inadequacy of schol.'s πολυκηδείαις i.e. λύπαις. ἀκηδείη in verse elsewhere only Q.S. 3.524 ('négligence, absence de soins' Vian and Battegay, *Lexique* s.v.). [Toohey, *Glotta* 70 (1992), 239f., takes a different, and altogether implausible, line.]

299-303 μή τι φιλοξενίην ἀγόρευε exclaims Medea later on with reference to her father's temperament (1108). Initially Aeetes is solicitous enough (cf. Rose 1984.120), providing the newcomers, three of whom are unknown to him, with a handsome meal before asking the Phrixids to explain themselves: lit. on this practice in Most, *TAPA* 119 (1989), 26 n.56; but it is not always observed in the *Odyssey*, West on 1.123-4, and not normally observed in the *Argonautica*, cf. i.961f., al., with Vian, *Gnomon* 46 (1974), 350. They enjoy a bath too, a luxury not offered automatically, West on *Od.* 3.464f.; λοετρά are not specified anywhere else in the *Argonautica* in connexion with the reception of visitors.

299-300 δμῶες δ' ... harks back to 271f., where the palace-staff started to prepare a meal and baths for the newcomers (cf. *Noten* 342); once they for their part (αὐτοί) have finished, the meal can go ahead. There has been plenty of time for Medea to take in the sight of Jason: such a sumptuous meal (271-2) will not have been got ready in minutes (note δή), and bath-water has had to be heated for and distributed among seven people.

299 δμῶες δ' ὁππότε ... The run /Κόλχοι δ' ὁππότε ... marks a major transition in iv.507. Ctr. here *Od.* 17.320 /δμῶες δ' εὖτ' ... (not in narrative).

δμῶες δ' ... σφιν .. θῆκαν ἐδωδήν But *Od.* 5.199 (196: see below) /τῇ δ' ... δμῳαὶ ... ἔθηκαν/; *Il.* 8.504 ... δέ σφισι βάλλετ' ἐδωδήν/ (for horses; /δόρπα .. ἐφοπλισόμεσθα 503).

ἐπαρτέα θῆκαν Cf. [Orph.] *A.* 275 corr. οἱ ἐπαρτέα θῆκαν. Similarly ii.1177 /αὐτὰρ ἐπεὶ .. -εα δαῖτα πάσαντο/, i.234 αὐτὰρ ἐπεὶ δμώεσσιν -έα πάντ' ἐτέτυκτο, i.333 (/πάντα ...); as so often in this poem, we are afforded a glimpse (but only a glimpse) of possible 'alternative' systems. In *Od.* ἐπαρτής is applied to persons. Cf. further *HyDem* 127f. αὐτοί/ δεῖπνον ἐπηρτύνοντο then δόρποιο .. ἤρατο θυμός/, and the use of ἐπαρτίζειν in i.1210.

θῆκαν ἐδωδήν Ctr. *Od.* 5.196 ἐτίθει πάρα .. ἐδωδήν/ ('to eat and to drink' 197; 'food and drink' 201); id. 6.76 ἐν κίστῃ ἐτίθει .. ἐδωδήν/.

ἐδωδή here denotes sustenance in both solid and liquid form (τροφή schol. D on *Il.* 24.475), cf. *Od.* 5.196f. above, and *AH* Q56. So elsewhere in our poem: ii.196 al. with ref. to Phineus' diet, ii.1013 (husbands nourished by wives at a trying time). Ctr. the sole Callimachean example, *fr.* 688.

300 αὐτοί 299-300n. We do not need this pronoun to see that the familiarity and lack of privacy associated with most Homeric households, where bathing is carried out with female help (Kirk on *Il.* 5.905; West on *Od.* 3.464f., who remarks 'It is not clear where the poet imagines this activity taking place, whether in a side-room or in the megaron itself'; Hainsworth on id. 6.217-22) are not in evidence here. [*Il.* 10.576 dispenses with assistance, but there the poet is clearly striving for economies: there are two bathing-operations in close succession, and a rapid denouement is in order. Hainsworth on 576-9 deals too severely with the passage.]

τε λιαροῖσιν The lengthening of the epsilon (S offers λλ-: Fränkel *Einleitung* 70; cf. Merkel *Proleg.* 104f.) has a parallel in the Homeric τε λιαρῷ, in the context of washing; similarly infr. 876, where, as here, the sense is 'pleasantly/refreshingly warm' (see n. ad loc.). For Ap.'s (not especially adventurous) employment of this epithet see Livrea on iv.572; nowhere else in 3[H].

ἐφαιδρύναντο λοετροῖς This time Ap. adapts a Hesiodic model, cf. the middle use of this verb but with direct object in WD 753 λουτρῷ χρόα φαιδρύνεσθαι/ (see West there); with personal object Nonn. D. 38.147 υἱέα παππῴοισιν ἐφαιδρύναντο λοετροῖς. On other occasions active, with λ. (a) plur.: Aesch. Ag. 1109, Ezech. TGF 128.20 (χρῶτα), Nonn. D. 16.7 (δέμας), 24.44; (b) sing.: Nonn. Par. 13. 66 and (δέμας) 5.8, D. 10.143. Cf. on 46-7 (GVI 1163).

301 ἀσπασίως Cf. i.1173 (... δόρποιο); Od. 13.33-4. Not an idle detail: we last heard of a proper meal at ii.1227: see *Noten* 342.

ἀσπασίως ... θυμόν Ctr. Od. 8.450 (451 'warm bath').

δόρπῳ τε ποτῆτί τε Linked also in ii.307 ἐπεὶ δόρποιο κορέσσαντ' ἠδὲ ποτῆτος/, see *Echoes* there; not an Homeric combination for 'food [see below] and drink': ctr. Od. 17.603 πλησάμενος δ' ἄρα θυμὸν ἐδητύος ἠδὲ ποτῆτος, al. (LH s. ποτής). Further variations: ii.861-2 ~ Il. 19.306; iv.619 ~ Od. 10.379. Cf. Marxer 35.

[Orph.] A. 406 ἀλλ' ὅτε δὴ δόρποιο ποτοῦ θ' ἅλις ἔπλετο θυμῷ (corr.; cf. id. 233, with Vian's *loci similes*) was possibly inspired by our passage.

δόρπῳ Normally a late evening meal in Ap.: cf. Hom., Erbse on schol. Il. 2.381a-b ~ Lehrs 127f./Schmidt 1976.191f., AH Q57f.; but ctr. ii.226 (~ Ap. CA 5.4) and also (Garson 4) ii.307 cited above. So (= food/any meal) HyDem 129 (Richardson ad loc.) ~ Matro SH 534.104, HyAp 511, Call. Hec. fr. 120 (prob.), Theoc. 24.139 (Gow ad loc.), Alex. Aet. CA 1.1, Euphor. SH 415 ii.11, and other examples in Lehrs 129-30.

θυμὸν ἄρεσσαν The double-sigma form of this aorist active (so συν- iii.901, iv.373) is wholly unremarkable (353n.); Hom. only ἀρέσαι, but middle ἀρεσσάμενος and so on. Sense: 'please, satisfy': LSJ s.v. ἀρέσκω III. *Scutum* 255-6 (cited by Ardizzoni) φρένας .. ἀρέσαντο/αἵματος (ἐκορέσαντο schol.) is not so very different. There may however be a closer parallel lurking in a passage of Call., *Aetia fr.* 59.17 = SH 265.17 θυμὸν ἀρε[σσάμενος – the source of Nonn. D. 25.370-1 ἀρεσσάμενος δὲ τραπέζῃ/θυμόν.

Homer's ἤραρε θυμὸν ἐδωδῇ/ (Od. 5.95, 14.111) is obviously relevant: 'supplied' amounts to 'satisfied,' cf. LH s.v. ἀραρίσκω p. 165(b)12f., and also the Homeric θυμαρής/θυμήρης, defined by schol. Od. 23.232 as τῇ ψυχῇ ἀρέσουσαν (similar explanations were advanced elsewhere). Ctr. Il. 19.179 σε δαιτὶ ... ἀρεσάσθω/.

302 ἐκ δὲ τοῦ Aeetes now gets right down to the job of finding out what has happened. The single line devoted to the consumption of food and drink is followed up with a terse and dry 'and following on from that,' in preference to a leisurely sequence in Homeric style (ctr. in particular *Od.* 5.92-6 [95: 301n.] capped with a /καὶ τότε δὴ ...) specifying the act of eating/drinking and (*via* a temporal clause) satisfaction therewith (see Arend 68f., and in Ap. himself ii.307, al.: Peschties 90).

An identical *incipit* occurs in *Od.* 23.199, but the sense is different.

σφετέρης .. θυγατρός But i.813 ἐῆς .. θυγατρός/; iv.1094 θυγατρὸς ἐῆς ~ *Il.* 21.504, *Od.* 19.400 θυγατέρος ἧς/. Cf. iv.1493 /θυγατέρα σφετέρην ('his own,' as here), but *Il.* 5.371 al. θυγατέρα ἥν/.

ἐρέεινε 'set about questioning'; this verb can preface direct speech in enquiries addressed to or on the subject of newcomers in *Od.*, cf. ii.1134; it is used of mutual interrogation by host and guests in i.980. ἐρέεινε ../υἱῆας ... ἐπέεσσι builds in particular on *Od.* 4.137 ἔπεσσι (for Ap. rather ἐπέεσσι, as *codd.*) πόσιν ἐρέεινεν (οἵτινες οἵδε/ἀνδρῶν 138-9 ~ infr. 315-6).

303 υἱῆας 196n.

τοίοισι παρηγορέων ἐπέεσσι 24n. Cf. Musae. 244 /τοίοις ... παρηγορέων .. μύθοις/, and for ἐπέεσσι i.294; iii.610, iv.1740 παρηγορέεσκεν ἔπεσσιν/ ~ Q.S. 14.161 -έοντες ἔπεσσιν/.

παρηγορέων In ii.64, 1196 (cf. *Noten* 308 n.405), iii.610 urge, press, exhort, in i.294, ii.622, iv.1740 address with words of consolation or comfort, in iv.1410 = ἱλάσκεσθαι. It is certainly true that Aeetes is pressing for information; but the notion of friendly reassurance cannot be excluded entirely, for the king, though adopting an 'I told you so' attitude, none the less deals amicably enough with his grandsons, addressing them with a flourish, taking an interest in what has befallen them, and subordinating his own weighty reminiscences to the matter in hand. He wants information, and so he will naturally seek to put his audience at their ease, as best he can.

The verb does not occur in archaic verse. In Ap. only of Hellenistic poets; reasonably common later: *Apolloniana* include i.294 -έων προσέειπεν/ = Q.S. 14.184; ii.64 /πολλὰ παρηγορέοντες = id. 1.777 + 2; ii.1196/ἴσκε -έων: cf. id. 5.612; Nonn. *D.* 11.72 al.

304f. A formal and fulsome opening address; perhaps an echo of the stage-tyrant. Aeetes starts by advertising his magnanimity in terms recalling Argos' account of ii.1147f. (picked up by Jason at iii.190f.): itching for information, he is careful to create a good impression by giving the newcomers to understand that he is a hospitable type, πάντων hinting (somewhat implausibly, it might be thought) at a generous stream of ξεῖνοι 'honoured' in his halls. At the same time, although his hypocrisy will only be exposed later, and then not universally (584f.), Jason has not been exactly sanguine about the prospects of settling amicably (nn. on 167-95(6), 190), and cannot feel entirely comfortable now about being totally ignored until the last moment, when 'these men here' are lumped together with 'the ship,' the whereabouts of which Aeetes is clearly anxious to ascertain.

304 παιδὸς .. κοῦροι *Variatio*: Aeetes does not employ the neutral language of the narrator (302-3). Both terms serve as reminders of his senior status.

παιδὸς ἐμῆς But *Il.* 24.214 /παιδὸς ἐμοῦ (+ pause).

304-5 τὸν .... ἔτισα Echoed in 584-6 Φρίξον .../δέχθαι ἐνὶ μεγάροισιν .. ὃς περὶ πάντων/ξείνων κτλ., where the matter is put in an entirely new light. For the wording cf. *Il.* 10.88, [Hes.] *fr.* 70.39 (name +) τὸν περὶ πάντων/...; *Il.* 18.81 (name +) τὸν .. περὶ πάντων τῖον ἑταίρων/, similarly Hes. *Theog.* 411-2 τὴν περὶ πάντων/... τίμησε ~ Kaibel *EG* 875.4-5 ὃν περὶ πάντων/τίμησαν; *Il.* 17.583-4 ὅς .. ἁπάντων/ξείνων ...

305 ἡμετέροισιν ... ἔτισα On the verb see 181n. Homer has (1) ἐνὶ μεγάροισι .. ἡμετέροισι/ *Od.* 3.186; *pluralis majesticus*, spoken by Nestor, cf. Floyd, *Glotta* 47 (1969), 116f.; this possessive adj. is so used elsewhere in *Arg.* by royals, i.664 al., and by the leader Jason, i.412 al. Cf. 536n. (2) ἐνὶ μεγάροισιν [cf. ii.304 ~ *Od.* 4.624, 24.412; iv.1085] ἄκουσα/ *Il.* 1.396 and sim. (3) μιν ... τίεν ἐν μεγάροισιν/ *Od.* 1.432; later: Greg. Naz. 1497.236 τίεις μεγάροισιν.

306 Aeetes asks: 'How come you are rushing back here? Can it indeed be the case that [ἦε: 12n.] ...?' Chalciope had taken it for granted that her sons had not reached Hellas (260f., note τηλόθι: they could not have been away for very long). Aeetes later (375f.) asserts that they have – but by then he has lost his composure and represents the approach in the blackest terms, as an Hellenic *Komplott*. Here the implication is that it comes as no surprise that they did not reach their destination – something was bound to stop them. Fränkel's repunctuation ... νέεσθε; παλίσσυτοι, ἦέ ... (1928.568; *Noten* 343), designed to make Aeetes suggest right away that the Phrixids had been to Hellas, blunts the edge of his coming outburst. The resultant sequence is in any case forced and just *too* compressed: '<Have you

come> speedily back [scil. without incident] <from your destination>, or did some ...?' And παλίσσυτοι cannot really be dissociated from νέεσθε: cf. 373, i.1206, VDB 2.27 n.5.

πῶς ... Fränkel (*Noten* 343) compared the question put by the startled Aeolus and company to the returning Odysseus in *Od.* 10.64 (from a story recently revived and, apparently, radically recast by Philetas, see *CA* 5: Odysseus, wandering in the west [compare Ap. 311f./iv.764f.!], got involved romantically with one of his host's daughters). Hunter (n. on 299-438) added a detail or two. Further imprints include: *Od.* 10.5-6 παῖδες + θυγατέρες + υἱέες + ἐνὶ μεγάροις cf. Ap. 303-5; 23 ~ 316; 25 ~ ii.1098; ?48f.54f. storm-winds cf. 308n.; 58 ~ 301; 59f. ~ 177-8; 74 ~ 381. The same episode has already been raided for the account of Cyzicus in i; it will provide further food for thought in iv (Hutchinson 102-4).

Αἶάνδε Here only; cf. 313n. Perhaps the poet is playing on the name's inherent indefiniteness: the seafarers, off on a long voyage (308, cf. 602), have come speeding back to land (αἶα) as well. See on 373, and cf. Leon. Alex. *FGE* 1948 ('offenbar spielerisch' Dräger 59 n.163).

παλίσσυτοι 112n.

ἠέ τις ἄτη reappears in Q.S. 4.201, Agath. *AP* 7.596.3. The know-all Aeetes (cf. 309), who ironically was himself living under an ever-present threat of ἄτη (600), may be imagined as having been ready enough at the stage of planning and preparation to warn repeatedly of the possibility of 'some catastrophe,' secure in the knowledge that his grandsons were absolutely committed to this venture (cf. 601-2).

Argos responds to this query at once, and he blames the ship (320f., cf. 340f.).

ἄτη 56n.

307 σωομένοις In iv.197 the Homeric active, σώετε 'save,' in ii.610 σώεσθαι, 'be saved.' Here σώομαι represents σεύομαι (cf. -σσυτοι in 306): for possible origins see Vian ed. 1961, and Schulze *KS* 378f., Wackernagel *KS* 221; perhaps σο- led to σω- on the analogy of Homeric σόω/σώω (cf. on that LSJ s.v. σῴζω 4-5, Erbse at schol. *Il.* 9.393 and 681). The contracted Doric form σῶσθαι must be related (Boesch 37): cf. Epilycus *PCG* (V) 4.1 σῶμαι, and the Hesychian σῶμαι· ἕρπω Δωριεῖς and σῶται· ὁρμᾶται, ἔρχεται, πορεύεται, with Bulloch on Call. *h.* 5.4 [cf. FJW on Aesch. *Suppl.* 836, Davies on Soph. *Trach.* 645], who conjectures σῶσθε for σοῦσθε there. Note also Budé TEST. at ii.296 (σώω = ὁρμῶ, cf. the Hesychian ?σώοντο· ὡρμῶντο). This must be the sense of σώεσθαι ii.296 (cf. ἀίξαντε 427; an echo in Max. 569), σώοντο 1010 (cf. for 'speeding' iv.595, al.). [This said, I have long felt that there may also be a touch of sarcasm lurking here. The verb *could* be interpreted 'as you were making secure progress' (σῴζεσθαι is common in the sense 'journey safely/unharmed,' LSJ s.v. II2). This would produce a forceful contrast with ἄτη; cf. in the context of voyaging σωότεροι in i.918.]

μεσσηγύς Like μεταξύ, 'in mid-course,' as at *Il.* 11.573 al., *Od.* 7.195, ii.337 and often. Note also *Il.* 20.370 μεσσηγὺ κολούει/ (where schol. T compares *Il.* 8.408: below), with Rengakos 1992.40.

ἐνέχλασεν *Il.* 8.408 (cf. id. 422) μοι .. ἐνικλᾶν ὅττι κεν εἴπω/ (νοήσω *vulg.*, cf. Call. *h.* 1.90 with McLennan's note), 'thwart to my detriment whatever I say' (cf. *Il.* 8.8, with Paley ad loc., and ἐνικλᾶν + dat./ accus. in Call. *fr.* 75.22) could be interpreted (Wifstrand 1928.2553-4) as 'thwart me – whatever it is I say' (schol. D ἐμποδίζειν, cf. Erbse on schol. AbT; *LH* s.v.). Here 'broke in on you, stopped you in your tracks': cf. infr. 314 ἐν ποσὶν ..., and see Linsenbarth 52.

307-8 οὐ μὲν ... 'You just would not listen to what I told you (all those times) ...' – not that Aeetes is *really* the kind of man to take no for an answer. He speaks like Halitherses in *Od.* 24.456, though he does stop short of scolding his grandsons for their folly. οὐ μέν = οὐ μάν, as e.g. *Il.* 22.13, the remonstrating Apollo, 'Well, you certainly won't kill me,' with an adversative implication (preferable to a bland 'won't however ...'); *GP* 362 (in need of more careful sifting).

ἐμεῖο/πείθεσθε The pronoun in 'πείθεσθαι me' is often expressed by the genitive in Herodotus and elsewhere (Headlam and Cunningham on Hds 1.66); for Homer cf. on 91-2. Q.S. 2.59, 5.152 ἐμεῖο πίθεσθε.

308 Clearly written with an eye on *Od.* 20.64 (μ' .. θύελλα: on the picture see 306n., Aeolus-episode) προφέρουσα κατ' ἠερόεντα κέλευθα/, but the verb here means 'bring forward as an objection.'

μέτρα κελεύθου An Odyssean expression, 4.389 ... εἴπῃσιν ὁδὸν καὶ μ. κ./, scil. Proteus, ... οἶδε 386, sim. 10.539, the knowledgeable seer Teiresias; also in epigr. *ap.* Plut. *Aem.* 15, verse 5, Nonn. *D.* 38.243 (παλίλλυτα μ.), Jo. Gaz. 1.34 (ὁμόζυγα μ.), cf. id. 2.169 (σαόφρονα μ. -ων/). μέτρα are the measurable 'distances' involved in 'traversing' (μετρεῖν -εῖσθαι) a route – only these μέτρα are ἀπείρονα, i.e. so vast as to be beyond the scope of measurement, as Aeetes can verify from personal experience (309); this from an individual descended from map-makers (iv.279f.) skilled in the science of γεωμετρία! The strangers, of course, *have* traversed these immense distances to reach πείρατα γαίης.

The term, the connotation of which varies with context, has been discussed recently by West on *Od.* 4.389-90, Heubeck on id. 10.539-40 (p. 73), West on Hes. *WD* 648 (note the element '(I) know'); see also Gow on Theoc. 16.60, with Prien, *CW* 70 (1976), 161f.

309-13 Cf. *Studies* 29. Aeetes is out to impress his visitors. He is a son of Helios, *and* he has been specially favoured. His father's chariot travels from east to west and back again (δινεύσας 310, whirled along on a round trip: cf. δινηθήτην in *Il.* 22.165). Circe was transported to her western home on one of these regular journeys; Aeetes went along for the ride and evidently (309) for enlightenment: cf. Lesky 36, *Noten* 539 n.172, *Studies* 104 n.1 (against Livrea's ἐκόμιζον, anticipated by Chrestien: Vian 1972.478). But Aeetes is no Phineus. The reader has missed out in ii, where Ap.'s Boreads were not permitted to relive the whirlwind aerial surveys conducted in the Hesiodic *Catalogue* (*ffr.* 150f.; West 1985.84-5); here too the lover of leisurely exposition is going to be disappointed (314).

For a succinct treatment of the literary background see VDB 2.122 (on 313), and also the bibliography in Heubeck's note on *Od.* 10.133-574; further: Hatzantonis, *RBPh* 54 (1976), 5f. (esp. Circe in *Arg.*); Bömer on Ov. *Met.* 4.205 ~ Fordyce on Virg. *A.* 7.10 (Monte Circeo); Vian in *Peuples et pays mythiques: Actes du Ve Colloque du Centre de Rech. Myth. de l'Univ. de Paris X* (1986), 182 (a version locating Circe in the *extreme* west? But in fact Aea itself, popularly thought to lie at the οἰκουμένη's limits, is not so regarded universally in the poem: VDB 1.197 n.1).

The moment Circe is mentioned in *Od.* 10 (135f.), the poet takes the opportunity to link her name with that of her brother Aeetes son of Helios (243n.), both of them being localised in the east (Lesky 36f., Heubeck on *Od.* 10.135-9). It is hard indeed to believe that archaic *Argonautica* failed to associate the two (see for differing viewpoints e.g. Livrea's note on iv.662), or that Circe was not in some way implicated in the fate of Argo and her crew (cf. her remarks at *Od.* 12.69f., and see Meuli 112f.). If she was, it would be interesting to know the respective functions of Circe daughter of Perse/Perseis and Medea priestess and pupil of Hecate daughter of Perses. Originally perhaps the former played a prominent part in Jason's salvation, to be supplanted in due course by Medea (called in from a different area of the world: E. Will, *Korinthiaka* (Paris 1955), 85f.), who could lend some meaningful romantic interest as being rather less scary: there is not really room for two attractive πολυφάρμακοι (27n.) at the centre of such a story; see in general Parry 48, 51f. (This seems to me far more likely than the commonly held view of an *Homeric* Circe modelled on an *Argonautic* Medea.) It may be significant that according to Diodorus Siculus (4.45 ~ Dion. Scyt. *fr.* 20 Rusten, cf. id. *fr.* 21) *Circe* came to surpass her mother and mentor *Hecate* in the art of φαρμακεία: an obvious recipe for conflict, and perhaps a contributory factor in Circe's uprooting (cf. VDB 2.122); Hecate for her part περίαλλα .. δάε Medea (529 infr.): loaded?

Ap. does not tell us why Circe moved house: she is after all a thoroughly inscrutable character. It is important to note that he himself does not talk of 'exile' (*pace* a number of critics): *Circe* in iv.748 will disapprove in the strongest terms of *Medea*'s ἀεικὴς φύξις [ctr. Val. Flacc. 7.231]. Ironic indeed, if the story told by Diodorus 4.45.4 (cf. Rusten p. 118; Parry 51-2, 54) or something like it was in circulation in the third century.

309 ᾔδειν ... But *Il.* 14.71 /ᾔδεα [schol. D ᾔδειν] μὲν γὰρ ὅτε ... Cf. on the form of the verb Marxer 21, and KB 2.242, H. Rix, *Historische Grammatik des Griechischen* (Darmstadt 1976), 258. It means 'get to know about by direct observation' (cf. ἴδοντο in *Od.* 7.322); on the flavour of this and related verbs of cognition see the lit. in Clay 12-13.

πατρὸς ἐν ἅρμασιν ... The chariot is naturally an important element in this myth. Medea has access to a chariot from Helios in Euripides' play [?snakes: cf. Circe in Val. Flacc. 7.120, 218f.; see on the motif Parry 252] ... ὄχημα πατρὸς Ἥλιος πατήρ κτλ. (1321), and Aeetes evidently has a replica (245-6n.), cf. Apsyrtus in Val. Flacc. 6.517f. Circe has stock stolen from the Sun-god <to draw her chariot>, Virg. *A.* 7.280f. A likely model here is Phaethon's ride (*Noten* 343, *Studies* 21), cf. Medea in Sen. *Med.* 32f.; iv.598 (likewise prefaced by ποτε) uses similar phraseology: πέσεν ἅρματος Ἡελίοιο [Eur. *Phoen.* 1562-3 ἅρματα .. ἀελίου or better Ἀελίου]/... (there follows ἡ δ' ἔτι νῦν περ/ ~ infr. 312); cf. in addition Ov. *Met.* 2.142 *Hesperio*, 325 *Hesperiae*, and Nonn. *D.* 39.5 ἑσπερίῳ ref. Phaethon ~ Ap. 311.

Another possible source of inspiration is Simias' account of the aerial journey of one Cleinis (*CA* 1, see Fränkel 1915.25f.) who when he visited the Hyperboreans <? in Apollo's airborne chariot: cf. Alc. *PLF* 307(c)> personally witnessed (ἐνόησα 9) a number of marvellous sights from above: cf. /ἐκ δ' ἱκόμην in 7 with ἐκ δ' ἱκόμεσθα/ in Ap. 311 (Simian influence: 6n.).

πατρὸς ... Ἠελίοιο Used by Aeetes again in 598; cf. Medea in Eur. *Med.* 406, and Acsch. *fr.* 68 corr. πατρὸς Ἠελίου (from *Heliades*).
ἐν ἅρμασιν *HyDem* 431 (-ι; divine).

310 δινεύσας 309-13n., cf. Willink on Eur. *Or.* 982-4 (p.247). No doubt picked up from the Phaethon-story (Nonn. *D.* 38.321 δινηθέντες, cf. 162 δινωτῇ, 351 δινήεντι).

310-11 ἐμεῖο κασιγνήτην ../Κίρκην Cf. iv.683-4.
ἐκόμιζε/... εἴσω Tragic: e.g. Soph. *OT* 678. [-ζον is abandoned in VDB 2².]

311 ἑσπερίης .. χθονός The 'evening-/western land' is where Helios heads from his place of rising in the east. We do not know whether ἑσπερίη/'Εσπερίη (χθών) = 'Italy' was in regular use by now: it occurs thus in Agathyllus *SH* 15.3 (2nd/1st cent.?), cf. Parthenius *SH* 645 ἀλλ' ὅτ' ἀφ' ἑσπερίης Ἑρκυνίδος ὤρετο γαίης with the editors ad loc., and later Kaibel *EG* 905.1 (Gortyn, 4th cent.) /ἑσπερίης πάσης χθονός; from Ap. (?): Anon. *AP* 9.210.7 (v.l.) μετ' ἐμεῖο .. ἑσπερίης χθονὸς... Lat. *(terra) Hesperia*: NH on Hor. *Carm.* 1.28.26, Fordyce on Virg. *A.* 7.4 ['Stesichorus': *Tab. Il.* is to be used with extreme caution, in this regard as in others: Horsfall, *JHS* 99 (1979), 39].
εἴσω χθονός In Eur. *Or.* 1231 ("perhaps 'epic' in flavour", Willink ad loc.), Q.S. 14.585, Nonn. *D.* 30.177 ἔσω χθονός means 'below the ground.' On the use of εἴσω/ἔσω with gen. cf. McLennan on Call. *h.* 1.34 (but only a partial picture of Hellenistic practice).

311-2 ἐκ .... Τυρσηνίδος Cf. iv.849-50 -ος, ἔστ' ἀφίκανεν/ἀκτὴν Αἰαίην Τυρσηνίδος ἠπείροιο (*Od.* 15.36 ἀκτὴν .. ἀφίκηαι/ scil. νήσου see below!); Simias cited in 309n.; [Orph.] *A.* 713-4 ἐξικόμεσθα/ἀκτήν (? See Vian ad loc.) ~ 681 al. ἐξικόμεσθα/, id. 1249 *codd*. Τυρρηνὰς δ' ἱξόμεθ' [ἱκόμεθ' Stephanus; ἵξομεν Vian] ἀκτάς/.
Ctr. *Od.* 14.290-1 ὄφρ' ἱκόμεσθα/Φοινίκην, ὅθι ... (iv.1474-5 τέως ἐξίκετο γαῖαν/..., τόθι ...).

ἀκτὴν ἠπείρου But *Od.* 24.378 /ἀκτὴν ἠπείροιο. Cf. iv.850 above, and *Od.* 13.234-5 ἀκτή/... ἠπείροιο/; i.584-5 ἠπείροιο/ἀκτή (Magnesian peninsula).

Circe inhabited an Αἰαίη νῆσος in the east according to Homer

(*Od.* 12.3-4), but it is clear that strenuous efforts were made in some quarters to locate her, together with this particular island-home, in the west (schol. on *Od.* 12.3-4 and 10.135; Lesky 51f.; for an interesting recent discussion see A. Ballabriga, *Le soleil et le Tartare* (Paris 1986), 110f.). So perhaps there is light-hearted literary point-scoring here: Aeetes as an (early!) eye-witness can accurately describe the locality occupied by this μετανάστης, and thus put right, for those who want to know, a persistent misconception: cf. Medea at 1074, echoed by Jason at 1093, and the (*Homeric*: Thomas, *PLLS* 5 (1985), 65) seer Helenus in Virg. *A.* 3.386, who makes Circe inhabit an *island* in western waters, whereas in 7.10f. the voyagers clearly skirt the shores of a *mainland* habitation. It may be relevant that Monte Circeo might easily be taken for an island (cf. Strabo 5.3.6 and Fordyce on Virg. *A.* 7.10), and that it was, allegedly, an island once and later [but see above!] became a promontory (cf. Theophr. *HP* 5.8.3 etc., Phillips, *JHS* 73 (1953), 55, Solmsen, *HSCP* 90 (1986), 98, *RE* 3.2566-7). What is *not* relevant in my view is the consideration that νῆσος may be used loosely to denote a 'Halbinsel' (*Noten* 343; Vian 1978b.97 n.99): the Odyssean models render any such implicit equation, unlikely on general grounds, most implausible: 13.234-5 island or ..., 24.378 spoken by an islander, interestingly enough about an area which, from a historical standpoint, was once connected to the mainland but was later detached from it (Wace and Stubbings 400, Heubeck on 377-8).

Τυρσηνίδος Add to the above iv.660, 856 ἀκτὰς -ίδας, ἀκταῖς -ίσιν (for schol. at 850, 856 to do with Αἰαίη νῆσος). Τυρσηνίς already Eur. *Med.* 1342; fairly common in later verse (no *Apolloniana*).

Cf. [Hes.] *Theog.* 1011f. Circe, 1015 μάλα τῆλε, ibid. νήσων (!), 1016 Τυρσηνοῖσιν.

312-3 ἔνθ' ἔτι νῦν περ/ναιετάει The Argonauts are going to be put in the position of verifying this claim at least. περ intensifies ἔτι νῦν: bequeathed by the logographers perhaps. Like Hypsipyle in i.825 (... ναιετάουσι/) and Argos in ii.1214 (ἵκετο ...), Aeetes borrows one of the poet's expository tags: i.1061, iv.480; also ἡ δ' ἔτι ... iv.599, οὐδ' ἔτι ... i.644, /τούνεκεν εἰσέτι νῦν περ i.1354. The only other example known to me is Q.S. 10.131 ἧς ἔτι νῦν περ/ (.. σῆμα ~ Ap. i.1061-2).

... ναιετάει Hes. *Theog.* 775 /ἔνθα δὲ ναιετάει.

313 μάλα ... After *Od.* 4.810-11 κασιγνήτη (cf. supr. 310) .. ἤλυθες (cf. 311 *ad fin.*); οὔτι πάρος γε/πώλεαι, ἐπεὶ μάλα πολλὸν ἀπόπροθι δώματα ναίεις, cf. *Il.* 23.832; suppl. in Anon. hex. (pap. 2nd cent. AD; hardly Rhianus) *SH* 923.2.

ἀπόπροθι + gen.: Hes. *WD* 389-91 ἄγκεα ../πόντου .. ἀπόπροθι .../ναίουσιν (ναιετάουσ' 389), cf. infr. 372, 1065. The word is recalled by the poet in iv.555.

Κολχίδος Αἴης The ἀκτή specified in 312 is ἀκτὴ Αἰαίη (iv.850), 'of Aea': i.e. Circe lives 'a very long way from *Colchian* Aea' (cf. ii.417 and earlier Hdt. 7.197.3, with Allen 90; Ovid was to exploit the ambiguity: McKeown on *Am.* 1.8.5-6); on top of that, *Homer's* Circaean 'island of Aea' was situated where Helios *rose* (*Od.* 12.3-4) prior to starting on his westward journey (ctr. 310f.), see 311-12n., and on Aea generally, in addition to Lesky's classic treatment, W. Burkert, *Structure and History in Greek Mythology and Ritual* (Berkeley and Los Angeles 1979), 10. Against this clausula may be set not only Homer's πατρίδος αἴης but also the following examples of the pattern –‿‿ (proper adj.) αἴης (cf. already Aesch. *Pers.* 59 Περσίδος αἴας in a dactylic run; *Od.* 13.249 Ἀχαιίδος .. αἴης/): iv.337 Νέστιδος, Call. *h.* 4.287 Μηλίδος, *GVI* 1451.1 (Rhodes, *c.* 200 BC) Δωρίδος, *Or. Sib.* 14.238 Ἑλλάδος, D.P. 20 + 5 and Cougny 6.233.3 Ἀσίδος, D.P. 805 Μυσίδος, 957 and 1038 Περσίδος, 1148 Κωλίδος. Also – –‿‿: iv.131, 568 (ἑκάς), cf. D.P. 46, orac. in Porph. *ap.* Eus. *PE* 9.10, verse 5; ‿‿–‿‿: D.P. 25, suppl. in Anon. hex. (pap. 2nd cent. AD) *SH* 913.10.

In archaic epic αἶα (etc.) always occupies the final foot: cf. Haslam, *Glotta* 54 (1976), 207f.; so in Ap. 4 ×, and in 3[H] generally: Call. *h.* 4.287 [id. *Hec. fr.* 70.23: Γαῖα should be read], Theoc. 17.91, Euphor. *CA* 50.1 and *SH* 432.3 [suppl. in undatable *SH* 913.10; id. 938.14 is definitely Imperial]. Internally i.580, not so otherwise in 3[H] (dub. conj. in Eratosth. *CA* 16.12). Αἶα as a name is more mobile: clausular 5 ×, otherwise 8 ×.

314 ἀλλὰ ... ἦδος For such a rhetorical flourish designed to discontinue μῦθοι, discourse or storytelling, cf. e.g. *Od.* 12.450 (μυθολογεύω; for the opposite tendency see West on id. 4.595-8), Eur. *Hel.* 143, *Hcld.* 951-2, i.648f. (spoken by poet). The capping 'aetiological' sequence of 312-3 should already have alerted us to the fact that Aeetes will not prove to be an after-dinner orator like Nestor (cf. Beye 1982.16; but rather more voluble types frequent the pages of this poem: Phineus in ii.311f., Levin 162 n.1; Lycus in ii.774f., Webster 75). In fact, he has said enough to impress the newcomers with his knowledge of distant places and with his family connexions (cf. Argos' report at ii.1204, n.b. στεῦται): anxious for information himself, he is not inclined to enlighten his audience further.

For the wording cf. i.1294 (with Fusillo 254), the angry and impatient Telamon: ἀλλὰ τί μύθων [4 lines of them] ἦδος, ἐπεὶ καὶ νόσφιν ἑταίρων ...; after Il. 18.80 ἀλλὰ τί μοι τῶν ἦδος [sim. Od. 24.95], ἐπεὶ φίλος ὤλεθ' ἑταῖρος ... (clausular ἑταίρων: 81); similarly Theoc. 16.40 /ἀλλ' οὔ σφιν τῶν ἦδος, ἐπεὶ ... Agathias later borrows directly from Homer: AP 5.292.7; μῦθον ibid.

ἦδος here is not so much *enjoyment* as *point, use* (Vian ed. 1961): glosses on Homer commonly take the form of ὠφέλημα sim. (Henrichs 246 n.21); in fact, *profit, satisfaction* is appropriate in Il. 11.318 (ὠφέλεια schol. D, cf. id. at Il. 18.80 cited above) and elsewhere.

δ' With ἀλλὰ ... ἦδος Aeetes has put a stop to his personal reminiscences. Now with δ', 'expressing a break-off, like ἀτάρ' (*GP* 167), he turns directly to the Phrixids whom he addressed at the start. The sequence in Eur. *Hel.* 143-6 is not dissimilar: ἅλις δὲ μύθων then ὧν δ' οὕνεκ' ἦλθον .... σὺ προξένησον κτλ.

... ἐν ποσὶν .. ὄρωρεν Cf. the clausula of 836 below. Given the question put by Aeetes at 306-7 (see 307n.) and Argos' response (320f.), it is natural to interpret '"the obstacles which have arisen in your path'; ἐν ποσίν = ἐμποδών" (Mooney) rather than 'your immediate position/concern' (so Fränkel, *Noten* 343-4, with illustration, cf. Crees and Wordsworth, ed. 1927, 'what lies before you,' 'what is your errand'; add from Hellenistic verse τὰ δ' ἐν ποσίν [the same run in ?Eur. *Andr.* 397, id. *IT* 1312] Arat. 252, 'what lies right before his feet'). But ἐν ποσί *can* = ἐμποδών, cf. Hdt. 3.79.1 τὸν ἐν ποσὶ γινόμενον beside 1.80.3, 3.147.2 τὸν ἐμποδὼν γινόμενον; for the perfect ὄρωρεν, 'have presented themselves' (59n.), cf. id. 6.82.1 οἱ ... ἐμποδὼν ἔστηκε.

ὑμῖν or ὔμιν here only in the poem; on ἡμῖν ἥμιν (e.g. infr. 487, 1111) see VDB I.LXXIV; a papyrus (2nd-3rd cent.) at ii.1160 evidently had this form, but the scribe had second thoughts: Musso, *ZPE* 62 (1986), 45. These datives (*GH* 1.270, Meier-Brügger, *Glotta* 64 (1986), 135, 137f.) were much discussed in antiquity: La Roche *HTA* 274-8; Erbse on schol. *Il.* 1.147; Vian 1962.38 (against ὔμμιν adopted here by Ardizzoni).

315 εἴπατ' 1106n.

ἀριφραδέως Like σαφῶς (e.g. Bond on Eur. *HF* 55), 'clearly and reliably.' A host can expect a precise answer to his queries (e.g. *Od.* 8.572f., cf. Jason to the Phrixids at ii.1137), but Aeetes has real reason to press for a clear and open statement: see 599-600. This adverb, first reliably attested in the third century (the date of Homer's Π¹²: -έως at *Il.* 23.240, West *PP* 187), is not especially common: Maiist. *CA* 21 καταλέξαι (cf. v.l. *Od.* 23.225?; + ὅππῃ) ~ [Orph.] *A.* 936; [Theoc.] 25.175 ἀγορεύει ~ D.P. 1168, [Apolin.] 144.10, 15; others: *GVI* 2026.7 (Thasos, 2nd ccnt. AD); Q.S. 2.43, 3.724 (/φαίνετ' ἀ.); [Orph.] *A.* 1362 con. Vian]. Cf. Homer's (/σῆμα ...) εἰπὲ ἀριφραδές (*Od.* 24.329).

315-6 οἵτινες ... /ἀνέρες With οἵδ' he points, cf. *Od.* 4.138-9 (302n.), about ξεῖνοι: ... οἵτινες οἵδε/ἀνδρῶν εὐχετόωνται κτλ., and ὅδ' in *Od.* 16.57; for the wording also id. 9.89 = 10.101 /οἵτινες ἀνέρες εἶεν, 16.236 οἵτινες ἀνέρες εἰσί/.

οἵτινες implies that the questioner wants more than just names: compare schol. bT's remark on οἵτινες in *Il.* 2.488(*a*) τίς καὶ πόθεν καὶ τίνων πατέρων καὶ προγόνων. Argos obliges: 354-66.

οἵδ' ἐφέπονται A similar clausula in Call. *h.* 4.75. Aeetes assumes that the Phrixids have come back in their ship with 'these' strangers in attendance; in reality, his grandsons are now among those who 'accompany' (infr. 365) Jason in his quest for the Fleece (ii.1192f.).

316 ὅππῃ τε Cf. *Studies* 105 n.5. The paradosis (on which see Speake 1975.110) points to ὁππότε <τε>, but *where* (nobody has seen a ship) makes sense, *when* does not, for Aeetes would have no reason to suppose that their approach was anything other than instantaneous. ὅππῃ is in fact put beyond any doubt by the clear echo of *Od.* 9.279, see on 176f.(3); cf. too *Od.* 24.298f. mentioned below.

γλαφυρῆς ... ἔβητε *Od.* 9.548 al. γλαφυρῆς ἐκ νηός, 13.116 ἐκ νηὸς βάντες (γλαφυρῆς ἐκ νηός 117), 24.301 ἔβησαν/ scil. νηός ~ 299 'where is the ship ...?'

γλαφυρή is one of the commonest epithets for νηῦς in Homer: West on *Od.* 3.287, J. S. Morrison and R. T. Williams, *Greek Oared Ships* (Cambridge 1968), 45, cf. also Càssola on *HyAp* 405; so iv.582, but not otherwise in 3ᴴ. 'Das preisende Beiwort im altepischen Stil ist höflich, denn noch gibt sich Aietes, in der Gegenwart der fremden Herren, urban' *Noten* 344. See further on 176f.(3).

317/319 μιν ἐξερέοντα .... προσέειπεν Cf. i.710-11 (and iii.1167/ 1168 ~ *Od.* 10.109f.).

317 τοῖά μιν ... προπάροιθεν Like *Il.* 22.197 /τοσσάκι μιν προπάροιθεν ...

τοῖα marking speech-closure: 367, iv.1029 (/τοῖα μὲν, μὲν f.v.l. here); Führer 39 n.30.

μιν ἐξερέοντα Ctr. *Od.* 10.249 μιν ... ἐξερέοντες/ (a story: 251f.). ἐξερέω -έομαι of questioning visitors: *Od.* 3.116, al.

κασιγνήτων προπάροιθεν ii.1122 Ἄργος δὲ παροίτατος ἔκφατο μῦθον/, i.e. Argos (rather than any of his brothers) was the very first to speak (cf. παροίτατος in ii.610, iv.494). So here he addresses Aeetes 'in advance of' his brothers: he naturally (319) takes the initiative. προπάροιθεν is a temporal adverb in Homer [Lehrs 115, Erbse on schol. *Il.* 2.92*a*] etc., and a temporal preposition in Aesch. *Theb.* 334, Arat. 938, 1010, 1065, ii.527 and later (cf. tragic πάροιθε, πάρος). Since in so doing Argos is taking on the role of spokesman, one might alternatively translate προπάροιθεν as one would πρό at Soph. *OT* 10, ~ γεραιέ 9 (*Noten* 290); but there is no real need for this.

318-9 Ἄργος .... προσέειπεν Cf. ii.1140 /τὸν δ' Ἄργος προσέειπεν, iv.393-4 τοῖα .../μειλιχίοις ἐπέεσσιν ὑποδδείσας προσέειπεν (drawing on *Od.* 24.393), ii.467 /μειλιχίως ... μετηύδα/.

318 Ἄργος, He now takes centre-stage.

ὑποδδείσας 'ὑπό s'est prêté à souligner l'amorce d'un procès' *GH* 2.138. In the so-called 'absolute' use of this verb at *Od.* 9.377 an object can be readily understood (as with ὑποτρομέουσιν at *Il.* 22.241). Ap. may not have thought so: cf. iv.394; with infin. infr. 435 ('be filled with fear at the idea of ...').

The responsibility for explaining the situation must fall on Argos' shoulders by virtue of his seniority. His reaction here recalls that of ii.1198f., where he had expressed his fears about the expedition's outcome (1203, *Noten* 311) in the light of Aeetes' ἀπηνείη. It is as if the king has already vented his anger and needs to be mollified: cf. iv.391 χόλον, then 394 μειλιχίοις ἐπέεσσιν ὑποδδείσας προσέειπεν (a sequence inspired by *Od.* 16.425). The outlook is not promising (cf. on 15), and Argos must know it.

ἀμφί + dative with δέδια *PV* 182. Cf. *Noten* 344-5.

(-)ῳ Αἰσονίδαο 86. See on 175.

319 μειλιχίως ii.467, iv.732; the only other example appears to be Nossis *HE* 2820. The employment of adverbs in -ως by Ap. and other Hellenistic poets is still in need of thorough investigation: see in general Rossi, *RFIC* 96 (1968), 157-8.

προσέειπεν ... ἦεν After *Od.* 7.155-6 (159 /'Ἀλκίνο', οὐ μέν ...), 11.342-3 μετέειπε ...'Ἐχένηος,/ὃς δὴ Φαιήκων ἀνδρῶν προγενέστερος ἦεν (speeches about hospitable treatment/gift-giving), *Il.* 2.555 ὁ γὰρ προγενέστερος ἦεν/. προγενέστερος here means 'older <than the rest of his brothers>': cf. i.165 /τῶν ἄμφω γνωτὸς προγενέστερος, and perhaps (see Vian 1970.81) ὁπλότερος in i.43 ('younger than <his fellow> Lapiths'); so γεραίτερος and πρεσβύτερος from time to time in prose, though some have felt impelled to emend (Seaford on Eur. *Cycl.* 101). Virgil imitates with *maximus* [cf. Sil. It. 7.428] *Ilioneus placido sic pectore coepit* (*A.* 1.521).

Perhaps the stress placed on Argos' seniority has an ulterior motive: Ap. does not take on board another brother, who sported the name Πρέσβων (Epimenides DK3 B12, cf. Robert 764, Dräger 213 n.204)!

320-66 For differing assessments of Argos' performance as spokesman see *Studies* 29f. (another admirer: Hübscher 54; cf. also PF on 320-66, whose analysis seems to me to skate past some unwelcome truths; and, in brief, Beye 1982.131). His is an unenviable task, particularly when we recall that he is ignorant of a number of key facts (*Studies* 29-30). Even so, his speech, though eloquent (if at times unappealingly florid and circumlocutory) and conciliatory to some degree, must be regarded as striking the wrong note in several respects:

(1) He is over-zealous in presenting the newcomers in the best possible light: Jason outstanding among his peers – and banished; Colchian ship compared most unfavourably with superb and divinely-constructed Argo; offer of compensation capped with a confident prediction of victory (by a ship's crew) over an obviously troublesome national enemy; playing-up of Argonauts' divine descent – Aeetes' rejoinder to this is in tune with what we have been led to expect from Argos' own description of him at ii.1202f.

(2) His account of king and outcast, of the latter's 'offence,' and of Zeus and the rest (333-9) is just *too* wooly.

(3) If his omission to divulge the ship's whereabouts is understandable, the failure to identify the expedition-leader until the last gasp seems ill-advised: before 357 Aeetes is treated to: 326f. 'these men here,' 'their ship,' 'them,' 'they ...' etc.; 333f. 'this man here' etc.; 345 'the men' aboard Argo; 347-53 'he' and so on.

(4) His reluctance to put a straight request can only generate a suspicion of deviousness (full marks to Argos here). Fleece: need for removal from Colchis alluded to hurriedly in the subordinate clause of 339 [cf. Hübscher 53]; term drops from view when question of Aeetes' 'giving' arises in 349; = 'present' from Aeetes 352. — 356f.: a wealth of genealogical detail, inviting the conclusion that Aeetes

should help, as being 'related' to the members of the crew indirectly, directly, or (as being of divine stock himself) generally: but Argos cannot bring himself to come out into the open, and there is no appeal. —

I see no grounds for supposing that Argos is delivering an agreed speech word for word, even if certain of the details have been settled in advance. He shows none of the adroitness exhibited by Jason in his dealings with the Phrixids, in the course of which Argos had been portrayed (good-humouredly) in a none too flattering light (see the fine analysis of part of the encounter in VDB 1.172-3).

A snappier, more direct approach, even if it provoked a ferocious reaction, would have prevented Aeetes from concluding that the story of his grandsons' involvement with these men, allegedly engineered by higher powers (323, 328), sounded decidedly fishy; that he felt threatened comes as no real surprise. Argos simply does not deserve to be given a clean bill of health (Fränkel *Noten* 347, on 367-70, mentions the *contribution*, but neglects the *presentation*).

320f. The story of the shipwreck [ii.1093f.] ~ *Od.* 9.283f.: see on 176f.(3). Unlike Odysseus, Argos does not resort to deceit with his formidable interlocutor, though he is prepared to be evasive more than once. Ctr. also 319/320f. with *Od.* 9.363f.: the gift-seeking Odysseus' μειλίχια ἔπεα in response to a direct question are downright mendacious.

320-1 Aeetes has wondered about the whereabouts of 'the ship' (316), by which he meant the Colchian ship recently dispatched (*Noten* 344). Argos responds at once with a dismissive κείνην .. ἄφαρ ..., but he takes his time about identifying 'the ship' (327) that conveyed them back to Colchis. When he comes to deal with this in detail (340f.), he conveniently omits to pinpoint the location of a vessel which clearly carries a full complement of armed warriors (347f.351f.), a move which is not lost on Aeetes.

κείνην ... Argos echoes his own description at ii.1125-6 (ἄελλαι), but he also borrows from Jason, who, after telling the Phrixids what a marvellous ship Argo, co-built by Argos (!: 340f., 340nn.), was, turned to the subject of the Colchian vessel: ii.1189f. ἀτὰρ κείνην γε κακὸν διὰ κῦμ' ἐκέδασσε before she even got anywhere near the Symplegades (this ship could not even survive lesser perils!). With ἄφαρ Argos of course exaggerates somewhat – understandably given the

COMMENTARY 321

shock of it all. Still, Aeetes cannot have liked being told that in the presence of visitors. But there is more to come.

ἄφαρ .. ἄελλαι Cf. *Od.* 8.409 (but different context).

διέχευαν Cf. διασκιδνᾶσιν in *Il.* 5.526 in conjunction with ζαχρειῶν 525, and ii.1189 cited above. This is a colourful word, in Homer 'carve up,' 'dismember' (cf. West on *Od.* 3.456). For its use here compare *GVI* 1760.1-2 (Ephesus, 1st cent. AD?) σάρκας ἐμὰς σπιλάδες διέχευαν/ὀξεῖαι ..., Q.S. 14.504 /πάντα ... κακαὶ διέχευον (-αν Spitzner) ἄελλαι/. There is perhaps some connexion with Theoc. 22.202-3 ἔγκατα δ᾽ εἴσω/χαλκὸς (sword) ἄφαρ διέχευεν: ctr. *Od.* 3.456 /αἶψ᾽ .. μιν διέχευαν, ἄφαρ δ᾽ ...

ἄελλαι/ζαχρηεῖς So already i.1094-5, sim. θύελλαι iv.834-5, but i.1159 -έσιν αὔραις/; *Il.* 5.525 /ζαχρειῶν [but both -ει- and -η- are attested for Hom.] ἀνέμων, Opp. *Hal.* 1.221 ἀνέμου ζαχρηέος. This adjective, related to ἔχρα(ϝ)ε (*LfgrE* s.v., also Kirk on *Il.* 5.522-7, Hainsworth on id. 12.347; cf. ἐπέχραον in ii.498) recurs in Nic. *Ther.* 290, Dion. Bass. 20vi (cf. Livrea's ed., pp. 67-8).

Ap. may be thinking of Odysseus with δόρυ (*Od.* 5.371): ἄνεμος ζαής 368, διεσκέδασ᾽ 369.

321 αὐτούς i.e. ἡμᾶς [cf. Aesch. *Ag.* 661] αὐτούς (see Marxer 64): κείνην is the ship, αὐτούς the people manning it (cf. e.g. *Od.* 3.11 τήν/ αὐτοί; infr. 345). Ap. must also be remembering *Il.* 13.684 /ζαχρηεῖς then αὐτοί τε ...

ὑπὸ δούρασι πεπτηῶτας codd. Ardizzoni's δούρατι (1956.375f. and ed.; conjectured independently by Fränkel, OCT) earned instant approval from Vian ed. 1961, Keydell 35, van Krevelen 1961.157, Irigoin, *REG* 75 (1962), 300 (Soph. *Ant.* 715f., adduced by Lloyd-Jones 1963.157 in favour of the transmitted text, does not seem helpful). 'Les naufragés s'agrippent à la poutre *sous* ou *contre* laquelle ils se blottissent, leur tête seule émergeant' VDB 2.122, who remark that the singular would point up the interest that heaven must have taken in their salvation: cf. the sequence of ii.1118f. τοὺς δ᾽ ἄμυδις (scil. all four of them together) κρατερῷ σὺν δούρατι κύματος ὁρμή/... μετ᾽ ἠιόνας βάλε νήσου/νύχθ᾽ ὑπὸ λυγαίην following on from 1110f., Phrixids πίσυρές περ ἐόντες/δούρατος ὠρέξαντο πελωρίου, οἷά τε πολλὰ κτλ. I am not convinced. In Argos' own truncated report (ii.1125-6) ἄελλαι/νηὸς .. διὰ δούρατα πάντ᾽ ἐκέδασσαν/. δούρασι follows on naturally here from διέχευαν in this highly compressed version of what befell the voyagers: 'a plank' would require clarification (cf. ii.1110f.1118f.), and Argos does not concern himself with any of the extraordinary happenings. 'Planks' gets his immediate message across effectively enough.

ὑπὸ: 'ἐπὶ Bigot, Hoelzlin praeeunte, et denuo Madvig' Vian 1975.91. One might feel inclined to see in ἐπὶ δούρασι πεπτηῶτας a corruption waiting to happen (cf. Mooney): ὑπὸ δούρασι is a familiar expression (e.g. infr. 1375), and there is another ὑπό coming very soon (323); and to agree with Livrea (1975.655; he adduces Ach. Tat. 3.5.1) that all talk of submerged Phrixids is gravely implausible. ἐπί would suggest not that they were swept to shore (eventually) while just holding on, but rather that they climbed aboard, like Odysseus in *Od.* 12.444 (cf. id. 424f.) and, fleetingly, in id. 5.371, and stayed there either 'prostrated' (πίπτειν; or cf. Aratean usage, discussed below??) or 'huddled' (πτήσσειν cf. ἀσχαλόωντας ii.1114?). On the other hand, Argos is not the most unaffected of speakers, and perhaps ὑπὸ δούρασι πεπτηῶτας is being converted from a straightforward battlefield-image 'fallen beneath *spears*' (the war-god is lurking in 322) into a contrived 'fallen/prostrated under *planks*,' the brothers effectively being pinned under or down by them as they were swept to *terra firma*. Indeed, many of the components of the storm-scene in ii.1097f. are borrowed from Iliadic martial contexts; a number of them are listed in M. F. Williams, *Landscape in the* Argonautica *of Apollonius Rhodius* (Diss. Univ. of Texas at Austin, 1989), 187-8. In any event, it is hard to see just what inference, if any, may be drawn from *Od.* 14.474 ὑπὸ τεύχεσι πεπτηῶτες/.

πεπτηῶτας Obviously from πτήσσειν in ii.535 (δείματι, τρήρωνος 534), otherwise I think from πίπτειν (cf. in general Ardizzoni 1956.378f., Vian ed. 1961 ad loc., *GH* 1.428/430, F-G on *Od.* 22.362-3): i.1056 (~ *Od.* 22.383-4), ii.832 (-κάππεσε 831), iii.973, 1312, iv.93 ('knees' often associated with πίπτειν and compounds, note esp. Eur. *Suppl.* 278; cf. ἀναειρόμενος in the next line), 1263 (ὑπ᾽?, shipwreck: see VDB 3.189), 1298, 1454 (flies that have thrown themselves, swooped round a drop of honey, in a swarm: hardly from πτήσσειν). Other Hellenistic poets: πίπτειν Eratosth. *CA* 16.9 (v.l.), Antip. Sid. *HE* 398 (also to be included, perhaps: 'Simon.' *HE* 3320 = *FGE* 962), Nic. *fr.* 81/82.2; Aratus seems to go his own way: see Martin on 324, Campbell *Index Arat.* s. πίτνημι; he is followed, I believe, by Euphorion, *CA* 51.5. In later poetry generally from πίπτειν.

322 νήσου Ἐνυαλίοιο Cf. *Studies* 105 n.4. More florid language ('belonging to/of Ares' suffices in ii.1031, 1047; 1230). This imposing title recurs in 560 (Idas, disparagingly setting his god against 'the

COMMENTARY 323

Cyprian,' ctr. Mopsos' 'Cythereia' [108n.] in 553) and 1366(n.) (here Ἐνυαλίου .. Ἄρεος after *Il.* 17.210-11 in connexion with the huge stone thrown by Jason in the course of his glorious *aristeia*: *Studies* 87). Cf., from contemporary poetry, the use of Ἐνυάλιος in elevated surroundings, Simias *CA* 14.2, and of ἐνυάλιος similarly, [Theoc.] 25.277; it also occurs in a number of ornate Hellenistic epigrams.

ποτὶ ... κῦμα From *Od.*: 5.402 the shipwrecked Odysseus, adrift in the water, /ῥόχθει ... κῦμα ποτὶ ξερὸν ἠπείροιο/; 19.278 Odysseus reaching the land of the Phaeacians (where two shipwrecks become one) /τὸν δ' ... ἐπὶ (!?) τρόπιος νεὸς ἔκβαλε κῦμ' ἐπὶ χέρσου/ (ξερόν is equated with χέρσος by Hesychius, ξ56).

ξερόν On this Homeric hapax see Hainsworth on *Od.* 5.402, and also Janko, *Glotta* 57 (1979), 21, Ruijgh 1991.618. ποτὶ ξερόν also Phanias *HE* 3002. Less grandiloquently the narrator in ii.1119 μετ' ἠιόνας βάλε νήσου/.

323 λυγαίῃ ὑπὸ νυκτί Infr.1361, ἐνὶ 863; but /νύχθ' ὑπὸ λυγαίην ii.1120, iv.458: cf. Eur. *IT* 110 νυκτὸς .. λυγαίας (a high-sounding line). In i.218 (*codd.*, which must be right: VDB ad loc.) λ. + νεφέεσσι, cf. Soph. *fr.* 525 (but the text has often been questioned), Eur. *Hcld.* 855 (in the course of a messenger-speech replete with elevated diction). This epithet, taken over from tragedy by the γλωσσοτέχνης Lycophron, is not common. Add to LSJ: *GVI* 1912.4 = *CEG* (2) 680.5 (Cyrenaica, 4th cent. BC) [the Imbros inscr. is *GVI* 1988.10]; orac. *ap.* Porph. *Plot.* 22 (PW 473.27): + σκοτίη, to be added to Livrea's note on iv.1698.

ὑπό *under cover of* or *in*: see Haggett 57, LSJ s.v. B4.

νυκτί .. δέ ... ἐσάωσεν Ctr. *Il.* 5.23 σάωσε δὲ νυκτὶ ... (22 /οὐδὲ γάρ ~ Ap. 324).

θεὸς ... For the attribution of rescue from the perils of the sea to 'some god' there is a nice parallel in the messenger-speech of Aesch. *Ag.*, 663 θεός τις, then (~ Ap. 328) Τύχη .. σωτήρ, cf. Nisetich in *TAPA* 107 (1977), 240 *et circa*, and also NH on Hor. *Carm.* 1.35.6, J. Péron, *Les images maritimes de Pindare* (Paris 1974), 124; see Headlam-Thomson on Aesch. *Ag.* 661-4 for illustration. Unlike Jason (ii.1183-4 ... ἐξεσάωσε/χείματος), Argos does not refer to a particular god until the all-important topic of the Argonauts' contribution is broached (326). For the wording cf. in Homer *Il.* 15.290 /ἀλλά τις .. θεῶν ἐρρύσατο καὶ ἐσάωσεν/ echoed, minus the hiatus, in iv.917-8 (rescue at sea) /ἀλλά μιν .. θεὰ .... ἀνερέψατο (ἀνερύσατο cod. E here, from Homer) καί ῥ' ἐσάωσε/.

324 οὐδὲ γάρ *et circa*: cf. *Il.* 19.408 σαώσομεν, 410 θεός, 411 /οὐδὲ γάρ, 413 /ἀλλὰ ... Snatches of Amphidamas' speech to the Argonauts in ii are detectable here: 1047-8 νῆσος + 'Αρητιάς + ὄρνιθας, 1052 /οὐδὲ γάρ ..., 1059 τὸ πάροιθεν.

αἳ τὸ πάροιθεν Again infr. 895.

ἐρημαίην Hom. ἔρημ- *Od.* 3.270 and (326-7n.) 12.351; [Scymn.] 912-3 ἔρημος .... νῆσος Ἄρεως, Müller ad loc. — ἐρημαῖος: Campbell on Q.S. 12.489 (/νῆσον -αίην this island ii.385).

κατὰ νῆσον Cf. ii.771; not in Hom.: κατὰ νήσους claus. *HyAp* 251, 291.

325 ηὐλίζοντ' of birds (αὖλις Hom.+): see LSJ, and Apollonid. *GPh* 1259; cf. infr. 929. Contrast *Od.* 5.65 ὄρνιθες τανυσίπτεροι εὐνάζοντο/.

ὄρνιθες Ἀρήιαι Here (Giangrande, *CR* n.s. 23 (1973), 87) and even more obviously at ii.1033-4 Ἀρήιον .... ὄρνιν (gender: VDB 1.227 n.1; cf. the alternation with Nestor's horses, Hainsworth on *Il.* 11.597, and see 1058n.) carrying a suggestion of ἀρήιος i.e. πολεμικός; repulsed (326) by the heroes.

On the postp. epithet cf. Wifstrand 1933.104-5 (discussing ἀρήιος in ii.397 al.): priority is given to identifying the creatures in question, their habitat having been specified already (322).

325-6 οὐδ' .../εὕρομεν ... Another snatch from Odysseus' brush with Polyphemus (see on 176f.(9)): *Od.* 9.216-7 οὐδέ μιν ἔνδον/εὕρομεν, ἀλλ' ... (ἐξελάσαντας 227). These birds were gone for good – but the newcomers have found somebody just as dangerous as the Cyclops 'at home.'

οὐδ' ἔτι κείνας A similar clausula infr. 1346 (but κεινάς).

326 οἵδ' He points (cf. 315); οἵγ' (offered by Ω) is out of the question, as Wilamowitz stressed, *HD* 2.253.

ἀπήλασαν This compound, found here only in the poem, is not Homeric; no doubt from a prose, or a tragic, source (literary background: VDB 1.169-70). Aeetes is clearly unimpressed: he will presently come up with formidable creatures of his own, from Ares' Plain (409f.); and μῆτις (cf. ii.383f.1049f.1058f.) will again win the day.

326-7 ἐξαποβάντες/νηὸς ἑῆς 199n. νηὸς ἑῆς = Q.S. 7.571, cf. [Orph.] *A.* 356; Hom. /νηὸς ἐμῆς ἐπιβᾶσαν (*Od.* 13.319).

There are wry echoes hereabouts of the tale of Odysseus' comrades in *Od.* 12: on a desert island (351), they ἐξαπέβησαν ../νηός (306-7), and proceeded to 'drive off' (343, 353, 398) the cattle [cf. Aeetes at iii.592-3] of Helios (!).

327 προτέρῳ ἐνὶ ἤματι See ii.1032/1097/1100/1121f.; *Noten* 280.

προτέρῳ .. ἤματι But *Il.* 21.5 (Max. 242) /ἤματι .. προτέρῳ. Opp. *Hal.* 3.416 προτέροισιν ἐν ἤμασιν.

ἐνὶ ἤματι No exact Homeric parallel for such an hiatus at this point, but compare *Il.* 22.206 ἐπὶ Ἕκτορι, id. 18.501 ἐπὶ ἴστορι, *Od.* 17.454 ἐπὶ εἴδεϊ. Later in the verse ἐνὶ ἤματι iv.236, 1479, 1502, ἐπὶ ἤματι (text: Campbell 1973.78) ii.660: Hom. ἐπὶ ἥμισυ *Od.* 13.114, but cf. the digammated ἐπὶ οἴνοπα, ἐπὶ ἕσπερος -ον etc., and note *Cypria EGF* 4.4 ἐνὶ ἄνθεϊ, Philetas *CA* 9 ἔπι ἤθεσιν, Arat. 962 ἐπὶ ὕδατι, 1027 ἐπὶ ὄψιον.

Later examples of ἐνὶ ἤματι: [Orph.] *fr.* 274.1, *Vis. Doroth.* 4, Greg. Naz. 491.37 and often, Max. 171.

σφ' ἀπέρυκεν scil. ὁδοῦ, kept them where they were, detained them. An unusual use of the compound verb, but ἀπερητύειν in i.772 (n.b. ... ὁδόν earlier in the line) is exactly comparable (unlike iii.174, *pace* Giangrande 1973.7-8 and a number of others); cf. Xen. *Anab.* 3.3.3 ἢν δέ τις ἡμᾶς τῆς ὁδοῦ ἀποκωλύῃ and sim. The glosses adduced by Merkel *Proleg.* 165 (*EtM* 378.18, Hesych. α6029: *inter alia*, κατέχειν) may or may not be relevant.

There is of course nothing in the text to suggest that the Argonauts *would* have departed at some point during the 'previous day' or even at the crack of dawn (when they fell in with the Phrixids); on the contrary, they had had little respite recently, *and* they were expecting an ὄνειαρ to come their way at this very spot (ii.382f. cf. 1091f.). Perhaps Argos had been made aware of this, perhaps not. What is important here is the intimation that heaven took an interest in the Phrixids' well-being – "ein Wink an den König, sich dem göttlichen Willen nicht zu widersetzen sondern nach Kräften mit ihm zusammenarbeiten" (*Noten* 345).

σφ' 48n.

328 Jason for his part had attributed the arrival of the Phrixids ἐννεσίῃσι .../ἀθανάτων (ii.1166-7) and to Zeus in particular (ii.1179f., cf. Argos already in 1133), correctly in both cases (ii.1110f./1098f.).

οἰκτείρων Cf. οἰκτείρασα in iv.917 cited on 323 (with Paul 124-5), and Argos himself, once he has invoked Zeus Xenios before the Argonauts, in ii.1130. Zeus does feel pity in *Il.* 16.431f., al. – not that mortals are put in the picture about that (Rutherford on *Od.* 20.202-3). Argos reports it as a fact, with no softening που.

Ζηνὸς νόος A grand-sounding expression borrowed from Hes. *WD* 483 (~ Opp. *Hal.* 1.769), cf. *Il.* 16.103; id. 15.242, *Od.* 24.164 etc.; West on Hes. *Theog.* 613, Sullivan, *SIFC* n.s. 7 (1989), 158f.

ἠέ τις αἶσα i.e. what has happened may be attributed to calculated planning on the part of Zeus, or to the workings of a less easily definable but no less purposeful 'Destiny/destiny' (261n.) – the detention of the Argonauts can be slotted into the preordained 'scheme of things.' It is inappropriate to talk of 'le hasard (τύχη), par opposition au dessein réfléchi de la divinité' (Vian ed. 1961, thinking no doubt of passages such as Eur. *fr.* 901.2 εἴτε τύχα <τις> εἴτε δαίμων ...; 'or was it only chance?' Rieu in his usual racy style. In fact, the concept of τύχη itself needs sensitive handling: see e.g. Bond on Eur. *HF* 1393). Cf. infr. 660 τις .. μοῖρα, 'some stroke of fate' (the exact circumstances of death being immaterial), and 323n.

There is irony in all this of course: Argos could not know that Aeetes would have no reason to thank heaven (and would thank Zeus least of all) for his grandsons' salvation (*Studies* 29).

τις αἶσα For similar expressions see Campbell on Q.S. 12.527.

329 To 'because right away ...' (but infr. 1195 'the moment that ...'; both Homeric), i.e. as an *immediate* consequence of this divine sympathy (cf. ii.1166-7, 1179f.), Argos flatteringly adds ... εἰσαΐοντες ..., viz. '*the moment* they heard Phrixus' name and your own' (cf. ii.1141f./1160f., but no Aeetes there! Argos is quiet about his own fears, ii.1200f.).

βρῶσιν ... ἔδωκαν For the giving of food and clothes (an important aspect of hospitality in *Od.*: Rutherford on 19.317-22, Block, *TAPA* 115 (1985), 3) see ii.(1129), 1166, 1168, 1177f., 1227. *Odyssea*: 6.209, 246 δότ' ... βρῶσιν (in Homer always coupled with 'drink,' cf. Chantraine's discussion of the term in *BLG* 59 (1964), 11f.; nowhere else in 3^H); 6.144 καὶ εἵματα δοίη/, 7.238 εἵματ' ἔδωκεν/ (cf. 13.369), 7.295-6 σῖτον ἔδωκεν ἄλις (cf. 23.341, al.) .... καί μοι .. εἵματ' ἔδωκε/; after shipwreck (allegedly): 14.320 (clothing).

330 Φρίξοιο Argos was not to know that the linking of Phrixus' name with Aeetes' would not be appreciated (*Studies* 29); the latter has to wait to be told (and he is told only indirectly) *why* 'the name of Phrixus' is of momentous importance.

COMMENTARY 332 297

περικλεές i.1069 π. οὔνομα, 1322 π. ἄστυ, the latter combination already in Ibyc. *PMGF* S151.2, cf. M. Nöthiger, *Die Sprache des Stesichorus und des Ibycus* (Zürich 1971), 174-5. All the other occurrences of this uncommon epithet (Fränkel reminds us of the illustrious *name*: 1963.160) are in LSJ. Ap. also has ἐπικλεές, iv.1472, Livrea ad loc. (add: Simon. *IEG* 11.35, Maiist. *CA* 30).

εἰσαΐοντες (or rather εἰσαΐοντες: 352-3n.) 145n.

331 αὐτοῖο σέθεν But *Il.* 23.312 σέθεν αὐτοῦ. σέθεν is not used possessively in Homer (*GH* 1.244): ctr. in 3^H this poem 6 × in all; Call. *h.* 3.172 [pentam.: *ffr.* 24.2, 75.75]; Maiist. *CA* 1; Euphor. *CA* 123 ([Theoc.] 27.44 is later).

μετά 13n. So μετὰ πτόλιν (Αἰήταο/) ii.459, 890, 1093, iii.621, μετὰ πτολίεθρον ii.760.

τεὸν ἄστυ Cf. 348 (μετήλυθε), Nonn. *D.* 40.23, [Apolin.] 67.68 (μετεσσύμενοι); in reverse infr. 387. Argos now makes it plain that the strangers have business with Aeetes – but he takes a while to get to the point.

νέονται νέμ- E: cf. G at ii.1094 (damaged archetype).

332 Argos talks as if he is feeling his way with a complete stranger upon whom he depends for help or protection (cf. e.g. Jason at 1083f.); another preamble at 354f.

χρειώ 173n. A 'host' might be expected to show an interest in this (cf. Circe at iv.721, /χρειὼ ναυτιλίην τε ..., and ctr. Amycus at ii.8-9 χρειὼ .../ναυτιλίης ...). Aeetes has not thought to do so, being more concerned about what had befallen the unheeding Phrixids.

ἢν ἐθέλῃς Cf. i.891-2. *Il.*: 9.429, 692 ἢν ἐθέλῃσιν, sim. vulg. at 4.353 [404n.], 9.359, v.l. 8.471; Wåhlin 87.

ἐθέλῃς ἐξίδμεναι But *Il.* 13.728 ἐθέλεις περιίδμεναι.

ἐξίδμεναι Again in 1083, in a similar utterance; otherwise only Soph./Eur. I doubt if Ap. drew any sort of semantic distinction between ἐξίδμεναι and (cf. 355) ἴδμεναι: cf. Moorhouse III for Soph., and more generally Bond on Eur. *HF* 18; contrary views in Davies' note on Soph. *Trach.* 5. It does sound good though.

οὔ σ' ἐπικεύσω Aesch. *Ag.* 800 οὐ γάρ <σ'> ἐπικεύσω, see Fraenkel there, and cf. Linsenbarth 23; but this remedy is rejected by some. In Homer οὐκ (ii.312, Greg. Naz. 1265.41, *SEG* 34.1115.1, undated) or οὐδ' (see Kirk on *Il.* 5.816; Greg. Naz. 1508.39, 1567.208, Eudoc. *Hom.* 30, 104, 1936) ἐπικεύσω/. Ap. (iv.1105) also has the Homeric

(*Od.* 3.187, 23.273; also *HyAp* 66) οὐδέ σε κεύσω/, which recurs in Anon. didact. *GDK* 64.114; ctr. D.P. 270 (/εἰ δὲ ... ἐθέλεις ..) οὔτι σε κεύσω/.

333f. Pelias' usurpation of the throne (made explicit first in Pindar, *P.* 4.104f., cf. Matthews 206; Dräger 295f. wrongly seeks to deny any such suggestion in our poem) and misappropriation of property (... ἀπούραις ἀμετέρων τοκέων νέμεαι declares Jason roundly, id. 149f.) have been alluded to only very faintly and sporadically in the first book (VDB 2.122-3, cf. Braswell on *P.* 4.134-68, p. 220), in the course of which numerous opportunities to provide more in the way of background information were not taken up (as e.g. in 279 Alcimede's lament, 908 Jason's reference to his parents' position, 981 questioning of newly arrived Argonauts cf. ii.763); Jason himself at ii.624f. has high-mindedly refrained from offering any record of his *personal* grievances, focusing instead on the welfare of the *crew* under his command. To Argos, who must have been fed with a full version of events at Iolcus in the course of deep and protracted conversations (ii.1226), falls the job of giving these topics an airing (of sorts), before Aeetes of all people, a Pelias-clone if ever there was one, cf. Argos' own description at ii.1202f. Motivated by a desire to present Jason in the best possible light – a man of substance who had the authority and influence to assemble a pan-Hellenic force (347f., cf. 356, 363) capable (and worthy) of taking on a king's sworn enemy (353f.) and successful in voyaging from Hellas to Colchis thanks to divinely-manufactured transport of their own (cf. 340f. beside 309f.), Argos walks into trouble. He was of course unaware that his grandfather was living in fear of losing his throne; but he might have been expected to reflect that Aeetes, a king and proud of it, could not possibly take kindly to being confronted with a dispossessed stranger with an outstanding reputation for ἀλκή in his own right (334-5: the point is not lost on him: see the stinging 407 *et circa*): even the most benign of rulers might feel some disquiet on that score. See further 320-66, 333nn.

333 τόνδε ... 'This person before you' (he points to Jason, who arrived bearing a σκῆπτρον) is followed up with 'a certain individual,' then, with heavy emphasis before the main caesura of the next line, 'a king' (Argos resorts to a similar trick in 339 Αἰολιδέων γενεήν). If the account of Pelias' pronouncement in 336-9 is clothed in the profound obscurity of oracular utterance (Aeetes, who has been on the receiving-end of a riddling oracle relating to *his own* γενέθλη, 599-600, cannot have liked this), the studied wooliness of 333-4 (neither victim nor aggressor identified or precisely localised) can only have provoked the deepest suspicion or irritation or both. Argos' evasiveness (which Levin seems eventually to have discerned, 20 n.4) shines forth with all the brilliance of a beacon in the night.

ἱέμενος A strong term: not just *desiring* but *hell-bent on*. In fact, Pelias could not wait to get rid of Jason (i.15f.).

πάτρης .. ἐλάσσαι Cf. Medea in iv.385-6, and *GVI* 224.3 (Rome, 1st/2nd cent.) πάτρης ἀπάνευθε ⌣–×; [Apolin.] 140.20 ἀπάνευθεν ἐλάσσης/.

Argos is clear on one point: Pelias took this line because Jason represented a threat. If Argos believed that the conveyance of the Fleece to Hellas carried the promise or prospect of proper reinstatement (cf. Pind. *P*. 4.165f.; Jason's modest aspirations in i.902-3 need to be taken in context: he has just been offered royal status, and he must courteously decline!), he does not say so: indeed, ἀμήχανον might be thought to suggest the opposite. Perhaps he does *too* good a job of painting Jason as a once-powerful man now without a home or resources.

ἐλάσσαι then οὕνεκεν: Ap. may have had his own ideas about the sense of *Il*. 6.158 (Proetus/Bellerophon: 353n.) ἔλασσεν, ἐπεὶ πολὺ φέρτερος ἦεν/...

334 κτεάνων 266n.; cf. Pind. *P*. 4.290.

περιώσιον Fränkel's repunctuation (OCT) offers a clear improvement: cf. in general [Apolin.] 28.9 ἑῇ περιώσιος ἀλκῇ/, and, for the break after βασιλεύς, *Il*. 1.231 ... β., ἐπεὶ ... Ap. uses π. 12 ×, but it is not common in the Hellenistic era (add to the examples cited below Theoc. 17.23, Simias *CA* 1.8, Nic. *Ther*. 518). The adverb -ιον is Homeric; also i.466 π. ἄλλων/ = *HyDem* 362 (surely untouchable: contrast James in *JHS* 96 (1976), 168), Pind. *I*. 5.3, Opp. *Hal*. 1.448, 4.523, Greg. Naz. 1272.18, 1517.152; Maiist. *CA* 50 π. ἄλλος/. Adv. -ια (infr. 1326 θυμαίνεσκον/) is rare: *HyHom* 19.41, [Theoc.] 25.125, [Orph.] *A*. 62 (κυδαίνεσκεν/). Of the adjectival uses, ii.434 ἄντρον (text: Campbell 1973.76, 88-9), ii.1063 αὐτή, i.1307 (ἀνδράσι λεύσσειν/) & iv.1430 θάμβος, ii.865 θάρσος, i.590 λαῖφος, iv.1554 ξεινήιον, iv.554 σήματα, ii.394 φῦλα, only the third and the last can be paralleled: *GVI* 265.3 (Syria, 2nd/3rd cent.) θάμβος π. ἀν[θρώ]ποισιν/ cf. D.P. 829 π. ἀνδράσι θαῦμα/; D.P. 960 π. φῦλα.

In all cases the notion of size, quantity, intensity is entirely apt (ctr. *Noten* Index s.v.): Campbell 1973.76, VDB 3.169 (but the alternative proposed at id. 201 for iv.1555 is not attractive).

οὕνεκεν In hexameters as early as Parm., DK28 B8.32, 34 (however it is to be construed). Here and infr. 626, iv.793 (VDB 3.105 n.1) *because*; infr. 470 *that*; iv.1032 (Campbell 1973.85, VDB 3.114 n.4) re-inforcing prep. ἀμφί. In Hellenistic verse prep. in Lyc. 935, Hds 1.84; *the reason for which* id. 6.15; *that, how* [Theoc.] 25.167; otherwise *because or for which reason*: Aclep. *HE* 836, Posidipp. id. 3128 corr.; Call. *fr.* 51, *h.* 4.53; Lyc. 864, 1187; Theoc. 7.43, 13.74; Hds 2.21; Euphor. *CA* 176.2; [Mosch.] *Meg.* 73; Anon. *FGE* 1642 (v.l.).

335 σφωιτέρῃ See Livrea on iv.274, but add *his* ii.763, and *GVI* 635.6 (Smyrna, 2nd cent. BC); also Henrichs 133 n.5, Rengakos 1993.118. The word is not especially common in post-Hellenistic verse: Man. 2.190, Q.S. 12.89, 14.174, [Orph.] *L.* 3×, Nonn. *D.* 4×, [Apolin.] 15×.

πάντεσσι μετέπρεπεν ... 246n. The 'king' is one of the 'all,' as Aeetes will have gathered from the general drift (Pelias an Aeolid: mother Tyro, daughter of Salmoneus son of Aeolus). — Cf. Jason's preeminence in Dion. Scyt. *fr.* 14 Rusten, with Dräger 319 n.89.

Αἰολίδῃσι So the Phrixids have turned up with a fellow-Aeolid: and Aeolids are not good news (cf. 333n., the oracle; and the cutting Αἰολίδην Φρίξον from Aeetes in 584). The king has to wait to see how the genealogy works out (356f.).

336 πέμπει δεῦρο νέεσθαι Cf. *Od.* 4.8 πέμπε νέεσθαι/ and sim.; ii.814 ἔκπεμπε νέεσθαι/ = *Il.* 21.598; infr. 376 ~ *Od.* 16.132.

πέμπει Vivid present (cf. στεῦται in 337), 'is sending,' and not 'sent' or 'has sent.' Argos is speaking to a man who was ready to 'send' the Phrixids on their (fools') errand (601).

ἀμήχανον Better taken with τόνδε (cf. iv.1049, and (attributive) adj. followed up with an οὐδέ in ii.681 ~ *HyHerm* 257; also e.g. *Il.* 18.240 /πέμψεν ... ἀέκοντα νέεσθαι/, id. 21.48) than as 'neuter internal accusative' (Gillies, and so for instance Vian ed. 1961, VDB 2.64 n.5, Vian on [Orph.] *A.* 1228).

On Argos' use of the word see 333n. He means it to relate generally to Jason's helpless and hopeless position. But it harbours considerable irony: Argos cannot know (but we do) *to what degree* the imposition of the voyage has rendered Jason ἀμήχανος. On top of that, there is more ἀμηχανίη in prospect, induced this time by an ἄεθλος set by Aeetes (423, 432). Argos implies of course that Aeetes would not wish to be thought another Pelias (cf. Ibscher 163).

336-9 οὐδ' .... ἱκέσθαι Argos tells Aeetes in a roundabout way that the fleece, viz. *the* Fleece in his possession (not mentioned so far) has to go to Hellas (scil. conveyed there by the unnamed Aeolid of 333f.) and hopes for a sympathetic response: Zeus is angry (Aeetes might be expected to have some regard for him) in connexion with a maltreated Phrixus (Aeetes has shown benevolence towards him, ii.1147f./iii.304f.). Having got in a reference to the Fleece, he quickly changes the subject, though not for the better.

On the events at the back of this exceedingly obscure and compressed utterance see VDB 1.283, on ii.1194-5 Jason (improvising?) to Phrixids Φρίξοιο θυηλάς (scil. the attempted sacrifice of Phrixus, see Wifstrand 1929.86-7) /στέλλομαι ἀμπλήσων, Ζηνὸς χόλον Αἰολίδῃσιν, and also Fusillo 34f.; Riedweg, *CQ* n.s. 40 (1990), 133-4; Zeus ~ Phrixus elsewhere in the poem: VDB 3.266, C *ad init.* Here the motif of Zeus' wrath is pulled to the forefront for effect, and χόλον is stepped up to μῆνιν/καὶ χόλον (see 337-8n.). The 'unendurable pollution' (of which we hear nothing elsewhere in the poem) is that brought upon the line by what Athamas tried to inflict on Phrixus <on the altar of Zeus>; Φρίξοιο .. ποινάς means 'compensation/satisfaction/chastisement *for* <the attempted killing of> Phrixus,' ποινὰς Φρίξου ἀπολουμένου rather than ἀπολομένου in this case: see *LH* and LSJ s. ποινή for examples of the latter type of expression, and more generally Braswell's note on Pind. *P.* 4.63 (d). Ctr. Dräger (200-9n.).

One may compare on a broad level the variation in (explanations include fate, expiation, and the involvement of Zeus), and the obscurity sometimes attaching to, the motivation for Heracles' labours: Bond on Eur. *HF* 20f.

336-9 οὐδ' ὑπαλύξειν ... Cf. iv.1082-3 ὑπάλυξε/... χόλον, and *Or. Sib.* 14.241 κοὐκ ἔστι φυγεῖν χόλον οὐδ' ὑπαλύξαι/. Similar clausulae in *Il.* 11.451, 12.327, *Batrach.* [98], Ammon 13; cf. as well iv.1261.

I doubt if the unexceptional fut. infin. ὑπαλύξειν merits special justification: Ardizzoni 1956.379-80 appeals to the variant in *Il.* 10.371, but there ὑπὸ .. ἀλύξειν is not equivalent to ὑπαλύξειν.

337 στεῦται Not a colourless 'claims' or the like. στεῦμαι means 'declare, insist, pronounce in solemn, super-confident, forceful, boastful, aggressive, threatening language,' sim.: on the word's range see in general Leaf on *Il.* 18.191, Wackernagel *SU* 20if., Russo on *Od.* 17.525 (van der Valk 1.265-6: too narrowly focused). In Homer it is quite often glossed with διαβεβαιοῦσθαι, and so schol. Ap. ii.1204, where στεῦται (ref. Aeetes: cf. Ibscher 163) is an uncomplimentary εὔχεται, cf. *Il.* 2.597; with στεῦτο in 579 infr. (n.) cf. ἀπείλεε in 607.

ἀμειλίκτοιο Διός The epithet is not applied to persons in archaic epic; cf. here Nonn. *D.* 8.353 ἀμειλίκτου χόλον Ἥρης/. Since Zeus can be propitiated (generally, and as Ζεὺς Μειλίχιος), we are not dealing with a standing attribute – not at any rate on the face of it. I suspect that Argos here is made to allude for effect (in the wake of the theme of μᾶνις χθονίων in Pind. *P.* 4.159 mentioned below) to the formidable figure of Zeus Chthonios, who might truly be termed, like Hades (see on the interrelationship West on *WD* 465) ἀμείλικτος (*Od.* 9.158 'Ἀίδης .. ἀμείλιχος, Bion *fr.* 12.3 Gow ἀμειλίκτοιο ... 'Ἀίδαο/; cf. ἀμείλικτον in *HyDem* 259, Richardson ad loc.).

On the patterning of the pairs of attributive adj./subst. in this line (here lending weight to the utterance) cf. Bühler, ed. Mosch. *Eur.*, p. 215 (this example not mentioned).

337-8 Διὸς .... χόλον A reworking of the theme of μᾶνις in Pind. *P.* 4.159, cf. Braswell ad loc. and Faerber 49 n.5. The language is essentially Homeric: (1) *Il.* 5.34 al. Διὸς (δ' ἀλεώμεθα) μῆνιν/. (2) *Il.* 4.513 al. χόλον θυμαλγέα. Cf. later *GVI* 1610.3 (Cyzicus, 2nd/3rd cent.); -γέ' [Hes.] *fr.* 318. (3) *Il.* 15.122 (Διὸς ..) χόλος καὶ μῆνις; gen. *HyDem* 350, 410, accus. [Apolin.] 17.16; μῆν- first: '*Il.*' 1.2 *teste Aristox.* (Kirk, ed. *Il.* vol. I, p. 52) μῆνίς τε χόλος θ', Lucill. *AP* 11.279.2 (about *Il. init.*) μῆνιν καὶ χόλον, Q.S. 10.346-7 μῆνιν .../καὶ χόλον. (4) *Il.* 18.108 /καὶ χόλος.

On (3): van Krevelen 1953.53-4; cf. also Lehrs 132-3, Zumbo, *Helikon* 13/14 (1973/74), 474f., Kirk on *Il.* 6.166-7, Hainsworth on id. 9.426. Here, as in *Il.* 15.122, effective intensification, in '*Il.*' 1.2 pure padding; Schwyzer's 'hysteron proteron' (*RhM* 80 (1931), 214), i.e 'a fit of temper <resulting in> lasting resentment,' is bizarre.

On Homeric μῆνις and cognate words applied to gods/the demigod Achilles/humans see the lit. in Janko on *Il.* 13.459-61, Clay 65. In Ap. μῆνις is divine wrath i.802 v.l. and here (cf. ii.247, and in 3[H] Call. *fr.* 637 with Lloyd-Jones' brilliant correction ἐπεὶ χθονίων, [Theoc.] 25.200), in i.1339 it is Jason's (after Achilles'! 382-5n.), in iv.1205 Aeetes' (Frisk, *Eranos* 44 (1946), 33: but Aeetes is son of a god).

θυμαλγέα μῆνιν Or. Sib. 14.228 (θεοῦ).

338 -οἷό τε ποινάς Ctr. *Il.* 14.483 -οἷό γε ποινή/.

339 πρὶν ... ἱκέσθαι Like *Od.* 4.823 al. πρὶν πατρίδα (similarly infr. 775 Ἀχαιίδα, iv.33 Κολχίδα) γαῖαν ἱκέσθαι/. Cf. also i.904, ii.891 ἐς Ἑλλάδα [13n.] γαῖαν ἱκέσθαι/; supr. 29 [see 13n. again] ἐς Ἑλλάδα κῶας ἀνάξειν/.

340f. Argos comes up with another impressive name (340n.). As he must have been told by his boastful grandfather, Athena had had dealings with the Colchian king (iii.1183-4): this same goddess manufactured the ship which brought the newcomers to this part of the world. Ap. makes Argos echo – and trim – Jason's glowing account of ii.1187-9 (cf. i.111-2, and Fusillo 81-2 n.49: details about Argo's construction, a topic brushed aside at i.18-9, are scattered throughout the poem): Argo was built by Athena *and* her co-worker Argos. The reader must recall that in this poem the *Phrixid* Argos has lost out to Argos *son of Arestor* (*Studies* 105 n.8; VDB 1.244, 2.27 n.6), a pale, perhaps imported figure who is accorded star-status (cf. i.18-9, 111-2, 226, (724), ii.612f.)! Catullus (64.9) was later to suppress the name of the goddess' associate to make an etymological point: Thomas 149.

Another scrap of Argonautic lore may be relevant. Argos, no shipwright, none the less speaks with assurance, and with pride, about the build-quality of Argo: in particular, ἐνὶ γόμφοις/ἴσχεται (343-4). Recall the engaging story recounted by one Damagetus *ap.* schol. Ap. i.224-6*a* (= Demaratus *dub.* Jacoby, *FGH* 42 *fr.* 3; other thoughts in Wendel, *Hermes* 66 (1931), 465) about Argos' activities at Pagasae: ἐκέλευσεν ὁ Πελίας τὴν Ἀργὼ ἀραιοῖς γόμφοις παγῆναι, ἵνα ταχέως ἀπολέσῃ αὐτούς· ὁ δὲ Ἄργος τοὐναντίον πεποίηκεν ... Our Argos, so far from being involved in a story about flimsy construction-methods, is the victim of them (or considers he is)!

340 Ἀθηναίη Παλλάς A pretentious inversion (*Studies* 105 n.4) of Homer's Παλλὰς Ἀθηναίη (*Il.* 10.275 etc.) and Παλλὰς Ἀθήνη (on the other hand Ἀπόλλων Φοῖβος in i.759 is not especially striking, *pace* Faerber 80 n.3), well in keeping with this latter-day tragic messenger's penchant for the grandiose (cf. particularly the note on Ἐνυαλίοιο in 322). The only parallel for this order appears to be *CEG* (2) 849.6 (4th cent.?) Ἀθαν[α]ί[α]ς [Π]αλλ[άδο]ς.

κάμεν With νῆα(ς) *Od.* 9.126-7, i.18-9 (Argos), 111 (Athena), Colluth. 199 (Athena 200).

The very earliest epic accounts will have involved Athena (8n.) in

Argo's construction, just as she was cast in the role of (co-)builder/ overseer of the Trojan Horse (analogous to ship: Campbell on Q.S. 12.423f. and 428, Livrea, *RhM* n.s. 123 (1980), 235f.). Indeed in *Od.* 2.287f. (see the interesting observations of Detienne and Vernant, 219f.), where Athena plays an active part in fitting out a ship for Telemachus, the poet is clearly thinking of her association with Argo: there are other traces of Argonautic material in the episode, and among the (presumed) Odyssean echoes in Antim. *fr.* 57, Athena's equipping of Argo, is 2.389-90; see also 341-2n.

Faerber (82) considers i.19 and ii.612f. to represent the proper state of affairs: Argos built Argo under Athena's supervision. In fact, Ap. himself is at pains to counter any such impression: i.111-2 (see Campbell 1978.122) *combines* co-building *with* ὑποθημοσύναι (112 ~ 19, cf. 226); Tiphys' observation in ii.612f. does not preclude divine participation in the building-operations; and Athena is actively involved in i.526f./iv.582f., i.551, 723f., ii.1187f. Ap. perhaps sought to harmonize elements from a fluid tradition: compare the various approaches to Athena/Epeius: Trojan Horse (Campbell on Q.S. 12.104-21). [In i.724 the leader Jason, not unnaturally, played a part in the operations. Recall here the story of Paris building/getting built a fleet, at Aphrodite's suggestion: NH on Hor. *Carm.* 1.15.1.]

οὐ μάλα τοίην ... i.e. with a build-quality not at all/remotely like that of the ships which ... The Odyssean use of μάλα τοῖος -ον is quite different.

341-2 *Oppositio*: *Od.* 2.292f. Athena speaking (see on this episode 340n.) εἰσὶ .. νῆες/πολλαὶ ἐν .. Ἰθάκῃ .../τάων .. τοι ἐγὼν ἐπιόψομαι ἥτις ἀρίστη/κτλ. Contrast also *Il.* 10.113 /τῶν .. νῆες ἔασιν ...

341 Κόλχοισι ... Argos speaks like an outsider looking in; not that he is *pure* Colchian himself. We first met the Phrixids on their 'Colchian ship' (ii.1095), which promptly came to grief (ii.1108f., iii.320f., 342f.). There was no shortage of ships in this part of the world (iv.238f.), but none could match Athena's creation (cf. i.113-4, in connexion with Argos Arestorides!).

-οισι μετ' ἀνδράσι(ν) *Il.* 17.445 etc. cf. i.648 al.

342 αἰνοτάτης Those who see in Argos a model of tact will wish to join Fränkel (so VDB 2.25 n.2) in interpreting *ill-fated* (*Noten* 346, cf. already Platt 1914.22). Argos has just spoken unflatteringly about the quality of Colchian vessels (cf. Faerber 97 n.4), and he goes on to draw an unfavourable distinction between the storm-resistance of their ship and that of Argo. In ii.1126 he complained of his νηὸς ἀεικελίης, in a passage where he had no reason to exercise restraint: 'disreputable' i.e. 'shabby, shoddy, of indifferent quality,' εὐτελής, κακός (see *LfgrE* under schol.), φαῦλος. So here, 'the most fearful, awful, dreadful, dire': cf. e.g. αἰνότερον in *Od.* 11.427, αἰνότατος ('absolutely awful') in id. 4.441, and αἰνῶς often; with schol.'s κακίστης ctr. ἀρίστη cited in the note on 341-2.

Argos comes close to being aggressive here: he is definitely pushing his luck. There is nothing in the text to suggest that Aeetes had deliberately provided the Phrixids with anything approaching an unseaworthy vessel: he clearly relied (as did Pelias with Jason, according to most) on the dangers inherent in an immensely long sea-journey (cf. 307f., 600-1) to see them off. On the contrary, the Colchian ship seems to have been robustly constructed: VDB 1.206 n.1, 229 n.5; it did fall foul of an exceptionally violent storm, generated by Zeus.

αἰνοτάτης ἐπεκύρσαμεν αἰνοτάτῃ viz. -ῃ *w*. The genitive is preferable, cf. Aesch. *Pers.* 853 (Fränkel OCT) with Ardizzoni here, and e.g. Eur. *Med.* 1363 μητρὸς .. κακῆς ἐκύρσατε, LSJ s.v. κυρέω I2.

ἤλιθα γάρ μιν But *Od.* 14.215 (cf. 5.483) ... γάρ με ... ἤλιθα ...

ἤλιθα In ii.283 (*pace* Ardizzoni here) a straight equivalent of μάτην (281), it means something like 'with a phenomenal intensity' in iv.177, 'to a phenomenal distance' in iv.1265 (ἤλιθα δ' ὕδωρ/...; 'à l'infini' VDB 3.189; Faerber 36 n.1 advocates 'uselessly,' cf. Mooney's note), here perhaps 'with phenomenal violence' or, conceivably, closely with ὕδωρ (cf. below), 'water in a (one huge concentrated?) mass': the usual interpretation is 'comprehensively' *vel sim.* in the wake of schol.'s ἀθρόως (which might be meant rather in the sense 'all of a sudden' or 'at one fell swoop'). See on the word Thesleff 188-9 and esp. Hiersche, *Philologus* 102 (1958), 140f., with Bulloch on Call. *h.* 5.124; also Livrea on iv.177 (but in Nic. *Alex.* 140 ἤλιθα is adj., as LSJ Suppl. now recognises [cf. Gow, *CQ* n.s. 1 (1951), 102]; id. 423 ~ LSJ: cf. now Haslam, *Glotta* 70 (1992), 35 with n.3; in Philox. *PMG* 836(a)2 ἤλιθ' ὕδωρ, 'water in great abundance,' is a very attractive conjecture). After the Hellenistic period only Man. 2.3.

343 λάβρον ὕδωρ i.e. πόντου λάβρον ὕδωρ (i.541), cf. ii.1102-3, though we may also recall the rain sent by Zeus (ii.1099 ὕδατι), cf. λαβρότατον .. ὕδωρ/ in *Il.* 16.385. For this combination cf. [Opp.] *Cyn.* 4.169 (claus.), Q.S. 14.599 (framing verse), and ὕδατι λάβρῳ/ in Diosc. *HE* 1673, Opp. *Hal.* 1.575, [Opp.] *Cyn.* 2.139.

This expressive epithet (cf. Biehl on Eur. *Or.* 697) is elsewhere confined to the narrative (7 ×), as invariably in Homer.

πνοιή scil. ἀνέμου (ii.1098, 1108, 1114); Argo on the other hand could withstand πνοιαὶ παντοίων ἀνέμων: 344.

For λάβρον in association with πνοιή cf. *Il.* 16.624f. κῦμα .../λάβρον ... ἀνεμοτρεφές ~ ii.168 /πνοιῇ then 173 λάβρον scil. κῦμα.

διέτμαγεν *Il.* 1.531, *Od.* 13.439 -τε διέτμαγεν· ἡ. Here 'cut, smash to pieces' (sing. verb as e.g. *Od.* 5.111 ἄνεμός τε .. καὶ κῦμα πέλασσε/, cf. La Roche *HU* 187, KG 1.79), as Nonn. *D.* 36.450 διατμήξει νέας (ctr. διατμήξας in *Od.* 3.291). διέτμαγ- in Homer: (1) *Od.* 7.276 -ον, 'I cut a path through'; (2)(a) pass. -εν, literal: *Il.* 12.461, 16.354; (b) pass. -εν = 'were parted, took leave of each other' *Il.* 1.531, 7.302, *Od.* 13.439. In all the Iliadic passages there are variants -ον. The post-Homeric occurrences are: (1) transitive -ον and -εν: Opp. *Hal.* 3.146, Q.S. 8.319, Nonn. *D.* 22.211, 43.45, 45.291, Paul. Sil. *AP* 5.217.1, *Soph.* 719, Agath. *AP* 5.218.9; (2)(a) no example; (b) -ον 'they parted': Ap. ii.298, iii.1147, Nonn. *D.* 7.108; to be included here probably [Apolin.] 113.9 διέτμαγες, which seems to signify 'part company <with me>, take yourself off' (φεῦγε 5). On (2)(b) see Ludwich 1.199; Platt 1914.30; van Krevelen 1951.97; Giangrande 1976.277; Rengakos 1993.107-8.

343-4 ἐνὶ ../ ἴσχεται As both ἴσχεσθαι and ἐνίσχεσθαι can mean *be held fast* it is a matter of indifference whether ἐνί is regarded as an instrumental preposition (e.g. Oswald 129) or as *in tmesi*; more likely the latter: an echo in Opp. *Hal.* 1.194 εὐγόμφοισιν ἐνισχόμενος πινάκεσσιν/.

γόμφοις ... The part these play in producing a seaworthy vessel is stressed at an early point, i.369-70 ('Argos' 367!: 340f.n.), cf. ii.613-4 (singled out as crucial components, cf. e.g. Archimelus *SH* 202.3-4 = *FGE* 85-6) with VDB 1.206 n.1, 267 (on ii.82), FJW on Aesch. *Suppl.* 440-1. The Colchian ship, though secured with θοοὶ γόμφοι (ii.1112), was wrecked, like Odysseus' raft, whose γόμφοι (*Od.* 5.248) in the end (5.370/7.275) could *not* resist πάσας ... ἀέλλας/... (5.292, signalled in *Echoes* 47) ~ infr. 344 πᾶσαι .. ἄελλαι/.

ἥν καί For ἥν in generalisations see KG 2.475f., Wåhlin 87; *Od.* 16.276 /ἥν .. καὶ ... -ωσι ⌣−×.

πᾶσαι ἐπιβρίσωσιν ἄελλαι Cf. ii.1125 (spoken by Argos) /πόντῳ .. τρηχεῖαι ἐπιβρίσασαι ἄελλαι/ (and *Od.* 3.320 ἐλθέμεν, ὅν τινα πρῶτον ἀποσφήλωσιν ἄελλαι); Q.S.: 14.251 πᾶσαι ... ἐνόρουσαν ἄελλαι/ (1.488

ἐπιβρίσασα ... θύελλα/), 14.468 'Ανέμους .. πάντας ἐπιβρίσαντας. ἐπιβρίθειν subj. winds: so already Theophr. *Vent.* 34.
ἴσχεται then ἐπιβρίσωσιν: ctr. *Il.* 5.90 ἴσχει then ἐπιβρίσῃ 91.

345-6 Ἄργος (co-)builder of 'Αργώ has been left out of the reckoning; we are left then with the ship's *speed*: 'Αργώ is ἀργή, cf. Theoc. 13.23-4 with Campbell in *Owls to Athens: Essays* ... *Dover* (Oxford 1990), 117, and Robert 770, *RE* 2.723.10f., Braswell on Pind. *P.* 4.25(b) (in refusing to attach any particular significance to the epithet θοᾶς, he takes too narrow a view of ἀργός, cf. *LfgrE* under ἀργός, ἀργιπόδας and 'Αργώ), Thomas 150f. (who reckons that it might be a Callimachean etymology), Dräger 21. For the rapidity of Argo when (a) wind-driven and (b) propelled by oars see esp. ii.930f. and i.1156f.

Ovid no doubt had these lines in his head at *Trist.* 1.10.3-4 (*Minervae* 1), as well as Catull. 4.3f. (this cited by Hoelzlin here).

345 ἐξ ἀνέμοιο Ctr. *Il.* 11.308 (and 5.865). Lit. 'through the agency of,' when the wind acts upon her (cf. Vian ed. 1961, and ctr. i.600; iv.1624 ~ *Il.* 19.415): Q.S. 10.69-70 πόντος ../μαίνεται ἐξ ἀνέμοιο. One may compare in general the Homeric use of ὑπό + gen., used thus 'besonders für meteorologische Erscheinungen,' H. Jankuhn, *Die passive Bedeutung medialer Formen untersucht an der Sprache Homers* (Göttingen 1969), 106, with examples (cf. Ap. ii.741, iii.970; and iv.643!). With a passive verb i.520-1 ἐκ δ' ἀνέμοιο/... τινασσομένης ἁλός (so to be construed!), ii.1245 φορεύμενοι ἐξ ἀνέμοιο/, iv.215 κορύσσεται ἐξ ἀνέμοιο/, and so too Lucill. *AP* 11.107.1 πεφορημένῳ ἐξ ἀνέμοιο/, Opp. *Hal.* 1.779, Q.S. 9.271, Nonn. *D.* 3.38. But in iv.609 πνοιῇ .. ἐξ ἀνέμοιο/ = <propelled> by the blast issuing from ... (an unnecessary fuss has been made about this: Fränkel *Noten* 506, who maintained that πνοιή and ἄνεμος are identical; James 80 mistranslates. Cf. e.g. Diggle 28-9 on prepositional phrases dependent upon a noun).

ὅτ' rather than ὅταν to enunciate a general truth: cf. *GHD* 263-4, *GH* 2.256.

ἀνέρες αὐτοί See 321n.; *Od.* 15.302 ἀνέρες ἄλλοι/. αὐτοί then ἐρετμοῖς (see below): cf. *Od.* 12.180.

346 νωλεμέως Perhaps just 'with might and main' (VDB 1.274; cf. above on 147), though the adverb may combine the notions of vigour/power (so for instance ἐπικρατέως i.914, βίῃ i.1157) and uninterrupted effort (cf. e.g. the rowers in i.1154/1161, and ἀλίαστον in ii.649) both here and at iv.504-5 (n.b. '... *until* they arrived at ...'). Ctr. *Od.* 4.287-8 χερσί *then* /νωλεμέως (where many moderns offer 'firmly,' i.e. exerting powerful pressure, rather than a negative 'with no relaxation of effort').

χείρεσσιν .. ἐρετμοῖς Uncritically handled by Linsenbarth 71, and set upon by a number of unwary critics, who, like the authors of the conjectures ἐρετμά (*cod.* O) and ἐρετμούς (*cod.* E), have fallen into the trap of regarding this particular use of the 'double dative' as bad Greek. In reality, it is one more example of Argos' prediliction for high-flown language: cf., from a tragic chorus, χερὶ ... ξίφεσιν in Soph. *Aj.* 229f. (Campbell 1978.120-1, cf. Moorhouse 88-9), and, from a different one, θνατοῖς ... ἐρετμοῖς, 'to mortal men, viz. to the oars <they plied>,' Eur. *HF* 401-2; later, with 'hand' second: Opp. *Hal.* 5.653 δρεπάνη τάμε χειρὶ παχείη/ (so to be articulated). Related, though easier, are combinations like χερσὶ βίη in Hes. *WD* 321 (*GG* 2.170; Verdenius ad loc.), χερσὶ κράτει in 'Simon.' *FGE* 877; proecdosis i.543 (Campbell 1973.89-90, Livrea 1977.13) looks like an elegant variation on this type.

Livrea (1975.653-4) argues robustly for ἐρετμά, appealing to Ap. at i.552 ἥρωας χείρεσσιν ἐπικραδάοντας ἐρετμά, and also to *Od.* 12.205; ἐρετμοῖς is blamed on *Od.* 13.22 ὁπότε σπερχοίατ' ἐρετμοῖς/. However (cf. Wellauer), 'she runs ... speed <*her*> onwards with oars' is plainly preferable to 'she runs ... drive *their oars* speedily onwards'; cf. in general *Il.* 23.429 /κέντρῳ (instr. dat.) ἐπισπέρχων, where we must supply an accus. ἵππους. Opp. *Hal.* 5.544 νῆα κατασπέρχουσιν ἐρετμοῖς/, cf. id. 4.90-1.

ἐπισπέρχωσιν ~ ἐπιβρίσωσιν 344: on the assonance see *Noten* 346; Argos is truly 'putting on the style.'

347 Argos gets back to Jason, and not before time. Aeetes now learns that the unnamed outcast heads a distinguished company of heroes from every quarter of Hellas: but still no names.

ἐναγειράμενος All occurrences in LSJ – unless one should include Ar. in *Il.* 1.142 (Ludwich 1.182; nautical; *Od.* 16.349 presumably as well); ... ἡρώων: cf. i.124. ἀγείρειν is used of a recruiting drive in *Il.* 11.770, Hes. *WD* 652, al.

Παναχαιίδος 'All-Achaea' [601n.], that is to say the whole of Hellas/Greece (Walther 18, Delage 22) only here and i.243 (/ἡρώων ibid.; there with γαῖα, corresponding to the Homeric Ἀχαιίς beside the fuller Ἀ. γαῖα: see Griffiths 174); ~ Hom. Παναχαιοί, on which see Hoenigswald, *Language* 16 (1940), 187-8.

COMMENTARY 348-9   309

Phineus called the Argonauts Πανελλήνων προφερέστατοι in ii.209 (cf. on 13, and Kirk on *Il*. 2.529-30): so Telamon could talk of Heracles' κῦδος ἀν' Ἑλλάδα in connexion with a return home (i.1292f.), and Jason will undertake as expedition leader to spread Aeetes' good name Ἑλλάδι πάσῃ (iii.391f.); in iv.204f. Jason in a rousing address to his men will think in terms of 'Hellas'' disgrace or prestige, just as in i.242f. the inhabitants of Iolcus have expectations of a 'band of heroes' drawn from 'the land of Panachaea' (cf. iv.195; Theoc. 13.18 is not as specific). Herodotus evidently saw the enterprise in pan-Hellenic terms (1.2, cf. C. M. Dufner, *The* Odyssey *in the* Argonautica (Diss. Princeton 1988), 1.236f.), as he did the Trojan war (1.3, see for the idea NH on Hor. *Carm*. 2.4.9, Zagagi 24, 61), and in fact tragedy must have routinely presented the Argonauts as a pan-Hellenic élite penetrating a barbarian world. It is instructive to recall the complexion of the Euripidean Heracles' exploits (cf. Bond, ed. *HF* Index s. Heracles, lines 2-3); indeed, in his quest for the Amazon's Girdle, he 'assembles' companions from 'Hellas,' as Jason does: *HF* 408f. may well be drawing on an epic model of fairly recent vintage; see further Bond on 408-18, p. 170, Wilkins on Eur. *Hcld*. 215-9.

εἴ τι φέριστον ... The same clausula in *Or. Chald., fr. dub*. 214.2 des Places (where Mingarelli's εἴτε is quite unnecessary). Instead of a plain οἵ τε φέριστοι (this, and things like it, appear in certain strands of the transmission), a grandiloquent '<pre-eminent individuals,> if anything <is> pre-eminent among ...,' a turn of phrase (related to the use of the neut. plur. superlat.: KG 1.63, Gow on Theoc. 15.142) which may be closely paralleled in Theoc., 7.4-5 (see Gow/Dover ad loc.), *HE* 3442-3; another τι- expression in the same poet (13.18 Argonauts, πασᾶν ἐκ πολίων) has often been compared (deliberate downgrading of Ap.'s high-flown language? See on the phrase Gow ad loc., Fabiano, *GRBS* 12 (1971), 531). Note too Call. *h*. 1.70 αἰζηῶν ὅτι φέρτατον ~ iv.1593 (ὅττι φέριστον was proposed for iii.347 by Naber 31!).

The Argonauts are addressed as φέρτατοι iv.1031, 1383; cf. Phineus at ii.209, cited in the previous note.

348 τεὸν ἄστυ μετήλυθε echoes 331 (see n.; Nonn. *D*. 47.475 ἄστεα .. μετήιεν), a remark which led, eventually, to mention of the Fleece (339); this time round Argos is not so communicative (349n.).

348-9 πόλλ' ἐπαληθείς/ἄστεα Cf. (*Echoes* 47) *Od*. 4.81, 15.176 πόλλ' ἐπαληθείς/, and id. 16.492, 19.170 /πολλὰ .. ἐπὶ ἄστε' ἀλώμενος (ἐνθάδ' ἱκάνω/), all save the first of Odysseus. Argos throws a literary titbit Aeetes' way, recalling the celebrated weary and reluctant wanderer (cf. in general Bond on Eur. *HF* 1197) of *Od.* 1.1-4; in visiting numerous 'cities' our traveller has his eye on one 'city' in particular. Jason will see the need to spell out the point about his reluctance properly (388f.).

349 πελάγη .. ἁλός Posidipp. *HE* 3149 (corrected) ἐφ' ἁλὸς πελάγη/. In archaic verse (*Od.* 5.335, Archil. *IEG* 8.1, *HyAp* 73, *HyHom* 33.15) ἁλὸς ἐν πελάγεσσι(/). Cf. further Soph. *Ant.* 966 (??), Eur. *IT* 300, *Tro.* 88 ~ Men. *Pk.* 809, and see Braswell's note on Pind. *P.* 4.251(b); Diggle 80.

Archestr. Gel. *SH* 165.12 πολλὰ περήσαντες πελάγη βρυχίου διὰ πόντου.

-η Contracted form: cf. ii.1268, iv.274, 1217; Campbell on Q.S. 12.174-5 (see also Janko 144).

στυγερῆς ἁλός Unique combination? On the epithet in Ap. see Livrea on iv.8. Compare too Jason's στυγέων μὲν ἁλὸς κρυόεντα κέλευθα/νηὶ διαπλώειν κτλ., ii.628-9; 390n.

ὁπάσσαις 'Prudenter omittitur κῶας, vox Aeetae odiosa' Hoelzlin. In fact, Argos cannot bring himself to ask directly (in 352 he talks of a 'present'); he is direct enough with his offer of compensation, 353.

-αις -οις is defensible (cf. in general Campbell 1973.76; and 644n.). But only E has it.

350 αὐτῷ ... ἔσσεται The decision will be Aeetes': he will not be coerced. The formality of Argos' utterance echoes that of the seer Phineus in ii.345 /καὶ τὰ μὲν ὥς κε πέλῃ, τὼς ἔσσεται, cf. /τὼς ἔμεν ὥς κεν ... in iii.629.

αὐτῷ of course means 'you yourself,' as in i.476 (Marxer 64, KG 1.654; Gillies compared infr. 537, verb ἐφανδάνει), but the momentary ambiguity seems one that Argos might have taken steps to avoid (cf. *Studies* 105 n.9).

ὥς κεν ἄδῃ *HyAp* 75 ἤ κεν ἄδῃ οἱ/ (ἁλὸς .. πελάγεσσιν/ 73).

οὐ γὰρ ἱκάνει Cf. *Od.* 6.136, and Campbell on Q.S. 12.222.

351 χερσὶ βιησόμενος Orac. *ap.* Plut. *Mor.* 399c /χερσὶ βιησάμενοι (cf. the error in Ω here), Anon. *FGE* 1829, 1841 χερσὶ βιησάμενοι or βιασάμενοι/. In Nic. *Alex.* 362 /χειρὶ βιαζόμενος *cod.* Π has βιησάμενος.

-εν δέ ... Cf. *Od.* 20.383 -εν κέ τοι ἄξιον —×, and *Il.* 23.562, *Od.* 8.405. μέμονεν means 'he is extremely anxious' to ...

ἄξια τίσειν Similarly Anon. *HE* 3780-1 ἀντάξια βουλῆς/τεῖσαι, *SEG*

17.756.4 *(carm. hon.*, Syria, 4th cent. AD?) ἐπάξια τεῖσαν. Ctr. Theoc. 17.114 δωτίναν ἀντάξιον (/πολλὸν .. πτολίεσσι 111, ἵκετ' 113, ὤπασε 114).

τίσειν μέμονα/fut. infin.: often indistinguishable from pres. or aor.; here truly prospective: is anxious that he will be able to pay …

352 δωτίνης, Highlighted, none too diplomatically. /δωτίνης· in i.89 gives added weight to the theme of Eurytus' ingratitude. Here the close proximity of τίσειν is of interest: cf. *EtM* 294.7, δωτίνη derived by Alexander of Cotiaeum from δόσις + τίνειν, see Dyck, *ICS* 16 (1991), 327-8.

Il. 9.155-6 δωτίνῃσι then οἱ ὑπὸ σκήπτρῳ.

352-3 αἰὼν ἐμέθεν … Cf. Argos in 477f. Whether this gesture is sprung on Jason, or is part of a prearranged plan, one cannot say: the narrator has said nothing on the subject. When Jason comes to repeat the offer, he does not confine himself to one foe (392f.).

On the Sauromatae see the useful note in VDB 2.123. It is hard to see how Aeetes could have taken kindly to the confident tone adopted by Argos, whatever he thought of the substance: see *Studies* 30-1, also id. 105 n.9, referring to Wilamowitz, *HD* 2.235 n.1. The motif of a brush or brushes with local peoples is likely to go some way back in one form or another, and I see no justification for thinking of 'the crew as a mercenary army to do Aeetes' fighting in the Hellenistic tradition,' Beye 1982.131. For the theme recall Heracles in ii.786f., another passage where some have felt the influence of contemporary exploits: see VDB 1.160f.

αἰών So to be accented: see West on Hes. *WD* 9, and id. *BICS* 31 (1984), 175f. on what to do about κλύω. Adjustments need to be made elsewhere in Ap.; in the stretch of the poem covered by this volume see 145, 270, 330, 368.

μέγα δυσμενέοντας should have appeared in Bissinger 247. δυσμενέοντες is clausular in *Od.* 2.73, 20.314.

353 9 sigmas, with no obvious motive (? pressing offer home): cf. Clayman, *TAPA* 117 (1987), 84. See on 1005.

σοῖσιν … δαμάσσει *Il.* 6.159 οἱ ὑπὸ σκήπτρῳ ἐδάμασσε (is τούς Ap.'s response to the ἀπορία of the suppressed object there, viz. 'them' rather than 'him'? See on the question Dräger 92 n.272) – from the story of Bellerophon (cf. Wilamowitz *HD* 2.235 n.1, and nn. on 230f., 422f.), and this is not the only point of similarity: cf. *Il.* 6.150-1 ~ Ap. 354-5; 154f. (Αἰολίδης; τέκεθ', τίκτεν) ~ 360f.; 158 (φέρτατος rather than

-ερος for Ap.?) ~ 347; 166 ~ 367f. (note in the sequel, *inter alia*, 215f. ~ 359f., and see 409n.).

Cf. 395 infr.

σκήπτροισι On the plur. used like this (*Index* s.v.; not otherwise in 3^H) see Chiasson, *Phoenix* 36 (1982), 159f.

δαμάσσει Cf. iv.1654. The Homeric future is asigmatic (Meister 95f., *GH* 1.448). Marxer (8-9) surmises (half-heartedly) that Ap. may have taken δαμάσσομεν in *Il.* 22.176 for a future. In fact he is partial to the type: ἀτίσσει (181n.), δικάσσει (-σ- Hom., aor. -σσ-), κομίσσω (κομιῶ Hom., aor. κόμισσα), νοσφίσσομαι (aor. -σσ- Hom.); and the Homeric ὀπάσσ- φράσσ-.

354f. 354-5 echo ii.1154-5 (Argos to Jason) εἰ δὲ καὶ οὔνομα δῆθεν ἐπιθύεις δεδαῆσθαι,/τῷδε .. πέλει οὔνομα κτλ., while 356f. borrow elements from Jason's response of ii.1160f.; but Argos stops short of spelling out a message ('since a blood-tie can be established, help from the family is in order') and leaves Aeetes to draw his own conclusions.

354-5 On the type of formula used here consult Kost on Musae. 219. At the root of this passage lies *Il.* 6.150-1 (so, for Ap., ἐθέλεις and δαήμεναι belong together); see also *Il.* 20.213f. + sequel (plenty of genealogical detail).

οὔνομα ... γενεήν τε So Call. *fr.* 178.14 ἐδάην οὔνομα καὶ γενεήν/, Triph. 290 (εἰπὲ ...) /οὔνομα καὶ γενεήν; Virg. *A.* 10.149 *memorat nomenque genusque*/, and similarly Val. Flacc. 2.468. Differently i.20-1 νῦν δ' ἂν ἐγὼ γενεήν τε καὶ οὔνομα μυθησαίμην/ἡρώων (*Il.* 21.187 /αὐτὰρ ἐγὼ γενεὴν ...; id. 7.128 ... ἐρέων γενεήν τε ...; Hes. *WD* 10 ἐγὼ δέ κεν ... μυθησαίμην/; *Il.* 3.235 (κεν ..) γνοίην καί τ' οὔνομα μυθησαίμην/ (see on this verse Apthorp, *ZPE* 82 (1990), 18f.); *GVI* 1431.3 (Athens, 2nd cent. AD) γενεήν τε καὶ οὔνομα −∪∪−×), ii.762-3 γενεὴν καὶ οὔνομ' ἑκάστου/.. μυθεῖθ', whence Q.S. 7.234 /μυθεῖτ' .. γενεὴν καὶ οὔνομ' ἑκάστου/.

δῆθεν εἰ δῆθεν is the same as εἰ δή, 'if indeed,' 'if really': Argos speaks politely, not wishing to be seen to be pushy (Aeetes *does* want the information of course: 315-6), as in ii.1154 (cited above) ~ 1139. δῆθεν occasionally in Hellenistic verse: Ap. 8×, and Arat. 101, Call. *Hec. fr.* 70.8 (~ Ap. ii.384) and *fr.* 384.21 (?: Pfeiffer, Addenda II, p. 121); thereafter I think only Eudoc. *Cypr.* 2.263.

ἐπιθύεις Cf. ii.1154 (above), and i.1238. Whether or not ἐπιθύουσι + infin. (*GHD* 49, Schulze *QE* 339-40) means *be bent on* in *Il.* 18.175 (μέμονεν 176 cf. Ap. 351; Zenodotus eliminated the infinitival construction: Erbse 1953.164, Rengakos 1993.62-3), that is clearly the sense intended in *HyHerm* 475. A stronger version of the ἐθέλεις of *Il*. 6.150/ 20.213 (above); cf. supr. 332.

γενεήν ../ἴδμεναι Homer has /ἴδμεν ... γενεήν *Il*. 20.203 and sim.; ctr. *Il*. 13.728 ἐθέλεις -ίδμεναι.

355 οἵτινές εἰσιν *Od*. 3.70 (about ξεῖνοι), 17.363; similarly i.962-3 ... ἠδὲ γενέθλην/ἔκλυον οἵτινες εἶεν. Compare Aeetes in [Orph.] *A*. 820.

ἕκαστά .. μυθησαίμην Shaped like *Od*. 13.191 (ὄφρα ....) ἕκαστά τε μυθήσαιτο/. γε or (Brunck, and independently van Herwerden 115, Headlam 110) κε? If confronted with a lacuna we would automatically supply κε: cf. κε μυθησαίμην/ in *Od*. 21.193, and also i.20, Hes. *WD* 10 (West ad loc.), etc. But γε (emphatic, each and every detail: *GP* 120; Argos is eager to oblige – at last!) is almost certainly sound: so e.g. Wåhlin 21, Vian ed. 1961, Ardizzoni, Chantraine 1962.314. The optative finds a parallel in *Il*. 15.45 παραμυθησαίμην ('would be inclined, willing to'), cf. Leaf ad loc., *GHD* 272, *GH* 2.216 (comparing ἄν + optat. in *Il*. 9.417).

356f. Cf. Jason in Val. Flacc. 5.477f. Theme of 'genealogy in support of φιλία': Wilkins on Eur. *Hcld*. 207f.

356 οἷό περ οὕνεκ' Similarly i.1325 (Heracles/Polyphemus: Hylas) οἷό περ οὕνεκ' ἀποπλαγχθέντες ἔλειφθεν/. οὕνεκα with gen. also infr. 370: first in Solon, *IEG* 36.1 and 26; 3[H]: Theoc. 11.30. Ctr. *Od*. 3.140 τοῦ (neut.) εἵνεκα .. ἄγειραν/ (μυθείσθην ibid. cf. Ap. 355).

οἷο *whose* never in archaic epic; prompted here perhaps by the association of οἷο with εἵνεκα in *Od*. 15.251 al.

ἀφ' Ἑλλάδος Also ii.1141, iii.375; common in later verse. Hellas: 13n.

ὦλλοι 176n.

ἄγερθεν *Il*. 23.287 v.l., see Allen/Erbse schol. ad loc., *LfgrE* s. ἀγείρω schol. and p. 56.54-7.

357 κλείουσ' 246n. Ctr. κλεῖον ... υἷα/ in ii.163.

Αἴσονος υἱὸν ... [Hes.] *fr*. 40.1 /Αἴσων, ὃς τέκεθ' υἱὸν Ἰήσονα, Anon. *TGF* 188c Αἴσονος υἱὸς Κρηθέως ἀφ' αἵματος.

'Son of Aeson' must have figured in many an epic *Argonautica*. Patterns in Ap.: (1) (foot 2 ...) Αἴσονος υἱός (a) in a formula prefacing a speech: i.331, 899, 1336, ii.410 (/ἥρως), 885, 1134; (b) otherwise:

iii.1380. (2) Claus. Αἴσονος υἱός 443 infr. For (1)(b) cf. Q.S. 12.267; for (2) cf. [Orph.] A. 305, 491 codd., 1176. Other configurations: id. 989 ~ 1016; 65 ~ 297 (see Vian on 130).

-α Κρ- On the quantity of the end-syllable see Fantuzzi 159 n.16.

358f. Cf. on 354f. Argos echoes Jason's earlier pronouncement, ii.1160 ἦ ἄρα δὴ γνωτοὶ πατρώιοι ἄμμιν ἐόντες (ἰόντες Ω, *vix recte*: cf. ii.235, πέλοιτο infr. 359, and the Homeric model *Il*. 6.215-6 /ἦ ῥά νύ μοι ξεῖνος πατρώιός ἐσσι ..·/Οἰνεὺς γάρ ...), then 1162-3 Κρηθεὺς γάρ ῥ' Ἀθάμας τε κασίγνητοι γεγάασι,/Κρηθῆος δ' υἱωνὸς ἐγώ ... (γεγ. + υἱωνός: cf. infr. 366).

358 εἰ ἐτήτυμον (cf. Hopkinson on Call. *h*. 6.98-9, Stinton 238f., and εἰ ἐτεόν in *Od*. 3.122 [ref. parentage] and often; *si vera* ... in Val. Flacc. 2.559) does not carry the slightest suggestion of discourtesy, nor does it cast any doubt whatsoever on the veracity of the account. That does not stop Aeetes from throwing out a sour and barbed 'if really/genuinely' at 402.

... ἐτήτυμον ... Cf. *Il*. 13.111 /ἀλλ᾽ εἰ ... ἐτήτυμον .. ἐστιν/, *HyAp* 176 ἐτήτυμόν ἐστιν/, and for ἐτήτυμος -ον applied to descent *Od*. 4.157, i.142, Call. *fr*. 617.1; Headlam-Thomson and Garvie on Aesch. *Cho*. 948; see also Pfeiffer on Call. *fr*. 780.

ἐστι γενέθλης (-η in *Il*. 2.857 and elsewhere) The same clausula in orac. *ap*. Merkelbach, *ZPE* 88 (1991), 70 verse 3/Graf id. 92 (1992), 268, Q.S. 1.191, Greg. Naz. 461.64, Nonn. *D*. 27.190, [Apolin.] 38.27, Colluth. 299, Anon. *AP* 9.212.3 (Παιήονός ἐστι γ./). ii.521 Παρράσιον, τοίπερ τε Λυκάονός εἰσι γενέθλης is derived from *Od*. 13.130 Φαίηκες, τοίπερ τοι ἐμῆς ἔξ εἰσι γενέθλης and id. 4.232 Παιήονός εἰσι γενέθλης/.

359 Cf. *Il*. 11.382 al. /οὕτω κεν; id. 6.215-6 (n. on 358f.), a notable echo: no need for antagonism there, and no need here; and these variations on *Od*. 18.225 κ' ... -ι πέλοιτο/: iv.536 κεν ... -ι πέλοιτο/, iii.494 κεν ὕμμι .. -ι πέλοιτο/, 784 ἂν .. ἄμμι πέλοιτο/. — Cf. the use of optat. + ἄν in Eur. *Hcld*. 212.

οὕτω So *sic* in Virg. *A*. 8.142 (140 'if we put any trust in what we have heard,' cf. ἐτήτυμον 358), Aeneas to King Evander (see Clausen 119-20); Ov. *Met*. 13.28.

γνωτός *blood-relative*, cf. ii.1160 cited above; in i.165 of a brother (cf. Call. *h*. 1.58), i.53 a half-brother (cf. Call. *fr*. 110.52); on Homeric usage see *LH*/*LfgrE* s.v., and cf. Rengakos 1992.35.

360 Argos continues in the severe genealogical mode: [Hes.] *fr.* 10(a) 25-6 /Αἰολίδαι δ' ἐγένοντο .../Κρηθεὺς ἠδ' Ἀθάμας καὶ Σίσυφος ~ Eur. *fr.* 14.3 Αἰόλου δὲ Σίσυφος Ἀθάμας τε Κρηθεύς τε. On Athamas see VDB 1.11.

ἄμφω γάρ = *Il.* 18.329 etc.; also in iv.1769.

υἷες υἷε E, but cf. i.87, 176; clearly a conjecture: cf. VDB 2.125, on iii.496. υἷε (not otherwise in 3^H) in Ap.: only where metre disallows plur. (ctr. Hom.), i.118, 163, iv.81, 1465, 1483.

361 Φρίξος Argos rounds off his review of the Aeolid line with a mention of the man who had married one of Aeetes' daughters. The motif of an appeal to family ties with reference to Phrixus had been deployed in far different circumstances by Pindar, *P.* 4.160f.

δ' αὖτ' ... πάϊς = *Od.* 1.399 = 2.177, but not in genealogical discourse.

πάϊς Αἰολίδαο Similar clausulae in archaic epic are to be found at *Il.* 19.123, [Hes.] *fr.* 70.35; cf. *Il.* 13.698.

... Αἰολίδαο The link is not one that is going to bring Aeetes any joy: 335n.

Ctr. *Od.* 11.237 (... δὲ Κρηθῆος: cf. Ap. 358) γυνὴ ἔμμεναι (cf. Ap. 362) Αἰολίδαο/.

362-3 It may be that, despite the extraordinary productivity of a number of Greek gods, Argos considers that Aeetes *must* have heard of such a close relative. If he does, he is not prepared to speak with total assurance; he had been similarly tentative with the Argonauts at ii.1142 (δοκέω που ἀκούετε κτλ.).

On the articulation see Wifstrand 1929.92 (no punctuation at the close of 362). 'If you hear that there exists [have heard of the existence of: for the tense see Gow on Theoc. 15.23] a certain offspring of Helios <called Augeias>, it is Augeias that you are gazing at, here in front of you' (Aeetes will have directed his attention to the latter as Argos pointed to him). There is a close parallel for this sequence in Phil. *GPh* 3066 τὸν ἐκ Σινώπης εἰ κλύεις Δαμόστρατον then 3068 τοῦτον δέδορκας: cf. *hic tibi* in Stat. *Ach.* 1.732. For the use of ἀκούειν (so *audire* e.g. Ov. *Met.* 10.560) cf. iv.1560, and Call. *fr.* 64.5 εἴ τιν' ἀκούει[ς/ with Pfeiffer ad loc. + his Addenda, p. 500 (Greg. Naz.) and p. 502 (on 94): but add Eryc. *GPh* 2246 (see Page there; resembles iv.1560); Greg. Naz. 1462.143 (εἴ τιν' ἀκούεις/); Colluth. 70/72, 278 and 280-1 (~ 284: cf. Ap. 364).

Augeias: see on 196f. Son of Helios (i.172f.): VDB 1.247 (on i.175), Gow on [Theoc.] 25.54 (whence [Orph.] *A*. 214). Argos here recalls his own observation on Aeetes: ii.1204 /στεῦται δ' Ἠελίοιο γόνος ἔμμεναι. Any hopes he may be entertaining of a glimmer of interest will soon be dashed: Aeetes will make no attempt to acknowledge his relation (who in any case is clearly there in a subordinate capacity – the king deals directly with Jason alone) and indeed will let it be known that he does not necessarily believe what he has been told (402).

γόνον ἔμμεναι Based on *Od*. 18.218 (... φαίη) γόνον ἔμμεναι ὀλβίου [cf. 1.174?] ἀνδρός/.

εἴ τιν' ἀκούεις Cf. in archaic epic *Od*. 15.403 (τις ... -αι,) εἴ που ἀκούεις/, *HyAphr* 111 (named father).

δέρκεαι Not idly chosen: see Campbell 1974.44 n.19; the verb often of Helios himself of course: cf. e.g. Mugler, *REG* 73 (1960), 67.

363 Τελαμών See on 196f.
ὅδε ὅγε Ω: *correxi* (1971.416-7).
κυδίστοιο The hero who attracts this particular epithet in *Il*./*Od*. is Agamemnon king of men: he has close links with its other male recipient, Zeus king of the gods. An apt choice then for the Zeus-born king Aeacus.

364 Αἰακοῦ ἐκγεγαώς ... A similar sequence earlier in i.208 /Ναυβόλου ἐκγεγαώς, ξεῖνος δ' ... The line as a whole is based on *Il*. 21.189 (Achilles, boasting) ... Αἰακίδης· ὁ δ' ἄρ' Αἰακὸς ἐκ Διὸς ἦεν/; note too [Hes.] *fr*. 205.1 (Aegina) τέκεν Αἰακόν, Eur. *IA* 699 Ζεύς· Αἰακὸν δ' ἔφυσεν, Ov. *Met*. 13.25-8.

There is no suggestion in the poem that Zeus fathered *Aeolus* (Eur. *Ion* 63) or had any place in the Aeolid line (details: Braswell on Pind. *P*. 4.167(d)): in Ap. Zeus is a remote figure whose displeasure at Athamas' treatment of Phrixus is not keyed to a strictly personal interest. In any case, Ap. wants an *Aeacid* there for a particular purpose: 382-5n.

αὐτὸς ἔτικτεν Ctr. *Il*. 22.428. αὐτός means 'none other than': Bühler on Mosch. *Eur*. 12(c).

365-6 True in the sense that the Argonauts *collectively* could be termed /ἀνδρῶν ἡρώων θεῖος στόλος i.970 *et sim*., ἡμίθεοι (cf. Braswell on Pind. *P*. 4.12(b), 13, 169-87, and also Clauss 1990.138 n.22) /*semidei*, and 'sons/offspring of gods' (e.g. iv.1383, 1389 with Livrea ad loc.,

1773 corr., Catull. 64.23, Sen. *Med.* 227, Val. Flacc. 1.1 al.); Herter *JAW* 280.

As it happens, Argos has made Jason the exception (cf. 364n., Zeus/Aeolus!), though he is not of course the only one (VDB 1.7, Levin 30) – not that Aeetes is bothered about such niceties (402, n.b. plural ἐστε).

For the language employed cf. (1) *Il.* 21.371 ὅσσον οἱ ἄλλοι πάντες, ὅσοι Τρώεσσιν ἀρωγοί (cit. Svensson 45); Theoc. 22.178 [176n.] with id. 13.17 οἱ δ' αὐτῷ (Jason) ἀριστῆες συνέποντο/. (2) *Il.* 2.665-6 οἱ ἄλλοι/ υἱέες υἱωνοί τε (~ iv.277), and *Od.* 24.515, *GVI* 264.6 (Batanaea, 2nd cent. AD), 109.2 (Rome, 4th cent. AD?). (3) *Il.* 16.449 /υἱέες ἀθανάτων. (4) Nonn. *D.* 5.292 /υἱωνὸν γεγαῶτα ~ *Od.* 6.62 ... δέ ... υἷες ... γεγάασιν/.

365 ὣς δὲ καὶ ὧλλοι On this run see Campbell on Q.S. 12.173. ὧλλοι (176n.) forms a ring with 356 (start of the peroration).

συνέπονται Cf. Gillies here, with LSJ s.v. 1.

367 τοῖα 317n.

παρέννεπεν Here only, speak with a view to winning over: cf. 14-5n. on παραιφάμενοι, and, e.g., παραυδᾶν and παρειπεῖν; lyric source? Infr. 474 προσέννεπεν [51n.] Ἄργος; unHomeric too are Ap.'s ἐξ-, μετ- (1168n.), συν- (tmes.).

367-8 A taut piece of writing, cf. *Studies* 31; a simile might have been expected at this point to heighten the suspense: one appears at Val. Flacc. 5.519f., cf. [Orph.] *A.* 840.

ἄναξ ... /εἰσαΐων Recalled in two passages of Nonn. *D.*: 17.262-3 /εἶπεν ..., εἰσαΐων δέ/ .. ἄναξ κεχόλωτο, 44.17 ... δ' .. ἄναξ ἐπεχώσατο [the only other example of this compound] Βάκχῳ/.

ἐπεχώσατο See above along with 176f.(5)n., and cf. iv.8-9; Hom. (*Il.*) περιχώσατο, + gen.

εἰσαΐων 145n., accent 352-3n. Ctr. i.764 /εἰσαΐων then -ενέποντι. *Il.* 6.509 and 15.266 begin with κυδιόων· ὑψοῦ δὲ ...

ὑψοῦ ... ἠερέθοντο Schol. talk of (*inter alia*) 'swelling' with anger (383n.; cf. LSJ s. ἀείρω V2, and also schol. D on οἰδάνει in *Il.* 9.554: εἰς ὕψος αἴρεσθαι ποιεῖ), but the sense is rather 'was lifted on high,' 'surged high' (Mooney), seething with rage (cf. ζέω + compounds in association with θυμός and with χολή χόλος), in an uncontrollable state of agitation. Perhaps an adaptation through Homer (638n.) of a tragic model: cf. (*Studies* 31) Soph. *OT* 914-5 (Kamerbeek ad loc.) ὑψοῦ .. αἴρει θυμὸν Οἰδίπους ἄγαν/λύπαισι ..., with LSJ s. ἀείρω III1.

369-71 φῆ κτλ. External manifestations of Aeetes' anger (369a, 371) frame authorial comment on his feelings about who is most to blame. We have to wait a while for the speech to begin, as very occasionally elsewhere in the poem: the notable examples are i.886-7 ~ iii.1066-8 (less striking, because much more concisely expressed, are, e.g., iii.169-70 [n. ad loc.], 687). Comparable, and roughly comparable, instances of the technique in the Homeric poems may be elicited from Bolling's article in *CP* 17 (1922), 213f.

On φῆ introducing direct speech see 382n.

369 ἐπαλαστήσας See Kost on Musae. 202, but add *Il.* 15.21; Man. 2.183; Q.S. 5.584; Greg. Naz. 898.196 (τοῖον ἔειπεν ἔπος); Eudoc. *Cypr.* 2.461 (προσεφώνεε).

ἐπαλ- = ἐπαγανακτήσας, scil. at them (all of them, but the Phrixids in particular). The verb recurs in 557(n.), applied to the irascible Idas /δείν' ἐπαλαστήσας μεγάλῃ ὀπί, giving vent to his impotent rage/deep indignation at <their behaviour>, where δείν' perhaps takes account of the lexicographers' δεινοπαθήσας (e.g. Ap. Soph. 23.2).

ἄναξ then ἐπαλαστήσας: but Call. *h.* 4.239 δεσπότις then ἀλαστήσασα (+ speech).

369-70 The emphatic Χαλκιόπης reflects his indignation: 'and he was furious most of all with the sons of Chalciope <no less>': see infr. 605. I am not sure however that the aorist μενέηνε, 'vented his fury,' should be so lightly dismissed (the behaviour of L is interesting in this regard).

370 The word-order is no doubt designed to mirror the agitation.

τῶν .. σφε ... It was at *their* (the Phrixids') instigation [ctr. Argos' claim in 356] that they (the Argonauts) had ...

σφε 48n. σφι Ω: cf. Budé *app. crit.* at ii.1026, and Brunck's conjecture at iv.1410 [but σφι there means I think 'on their behalf,' like τοῖσιν in *Il.* 1.450 and 3.275, parallels overlooked by Platt 1920.84 and others].

οὕνεκ' 356n. In Hdt. postpositive εἵνεκα (slightly held over in *Od.* 11.438 [claus. εἵνεκα // πολλοί], as ἕνεκ' id. 24.251; more markedly in Call. *h.* 4.151) is often very distant from its substant.; examples from tragedy are assembled in Wackernagel *KS* 610-11, FJW on Aesch. *Suppl.* 1006-7 (p.300).

... ἐώλπει 'he was convinced' that; *Od.* 8.315 ... σφεας .. ἔολπα ...

-έμεν, *Il.* 19.328 ... γάρ ... ἐώλπει/. ἐόλπει (v.l. Hom.; cf. *GHD* 61, *GH* 1.480) Ω here, but not at iv.10; 3^H: [Theoc.] 25.115 ἐώλπει codd.

371 Ap. is careful to relate the ὀμμάτων ἔκλαμψις to Aeetes' present state of mind: descendants of Helios exhibit this characteristic in normal circumstances (see notably iv.726f., and VDB 2.66 n.2). He adapts *Il.* 15.607-8, the murderous Hector full of μένος (604 μεμαῶτα cf. ?μενέαινε here in 369) τὼ δέ οἱ ὄσσε/λαμπέσθην βλοσυρῇσιν ὑπ' ὀφρύσιν, choosing again (367-8n.) not to work in a simile: contrast *Il.* 19.365-6, Achilles μενεαίνων, τὼ δέ οἱ ὄσσε/ λαμπέσθην ὡς εἴ τε πυρὸς σέλας, echoed in i.1296-7 (cf. Herter *JAW* 295), iv.1543-5 (cf. Faerber 39 n.4); *Il.* 1.104 ~ μένεος 103, al.; Graz 239f.

ἐκ ... ἔλαμψεν Similarly Greg. Naz. 675.95 /αὐτὸς δ' ὄμματ' ἔλαμψε. ἐκλάμπειν not in early verse; tragic source? Cf. also iv.1437 ὄσσε δέ οἱ βλοσυρῷ ὑπέλαμπε μετώπῳ/.

οἱ ... ἱεμένοιο On the switch see *GH* 2.71f., 322f. The Apollonian examples are collected by Merkel, *Proleg.* 88-9; see also *Noten* 354f.

ἱεμένοιο ἱέμενος is usually associated with great haste or with deep longing, craving, determination, ardour; here it denotes furious impetuosity, impatience (Aeetes is most anxious to be rid of these troublemakers): A glosses with ὁρμῶντος μετ' ὀργῆς, Fränkel *Einleitung* 60. Cf. Vian 1973.95, and more generally F-G on *Od.* 22.256. Perhaps Ap. took *Od.* 2.327 thus. Van Herwerden's ὀφρύσι χωομένοιο (115) may serve as an illustration of the undisciplined approach to textual criticism.

ὄμματ' ὑπ' ὀφρύσιν Cf. Campbell on Q.S. 12.402, and on the facial expression generally Holoka, *TAPA* 113 (1983), 1f.

372-81 Faerber (99 n.4) suggested that the targets of Aeetes' fury shift (viz. 372-3 all, 374 Argonauts, 375-6 Phrixids, 377-81 all); but, details of interpretation aside, it seems unwise to scrutinise this demonstration of blind rage too closely. The speech reads like a sustained attack on the guests at his table: the whole band of conspirators *(Studies* 31) rather than just the Phrixids *(Noten* 349f.) or just the Argonauts (VDB 2.26f.). The introductory parenthesis of 369-70 elucidates his depth of feeling in relative terms (μάλιστα 'in particular'): what it does *not* do is indicate that the Phrixids are going to be the sole addressees (so Fränkel), or that his wrath is about to be deflected from them temporarily (VDB). Further discussion: PF on 367-81.

372 οὐκ ... Cf. *Studies* 105 n.13. An echo no doubt of Archil. *IEG* 19.4 ἀπόπροθεν .. ἐστιν ὀφθαλμῶν ἐμῶν (note 'tyranny' 3!), but closer to our passage is Pacuv. *trag.* 184 *non ... e conspectu* ...; cf. Headlam on Hds 8.59 for further illustration (he also recalls *Od.* 10.72: cf. 306n.). 'Eyes' (*the* curiosity in the anatomical make-up of individuals with such connexions) neatly picks up the 'eyes' of 371; see further the note on 176f.(5).

Ctr. θᾶσσον ἀπ' ὀφθαλμῶν in *Il.* 23.53, ὡς τάχιστ' ἐξ ὀμμάτων in Aesch. *Suppl.* 949.

On the indignant οὐ + future to express a command (often incorporating some word or words denoting rapidity of action) see KG 1.176-7, Barrett on Eur. *Hipp.* 212-4, Bond on id. *HF* 254.

ἀπόπροθι 313n.

λωβητῆρες Cf. *Studies* 105 n.14. As a general term of abuse, λωβητῆρες suits both Phrixids and Argonauts (*Studies* 31); this particular vocative recalls *Il.* 24.239 (target: 237, 'all the Trojans ...').

See *LH* s.v. (and Erbse on schol. *Il.* 24.239b) for this word in Homer, and the attendant glosses. Aeetes is no doubt thinking in terms of λώβας ποιοῦντες (cf. 375f.: 'workers of λώβη' is the usual sense of the substantive after Homer, for example Soph. *Ant.* 1074, Nic. *Ther.* 796, Kaibel *EG* 1007.1, 1008.1), but note also the glosses λωβᾶσθαι ἄξιοι (cf. 378f.) and ψεῦσται (cf. 381).

373 αὐτοῖσι δόλοισι 'and take your machinations with you,' cf. on 96: see 592 (Argonauts), 599f. (Phrixids) – a *Komplott* (375f., cf. *Studies* 31).

Homer in this sedes has κακοῖσι δόλοισι, *Il.* 4.339.

παλίσσυτοι 112, 306nn. Αἰάνδε [see n.] νέεσθε παλίσσυτοι in the latter line is now converted into νεῖσθ' ... παλίσσυτοι ἔκτοθι γαίης (!).

ἔκτοθι γαίης [Opp.] *Cyn.* 4.252 (so read), Nonn. *Par.* 21.51; subst. first in i.243 ~ Antim. *fr.* 72 (with verb of motion: 255n.).

Hom. ἄλλοθι γαίης/, *Od.* 2.131.

374 Cf. *Studies* 106 n.15. Lit. 'before somebody with disastrous consequences lays eyes on ...' i.e. 'before somebody bitterly rues the day he set eyes on *both* the Fleece *and* Phrixus!' (VDB reverse the last two elements; even so, the translation does not really square with the interpretation advocated in 2.66 n.4: Chuvin 331). Phrixus is dead and gone, but of course it is *Aeetes himself* who wishes that he had never set eyes on either (cf. 584f.). The language of passion can safely ignore 'hendiadys' (Vian ed. 1961, VDB above) and can do without

Fränkel's 'rational analysis' (*Noten* 350-1). Livrea's interpretation (1982.20) is singularly unconvincing. Dräger (209) just fantasizes.

It is hard to believe that this piece of ranting is directed solely at the grandsons, particularly as the question of Jason's interest in the Fleece *and* in Phrixus has just been aired (333-9, 347f.), or solely at the Argonauts – as if Argos and his brothers can be distanced from either the Fleece or the individual who brought it to Colchis.

Ap. clearly has in mind hereabouts the mocking *Od*. 17.447-8 (note τραπέζης ~ infr. 377 and the v.l. ἴδηαι): appeal for a gift, rudely rebuffed. Cf. also *Il*. 2.355 al. /πρίν τινα... and *Od*. 10.385 /πρὶν... ἰδέσθαι/. For the menacing τινα cf. *Od*. 13.427, 15.31 πρὶν .. τινα γαῖα καθέξει/..., Eur. *Andr*. 577 πρὶν κλαίειν τινα, and KG 1.662, Livrea 1977.14, Bond on Eur. *HF* 747f.

λευγαλέον 263n. An ugly word, used to good effect here.

τε See *Noten* 503 n.95, and West on Hes. *WD* 254.

δέρος 88n.

375-6 See *Studies* 31-3 for analysis/extended discussion of these (deliberately?) problematic lines. An outline (see further 375 and 376nn.):

αὐτίχ' appears to mean that the expedition set off from Hellas right away, i.e. a plot was cooked up between Phrixids and Argonauts which brought them here directly, the motive for the trip abroad now being conveniently forgotten by the irate king.

ὁμαρτήσαντες is best taken as ὁμαρτήδην ἐλθόντες (cf. ὁμιλαδόν in 596), 'having come as a joint force,' the verb combining the notion of movement with that of cooperation: see glosses in *LH* s.v., and 375n.

'From Hellas' sounds wild (VDB 2.26f.) in the light of Chalciope's observations in 260f., Aeetes' own in 306f., and the plain facts; the spluttering Aeetes is adverting to a real enough event – in a different version (Matthews 204f.; *Studies* 32; VDB 1.170-1). This is one element in the outburst that Jason has to ignore.

In 375-6 Ω has οὐδ' then τε then νέεσθαι: οὐκ, δὲ, νέεσθε corr. E. The second of these is hard to resist, unless Aeetes' state of mind is held accountable for a lapse in coordination. οὐδ' may perhaps stand as a fiercely emphatic negative: cf. Vian ed. 1961; *GP* 197-8; de Vries and Verdenius, *Mnemosyne* 32 (1979), 163-4. νέεσθαι (but -ε is hardly a change) may be an indignant exclamatory infinitive (Aeetes breaks off after Ἑλλάδος; I would hesitate to call ὁμ. an 'exclamatory nominative,' a label applied to the participle in iv.60 by VDB, 3.149, mistakenly in my view): 'to think that you came here *not* to get your hands on the Fleece – no! – but on ...!' So de Mirmont, cf. in similar vein Campbell 1982.15; the forceful οὐδ' would then replace the expected introductory pronoun: Fraenkel on Aesch. *Ag.* 1662f., V. Bers, *Greek Poetic Syntax in the Classical Age* (Yale 1984), 184f. [VDB 2².27 n.6 consider altering the termination of the participle; I am sceptical.]

ἐπὶ κῶας means (*Studies* 32) 'to get the Fleece,' cf. Hdt. 7.193.2 ('aus einem Argonautenepos,' Leumann 306): on Aeetes' lips, *pace* Dräger 29 n.65, the preposition has an uncomplimentary colouring (elsewhere in the poem the neutral μετὰ κῶας is employed). He implies that even the Fleece would be taken by force, for all Argos' assurances to the contrary (351f.), if its acquisition were really an issue.

When Aeetes talks of σκῆπτρα ... it is natural to think of the Phrixids as the guilty party – if we read ahead to 596-7. But the dispossessed Jason cannot be ignored (333-4).

375 αὐτίχ' ὁμαρτήσαντες Cf. Musae. 52. Ardizzoni compared the use of ὁμαρτεῖν in *Il.* 12.400 and *Od.* 21.188 (spelling: F-G ad loc., Barrett on Eur. *Hipp.* 1194-7; see in general Szemerényi, *Glotta* 33 (1954), 264f.), where the sense is 'act, move in unison, jointly,' in the latter case linked with βῆσαν, cf. νέεσθ- here, and see Gow on [Theoc.] 25.192. I see no merit in his proposal, taken up by VDB (and by VDB 2².27, with an altered translation), that this verb should be dissociated from ἀφ' Ἑλλάδος: a pause after ὁμαρτήσαντες does not naturally suggest itself, αὐτίχ' is then oddly isolated, and the forward transference of the element 'from Hellas' drains away much of its impact. Aeetes' point, I believe, is that the whole party set off without further ado from the homeland of Phrixus with no thoughts of the κτέανα – and no thoughts of the Fleece either!

Wilamowitz (*HD* 2.250) suggested that a verse has dropped out containing a run-up to 375: ? '<You Phrixids (with no thoughts for your patrimony) are approaching us in league with them,> having ...' Aeetes however goes on to show that he is not wholly in command of syntax; and 375-6 for me have an air of completeness, even if one or two uncertainties remain.

ἀφ' Ἑλλάδος 356n. On E's desperate ἐφ' Ἑλλάδα see schol. J (with αὖθις for αὐτίχ' into the bargain: cf. Fränkel *Einleitung* 86): the idea here is to get the addressees *back to* Hellas (remove, or lighten, punctuation at end of 374); cf. the optat. -ήσαιτε in J². If you think that bizarre, look at Brunck's note on 375 (Wellauer is good on this).

ἐπὶ κῶας See 375-6n., and Braswell on Pind. *P.* 4.178(d). I do not know what induced Livrea (1982.20) to speak of 'inconcinnitas' in this connexion.

Fränkel (*Noten* 349f.) insists that οὐδ' ἐπὶ κῶας can only be directed at the Phrixids. It is true that Aeetes goes on to deal (seriously) with *Jason*'s desire to take the Fleece away with him, but that is only when the question has been raised again by Jason – and by then Aeetes has cooled down, and is prepared to do a deal, on his own terms. For the moment the king, beside himself with rage, represents the approach as a conspiracy. (401f. and 434f. bristle with sarcasm and contempt. It is absurd to argue that the present outburst is so vitriolic that the Argonauts cannot be reckoned among the intended targets: *Noten* 350.)

376 σκῆπτρα ... τιμήν A weighty combination ('separates': *Il.* 18.505 /σκῆπτρα δέ, id. 3.459 καὶ τιμήν, same sedes): compare Prometheus of the great god Zeus, *PV* 171 σκῆπτρον τιμάς τ' ἀποσυλᾶται. Again, but in reverse order, infr. 596-7.

τιμὴν βασιληΐδα In Homer (*Il.* 6.193; second foot ...) τιμῆς -ίδος (the Bellerophon-story: handed over willingly by king!), in Hesiod (*Theog.* 462, 892, both 'threatening' situations) the clausula -ίδα τιμήν, which was to prove quite popular: Isyll. *CA* 64; [Orph.] *fr.* 101.2, cf. the supplement in *Deru. Pap.* column XI.13; Man. 1.1; Greg. Naz. 443.57, 1376.329; orac. *ap.* D.S. 8.29 and 35.13 (PW 71.3 and 431.1); *Or. Sib.* 3.120, 8.201; Kaibel *EG* 1028.53.

δεῦρο νέεσθαι (?) A clausula in *Od.* 16.132 (where infin. = imperat.). VDB's observation (2.28) that the verb is unlikely to refer to the Phrixids alone has some force; but it is apt enough in the context of an alleged concerted effort.

Schol. LJ on νέεσθαι: ἀπὸ κοινοῦ τὸ ἔολπα (see on this Wendel 1932.24, 38-9; VDB 2.27 n.1); cf. *Studies* 106 n.17. This is clearly an attempt (inspired by ἐώλπει, or rather ἐόλπει in Ω at 370: cf. Wendel, *Schol. app. crit.*, p. 231.2) to explain the troublesome infinitive. ἀπὸ κοινοῦ means that it is shared by two clauses, that is to say, either 370 + 376 (amounting to 'supply ἔολπα from above') or, more likely, 375 + 376: 'I believe you came not by any means to get the Fleece, but <I believe you came to get>' the throne.

Further discussion: Cantarella, *RIGI* 10 (1926), 54; Livrea 1982.20 (who takes a pessimistic view of the text's condition).

377f. See *Studies* 31. Aeetes here addresses all the newcomers, as he has done all along. Is is hardly relevant that the Phrixids had eaten at Aeetes' table on past occasions (and so cannot be included here): the whole embassy has enjoyed his hospitality on this. Compare 301/302, host questions Phrixids after meal.

We are reminded then in no uncertain terms that Aeetes does indeed, despite the vile talk issuing from his lips at this moment, have regard for the laws of hospitality (cf. VDB 2.28; Beye 1982.131, but he gravely misjudges the tone of this passage) – not that he can bring himself to appeal to Zeus Xenios openly. Jason's declaration of 192-3, less than whole-hearted as it was, has proved to be valid in this particular case. But from this point on things begin to go really wrong, with no breach of etiquette on Aeetes' part.

377/379 Cf. *Studies* 106 nn.18 and 19. More ragged syntax. κε strictly speaking has no place in a condition of this kind. In i.197f. εἴ κ' ἔτι .... μετετράφη Apollonius imitates the eccentric and isolated Homericism /εἰ δέ κ' ἔτι .. γένετο at *Il.* 23.526. Here the 'bad grammar' is born of a fusion of various Homeric elements housed in a novel context: *Il.* 1.137 al. /εἰ δέ κε μὴ ..., id. 21.567 /εἰ δέ κέ οἱ προπάροιθε ..., *Od.* 10.354 -η προπάροιθε .. -ε τραπέζας/, id. 17.447 [above on 374] ἐμῆς ἀπάνευθε τραπέζης/. On the construction see, besides the standard grammars, Gow on Theoc. 2.118-28; Howarth, *CQ* n.s. 5 (1955), 86f. (*Il.* 23.526 is best regarded as a clumsy reworking of the run at id. 490 ... κε .. προτέρω ἔτ' .. γένετ' ἀμφοτέροισιν/. εἰ δέ κ' ἔτι προτέρω may have been a ready-made *incipit*, cf. *Od.* 5.417. Chantraine, *GH* 1.283, suspects corruption, surely wrongly.)

As for the apodosis, the incensed Aeetes indulges in a further lapse: 377 'if you had not *first* ...' is followed up with 'I would *have* ...' rather than with 'I would ...'

377 ἐμῆς ἤψασθε τραπέζης Nonnos has a number of similar runs (see Vian on *D.* 2.668), e.g. *D.* 26.374, 40.237 μιῆς ἥπτοντο (ἥψαντο) τραπέζης/, 33.381 ἐμῆς ψαύσαντα τραπέζης/. Cf. as well Pampr. *fr.* iv22 μι]ῆς ἥπτοντο τραπέζης/ (see McCail, *JHS* 98 (1978), 46, Livrea, *RFIC* 106 (1978), 284).

On the table, a powerful symbol of hospitality, see *AH* P58, and Gould 79 n.35.

378-9 *Homerica*: Il. 5.292 (weapon in battle) ἀπὸ .. γλῶσσαν .. τάμε; *Od.* 12.442, 23.87 καὶ χεῖρε + *Il.* 21.115-6 (n.b. the grisly sequel), *Od.* 24.397-8 χεῖρε πετάσσας/ἀμφοτέρας (ἀμφοτέρας here is a grim addition: 'yes, both of them'; on enjambement involving this word see

COMMENTARY 381

Mineur on Call. *h.* 4.107f.). Cf. also (*Studies* 106 n.21) *Od.* 22.475-7 (punishment of goatherd), and the threat of id. 18.85-7, involving the ὑβριστὴς Ἔχετος of iv.1093, conjured up to illustrate Aeetes' cruel streak; *Il.* 21.453f.; the hybristic Pentheus later in Nonn. *D.* 45.75f. I suspect however that we are dealing here with a reflection of a stage Aeetes also, for this talk of dire mutilation accords well with representations of barbarian behaviour in tragedy: see e.g. E. Hall, *Inventing the Barbarian* (Oxford 1989), 158-9.

Cutting out of the tongue: Headlam on Hds 6.41.

... ταμών See on 176f.(5).

κεάσσας *chop off*: ἀπό does double duty, as in *Od.* 22.475-6 (above) ἀπὸ .../τάμνον, then /χεῖρας ... κόπτον 477. In ii.104 κεάσθη is used of a warrior's head split in two by a sharp blade; cf. *Il.* 16.411-2 and *LfgrE* s.v. κεάσσαι 2. See too n. on 176f.(5).

379 οἴοισιν .. πόδεσσιν A gruesome adaptation of /οἴοισιν .. ποσίν in *Od.* 8.230 (racing). For the dative compare τοῖς, that is to say πόδεσσιν [*sic* !], in *Od.* 20.367.

ἐπιπροέηκα Seen by VDB (2.26, cf. already Vian ed. 1961) as a pointer to the identity of the addressees: they would have been sent as messengers *to* (ἐπι-) *their companions* after being mutilated; the meaning could equally well be 'to <the rest of the band of conspirators>' (cf. ὅμιλον in 434: Argos leaves with the three Argonauts, and Aeetes makes no move to stop him).

It is better however to articulate as ἐπιπρο-, 'in a forward direction,' i.e. 'pitch head first,' 'send packing' (*Studies* 106 n.19). So for sure iv.1617, '*sent* the ship travelling *straight on*, into the sea,' cf. *Il.* 17.708 'I have sent him *out, on his way*, to the ships,' and id. 18.58 = 439 (not 'against' <the enemy>, as Edwards ad loc.).

D (see Speake 1969.92/1975.110, Speake and Vian, *GRBS* 14 (1973), 310 n.16) offers a blander compound: ἀποπροέηκα (con. van Herwerden 115, comparing *Od.* 14.26; accepted by Fränkel OCT).

380 ἐρητύοισθε Ap. alone among 3[H] poets uses both this verb (i.171, ii.835) and ἐρύκειν (i.346 al.) with infin. in the sense *prevent from*. Neither is Homeric: see Merkel *Proleg.* 177-8, McLennan 49.

καὶ ὕστερον ὁρμηθῆναι, scil. δεῦρο, is lifted from *Il.* 14.313 κεῖσε μὲν ἔστι καὶ ὕστερον ὁρμηθῆναι/, cf. *Od.* 12.126 (where ὁρμ. has an aggressive colouring, as here), μιν .. ἀποπαύσει ἐς ὕστερον ὁρμηθῆναι/.

381 Call. *fr.* 85.12 π]ολλά τε καὶ μακάρεσσιν ἀπεχ[θέα ... then]π ι.

οἷα ... for ὅτι τοῖα, (380) 'so that ..., and because ... such things,' the incorporation of δὲ καί being eased by the compression. 380 amplifies the point about 'hands' in 378, 381 harks back to 'tongues' ibid. So Wifstrand 1929.92-3 (rightly dismissing Platt's interpretation, 1914.30-1), cf. VDB 2.123, and see id. 3.170-1 for examples of dissymmetry in coordinated clauses.

Alternatively (and less fluently, though that is not necessarily a bad thing), οἷα may be regarded as exclamatory (cf. οἷον δέ in Ar. *Pax* 33); in that case, print a dash at the end of 380. The run οἷα δὲ καί ('as well') recurs in iv.1091, and there οἷα is definitely exclamatory.

However the lines are analysed, the sense is the same. The newcomers would have been prevented from embarking on such an aggressive enterprise again (scil. with a view to laying hands *on his throne*, 375f.); *and* they have told lies *against the gods* into the bargain (καί: hardly 'even,' as Mooney and others), so meriting the loss of their organs of speech.

μακάρεσσιν .. θεοῖσι Closed up in Homer, as claus., *Il.* 1.599 etc. But i.507 μακάρεσσι θεοῖς, = *Il.* 5.819 al.

ἐπεψεύσασθε means 'tell lies against' ('about' is too bland); cf. from contemporary poetry -επιψεύσονται scil. dat. pers. = goddess in Call. *h.* 3.223.

See *Studies* 106 n.16. I doubt if this line has anything to do with 336-9, as has sometimes been supposed (Fränkel *Noten* 349 adds the reference to Zeus in 328 and the claim made about Athena in 340f.). As a parting-shot Aeetes recalls the close of Argos' speech where divine ancestry is claimed for the Argonauts as a body (Argos, note, cannot be excluded as a target here: he is as implicated as anybody, *Studies* 31): he finds this hard to swallow, as 402f. plainly show (there the themes of divine pedigree and seizure, implicit here in 380-1, are presented in reverse). Cf. Gillies' commendably lucid note.

382f. Telamon: see on 196f. Here is one way of dealing with Aeetes, but it cannot be tried: the loaded ὀλοόν in 384 says it all. Telamon's fiery temperament will find a different outlet, 515f.; in 1174, his last solo appearance in the poem, ἀρηίφιλος Τελαμών is one of the two ambassadors sent on a purely formal errand to Aeetes.

382/385 HyDem 145 /φῆ ῥα θεά, τὴν δ' .. ἀμείβετο ... Cf. also, in speech-closure, Hes. *Theog.* 550 /φῆ ῥα δολοφρονέων, infr. 693, variation /φῆ ἄρα 718. On φῆ so used see Lehrs 96-7, Richardson on *HyDem* loc. cit./Hopkinson on Call. *h.* 6.45, adding iii.154, and, for φῆ introducing direct speech, iii.369, Timo Phl. *SH* 840.1, Theoc. 17.65, Epic. adesp. *CA* 4.1.

φῆ ῥα closes a speech in Π⁴⁰ (3rd cent.) at *Il.* 3.355, West *PP* 56. Ctr. *Od.* 11.538 /ὣς ἐφάμην, .. δὲ .. Αἰακίδαο/...

382 χαλεψάμενος 97n. Aeetes has expressed his anger at what he considers to be gross provocation.

382-5 Not 'Telamon' but 'the Aeacid': with the clausula of 382 Ap. evokes memories of the Aeacid *Achilles*, whose temper brought ruin in its wake (cf. ὀλοόν): *Il.* 9.184 μεγάλας φρένας Αἰακίδαο/. On top of that:

(1) *Il.* 9.646 (Achilles speaking) ... μοι οἰδάνεται κραδίη χόλῳ (so in the famous *exemplum* of Meleager: 9.553-4 ... χόλος, ὅς τε .../οἰδάνει ἐν στήθεσσι νόον ...).

(2) ἀντιβίην of violent face-to-face confrontation: *Il.* 1.278 ref. Achilles with the king. With ... ἔπος cf. id. 1.304 ἀντιβίοισι .. ἐπέεσσιν/ of the same pair, sim. 2.378 (+ χαλεπαίνων, the king: note χαλεψάμενος here).

(3) I have a strong feeling that we are also meant to recall the celebrated scene of Athena's intervention in the Achilles-Agamemnon dispute: 1.173f. Agamemnon: 'Clear off!' and so on; 188 ὣς φάτο, Πηλείωνι δ' ἄχος γένετο, ἐν δέ οἱ ἦτορ κτλ. [cf. infr. 396f.!]; then, 194f., but Athena arrived to stop him, πρὸ γὰρ ἧκε θεὰ κτλ. Here *not* ἀλλ' ἀπέρυκεν/Ἥρη [= iv.509-10! On the associations of (ἀπ)ερύκειν with *divine* activity see 250-2n.]. —

Telamon has already assumed the role of the younger-born *Aeacid* (cues in i.1301, 1330) in i.1296f. (see for some comments Beye 1982.87, Hunter 1988.44), but only fleetingly. *Jason* vows not to get caught up in μῆνις (i.1339), in this context undeniably ἡ ἐπιμένουσα ὀργή, as a result of conduct arising from a fit of temper (viz. *Telamon's* χόλος, described in less than a hemistich at i.1289). The 'irony' of which Beye speaks (irony is pervasive in this passage) must relate to the responses of the φιλόμηρος reader.

382-3 μέγα δὲ ... After *Il.* 1.103 and *Od.* 4.661 (compare later *Vis. Doroth.* 138/139) ... δὲ μέγα φρένες –⏑⏑–× (heralding angry outburst); *Il.* 9.184 (above). Similarly iv.92-3 ἴσκεν ἀκηχεμένη· μέγα δὲ φρένες Αἰσονίδαο/γήθεον. Cf. Q.S. 9.344-5 ... δὲ μέγα .../θυμὸν ἀνοιδήσαντο (Bissinger 246).

383 νειόθεν Homeric hapax (*Il.* 10.100, ref. warrior Agamemnon, followed up with φρένες ἐντός ~ Greg. Naz. 1367.198, 1453.20), also in the fragmentary Archil. *IEG* 89.14-5 θυμὸς [.../νειόθεν (? cf. Ap. i.1288-9). Ap. may have derived his fondness for the word (9 ×; not otherwise in 3^H) from Aratus: 234, 568, 659, 708.

It is interesting that Cicero at *Tusc.* 3.9.18 (~ p. 75 Morel) renders οἰδάνεται in *Il.* 9.554 (below) with *penitus turgescit*.

οἰδαίνεσκον Supply χόλῳ (as we may supply ἐκ κραδίης with the preceding adverb, from *Il.* 10.100), cf. Cunningham on οἰδῆσαι in Hds 4.49, Jocelyn, *PCPS* n.s. 16 (1970), 43, *Il.* 9.553-4 (~ i.478), 646 (above on 382-5), and the Hesychian (094) οἰδαίνεσθαι· θυμοῦσθαι. Hence no doubt Val. Flacc. 5.521 *tumet*. This verb first in Arat., 909 (see on νειόθεν above; iii.383 from one of his *Medica*??); later verse: Androm. *GDK* 62.29, 98; Opp. *Hal.* 1.772 (~ Arat.), al.; Greg. Naz. 1268.87; [Orph.] *A*. 365 *codd*.; Nonn. *Par.* 18.4 and *D*. 10 × (48.371 οἰδαίνοντι χόλῳ). οἰδαίνεσθαι crops up in schol. T's note on οἰδάνει in *Il.* 9.554.

The frequentative, unless it has an intensive (according to Gillies, inceptive) function, suggests that Telamon was having something of a struggle to restrain himself (cf. ἐέλδετο, 'was longing'). He did not explode there and then (ctr. i.1289), but might have done so before too long, had not Jason cut in. If this is what is envisaged, then here is another example of Apollonian economy: ? a stunned silence, with the angry Telamon entertaining murderous thoughts: but before his thoughts were translated into words, disaster was averted ...

ἐέλδετο ... θυμός Q.S. 13.277 ἔλδετο θυμός, otherwise θυμὸς ἐέλδεται *Od.* 15.66, Hes. *WD* 381, Q.S. 14.441, θυμός .. ἐέλδεται *Od.* 18.164, and /θυμὸς ἐέλδετο Q.S. 13.224. Clausula ἔνδοθι θ.: *Od.* 2.315, 19.377, infr. 1009, [Apolin.] 108.45.

384 ἀντιβίην 382-5n.; (ἐν)αντίβι(ος) often of *open* hostility. An expressive adverb (the recurrent gloss ἐξ ἐναντίας, cf. *LfgrE* s.v. schol., Henrichs 140 n.15, does not do it full justice): in *Il.* 1.278 the poet ἐπήνεγκε τὸ ἀντιβίην, τὸ μετὰ βίας καὶ φιλονεικίας δηλῶσαι θέλων, schol. T at 277-8. Elsewhere in the *Argonautica* it is employed in a strictly martial context: i.1002, ii.758, iv.409.

ὀλοὸν .. ἔπος ὀλοός often = holding out a positive prospect or threat or suggestion of ruin, destruction, annihilation (cf. ὀλοὰ φρονέων, ὀλοόφρων, 'with murderous thoughts/intentions,' sim.): ὀλοόν then complements ἀντιβίην and points to Telamon's desire to give voice to his murderous thoughts. There is also a suggestion that such a step would have been fatal (cf. Aeetes without such provocation in 398): so e.g. Vian ed. 1961, 'qui aurait été funeste.' See also *Od.* 9.302-3 [and Jason's pronouncement in iv.401-2], with the note on 176f.(6). The same layers of meaning are present in iv.410 οὐλοὸν ἔκφατο μῦθον/ (not 'horrible' VDB, sim. 'tremenda' PF): with Apsyrtus' projected murder Medea is herself (along with others) on the road to ruin (cf. iv.445-9: 446 οὐλόμεναι 'spelling death'; ἔριδες also looks far into the future). See also Q.S. 12.552, Campbell ad loc.

φάσθαι ἔπος So *Il.* 9.100 (θυμός 101), *Od.* 17.584; iv.1200 (see Fantuzzi 69 with n.50). φάσθαι/φᾶσθαι: VDB I.LXXVI; La Roche *HTA* 373. *Od.* 21.194 φάσθαι (scil. ἔπος, 193) .. με θυμὸς ἀνώγει/.

384-5 ἀλλ'... 382-5n. Cf. also i.494, iv.187, Jason exercising a restraining influence.

385 πρὸ γὰρ ... Similarly i.1245-6 οὐδ' ἐπέκυρσε/ποίμνῃσιν, πρὸ γὰρ αὐτοὶ ... There is little or no point in wondering whether the temporal πρό there, or here (προαμείβεσθαι does occur, though not in the sense 'respond prior to ...') or elsewhere (ii.1043, iii.1198, iv.84 ['by this time' rather than 'out into the open'], 560) is adverbial or *in tmesi;* but πρό in iii.1174 must be adverbial. Homeric usage: *LH* 2.225, LSJ s.v. C.

αὐτός *Od.* 20.165f. /αὐτὸς ... προσηύδα μειλιχίοισι·/"ξεῖν' ...

ἀμείψατο See n. on 31 (ἀμείβετο μ.). The aorist is natural in the wake of πρό (Jason got in before any damage could be done). Only once does the aorist of this verb introduce a speech in Homer, *Il.* 4.403: *GH* 2.192, Edwards, *HSCP* 74 (1970), 22; system-builders will be tempted to emend: Riggsby, *TAPA* 122 (1992), 107 n.21. But there are further examples in our poem, though nowhere else in 3[H]: ii.255 (matching aorist of 254); 1159; 1218 (φώνησέν τε/); see *Echoes* in all three places.

μειλιχίοισιν See on ὑποδδείσας in 318, and 15, 31nn. It is now Jason's turn to try to mollify the king (his own pronouncement in Eur. *Med.* 455f. has often been compared). His μειλιχίη is a quality to be admired, not deprecated, in Ap. (thus far at least: our perceptions will change in due course) as in Pindar. We hear of μειλιχίοισι λόγοις in *P.* 4.128 (cf. Beye 1982.48, Braswell ad loc. and on 101-2(b)), and of μ. ἐπέεσσι sim. in his dealings with his mother (i.294), with Tiphys (ii.621), with Medea (iii.1002 [cf. 985] and iv.394); only in the last of these passages is μειλιχίη πολέμοιο involved (cf. 396f.), and then only indirectly and in exceptionally threatening circumstances. As Braswell noted, for Pindar Jason's μειλιχίη, which was probably part of his make-up at a very early date (ctr. Carey, *Maia* n.s. 32 (1980), 146), will have stemmed from Cheiron: add *P.* 9.43, Cheiron/Apollo, on which see Woodbury, *TAPA* 103 (1972), 572 = Woodbury 1991.242. See also 189-90n.

386-95 The reader of this poem will expect something businesslike and to the point from Jason (and certainly nothing to match Argos' verbal diarrhoea: compare Val. Flacc. 5.471f., a truly verbose Jason). In the space of ten lines (Aeetes gets back what he has delivered) he (a) offers an assurance that the king has misunderstood the expedition's purpose: its members, and notably its leader, have come under duress; (b) puts in a polite but direct request, followed up with a promise of a satisfying reward in due course as well as tangible repayment in the shorter term.

The former point is put as diplomatically as it could be. Jason naturally refrains from countering explicitly the wild claim about 'sceptre and royal office' (376) and proceeds to focus attention on the single piece of property 'belonging to somebody else' (389): that he fully acknowledges. The statement that none of them, himself included, wanted to come at all is reinforced by an appeal to forces outside his own control, but also by condemnation, explicit this time round (ctr. 333f.), of the 'king' responsible for his plight. In fact the cunning Aeetes, who has been painted in the most uncomplimentary colours by both Argos (ii.1202f.) and Hera (iii.15), and who might be expected now to react outrageously, will not allow himself to be branded an ἀτάσθαλος in this particular negotiation: the ἄεθλος *he* sets is after all one he engages in himself, apparently as a matter of routine (408). If his treatment of the stranger is strongly reminiscent in a general way of Pelias' imposition (405-6n.), Aeetes none the less does not stray beyond the bounds of δίκη, as Jason himself will have to acknowledge (427).

Jason's second step is to appeal to the king's vanity by building on Argos' flattering reference to his οὔνομα περικλεές (330-1) with a promise of glorious renown throughout Hellas (he leads a pan-Hellenic expedition: 347), perhaps akin to that enjoyed by a god (392n.): he will attend to that personally. And the offer of an instant return is extended (see 351-3) to include a national enemy of Aeetes' own choosing.

Fränkel (*Noten* 352, on 386-90) is unduly hard on Jason here. Whatever he has said about himself as leader (and he *must* get the point across that his coming was unavoidable), he is careful to guard

COMMENTARY 386-8 331

against the impression that the Argonauts are a crowd of feeble and victimised individuals: so he presses the suggestion that they would be *ready and willing* (πρόφρονες 393: a strong word) to provide a *prompt* settlement by engaging *in warfare* on an ambitious scale. The Argonauts are not aggressive — but they are willing to show their mettle if asked to do so.

386 Αἰήτη No honorific address, and no attempt either to soften the effect of the plain vocative (ctr. e.g. the reproachful Diomede in *Il.* 9.32 Ἀτρεΐδη but then ἄναξ 33); Jason matches Argos' directness (320): he is no abject suppliant.

σχέο See on this *Studies* 106 n.23. (1) There can be no objection in principle to the sequence of datives: so, for instance, with 'ethic' pronoun, *Il.* 24.716 /εἴξατέ μοι οὐρεῦσιν. But it is hard to believe that τῷδε στόλῳ is the equivalent of περὶ τοῦδε τοῦ στόλου (thus schol., and, e.g., Ardizzoni, VDB), not just because the sense required, 'as far as ... is concerned' (a use of the dative not without parallel, see e.g. Denniston on Eur. *El.* 608-9, Wilkins on id. *Hcld.* 202) here sounds extremely crabbed and awkward, but also because σχέο should be unencumbered: its parent is *Il.* 21.379 (a polite request to desist from violence) /῾Ήφαιστε, σχέο, τέκνον ἀγακλεές, then οὐ γὰρ ...; cf. Hom. σχέσθε, ἄνσχεο, ἴσχεο, -εσθ᾽. (2) With a stop after μοι and none after στόλῳ, we must accept a late γάρ (but hardly exceptionally late: τῷδε στόλῳ οὔτι: see *GP* 95f., Dover, *CQ* n.s. 35 (1985), 338f.; ἐπὶ ξηρὴ γάρ ... in iv.1394 is if anything more striking) rather than emend, as μάλ᾽ Fränkel OCT; lacuna after μοι Piñero *ap*. VDB: most implausible. Such passages as Hdt. 6.39.2 στόλῳ ἀπικόμενοι lend weight to such an articulation: Svensson 9 n.1, q.v. for extended discussion; he points to Call. *HE* 1238 ἀφανὴς οὔτι γάρ ...

τῷδε στόλῳ Cf. Aesch. *Suppl.* 461. '*This* expedition' is *not* one organised 'for warlike purposes' (LSJ s. στόλος *ad init.*). Aeetes sees it in terms of a predatory venture, Jason is at pains to allay his anxiety, without being too explicit: ctr. Val. Flacc. 5.495f., [Orph.] *A*. 829 (and Ilioneus in Virg. *A.* 1.527f.).

στόλῳ 175n.

386-8 αὔτως .... ἰέμενοι αὔτως is picked up by ὡς (LSJ s.v. αὔτως I): i.e. 'in the actual way in which you seemingly suppose [scil. as predators/usurpers] nor indeed out of a burning desire [a strong term: 371n.] <to come at all>: and who *would* ...?' Given Jason's attitude to the voyage, as opposed to that of his crew (cf. Lawall 162-

3, Vian 1978.1027), ... ἱέμενοι is less than candid. But he is of course at pains to play down any suggestion of aggression. And he does direct attention to his own position promptly enough.

387 ἄστυ τεόν 331n.

δώμαθ' ἱκάνομεν Cf. *Echoes* at i.785, and supr. 213n.

... ἱκάνομεν ... Cf. supr. 84 /οὔτι (βίης χατέουσαι) ἱκάνομεν ..., and iv.1566 (subject the Argonauts) /δεῦρο γὰρ οὐκ ἐθέλοντες ἱκάνομεν.

που ἔολπας A softened version of the heavily sarcastic /ἦ δή που μάλ' ἔολπας of *Il.* 21.583.

388 οὐδὲ μέν 'nor indeed': Verdenius on Hes. *WD* 187.

ἱέμενοι See on 386-8. Mooney's 'through covetousness' is no doubt based on the mistaken suggestion of schol. P.

388-9 τίς δ' ... Ap. draws on Hermes' visit to the welcoming Calypso (see on 108f.) in *Od.* 5, where the god, rather tetchily (for Calypso's benefit: she is soon to be 'robbed'), declares that Zeus has *instructed* him (ἠνώγει) to come 'against his will': then (99-100) τίς δ' ἂν ἑκὼν τοσσόνδε διαδράμοι ἁλμυρὸν ὕδωρ/ἄσπετον; The epithets vanish in our version, and so does Zeus of course (ctr. 389 *ad fin.*), to whom Argos has referred in his hazy account of 336f.

According to PF on 388-9, with this question (they call it an 'adynaton') Jason 'riaffirma definitivamente lo statuto antieroico della spedizione.' Not so: the point is that *nobody*, hero or otherwise (or even god: see above!) would willingly venture such a long sea-journey: there is no glittering prize lying at the other end ready for the taking. No, his presence here is due to exceptional pressures (389-90).

τίς δ' ἂν τόσον ... Eur. *Hel.* 97 τίς σωφρονῶν τλαίη τάδ' ἄν; [Opp.] *Cyn.* 4.14-5 -οι; τίς δ' ἂν τόσον ὠπήσαιτο/θνητὸς ἐών; Ctr. *Il.* 10.307, 24.565 ... κε τλαίη.

We may recall Jason's question to Phineus (the tone and substance of which are hardly to be deplored: so Lawall 163) in ii.416 (τόσην ...), on which see Bühler, ed. Mosch. *Eur.*, p. 195.

τίς δ' Dismissively, like καὶ τίς, 'and who <anyway> ...?': *GP* 173f. /309f.

τόσον οἶδμα περῆσαι Cf. Pampr. *fr.* 3.100 Livrea τόσον οἶδμα, Nonn. D. 42.102 τηλίκον οἶδμα περήσας/, and *tantum aequor* in Val. Flacc. 4.541 al. After Ap.: Colluth. 295 τέτληκα καὶ οἴδματα τόσσα περῆσαι/. For the clausula οἶδμα περ- see as well iv.457, Anon. epic. *SH* 901(A)7 (prob.), and Kost on Musae. 203-4 (p. 401) and 203 (ibid.); note earlier Soph. *Ant.* 337, Eur. *IT* 417.

οἶδμα 'waves/waters' of the sea, 'sea' (so i.183 al.): Campbell on Q.S. 12.432.

τλαίη Cf. Jason in iv.192, 1360.

ἑκών Ctr. Pind. *P.* 4.165 + sequel.

ὀθνεῖον Cf. 591 /ὀθνείοις ἐπὶ ... κτεάτεσσιν, and Man. 4.565 /ὀθνείων κτεάνων. The word, attested in the form ὀθνέος as early as Archil. *IEG* 244 (cf. Bühler, *Hermes* 96 (1968), 232f.; Renehan 1982.106) is common in Hellenistic and later verse; for some account of its previous history see Chantraine, *BSL* 43 (1946), 50f.; Bowra, *Glotta* 38 (1960), 51. In Ap. 9×: note i.869 γυναιξίν ~ Eur. *Alc.* 646, Man. 4.[493-4].

ἐπὶ κτέρας picks up Aeetes' ἐπὶ κῶας 375. κτέρας: 186n.

389-90 ἀλλά με δαίμων ... For samples of the extensive modern literature on δαίμων see O. Tsagarakis, *Nature and Background of Major Concepts of Divine Power in Homer* (Amsterdam 1977), Darcus, *Phoenix* 28 (1974), 394 n.12, and for discussion, among Homeric commentators, Hainsworth on *Il.* 9.600, Janko on id. 15.461-70, Rutherford on *Od.* 19.10; fundamental of course is Jörgensen, *Hermes* 39 (1904), 357f. 'An unspecified supernatural agency invoked as the cause of the inexplicable' Hainsworth on *Od.* 5.396 – or in this case, as the cause of something which Jason would rather not attempt to explain. Argos had indicated something of the divine background to the quest for the Fleece (336f.), and of course a particular god was the prime mover (see notably Jason to Apollo, i.414). In this situation Jason chooses (very wisely) merely to hint at divine prompting, as he throws maximum emphasis on the unacceptable behaviour of the human instigator.

In ii.249 Zetes uses δαίμων as a vague term for 'a divine power,' 'the divine apportioner,' ignorant as he is of the precise involvement of <particular> 'gods' in this sorry business. In ii.421 Phineus talks cryptically of a δαίμων who will act as guide: he means Hera, iv.294f. In iv.64 the δαίμων is Eros, who is kept out of this whimsical scene: the gravity of the σχετλιασμός in iv.445f., where the god is represented as a loathsome and destructive carrier of misery, cannot be undermined. In iv.1040 the 'heavy' δαίμων alludes to the overwhelming power of Eros [cf. e.g. Theoc. 3.15: Eros is no heavyweight, but he comes down heavily on his victims! See in general FJW on Aesch.

Suppl. 651], whom the young Medea cannot bring herself to name (not 'un sort cruel,' VDB).

δαίμων ~ imposition of ordeal(s): cf. Heracles ('speaking vaguely,' says Bond on Eur. *HF* 20f.) in *Scutum* 94 αὐτὰρ ἐμοὶ δαίμων χαλεποὺς ἐπετέλλετ' ἀέθλους. We may also recall Odysseus in (for instance) *Od.* 24.306-7, ἀλλά με δαίμων/πλάγξ' ἀπὸ Σικανίης δεῦρ' ἐλθέμεν οὐκ ἐθέλοντα, this an example of the 'short sharp shock' commonly administered in *Od.* particularly, de Jong 158f.

For the configuration of the clausula ἀλλά με δαίμων consult Campbell on Q.S. 12.255.

390 Similarly already ii.210f., Phineus of the Argonauts 'whom Jason takes in search of the Fleece κρυερῇ βασιλῆος ἐφετμῇ/.' Even now, Aeetes is none the wiser about the identity of this 'king' (see 406, 419).

κρυερή = φρικτή (cf. *LfgrE* under κρυερός, κρυόεις), bringing one out in a cold shiver. Jason had talked of the ἁλὸς κρυόεντα κέλευθα/ in connexion with the mission imposed by Pelias (ii.628: cf. i.918), and Argos had labelled the sea traversed by Jason on his quest στυγερή (349), cf. στυγέων ... in ii.628 just mentioned, and ii.412 στυγ. describing the Symplegades. See on this field of metaphor L. L. Clader, *Helen: Mnemosyne* Suppl. 42 (1976), 18f., and N. Zink, *Griechische Ausdrucksweisen für Warm und Kalt im seelischen Bereich* (Heidelberg 1962), noting also the (figurative: see Woodbury, *TAPA* 111 (1981), 239 = Woodbury 1991.378) 'Orchomenos received a shipwrecked man ἐξ ἀμετρήτας ἁλὸς ἐν κρυοέσσᾳ .. συντυχίᾳ,' Pind. *I.* 1.36f. (cf. κρυερός of a shipwrecked corpse in 'Simon.' *FGE* 980, Zonas *GPh* 3465, and of a voyage which took a corpse to Hades, Perses *HE* 2896). See further the note on 422f.

The term may have been employed in earlier *Argonautica*: Pindar (*P.* 4.73) had described an oracular response delivered to Pelias as κρυόεν ... θυμῷ.

βασιλῆος ἀτασθάλου scales down [Hes.] *Theog.* 995-6 βασιλεὺς ὑπερήνωρ,/ὑβριστὴς Πελίης καὶ ἀτάσθαλος ὀβριμοεργός, where Pelias is mentioned in connexion with the imposition of ἄεθλοι. Cf. also Pind. *fr.* 140a.56-7 βασιλῆος ἀτασθαλία. On this strongly condemnatory term see West on *Od.* 1.7, and the lit. cited in *LfgrE* s.v., Verdenius on Hes. *WD* 134. In i.480 it is applied to the impious words of the outrageous Idas, in i.815 to the fiendishly cruel stepmother, in i.1317 to <the ἀλιτήμενος> Eurystheus who imposed ἄεθλοι on Heracles; iv.1092 (which recalls Hes. *Theog.* 164) /πατρὸς ἀτασθαλίῃσι of Danae's treatment at the hands of her father (with an eye on Aeetes!). Otherwise in 3ʰ: Theoc. 22.131 [Polydeuces was no βάρβαρος] and (subst.) 7.79 (... ἄνακτος/). – Dräger (153 ~ 135 n.391, 141 n.412) argues that this and similar labels relate in early accounts to Pelias' sinful behaviour toward Hera; things change with Pindar, who represents him as a violent usurper. I doubt this; in particular, it is very hard to believe that the string of uncomplimentary epithets in [Hes.] *Theog.* 995f. did not mean to describe the brutal tyrant-type (like Eurystheus for example).

βασιλῆος ... ἐφετμή In this sedes (-αῖς, -ῇ) Greg. Naz. 500.25, Paul. Sil. *Soph.* 706. Elsewhere -ῆος ἐφετμ-/: *HyDem* 358; i.279, ii.210, 615 (all three of Pelias: no doubt an old Argonautic tag, cf. ... ἐφημοσύνῃ ... i.3); Pampr. *fr.* ιυι (suppl.); [Apolin.] 118.214, 145.9; Paul. Sil. *Soph.* 340.

... ὦρσεν ἐφετμή *Il.* 21.299 θεῶν ὄτρυνεν ἐφετμή/.

391 At long last, a direct request, on behalf of suppliants. Aeetes will either oblige, or put himself in the wrong: that is the idea anyway.

δὸς χάριν ἀντομένοισι Cf. Eur. *HF* 321 δὸς χάριν .. ἱκνούμεθα, and Nonn. *D.* 27.264, 39.178 /δὸς χάριν ἀμφοτέροισι(ν). δὸς χάριν (often addressed deferentially to gods, like δός alone: Gerbeau on Nonn. *D.* 18.41) is a common *incipit* in later verse. Hom. χάριν .. δοῖεν/, *Il.* 23.650.

ἀντομένοισι 77n.

391-2 Ap. here wittily recalls *Od.* 17.415 (wandering beggar Odysseus to Antinous, who is 'like a king') /δός, 418 ἐγὼ δέ κέ σε κλείω κατ' ἀπείρονα γαῖαν/. Cf. also id. 8.496f. (note ἐγὼ πᾶσιν ... and πρόφρων), *HyAp* 174f. (where observe /ἡμεῖς .. ὑμέτερον κλέος οἴσομεν), AHS ad loc. (on 'bargains' struck by Odysseus). A Virgilian echo: Ilioneus to Latinus in *A.* 7.231-2.

σέθεν δ' ἐγώ Homeric unit, *Il.* 1.180, 8.477, found also in Theoc. 17.135 (note context), Arch. *GPh* 3770. See in general FJW on Aesch. *Suppl.* 923.

σέθεν as possessive: 331n.

Ἑλλάδι πάσῃ A clausula in Archestr. Gel. *SH* 132, suppl. in Anon. hex. id. 904.13, *Or. Sib.* 3.537, and in epigram: *CEG* (2) 468(ii) 1 (4th cent.?), Archimelus *FGE* 97 = *SH* 202.15, *GVI* 589.1 (Syria, 3rd cent. AD?), Anon. *APl* 292.1 (κλέος). Cf. Xenoph. *IEG* 6.3 /τοῦ κλέος

Ἑλλάδα πᾶσαν ἀφίξεται. Jason speaks as one who got together an expeditionary force from every quarter of Hellas (347n.).
Ἑλλάδι 13n.

392 θεσπεσίην The extent to which the broad definition θεῖος (Henrichs 249 n.16; cf. Hoekstra on *Od*. 13.363, Janko on *Il*. 15.637, and also Bechtel 165f., Fraenkel on Aesch. *Ag*. 1154) can be applied to this epithet in Homer is open to debate: contrast, for instance, the entries of Cunliffe *LHD* and *LfgrE*. Here, in line with lexicographical theory (e.g. schol. D at *Il*. 2.670, 9.12 πολύς, Hesych. θ388 θεσπεσίη· μεγάλη, πολλῇ ...), θεσπεσίην could be regarded as a heightened εὐρεῖαν: cf. Simon. *IEG* 16.2-3 σφιν ἀέξει/... εὐρεῖαν κληδόνα..., εὐρύ in Xenophanes cited on 391-2, and, e.g., *Od*. 19.333. The notion of immense quantity is clearly felt in, for instance, i.977 (i.q. ἀπειρεσίοις), Theoc. 15.66 (where see Gow), Anon. *SH* 1169, cf. Campbell on Q.S. 12.398.

On the other hand, the sense θεῖος well suits Jason's tone (391a might easily be addressed to a god, see n.), and VDB translate 'divine'; illustration of the idea in Hunter (but Jason of course is to be taken as operating subtly, avoiding as he does the conventional hyperbole 'as though you were a god' *vel sim.*, cf. 1124n.; Beye 1982.131 seems to me to view the offer from the wrong angle). See also 443n.

οἴσω See *HyAp* 174f. cited on 391-2. Ctr. κληδόν' ἤνεγκας in Eur. *Hel*. 1250; and *Il*. 7.81 ... δώῃ (subject *a god*: see above), 82 οἴσω.

κληηδόνα A sonorous form, borrowed from *Od*. 4.317. Not in this sense in Homer (the same goes for φήμη, its broad equivalent: Russo on *Od*. 18.117); this from a tragic model (the word here only in 3^H)?

καὶ ... ἤδη Cf. *Il*. 16.852 al. ἀλλά τοι ἤδη/, infr. 1051 καὶ δέ τοι ἄλλο ... — ἤδη means 'right now,' as opposed to what he will do when he gets back to Hellas.

393 πρόφρονες + infin.: *Il*. 17.353 (so taken by Ap. presumably; probably correctly); Greg. Naz. 1359.75f.

ἄρηι θοήν 'prompt ... with <our services in> war,' a resolution of the Homeric ἀρηΐθοος (~ i.1042), interpreted as 'fleet in war/battle' (*EtM* 139.57) rather than as 'running in battle' or 'warlike' (for these definitions see *LfgrE* s.v. schol.). One may think of the uncertainties attaching to e.g. APHIKTAMENΩI in *Il*. 22.72 (see Richardson there), BOH(I)ΘOON in id. 17.481 (see Erbse schol. ad loc.). Marxer (61) curiously suggested ἀρηιθοήν. With θοήν Jason hints at speedy success: but he avoids Argos' super-confident tone (353).

ἀποτῖσαι ἀμοιβήν Cf. iv.1327 ἀπὸ .. τίνετ' ἀμοιβήν/, 1353 μενοεικέα

COMMENTARY 396

τῖσαι ἀμοιβήν/ ~ *Od*. 12.382 τίσουσ' .. ἐπιεικέ' ἀμοιβήν/, and further: Eur. *HF* 1169; i.619, ii.475; Maiist. *CA* 40 τῖσαι ἀμοιβήν/; [Orph.] *A*. 1304; Nonn. *Par*. 10.114. The notion of strict reciprocity voiced here is perfectly in accord with the probability that Jason is treating Aeetes as though he were a god being asked for a favour (391, 392nn.).

394 εἴτ' οὖν A businesslike combination, not found in archaic poetry: *GP* 418-9; also in ii.1279, iv.716, 1412.

γε λιλαίεαι is founded on *Od*. 11.380 (Odysseus politely to Alcinous) /εἰ δ' ἔτ' ἀκουέμεναί γε λιλαίεαι (cf. later Max. 20); note also *Il*. 12.248 /εἰ ... -εαι, ἠέ τιν' ἄλλον/, *Od*. 10.267.

395 σφωιτέροισιν ... δαμάσσαι See on 335 and 353.

396 ἴσκεν *he spoke*: 11 × after a speech in Ap., once unelaborated (iii.555), elsewhere followed up with a word configured ⏑–⏑⏑– (name: ii.240; adverb: iii.439; participle: ii.1196, iii.484 i.q. iv.1586, iii.938, iv.92) or ⏑––– (iv.410/ἴσκεν ὑποσσαίνων; so here, but unstopped, cf. next) or ⏑––––⏑ (i.834/ἴσκεν, ἀμαλδύνουσα ...). Ctr. Theoc. 22.167 /ἴσκον τοιάδε πολλά, a decidedly unepic run.

For extended discussion and bibliography see Livrea on iv.92; also Edwards 167-8, Dyck 143-4, Russo on *Od*. 19.203, F-G on id. 22.31.

ὑποσσαίνων Forcefully put (for ὑπο- cf. ὑποτρέχειν [Willink on Eur. *Or*. 670], and ὑπιέναι, ὑποθωπεύειν; cf. Hutchinson 107, 112, 126). Jason's 'flattery' or 'fawning,' delivered in a suitable tone of voice (ἀγανῇ ὀπί) and designed to elicit a favourable and positive response (see in general Barrett on Eur. *Hipp*. 862-3, and on the word's range Harriot, *CQ* n.s. 32 (1982), 14), relates to his appeal to the king's sense of his own importance (391f.); so Jason, to Medea this time, in 974, and again in iv.410 (where as here he seeks to lower the temperature, but that is no reason to dilute to 'seeking to soothe <her violent anger>': Jason implicitly – and winningly – rejects her charge that she is not important to himself or the others). The question of his sugary tone then should not be dissociated from consideration of its intended targets – receptiveness to servile flattery is part of the conventional perception of βάρβαροι, and Jason is skilled at the verbal level in sizing up the opposition. Beye (1982.85) takes too dim a view of the approach adopted here.

The compound verb first in Ap.: ii.974 τοῖον -ων φάτο μῦθον/, and iv.410 ἴσκεν -ων· ἡ δ' οὐλοὸν ἔκφατο μῦθον in the wake of /μειλιχίοις ἐπέεσσιν 394 ~ supr. 385 μειλιχίοισιν/ (Bacch. 1.76-7 προσφώνει .../

–⏑– (? μειλίχῳ)] σαίνουσ' ὀπί). In later verse: Nonn. D. 3.228 -ων ... μύθῳ/, 42.362 τοίην -μυθον -ων φάτο φωνήν/, Paul. Sil. Soph. 927, 1022.

On the double sigma (see Budé *app. crit.* here and at 974), which Ap. will certainly have employed (see Rzach 487), cf. Hoekstra on *Od.* 16.4, Perpillou, *RPh* 50 (1976), 54-5.

ἀγανῇ Cf. Jason at Pind. *P.* 4.101, with Braswell on 101-2(b); 78, 385nn.

-ῇ ὀπί See Campbell on Q.S. 12.58.

396-400 Recalled here, uniquely in the poem (so it is with a number of Homeric type-scenes), are various sequences involving a hero's/warrior's choice between two possible courses of action at a critical point:

(1) *Il.* 1.188-92, which features the incensed Achilles, no friend of diplomacy, and Agamemnon (see 382-5n.!): /ὣς φάτο ... ἐν δέ οἱ ἦτορ/ στήθεσσιν λασίοισι διάνδιχα μερμήριξεν,/ἢ ὅγε .... Ἀτρεΐδην ἐναρίζοι,/ ἦε ...

(2) *Il.* 13.455-8 (sim. *Od.* 4.117-9, 24.235-9) ὣς φάτο· Δηΐφοβος δὲ διάνδιχα μερμήριξεν,/ἤ ...., ἤ πειρήσαιτο .../ὧδε δέ οἱ φρονέοντι δοάσσατο κέρδιον εἶναι. Here however the πεῖρα contemplated by the subject is rejected in favour of the first option.

(3) *Il.* 14.20-3 ὥρμαινε δαϊζόμενος κατὰ θυμόν/διχθάδι', ἢ .../ἦε .../ ὧδε δέ οἱ κτλ. Note the πορφύρειν image in 16f., on which see C. P. Caswell, *A Study of Thumos in Early Greek Epic* (Leiden 1990), 46.

See further Arend 106f.; Voigt 30f.; Russo on *Od.* 20.30, Heubeck on id. 24.235-40; Virg. *A.* 4.285-7, Pease ad loc.; Stat. *Theb.* 3.444-51.

396-7 τοῖο δὲ θυμός ... Cf. *Il.* 23.597 τοῖο δὲ θυμός/, and id. 4.289 al. θυμὸς ἐνὶ στήθεσσι ⏑–×. ἐπὶ (Ω: ἐνὶ E only) must be an old error: the notion 'against' may have occurred to someone who thought of πόρφυρεν in terms of 'heave,' 'surge' without looking too closely at the accompanying accusative (it is hard to see how *Il.* 9.490 al. could have influenced anybody); but confusion between the two is of course common enough.

397 διχθαδίην ... μενοινήν is picked up by Nonn. *D.* 11.96-7 μενοινήν/διχθαδίην, cf. id. 4.65. Gillies noted *Il.* 16.435 διχθὰ δέ μοι κραδίη μέμονε φρεσὶν ὁρμαίνοντι ...

πόρφυρεν 23, 396-400nn.

μενοινήν μενοινή (> μενοινᾶν, cf. Meister 89, Marxer 38, and see in general *GG* 1.725-6) is not attested before the Hellenistic era (Call.

h. 1.90, Ap. 7 × in all); extremely common thereafter; *Apolloniana*: only Nonnos above and [Orph.] *fr.* 332.2 as corrected by Wilamowitz ἐν στήθεσσιν .. μενοιναί/; [Apolin.] 7.33 κακῇ δ' ἔσκαψε μενοινῇ/ cf. iv.413.

398 The murderous thoughts of this killing-machine (415f.) are expressed in language familiar from the Iliadic battlefield: 5.151 σφεας ... ἐξενάριξε/, 13.562 al. ὁρμηθείς, id. 496 al. αὐτοσχεδὸν (there scil. αὐτοσχεδίη μάχῃ: see 148n.) ὡρμήθησαν (-ήτην)/.

(ἢ) σφεας ὁρμηθείς Cf. iv.49; on ἤ/ἦ: Rengakos 1993.102-3.

σφεας The focus has shifted *via* Telamon's threatened outburst and Jason's claims about the expedition's purpose from Argonauts and Phrixids to Argonauts alone – though one may doubt whether *Aeetes* at this point is in any mood to draw fine distinctions. Cf. *Studies* 33.

ἐξεναρίζοι then πειρήσαιτο: alternating present and aorist optatives (on the mood see *GHD* 275f., *GH* 2.224), as in one of the main models, *Il.* 1.191 ἐναρίζοι, 192 παύσειεν ...; for πειρήσαιτο specifically see Hom. in 396-400n. In fact, optat. ἐξεναρίξαι (this -αι: Rzach 576) does not occur; *w*E seek to tidy up with -ίξοι (see 349n.).

399 ἢ ὅγε in the second part of a disjunction is deployed in the course of a similar sequence at *Il.* 5.673, and cf. *Od.* 4.790. — i.308 (sim. iii.1241) finds a precise analogue in *HyHom* 7.28. Note further Call. *h.* 3.150, Man. 3.286, Greg. Naz. 559.488, and see West on Hes. *WD* 246.

βίης scil. τῶν ἡρώων (schol. P), note σφεας in 398. So we are led to suppose: in reality Aeetes has his eye on the leader <whose defeat and death in the wake of a 'gentleman's agreement' should (in theory) remove the general threat>. Even in 405 it is looking as if the πεῖρα *could* relate to the whole company: then (407) comes the surprise. Jason was right to think in terms of βίη (181), but its perpetrator will turn out to be none other than himself.

399-400 τό 'which thing,' the test just referred to. Model: *Od.* 19.283 ἀλλ' .. οἱ τόγε κέρδιον εἴσατο θυμῷ/.

... ἄρειον ... *Od.* 23.114 /πειράζειν then φράσεται then ἄρειον/.

φραζομένῳ ... iv.494 ... φραζομένοις· Πηλεὺς δὲ παροίτατος ἔκφατο μῦθον.

400 καὶ δή μιν i.1120; this run heads the verse in *Il.* 6.52, 22.457.

ὑποβλήδην προσέειπε Infr. 1119 τὴν δ᾽ .. δῆθεν ὑποβλήδην προσέειπε/, i.699 καὶ τοῖον ὑποβλήδην ἔπος ηὔδα/ (Q.S. 2.147 καὶ τοῖον ὑποβλήδην φάτο μῦθον/).

ὑποβλήδην: 'by way of prompting,' i.e. advancing a positive suggestion or proposal (see VDB 2.67 n.4) suits all three occurrences; 'in response,' 'by way of a rejoinder,' is a viable, if rather bland, alternative; another option is 'by way of interruption,' in i.699 if we are prepared to believe that the θρόος of the assembly (Ap. perhaps here recalls *Il.* 19.80/81f.) is still in evidence as Hypsipyle 'cuts in,' 'right away,' here in iii.400 (Hoelzlin pressed for this) if we take the adverb in conjunction with Aeetes' dismissive opening salvo in 401, in iii.1119 (1120f. are likewise dismissive) if we imagine that Jason effectively 'breaks in on' Medea's tearful display (there is indeed some laxity in the use of the word at *Il.* 1.292, according to Kirk ad loc.).

It is not unreasonable to suppose that the poet does not wish to be pinned down (cf. on παραβλήδην in 107): there was room for disagreement on the interpretation of ὑποβλήδην/ὑββάλλειν in *Il.*, cf. the entries in *LH* together with Erbse on schol. *Il.* 19.80a/b, Henrichs 141 nn.2-3, Rengakos 1993.74-6. For further discussion see in addition to the commentaries Merkel *Proleg.* 166, Seaton 1891.11-12, Fränkel 1928.568-9, Belloni 66-8, and more generally Fantuzzi 78-9.

All other examples of ὑποβλήδην save Babr. 95.65 in LSJ.

401-21 Certain stylistic features point firmly in the direction of a tragic source for this account of the imposition, viz. Sophocles' *Colchides*: see *Studies* 107 n.24 for a summary, and the commentary for the details; also, more generally, VDB 2.7-8.

401 ξεῖνε With the information at his disposal Aeetes might have responded to Jason's Αἰήτη (386) with an Αἰσονίδη. Instead, a two-edged mode of address (cf., in a mellower tone, Hypsipyle to Jason in i.793): Jason is his 'guest' and will be treated accordingly, but he is also a 'stranger' (cf. Pelias in Pind. *P.* 4.97), and Aeetes evidently looks upon foreigners with suspicion and distaste. Medea too will spit out this word in iv.33, and use it to Jason's face in the course of a fervent plea to be admitted into the 'family' at id. 89 (see VDB 3.150, on 91). Cf. Faerber 99.

τί κεν ... Cf. *Studies* 107 n.1; i.e. 'why should I have to listen to you treating me to a continuous blow-by-blow account of each and every detail <concerning your arrival here and your personal circumstances>?' Hardly fair, since Jason has shown no inclination to follow

COMMENTARY 402-3

in Argos' (and still less in Odysseus'! Beye 1982.16) footsteps. It is of course Aeetes' way of saying that he is just not interested in the personal details (no Alcinous this!) – he will get the Fleece <without discussion> if the terms are met. According to Beye, who however expresses no opinion on the behaviour of Aeetes here, Jason 'is made to look ridiculous' (1982.31).

τὰ ἕκαστα Cf. ii.391 τὰ ἕκαστα διηνεκὲς (corr.) ἐξενέποντα/, Greg. Naz. 1549.95 (sim. 1559.110) τί μοι τὰ ἕκαστα διακριδὸν ὧδ' ἀγορεύειν;/. — Ap. has τὰ ἕκαστα 19 ×: note i.394 ~ HyHerm 313; i.1097 τὰ ἕκαστα πιφαυσκομένη copied by Eudoc. Cypr. 1.93, infr. 1165 and iv.1346 πιφαυσκόμενος τὰ ἕκαστα/ = D.P. 173 ~ Od. 12.165 τὰ ἕκαστα ... πίφαυσκον/; iv.463 /καὶ τὼ μὲν τὰ ἕκαστα cf. Od. 14.375 and [Orph.] A. 767, 1155. Other Hellenistic poets however did not share his fondness for it: [Theoc.] 25.195, Nic. Ther. 837. It is pretty common subsequently. Apollonian usage: Svensson 38.

διηνεκέως ἀγορεύ- Similarly Od. 4.836 al., i.649, 847; naturally these and related Apollonian passages have attracted the attention of the (anti-) ἄεισμα διηνεκές brigade: e.g. Beye 1982.15-6, Dickie 281.

... ἀγορεύοις So FNQ (cf. Speake 1975.110): ἀγορεύεις Ω, the result presumably of early miscopying rather than of accommodation to Od. 1.306-7 ... ηὔδα·/ξεῖν', ... ταῦτα ... ἀγορεύεις/, 8.235-6 ... προσέειπεν·/ξεῖν', ... ταῦτ' ἀγορεύεις/.

Trash-collectors will always find something to support the insupportable: Giangrande, Hermes 98 (1970), 266; for warranted scepticism about giving such aberrations a good home see LH s.v. κε p. 698, KG 1.210, and, among commentators, e.g. Janko on Il. 14.484-5.

Ctr. Il. 2.250 (248-9 /οὐ ... σέο χερειότερον .... ὅσσοι ... ἦλθον/ cf. Ap. 403 /οὐδὲν ἐμεῖο χέρηες ... ἔβητε/), Od. 18.380 ἂν ... ἀγορεύοις/.

402-3 Cf. Studies 107 n.1. (a) If you are genuinely of divine stock ['you' plural, a scathing reference to the entire company, picking up Argos' report of 365-6] (in that case you will be able to perform what I, the son of a god, can perform); (b) or if alternatively you are in no way my inferiors in another/a different respect [ominous: Aeetes is thinking forward to the need for the 'stamina and valour' he himself displays], you who have come... Despite the switch to Jason himself in 404, it is looking at the moment as if the preconditions for the surrender of the Fleece are to be met by the Argonauts as a body (by the exercising of βίη along the lines suggested by Jason in 392f., one might suppose). The reality turns out to be far different. See further 405-6n.

402 εἰ .. ἐτήτυμον harks back sarcastically to 358, see n. In Val. Flacc. 7.50-1 Aeetes voices his doubts less subtly.

Ctr. *Il.* 13.111 /ἀλλ' εἰ ... ἐτήτυμον .. ἐστιν/.

ἐστε .. γένος Cf. *Od.* 4.63 ἀνδρῶν γένος ἐστὲ ...; Tyrt. *IEG* 11.1; orac. *ap.* West, *ZPE* 1 (1967), 185, II(b) 17.

θεῶν γένος So Q.S. 6.205, 11.137, *SEG* 18.295.1 (Moesia, 4th cent., *carm. dedic.*); an *incipit* in Hes. *Theog.* 44 (in a different sense), and cf. Pind. *N.* 6.1. See further Fränkel *Einleitung* 135-6.

ἠὲ καὶ ἄλλως *Od.* 9.267 (preceded by εἰ ..., but in the sense 'in the hope that'; see n. on 176f.), 17.577.

403 χέρηες occurs at *Od.* 15.324 (on the form see La Roche *HTA* 378f./Erbse on schol. *Il.* 1.80c; Risch 90 n.78 with Ruijgh 1991.494), but there of individuals inferior in respect of *birth* (Ap. 402a); perhaps Ap. read χέρηα in *Il.* 4.400, εἷο χέρεια (μάχῃ). In ii.1220 on the other hand he writes χερείους not χέρηας. χέρη- nowhere else in 3^H.

ὀθνείοισιν Not merely a loose pluralising of Jason's ὀθνεῖον .. κτέρας (389 and n.): Aeetes believes that there is more at stake than that (cf. 591).

404 δώσω ... Homerica: *Od.* 4.615, 15.115 (but both of offers generously made, with no strings attached) /δώσω τοι, id. 3.50 σοὶ (τοι Zen.) .. δώσω χρύσειον ἄλεισον/ (cf. iv.87 cited below), *Il.* 22.117 /δωσέμεν .. ἄγειν *et sim.*

χρύσειον ἄγειν δέρος Cf. note on 88, and i.889; iv.87 (/δώσω .. χρύσειον .. δέρος, Medea with a condition); Pind. *P.* 4.161.

ἤν κ' ἐθέλῃσθα In i.706/715 we have the regular αἴ κ' ἐθέλωσι -ητε/; Π⁷ (1st cent. AD; see Henrichs, *ZPE* 5 (1970), 53-4) carries supralinear/marginal variants ἤν κ', no doubt influenced by the reading of Ω here (αἴ κ' D: Speake 1969.89/1974.126-7). Given the quest for variety in this poem alteration either way for the sake of uniformity is unwise. In *Il.* 4.353 the vulgate has ἤν ἐθέλῃσθα, with ἤν κ' offered only by a 3rd cent. AD papyrus and by *codd*. AT (elicited no doubt from the following αἴ κεν); cf. also Allen at *Il.* 9.359, and Rengakos 1993.130-1. On the other hand *Od.* 18.318 /ἤν ... κ' ἐθέλωσιν, even if it actually represents a 'modernisation' (see e.g. *GHD* 331, *GH* 2.282; Janko on *Il.* 15.502-6 is right to be sceptical), was very probably there in Ap.'s own repertory of 'Homeric peculiarities' (so classified by Goodwin *MT* 167). See further Platt 1914.31 (a good specimen of his robust style), Gillies ed., pp. 139-40 (but Arat. 562 must go!), and cf. Campbell on Q.S. 12.226. Ctr. *Il.* 9.288 ... ἤν κ' ἐθέλησθα... ἄγεσθαι/. I have often wondered about Ap.'s perception of HN κ' ἐθέλησθα/ in *Il.* 21.484 (/εἰ δ' ἐθέλεις 487).

405 πειρηθείς Emphatic: <but only> after ... Aeetes in [Orph.] *A.* 852 is more explicit: πειρηθεὶς ἀέθλων ('Golden Fleece' 853). We may recall here Jason's πειρήσω in 179: 'the biter bit.' Cf. *Od.* 9.174/281, with Hogan, *TAPA* 106 (1976), 201; and the 'tester' Odysseus caught out later on Ithaca by his πειρωμένη wife: Rutherford, *JHS* 106 (1986), 160.

405-6 ἐσθλοῖς ... Ironic indeed: Aeetes, however careful he has been to set what is on the face of it a 'fair' task (386-95n.), *is* very much a Pelias-figure, as he is soon to show (cf. Faerber 99, *Noten* 352; also Braswell on Pind. *P.* 4.94-120, Pelias the 'stage-tyrant'), both in his imposition of a seemingly 'unrealisable' (502) ordeal and in his general demeanour.

After the plurals of 402-3 Aeetes has turned his attention to Jason personally (404-5 init.), but he has not said in so many words *who* is to undergo the πεῖρα. In 405f. he talks again in terms of a plurality ['you' plur.: viz. Argos + Jason, in actual fact], and it is only with τοι in 407, balanced by αὐτός in 408, that the king's intentions start to come through loud and clear: he wants a solo-effort. If there *should* be any lingering doubt, the abrupt σὺ δ' ... which comes in at mid-verse after Aeetes' boast (418) will settle the question.

ἐσθλοῖς ... ἀνδράσιν Cf. e.g. Eur. *Hcld.* 201 παρ' ἐσθλοῖς ἀνδράσιν, Maiist. *CA* 4-5 ἐσθλοῖσιν .../ἀνδράσιν, Hom. *Od.* 3.471 ἀνέρες ἐσθλοί *et sim.*; ἐπ' ἀνδράσιν is Homeric (cf. infr. 1352).

ἐπ' 'against' (cf. ἐπι-φθονεῖν; so apparently the preposition-specialists, Haggett 45, Oswald 182), or better (like ἀμφί + μεγαίρω in *Il.* 7.408), 'in the case of' (Hom. e.g. *Il.* 19.181, but we may be dealing here with tragic adaptation: I note Eur. *fr.* 814.2 φθονεῖσθαι ... ἐπ' ἐσθλοῖς, s.v.l.).

οὔτι μεγαίρω Infr. 485, iv.419; Homeric claus., also *HyHerm* 465, orac. *ap.* Hdt. 1.66.1 (PW 31.3), Q.S. 2.44, 14.222, Greg. Naz. 616.480, 980.134.

406 ὡς .. μυθεῖσθε But *Od.* 8.180 /ὡς σύγε μυθεῖαι.

τὸν .. κοιρανέοντα Cf. *Studies* 107 n.24. 'That ruler of yours in Hellas': Argos and Jason of course have both omitted to put a name to this 'king' (334/390). In Homer the combination article + participle (note here *PV* 958, τὸν νῦν κοιρανοῦντ') takes the form *a* + *b* or *a* + particle(s) + *b*, *GH* 2.321, Svensson 31f.: ctr. supr. 174.

Ἑλλάδι 13n. Aeetes is in no position to be any more precise.

κοιρανέοντα *c. dat. loci* (i.34) is not Homeric (but cf. notably the use of ἀνάσσω). Ap. goes for variety, as so often: ii.998 dat. pers. (trag.+), iv.547 absol. (Hom.). There is no doubt a sneering suggestion of 'ordering about,' 'pulling rank on' people, like Agamemnon κοιρανέων in *Il.*: cf. 333f.

407 Cf. [Orph.] *L.* 204 πεῖρα δέ τοι καὶ τοῦδε παρέσσεται, αἴ κ' ἐθέλησθα (~ 404 supr.).

πεῖρα 16n. In this detail as in others we recall the unpleasant Amycus (ii.16f.): cf. Rose 1984.121.

μένεός τε καὶ ἀλκῆς *Il.* 22.282 (of Hector, soon to be killed; cf. in addition id. 6.265, with the variant) μένεος ἀλκῆς τε, *Od.* 22.237 (Athena/Odysseus and son) σθένεός τε καὶ ἀλκῆς πειρήτιζεν/. Cf. ii.44-5 with *Il.* 9.706, 19.161.

408 Strained and pompous language: 'one in which, as one would expect [ῥ'], I personally and unaided [cf. *solus* in Val. Flacc. 7.69, also μοῦνος in Pind. *P.* 4.227] am triumphant with the help of my two hands.' Cf. here Soph. (?) *Theseus* (?) [a Jason-like figure in many ways: see e.g. Vian ed. 1961 on 418, adding to 'Sinis' etc. 'a bull'!] *fr.* 730c 10-11 Radt καὶ πρόσθε δὴ 'γὼ πολλάκ[ις/καθεῖλον αὐτὸς ταῖν ἐμ[αῖν, which must have been followed up with χεροῖν; *Studies* 107 n.24.

τόν Unhomeric use of relative: Mugler, *REG* 54 (1941), 12.

τόν ῥ' αὐτός The same run, but in different sedes, at *Il.* 2.309, *Od.* 23.178.

περίειμι Recall the boastful Amycus in ii.58 (after *Il.* 8.27), cf. 407n.

χεροῖν 50n.

ὀλοόν Cf. infr. 906, '<potentially> lethal,' and see 384, 436nn. Schol. P offers a diluted explanation, and many translators follow suit.

409f. A remarkably jejune description of the bulls, even by Apollonian standards, lacking the epic colouring in evidence in Val. Flacc. 7.62f.; after Sophocles perhaps, cf. above on 401-21. When Jason reports back to his men at 495f., he reproduces 409-10 pretty faithfully, but abridges the ensuing account of ploughing, sowing and combat, after due notice (493-4).

409 The asyndeton is noteworthy: Aeetes gets down to the details with evident gusto.

πεδίον τὸ 'Αρήιον So ii.1268, iii.495, 1270. After the Homeric πεδίον τὸ 'Αλήιον (*Il.* 6.201, = D.P. 872), cf. Svensson 18; perhaps this particular run was concocted by Ap. himself, as elements drawn from the Bellerophon-story are detectable in other places: see on 353, and also on 422f.

πεδίον ... ἀμφινέμονται It is natural here and in 495 to think in terms of 'pasture, graze (all) over' (ἀμφι- commonly means '(überall) in,' Verdenius, *Mnemosyne* 24 (1971), 297; [Orph.] *A*. 742 πεδίον περιναιετάουσι/, 'habitent la plaine' Vian), cf. νέμεσθαι + ἀμφί of μῆλα in ii.513-4, and also ἀμφιν- of bulls in [Opp.] *Cyn.* 2.101. Ap. uses this Homeric verb elsewhere of human/nymph habitation (cf. Hom. νέμεσθαι, and see Kirk on *Il.* 2.496), whether with accus. (i.947 πεδίον, 1224, ii.988 πεδίον, 1117, 1150) or with object unexpressed (ii.999: ctr. *Il.* 2.655, *Echoes* ad loc.), see Vian 1978b.103-4; 3[H] otherwise: Arat. 282 ('sont installés' Martin).

410 Repeated by Jason in 496 (... -τας), but it is not granted 'formulaic' status; later: 1303-4 τώγε θοὴν φλόγα φυσιόωντες/ἐκ στομάτων, cf. Pind. *P.* 4.225f. (φλόγ'). See further on 411.

χαλκόποδε 230n.

φλόγα φυσιόωντες Expressive alliteration (see Hunter here), cf. *Il.* 23.217-8 cited in next note, *HyHerm* 113-4 φλόξ/.. φύζαν (? or φῦσαν), and also many examples of φῦσ(α) + φυσ(άω) sim. from *Il.* 18.470 on (φῦσαι ... ἐφύσων framing the verse). — The quest for 'strong plosive alliteration,' Richardson on *Il.* 23.333, accounts for the unique φῆ (for ἦ) πυρὶ καιόμενος ... ἔφλυε ... in *Il.* 21.361.

φυσιόωντες For the plural rather than the dual see the Budé *app. crit.* here and at 496, 1303 (cf. 1292 plur. Π²⁷ + Ω); VDB 2.125, on 496.

φυσ. transitive, like (ἐκ)φυσᾶν, ἐκφυσιᾶν, ἀναφυσᾶν -ιᾶν (cf. ii.431); also ii.87. Ctr. *Il.* 23.217-8 φλόγ' ἔβαλλον,/φυσῶντες.

411 στυφελὴν κατὰ νειὸν ''Άρηος 1053 στυφελὴν διὰ νειὸν ἀρόσσης/ (ζεύξῃς βόας 1052); 754 κατὰ νειὸν (778) ''Άρηος/. A token amount of repetition for details relating to the hero's *aristeia*: see 230, 231, 232, 410nn., and the examples from book iii cited on τετράγυον in 412.

στυφελήν Only καταστυφ- in archaic epic. This perhaps from Sophocles: στυφελός στύφλος chiefly tragic, cf. in general Erbse 1953.185. ἀκτή ii.323, Aeschylean; in Phineus-episode. — ii.1005 χθών in connexion with working the land, Soph. *Ant.* 250 γῆ. — ii.1248 πάγοι ref. Prometheus, cf. *PV* 748 [and Anon. *SH* 1107]; spoken *to* Prometheus. — Cf. 401-21n.

νειόν So, of course, hardest to work: see 1331f.

412 τετράγυον Strategically positioned; pause: Aeetes is out to impress. This word twice in *Od.*, see 7.112-3 (Hainsworth ad loc.) ὄρχατος.../-υος (~ Nonn. *D.* 3.140, 142), and more pertinently 18.374 τετράγυον δ' εἴη, εἴκοι δ' ὑπὸ βῶλος ἀρότρῳ ~ Call. *h.* 3.175-6 (see Bornmann there and, speculatively, Bing, *ZPE* 54 (1984), 7-8; 'the typical heroic field' remarks Mair) /μὴ νειὸν τημοῦτος .. βόες .../τετράγυον τέμνοιεν ὑπ' ἀλλοτρίῳ ἀροτῆρι, and so infr. 497 /τετράγυον ... νειὸν ἀρόσσαι/, 1343-4 τῆμος ἀρήροτο νειὸς ὑπ' ἀκαμάτῳ ἀροτῆρι/τετράγυός περ ἐοῦσα (on these repeated elements see 411n.). Cf. later [Orph.] *A.* 871 (Jason subdued the bulls) /τετραγύῳ (corrected, cf. Vian ad loc.) θέμενος σπόρον αὔλακι.

See further VDB 2.68 n.2, who draw attention to Pherecydes' more ambitious specification (cf. *Il.* 9.579! Not in the least surprising in a culture that could, say, give the Hydra 9, or 100, or an indeterminate number of heads, and deal with Cerberus in much the same way).

... ταμὼν ... ἀρότρῳ Compare i.1215 νειοῖο γύας τέμνεσκεν ἀρότρῳ/.

ταμών As VDB note (2.124), the aorist participle is strictly speaking describing an action which is coincidental with that of the main verb (contrast *Od.* 12.11 αἶψα ταμόντες): see e.g. Barrett on Eur. *Hipp.* 289-92, Braswell on Pind. *P.* 4.36-7. Aeetes though is plainly bent on representing his effortless victory as a rapid *succession* of 'jobs to be got through,' n.b. the elaborate chiasmus, ἐλάω ζεύξας ~ ταμὼν .... ἐνιβάλλομαι.

τέλσον 'turning-point,' 'headland' at the end of the furrow. Etymology and Homeric usage are examined at length by Pisani, *Athenaeum* n.s. 18 (1940), 3f., but see on the former also Forbes, *Glotta* 36 (1957), 260-1, Wyatt, *GRBS* 16 (1975), 253.

Cf. *Il.* 13.707 τέμει (τέμνει *vulg.*, see Janko ad loc.; the text has sometimes been emended to bring it into line with Ap.: see e.g. Seaton 1891.7) ... τέλσον, 18.544 and (νειοῖο ...) 547; applied to ploughland elsewhere only in Cougny 6.264.34. Otherwise *edge, perimeter, boundary*

Nic. *Ther.* 546 (Gow, *CQ* n.s. 1 (1951), 109), plur. Crin. *GPh* 1819, Paul. Sil. *Soph.* 149, 424 ~ 820; metaph. *pinnacle* Greg. Naz. 674.86 ἀρετῆς ἐπὶ τ., 1542.282 καλοῦ; Hesych. has the entry τέλσα· στροφάς, τέλη, πέρατα (schol. D on Hom. had the last two on tap).

413-5 Not easy Greek, but Ω's text is defensible. Neither West's ἀκτῆς nor E's ἀκτήν is convincing. σπόρον looks comfortable on its own: it is not complemented by a genitive in either 498 or 1173, and cf. the passages cited in 413n.; a change to the accusative, though easy enough in itself (such corruption is far commoner than Platt says, 1914.37, and ἀκτῇ might easily have suggested itself in the wake of ἐνι-) does nothing, any more than does ἀκτῆς, to explain the ensuing dative ἀνδράσι. But there is no need to throw in the towel (Fränkel OCT marks a one-line lacuna after 414: but do we want any more detail at this point? Erbse 1963.24/*Gnomon* 38 (1966), 160 rightly deplored Fränkel's readiness to leave voids in the text). ἀκτῇ may be retained as a dative of purpose (413n.), without recourse to an idiosyncratic (and incredible) interpretation of *Od.* 18.70/24.368, as Livrea suggested (1982.20); the other dative in 413, located as it is out of the way before the main caesura, is hardly an obstacle. ἀνδράσι fulfils exactly the same function: 'I do not throw in the furrows seed to produce Deo's grain, but rather <I throw in> the teeth of a terrible serpent which sprout in a transformed state [cf. Hoelzlin here], to produce men who are armed warriors in their physical make-up [*or*: 'bodily appearance']' (cf. acc. relation δομήν applied to the Earthborn in 1395). So, essentially, VDB 2.124.

That δέμας can be taken in conjunction with the dative ἀνδράσι in the sense 'like' (so Naber 31, cf. on that Seaton 1908.19), or that μεταλδήσκοντας can bear the sense 'growing in a metamorphised form bearing the likeness of' (schol. L⁵, echoed by Ardizzoni, ventured ἐξισουμένους, a blind stab indeed), I do not believe. Nor can μεταλδήσκοντας ἀνδράσι be regarded as a straight equivalent of μετ. εἰς ἄνδρας (so e.g. Linsenbarth 56, in the midst of an ill-assorted collection of 'verbs governing dative'); the metamorphosis terminology of Mosch. *Eur.* 52 (Campbell ad loc.) is of a wholly different order; and [Orph.] *A.* 1290 /πέτραις δ' ἠλλάξαντο δέμας μορφήν θ', 'they exchanged their bodily shape and outward form/beauty for rocks,' i.e. they turned into rocks, is of no real help here. Damsté's interpretation (8) is fantastic: 'qui viris armatis vitam corpusque darent' — ἀνδράσι .. δέμας in apposition to ἰδόντας!

Cf. generally Eratosth. *CA* 16.17-8 (had Ap. written a didactic poem, it would surely have read much like these lines) ἀλδήσκουσαι/ καρπὸν .. Δημήτερος ... ἄνδρες/...

413 σπόρον Cf. Chryssafis on [Theoc.] 25.25; this (and ὁλκοῖσιν?) from Soph. (cf. 401-21n.)?

ὁλκοῖσιν 1378n.

Δηοῦς .. ἀκτῇ In archaic epic Δημήτερος (..) ἀκτήν/, and similarly Eur. *Hipp*.138 and *fr*. 892.2, Epinicus *PCG* (V) *fr*. 1.9, [Orph.] *A*. 323. Δη(ώ) (Richardson on *HyDem* 47, Hopkinson on Call. *h*. 6.17; not in Hom./Hes.) was much affected by Hellenistic poets: e.g. Ap., iv.896 (cf. Jackson, *LCM* 15 (1990), 56), 986, 988; Call. 7 ×; Theoc. 7.3; Euphor. *CA* 9.14. Ap. does not use Δημήτηρ.

Aeetes chooses his image well: Demeter's grain is by convention life-giving (e.g. Aesch. *fr*. 300.7), the warrior-crop seeks to deal out destruction.

... ἐνιβάλλομαι Possible reminiscences in [Theoc.] 25.25-6 σπόρον ἐν νειοῖσιν/... βάλλοντες .. τετρα- [unusual detail, see Gow: influenced by Ap. 412 init.?], Nonn. *D*. 2.64 /οὐ σπόρον ἀμφεκάλυψε πέδῳ ..., 32.72 βαλὼν σπόρον αὔλακι [cf. [Orph.] *A*. 871 cited on 412] γαίης/, Agath. *AP* 11.365.1 σπόρον ἔμβαλε γαίη/. Cf. also Call. *SH* 276.8 βάλοις .. ἐνὶ σπόρον ...

-βάλλομαι: we might see in the middle a suggestion of 'for my own benefit' – Aeetes, unlike the cultivator, does this for his own entertainment. On the other hand, σπέρματα πάντα βαλέσθαι/ in Arat. 9 (cf. Max. 499-500) has no such colouring. [I am not taken with labels like 'dynamic,' 'expressive' ...]

ἀκτῇ On the dative of purpose see *GG* 1.139f., and also Gonda, *Mnemosyne* 10 (1957), 2-3, Schenkeveld, id. 42 (1989), 474f., Verdenius on Hes. *WD* 329, VDB 2.124. I cannot credit Vian's suggestion (1962.38) that the dative is meant as a positive pointer to the espousal of the Homeric significance of ἀκτή.

414 ὄφιος δεινοῖο ... A hackneyed combination, cf. especially (see Wifstrand 1933.106) Hes. *Theog*. 825 (variant) ὄφιος δεινοῖο δράκοντος/ [cf. infr. 1178]. In iv.1506 /δεινὸς ὄφις, = [Hes.] *fr*. 204.136, orac. *ap*. Hdt. 6.18 (PW 84.5), *Or. Sib*. 5.29 + 3, [Orph.] *A*. 928.

For ὄφιος ... ὀδόντας cf. infr. 1005 and earlier Eur. *Suppl*. 703 (δεινός 704!); infr. 1177-8 ὀδόντας/.. δράκοντος ([Orph.] *A*. 873 δρακοντείων .. ὀδόντων/).

μεταλδήσκοντας Absolute hapax; μετ- as in μεταφύομαι, μεταβλαστάνω (hardly a redundant preverb: Fraser 2.898 n.168). ἀλδ- is intrans. in *Il.* 23.599 [n.b. φρίσσουσιν ibid., cf. Ap. iii.1355], Damocr. *ap.* Gal. 14.101, [Opp.] *Cyn.* 1.318, 3.181, ἀναλδ- infr. 1363 (Earthborn), [Opp.] *Cyn.* 2.397.

-οντας ὀδόντας The harsh jingle (harsher than that of *Od.* 18.28 fin.) contributes to the air of menace.

415 ἀνδράσι τευχηστῇσι Aesch. *Th.* 644 [*Theban* saga, cf. teeth; from epic no doubt] ἄνδρα τευχηστήν (but ἀνδρῶν τευχηστήρων id. *Pers.* 902; consult on both of these Sideras 153, Belloni on *Pers.* loc. cit.). See further McLennan on Call. *h.* 1.77 (add perhaps Call. *SH* 296.4). For the configuration of the *incipit* cf. *Od.* 1.349.

... δέμας Ctr. *Il.* 21.285 δέμας δ' ἄνδρεσσιν ἐΐκτην/.

τοὺς δ' αὖθι An identical run, but earlier in the verse, occurs at *Il.* 11.701; there αὖθι is purely local, here it means 'there and then,' as sometimes with verbs of killing in Homer: *LfgrE* s.v.3, cf. West and Verdenius on Hes. *WD* 35.

δαΐζων then δουρί: cf. *Il.* 18.195 /ἔγχεϊ δηϊόων. The verb (see in general FJW on Aesch. *Suppl.* 680, Cheyns, *AC* 48 (1979), 605f.) is aptly conjoined with κείρω. Cf. *Il.* 7.247 δαΐζων χαλκός of a spear shearing through a shield's protective layers, 14.518 id. slitting open the body and disembowelling the victim, as well as 11.71 δῄουν of spear-throwing (85) combatants compared to 'reapers' (67); δαΐξαι in i.758; δαϊζομένων ὑπὸ δουρί/ in Timolaus *SH* 849.6.

416 κείρω ... Cf. /"Ἄρεος ἀμώοντος .. ὑπὸ δουρί in 1187: similarly κέρσειεν in Aesch. *Suppl.* 666 applied to Ares, the reaper, 637f., see FJW on 637-8 and 666 for copious illustration of the image, with the remarks of P. R. Hardie, *Virgil's* Aeneid: *Cosmos and Imperium* (Oxford 1986), 288, and R. O. A. M. Lyne, *Words and the Poet: Characteristic Techniques of Style in Vergil's* Aeneid (Oxford 1989), 140f.

Campbell 1990.482 discusses the distinctive spear employed in combats of this complexion (cf. too Dräger 186). There is nothing extraordinary about the fact that Aeetes proudly claims to cut down the <spear-carrying> Earthborn who encircle him with his own <boastworthy: 1231f.> spear, particularly as the spear is *the* weapon of the fighting man in the *Iliad* (Hainsworth on 11.67-9 and 263, Edwards on 18.609-13), so much so that it can at times assume the sword's functions (Hainsworth on 11.95-6, Janko on 14.465-9; conversely, a sword behaves like a thrusting-spear in 12.190f.); note δορός in the reaping-image (Bond ad loc.) in Eur. *HF* 164, and δόρυ in the account of the hoplite Giants in id. 1191 (Bond's 'to *battle*' does not do justice to the sharp visualisation of spear-bearing creatures). Jason will use a *sword* κείρειν his opponents (cf. e.g. Soph. *Aj.* 55, Stanford ad loc.; recall here the highly coloured use of κατακείρειν in *Od.* 23.356) – and when he does the image of the 'reaper' (cf. 418) mowing down his 'crop' is fully developed: 1389 ~ 1391 [~ Lyc. 214-5], cf. iv.1033-4 (θέρος).

Homer in contrast uses κείρειν in conjunction with ἀπό when spears are in question: *LfgrE* s. κείρω III, Janko on *Il.* 14.545-7.

ἐμῷ ὑπὸ δουρί *Il.* 11.433 (warrior on battlefield) etc.

περισταδόν ii.206; only once in Homer, *Il.* 13.551 (encircling enemy with thrusting-spears; παρασταδόν Zen. Aristoph., cf. Duentzer 87, Erbse 1953.164, Rengakos 1993.71-2, Janko on *Il.* 13.550-3), but common enough subsequently: Hollis on Call. *Hec. fr.* 69.14 (but for [Theoc.] 25.103 see Gow ad loc., Garvie on Aesch. *Cho.* 983), Campbell on Q.S. 12.362.

ἀντιόωντας As *Il.* 15.297 ἀντιάσαντες/, scil. with spears at the ready.

417 Asyndeton once more, as Aeetes sums up his triumphant working-day.

ἠέριος (ἦρι) cf. 915. Homeric in this sense (*LfgrE* s.v., Kirk on *Il.* 1.497, Heubeck on *Od.* 9.52), though not all the examples are clear-cut: in fact ancient explanations were many and varied (Merkel *Proleg.* 179), and there is no firm agreement among modern philologists: see e.g. Jones, *Glotta* 39 (1961), 123f., Kiparsky, *Language* 43 (1967), 625f.

But (cf. Erbse 1953.176-7, though there are one or two inaccuracies): i.580 (~ ἠερόεν i.1114, ἠεροειδέα iv.575) 'in the hazy distance'; iv.1239 'into the dim distance' or better (cf. VDB 3.189, and more generally LSJ under ἀέριος/ἠέριος, with Giangrande, *CR* n.s. 13 (1963), 255) 'coextensively with the sky' (cf. 1246, and also ἄμμου μέγεθος ἀέριον in Diod. Sic. 1.33.3); similarly ὑπηέριον in iv.1577 is perhaps not 'sous la brume' (VDB) but '(extending) under the canopy of an open sky' (to ..., beyond ...).

For the association with ἀήρ *mist* sim. note already ?[Hes.] *fr.* 26.20 (from *Theog.* 9-10 by the look of it: see West 1985.129), Eur. *Phoen.* 1534, Arat. 349, and cf. Nonn. *D.* 2.662 al., Cougny 6.144.5, 159.9, (metaph.) Greg. Naz. 1234.86; so also, to judge by ἠέρα ἑσσάμεναι of verse 6, Anon. hex. *SH* 938.8.

ζεύγνυμι βόας The expression will naturally recur, but with varia-

COMMENTARY 418

tions: 626 on its own, 508 plus 'of Aeetes,' 1052 with epithet (prepositive: ctr. *Il.* 20.495).

δείελον ὥρην Nonn. *Par.* 19.161, *D.* 7.284. Shaped like δείελον ἦμαρ/ *Od.* 17.606, see Kastner 33. Aeetes starts at first light, and goes on till late evening (the contrast he draws leaves us in no doubt about the significance of δείελον: cf. e.g. the Aristotelian ἕωθεν καὶ δείλης, 'early in the morning and late in the evening,' *fr.* 531): Jason will do likewise, for he is finished with the Earthborn by sunset (1340f. ~ 1407).

δείελον Adj. δείελος Hom. (above) +; Ap. has also subst. δείελος i.1160 (Hom.+), adj. δειελινός i.452 (Theoc. 13.33, Argonautic context; Call. *fr.* 75.12), a poetic version of the everyday δειλινός (see Schmitt 111 item 23).

ὥρην Accus. as e.g. infr. 899, Strat. *AP* 12.250.1 (going out on a revel) νυκτερινὴν ... μεταδόρπιον ὥρην, see LSJ s.v. ὥρα B4, with Platt, *JPh* 31 (1910), 234-5/ 33 (1914), 24-5.

418 παύομαι ἀμήτοιο Anon. *AP* 9.384.23 /παύσασθαι νειοῦ (other *Apolloniana* are present). Ctr. *Il.* 8.295, *Od.* 4.103 *incipit* παύομαι followed up with a pause.

ἀμήτοιο ἀμητοῖο E, and so Ω at 436: see West on Hes. *WD* 383-4. The term is employed figuratively (and somewhat cryptically: review in Edwards on 221-4) in *Il.* 19.223 (~ Anon. *SH* 1057?); cf. infr. 436, and on κείρω in 416, ἀμώων in 1382; Chuvin on Nonn. *D.* 4.442.

τάδε τοῖα 'cette tâche dans de telles conditions' VDB, somewhat optimistically adducing *Od.* 4.485; cf. perhaps rather id. 16.205 ὅδ' ἐγὼ τοιόσδε, i.e. 'this man am I, such as you see before you.' Fränkel however obelised (OCT, cf. Speake 1974.130-1). One might consider, without venturing too far into territory trodden by Gilbert Wakefield, τάδε δοιά, = τάδ' ἀμφότερα, 'these two tasks' – if one is prepared to throw away some crisp alliteration: derived from Sophocles?? Cf. e.g. *Aj.* 528, involving τελεῖν; Todd, *CQ* 36 (1942), 29f., lit. in Mineur on Call. *h.* 4.88 (admittedly there are Homeric examples, e.g. *Od.* 18.334).

In any event, there is no point in dragging in the 'glossographers'' τοῖοι ἀντὶ τοῦ ἀγαθοί (Erbse on schol. *Il.* 7.231a, 23.16a, 24.164a; Pfeiffer on Call. *fr.* 627, FJW on Aesch. *Suppl.* 400, Dyck 157f.), as does Giangrande, *CR* n.s. 13 (1963), 154.

... τελέσσεις 'if <it turns out that> you will <actually manage to> carry out ...'; suppressed here is the 'truly' which often accompanies prospective conditions of this kind: e.g. iii.1080-1, iv.834-5; *Il.* 13.375 /εἰ ἐτεὸν δὴ πάντα τελευτήσεις ...

419 αὐτῆμαρ 'that very same day' (Medea uses this same adverb in connexion with the execution of the ordeal at 788): Jason can depart there and then with the Fleece for all he cares – not that Aeetes considers this a likely outcome (cf. 1189-90).

There is a wry echo of i.244 here: in fact it is Aeetes who proves to be calling the tune, not Jason or the Argonauts.

τότε (?) So Fränkel, who saw in *codd.*'s τόδε an *Echoschreibung* of τάδε in 418: see *Einleitung* 39. This may be right ('then' looking forward forcefully to the 'but before that' in 420), but 'this Fleece <which we are talking about and which is of immediate concern>' (cf. e.g. [Theoc.] 25.181, and see Campbell *ap.* Vian 1973.87 n.2) is unobjectionable in itself; and I wonder if we should be wiping out the possibility that Ap. is indulging in his common trick of using a character to advert to a storyline divergent from that of the 'main text': according to *Naupactia EGF fr.* 8 (see Matthews 201) and [Hes.] *fr.* 299 the Fleece was stored *in Aeetes' palace* (419 fin.: 'king's <dwelling>'!). Aeetes then will be mentioning the Fleece with a knowing wave of the hand – a good Mediterranean gesture!

τόδε (?) κῶας ἀποίσεαι Infr. 1060-1 τὸ δὲ κῶας ἐς .../οἴσεαι.

ἀποίσεαι Cf. e.g. Theoc. 1.3; middle post-Homeric.

εἰς βασιλῆος Like εἰς Ἀίδαο at ii.353 (Homeric). I have not noticed this particular expression elsewhere. Contrast *Od.* 4.621 ἐς δώματ' ... βασιλῆος/, id. 8.257 /οἴσων ... δόμου ἐκ βασιλῆος/.

420 πρὶν ... δοίην Like *Od.* 14.155 /πρὶν (before the condition I have stipulated is met) δέ κε ... οὔτι δεχοίμην/ (εἴκων 157). Cf. also id. 15.449 /καὶ δέ κεν ... δοίην/ (+ γάρ).

μηδ' ἔλπεο *Il.* 20.200-1 = 431-2 μὴ .../ἔλπεο (but with infin.) .., ἐπεὶ ...

420-1 With this closing generalisation (see Faerber 99) Aeetes gives voice to his utter scorn for Jason and his request, on two fronts: ἀγαθός/κακός advert not only to fighting capabilities but also to social standing (Jason is after all a homeless outcast), and specifically to the status conferred by birth (n.b. γεγαῶτα), cf. 402f., and also, in the context of a πεῖρα, *Od.* 21.322f./335 (noted by Hunter 1993.23). That the 'good' man should 'give in to' one who is his inferior in these respects is degrading indeed: ἀεικές also is a term associated with discredit in both the military and the social sphere, A. W. H. Adkins, *Merit and Responsibility* (Oxford 1960), 42f. Aeetes has a further dig at 437-8.

I suspect that hereabouts (cf. 403, 438) Ap. offers a tongue-in-cheek reminder of the villain Eurystheus, imposer of ἄεθλοι, labelled by Heracles χείρονι (!) φωτί, *Od.* 11.621; cf. id. 623 ~ infr. 429 and 431, 625 init. ~ infr. 428.

421 Cf. [Orph.] *A*. 410 (οὐ ... γάρ ...) ὁπλότερον γεγαῶτα γεραιτέρῳ ἰσοφαρίζειν.

ἄνδρ' ἀγαθὸν γεγαῶτα ἄνδρ' ἀγαθόν heads a hexameter in Thgn. *IEG* 173, a pentameter in Tyrt. id. 10.2. Ctr. Simon. *PMG* 542.1 ἄνδρ' ἀγαθὸν ... γενέσθαι.

κακωτέρῳ ἀνέρι εἶξαι Cf. Eur. *Ion* 637, and for the form [Theoc.] 27.22 κακωτέρῳ ἀνέρι δώσει/; on Homeric κακώτερος see F-G on *Od.* 21.324.

ἀνέρι εἶξαι But *Il.* 13.321 /ἀνδρὶ ... εἴξειε.

422f. For a generally well-balanced assessment (there is little else to recommend at the moment: see below) of Jason's ἀμηχανίη (423, 432), which is matched by that of his comrades (504, cf. ii.408-10; ii.860f. ~ 885; iv.1308 ~ 1318; Levin 49 n.2) in the face of an unachievable demand (502: cf. iv.1307/1308; n.b. ὀψέ 426 and 504f.), see Vian's paper 'ΙΗΣΩΝ ΑΜΗΧΑΝΕΩΝ' (1978.1025f.), and also Vian, *RPh* 48 (1974), 131, VDB 2.32f. Critics have often found the temptation to construct a profile of 'heroism,' or the lack of it, on the basis of ἀμηχανίη, sometimes to the exclusion of practically every other behavioural trait, irresistible: cf. lately Natzel, 'Iason, der neue Heldentypus, ist ἀμήχανος' (188) – his ἀμηχανίη being a development of the *Odyssey*'s heroic ideal of πολυμηχανίη (208 n.127). — I regret to say that I find Rosenmayer's paper of 1992 flawed in every important respect: 'epic' modes of conduct are severely underrepresented; p. 183 harbours a staggering misrepresentation of the situation; inaccuracies abound.

Our heroes, like their counterparts in Homer, may be assured, or may even be certain about, the favourable outcome of long-term objectives, but they are not thereby exempted from despair (at times intense despair) when things go badly: Duckworth 1933.94f. So here Jason, completely thrown, does not know which way to turn: a temporary, stunned introversion is the immediate symptom of his numbing panic. The ordeal imposed by Pelias had inspired this same, wholly natural (Lawall 134f., Beye 1969.52, Rose 1984.127) reaction in him prior to departure (i.460f., where ἕκαστα must refer to the sum total of the awesome responsibilities heaped upon Jason as leader: they are now beginning to sink in; the use of ἀμήχανον in ii.623, where Jason goes on to state that he should have *refused* Pelias' demand, is particularly piquant) – a reaction which the crass Idas misguidedly attributes to fear and cowardice (i.464-5; Telamon commits a similar blunder at i.1289f.). Argos had conjured up the apt, but hardly pejorative label ἀμήχανος in connexion with Pelias' treatment of Jason in iii.336(n.), and the cruel Aeetes now apes his Hellenic counterpart by compelling the hero once again to shoulder an apparently hopeless task (one quite unlike Amycus' challenge in ii init., which was at least within the bounds of normal experience: cf. in part Lawall 134-5), clearly in the expectation that he will lose his nerve altogether.

There are, as so often in such fraught situations, powerful Homeric resonances (see too 422-6n.): the ἀμηχανίη that gripped Odysseus and his companions in the clutches of the barbarous Cyclops (*Od.* 9.125: see note on 176f.(8)); Odysseus' nervy reaction to the sight of the suitors arming themselves: μέγα δ' αὐτῷ φαίνετο ἔργον/ (id. 22.149); the hero Odysseus' appeal to the force of 'necessity' in undertaking a formidable challenge (id. 10.273: see on that the useful remarks of Hugh Parry, *Phoenix* 40 (1986), 258).

Certain aspects of Jason's behaviour (*and* that of his crew!) may be related to the condition μελαγχολία. The atrabilious reaction of Heracles in i.1262 (on the imagery see NH on Hor. *Carm.* 1.13.4 and 1.16.22) shows one side of it; this, together with its milder, 'cold'-related manifestation, has been illustrated from ancient sources by Toohey, *ICS* 15 (1990), 143f. There is more to be said though, both generally and on specific points. Consider, for instance, Jason's reference to κρύος in context at ii.628 [cf. above on 390!]. And what of Bellerophon [see on 230f., 353]? He was an identified '*hot*' melancholic (Toohey 152), who had to do with πεδίον τὸ Ἀλήιον, just as Jason was to operate on πεδίον τὸ Ἀρήιον (see 409n.): Jason, ἀμήχανος at i.1286f., sat /ὃν θυμὸν ἔδων 1289: like Bellerophon, /ὃν θυμὸν κατέδων, *Il.* 6.202. [On the condition see now van der Eijk, 'Aristoteles über die Melancholie,' *Mnemosyne* 43 (1990), 33f.] One may compare (most obviously) Ap.'s interest in the symptomatology of Phineus' καταφορά (see Erbse 1953.186-7).

422-6 Here is a truly heroic challenge. Ap. recalls *Il.* 7.92-4 (warriors scared of Hector) /ὣς ἔφαθ', οἱ δ' ... ἐγένοντο σιωπῇ·/... δεῖσαν δ' ὑποδέχθαι·/ὀψὲ δὲ ... μετέειπε/κτλ. (Bulloch 1985.591 presumably had this in mind when he adduced *Il.* 7.161f., taken up infr. 515f.). Note later Musae. 160 ἄφθογγος ἐπὶ χθόνα πῆξεν ὀπωπήν/, 172 /ὀψὲ δὲ ... ἀνενείκατο φωνήν/, Colluth. 303-5 /ἔννεπεν· ἡ δ' .. ἐπὶ χθονὶ πῆξεν ὀπωπήν/δηρὸν ἀμηχανέουσα .../ὀψὲ δὲ ... ἀνενείκατο φωνήν/.

422 Infr. 1063 ὣς ἄρ' ἔφη καὶ σῖγα ποδῶν πάρος ὄσσε βαλοῦσα ...
ὣς ἄρ' ἔφη· ὁ δέ = iv.1571. See 30n.
ὁ δὲ σῖγα ... πήξας 22, 123, 174nn. 422-3 ὄμματα πήξας/ἧστ': ctr. *Il.* 3.217 /στάσκεν ... ὄμματα πήξας/.
For σῖγα in association with ἄφθογγος cf. Eur. *Phoen.* 960, and note as well id. *Ion* 582-3 σιγᾷς; τί πρὸς γῆν ὄμμα σὸν βαλὼν ἔχεις/ἐς φροντίδας τ' ἀπῆλθες ...;

423 ἧστ' αὔτως i.794 /ἧσθ', 1290 (Jason) /ἧσ' and so *Il.* 1.133-4, *Od.* 13.336-7 αὔτως/ἧσθαι (ἧσται), *Certamen* 124 corr. αὔτως (53n.) here means not 'absolutely' but 'just as he was,' eyes down in an attitude of deep thought; cf. Bulloch on Call. *h.* 5.83 (p. 191 n.4).
ἄφθογγος As *HyDem* 198 (the grieving Demeter) /δηρὸν δ' ἄφθογγος .. ἧστ' (note also 194 downcast eyes, 197 sitting), Richardson on 197-201; id. 282 (χρόνον, οὐδὲ ...); Soph. *Aj.* 311 (bewildered hero) τὸν .. ἧστο πλεῖστον ἄφθογγος χρόνον. Note too Hdt. 1.116.1 ἐκπλαγεὶς δὲ τούτοισι ἐπὶ χρόνον ἄφθογγος ἦν· μόγις δὲ δή κοτε ἀνενεχθεὶς εἶπε ..., and also the partially corrupt Ibyc. *PMGF* 283.
ἄφθογγος, ἀμηχανέων Cf. the shocked Lemniades in i.638-9 ἀμηχανίῃ .../ἄφθογγοι, the stunned Teiresias in Call. *h.* 5.83-4 (note 82: ἔφα + δ' ὄμματα) ἄφθογγος .... φωνὰν ἔσχεν ἀμαχανία/, Bulloch ad loc.
ἀμηχανέων κακότητι Also ii.410 (ὀψέ 409; Jason), 1140 (Argos); iv.1259 (Ancaeus) ἀμηχανίη κακότητος/ ~ Maced. in 126n. For the dative cf. Aesch. *Ag.* 1113 (Linsenbarth 69) – perhaps.
κακότητι Applied to the desperate plight of Jason and/or the Argonauts in ii.410, iii.476, 1127, iv.1259; so recurrently in *Od.* of the hero (5.290 al.) and the hero and his companions (9.489 al.). Hunter (1993.22-3) tries a different tack (Ancaeus in iv is apparently spared the indignity; ii.410 relates to Jason, not to the Argonauts).
Jason's expectation of κακότης at the hands of Aeetes has proved well-founded, though not in the terms he envisaged (182).

424 ἀμφὶ .. στρώφα The question whether ἀμφί is a preposition (so Haggett 39; ἀμφὶ χρόνον Pind. *O.* 2.30) or a preverb may be answered quite simply: whereas the former adds nothing to the sense, the latter adds much: cf. Nonn. *D.* 41.264 περιστρωφῶσα μενοινήν/. That Christodorus may have thought differently (26-7 βουλήν/ ἐστρώφα, cf. LSJ s. στρέφω VI) need cause us no concern. Ctr. in Homer *Il.* 8.348 ἀμφιπεριστρώφα, of the warrior Hector busily wheeling his chariot.

πολὺν .. χρόνον Always closed up in Homer, *Il.* 2.343 etc. (*Od.* 11.161 al. π. χρ., οὐδὲ, cf. *HyDem* cited on 423).

οὐδέ πῃ εἶχε Lifted from the battlefield scene in *Il.* 16.110-1 (Ajax up against it) πολὺς .., οὐδέ πῃ εἶχεν/ἀμπνεῦσαι.

425 θαρσαλέως Jason *will* find the necessary θάρσος – and without a Hera to implant it (ctr. ii.865-6, after *Il.* 21.547). The adverb is echoed in 505, Peleus offering to shoulder the task.

ἐπεὶ ... ἔργον See note on 422f. (*Od.* 22.149). Other relevant *Homerica* are: *Od.* 10.79 ἐπεὶ οὐκέτι φαίνετο πομπή/, id. 22.408 (ὀλολύξαι, ἐπεὶ ...), *HyDem* 351 ἐπεὶ μέγα εἴσιδεν (or μήδεται) ἔργον/ [cf. i.662], *Il.* 12.416 μέγα ... φαίνετο ἔργον/.

426 *Od.* 4.706 (ἀμφασίη 704) /ὀψὲ δὲ ... ἔπεσσιν ἀμειβομένη προσέειπεν/.

προσελέξατο Also iv.833 (τοίῳ -ατο μύθῳ/). Not a *very* common verb: Hes. *WD* 499 (of self-address, West ad loc.), Call. *h.* 3.80, Theoc. 1.92, [Theoc.] 25.192 (τοίῳ -ατο μύθῳ/, cf. Perrotta 250), (uncertain in Anon. epic. *CA* 2.54), *Galeomyomachia* 25 (*ZPE* 53 (1983), 14), Q.S. 1.99, 10.423, Anon. encom. *GDK* 34.141 (5th cent.) φίλῳ προσελέξατ[ο μύθῳ/, [Apolin.] 88.37. Musaeus has προσέλεκτο, derived from ancient speculation on *Od.* 12.34.

κερδαλέοισιν I no longer entertain doubts about the aptness of this word (Campbell 1971.417): see Vian and VDB cited in the note on 422f., and also Gillies here. In archaic verse κερδαλέος is used predominantly in the sense 'crafty,' 'artful,' sim.: cf. Call. *h.* 3.152, and the subst. κερδοσύνη at ii.951. It may be (cf. Beye 1969.52) that Ap. employs the word teasingly to imply that Jason's heroism is to be aligned (as it will be increasingly) with the Odyssean 'crafty success' (Hainsworth on *Od.* 5.173-9); I think in particular of Odysseus' way of dealing with the Cyclops, an episode which forms part of the sub-text hereabouts, cf. the remarks of Friedrich, *JHS* 111 (1991), 25. 429 init. is in line with an evocation of this Homeric hero: recall his celebrated τλημοσύνη (briefly but effectively sketched by Crane, 1988.148-9). But as far as the immediate context is concerned, one may compare, *pace* Hutchinson 108 n.35, *Il.* 10.43-4 βουλῆς .../κερδαλέης, a plan which will bring κέρδος by averting imminent disaster (schol. D συνετῆς, ὠφελίμου ..., schol. AT ἐπωφελοῦς, i.e. prudent as being tactically advantageous [cf. e.g. κέρδος in *Il.* 10.225, Hainsworth on 224-5: 'κέρδος and related terms ... imply the skilful assessment of a situation and getting the most out of it'; see further Roisman, *TAPA* 120 (1990), 23f.], profitable (*Il.* 9.76 /ἐσθλῆς καὶ πυκινῆς, scil. βουλῆς; opp. νηκερδής, id. 17.469); cf. the use of κερδαλέος in classical writers, LSJ s.v. I2.

Jason's response is well-advised, as it confers the positive advantage of keeping Aeetes at bay (note the menacing 435f.): he *has* plucked up courage to undertake the ordeal, even though his own chances of survival look bleak (429). Events will show this to have been a 'wise' move. In addition, he prudently suppresses a wholly natural impulse to protest about the severity of the challenge: 427-31n.

For the wording compare *HyHerm* 162 al. μύθοισιν ἀμείβετο κερδαλέοισιν/.

427-31 A controlled, low-key response: not for Jason anguished appeals or protests to the gods above: cf. Hübscher, 82 n.26. He assures (μάλα τοι) Aeetes that he recognises the legitimacy of the challenge: the Fleece has to be earned, and there has been no unwarranted show of βίη as envisaged in 181. None the less, he is being pressured 'to an exceptional degree' (427), and the task imposed is ὑπερφίαλος, 'going beyond the bounds' (of what, is left dark: 428n.); the 'evil necessity/compulsion' <applicable to the present demand> is comparable (καί 431) to that exerted by Pelias in making him come to Colchis in the first place – and Jason has already intimated what he thought of that (390, κρυερή echoed by ῥίγιον 430). Reading between the lines then, we recognise that Jason is conscious of having been cornered by another Pelias; but he prudently (cf. 426n.) refrains from saying so outright: ctr. Val. Flacc. 7.91f.

427 ... μάλα τοι ... Ap. mirrors the form of *Il.* 23.543 (that a good-humoured disagreement) /ὦ Ἀχιλεῦ, μάλα τοι ..., note δίκη 542 (variously interpreted: δικαίως schol. D), ἄεθλον 544.

δίκη Cf. 66-74n., and εὐδικίη in connexion with Jason's ἄεθλοι at iv.343.

περιπολλὸν ἐέργεις The verb means 'fence in' (cf. schol. L&P: συγκλείεις): Aeetes locks Jason, who acts under compulsion (430), into a situation from which there is no escape: cf. ἀμφὶς ἐέργει subject Ἀνάγκη in Parm. DK28 B8.30f. περιπολλόν 'to a very great extent,' hinting at 'excessively,' cf. 427-31n. (Fränkel *Noten* 353 misses the point completely): the adverb also in ii.437, 472, Musae. 67; presumably from Aratus, 914 περιπολλά (on the analogy of ὑπέρπολυς, περιπληθής, or (??) prompted by a misinterpretation of Hes. *Theog.* 59 περὶ δ' ἤματα πόλλ' ἐτελέσθη/).

-πολλὸν ἐέργεις Hdt. 6.102 κατέργοντες .. πολλόν.

428 τῷ καὶ ἐγώ Man. 6.224, cf. earlier Pind. *I.* 8.5 ἀέθλων ... τῷ καὶ ἐγώ, καίπερ ...

τὸν ἄεθλον The article with ἄεθλ. is Homeric: in this sedes *Od.* 23.261, and so [Theoc.] 21.52, Maced. *APl* 51.3, Agath. *AP* 4.4.57 /σοὶ γὰρ ἐγὼ τὸν ἄεθλον ἐμόχθεον.

ὑπερφίαλόν περ ἐόντα Theoc. 22.97 (cf. Faerber 62, Köhnken 94) παῖδα Ποσειδάωνος ὑπερφίαλόν περ ἐόντα (Amycus: could describe Pelias as well, interestingly enough!). Here 'going beyond the bounds' of his capabilities, one might say: cf. par. schol. 427-31a, Vian ed. 1961; ὑπερφίαλος 'overwhelming' in Pind. *fr.* 92.1, sim. ὑπέροπλος LSJ s.v. III. But the usual uncomplimentary nuance simmers below the surface (427-31n.): the individual who imposes the ἄεθλος is himself ὑπερφίαλος (14-5, 15nn.).

429 τλήσομαι Cf. Anon. *AP* 9.678.1 ἔτλης ... ἆθλον/, and Call. *h.* 4.129-30 /τλήσομαι ... καὶ εἰ μέλλοιμι .... ἔρρειν/ (noting 'Αναγκαίη 122 cf. Ap. 430), Mineur ad loc.; also *Il.* 11.316-7 /τὸν δ' ἀπαμειβόμενος προσέφη .../.. ἐγὼ ... τλήσομαι.

εἰ καί 'The distinction between εἰ καί and καὶ εἰ is ... one that cannot be very strongly pressed' *GP* 301, cf. also E. J. Bakker, *Linguistics and Formulas in Homer* (Amsterdam 1988), 224. Here is a case in point (ctr. e.g. Ar. *Lys.* 123, *Plut.* 216-7); another is εἰ καί in ii.625f., a passage echoed now (the gruesome picture evoked there relates of course to the fate of *Pelias himself*, who is staring the reader in the face at 624!! On *his* dismemberment see C. Uhsadel-Gülke, *Knochen und Kessel* (Meisenheim-am-Glan 1972), 38-9; Parry 117); see further examples in *Index* p. 142 entry καί, 13-5.

μοι θανέειν μόρος Taken over from *Il.* 19.421 μοι μόρος .. ὀλέσθαι/, the doomed but defiant Achilles. Ctr. id. 7.52 τοι μοῖρα θανεῖν. Ap. no doubt remembers as well the ἐπὶ καὶ θανάτῳ of Pind. *P.* 4.186. An echo too of Eur. *Med.* 393 (ἀμήχανος 392, τόλμης 394)?

θανέειν Simply and tellingly put: Medea will soon be haunted by the prospect of Jason's 'death.' In Val. Flacc. 7.427f. Jason puts this eventuality directly to Medea.

'Jason *was also noble enough* to express the same sentiment [scil. as

Telamon at 513-4] when he accepted the challenge from Aeetes' Lawall 139 n.27, italics mine. One wonders why he did not say 'Even Jason was …' and be done with.

429-31 Ω's ἐπικείσετ' should be retained (compare Campbell 1990.483), though not by the application of meaningless labels (White, *AC* 60 (1991), 216). Instead of voicing a banal generalisation (ἐπίκειται Lloyd-Jones *ap*. Fränkel OCT; ἐπικεῖται *cod*. Z), Jason, just faced with the prospect of his own certain death, speaks with all the fervour of a prophet of doom, branding 'evil necessity/compulsion' the most chilling thing that will be imposed in the future (for ἔτι see e.g. Pearson's note on Eur. *Hel*. 57) upon mankind (ἀνθρώποισι, i.e. coming generations): he borrows elements from the gloomy forecasts of Hesiod (more of him below), *WD* 195-6 (/ζῆλος δ' ἀνθρώποισιν .... κακό- ὁμαρτήσει), 200-1 (... λείψεται ἄλγεα .... ἀνθρώποισι, κακοῦ δ' ...), cf. Arat. 125-6 (... αἷμα/ἔσσεται ἀνθρώποισι, κακὸν δ' ἐπικείσεται ἄλγος. On the text here see Ludwich, *Hermes* 91 (1963), 441 n.1). His motive for projecting the 'imposition' into the future is plain: he avoids a *direct* confrontation between *the present* compulsion (viz. duress) and that visited upon him by Pelias *on a past occasion*: see 427-31n. VDB 2.124, supported by Livrea 1982.20, detect a reference to Jason's attitude to the death that awaits him in comparison with the exile already inflicted: '… than *that* cruel necessity which …' But, the awkwardness of ἀνθρώποισι apart (Hutchinson 108 n.36), *the* ἀνάγκη must surely be related (however evasively) to the inescapable predicament described in 427f., 431 indicating that Jason was a victim of the same sort of treatment on a past occasion also (καί), viz. that same <necessity> which brought him here in the first place. But human nature being what it is, I am willing to bet that we have not seen the last of a perfect/present tense, in one form or another.

429-30 οὐ .... κακῆς Further Hesiodic elements (see 429-31n.): *WD* 157 ἔτ' ἄλλο, 702f. /οὐ .. γάρ .... κακῆς οὐ ῥίγιον ἄλλο/.. ἤ … (Semon. *IEG* 6.2 ... οὐδὲ ῥίγιον κακῆς, [Orph.] *fr*. 234 οὐ ... ῥίγιον ἄλλο).

οὐ γὰρ ἔτ' ἄλλο Similar clausulae in *Il*. 6.411 al., Bianor *GPh* 1711; *GVI* 1573.3 (Knossos, 2nd/1st cent.), 1992.7 (Athens, 1st cent. AD).

ῥίγιον A strong term: compare Kirk on *Il*. 5.872-4, Russo on *Od*. 17.430, Mawet, *AC* 41 (1972), 448f.; recall Jason's κρυερή at 390(n.), and his ῥίγιον in the stiffly worded warning to Medea at iv.402.

κακῆς .. ἀνάγκης See Campbell on Q.S. 12.388.

ἐπικείσετ' ἀνάγκης But *Il.* 6.458 ἐπικείσετ' ἀνάγκη/, scil. upon you at the hands of a cruel overseer.

ἀνάγκης Aeetes' involvement is alluded to with a general (and grand-sounding) 'necessity/Necessity'; Jason does not give voice to his feeling that a specific act of *coercion* has been perpetrated, just as in the case of Pelias (431, cf. 427-31n.). On the range of this word see H. Schreckenberg, *Ananke* (Munich 1964), with Richardson on *HyDem* 216-7; also Griffith on *PV* 515.

431 ἐπέχραεν For scholarly theorizing on this Homeric verb (well treated by Ruijgh, 1957.131) see Erbse 1953.176, van der Valk 1.264-5, Livrea on iv.580. In *Il./Od.* the sense is 'press hard upon,' 'come into violent contact with,' 'assail': so ii.283 'tried to make (violent) contact with' (not 'grazed'), 498 (onset of winds), iv.508 a strong ἐπιβάλλεσθαι, 'apply oneself aggressively to the task of.' Here 'pressed me hard,' 'coerced,' with consec. infin. as χράω in *Il.* 21.369; *Od.* 21.68-9 (schol. V there ἐβιάσασθε); or perhaps Ap. was thinking of a gloss ἐπέσκηψε (so schol. HPV on ἔχραε in *Od.* 5.396), i.e. 'lean upon' one to do.

This compound is much affected by later poets. With the exception of Q.S. 10.97 ('launch *x* against') and 11.480 ('graze against'), 'assail,' 'launch an attack on' sim., in a variety of applications: Nic. *Ther.* 14; [Opp.] *Cyn.* 1.415, 2.433; Q.S. 8.74, 9.128, 14.522, 602; Greg. Naz. 476.7, 581.37, 986.215, 1002.434, 1237.128, 1503.328, id. *AP* 8.117.1, 232.1; Anon. *Blem.* 67 Livrea; Nonn. *D.*, 22 ×; [Apolin.] 37.32, 73.11, 77.52, 101.26, 106.71; Paul. Sil. *Soph.* 222a, 602; Anon. *AP* 14.3.2.

ἐκ βασιλῆος A clausula in *Od.* 8.257 and, e.g., Samius *HE* 3262, Phil. *GPh* 2650, Opp. *Hal.* 1.69.

432-3 ἀμηχανίη and ἀσχαλόωντα reinforce the point that Jason is completely thrown; his comrades are soon to follow suit (502f.): ἀσχαλόωντες in 448 serves as an effective bridge.

ὣς φάτ' marks speech-closure 8 × in the poem: (1) followed by a pause/stop 2 ×; (2) rounded off with (a) adverb 1 × (b) patronymic 2 × (c) participial clause extending to the end of the fourth foot 3 ×. Parallels in Homer: only (1) *Il.* 21.423 al. ((2)(c): ctr. *Il.* 12.442 *et sim.*; *Od.* 22.210). 3[H]: no further examples.

ἀμηχανίῃ βεβολημένος Cf. infr. 893 ~ iv.1318, and Q.S. 7.537, 14.497; metaph. βεβ. (as Homer: Hainsworth on *Il.* 9.3, Lehrs 65-8, Livrea, *GIF* n.s. 8 (1977), 30; morphology: K. Strunk in *Studies L. R. Palmer* (Innsbruck 1976), 391f.) also i.1216 ἀνίη (Q.S. 3.763, 10.276, 11.325), ii.409 ἀμφασίη (Q.S. 2.585, 7.726, hymn in *GDK* 56.6).

It is used literally however in i.262 (see on this Vian 1970.84, and also Campbell, *GIF* n.s. 9 (1978), 288-9), 1269 (see Zumbo 1975/76.472f.; κακῷ βεβολημένος οἴστρῳ/bull ~ τετυμμένος 1265, whence Nonn. *D.* 42.188; but metaph. in *Or. Sib.* 1.150 and [κακῷ] 368, Musae. 133), infr. 1310; so too in Arat. 609 and often enough in later verse.

αὐτὰρ .... ἀσχαλόωντα ii.620-1 αὐτὰρ ὁ τόνγε [cf. i.1216; and ii.54, 443]/μειλιχίοις ἐπέεσσι .. προσέειπεν/, i.791-2 ἔμπα δὲ τόνγε/.. μύθοισι προσέννεπεν αἱμυλίοισι/, iii.710 corr. /τὴν δὲ ... προσέννεπεν ἀσχαλόωσαν/. On the localisation of the unit αὐτὰρ ὁ, ὅγ' in Ap., and on this particular pattern, see Ruijgh 1957.53.

σμερδαλέοις ἐπέεσσι Shaped like *Il.* 20.109, cf. ii.639 ~ 1218 (corr.! iii.696, adduced by VDB in favour of the transmitted text, is not an acceptable parallel). σμερδαλέοις = ἐκπληκτικοῖς, καταπληκτικοῖς, 'terrifying,' 'frightening out of one's wits' (see ii.1206!), 'completely confounding/intimidating.'

ἐπέεσσι προσέννεπεν 51, 78nn.

ἀσχαλόωντα Of demoralization, see VDB on 710 (2.80 n.1), adding ii.888 ~ ἀμηχανέων 885, iv.1277 ~ ἀμηχανίη 1259, iv.1703 ~ ἀμηχανέοντες 1701.

434f. This is the extent of Aeetes' hospitality: Jason is now dismissed. Cf. *Noten* 353. Ap. gives a sinister twist to Zeus' words to Thetis in *Il.* 1.522-3 /ἀλλὰ σὺ μὲν νῦν .. ἀπόστιχε .... ἐμοὶ δέ κε ταῦτα μελήσεται, ὄφρα ...

434 ἔρχεο νῦν // μεθ' ὅμιλον A combination of Homeric units (note in particular *Il.* 15.54 /ἔρχεο νῦν μετὰ φῦλα, id. 221 /ἔρχεο νῦν ... μεθ' Ἕκτορα, and 20.47 μεθ' ὅμιλον .. ἤλυθον) – the latter also infr. 952.

ὅμιλον .. μέμονας Ctr. *Il.* 13.307 μέμονας .. ὅμιλον/.

ὅμιλον ὅμιλος, often denoting an adventitious group of individuals (cf. West 1990.143), can have an uncomplimentary colouring (as i.680, the nervous Polyxo), and Aeetes thinks of the Argonauts as a gang of pirates in 589f., note the caustic ὁμιλαδόν in 596. It is used of the Argonautic στόλος in i.48 and often (cf. infr. 1166).

μέμονάς γε πόνοιο Peleus is made to borrow Aeetes' language in 509 ... μέμονάς τε πόνοιο/. For the form compare ii.489 ἐπεὶ μέμονέν γε ~ *Il.* 9.247 εἰ μέμονάς γε (spoken to the warrior Achilles).

μέμονας In Hom. μεμα(ώς) with gen. ἀλκῆς, ἀυτῆς, ἔριδος.

πόνοιο signifies 'battle-toil,' πολεμικοῦ ἔργου (see Lehrs 74), 'combat.' But there is a touch of sarcasm in the term, since Jason's ordeal will involve strenuous physical exertion, as Aeetes has explained (411f.). πόνος resurfaces tellingly when *Aeetes* has been proved wrong in his expectations (1401n.).

435-6 ὑποδδείσαις .... μεταχάσσεαι On this sequence, and on the placement of the optat. -αις, see Campbell 1990.483. The tentative 'were to' is followed up with an 'or if (as is more likely) you are going to': μεταχάσσεαι is a future, after *Il.* 5.350 /εἰ δὲ σύγ' ἐς πόλεμον πωλήσεαι (where φοιτήσεις schol. D: see on the form *GH* 2.284), ῥιγήσειν 351 ~ Ap. 438. Cf. infr. 1189-90 (where note the run ἐπὶ ζυγὰ βουσὶ ...).

435 εἰ δὲ σύγε So ... σύγ' *Il.* 4.34 al., cf. above. The strengthened pronoun is matched by αὐτῷ ... μοι in 437: 'if *you* ..., *I personally* ...'
ὑποδδείσαις + infin.: 318n., McLennan 55.
ἐπαεῖραι + dat.: differently Homer: Vian ed. 1961, *LfgrE* s. ἀείρω II4.

436 οὐλομένου A crucl rcminder of the nature of the task set. For Ap. (so, in Homeric exegesis, e.g. schol. D at *Il.* 14.84, cf. Erbse on schol. *Il.* 1.2*a*, and for discussion of Homeric usage the bibliogr. in Braswell on Pind. *P.* 4.293(c)) οὐλόμενος = ὀλοός (*Noten* 107-8, cf. Bond on Eur. *HF* 1061), 'lethal,' 'pernicious' *et sim*. Cf., with reference to Jason's *aristeia*, ὀλοός in iii.408, 906, 1028, 1049, 1301, 1388, οὐλοός in iv.1033. In 3[H] otherwise: Theoc. 24.29 (ambiguous it would appear: λυγρά points in one direction, τὰ καὶ ... in another).
μεταχάσσεαι Like μεταχωρεῖν, *retire, withdraw from*; here only (μετα-: see in general Boesch 65). χάζεσθαι + gen. is Homeric (e.g. *Il.* 15.426 μάχης, cf. iii.1051 ἀέθλου, of Jason); so ἀναχ- iv.1241.
ἀμήτοιο 418n.

437 τὰ ἔκαστα ... See 401n.; i.339 /ὄρχαμον .. ᾧ κεν τὰ ἔκαστα μέλοιτο/, of which this utterance is an ironic echo: Aeetes may be counted upon to see personally to every last detail, for Jason by then will have forfeited any right to determine how he and his men should be treated.

437-8 ὄφρα .... μετελθεῖν μετελθεῖν means 'to approach' someone with a request, scil. as a ξεῖνος: the host-guest relationship figures explicitly in *Il.* 3.353f. ὄφρα τις ἐρρίγῃσι καὶ ὀψιγόνων ἀνθρώπων κτλ. (Menelaus, like Aeetes, is soon to be disappointed), used here in tandem with 8.515f. ἵνα τις στυγέῃσι καὶ ἄλλος κτλ. (the confident Hector, likewise to be thwarted in due course) and 1.185f. ὄφρ' ἐὺ εἰδῇς/ὅσσον φέρτερός εἰμι σέθεν, στυγέῃ δὲ καὶ ἄλλος κτλ. (the domineering Agamemnon, who will eventually be the loser).

ὄφρα καὶ ἄλλος Cf. *Od.* 14.400 /ὄφρα καὶ ἄλλος .. ἀλεύεται, claus. ὄφρα καὶ ἄλλῳ id. 8.241.

ἄλλος Similarly ἄλλῳ in Amycus' threat at ii.57 (on the interrelationship see Rose 1984.121 with n.17).

... ἐρρίγῃσιν ... Note later Nonn. *D.* 36.159 (and Q.S. 14.441-2).

ἀρείονα φῶτα is a clausula in Hes. *WD* 193. Recalling the Agamemnon-Achilles confrontation (above), we may reflect that the former dealt harshly with ἕο μέγ' ἀμείνονα φῶτα (*Il.* 2.239); in our poem too the bully will be worsted. (Cf. also *Il.* 7.111-2, of Hector). Hurst's definition of ἀρείων here (86) is too narrow.

For related sentiments about the inadvisability of vying with (etc.) one's 'betters' see West on Hes. *WD* 210-11, Gerbeau on Nonn. *D.* 19.316.

439 ἴσχεν 396n.
ἀπηλεγέως 19n. Aeetes' blunt and brutal speech leaves no room for further discussion, and it is time to disperse.

ὁ δ'... Built like *Il.* 5.13 ὁ δ' ἀπὸ χθονὸς ὤρνυτο πεζός/, and cf. id. 23.488 al. /ὣς ἔφατ', ὤρνυτο δ' αὐτίκα (! See on παρασχεδόν 440) ... Cf. also 47-50n.

440 Αὐγείης Τελαμών τε 363 Αὐγείην· Τελαμὼν δ' ... Ctr. 196-7.
Αὐγείης 197n.
παρασχεδόν for παρεγγύς first in Ap. Although a local sense would fit here ('at his side': so e.g. Ardizzoni; but an *immediate* departure is equally, if not more, to the point) and in i.1091 (? cf. παρστάς *Il.* 10.157: Campbell 1969.284), a translation 'at once,' 'directly' sim. is preferable or obligatory in i.354, 698, ii.10 (cf. 8f.), 859 (Campbell 1973.81; ctr. Zaganiaris 322), iii.667, iv.99 (cf. αἶψα in 93), 230, 1331, and should perhaps be applied across the board: so VDB 1.279.

Other examples: (a) local: epigr. *ap.* Foss, *ZPE* 26 (1977), 161, verse 6, another *ap.* Robert, *Hellenica* 4 (1948), 7 n.2, verse 1; Opp. *Hal.* 3.364 + 4; *Or. Chald.* 37.12; [Apolin.] 140.18; (b) temporal: Nic. *Ther.* 800, *Alex.* 207.

εἵπετο ... A comparable clausula infr. 1334.

441 οἷος, ἐπεί Like *Od.* 1.244 al. /οἷον, ἐπεὶ ...;

μεσσηγὺς ... λιπέσθαι Lit. 'leave themselves [i.e. 'stay behind': so λιπέσθαι in *Od.* 17.187 (v.l.) *et sim.*: ~ infr. 825-6 κασιγνήτους .. ἔτ' αὐτόθι μεῖναι ἀνώγει/"Ἄργος] still on the spot in the meantime [infr. 723 /μεσσηγὺς ... λίπον].' μεσσηγύς, local in Homer, can also function as a temporal μεταξύ in Ap. (*Index* s.v.): cf. LSJ s. μεσηγύ II (prose).

αὐτόθι .. λιπέσθαι Cf. *Il.* 10.443, 21.201 *et sim.* (*Echoes* at ii.832).

νεῦσε The accompanying infin. finds an Homeric precedent in *Il.* 9.620-1 (embassy scene; departure of visitors; somebody stays behind). After Chalciope's outburst Argos wisely decides to leave his 'very own brothers' (αὐτοκ-: they are all sons of the same mother [see in general *LfgrE* s.v.], and she has already made her displeasure clear) where they are: another mass exit is not on! Jason and co. can then depart without further incident. 'They were to enlist the sympathies of Chalciope on behalf of Jason' says Mooney, inattentively jumping the gun.

Aeetes is happy to let Argos wander off with the strangers: he has sized Jason up, and knows, or thinks he knows, that he has him where he wants him.

442 Cf. *HyDem* 80 /αὐτοκασιγνήτῳ· ὁ δ' (and so τοὶ δ' Mosch. *Eur.* 122); *Il.* 24.647 al. /αἱ δ' ἴσαν ἐκ μεγάροιο, *Od.* 20.6-7 ταὶ δ' ἐκ μεγάροιο ../ἤισαν.

ἤεσαν 'started to make their way'; so *codd.* here (see on the form *GG* 1.674, and P. Chantraine, *Morphologie historique du grec* (2nd ed., Paris 1961), 204), but ἤισαν infr. 1331, κατήισαν ii.812. ἤεσαν should not be lightly dismissed (ἤισαν Rzach 593, cf. Boesch 23, who embraces some post-Homeric forms wholeheartedly, and rejects others out of hand): cf. Xenoph. *IEG* 3.3 (ἤισαν Meineke), [Theoc.] 25.136 (id.), *Or. Sib.* 1.279, Q.S. *ap.* Campbell 1973.74 n.4. Ap. may well have had access to copies of Homer carrying this very form (note Plato at *Od.* 24.9).

ἐκ μεγάροιο 285n.

443f. A brief mention of Jason's physical attractiveness, the first in a series of general descriptions in iii/iv (Griffith, *CPh* 80 (1985), 310), heralds a vivid account of Medea's recollections (453f.). Ap. now sets about highlighting the impact made by Jason as an individual; previously Medea had been sent reeling by Eros, and the focus of her passion had receded from view (287f. 'Aesonides,' then over to Medea).

443 θεσπέσιον 'marvellously,' 'phenomenally,' teasingly hints at the interested presence of Jason's divine 'shadow' (see 392n.): cf. Athena *Od.* 6.229f. (the sequel echoed infr. 444) and θεσπεσίην + χάριν in 2.12/17.63, 8.19 [imit. Colluth. 248] ~ θηεῦντο 2.13/17.64, ἐθήησαντο 8.17, with Clay 161-2. In the event, Ap. reserves a formal beautification-scene for the occasion of Jason's face-to-face meeting with Medea, infr. 919f. In iii.1064 (hardly adj.!), iv.207 adverbial θεσπέσιον (LSJ s.v. III; common in Imperial verse, e.g. Q.S. 9.297) carries no such overtones.

ἐν πᾶσι μετέπρεπεν See 246n. Cf. Campbell on διέπρεπεν in Mosch. *Eur.* 71. — ἐν πᾶσι: cf. Aeneas in Virg. *A.* 4.141.

Αἴσονος υἱός 357n.

444-5 Infr. 925 (where note ἐθάμβεον) Jason /λαμπόμενον χαρίτεσσιν (~ Anon. *AP* 5.26.3; cf. Richardson on *HyDem* 276, and Gerber, *QUCC* n.s. 25 (1987), 16), i.1230 the irresistible Hylas, about to be taken (cf. Beye 1982.93, and 121-2n.) κάλλεϊ καὶ γλυκερῇσιν ἐρευθόμενον χαρίτεσσιν. Ap. here recalls Nausicaa's admiration for Odysseus: *Od.* 6.237 κάλλεϊ καὶ χάρισι στίλβων· θηεῖτο δὲ κούρη (cf. ἐθεῶντο in Plato *Charm.* 154c, al., of individuals gazing in unfettered admiration at a beautiful young man, θηέσκετο in ?Ap. *CA* 12.8, and see in general Mette, *Glotta* 39 (1961), 49f.): Medea though has to wait (in torment) before she confronts the handsome stranger directly.

χαρίτεσσιν '... includes manner and bearing as well as beauty,' Bond on Eur. *HF* 134.

ἐπ' αὐτῷ δ' −∪∪−× = *Il.* 4.470.

ὄμματα κούρη Cf. 886 and n. There is word-play here for sure: cf. Hds 4.71 ἐπιλοξοῖ ... κούρῃ (with Borthwick, *CQ* n.s. 30 (1980), 255). So, no doubt, Hegesian. *SH* 466.2-3.

λοξά Her brazenness (hardly too strong a term to apply to her behaviour in 287-8: she is the victim of a sudden overpowering fixation, cf. Buccholz 93) in looking Jason full in the face melts away just as the source of the temptation is himself in the act of departing. Now all she can do is send sidelong, furtive glances in his direction: she is beginning to feel guilty, and she takes steps to conceal the urges welling up inside her.

For the diction cf. ii.664-5 (oxen) ὄμματα δέ σφι/λοξὰ παρα- ..., iv.475-6 (Erinys) λοξῷ ἴδεν .../ὄμματι. λοξ. ὄμμ. occurs also Call. *fr.* 1.37-8, Damag. *HE* 1433-4, Nonn. *Par.* 18.78 and *D.* 5.308 al., Anon. *FGE* 1255, Cougny 4.111.4; see further Hollis' note on Call. *Hec. fr.* 72.1-2. The association of the epithet with lovers is amply documented by Kost on Musae. 101; cf. also Hudson-Williams, *CQ* n.s. 30 (1980), 125.

λοξ. also with καρήατα, ii.582: cf. Arat. 58 and later Jo. Gaz. 2.234.

παρὰ λ- Comparable lengthening before this epithet in *Il.* 2.44 etc. ὑπὸ λιπαρ-, where ὑπαὶ is an occasional variant (La Roche *HTA* 370): παραὶ SD here, cf. Campbell 1973.75.

λιπαρὴν ... καλύπτρην Derived from *Il.* 22.406 λιπαρὴν ⏑⏑⏑ καλύπτρην/ (see 448n.). λιπαρήν (in Homer 'shiny' ἀπὸ τοῦ ἐλαίου, schol. D on λιπαροκρήδεμνος at *Il.* 18.382: cf. E. B. Abrahams, *Greek Dress* (London 1908), 35; Lorimer 371f., 386; Edwards on *Il.* 18.595-6; lit. in *LfgrE* s.v.) was probably equated by Ap. specifically with ἀργυφέην (see iii.834-5/iv.473-4), i.e. 'shining white': schol. D on λιπαρός offer at various times λευκός and λαμπρός, on ἄργυφος at *Il.* 24.621 λαμπρὸν ἢ λευκόν; cf. *Il.* 14.185 (where λευκόν is both 'bright' and 'white' – a matter of common observation). In any event, Ap. plainly transfers the eye-catching sheen of the male's oiled body in his model (στίλβων *Od.* 6.237 ~ 227 anointing with oil) to Medea's mantilla, which may be thought of not merely as light-reflecting in a general way (see FJW on Aesch. *Suppl.* 1028) but as picking up the radiance emitted by Jason.

σχομένη n.b. aorist [ctr. Eur. *IT* 372-3]: having directed her eyes sideways at him she kept gazing at him in wonderment *past* (round the edge of: Ar. *Av.* 390 παρ' .. τὴν χύτραν ἄκραν ὁρῶντες, 'looking past/over the edge of ...') the mantilla or wimple draped over her head and shoulders. The καλύπτρη is not of course a veil shrouding the face ('Medea draws aside her veil to get a better look' Rose 1985.35, cf. Gillies; see on the broad construction Ardizzoni ed. and 1956.380f.). Contrast *Od.* 1.334 al. (cited by Hoelzlin) ἄντα παρειάων σχομένη λιπαρὰ κρήδεμνα, i.e. 'having positioned her mantilla before her cheeks,' her face not usually being concealed (I am not persuaded by the interpretation advanced by Haakh, *Gymnasium* 66 (1959), 374f.). The echo is significant: Penelope uses her mantilla to advertise her determination to resist sexual violation (see on this and other aspects of κρήδεμνον/καλύπτρη symbolism Nagler, *TAPA* 98 (1967), 299f.; also Armstrong and Ratchford 5f.); Medea, unable to sustain direct eye-contact, uses hers to screen her sexual fixation. Nausicaa on the other hand (together with her companions) tosses her κρήδεμνον aside, see Hainsworth on *Od.* 6.100.

446 κῆρ ἄχεϊ σμύχουσα Based on *Od.* 10.247, here given an erotic slant (Eurylochus' reaction to the loss of his comrades, enticed by

COMMENTARY 446-7 367

Circe): /κῆρ ἀχεϊ .. βεβολημένος. — Greg. Naz. imitates Ap.: 765.132 /κῆρ ἀχεϊ σμύχων.

ἀχεϊ The shifting term ἄχος (see in general F-G on *Od.* 21.412, and Tichit, *REG* 97 (1984), 189f.) is recurrent in the depiction of Medea's torment (Palombi 81f., cf. also Buccholz 93f.): the 'anguish' or 'pain' (i.q. Sappho's ὀνία: cf. Theoc. 2.39 al., iii.290 al., Vetta on Thgn. 1337) induced by passion will soon manifest itself as 'grief' (i.q. πένθος, cf. e.g. Laertes/Odysseus at *Od.* 24.315) for one who is as good as dead already (459f. ~ 464).

σμύχουσα, νόος ... Cf. 296-8. σμύχειν, 'a particularly ugly and gloomy word,' Richardson on *Il.* 22.410-11: cf. 762 (subject ὀδύνη), and Gow on Theoc. 3.17, Faerber 40 (who insisted that Theoc. loc. cit. preceded Ap. 762); Anon. eleg. (pap. 2nd cent. AD) *SH* 964.20 κατασμύξας subject Eros. It will have meant originally something like 'réduire en cendre avec beaucoup de fumée' (see Ruijgh 1991.484 and 616 on build and etymology). 'Smouldering' is eminently suitable both here and in 762; a neutral 'burning' (so schol. D at *Il.* 9.653, 22.411; see on Homeric usage Graz 250) can be confidently ruled out: cf. ii.445 ὑποσμύχονται = ὑποτύφονται (see schol. there), and the epigrammatists' τύφεσθαι (with schol. AbT at *Il.* 9.653c, Erbse ad loc., NH on Hor. *Carm.* 1.13.8).

446-7 νόος ... The lover's soul (ψυχή) can be said to vacate the body (e.g. Meleag. *HE* 4074f., a beautifully crafted piece; id. 4086f.; cf. in general Zagagi 135f.) and under Eros' influence to run off in search of the object of its desire, leaving its owner half-dead in the process (Call. *HE* 1057f.). Ap. may well have been inspired by such a motif (the *soul* figures in the Homeric line underpinning the images of 'dream' and of 'aerial flight,' *Od.* 11.222 ψυχὴ δ' ἠύτ' ὄνειρος ἀποπταμένη πεπότηται) to experiment with a picture far removed from the self-mocking frivolity of the epigram (Hutchinson preaches a different impression: *JHS* 111 (1991), 221): it is Medea's 'mind' (which has a will of its own, 298) that takes wing and follows in the *eromenos*' footsteps. One can of course be said to have one's mind 'somewhere else' sim.: Davies on Soph. *Trach.* 272-3; cf. the celebrated *Il.* 15.80f. + imitations, and also (πέτεσθαι) Thgn. *IEG* 1053, Ar. *Vesp.* 93, along with K. Sier, *Die lyrischen Partien der Choephoren des Aischylos* (Stuttgart 1988), 137, 205. Later, tamer instances of the νόος accompanying the loved one: Kost on Musae. 72 (add Nonn. *D.* 42.439-40).

Like a dream, the mind possesses no corporeal reality. In theory, unshackled by physical impediments, it can, again like a dream, move at great speed: see for this notion VDB on ii.546 (1.273), Campbell on Q.S. 12.202; rapidity of dream: iv.877 ἠΰτ' ὄνειρος/ ~ 878 θοῶς; Bion 1.58 (ἕπτα) with Fantuzzi ad loc.; Faerber 9; I. Kulessa, *Zur Bildersprache des Apollonios Rhodios* (Diss. Breslau 1938), 44. But a dream may also suggest feebleness: the image of the mind's free flight is undercut by ἑρπύζων, 'creeping,' i.e. 'moving laboriously, with immense effort' (Eur. *fr.* 25.3 old men ὀνείρων .. ἕρπομεν μιμήματα. Illustration of this idea: Bond on Eur. *HF* 111f.; cf. Ap. ii.197f., the aged and infirm Phineus), here under the oppressive weight of grief/dejection (~ ἄχεϊ 446, cf. with ref. to ἑρπύζειν schol. T/b at *Il.* 23.225 with Leaf's note on the line λύπη, schol. M/Q at *Od.* 1.193 ὀδύνη καὶ ἀνία); like the Argonauts in iv.1289. *Medea* cannot follow in Jason's footsteps: *her mind* can 'fly' in pursuit of him, but only falteringly and painfully, due to the debilitating effects of the emotional turmoil that springs from love's 'cares,' 'anxieties' (452 ~ 471, νόον).

Il. 22.199f., adduced by VDB (2.69 n.3) and others (cf. lately Natzel 51), may also have exerted an influence, though the dream-situation envisaged there is far more ordinary.

The mind's dream-like detachment from the body strikingly prefigures the 'externalised' images of 453f. Although Medea ponders deeply (452, 456) 'in her heart' (451), a rapid succession of visual impressions recapturing the departed Jason present themselves in cinematographic fashion 'in front, in front ... of her eyes' – she is reenacting a 'dream-experience.' A variation on the motif: infr. 1151(n.), where Medea's ψυχή has 'winged its way high up among the clouds': totally self-absorbed, she is in a dreaming – indeed a sleepwalking, 1152 – state.

νόος ... ὄνειρος Cf. *Od.* 2.92 al. (-σα) νόος δέ οἱ (often later: note in particular Mosch. *Eur.* 106 νόος δέ οἱ ἠΰτε φωτός/, and Opp. *Hal.* 3.505), *Od.* 11.222 above (see also Livrea on *Blem.* 3); ἠΰτ' ὄνειρος is clausular also in iv.877, Opp. *Hal.* 1.36, and cf. ii.197.

ἑρπύζων On the etymology of this expressive verb see Ruijgh, *Mnemosyne* 42 (1989), 153.

πεπότητο See above, and 684n. 'The verb recalls the Stoic use of *ptoia*' Pavlock 59: why should it?

μετ' ἴχνια νισομένοιο i.741 μετ' ἴχνια νίσετο, Q.S. 14.46 νισομένοιο κατ' ἴχνιον. For μετ' ἴχνια cf. also *Od.* 2.406 al., Matro *SH* 534.38, Call. *h.* 4.19, id. *HE* 1287, Greg. Naz. 1488.112, [Orph.] *L.* 443, [Apolin.] 33.28, Cometas *AP* 15.40.34. In i.575 the rarer κατ' ἴχνια should be read (Campbell 1971.408 n.1; VDB ad loc.).

νισομένοιο Similarly ii.199, iv.178 (in the plural at ii.1284 ~ Hes. *Theog.* 71); 3^H: Theoc. 7.25.

448 "'Alors donc, eux, comme on l'a dit': retour au v.442" Vian ed. 1961. Cf. *Il.* 10.541 /καί ῥ' οἱ μὲν ..., τοὶ δὲ ... (ἤλυθον 540), with Campbell on Q.S. 12.169, + *HyHerm* 182 /ὣς οἱ μέν ῥ'. Coupling of formulae often produce such effects in Homer: e.g. *Od.* 16.213 /ὣς ἄρα φωνήσας κατ' ἄρ' ἕζετο, Hoekstra ad loc. (but add *HyHerm* 365).

δόμων ἐξήλυθον But *Od.* 20.371 ἐξῆλθε δόμων. δόμων here = the whole palace-complex.

ἀσχαλόωντες See note on 433. *Il.* 22.412 /λαοὶ μέν ῥα ... -ον ἀσχαλόωντα/ (λιπαρὴν .. καλύπτρην/ 406, σμύχοιτο 411, /ἐξελθεῖν 413): the air of gloom is intensified by powerful literary reminiscence.

449 An important sub-plot is hereby signalled. Thoughts of Aeetes' anger, upon which the poet has placed maximum stress (Rose 1984.120 n.13), will pass through Chalciope's mind again in 614.

χόλον πεφυλαγμένη Cf. Nonn. *D.* 42.391 al., and earlier Aesch. *Suppl.* 427 φύλαξαι κότον.

χόλον .. Αἰήταο reappears with variations in iv.512, 740.

450 *Homerica*: (a) *Od.*: 21.8 /βῆ δ' ἴμεναι θαλαμόνδε [but not a bedroom] σὺν ... (v.l. 1.360 θαλαμόνδε βεβήκει/, *Echoes* 49, Rengakos 1993.137-8), 3.32 (/καρπαλίμως 30, μετ' ἴχνια ibid., ἧστο [~ Ap. 454??] 32) al. σὺν υἱάσιν; (b) *Il.*: 24.248 υἱάσιν οἷσιν.

καρπαλίμως ... βεβήκει 271, 280nn.

θαλαμόνδε 9n.

υἱάσιν *w* Atticises (see *GH* 1.228); cf. AE at 692. This form in 3^H: Call. *h.* 3.126 (692n.), Euphor. *CA* 96.1.

451 αὔτως δ' αὖ for /ὡς δ' αὔτως also i.1321, Q.S. 7.148, Eudoc. *Cypr.* 2.171, Max. 297. Medea too makes herself scarce.

μετέστιχε First in Eur. (*Hec.* 509, *Suppl.* 90), where μετα- = 'in search of' a person: here 'went in their footsteps, followed behind.' In Call. 'follow, track' (ἴχνια, *h.* 6.9); in Nonn. *D.* (Peek *Lex.* s.v.) 'go to join,' 'repair to/seek out' a place, 'pursue' on battlefield; in [Apolin.] 'go to' a place 77.102, 104.24, 59, metaph. 'pursue, come in pursuit of' 77.71, 114.5. Ap. has the Homeric ἀποστ-, but only 2 ×. See in general Letoublou, *RPh* 53 (1979), 93 n.4.

Chalciope has gone to her bedroom with three of her sons; Medea follows them out of the megaron, but obviously goes to her own bedroom, the scene of the coming monologue as of others.

451-2 πολλὰ .../ὥρμαιν' *Od.* 7.82-3, 23.85-6 (ἵε.., κατέβαιν'..) πολλὰ δέ οἱ κῆρ/ὥρμαιν', cf. *Il.* 10.4 (πολλὰ φρεσίν), 1.193 al. (κατὰ θυμόν/), 21.137 al. (ἀνὰ θυμόν).

ὥρμαιν' See 18n. Of a sleepless lover suppl. in ?Ibyc. *PMGF* S257(a), col. i.16.

452 ὅσσα τ' See Ruijgh 1971.950.

Ἔρωτες ἐποτρύνουσι Infr. 653 ἵμερος ("Ἵμερος) ὀτρύνεσκε/ ~ Aesch. *Th.* 693 ἵμερος ἐξοτρύνει. *APl* 202.4 ἐποτρύνων scil. Ἔρως, but different in application.

Ἔρωτες See 296-7n., and also *Studies* 130-1; Lasserre 78f.; Rosenmayer, *Phoenix* 5 (1951), 11f. Of the four contributions from 'the Erotes' (here, 687, 765, 937), only the last (in the mouth of a crow-preacher) approximates to the playfulness and irreverence of the epigram (cf. 446-7n.). When they have to do with Medea, there is nothing mannered or shallow or whimsical about their behaviour, nor do they function as 'a characterless divine entourage' (Beye 1982.127), or as one of 'the banalities of erotic literature' (Couat 326): they are fearsome creators of misery, generating in their victims acute anxiety, brazen deceitfulness, excruciating pain. That *Eros* has gone back to his home on Olympus is hardly a relevant consideration (cf. Buccholz 95). In fact, these pluralised beings (it is wrong to depersonalise them, as does, e.g., Paduano 100f.; PF go for a blend) may be thought to provide a very effective substitute at moments of great stress: Ap. can remind us of divine involvement without having to drag the boy-wonder back into the action by the scruff of the neck.

ἐποτρύνουσι μέλεσθαι Cf. for the form *Od.* 7.262 ἐποτρύνουσα νέεσθαι/ *et sim.*

μέλεσθαι 4n. Rounded off with μεληδήμασι (471). The notion that as a lover one cares or concerns oneself about another is particularly piquant in Medea's case, as Jason's plight gives exceptionally strong grounds for anxiety. On the use of the verb in erotic writing see Vetta on Thgn. 1320.

453f. A remarkably vivid account of Medea's lingering memories, delivered with a Sapphic directness. See a large number of the passages illustrating the φαντασίαι that present themselves to (dreaming) lovers in Pease's note on Virg. *A.* 4.83 (also id. on 3, 4, 11), and cf. above on 446-7. Medea, whose mind has just taken wing 'like a dream,' experiences the visual and aural stimuli associated with an actual dream: before her eyes 'still' (cf. εἰσέτι in Mosch. *Eur.* 19, with Campbell on 18) course images, in serial order, of 'the sort of man he was' (οἷος is deftly rounded off with a τοῖον to mark her conclusion), his mode of dress, his manner of speech, his bearing when stationary and in motion: cf. for this last element Ov. *Met.* 6.491, and Sappho's βᾶμα, *PLF* 16.17, with Fedeli on Prop. 1.18.11-12; but here I imagine there is a specific suggestion, in the wake of the grandiloquent plural φάρεσιν and the picture of Jason sitting 'upon the θρόνος' (I disagree here with Cairns 43 n.54), of 'regal' movement θύραζε, matching that of Aeetes in 268, where the same adverb occurs. These impressions are drawn together with a classic expression of 'hero-worship' (456-7). All the while (n.b. αἰέν in 457: this phenomenon has no fixed place in the sequence) she recalls <the sound of> his voice, and the tonal quality of the words conveyed by that voice. Admiration then gives way to an acute anxiety-attack, with a drastic outcome: she finds herself in the position of a mourner, who can now only indulge in lamentation and intense pity for the deceased object of her affections. The succeeding monologue puts on record the reactions of the 'dreamer': cf. 463 ἀνενείκατο ~ infr. 635, 464 δειλαίην κτλ. ~ infr. 636.

There can be little doubt that Ap. had in his mind a striking scene near the beginning of *Odyssey* 20: Penelope's dream (81 ὀσσομένη, interpreted as 'seeing before one's eyes' rather than as 'with an image in the mind,' τοῖος and οἷος 89 recalling 19.219, imitated in 454 below) and Odysseus' 'half-dream' (93 μερμήριξε 'he got down to musing/ pondering deeply,' and saw a vivid image of his wife, cf. Ap.'s πορφύρουσα in 456). Cf. also *Il.* 23.67, dream-figure!

453 προπρό A splendid touch, suggesting the idea (cf. schol.) of a continuous succession of sharply defined images; see on 446-7. προπρό is adverbial infr. 1013 (see Campbell 1990.484), iv.1235 (Livrea ad loc.); elsewhere only Euphor. *CA* 94.1. (It may be that Ap. regarded Homeric προπρο- as separable: we print by convention προπροβιαζόμενοι in i.386, προπροκαταΐγδην in ii.595 [see VDB *app. crit.*].) Cf. in general Boesch 66.

δ' ... οἱ ἰνδάλλετο πάντα Ctr. *Il.* 17.213 ἰνδάλλετο δέ σφισι πᾶσι/.

ἰνδάλλετο These images (ἰνδάλματα, = φαντάσματα) are not so much implanted in the mind through the vehicle of the eyes (cf.

Arist. *Mu.* 397b18f. τὰ δι' ὀφθαλμῶν ἰνδαλλόμενα ἡμῖν) as enacted directly in front of them (cf., in a different connexion, the δείκηλα, projected hallucinations, of iv.1672, discussed by Dickie 272f.).

ἰνδάλλεσθαι of a mental picture (LSJ s.v. 1) is certainly Homeric: *Od.* 19.224 (run-up imitated infr. 454f.), cf. Stanford ad loc., and *LH/ LfgrE* s.v. for uses and interpretations in archaic epic; the relevance of the Aristarchean treatment of *Il.* 17.213, highlighted by many (e.g. Merkel *Proleg.* 101, Seaton 1891.6, Erbse 1953.167, Rengakos 1993.34 n.3), eludes me. So too ii.545, infr. 812, and in other verse-types e.g. Lyc. 254, *Vis. Doroth.* 16. In i.1297 however 'shine, flash' (~ λαμπέσθην *Il.* 19.366; *oppositio* maybe: Euphor. *CA* 50.3 πυρὶ ... ἰνδάλλετο) rather than 'look like' (as e.g. Opp. *Hal.* 2.233 πέτρῃσιν ὁμοίϊοι ἰνδάλλονται/, this a variation on or a misunderstanding of Arat. 939).

454 A reworking of *Od.* 19.218-9, Penelope to the disguised ξεῖνος, about her lost husband (she weeps 249f.: cf. Ap. 460f.): εἰπέ μοι ὁπποῖ' ἄσσα [nothing as general in Ap.!] περὶ χροῒ εἵματα ἕστο,/αὐτός θ' οἷος ἔην, καὶ ...

φάρεσιν The plural somewhat grandly (453f.n.) of a single individual's garment (so e.g. Eur. *El.* 1221, infr. 863, 1031, Nonn. *D.* 4.333 al.), reflecting the εἵματα of *Od.* 19.218 (above). I see no reason to suppose that Jason came dressed for the occasion (so Rose 1985.35), even if a φᾶρος is not worn by just anyone (Heubeck on *Od.* 23.155).

For the dative cf. *Il.* 15.389 (Linsenbarth 67, Ardizzoni ed. and 1956.382f.); but note also the use of καταέννυμι and (LSJ s.v. I2) of ἀμφιέννυμι.

ἧστο The case for this 'forme à augment temporel analogique' (VDB 2.69 n.5) is succinctly put by Vian ed. 1961. See *Od.* 11.191, clausular εἶται: 'ἧσται Zen. *vulg.*: ἧστο Ar.' Allen ad loc. That is to say, there is a more than reasonable case (*pace* Haslam 58) for accepting the proposition that Ap. considered ἧστο to fall within the province of both ἕννυμι and ἧμαι. A translation 'in what sort of robes he was sitting' is hardly credible: but ἕζετ' in the next line, recalling ἧστ(ο) in 423, serves to remind us of the latter, and the normal, usage. Ctr. E: εἷτο supported by, e.g., Ardizzoni ed. + 1956.382, Fränkel OCT (hesitantly), Keydell 35, van Krevelen 1961.157; D: ἕστο ~ iv.1438, ἕεστο iii.1225 ~ Call. *Hec. fr.* 43, and so, e.g., Rzach 555, Mooney, Gillies. [Mosch.] *Meg.* 102 reproduces the Homeric εἵματα ἕστο/.

455 οἷά τ' ἔειφ' See on 453f., and VDB 2.458.

... ἕζετ' ... Cf. *Od.* 18.157, al. κατ' ἄρ' ἕζετ' ἐπὶ θρόνου −⏑⏑−×, and ctr. *Il.* 1.536 /ὣς ('so') .. καθέζετ' ἐπὶ θρόνου —⏑⏑—×, *Od.* 7.153 /ὣς εἰπὼν κατ' ἄρ' ἕζετ' ..., *Il.* 23.350 /ἕζετ' then ἔειπε/.

455-6 θύραζε/ἤιεν ii.198 ἦε θύραζε/ ~ *Od.* 21.89 ἠὲ θύραζε/; id. 19.69, 21.422 εἶσθα (ἦλθε) θύραζε/.
ἤιεν ... πορφύρουσα But *Od.* 4.427 al. /ἤια ... πόρφυρε ...

456 οὐδέ τιν' ἄλλον A clausula in *Od.* 16.361, 18.48.
ὀίσσατο This much discussed form with gemination (Rzach 448, 568-9, Schulze *QE* 354, Marxer 31, Livrea on iv.14; cf. also Campbell on Mosch. *Eur.* 8), no doubt present in Ptolemaic papyri of *Od.*, is almost constant in our MSS: VDB I.LXXV. A notable example: Anon. epic. *CA* 2.41; perhaps -σσ- should be read in Arat. 896, 1006.
πορφύρουσα 23n. The spondaic clausula (see Fantuzzi on Bion 1.27) 'zwingt uns gleichsam in die Seele des Mädchens hinein' Faerber 68; cf. infr. 1161.

456-7 ὀίσσατο ../ἔμμεναι ἀνέρα τοῖον But *Od.* 10.232 al. ὀισ(σ)ά-μενος .. εἶναι/, *Il.* 22.418 /— — ἀνέρα τοῦτον. Q.S. 8.37-8 is no doubt a reminiscence: ἐώλπει/ἔμμεναι ἀνέρα κεῖνον.

457-8 The words are still ringing in her ears, as if she had just stirred from a dream (453f.n.): cf. e.g. *Il.* 2.41, Luc. *Somn.* 5.
Echoes in Q.S. 1.458 αἰὲν ὄρωρεν/ ~ 6.168 πολὺς δ' ἐνὶ μῦθος ὀρώρει/, Nonn. *D.* 40.502-3 οὔασιν αἰὲν ἑκάστου/... ἐπεβόμβεε μῦθος.
ἐν οὔασι Cf. Aesch. *Pers.* 605 (female experiencing 'visual and aural hallucinations,' Broadhead on 603-6); Meleag. *HE* 4050 (αἰεί, Eros).
αἰὲν ὄρωρει α<ἰ>ὲν ὄρωρε/ a Ptolemaic papyrus at *Il.* 11.827 (West *PP* 109).
ὀρώρει Lit. presented themselves, made their presence felt; 59n. For the singular verb cf. *Il.* 9.573 ὅμαδος καὶ δοῦπος ὀρώρει/, id. 12.348, 361, with La Roche *HU* 187f.
τε μῦθοι For the lengthened τε see Rzach, *Wiener SB* 95 (1879), 706.
μῦθοι ... οὓς ἀγόρευσε Nonn. *Par.* 6.195 /μύθων ... οὓς ἀγορεύω/ (*Il.* 8.492-3 μῦθον ../τόν ῥ' .. ἀγόρευε, perhaps the source of *d*'s ἀγόρευεν here, though cf. *d* at i.475, iv.256 and D at ii.879, iv.1653).
μελίφρονες echoes 385, cf. Nyberg 130. μελίφρων: 'qui mellea dulcedine animum pertundit et oblectat' *Thesaurus* (see on this de Vries, *Mnemosyne* 24 (1971), 297); αὐδή ... μελί-: cf. *Il.* 1.249, Pind. *Paean* 8.78 μελ[ί]φρονι αὐδ[ᾷ, and on the image generally Scheinberg, *HSCP* 83

(1979), 22f. An embittered Medea is later to refer to Jason's promises as μελιχραί (iv.359).

In archaic verse this epithet is more often to be found before than after its subst., in Ap. only after: ii.1003 (καρποῖο like σίτοιο δόρποιο), [f.v.l. iv.1132]. Cf. here Homer's — — [subst.] δὲ μελίφρονα. Nowhere else in 3^H.

459 τάρβει ... αὐτῷ Shaped like *Il.* 4.493 etc. ταρβεῖν + ἀμφί here only, I believe. *Od.* 16.179 /ταρβήσας δ' ... μὴ .. εἴη/, iv.16 /τάρβει δ' Medea.

459-60 μή .... φθείσειεν She has been listening attentively to Aeetes' menacing parting shot, 437f.

ἠὲ καὶ αὐτός *Il.* 12.305, *Od.* 16.100; again in Nonn. *Par.* 7.62. Cf. iv.341-2 αὐτὸς ὑπέστη/Αἰήτης.

φθείσειεν (VDB I.LXXVI) rather than φθίσ-: cf. Vian ed. 1961 here, Campbell on Q.S. 12.351.

460-1 ὀδύρετο .... τεθνειῶτα Cf. i.1066; and *Od.* 4.110 ... τέθνηκεν. ὀδύρονται ... — ὀδύρετο: so 804 Medea ~ ἔρρεεν (δάκρυα) 805, /αἴν' 806.

ἠΰτε = ὥσπερ, ὡς, here with the participle, 'in the belief that, as though,' cf. iv.1738-9 ὀλοφύρετο δ' ἠΰτε κούρην/ζευξάμενος, with Fränkel 1950.133 n.40/*Noten* 618 n.349.

πάμπαν ... From the pathos-laden *Il.* 19.334-5 /ἤδη ... κατὰ πάμπαν/τεθνάμεν.

ἤδη τεθνειῶτα Like ἤδη τεθνᾶσι (-νηκε) *Il.* 22.52 etc.

τεθνειῶτα For differing views about Homeric τεθνειώς/-ηώς (Aristarchus) see bibliogr. in Heubeck on *Od.* 10.493-5, and Merkel *Proleg.* 118, West on *Od.* 1.289, Janko ed. *Il.* 13-16, p. 36, Ruijgh, *Mnemosyne* 38 (1985), 174, 399 and Ruijgh 1991.593. (Matro's transcription of (the bulk of) *Od.* 10.494, *SH* 540.6, presents -ει-, but that is expected.) — 3^H otherwise: -ει- [Theoc.] 25.273.

461-2 The theme of pity [Paul 5] for a loved one sure to die (752f.) resurfaces with even greater force in 761 /δάκρυ [Q.S. 2.623, 7.57, 14.269] δ' ... ἐλέῳ ῥέεν ~ *Il.* 17.437-8 δάκρυα δέ .... ῥέε κτλ.

τέρεν [Kirk on *Il.* 3.142, τέρεν .. δάκρυ, ref. Helen setting out to witness combat involving husband and lover] .../δάκρυον: cf. *Il.* 16.11, 19.323, *Od.* 16.332.

δέ οἱ ἀμφὶ παρειάς = supr. 121.

αἰνοτάτῳ 'extreme' (Vian ed. 1961), 'most intense/acute': cf. ii.577 αἰνότατον δέος, and 342n.

ἐλέῳ .. κηδοσύνῃσιν 'out of pity occasioned by her solicitous concern for him/mourning for a loved one': cf. for the successive datives Eur. *Hipp.* 1142, and see Campbell 1990.483.

κηδοσύνῃσιν First here (κηδόσυνος Eur. *Or.* 1017), see on the formation of the word Chantraine *FN* 210-3, Boesch 58/Giangrande 1976.274, Marxer 38, Fantuzzi 69 n.51; i.q. κῆδος, often used of profound concern for a loved one, which may be expressed in formal mourning, a nuance shared by a number of cognate words: see e.g. Kirk on *Il.* 6.241, Edwards on 19.292-4, Richardson on 21.122-3, 22.464-5, 23.160, and in Ap.: κηδείη 2×, κηδεμόνες iii.1274, κῆδος ii.858, iii.692. Also in i.277 (Alcimede, who, like her husband, has effectively given up her son for dead: cf. above 460-1); iv.1473 (i.e. νόστου κήδετο: because he was anxious to return to his comrades on Argo, whose loss he felt keenly; but other interpretations are possible); Cougny 3.288.4; schol. Eur. *Or.* 1017 records the singular.

463 Needless difficulties have been raised here (see VDB 2.125 on λιγέως, and cf. Campbell 1990.483). 'Zu Medeas "sanftem" Weinen gesellt sich ein "helles" Sprechen' *Noten* 354. Medea indulged in muted (and inarticulate) expressions of sorrow, but she did manage to 'bring up <from her chest: 684n.> speech in a clear-voiced fashion,' the content of which is put on record. From this point on she will give vent to her grief in unspecified ways, until, eventually, she falls asleep (616f.). The emphasis here is on the clarity and crispness (cf. in general Woodbury, *TAPA* 86 (1955), 37 = Woodbury 1991.77) of her utterance rather than its pitch, volume or audibility *per se*, as in *Il.* 3.214, 'he spoke παῦρα μέν, ἀλλὰ μάλα λιγέως,' i.e. 'with an extremely clear flow of words,' id. 1.248 'Nestor, the clear-toned orator ...' etc. (Kaimio 42f. deals most unsatisfactorily with λιγύς and related words: see further Verdenius, *Mnemosyne* 36 (1983), 16 n.3.)

ἦκα Of sound also infr. 565, see Pfeiffer on Call. *fr.* 177.11. Nonn. *D.* 2.88-9 δάκρυσε .../πυκνὰ δὲ μυρομένη ...

μυρομένη This verb is used with reference to a subdued display of sorrow from Medea again in 665 (~ 657, σῖγα... 662), 1065 (σῖγα 1063).

μυρομένη, λιγέως Ctr. *Il.* 19.5-6 λιγέως then μύρονθ'.

ἀνενείκατο μῦθον See Bühler/Campbell on Mosch. *Eur.* 20, Livrea/VDB [3.209] on iv.1748. (The Hermann-collection may be rounded off with Eudoc. *Cypr.* 1.151 δόλῳ δ' ἀνενείκατο μῦθον/).

464-70 The first of three (see Beye 1993.205) monologues in the third book: here Medea comes to realise where her sympathies lie. The second, which, like the first (this a seven-liner, matching the first monologue of *Il.*, 11.404f.), cultivates the utmost brevity (636-44), results in a decision to take positive action on Jason's behalf. In her final, sustained outburst of 771-801, one of the great showpieces of the poem (the only one of her monologues considered, in somewhat bland terms, by R. Scholes and R. Kellog in *The Nature of Narrative* (Oxford 1966), 181f.), Medea's thoughts move from an externally imposed death in the past (773f.) to a self-inflicted death in the future (788f.) and finally to the taking of her own life there and then (798f.). She is throughout a prey to indecision, signalled by the frequent use of asyndeton. But these, like the monologues in *Il./Od.* (conveniently assembled in Scully, *TAPA* 114 (1984), 11f.), are all essentially eloquent, controlled compositions (see in general Macleod on *Il.* 24.721-2, Homer's laments), free of forced or broken syntax, extravagant outpourings of grief, flamboyant imagery, stilted rhetorical poses (contrast Nonn. *D.* 4.182f., 47.320f. esp. 370f.; or Ov. *Met.* 7.11f., with Otis 1970.59f.172f.). The few statements of fact, defining her attitude to the stranger (470, 638) and acknowledging her own perplexity and anguish (772-3, 776f., 783f.), stand out in sharp relief, as does the vivid prediction about the gossip arising from her death (791f.). She throws out anxious questions (464, 771 [*sic*!], 797; in series 779f.) and exclamations of disquiet (636, 771, 783, 798), directs third-person imperatives at the absent Jason (466, 639, 778; otherwise 785-6), relates wishes or prayers through the medium of the optative or of ὄφελλεν/ὄφελον to Jason (467-8, 469, 787; 466) and to herself (640, 789; 773) and considers various eventualities (potential optatives 644, 784f., 798f.; conditional clauses 468f., 778f., cf. the fearing-clause of 637f.). Homer's monologues are in general rather less indirect, though they do contain most of the modes of utterance outlined above (see for example Clay 193, on *Od.* 13.200f.; more on style in the commentary on the succeeding speeches).

In 771f. the theme of her own misery overshadows everything else. Here she moves rapidly from that (464) to a statement of her own attitude towards, and concern for, 'that man' (464 again). If he is to vanish from her life, let him do so in safety, reaching home with his mission accomplished (468): only later will the thought occur to her directly that Jason might actually take her home with him (622f., an eventuality that comes out into the open, after much equivocation, in 1122f.). Her desire to see him dead (464-6) is as short-lived now as it is later (778-9). She wants him to survive, or failing that (469f.), to know that she at least takes no malicious pleasure in his destruction. She will soon come out on Jason's side, unaware that others are working towards this same end.

Val. Flacc.'s epic is littered with monologues. Medea's half dozen, which do not present a progression but rather focus on Medea's emotional state at various stages of the action, are well handled by U. Eigler, *Monologische Redeformen bei V.F.* (Frankfurt 1988), 78f., despite the (seemingly obligatory) Otis-inspired Ap.-bashing.

464 τίπτε ... ἄχος; τίπτε με is Homeric (*Il.* 11.606 al.), and recurs infr. 975; the interrogative neatly catches her utter lack of comprehension, which will resurface repeatedly (cf. Feeney 84). δείλαιος (first in Hipponax, *IEG* 36.4), here only in *Arg.*, is much affected by Hellenistic poets: Philet. *CA* 2.4, Arat. 946, Call., Theoc. and Herodas, Bion 1.4; *HE* 2052 (Leon. Tar.) etc.; also *GVI* 705.3, 844.5, 1870.2 (2nd/1st cent.); widespread subsequently. For the rest cf. *Il.* 8.147 al. τόδ' .. ἄχος, *HyAphr* 198-9 μ' ../ἔσχεν ἄχος (erotic context, elucidated by van der Ben, *Mnemosyne* 39 (1986), 23, cf. also J. S. Clay, *The Politics of Olympus* (Princeton 1989), 184-5; I share Wellauer's puzzlement as to why Brunck thought Ap.'s expression 'durum'), Alcm. *PMGF* 116 ἔχει μ' ἄχος ὦ ὀλὲ [Ruijgh, *Mnemosyne* 42 (1989), 169] δαῖμον [??Eros]. On ἄχος see 446n.

με δειλαίην = Nonn. *D.* 47.410 (speaker Ariadne, monologue: 464-70n.).

464-6 Both elements of this resoundingly emphatic 'polar expression' draw on explicit value-judgements: just as φθείσεται echoes φθείσειεν in 460 (fear about whether he *would* perish is converted *via* 460-1 into the certainty that he *will*), so πάντων ... προφερέστατος recalls her own appraisal of Jason in 456f., while χερείων harks back to Aeetes' cutting χέρηες (403) and κακωτέρῳ ἀνέρι (421, opp. ἀρείονα φῶτα of himself, 438). He will die, and let him! His heroic capabilities are of no concern to her. This particular show of self-deception proves to be very short-lived indeed.

Paduano's diagnosis of Medea's mental state is poor in my view, and his attempt to relate her utterance to a wider assessment of Jason's heroic status unwarranted (20f.).

ὅγε γε may mark the more important or (in the speaker's mind) the more convincing, valid, likely alternative (KG 2.173, but some of the examples they list do not come under this category), and it could here signpost Medea's own preferred view (so Hunter). More likely it serves to 'beef up' the light demonstrative: '*that man*,' the subject of all her anxiety; cf. *GP* 119, 121f., and note τόνγ' from Medea in 775 (a switch to κεῖνος in 785 once she thinks of him as actually dead and gone). For the use of the plain pronoun cf. *eum* and *eo* at Virg. *A*. 4.479, Pease ad loc.; Homeric examples: Macleod on *Il*. 24.702/ Rutherford on *Od*. 19.354.

πάντων ... προφερέστατος Closed up in *Od*. 8.128.

φθείσεται On the spelling see 459-60n.

-ατος εἴτε χερείων Cf. the clausula of ii.77, and also *Il*. 12.269-70 Ἀργείων ὅς τ' ἔξοχος .../ὅς τε χερειότερος ... For χερ- cf. 403n., and Ruijgh 1991.642.

ἐρρέτω A somewhat coarse word (cf. Macleod on *Il*. 24.239) to express her desire to be rid of him, here more than just a peevish imprecation (as in Homer: *Il*. 9.377, 20.349, *Od*. 5.139): she means φθειρέσθω (so schol.), literally, n.b. φθείσθω at 778; *contra*: Beye 1982.28. Cf. Atalanta in Ov. *Met*. 10.623f.

ἐρρέτω is used again by Medea, but in a different connexion, at 785-6(n.).

466 ἦ μὲν ... 460f. have prepared us for this development: Medea has converted a reasonable expectation into a past event, and, shocked by what she has allowed herself to say (his demise has had her blessing), she voices her heartfelt regret: 'I mean this really and truly [cf. i.689, al., *GP* 389] – would that he had made his escape ...!' For comparable examples of unattainable wishes 'for the restoration of someone or something that is (or is believed to be) irretrievably lost' see Pelliccia, *HSCP* 91 (1987), 51f.; an emphatic inversion here of the much more commonly expressed wish that an individual *had perished*: e.g. *Od*. 18.401 /αἴθ' ὤφελλ' ... ὀλέσθαι/, *Il*. 3.40, 428, 24.253-4, *vulg*. 764. Ovid (*Met*. 7.24) was to make his Medea follow a smoother train of thought with her ... *vivat tamen!*

Some misconstrue badly, in various ways: e.g. Wåhlin 38, Seaton, *CR* 17 (1903), 71, Beye 1982.28, Fowler 1990.158.

ἀκήριος ἐξαλέασθαι Cf. i.490 σόος ἐξαλέοιο/ with *Od*. 23.328 ἀκήριοι ... ἄλυξαν/, Nic. *Ther*. 190-1 ἀκήριος .... ἀλεύεται, and ctr. ἀκήριος in ii.197, where see schol. and *EtG/EtM*. On the various senses of the adjective (see in general Risch 113 n.100, Lee, *Glotta* 39 (1961), 192f.) consult *LH/LfgrE* and *LSJ/DGE*, adding: Nic. *fr*. 78-79.6, *Vis. Doroth*. 298, Anon. *AP* 1.56.2, Cometas *AP* 15.40.13.

467-8 Jason, she has imagined, is dead, or as good as dead. With a fresh strong asseveration she changes tack once again, praying that he may after all escape, and invoking her goddess in support of the prayer. She does not think of calling upon Hecate to assist Jason, or herself for that matter (cf. *Noten* 354, and Händel 116f.), any more than Circe has recourse to magic to capture a male's affections in Ov. *Met.* 14.12f., 312f. (Ovid made much of the witch Medea's helplessness, in a variety of ways: *Ars Am.* 2.101f., cf. *Rem. Am.* 261f.; *Heroid.* 12.165f., ctr. Hypsipyle in id. 6.83f.). Cf. Mene's sarcastic remark at iv.64-5, which should be viewed against the commonly voiced view that love cannot be cured by magic: see Gow on Theoc. 11.1, NH on Hor. *Carm.* 1.27.21. The decision to take positive action lies in the future – but with this sudden impassioned address to her mentor in connexion with Jason's safety and ultimate success she is at least moving in the right direction: in fact, her nephew is very soon to put to Jason the possibility that Medea, who practises magic under the direction of 'Hecate daughter of Perses,' might assist (477f.).

467 ναὶ δὴ ... *Od.* 20.37 /ναὶ δὴ ταῦτά γε [ναὶ δὴ τοῦτό γε some late MSS in *Il.* 18.128] πάντα θεά (a /τίπτε-sequence precedes, but in the mouth of a different speaker: 33] + *Od.* 5.215 al. (/)πότνα θεά (cf. supr. 79 ... πέλοιτο/ and n.). Cf. Pampr. *fr.* 3.104 Livrea /ναὶ .. πότνα... This utterance of Medea may be a reflection of the language of magic (!), see the examples of ναί (δέσποτα) collected by Festugière in *SO* 28 (1950), 89f.

πότνα Cf. Simaetha's πότνια in Theoc. 2.43 (εἴτε + εἴτε 44). So in Eur. *Med.* 395 Medea swears by Hecate τὴν δέσποιναν.

Περσηί *daughter of Perses* (Hes. *Theog.* 409f.; vocat. *Persei* Sen. *Med.* 814, Stat. *Theb.* 4.482), cf. iii.478 [~ Ov. *Met.* 7.74] ~ 1035; iv.1020 Περσηίδος .. κούρης/ ~ Nonn. *D.* 13.401; Quandt on [Orph.] *h.* 1.4, also Richardson on *HyDem* 24-6 and 24, Pfeiffer on Call. *fr.* 474. On an alleged 'Hesiodic' Hecate Perseis see West, *CR* n.s. 12 (1962), 200-1.

The pi-alliteration is not particularly pronounced, but it could conceivably be construed as representing a sudden surge of excitement/ agitation/sense of urgency (cf. e.g. *Il.* 24.352f., infr. 792, and in general Fraenkel on Aesch. *Ag.* 268, Groeneboom on *PV* 131-2, FJW on *Suppl.* 696-7, Davies on Soph. *Trach.* 947f.) or fervour (note the accumulation of μ and π/φ in the prayer of *Il.* 10.288f.) or as reflecting the language of magical incantation.

πέλοιτο buys an extra π (see above); Homer would have said γένοιτο (and so S here), cf. i.900 (adapting *Il.* 8.26).

468 οἴκαδε ... μόρον i.e. may he survive the ordeal (which holds out the prospect of a violent death) *and* get home safely with his mission accomplished. Mention of Jason's home (see 464-70n.) carries Medea way beyond the immediate predicament: it cloaks a desire, as yet unformulated, to be taken back with him. She is quiet here about the all-important Fleece: that she is soon to dismiss (620f.) in no uncertain terms.

οἴκαδε νοστήσειε *Od.* 2.343 (ref. Odysseus; but not an optative expressing a wish), and again in *Certamen* 136.

φυγὼν μόρον partly recalls Jason's resigned ... μόρος (429). The expression is Homeric (*Od.* 9.61 φύγομεν ... μόρον, cf. Hoekstra on 16.421); often thereafter: Aesch. *Pers.* 369, Lyc. 960, Q.S. 14.627, Nonn. *D.* 30.130 etc.

προφυγὼν μόρον later Jason to Medea at 1080 (~ Alc. *HE* 142 ἐκπροφυγὼν .. μόρον).

468-9 εἰ .... βουσί Medea then is prepared to entertain the *possibility* that Jason might survive, but she clearly regards his prospects as bleak; that feeling will persist.

Homer's Priam is a fruitful source of pathos: Medea echoes his εἰ δέ μοι αἶσα/τεθνάμεναι παρὰ νηυσὶν ..., *Il.* 24.224-5.

469 προπάροιθε 317n.

470 *Il.* 1.298 -ἐν οὔ τοι ἔγωγε -ομαι εἵνεκα ...
οὕνεκεν 334n.

οἱ *his*, with ἄτη, the subst. being delayed, as often, e.g. *Il.* 17.196 ἅ οἱ .../πατρὶ ...: cf. *Noten* 354-5.

ἔγωγε As Medea has seen, her father, representing the Colchian view of things, plainly harbours ἐπιχαιρεκακία about the inevitability of Jason's destruction (or capitulation, which will come to the same thing), and she wishes to be dissociated from that. The jump to sympathy in the form of positive help has yet to be made. Cf. Buccholz 97.

κακῇ .. ἄτῃ In Homer only a variant in *Il.* 9.21 (κακὴν ἀπάτην). Cf. Soph. *Aj.* 123 and, e.g., Nic. *Ther.* 352 -ε κακῇ ἐπαλαλκέμεν ἄτῃ/; ii.623 κακὴν καὶ ἀμήχανον ἄτην/ ~ Nic. *Alex.* 196 κακὴν καὶ ἐπώδυνον ἄτην/; ii.889; Man. 6.729; Q.S. 5.469. On ἄτη see 56n.

ἐπαγαίομαι Schol. ἐπιχαίρω, *take a fiendish delight in* (Paduano 22 n.18 talks mistakenly of 'l'uso erotico ...,' cf. Köhnken, *Gnomon* 48 (1976), 447), as in ?Ap. *CA* 12.18 (on which van Groningen, *Mnemosyne* 4 (1951), 111, seems to me to go badly astray), of the traitress Peisidice, besotted with her country's enemy Achilles; infr. 1262 *exult in*. The compound nowhere else in literature (see LSJ); ἀγαίομαι (Risch 284f., but see also Shipp 105 n.1, Wyatt 180 n.12): see Vian ed. 1961 here, id. 1978.1026; and my note on 1016.

The Peisidice passage raises the interesting possibility that the verb functioned here as a cue; it is certainly the case that "the theme of betrayal is implicit; Medea is being led to betray her family because of the overpowering emotion she feels for Jason," P. Toohey, *Reading Epic* (London and New York 1992), 83, cf. id., *ICS* 17 (1992), 276 (this paper however does not shed much light on Medea's overall condition, and there are far too many bits of mistranslated Greek).

471 ἡ μὲν ἄρ' ὥς Homer *passim*, but not immediately after a speech unless accompanied by ἀγορεύειν (cf. Führer 44). For ὥς used as it is here see Campbell on Q.S. 12.551a.

ἐόλητο means something like 'was in turmoil and torment,' a striking word with which to leave the account of Medea's sufferings in abeyance, more expressive than the standard ὁρμαίνειν used (with or without κατὰ φρένα καὶ κατὰ θυμόν) to mark a return to narrative in *Il./Od.* (cf. Scully op. cit. on 464-70, pp. 13f.). Mosch. *Eur.* 74-5 (Zeus, love-smitten: playfully overdrawn) ὣς εόλητο/θυμόν, see Bühler and Campbell ad loc., and also Braswell on Pind. *P.* 4.233(d). Buttmann *Lexilogus* 2.78 (cf. Mawet, *REG* 100 (1987), 112) posited a link with εἰλέω, and perhaps Ap. thought of the verb in such terms: cf. εἰλεῖτο in iv.1067?

μελεδήμασι Paul. Sil. *Soph.* 1018 νόον μελεδήμασι θέλγων [~ supr. 4, see note there and on 452]/.

κούρη closes this scene, κούρην opens the next phase of the struggle (616).

Addenda

I am indebted to Professor Ruijgh for these references:

28-9 ἄν 'in that case': see Ruijgh's paper in *Actes du colloque Pierre Chantraine* (Grenoble 1989), 75f.

75 εἰ (μή) + fut. indic.: Goodwin *MT* 165-6.

261 μέλλω + infin.: cf. Ruijgh, *Lingua* 65 (1985), 323f. πλάγξασθαι now seems to me to be most unlikely.

398 Ruijgh would regard pres. ἐξεναρίζοι as 'inceptive': see his article in *Mnemosyne* 38 (1985), 1-61.

INDEXES

Prefatory Note

Omitted here is analysis of Ap.'s manipulation of the Homeric texts; the final volume will incorporate a series of descriptive indexes (including material on textual variants, ancient exegesis and related matters) drawing on data presented in the course of the commentary in its entirety.

INDEX I
GREEK WORDS

-άας 129
ἀβλής 279
ἀγαθός 420-1
ἀγαίομαι 470
ἀγανός 78, 148-9, 396
ἄγε to Muse(s), in *didactica* 1
ἀγέραστος w. gen. 65
ἀγκύλος 157
ἀγοράομαι 168
ἀγορεύω (imperf./aor.) 83, 457-8
ἄγος 200-9, 203, 336-9
ἀγοστός 120
ἄγραυλος 276
ἄγρη 69
ἄγχι 'temporal' 294
ἀδάμας, ἀδαμάντινος 230f., 232
ἀδικία, erotic 130
ἀδμής 4-5
ἀεικέλιος 342
ἀεικής 420-1
ἀείρω, pass. of heavenly bodies 162
-άεις 129
ἀέναος -νάων 222
ἄημι 288-9
ἀήρ 141, 207f., 211, 275, 417
ἀθερίζω 80
ἀθέσφατος 294-5
Ἀθηναίη Παλλάς 340
αἴ + κε, no doubt implied, 26-8; cf. εἰ
αἶα/Αἶα 306, 313 -ίδος αἴης, 373
Αἶάνδε 306
Ἀίδης, acc. Ἄιδα, 61
αἰδώς in eyes 93
αἰθέριος 159-63, 159, 160-1
αἰθήρ 159-63, 166
αἴθομαι 296
αἴθουσα 39, 237
αἰμύλιος 51
αἰνός 342, 461-2
αἰνῶς 15
αἰπύς of building 238
αἱρέω, middle used idiomatically, 263-4
αἶσα/Αἶσα 3-4, 207f., 261, 328

Αἴσονος υἱός 357
ἀίσσω 36, 275, 286a
ἀίω, accent of aor., 270, 352-3
ἀκέων 85
ἀκηδείη 260, 297-8
ἀκήριος 466
ἀκηχέμενος 101
ἄκοιτις 38, 41f.
ἀκούω, εἴ τιν' -εις sim., 362-3
ἄκριες 166
ἀκτή of Demeter 413
ἀλδήσκω 414
ἀλεγίζω 193
Ἀλήιον πεδίον ~ Ἀρήιον π. 409, 422f.
ἅλις 103, 271-2
ἀλκή 185
ἄλληκτον adv. 74
ἄλλος in threat 437-8; cf. ὦλλοι
ἄλλοτε suppressed in the first member 297-8
ἄλλως, καὶ δ' ἄ. 66
ἀλοιφή 224
ἀλωή 114, 158
ἀμαθύνω 294-5
ἀμαρυγή, ἀμάρυγμα 287-8
ἀμβολίη 144
ἀμείβομαι, aor./imperf., 385
ἀμείλικτος Ζεύς 337
ἄμητος, image/accent, 418
ἀμηχανίη, ἀμήχανος 123, 126, 176f. (8), 284, 333, 336, 422f., 422-6, 423, 432-3
ἀμοιβαίη χάρις 82
ἀμοιβηδίς 225-6
ἀμορβός 277
ἀμπνείω w. acc. 231
ἀμύμων 190
ἀμφαγαπάζω 258
ἀμφαδίην 97
ἀμφασίη 284
ἀμφί w. dat., *for the prize of*, 117b
ἀμφιγυήεις 37
ἀμφιμάρπτω 146-7
ἀμφινέμομαι 409

ἀμφιπένομαι 271-2
ἀμφίπολοι 235-6
ἀμφιπονέομαι 251
ἀμφιστρωφάω (tmes.) 424
ἄν w. fut. infin. 28-9
ἀνά w. acc., 44; w. gen., 198; w. dat. (doubtful), 166
ἀναβλύω 220f., 223, 225-7
ἀνάγκη 429-31, 429-30
ἀναδέομαι 45-7/50, 50
ἀναίδητος 92
ἀναΐσσω 36
ἀνακηκίω 227
ἀναλδήσκω 414
ἀνάπτω 5
ἀναφέρομαι (ἀνενείκατο) 453f., 463
ἄνδιχα 23
ἀνεγείρω 294, 294-5
ἀνεοστασίη† 76
ἀνέχω 159-63, 161; intrans., 216-7
ἀνιάχω 253-6, 253
ἀνίη 290, 446
ἄντην w. dat.?? 100-1
ἀντιάω *request* 34-5
ἀντιβίην 382-5, 384
ἀντιβολέω 68, 179
ἀντίος 127, 286b-7, 287-8
ἄντομαι *implore* 77
ἀνωϊστως/-ί 6-7, 6
ἁπαλός 297-8
ἀπαμείρω 186
ἀπάνευθε 114
ἀπατάω 152
ἀπαφίσκω 130
ἀπελαύνω 326
ἀπερητύω 327
ἀπερύκω 174, 250-2, 327, 382-5
ἀπηλεγέως 19
Ἀπόλλων Φοῖβος 340
ἀπόπροθι w. gen.313
ἀποπρολείπω 267
ἀποσκεδάννυμι, sim., with ref. to meteorological phenomena 214
ἀποτρωπάομαι w. acc. 16
ἀπούρας 175
ἅπτομαι + τραπέζης 377
ἄρα/ῥα 14-5, 37, 41f., 115, 119-21, 119, 154, 223, 233-4, 242, 252, 260, 261, 408, 448

ἀραρίσκω (ἤραρε) 301
ἄργος? 210-4, 211
ἀργύφεος 444-5
Ἀργώ ~ ἀργή 343-4
ἀρείων 437-8
ἀρέσκω (with aor. ἄρεσσα) 301
ἀρηίθοος 393
ἀρήιος/Ἀρήιος 325; cf. Ἀλήιον
ἄρης, quant. of alpha in ἄρηι, 183
ἀρήτειρα 252
ἀριστῆες/ἄριστοι 7a
ἀριφραδέως 315
ἆσσον = ἐγγύς 17, 253
ἀστήρ of person 245-6
ἀστράγαλοι 117f., 117/124, 117b, 118, 119-21, 123-4
ἀσχαλάω 432-3, 448
ἀτάσθαλος 190, 390
ἄτε, like οἷα, 118
ἀτέμβομαι 99
ἄτη 56
ἀτίζω 181
Αὐγείης/-ας 197
αὐδάω (ὣς ηὔδα) 76
αὖθι 415
αὐλίζομαι of birds 324
αὐτὰρ ἔπειτα, a tag, 159; αὐτὰρ ὁ/ὅγ' 432-3
αὐτή 184
αὐτῆμαρ 419
αὐτίκα 23f.
αὐτόγυος 232
αὐτός, various uses, 11, 70, 96, 103, 112, 257, 285, 321, 350, 364, 373, 408
αὐτοσχεδόν 148, 398
αὔτως 53, 85, 123-4, 129, 185, 386-8, 423, 451
ἄφαντος 275
ἀφασία 284
ἄφατος 129
ἀφαυρός 144
ἄφθογγος 423
ἀφνειός 265-6
ἄχος 446, 464
ἄψηκτος 50
ἀψῖδες 135-41, 138

βαθυπλόκαμος 45-7/50
βαιός/ἠβ-; assoc. with Eros, 281

GREEK WORDS

βάλλομαι as middle 413
βασιληὶς τιμή 376
βεβολημένος 432-3
βέλος of shafts of light 287-8
βλύω, quantity of upsilon, 223
βολίς 140
βουσόος 277
βρῶσις 329

Γανυμήδης, etym.? 115
γάρ 2, 97; postponed 386
γε, various uses of, 14-5, 99, 112, 135, 152, 200, 355, 435, 464-6
γέλως 102
γέρας 3-4, 65
γηθόσυνος 259
γλαυκός 275
γλαφυρὴ νηῦς 316
γλυκερὴ ἀνίη 290
γλυφίδες in architecture, 217-8; in archery, 282
γλῶσσα cut out 378-9
γναθμός 128
γνωτός 359
γόμφος 340f., 343-4
γυῖα 63

δαῆναι 182
δαίδαλα 42-3
δαιδαλέος 237
δαΐζω 415
δαίμων 389-90, 464
δαλός 291f., 291
δαμάζω 4-5; form of fut. 353
δάμαρ 269
δέ 314, 388-9
-δε, or *separatim* ? 9
δειελινός/δείελος 417
δείκηλα 453
δείλαιος 464
δεινὸς ὄφις 414
δέμας acc. relation 413-5, 415
δενδίλλω 281
δεξιόομαι 258
δέρκομαι 362-3
δέρος/-ας 88
δεσμοί 62
δή (τόγε δή) 200
δῆθεν 354-5

δηιοτής 233-4
δηναιός 53
Δηώ 413
διά i.q. δίχα, in anastrophic tmesis 46
διατμήγω (διέτμαγεν -ον) 343
διαχέω 320-1
διέκ w. acc. 73, 158, 159
διέχω, middle, 283
δίζημαι/-ομαι 113-5
διηνεκέως 401
διιπετής 285
δίκη 66-74, 130, 209, 386-95, 427
δικλίς 235-6
Δικταῖος ~ Ἰδαῖος 133-4
δινεύω 309-13, 310
δινωτός 44
δολόεις 12, 86-9, 89, 191
δόλος sim. 12, 89, 191
δόρπον 301
δόρυ used to 'mow down' 416
δύομαι with initial longum 225-6
δυσηχής 96
δωτίνη 352

ἐγγελάω 64
ἐγκαταναίω 116
ἐγκάτθετο see ἐνι-
ἐγκλάω 307
ἐγώ/-ών 262; ἧμιν/ἥμιν 314
ἑδριάω -άομαι 170
ἐδωδή 299
ἐέργω metaph. 427; pass. w. gen. 184
ἕζομαι of wool-worker 294
ἔθνος + nation-name 212
εἰ, various uses, 61, 75, 80, 113, 180, 347, 358, 377/379, 429
εἰ δ' ἄγε νῦν 1
Εἴδυια (significance, spelling and accent) 243
εἰλέω 471
εἰλύω see ἐλύω
-ειμένος 45
εἶμι 25 (ἴομεν), 442 (ἤεσαν and ἤισαν)
εἵνεκα as late postp. 370
εἴρυσ(σ)α 149
εἰς w. gen. pers. 419
εἰσαΐω (+ accent) 145
εἰσέτι νῦν (περ) 203, 312-3
εἴσω w. gen. 311

εἴτε/εἴτε in indirect question 183
ἐκ 302, 345; w. no gen. expressed 231, 280
ἕκαστος (τὰ -α) 401, 437
ἕκηλος 176, 219
ἕκητι 266
ἐκλάμπω 371
ἐκλαχαίνω 222-3
ἐκπάγλως 60
ἐκπλέω w. acc. 159
ἔκποθεν 262
ἔκτοθι 255, 373
ἔκφημι (ἔκφατο μῦθον) 24
ἐκφύομαι, f.v.l., 201
ἐλαύνω *forge* 233, 235
ἕλιξ 135-41, 139-40
Ἑλλάς 13, 347, 391-2
ἕλος 168
ἔλπομαι see ἔολπα
ἐλύω (ἐλυσθείς, εἰλυμένος) 281
ἔμμορον 3-4, 4
ἐμός (crasis τἀμά) 102
ἔμπης 260
ἔμπλειος/-εος 119
ἐμφύομαι 201
ἐναγείρομαι 347
ἐνδαίω 286b-7
ἐνεοστασίη 76
ἐνεόφρων 76
ἔνθα δέ 235
ἐνθάδε 'performative' 2
ἔνθεν reflecting standpoint of narrator 2
ἐνί 140; ἐνὶ ἤματι sim. with hiatus 327
ἐνιβάλλομαι use of middle 413
ἐνικάτθετο/ἐγκ- 282
ἐνίπλεος/-πλειος 119
ἐνισκίμπτω 153
ἐννέπω colouring, aor. imperat. sing., 1; compounds 367
ἐννεσίαι 28-9
ἕννυμι, ἧστο and various other forms, 454
ἐννύχιος 294
ἐνοσχερώ 170
ἔντεα 176
ἐντύνω λέχος 40; -ομαι 293
Ἐνυάλιος/ἐν- 322
ἐξαποβαίνω 199
ἐξαῦτις 31

ἐξέμμορον 4
ἐξέρχομαι w. acc. 159
ἔξοιδα 332
ἐξότε 67
ἔοικε 16, 189-90
ἐόλητο 471
ἔολπα (ἐώλπει/ἐόλπει) 370
ἑός involving hiatus 26
ἐπαγαίομαι 470
ἐπαινέω 194
ἐπαλαστέω 369
ἐπαρτής 299
ἐπειρύω 149
ἐπήρατος 5
ἐπί w. acc., 375-6, 375; w. dat., 27-8, 405-6; ἐπὶ ἤματι *et sim.* involving hiatus 327
ἐπιβρίθω 343-4
ἐπιδοιάζω 21
ἐπιειμένος see ἐφίημι
ἐπιθύω w. infin. 354-5
ἐπικέ(κ)λομαι 85
ἐπικεύθω 332
ἐπικλεής 330
ἐπικλύζω 290
ἐπικύρω w. gen. 342
ἐπιμαίομαι 106
ἐπιμειδιάω 123, 129
ἐπιπέλομαι 25
ἐπιπροίημι 123-4, 379
ἐπίρροθος 184
ἐπισπέρχω 346
ἐπισχερώ 170
ἐπιτέλλομαι 277
ἐπιτέλλω/-ομαι 264-5
ἐπιφραδέως 83
ἐπιχέομαι, middle for the usual active, 205
ἐπιχράω 431
ἐπιχώομαι 367
ἐπιψεύδομαι 381
ἐπωνυμίη 245
Ἐρατώ, vocat. form, etymology, 1, 5
ἔργον 59, 81-2, 81
ἔρδω, ἔρξω/ἔρξον 109
ἐρεείνω 302
ἐρεύθομαι/ἔρευθος 121-2, 163, 297-8
ἐρημαῖος 324
ἐρητύω w. infin. 380

GREEK WORDS

ἐριδμαίνω 94
ἔρις ~ ἔρως 91f., 136
ἕρκος/-εα 215f.C(2), 215
ἕρμα 278f.
ἑρπύζω 446-7
ἔρρω, -έτω 464-6
ἐρύκω 250-2, 380, 382-5
ἔρως/Ἔρως 296-7, 297; Ἔρωτες 452
ἑσπερίη χθών 309, 311
ἔσω w. gen. 311
ἐτεόν/ἐτήτυμον, linked with εἰ, 358
ἔτι 123-4, 429-31; ἔτι νῦν (περ) 312-3
εὔκηλος 219
εὐμενέω 87
εὐνομίη 68
εὐπηγής/εὔπηκτος 235-6
εὐρύς, 'wide gates,' 216
εὐτρόχαλος 135
ἐφέστιος 116
ἐφετμή 390
ἐφίημι, in middle, object 'hair,' 45
ἐφίσταμαι 119-21
ἐφομαρτέω 111
ἐφύπερθε w. gen. 217-8
ἔχω ἕξω for σχήσω 99; σχέο μοι 386;
    (-)σχόμενος passive 95
ἐψιάομαι 118

ζαχρηής 320-1
Ζεύς as claus. 115
ζέω/ζείω trans. 273
ζυγόν nautical 167

-η for -εα 349
ἦ, ἦ μέν 152, 466; ἦ τε 34-5
ἢ καί 181
ἦ *spoke* 22, 111
ἡβαι(όν) 281
ἦδος 314
ἦε interrog. 12
ἠερέθομαι 367-8
ἠέριος 417
ἠθεῖος 51f., 52
ἠίθεος 246
ἦκα 107, 463
ἥκω 275
ἠλίβατος 162
ἤλιθα 342
ἧμαι 43-4, 423

ἡμερίς 220
ἡμέτερος 305
ἡμί see ἦ
ἡμίθεοι 365-6
ἤν κ' w. subj. 404; ἤν καί in generalisations 343-4
ἠνορέη 189
ἠπεδανός 82
ἠρέμα/-έω 170
ἦρι 41
ἥρωες 167
ἤτοι μέν 15, 59-60
ἠύτε w. partic. 460-1
Ἡφαιστότευκτος 230f.
ἧχι/ἧχι (τε) 162

θάλαμος 8-10, 9, 38, 215f.C(4), 235-6,
    237, 238, 247, 248, 249, 450
θαλερός 114
θάλλω of complexion 114, 121-2
θαμίζω 54, 250-1
θεή 252
θέλγω etc. 4-5, 27, 27-8, 33, 131f.
θελκτήριος 27, 33
θέμις 193, 203, 205
θεός 323
θέσκελος 229
θέσμος, θέσμια 209
θεσπέσιος 392, 443
θηέομαι 444-5
θηλέω 221
θηλύτεραι subst. 209
θήρη 69
θνήσκω, τεθνειώς -ηώς 460-1
θοός, ἄρηι θ- 393
θριγκός, spelling, 217-8
θρόνος 36f., 44, 47-50, 453f.
θρωσμός 199
θύεα 65
θυηλή 191
θυμός 98; periphrastically 20-1
θύρη 216
θῶκος 111

-ιάω formations 123, 129, 170
Ἰδαῖος ~ Δικταῖος 133-4
ἵεμαι 333, 371, 386-8, 388
ἱερός of rivers 165
ἴκρια 198

ἵκω, ἷξεν 275
ἱμείρω, ἱμερθείς 117a
ἰνδάλλομαι 453
ἰοδόκη/-κος φαρέτρη 156
ἵπποι horse-drawn vehicle 233-4
ἴσκω speak 396
ἶσος in compendious expressions 207f.
ἵσταμαι, ἵστα(σ)ο 1; (-)εστηώς 121; ἔσταν in Pindar 1, in visiting scenes 215; ἔστασαν ἔστ- 238
ἰτέα 201
ἴχνιον/-ια, μετ'/κατ' ἴ. 446-7

κάγκανος 272-3
καγχαλάω 124, 286a
καθίημι hair 45
καί, various uses of, 3, 5, 18, 95, 115, 181, 202, 365, 429
κακόν 129
κακός 420-1, 421
κακότης 95, 171-95(3), 182, 423
καλύπτρη 444-5
κάματος 233-4, 274, 288-9, 291f., 291
κάμνω 82, 230, 340; κεκμηώς 233-4
καναχηδά/-όν 71
κάρη ~ oath 151
καρπάλιμος/-ίμως 280
κάρφεα 291
καταειμένος 45
καταιβάτις 160-1
κατακτεατίζομαι 136
καταμάομαι 154
καταστεφής 220
κατατίθεμαι don not doff 156
κατείβω 290
κατέχω and middle 128
κατηφιάω etc. 123
κε in that event 34-5, 132, 144, 265-7; in unusual constructions, 34-5, 377/379, 404; in unacceptable constructions, 401; supplanted in MSS, 293
κεάζω 378-9
κέαρ 56
κεῖνος as emphatic pronoun 28-9
κείρω 416
κέ(κ)λομαι 85
κελεύω/κέλομαι, referents in the poem, 195
κενεαὶ χεῖρες 126

κερδαλέος/κέρδος 426
κερκίς 41f., 43-4, 45-7/50, 46
κερτομέω 51f., 56
κεύθω 332
κηδοσύνη/κῆδος etc. 461-2
κηκίω 227
κινύρομαι 259
Κίρκαιον (accent) 200
κλείω/κλέω call by name 245
κληηδών 392
κληῗδες nautical 167
κλισμός 47-50
κλωστήρ 255
κοίλη πέτρη 227
κοιρανέω 406
κόλπος 154-5
κόμη 45-7/50
κόπτω (ξύλα) 272-3
κορυφαὶ χθονός 158f., 159-63, 162
κούρη ~ 'eyes' 444-5
κουρίδιος 243
κουρίζω 133-4, 134
κραίνω 172
κρείων/-ουσα 240
κρήδεμνον 444-5
κρήνη viz. τυκτή 222
κρυερός/κρυόεις 390, 422f., 427-31, 429-30
κτέανον 266, 334
κτεατίζω/-ομαι 136
κτέρας 186
κύανος/-εος 135-41, 139-40
κύδιστος 363
Κυθέρεια 108
κύκλα of ball 135-41, 137
κυλίνδομαι 71
κυνέω, spelling of aor., 150
κύντερος/-τατος 192
Κύπρις ~ κύπρις 5
Κυταιεύς etc. 228-9

λάβρος 343
λαγχάνω 3-4, 4
λάθρη sim. of love 296
λάινεος/λάινος 217-8
λαιός 120
λαχαίνω and compounds 222-3
λείπω, ἔλλιπ- 111; λιπέσθαι = μεῖναι 441
λελοχημένος 7a

GREEK WORDS

λευγαλέος 263, 374
λευκός of skin-tone 45
λέχρις 238
λιαρός 225-7, 300
λιγέως 463
λιλαίομαι 80
λιπαρός 444-5
λίσσομαι 148
λοετρόν 299-303, 300
λοξός 444-5
λόχος, heroic, 6-7
λυγαῖος 323
λύω and middle 62
λώβη 74-5
λωβητήρ 372
λωίτερος/-ον 187

μάλα + superlat. 192
μαλακός 291
μαλερός 291
μάλιστα with comparative nuance 91-2
μάργος Ἔρως 120
μαρμαρυγή 287-8
μεγαίρω (οὔτι μ.) 405-6
μέγαρον/-α 215f.C(1), 228-9, 250-1, 285
μέγας and adv. μέγα 36, 66, 158, 221, 271-2, 352-3, 382-3
μείλιον 135, 146
μειλίσσομαι 105
μειλιχίη/μειλίχιος 15, 31, 78, 105, 196f., 320f., 385, 396
μειλιχίως 319
μελαγχολία 422f.
μεληδήματα, erotic/etymology, 4-5, 452
μελεδῶναι ~ μελεϊστί 4-5
μελίφρων 457-8
μέλλω w. fut./aor. infin. 261
μέλομαι in erotic writing 452
μέμονα 351
μέν 61, 264-5; οὐ μέν 307-8, οὐδὲ μέν 388; ἦ μέν 152, 466
μενεαίνω 95
μενοινή 397
μέσσαυλος 235
μεσσηγύς 307, 441
μετά w. acc. 13/331, 58; adv. 115
μεταλδήσκω 413-5, 414
μεταλλήγω 109-10

μεταπρέπω 246
μεταστείχω 451
μετατρέπω in tmesis 261
μετατρωπάομαι/-τρέπομαι 297-8
μεταφωνέω 169
μεταχάζομαι 436
μετέειπε 17
μέτειμι/-έρχομαι 181, 437-8
μέτρα κελεύθου sim. 308
μήδομαι 229
μήν, καὶ μ. 125
μηνιάω 123
μῆνις (~ χόλος) 336-9, 337-8, 382-5
μητιάω/μῆτις 12, 24, 30, 171-95(3), 176f.(8), 183-4, 210, 326
μητρυιή 191
μίτρη *baldric* 156
μνῆστις 289-90
μοῖρα 3-4, 261, 328
μολοῦσα sim. as claus. 9
μόρος 429
μῦθος 34, 171-95(1), 173
μυχός 42
μύωψ 276, 277

ναί 467
νάω/ναίω 224; cf. on 225-7
νειόθεν 383
νειόθι 62
νέοι Argonauts 194
νεύω w. infin. 441
νῆις, colouring of, w. sing. forms, 32
νήματα 255
νῆσος 311-2
νίσομαι, spelled νίσσ- 210; partic. 210, 446-7
νιφετός 69
νοέω/νόος 6, 7b, 19-20, 297-8, 309, 328, 446-7
νομεύς 277
νόστος 175
νύκτωρ 293, 294
νῦν in invocation 1
νωλεμές/-έως 146-7, 346

ξεῖνος, in vocat. -ε, 401
ξερόν 322
ξυνός in anaphora 173-4

ὁ 10, 70, 406, 432-3; crasis τἀμά, ὤλλοι, qq.v.
ὅγε 14-5, 78, 113-5, 200, 248-9, 280, 399, 432-3, 464-6
ὅδε 81, 113-5, 186, 315-6, 326, 333, 363, 418 (τάδε τοῖα?), 419
ὄθματα 93
ὀθνεῖος 388-9
ὄθομαι 93, 94
οἶδα 175, (ᾔδειν) 309
οἰδαίνω sim. of anger 382-5, 382-3, 383
οἶδμα 388-9
οἰκτείρω subject gods 328
οἶνος undigammated 224
-οιντο 13
οἴομαι see οἴω
οἷος, οἷόν τε (δέ) w. finite vb in simile introd., 276; οἷα = ὅτι τοῖα, or exclam., 381
ὀιστεύω with βέλεσσι sim. 27-8
οἶστρος 276, 277
οἴχομαι of deceased 204
ὀίω, shades of meaning, 28-9; in form ὀίσσατο 456
ὀκλαδόν/ὀκλάς 122
ὀλίγος, 'big ἐξ ὀ.' 294-5
ὀλοός 382f., 382-5, 384, 408, 436
ὀλοφύρομαι 72
ὅμαδος 270-1
ὁμαρτέω 375-6, 375
ὠμήθης 118
ὅμιλος 434
ὄμματα harbouring αἰδώς, ~ ὄθματα, 93
ὀνίνημι 20-1
ὀξύς, -ύ of hearing 253; -έα of vision 281
ὁπλότερος/-τατος 244, 319
ὅπως in Muse-contexts 2
ὄρθρος 41
ὀρίνω erotic 56
ὁρμαίνω 18, 451-2, 471
ὄρνυμι in perfective 59, 203, 314, 457-8
ὄρρα/ὅ ῥα sim. 37
ὅς, form οἶο, 356
ὄσσομαι 453f.
ὅστις 193, 195, 315-6
ὅτε w. subj. in generalisations 345
οὔ, ἑοῖ αὐτῇ *yourself* 99; οἱ possessive with delayed subst. 470
οὐ, ἦε καὶ οὔ 181

οὐδέ 102, 130, 375-6
οὐδός 215f.C(3), 280
οὐλόμενος/οὐλοός 384, 436
οὖλος 107, 297
οὖν, εἴτ' οὖν 394
οὕνεκα w. gen.356; late postp. 370
οὕνεκεν 334
οὔνομα 5, 354-5
οὐράνιος 159-63, 159, 160-1
οὐρανός ~ αἰθήρ 159-63
οὕτω inferentially 359

πάγκαρπος 114, 158
πάις 241
παλιμπετές 285
παλίσσυτος 112, 306
Παλλάς see Ἀθηναίη
παλύνω 69
Παναχαιίς/-οί 347
Πανέλληνες 13, 347
πανήμερος/-ιος 251
πανοπλότατος 244
πανσυδίη see πασσο-
παπταίνω 281
παρά w. acc., *past*; w. acc. pers., 1
παραβλήδην 107
παραί 38, 444-5
παραιφάμενος 14-5
παρᾶσσον 17
παρασχεδόν 440
παρεννέπω 367
παρέξ 237; with ἄλλο 195
παρηγορέω 303
παρθενική 4-5, 5, 86
παρθένος w. gen. parent 86
παρίσταμαι applied to Muse 1
πάροιθεν 186
παροίτατος/-ερος, -έρω 24, 179
πάρος w. gen. 22
πᾶς, πάντες ... πάντῃ sim. 192
πασσυδίη/πανσυ- 195
πείθομαι, contructions involving, 26-8, 307-8
πεῖρα etc. 16, 18, 113-5, 168f., 176f., 179, 405, 405-6, 420-1
πειράζω sim. w. acc. pers. 10
πέλαγος ἁλός 349
πέλας 59
πέλομαι, ~ γίγνομαι 467; aor. *is* 63

GREEK WORDS

περ 61, 242-3, 312-3
περί/πυρί confused 291
περι//δείδια 60
περιέχομαι 95
περιηγής 135-41, 135, 138
περικατατίθεμαι 156
περικλεής 330
περιμήκης 70
περιπέλομαι 25
περιπολλόν/-ά 427
περισταδόν 416
περιτίομαι 74
περιώσιος + advs 334
Περσηίς 467
πινυτή of witch Medea 288-9
πίπτω, πεπτηώς 321
πίσυρες 222
πίτνημι, πεπτηώς 321
πλάζομαι, colouring, ? aor. infin., 261
πλέκω and middle 46-7
Πλήιαδες 225-6
πλόκαμος 46-7
ποθεν in expression ἐκ (gen.) π. 262
ποθι 220f., 225-7, 225
πόθος 33, 262, 263-4
ποικιλόθρονος 44
ποινή w. gen. 336-9
πολιός 275
πολλάκι, w. aor., generalising, 188
πόλος 159-63, 160-1, 161
πολύθρονος 27
πολύς, πολέας etc. as fem. 21; form πολλόν 166, 275; πουλύν 166, 211
πολύστονος 279
πολυφάρμακος 27
πόνος 434
πόντος/Πόντος 159-63
πορφύρεος 275
πορφύρω 18, 23, 396-400, 396-7, 453f., 455-6, 456
πόσις (masc.) 41f.
ποτάομαι ref. mind sim. 446-7
ποτε in exempla 115-7, 190f.
ποτής 301
ποτι-σχόμενος 148-50, 150
πότνα 79, 467
πού imported 200
πούς, ἐν ποσίν 314
πρήσσω ~ πρηστήρ 274

πρηύνω 189-90
πρίν not until that point 420
πρό adv. or in tmesis 385
προαλής 73
προβολή 215
προγενέστερος 319
πρόδομος 39, 215f.C(3), 278
πρόμαλος 200-9, 201
προμολή 215
προπάροιθεν w. gen. 317
προπρό 453
προρέω trans. 225
πρὸς δὲ καί 232
προσέειπε 17
προσεννέπω 51
προσλέγομαι 426
πρόφρων 131, 176f.(9), 386-95, 393
προχοή 67
πτήσσω, πεπτηώς 321
πτύχες of Olympus 113, 114
πυκινός 6-7, 30, 288-9
πύλαι of Olympus ~ sky 159-63, 159; of palace 216
πῦρ of love 286bf., 291f.

ῥα see ἄρα
ῥαδινός 106
ῥαφαί 135-41, 139
ῥίγιον 429-30
ῥιπή 43
ῥόος/ῥοή and plurals 165

σέλας 231, 293, 294-5
σέλμα 167
σθένος, ὅσσον σθ. 63
σῖγα 123, 422
σκῆπτρον/-α 196f., 197, 197-8, 353, 376
σκοτίη 323
σμερδαλέος 432-3
σμύχω 446
σπόρος 413-5, 413
-σσ- in futures 353
στέλλω for περι- 205
στεῦμαι 337
στιβαρός 232
στόλος 175
στονόεις 279
στυγερός 349, 390
στυφελός 411

σύ, σεῖο/σέθεν possessive, 151, 331; ὗμιν/ ὕμιν 314
σύγε 435
συμφράζομαι 87
σύν + πάντα sim. 294-5
συναμάομαι 154
συνανδάνω 30
συνέστιος 116
συνηβολίη 144
συνορίνω 56
σφαῖρα 135-41, 135, 139
σφε sing./plur./dual 48
σφέτερος 186
σφωίτερος 335
σχεθεῖν i.q. ἐπι- intrans. 48
σώομαι *speed* 307

ταλαεργός 292
ταλασήιος 292
ταράσσω cf. s. τετρηχώς
ταρχύω 208
τε 37, 209, 374
τέθηπα 215
τείως 275
τέλλομαι 277
τέλος in relation to decision-making 172
τέλσον 412
τέρην 461-2
τετράγυος 412
τετρηχώς 276-7, 276
τευχηστής/-ήρ 415
τεχνήεις applied to Hephaestus and others 229
τηλόθι 255, 261
τιμή 3-4, 181, 207f., 376
τίνω χάριν 230f., 233-4
τίπτε 464
τις in threats 374
τοῖος, prefacing direct speech, 24, 51, 55, or indicating speech-closure, 317; τοῖ' ἄρα used resumptively, 228-9; crux τάδε τοῖα? 418; allegedly = ἀγαθός, ibid.
τόφρα 275
τράπεζα 377
τρηχύς metaph. 276
τρίτατος 224
τροχάλεια, τροχαλόν, τροχάω 135
Τυρσηνίς 311-2

τυτθός, fem. -ή, 93
τῷ καί 5

υἱός, use of dual in poem, 360; form υἱάσιν 450; υἱῆες etc. 178, 196; Αἴσονος υἱός 357; Κόλχων υἷες 245
ὑπακούω 169
ὑπείροχος 239
ὑπερηνορέη 65, 68
ὑπερφίαλος 14-5, 15, 427-31, 428
ὑπήεριος 417
ὑπό, w. acc., 278; w. gen., 345; w. dat., 2-3, disputed 321, 323
ὑποβλήδην 400
ὑποδδείδω 318, 435
ὑποδρήσσω 274
ὑποϊσχάνω 120
ὑποσ(σ)αίνω 396
ὑποτέλλομαι 277
ὑπωρόφιος 293
Ὑψιπύλη 216
ὑψόθι 255
ὑψόροφος 285
ὑψοῦ and ὑψόσ(ε) 221; ὑψοῦ fig. 367-8

φαεινός of clean appearance 154-5
φαιδρύνομαι 300
φᾶρος, in plur., 453f., 454
φερέσβιος 164
φημί, φῆ introducing or closing direct speech, 154, 382/385, 410; type φάτο μῦθον 259; ὣς φάτο and similar types of closure-formulae, 17, 30, 83, 432-3; φάσθαι φᾶσθαι 384
φθίνω, φθείσ- not φθίσ-, 459-60
φιλέω, -ασθαι passive 66
φίλος 151, 171
φιλότης 180
φλεγέθω 141
Φλεγραῖος 215f.(Α), 230f., 233-4
φλιή 278
φλόξ, φλογὶ εἴκελ- 287
φοιτίζω 54
φορβάς 276
φρήν, πυκιναὶ φρένες 288-9
φυσιάω trans. 410

χαίτη 45-7/50
χαλέπτω/-ομαι 97

GREEK WORDS

χάλκεος of architecture 217-8; w. ref. to Bronze Race 230f.
χαλκόπους 230
χάριτες of physical attractiveness 444-5
χείμαρροι subst. 71
χείρ 84, 136, 346; χερ- 50
χέρηες and other forms 403
χερνῆτις 291f., 292
χέρσονδε 199
χέω, aor. χεύετο, 291
χιτών 146-7, 154-5
χλοερός 220, 297-8
χλόος/-χλοος 297-8
χλωρός 297-8
χόλος (~ μῆνις) 336-9, 337-8, 382-5
χράω 431
χρειώ 52, 173, 332

χρέος 12, 108, 131, 189-90
χροιή 121-2
χρύσεος of gods' possessions 118, 156
χώρη ~ χῶρος 170

ψήχω 50
ψυχή vacates (lover's) body 446-7

-ώ vocat. 1
ὦλλοι 176
ὥρη, in accus. -ην, 417
-ως, adverbs in, 319
ὥς, postp., 141
ὥς in speech-closure, no verb of speaking, 471; ὣς οἱ μέν *et sim.* resumptively, 6

INDEX IIA
GREEK AUTHORS

Aeschylus
Ag. 85: 12
    663f.: 323
    800 suppl.: 332
    862: 41f.
    1133: 277.
Pers. 59: 313
    605: 457-8.
Suppl. 165f.: 211
    307-8: 277
    607-8: 195
    624: 172
    666: 416
    1041: 3-4.
Theb. 388: 135-41
    644: 415
    693: 452.
Fragments (Radt)
    69: 230f.
    281a3if.: 120

[Aeschylus]
PV 171: 376
    279: 111
    429: 159-63
    649-50: 286b-7
    722: 159-63
    958: 406

Agathias *AP*
    4.4.57: 428
    7.596.3: 306
    11.365.1: 413

Agathyllus *SH*
    15.13: 311

Alcaeus *PLF*
    307(c): 309
    327: 275

Alcaeus *HE*
    142: 468

Alcman *PMGF*
    1: 4-5
    27: 1
    27.2-3: 11
    58.1: 120
    59(a): 290
    116: 464

Alexander Aetolus *CA*
    10: 117/124

Alpheus *GPh*
    3528f.: 159

Anacreon *PMG*
    358: 135-41
    398: 117f., 117/124, 276

Anacreontea
    33.27f.: 276

Anonyma
AP 3.16.2: 267
    5.26.3: 444-5
    9.210.7 v.l.: 311
    9.363.3-4: 221
    9.384.23: 418
    9.656.2: 239
    9.678.1: 429
    14.62.1: 135-41
APl 372.5: 134
CA 2.41 (p. 74): 456
    4.1 (p. 78): 382/385
    7 (p. 80): 62
    7.11 (p. 80): 229
FGE 1829 & 1841: 351
GDK encom.
    16.7: 277
    16.21: 91-2
    34.141: 426
GDK epic.
    24v5: 275
HE 3684f.: 290

    3778-9: 32-3
    3780-1: 351
orac. ap. Porph. *Plot.* 22: 323
    ap. Plut. *Mor.* 399c: 351
SH 923.12: 293
    928.2: 233-4
    938.8: 417
    939.1-5: 278f.
    939.4: 96
    964.20: 446
    970i7: 61-3
    992.6-7: 115-7
    1018: 77
    1031: 290
    1057: 418
    1087: 291
    1153: 229
    1169: 392
TGF 680a9: 61-3

Antagoras *CA*
    1: 136

Antimachus (*Wyss*)
Lyde: 2
    fr. 34: 235
    fr. 44.1 corr.: 238
    fr. 57: 340
    fr. 62: 230f.
    fr. 72: 373
SH 69.4: 111

Antipater of Sidon *HE*
    184-5: 255
    193: 255
    194-5: 46
    334 v.l.: 215
    510-11: 50

Antipater of Thessalonica
GPh 355: 211
GPh 627-8: 59

GREEK AUTHORS

[Apolinarius]
  7.33: 397
  17.16: 337-8
  28.9: 334
  64.3 *praef.*: 267
  77.27: 274
  91.6: 4-5
  103.69: 287-8
  106.53: 290
  113.9: 343
  140.20: 333

[Apollodorus]
  1.6.3: 233-4
  1.9.1: 191

Apollonides *GPh*
  1180: 205

Apollonius Rhodius
Argonautica i
  1f.: 1-5
  3: 390
  8-11: 66-74
  9: 67
  14: 64-5
  15f.: 333
  18-9: 340f., 340
  20-1: 354-5
  20: 355
  21: 2
  22: 1-5
  23: 115
  34: 406
  43: 319
  53: 210, 359
  78f.: 261
  89: 352
  100: 245
  101f.: 216
  111-2: 340f., 340
  113-4: 341
  123: 80
  128 corr.: 215
  159 c.v.l.: 293
  165: 319, 359
  174: 362-3
  175: 196f.
  177: 8-9
  186: 265-6
  195: 134

197f.: 377/379
201: 111
204: 37
218 *codd.*: 323
221-3: 45
226-7: 270-4
226: 340f., 340
229f.: 265-6
234: 299
242f.: 347
243: 347, 373
244-5: 213-4
244: 419
260: 215
261f.: 291f.
262: 432-3
265: 189-90
267: 123
274: 56
277: 461-2
279f.: 259
279: 390
292: 259
294: 189-90, 303, 385
295f.: 259
298f.: 188-90
308: 399
312: 252
320 c.v.l.: 215
323: 195
332f./336: 171
336-7: 173-4, 175
339: 437
347: 270-1
350: 259
354f.: 275
369-70: 343-4
374 c.v.l.: 222-3
382: 194
384: 206
386: 453
394: 401
414: 389-90
424: 15
452: 417
458: 194
459: 118
460f.: 422f.
466: 334
476: 350

480: 390
494: 384-5
496-511: 134
501f.: 165
508-9: 133-4
508: 134
514: 170
526f.: 340
528f.: 170
542: 227
543 proecd.: 346
544: 287
546: 220
547f.: 159-63
551: 340
552: 346
565: 291
575: 464-7
580: 313, 417
584-5: 311-2
599: 233-4
613: 276
614-5: 64-5
615: 65
625-6: 242
637: 256
638-9: 423
642: 197-8
648f.: 314
649: 401
650: 196f.
656f.: 10f.
664-6: 171-95
667f.: 111
668: 133, 217-8
671-2: 4-5
671: 114
680: 434
692: 182
699: 400
702: 17, 253
706 c.v.l.: 404
713: 59
715 c.v.l.: 404
722: 158
723f.: 340
724: 340
729 corr.: 42-3
734: 273
739: 162
741: 446-7

742f.: 41f.
742: 45-7/50, 108
749: 186
759: 340
764: 367-8
772: 327
778: 163
784: 22
786 c.v.l.: 216
791-2: 432-3
792: 51
793: 401
802 v.l.: 337-8
813: 302
815: 390
825: 312-3
835: 107
847: 401
869: 388-9
873: 251
883: 259
886-7: 369-71
897: 188
900: 467
902-3: 333
908: 333f.
918: 390
961f.: 299-303
962-3: 355
977: 392
981: 333f.
993-4: 278
1037: 262
1042: 393
1051: 270-1
1060f.: 205
1061-2: 312-3
1069: 330
1081f.: 176
1091: 440
1097: 401
1103: 145
1110f.: 159-63
1116: 133-4
1117/1121: 220
1129f.: 133-4
1146 c.v.l.: 224
1156f.: 345-6
1174: 215
1182f.: 270-4
1182: 272-3

1194-5: 96, 156-7
1194 Ω: 156
1216: 432-3
1218-9: 263
1220: 2, 261
1230: 121-2, 163, 444-5
1232-3: 126
1238: 354-5
1245-6: 385
1245: 296
1262: 422f.
1265f.: 276, 277
1265: 277
1269: 432-3
1285: 267
1286f./1289: 422f.
1288-9: 383
1289f.: 196f.,422f.
1289: 382-5, 383
1292f.: 347
1294: 314
1296f.: 382-5
1296-7: 371
1297: 453
1301: 382-5
1307: 334
1315: 158
1317: 390
1319: 116
1321: 451
1322: 330
1325: 356
1329: 270-1
1330: 382-5
1339: 337-8, 382-5

Argonautica ii
1f.: 171-95, 422f.
8-9: 332
9: 181
16f.: 407
44-5: 407
54: 14-5
57: 437-8
58: 408
60: 107
61:107
64: 303
83: 277
104: 378-9
138: 158

159: 45
168/173: 343
169: 162
197f.: 446-7
197: 466
198: 455
206: 416
209: 13, 347
210f.: 390
210: 390
219: 260, 297-8
226: 301
231: 233
239: 38
247: 337-8
249: 389-90
255: 385
273f.: 309-13
278: 69
283: 342, 431
284: 48
287: 250-2
289: 158
296: 307
298: 343
307: 301, 302
311f.: 314
312: 203
323: 411
326f.: 185
336: 250-1
345: 350
353: 160-1
361: 246
369: 239
376: 292
381A: 235-6
382f.: 327
383: 183-4
384: 8-9, 354-5
385f.: 200-9
386: 217-8
391: 401
394: 6, 334
399: 228-9
400: 200
401: 6
403: 228-9
408-10: 422f.
409: 284, 432-3
410: 423

412: 390
416: 388-9
423f.: 12
423-4: 74-5, 89, 183-4
432: 250-2
434: 334
438-9: 263
441-2: 28-9
445: 446
448: 107
453: 239
465: 239
489: 434
498: 320-1, 431
513-4: 409
521: 358
535: 321
540: 210
541f.: 159-63
545: 453
547: 36
582: 444-5
595: 453
598: 232
612f.: 340f., 340
613-4: 343-4
615: 390
620-1: 432-3
621: 107, 385
623: 422f., 470
624f.: 333f.
625f.: 429
626-7: 4-5
628-9: 349
628: 390, 422f.
634f.: 171-95
642f.: 61-3, 61
645: 159
653f.: 191
660: 327
662 c.v.l.: 276
664-5: 444-5
667: 251
671: 277
675: 6
679: 156
681: 336
698: 69
731: 162
733: 202
734f.: 225-7

741: 345
743: 235
756: 258
762-3: 354-5
763: 333f.
772: 4-5
774f.: 314
784: 246
786f.: 352-3
811: 118, 251
821-2: 116
823 *et circa*: 199
836f.: 205
840: 204
851f.: 205
858: 263-4
859: 440
860f.: 422f.
861-2: 301
865-6: 425
881: 225
885: 422f.
889: 470
910: 245
926: 291
930f.: 345-6
938: 69
955: 263
964-1029: 200-9
964f.: 200-9
967: 6-7
991: 183
996: 200-9
998: 406
999: 409
1002f./1006f.: 200-9
1003: 457-8
1005: 411
1010: 307
1018: 209
1019: 205
1023f.: 200-9
1033-4: 325
1036: 284
1038: 285
1042-5: 278f.
1043-4: 283
1047f.: 324
1049-50: 183-4
1068: 184
1077: 270-1

1083-4: 211
1090f.: 2
1091f.: 327
1093f.: 264-5
1093-4: 228-9
1096: 263-4, 264-5
1097f.: 321
1098f.: 327
1110f.: 321, 327
1110: 222
1112: 343-4
1114: 321
1115: 294-5
1118f.: 321
1122f.: 10f.
1122: 317
1123: 77
1125-6: 320-1, 321
1125: 343-4
1126: 342
1127 corr.: 189-90
1128f.: 26-8
1130: 328
1131f.: 176f., 193
1131-2: 193
1137: 315
1140: 423
1141f.: 329
1142: 362-3
1146f.: 171-95, 176f.
1147-8: 190f.
1153: 266
1154/1159: 354-5
1154-5: 354f
1156: 34-5
1159: 31, 385
1160/1162-3: 358f.
1160f.: 329, 354f.
1160 c.v.l.: 314, 358f., 359
1166-7: 327
1166: 329
1169f.: 200-9
1174: 205
1177: 299
1179f.: 190, 327
1179-80: 188-90
1180: 66-74, 130
1182: 191
1183-4: 323
1186: 265-6

1187-9: 340f., 340
1189f.: 320-1
1191: 251
1192f.: 315-6
1194f.: 200-9
1194-5: 336-9
1194: 190, 191
1196f.: 6-7
1196: 303
1198f.: 318
1202f.: 14-5, 171-95, 176f., 333f., 386-95
1204f.: 171-95, 210-4
1204: 337
1207f.: 171-95
1207-8: 188
1214: 312-3
1216: 297-8
1218 (corr.!): 385, 432-3
1219-25: 171-95
1219: 52
1220f.: 184
1220: 185, 403
1221: 171-95
1222: 184
1224: 171-95, 180
1225: 171-95
1226f.: 148-50
1226: 333f.
1233-4: 133-4
1245: 345
1248: 411
1250: 285
1260f.: 6-7
1267: 228-9
1271f.: 6-7, 196f.
1271: 169
1279-80: 171-95, 183
1279: 15
1282: 195
1284: 446-7
1285: 6
Argonautica iv
1f.: 1-5, 6
1: 11, 288-9
2: 1
3: 284
7-9: 228-9
10: 370

11: 8
17: 286b-98
18: 106
24-5 corr.: 154
26-7: 278
27-8 corr.?: 46-7
31: 166
33: 401
36: 261
37 *et circa*: 288-9
41: 216
53: 286b-98
58: 286bf.
60: 375-6
62: 4
64-5: 467-8
64: 389-90
65: 279, 288-9
67: 199
78-80: 198, 199
84: 385
86: 6
87: 404
89: 401
92-3: 382-3
93: 321
95f.: 200-9
113: 153
125-6: 163
127: 70
141: 123-4
144: 6
168 corr.: 293
170f.: 121-2
175: 277
177: 342
179: 45
187: 384-5
190: 171
191: 173-4
195: 347
198: 270-1
199f.: 170
204f.: 347
205: 123
207: 443
214f.: 212
214: 176f.
219f.: 233-4
219/224f.: 245-6
222: 44

229: 200-9
237: 149
238f.: 212, 341
241f.: 86-9, 211
241: 10
251: 37
257: 265-6
275: 225
276: 181
277: 365-6
294f.: 211, 389-90
319: 225
338: 263
345: 200
354: 279
359: 457-8
362: 288-9
368: 209
372: 130
383: 129
385-6: 333
391f.: 95
391/394: 318
392 corr.: 97
394f.: 385
394: 318
402: 429-30
410: 384, 396
413: 397
422: 192
430-1: 67
438-9: 12-3
444: 162
445f.: 136, 286bf., 296-7, 297, 389-90
445-9: 384
445-6: 291f.
445: 129
446: 91f., 136, 279, 384
447: 276-7, 276
448: 7-166
449: 276-7
450f.: 2
450 *pap.*: 5
451 corr.?: 170
457: 388-9
460f.: 245-6
463: 401
464: 6-7
468: 271-2

473-4: 444-5
475-6: 444-5
478-80: 200-9
503: 194
504-5: 346
508: 431
509f.: 211
509-10: 250-2
530: 189-90
536: 359
547: 406
551: 276
552: 2
555-6: 52
555: 313
556: 48
574: 240
576f.: 211
582f.: 340
593: 257
597f.: 245-6
598: 233-4, 309
599f.: 225-7
600: 227
604 corr.: 45
609: 345
619: 263-4, 301
629f.: 159
636: 294-5
640f.: 211
643: 345
645f.: 210-4
646: 212
647-8: 211
657: 229
661: 198
665: 215
670-1: 294
677, 679: 1
694: 209
719-20: 47-50
721: 332
726f.: 371
728: 287-8
731-2: 27
748: 309-13
753f.: 211
756 V: 83
762: 232
773f.: 224
783f.: 7-166, 64-5
785: 58

794: 292
819: 274
833: 426
849-50: 311-2
852: 248-9
857: 287-8
859: 195
877: 446-7
888-9: 189-90
896: 413
917-8: 323
929: 42
950: 135
958: 166
959f.: 111
991: 257
996: 124
1009: 240
1018: 288-9
1020: 467
1032: 334
1033-4: 416
1033: 436
1040: 389-90
1049: 336
1058f.: 291f., 294
1062f.: 291f., 291
1062: 255, 292 *bis*
1063: 259, 294
1067: 471
1069-70: 268-70
1069: 240
1080-1: 33
1085: 243
1091: 381
1092: 390
1093: 378-9
1094: 302
1105: 332
1131 v.l.: 116, 134
1140: 294-5
1147: 286b-7
1160: 215
1166f.: 290
1182-3: 255
1199: 3, 250-2
1205: 337-8
1228 corr.: 225
1235: 453
1239: 417
1246: 207f.
1259: 423

1260 Ω: 10, 101
1263: 321
1265: 342
1279: 297-8
1280: 276
1289: 446-7
1291: 23
1297: 247
1300: 224
1307/1308: 422f.
1315: 285
1318: 422f., 432-3
1343 v.l.: 85
1346: 401
1363: 195
1394: 386
1410 *codd*.: 370
1423, 1425: 1
1428: 201
1433-4: 175
1433: 192
1437: 371
1438: 454
1439: 232
1443: 225
1449: 276
1454: 321
1472f.: 200-9
1472: 330
1473: 8, 461-2
1474-5: 311-2
1482 c.v.l.: 257
1493: 302
1500: 208
1506: 414
1509: 164
1513: 6
1516: 139-40
1543-5: 371
1550: 186
1555: 334
1560: 362-3
1562 corr.: 120
1563: 107
1577: 417
1593: 347
1617: 123-4, 379
1672: 453
1695: 277
1699: 61
1709: 255, 257
1719 c.v.l.: 293

1726 corr.: 286b-7
1734: 119-20, 120
1738-9: 460-1
1740: 303
1773-4: 176
1781: 2
Fragment CA
5.4: 301

?Apollonius Rhodius *CA*
12: 8: 444-5
18: 470
21: 195

Aratus
4: 192
9: 413
23f.: 159-63
27: 135
32f.: 133-4
32: 134
58: 444-5
65: 129
79-80: 139-40
125-6: 429-31
234: 383
239 v.l.: 215
252: 314
282: 409
309: 225-6
324: 321
346: 270-1
349: 417
401: 135-41, 138
451: 277
476: 135
478: 222
517 Hipparch.: 122
522 c.v.l.: 186
529: 136
543 v.l.: 277
609: 432-3
649: 195
653: 112
714: 195
723 v.l.: 277
774: 270-1
834-5: 163
909: 383
914: 427
939: 453
950 corr.: 199

962: 276, 327
1009: 162
1027: 327
1032: 285

Archestratus *SH*
165.12: 349
171.3 corr.: 215
192.4: 291

Archias *GPh*
3589: 282

Archilochus *IEG*
4.6: 167
19.4: 372
32: 73
89.14-5: 383
191: 281, 286b-98, 287, 288-9, 296, 297-8
244: 388-9

Aristeas
T19 Bolton: 159-63

Aristophanes
Av. 390: 444-5
Plut. 973: 56
Ran. 1333 con.: 215

Aristotle
Cael. 290a: 135
Meteor. 342a30: 140
350a18f.: 159-63
Mu. 397b18f.: 453

Asclepiades *HE*
860: 235-6
877f.: 117/124, 117b
882: 156
906-7: 117f.

Athenaeus
200c: 220f.
555b: 1-5

Bacchylides
1.76-7: 396
5.16f.: 158f.
5.74f.: 278f., 279
13.188-9: 164

18.16-17: 280
fr. 20B8: 288-9

Bion
1.58: 446-7
fr. 1.1 Gow: 284

Callimachus
Aetia Books 1-2/1 init./4 init.: 1-5
Fragments, Pfeiffer
1.37-8: 444-5
7.25-6: 2, 228-9
7.25: 167
43.48-9: 273
64.5: 362-3
70: 27
75.12: 297-8, 417
75.22: 307
75.24: 69
80.9: 288-9
85.12: 381
110.52: 359
115.17: 41
178.14: 354-5
186.29: 93
Fragments, SH
238.8: 1-5
239.7/10: 93
265.17: 301
276.8: 413
Hecale Fragments, Hollis
3: 27
43: 454
70.8: 354-5
70.10-11 *et circa*: 8-9
74.22f.: 294
114: 291f.
117: 277
fr. ??: 292
Other fragments, Pfeiffer
194.40-1: 205
195.23f.: 291f.
407 (XVI): 225-7
492: 277
500.1: 54
637 corr.: 337-8
676: 117/124
688: 299
763 (*incert.*): 227
SH 296.4: 415

Hymn 1
  5: 136
  38: 225
  46f.: 133-4
  54: 134
  58: 359
  70: 347
  90: 307, 397
Hymn 2
  47-8: 67
  49: 2-3
  72f.: 224
Hymn 3
  generally: 1
  5: 134
  42: 21
  77: 203
  98: 2
  99: 215
  142: 215
  150: 271-2
  158: 271-2
  175-6: 412
  186: 1
  205: 245
  223: 381
  268: 240
Hymn 4
  75: 315-6
  80: 297-8
  122: 429
  129-30: 429
  142/144: 42
  151-3: 82
  151: 370
  159 c.v.l.: 195
  160-1: 42
  209-10: 157
  219: 240
  239: 369
  271: 240
  324: 134
Hymn 5
  21-2: 51f.
  27-8: 121-2
  31f.: 46
  82-4: 423
Hymn 6
  42: 252
  99: 93
  138: 240

Epigrams, HE
  1057f.: 446-7
  1069-70: 115-7
  1081-6: 291f
  1238: 386

Certamen
  119 Allen: 251

Choerilus Samius *SH*
  316.1: 2

Christodorus *AP*
  2.26-7: 424
  199: 149
  281-2: 287-8
  284: 139-40

Claudian *Gig.* (2)
  45 corr.: 50

Colluthus
  1f./17: 6
  15: 170
  41f.: 276
  43: 277
  70/72: 362-3
  104: 67
  158: 51f., 51
  278/280f.: 362-3
  295: 388-9
  303-5: 422-6
  310 v.l.: 215
  322: 167

Cypria EGF
  fr. 4.4: 327

Damagetus *HE*
  1379: 215
  1433-4: 444-5

?Demaretus *FGH*
  42 fr. 3: 340f.

Demetrius of Scepsis
  fr. 53 Gaede: 133-4

Demosthenes Bithynus
  CA 6: 116

Didorus Siculus
  1.33.3: 417
  4.45: 309-13
  17.7: 133-4

Dionysius Bassaricus
(Livrea)
  fr. 20v4: 271-2
  fr. 35.8: 73

Dionysius Periegetes
  67-8: 162
  150: 161
  151: 246
  173: 401
  389: 162
  489: 245
  508-9: 5
  539: 166
  691f.: 200
  829: 334
  950: 203
  960: 334
  1009-10 corr.?: 200
  1013: 215
  1022: 247
  1029: 203
  1109-10: 163
  1118: 215

Dionysius Scytobrachion
(Rusten)
  fr. 14: 335
  fr. 20: 242-3, 309-13

Dioscorides Medicus
  4.85 v.l.: 217-8

Diotimus *HE*
  1737: 205
  1740: 216

Dorotheus *Cat. cod. astr.*
  6.157: 144

Empedocles DK31
  B17.27f.: 207f.
  B35.1: 177
  B54: 225-6
  B62.1-2 et seq.: 1
  B131.3: 1
  B136.2: 297-8

Eratosthenes *CA*
  10.1: 292
  16: 135-41, 159-63
  16.17-8: 413-5

Erycius *GPh*
  2246: 362-3

Eudocia *Cypr.*
  1.93: 401
  1.151: 463
  2.22: 200
  2.171: 451
  2.263: 354-5
  2.461: 369

Euphorion
CA 8: 175
  14.3: 228-9
  50.3: 453
  51.5: 321
  94.1: 453
  96.3-4: 277
SH 442.6: 227

Euripides
Alc. 646: 388-9
Andr. 532: 290
El. 1: 211
  1150-1: 217-8
Hel. 97: 388-9
  143-6: 314
  244: 220
Hcld. 95: 12
  207f.: 356f.
  212: 359
  855: 323
HF 164: 416
  321: 391
  401-2: 346
  408f.: 347
  1191: 416
Hipp. 347-8: 290
  447: 159-63, 166
  454: 115-7
  509f.: 33
  525f.: 91f.
  969: 276
  1142: 461-2
  1272f.: 159-63
Ion 121f.: 251

  582-3: 422
  637: 421
IA 547f.: 276
  584f.: 287-8
  585f.: 91f.
  699: 364
  1594: 91-2
IT 110: 323
Med. 5: 88
  7-8: 2-3
  392-4: 429
  395: 467
  455f.: 385
  478: 230f.
  526f./530f.: 8
  530f.: 27-8
  1012: 123
  1321: 309
Or. 1465: 253
Phaethon (Diggle)
  2f.: 163, 245-6
Phoen. 515-7: 188-90
  960: 422
Suppl. 258-9 corr.: 220
  703-4: 414
Fragments
  14.3: 360
  25.3: 446-7
  814.2 s.v.l.: 405-6
  911.3: 166

Glaucus *HE*
  1811-2: 139

Gregory of Nazianzus
  Carmina (Migne,
  page no/line)
  491.37: 327
  500.19: 117a
  500.25: 390
  629.650: 173-4
  675.95: 371
  765.132: 446
  898.16: 369
  1228.7 corr.: 170
  1359.75f.: 393
  1366.190: 210
  1370.239-40: 229
  1462.143: 362-3
  1493.182: 215
  1520.198: 5

  1527.85: 72-3
  1549.95: 401
  1576.318: 93
  AP 8.206.1 corr.: 70

Hegesianax *SH*
  466.2-3: 444-5

Hermesianax *CA*
  2.83-4 corr?: 276
  7.15: 65

Herodas
  1: 7-166
  3: 7-166
  4.71: 444-5

Herodorus *FGH*
  31*fr.* 53: 8

Herodotus
  1.2: 347
  1.3: 347
  1.116.1: 423
  1.199.4: 205
  2.35.2: 209
  2.90.1: 205
  2.156.3: 201
  3.16.2: 207f.
  3.38.4: 204
  3.79.1: 314
  4.23.2: 209
  5.8: 205
  6.39.2: 386
  6.82.1: 314
  6.102: 427
  7.193.2: 375-6
  7.197.3: 313

Hesiod
Theog. (see also under
  [Hesiod])
  44: 402
  55: 4-5
  59: 427
  67: 5
  71: 446-7
  78: 1
  122: 174, 288-9
  164: 390
  201: 111

GREEK AUTHORS

203f.: 3-4
205-6: 4-5
205: 152
254: 189-90
337/340: 244
351-2: 242-3
352: 243
362-3: 244
364: 244
386: 114
409f.: 467
411-2: 304
414: 3
421-2: 3-4
426-7: 4
483: 134
522: 159-63
546-7: 107
550: 382/385
581f.: 42-3
654 *codd.*: 31
664: 168f.
693: 164
749: 280
775: 312-3
792: 225
801: 186
809f. c.v.l.: 217-8
825 v.l.: 414
886f.: 30
WD 10: 354-5, 355
63: 5
66: 4-5
145f.: 230f.
157-8: 136
157: 429-30
193: 437-8
195-6: 429-31
200-1: 429-31
383-4: 225-6
389f.: 313
433: 232
483: 328
499: 426
641-2: 59-60
702f.: 429-30
753: 300
766: 270-4

[Hesiod] *Theog*
324: 230f., 231

934: 108
945-6: 244
956-7: 243
960: 243
989: 245-6
992: 27
993-4: 183
995-6: 390
995: 65
997: 2
1000: 4-5, 27-8
1002: 10
1011f.: 311-2
1015: 42

Scutum
34: 229
94: 389-90
255-6: 301
315: 70
357-9: 183
451: 287
477-8: 67

Fragments
1.6: 173-4
10(a)25-6: 360
26.20: 417
40.1: 357
150 et seq.: 309-13
171.7: 115
204.96: 229
204.136: 414
205.1: 364
257.3-5: 266
299: 419

Hippocrates
varia: 297-8
ap. Gal. 19.155: 297-8

Hymni Homerici
HyDem
116: 244
127f.: 299
145: 382/385
169-70: 154-5
187-8: 256
188: 280
194-8: 423
231: 154
282: 423

350: 337-8
358: 390
362: 334
379f.: 158
380f.: 158f., 159-63
436-7: 258

HyAp
28: 199
73/75: 350
99: 250-2
103-4: 135-41
168: 2
174f.: 391-2
331: 32
340: 106
380: 225
487: 206
503: 206

HyHerm
45: 287-8
113-4: 410
138: 189-90
155f.: 129f.
162: 426
182: 448
197: 225-6
257: 336
313: 401
365: 448
380: 219
417: 189-90
462: 152
475: 354-5
480: 219

HyAphr
7: 152
38: 130, 288-9
198f.: 96
198-9: 464
202-3: 115-7
204f.: 115-7
214: 115-7
243: 288-9
247f.: 96
283: 103

Alii 6.15-6: 258
7.28: 399
19.14: 281
19.15 corr.: 69
31.1: 11

Ibycus *PMGF*
  S151.2: 330
  S223(a): 158f.
  S257(a), col.i.7f.: 114
  id. 16: 451-2
  283: 423
  286.6: 114
  286.8f./12-3: 288-9
  288: 114
  289: 158f.
  314: 141
  324: 136

Ilias Parva EGF
  fr. 6: 115-7, 220

Inscriptions, Verse
CEG (II)
  849.6: 340
GVI 114.4: 205
  200.1: 26
  224.3: 333
  265.3: 334
  293.1-2: 243
  635.6: 335
  785.3-4: 73
  1163.10-11: 46-7
  1431.1-2: 205
  1431.3: 354-5
  1519.5: 246
  1726.2-3: 173-4
  1760.1-2: 320-1
  1945.3: 224
SEG 17.756.4: 351
  20.85.2: 246
  28.973.3: 116
  38.1102.2: 66

Joannes Gazaeus
  1.42: 139-40
  1.208: 287-8
  2.234: 444-5

Julianus Aegyptius *APl*
  388: 128

Leonidas of Tarentum
HE
  2073: 82
  2411f.: 291f.

Leonides of Alexandria
FGE
  1870-1: 132-3
  1948: 306

Longus
  1.17.4: 297-8

Lucillius *AP*
  11.107.1: 345
  11.279.2: 337-8

Lycophron
  90-1: 160-1
  174: 228-9
  214-5: 416
  1024: 243

Macedonius *AP*
  5.225.3: 126

Maiistas *CA*
  17: 131
  30: 330

Manethoniana
  (single book nos)
  2.3: 342
  4.565: 388-9

Marianus *AP*
  9.626.5: 273

Matro *SH*
  534.77: 224
  540.6: 460-1

Maximus
  171: 327
  297: 451
  569: 307

Meleager *HE*
  4028f.: 91f.
  4038f.: 136
  4050: 457-8
  4074f.: 446-7
  4076-7: 154-5
  4076: 117/124
  4080-1: 291f.
  4086f.: 446-7

  4204: 281
  4205: 91f.
  4268f.: 135-41
  4456: 261
  4718: 286b-7

Menander
Dysc. 54: 56

Menophilus *SH*
  558.6: 284

Mimnermus *IEG*
  11.1: 2
  11a: 244
  11a2: 159-63
  12.6-7: 235
  12.6: 230f.

Moero *CA*
  1: 116

Moschus
  1: 91f., 281
Eur. 6: 293
  19: 453f.
  31: 67
  47: 139-40
  74-5: 471
  94: 4-5
  106: 446-7
  164: 40
HE 2684: 297

[Moschus] *Megara*
  31: 240
  52: 112
  92-3: 60
  102: 454
  116: 149

Musaeus
  56: 287-8
  133: 432-3
  160/172: 422-6
  244: 303

Naumachius *GDK*
  29.1-2: 4-5

Naupactia EGF
  fr. 4: 7a
  fr. 7A: 8, 12
  fr. 8: 419

Nicaenetus *HE*
  2700: 138
  2706f.: 201

Nicander
Alex. 140: 342
  196: 470
  346: 277
  474: 297-8
  488: 4
  579: 297-8
Ther. 104 corr.: 246
  190-1: 466
  352: 470
  546: 412
  554: 277
  791: 4
  805: 32
  837: 401
Fragments
  72.3-4: 271-2
  74.24: 220
  75.1: 135

Nonnos
Dion. 1.364: 161
  2.64: 413
  2.88-9: 463
  2.662: 214
  3.86: 292
  3.124f.: 215f.(E)
  3.182: 217-8
  3.228: 396
  3.397-8: 119-20
  4.15: 280
  4.182f.: 464-70
  4.372: 121
  5.292: 365-6
  5.342: 287-8
  5.591-2: 294-5
  6.142: 292
  7.108: 343
  7.192f.: 278f.
  7.198: 141
  7.201: 282
  7.249: 287-8

  7.271/274: 281
  7.284: 417
  8.227: 2-3
  8.275: 69
  8.353: 337
  10.26: 297-8
  10.316: 287-8
  10.326: 118
  10.337: 120
  11.72: 303
  11.96-7: 397
  11.245: 297-8
  12.3: 210
  13.248: 212
  13.401: 467
  14.129: 206
  16.88: 72-3
  16.133: 86
  17.262-3: 367-8
  18.62f.: 215f.(E)
  18.93f.: 270-4
  18.136: 50
  21.342: 297-8
  22.120: 281
  23.233/233a: 98
  24.263-4: 255
  25.370-1: 301
  26.374: 377
  27.242-3: 168f.
  27.264: 391
  29.70f.: 278f.
  29.202-3: 230f.
  31.104: 210
  32.43: 52
  32.72: 413
  33.61f.: 113-5
  33.180f: 120, 154-5
  33.270/275: 292
  33.381: 377
  36.123 c.v.l.: 233-4
  36.428-30: 168f.
  36.450: 343
  37.531: 199
  38.147: 300
  38.321: 310
  39.178: 391
  40.237: 377
  40.502-3: 457-8
  41.264: 424
  41.305f.: 253-6
  41.405f./422f.: 113-5

  42.102: 388-9
  42.185f.: 276
  42.188: 276-7, 432-3
  42.200/202: 288-9
  42.242: 117a
  42.265: 102
  42.362: 396
  42.391: 449
  42.439-40: 446-7
  44.17: 367-8
  45.49: 253-6
  45.75f.: 378-9
  45.121: 118
  45.141: 220
  46.85: 278
  46.93: 233-4
  47.245: 2-3
  47.320f.: 464-70
  47.370f.: 464-70
  47.410: 464
  47.475: 348
  47.699: 159
  48.277: 120
  48.371: 383
Par. 6.195: 457-8
  9.46: 287-8
  11.138: 293
  12.47: 64
  17.34: 262
  18.32: 144
  18.147: 129
  19.61: 285
  19.150: 253
  19.161: 417
  20.54: 287-8
  21.51: 373

Nossis *HE*
  2820: 319

Nosti EGF
  fr. 6.2: 243

Numenius *SH*
  583.2: 16

Nymphodorus
  varia: 200-9, 202-3,
    205, 207f., 209

Oppian *Hal.*
  1.194: 343-4
  1.405: 199
  1.760 corr.?: 32
  1.787 corr.: 200
  2.97: 211
  2.233: 453
  2.521-31: 276
  2.611: 294-5
  3.16: 233-4
  3.296: 270-1
  3.505: 446-7
  5.66: 71
  5.466: 246
  5.544: 346
  5.653: 346

[Oppian] *Cyn.*
  1.386: 276
  2.101: 409
  2.134 v.l.: 215
  2.151: 114
  2.187: 276
  2.397: 414
  3.80: 203
  3.200: 294
  3.348-9: 287-8
  3.519: 225
  4.14-5: 388-9
  4.169: 343
  4.252: 373

Oracula Chaldaica
  fr. dub. 214.2: 347

Oracula Sibyllina
  1.368: 432-3
  3.651: 272-3
  6.9-10: 160-1
  14.228: 337-8
  14.241: 336-8

Orphica
Arg. 62: 334
  169: 246
  214: 362-3
  263 corr.: 267
  275 corr.: 299
  290: 173-4
  305: 357
  373: 198

  406 corr.: 301
  410: 421
  660: 193
  713-4: 311-2
  742: 409
  767: 401
  769-71: 177
  771: 14-5
  795: 297-8
  797 corr.: 241
  804: 170
  806: 246
  807: 74
  820: 355
  829: 386
  840: 367-8
  852: 405
  860: 177
  871 corr.: 412, 413
  873: 414
  890-1: 88
  905: 252
  1030: 2-3
  1132: 225
  1155: 401
  1249 *codd.*: 311-2
  1362 *codd.*: 83
Lith. 153: 233-4
  160: 220
  192: 119
  195: 246; 204: 407
  573: 284
  774: 189-90
Fragments
  178.2: 292
  274.1: 327
  332.2 corr.: 397

Palladas *AP*
  11.307: 136

Pamprepius (Livrea)
  fr. 1v22f.: 377
  fr. 3.100: 388-9
  fr. 3.104: 467

Pancrates *HE*
  2856: 225-6

Panyassis *EGF*
  fr. 12.11 corr.: 76

Parmenides DK28
  B1.11, 13: 159-63
  B6.7: 159-63
  B8.28: 261
  B8.43: 135

Parthenius *SH*
  645: 311
  646.4-5: 156

Paulus Silentiarius
Amb. 77: 162
  161-2: 163
  257: 138
Soph. 270: 274
  419: 139-40
  706: 390
  998: 287-8
  1018: 4-5, 471
AP 5.259.3: 287-80

Perses *HE*
  2889: 106
  2896: 390

Phanias *HE*
  3002: 322

Phanocles *CA*
  1.28: 203

Pherecydes
  242-3
  FGH 3 *fr.* 105: 8, 66-74
  3 *fr.* 112: 230f.

Philetas *CA*
  5: 306
  9: 327

Philip *GPh*
  3066: 362-3

Philostratus Junior
Imag. 8: 6, 123-4, 135-41, 146-7

Philoxenus *PMG*
  836(a)2 corr.: 342

[Phocylides] *Sent.*
  144: 294-5

Phoronis EGF
  fr. 2: 133-4

Pindar
O. 1.41/45: 115-7
    1.46-9: 273
    3.4: 1
    5.20: 134
    9.90: 117b
P. 2.41: 63
    4.1f.: 1
    4.25: 345-6
    4.58: 30, 167, 288-9
    4.68: 58
    4.73: 390
    4.97: 401
    4.101: 396
    4.104f.: 333f.
    4.128: 385
    4.134f.: 268-70
    4.136f.: 189-90
    4.139f.: 188-90
    4.140: 66-74
    4.149f.: 333f.
    4.159f.: 200-9
    4.159: 337-8
    4.160f.: 361
    4.161: 404
    4.162: 191
    4.165f.: 333, 388-9
    4.184f.: 8
    4.184: 286b-7
    4.186: 429
    4.187: 194
    4.213f.: 8
    4.214f.: 33
    4.218: 262
    4.224: 230f., 232
    4.225f.: 410
    4.227: 408
    4.233: 27
    4.290: 334
    5.117: 131
    9.43: 385
N. 1.42: 42
    11.8f.: 193
I. 1.36f.: 390

Fragments
  Dith. 2.15: 231
  Dith. 4.20: 162
  fr. 140a56-7: 390

Plato
  Charm. 154c: 444-5
  Crat. 410a: 5
  Ion 535c: 1
  Phaed. 110bc: 135-41
  Phdr. 244d: 262
  Phdr. 255c: 115-7
  Phdr. 259c: 5
  Symp. 178b: 136
  Symp. 196a: 296
  Symp. 196b: 114, 121-2

Posidippus *HE*
  3076: 80
  3102: 70
  3149 corr.: 349

Quintus Smyrnaeus
  1.41: 246
  1.431-2: 144
  1.442: 104
  1.445-6: 253-6
  1.458: 457-8
  1.777: 303
  2.59: 307-8
  2.117: 244
  2.147: 400
  2.283: 162
  2.411: 128
  2.554: 275
  2.585: 432-3
  2.665: 112
  2.666: 159
  3.524: 297-8
  3.763: 432-3
  3.780: 109-10
  4.201: 306
  4.300: 100-1
  4.432: 134
  5.237: 107
  5.432-3: 168f.
  5.612: 303
  6.168: 457-8
  6.229: 275
  6.230-1: 123-4
  6.476-7: 227
  6.576: 264-5
  7.66: 101
  7.148: 451
  7.164: 257
  7.234: 354-5
  7.537: 432-3
  7.571: 326-7
  8.37-8: 456-7
  9.22: 109
  9.36 corr.: 204
  9.344-5: 382-3
  9.471: 121-2
  10.69-70: 345
  10.131: 312-3
  10.282: 290
  10.335-6: 114
  10.346-7: 337-8
  11.209: 276
  11.490: 162
  12.24, al.: 24
  12.173: 365
  12.226: 404
  12.255: 389-90
  12.267: 357
  12.348: 176
  12.388: 429-30
  12.402: 371
  12.526: 145
  12.527: 328
  12.552: 384
  12.567: 95
  13.48: 219
  13.150: 273
  13.277: 383
  13.410: 243
  13.556: 43
  14.5-6: 71
  14.46: 446-7
  14.161: 303
  14.184: 303
  14.251: 343-4
  14.468: 343-4
  14.504: 320-1
  14.599: 343
  14.645: 294-5

Rhianus
  CA 1.21 corr.: 240
  HE 3228: 126

410 INDEX IIB

Rufinus *AP*
  5.60.3: 138

Sappho *PLF*
  1.1: 44
  1.3-4: 290
  1.14: 130
  16.17: 453f.
  16.18: 287-8
  31: 286b-98
  31.7f.: 284
  31.14: 297-8
  43.6: 288-9
  43.9: 294
  47: 288-9
  54: 158, 275
  130.2: 126
  192: 114

[Scymnus]
  912-3: 324

Semonides *IEG*
  6.2: 429-30

Simias
  CA 1: 6, 309
  CA 14.2: 322
  Wings 8-9: 136

Simonides
  IEG 11.35: 330
    16.2: 392
  PMG 575: 136

Simylus *SH*
  724.5: 212

Solon *IEG*
  13.14 corr.: 294-5

Sophocles
  Aj. 123: 470
    229f.: 346
    311: 423
    528: 418
    972-3: 264-5
  Ant. 781f.: 91f.
    791f.: 130
  OT 9-10: 317
    914-5: 367-8

Phil. 662: 205
Trach. 441-2: 91f.
  585-6: 27-8
  639 corr.: 246
  660 f.v.l.: 251
Fragments
  345: 115-7
  474.4: 287-8
  525: 323
  546: 242-3, 243 -
  ? Soph. *fr.* 730c10-11
  Radt: 408

Stesichorus *PMGF*
  278: 5

Theaetetus *HE*
  3365: 173-4

Theocritus
Id. 1.31: 139-40
  1.42: 63
  1.85: 126
  2.26 *et circa*: 294-5
  2.39: 446
  2.43: 467
  2.82: 286bf.
  2.88: 297-8
  2.104f.: 280
  2.108-9: 284
  2.112-3: 22
  2.113: 259
  2.125: 246
  3.15: 389-90
  3.17: 286bf.
  3.34/36: 152
  5: 142: 124
  7: 4-5: 347
  7.8-9: 220
  7.25: 446-7
  7.35: 173-4
  7.79: 390
  11.15-6: 287
  11.51: 291f.
  13 gen.: 2-3
  13.16: 2, 13, 58
  13.17: 7a, 58, 365-6
  13.18: 347
  13.19, 21: 2
  13.19: 2, 265-6
  13.23-4: 345-6

13.28: 167
13.33: 417
13.48: 288-9
13.54: 78: 55: 276
14.35: 149
14.42: 235-6
15 gen.: 7-166
15.1: 53
15.66: 392
15.112f.: 223-7
16.40: 314
17.19: 170
17.21: 232
17.37: 106
17.65: 382/385
17.105: 136
17.111-4: 351
17.132: 240
17.135: 391-2
18.17 *et circa*: 176
22.37f.: 222
22.49-50: 71
22.78: 167
22.97: 428
22.99: 7a
22.129-30: 257
22.131: 390
22.167: 396
22.176: 244
22.178: 176, 365-6
22.202-3: 320-1
24.29: 436
24.58: 22
24.70: 255
24.89: 272-3
26.10: 162
29.37f.: 61-3
HE 3442-3: 347

[Theocritus]
Id. 25.25-6: 413
  25.36: 197
  25.51 v.l.: 31
  25.54: 362-3
  25.115: 370
  25.136 *codd.*: 442
  25.139 *et circa*: 245-6
  25.156: 188, 280
  25.181: 419
  25.192: 426
  25.195: 401

25.200: 337-8
25.207-8: 235-6
25.213f.: 279
25.222: 185
25.273: 460-1
25.277: 322
27.22: 421

Theognidea IEG
173-4: 91-2
173: 421
1275: 277
1345f.: 115-7

Theopompus of Colophon
SH 765.2 corr.: 201

Timaeus *FGH*
566 *fr.* 39: 228-9
566 *fr.* 84: 200

Timo *SH*
825.1: 192
833.5-6: 192
840.1: 382/385

Timolaus *SH*
849.6: 415

Timonax *FGH*
842 *ffr.* 2/3: 245-6

Triphiodorus
37: 214
71: 287-8
262: 253
290: 354-5
345-6: 255
358f.: 276

Xenophanes *IEG*
3.3 *cod.*: 442
6.3: 391-2, 392

Xenophon *Oec.*
7.6: 292

INDEX IIB
LATIN AUTHORS

Apuleius *Met.*
4.31: 128
5.30: 91f.
6.22: 128

Catullus
4.3f.: 345-6
64.9: 340f.
64.86f.: 287-8
64.91-3: 286bf.
66.24-5: 288-9

Cicero *Tusc.*
3.9.18: 383

Ciris 158f.: 278f.

Claudian *Nupt.*
102f.: 43f.

De ave phoenice 35: 163

Ennius *Ann.*
18: 275

Horace *Carm.*
1.4.5f.: 41
1.13.5-6: 297-8

Lucretius
1.23: 1

Moretum
8f.: 291f.

Ovid
Am. 1.5.10: 41f.
Ars Am. 2.101f.: 467-8
Fast. 4.195f. 5/6 init.: 1-5
Heroid.
12.42-3: 230
12.165f.: 467-8
Met. 1.466f.: 278f.
1.492f.: 291f.
2.4f.: 215f.(E)
2.5f.: 230f.
2.22: 215
2.106: 230f.
3.373f.: 291f.
4.229: 253-6, 255
5.379f.: 278f.
5.381: 279
6.456f.: 291f.
6.491: 453f.
7.11f.: 464-70
7.24: 466
7.74: 467

7.78: 297-8
7.79f.: 291f.
7.158: 2
8.641f.: 291f.
10.623f.: 464-6
13.25-8: 364
13.28: 359
14.12f.: 467-8
14.312f.: 467-8
Rem. Am. 261f.: 467-8
Trist. 1.10.3-4: 345-6

Pacuvius *trag.*
184: 372

Propertius
3.3.33 corr.: 3-4

Reposianus
21, al.: 106
73: 46

Silius Italicus
3.669f.: 225-7
11.274f.: 270-4
14.397f.: 278f.

Statius
Silv. 1.2.155-7: 225-7
Theb. 1.515f.: 270-4
    3.444-51: 396-400
    4.274: 121-2
    7.34f.: 159-63
    11.7-8: 233-4

Valerius Flaccus
    2.115: 275
    2.136f.: 291f.
    2.468: 354-5
    2.651f.: 270-4
    3.534: 106
    5.325f.: 178
    5.329: 250-2
    5.373f.: 253-6
    5.399f.: 215f.(E)
    5.433-4: 230f.
    5.451-2: 228-9, 230f.
    5.471f.: 386-95
    5.477f.: 356f.
    5.495f.: 386
    5.519f.: 367-8
    5.521: 383
    5.556-7: 176
    6.433f.: 230f.
    6.517f.: 309
    6.657f.: 296
    6.663: 290
    7.50-1: 402
    7.62f.: 408
    7.69: 408
    7.91f.: 427-31
    7.231: 309-13
    7.427f.: 429

Virgil
G. 1.231f.: 135-41
    3.149: 276
A. 1.175-6: 291f.
    1.223-6: 159-63
    1.254-7/297: 108
    1.310f.: 176
    1.411f.: 215f.(E)
    1.411: 210
    1.412: 275
    1.413f.: 210-4
    1.495: 215
    1.521: 319
    1.527f.: 386
    1.613: 253-6, 284
    1.664f.: 128, 131f.
    1.703f.: 270-4
    3.386: 311-2
    4.67: 296
    4.141: 443
    4.246f.: 159-63
    4.256: 159-63
    4.285-7: 396-400
    4.357: 151
    4.479: 464-6
    5.83: 266
    5.312-3: 156
    7.10f.: 311-2
    7.56: 2
    7.231-2: 391-2
    7.280f.: 309
    8.142: 359
    8.387: 146-7
    8.407f.: 291f.
    9.476f.: 253-6
    9.622-4: 283
    10.149: 354-5
    12.224f.: 113-5

INDEX IIIA
COMPOSITION, LANGUAGE AND STYLE, METRE AND PROSODY

Accentuation 12 (ἦε), 57 (ἐνί), 71 (χειμάρρους), 81 (αΐδε), 145 al. (aor. ἀίω), 243 (Εἴδυια), 384 (φάσθαι), 418 (ἄμητος)

Accusative of relation 80; of fixed point in time 417; double accus. with verbs of depriving 175; with ἀμπνείω 230, ἀποτρωπάομαι 16, ἔξειμι sim. 159, ζέω 273, μείρομαι 4, πειράω 10, προρέω 225, τέθηπα 215, φυσιάω 410; w. ἀνά unusually 44, διέκ 73, μετά (of place) 13

Adverb cohering closely with subst. 62; in 'personal' construction with εἶναι 103; in -ως 319; -θι for -σε 255, 373

Allegorical interpretation of Homeric text 135-41, 211

Alliteration, assonance, rhyme, wordplay 1, 46-7, 51f., 71, 124, 192, 260-7, 275, 279, 346, 410, 414, 418, 467

Ambiguity 19-20, 33, 95, 96, 107, 135, 306, 307, 313, 325, 337, 350

Anachronisms, certain and probable in description of Aeetes' palace 215f., 220f., 222-3, 223-7, 225-7, 235, 238, cf. ad 270-4 (size of palace); note also 135-41B

Anacoluthon, unpromising 248-9, 375-6

Anaphora 230f.; paraenetic 173-4

Aoidos, Homeric 1, 4-5

Aporia, poetic/hymnic 1-5, 6; in Homer 66-74, 353; on a specific point of genealogy 136

Article, pronominal, interposed elements 70; + subst. 428, + partic. 406

Assonance see alliteration

Asyndeton 409, 417, 464-70; hair-raising specimen in MSS 208

Augment after word ending in a vowel 48; analogical temporal augment 454

Brevity (cf. s. compendious expressions, ellipse, epithets, narrator) compressed, economical style *passim*, e.g. 10, 36, 38, 97, 169, 198, 256, 268-70, 278f., 278, 279, 283, 297-8, 302, 381, ?383, 451

Cacophonous language 374, 446

Caesura, shift of scene at bucolic diaeresis 6; proclitic καί before main caesura 115; *versus tetracolos* 220

Chariot, poetic 1

Chiasmus 10-11, 412

Clausula involving monosyllable 115, patronymic 194; *spondeiazontes* 133-4, 197-8, 231, 252, 293, 456; end-stopped lines 37, runover in Ap. 20-1, 26-8, 28-9, 100-1

Clinical description 297-8, 422f.

Comparative, contrasting 209; 'younger than' effectively = 'the youngest' member 'of' a group 319

Compendious expressions 207f.

Conditional clauses (cf. s. subjunctive) 'if,' 'to see if,' 'if in truth' not implying real doubt about outcome or the facts 26-8, 113, 358; εἰ + ἀκούεις idiomatically 362-3; εἰ + pres. indic. 80; εἴ κε irregularly with aor. indic. 377/379; id. + optat. 'to see if ... *might* ...' sim. 180; εἰ μή + fut. indic. 75, 99

Contraction 193, 349

Correption before Πλ- 255-6, before Κρ- 357; unacceptable double correption 44

Crasis 102, 176

Dactylic bias 21; dactylic run arrested 2-3, 10, 146f.

Dative, concomitant/temporal 163, 225, 225-6, type αὐτοῖσιν τόξοισι 96, 373; instrumental, (clothed) 'with/in' 454, (play) 'with/at' 117b; of interest 370; locative, '(to a point) inside' (assoc. with κατα-) 154-5; of purpose 413-5, 413; of respect, 'as far as ... goes' 386 (doubtful ex.); 'double dative' 346, 461-2, cf. ad 413-5, alleged ex. 386; with ἐνικλᾶν 307; with ἀνά 44, ??166; allegedly with ἄντην 100-1

Diction, 3rd cent. hexam. (3^H see Abbreviations and Bibliography C), *passim*, as e.g. nouns 5, 144, 166, 175, 184, 233-4, 241, 266, 291, 313, 329, 337-8, 353, 360, 392, 397, 450; pronouns 48, 331; adjectives 52, 93, 162, 184, 222 *bis*, 229, 275, 280, 281, 294, 300, 316, 334, 390, 401, 403, 436, 457-8; adverbs 62, 97, 280, 281, 293, 334, 383; prepositions 22, 217-8, 266, 356; conjunction 67; particle 354-5; verbs 9, 14-5, 80, 99, 134, 193, 208, 224, 293, 370, 380, 385, 409, 426, 446-7, 460-1; speech-capping formulae 17, 22, 30, 83, 111, 259, 432-3

Didactica, influence exerted by, see esp. 135-41, 159-63, 160-1

Digamma neglected 201, 224

Dissymmetry in coordinated clauses 381

Dual participle = plural 206; dual introduced by conjecture 360 (subst.), 410 (partic.)

Ecphrasis in miniature 135-41; mannerisms of 137, 139-40

Elegy, amatory 2

Elision, unHomeric type 5

Ellipse of subject in gen. absol. 215; of object of verb 349

Epithets, prepositive 5, 13, 45, 148-9, 190, 229, 417, 2 × EN in series 158, 337; postpositive (cf. s. word order) 4-5, 5, 15, 37, 70, 135, 139-40, 162, 217-8, 263, 325, 414, 457-8; avoidance of epithet + name in run-up to direct speech 10, and of epithets/accumulation of epithets 36, 46-7, 47-50, 196f., 388-9; resolution of Homeric compound form 393

Erotic imagery/symbolism, see notably 163, 276, 280, 281, 286b-7, 287, 287-8, 288-9, 290, 291f., 294-5, 296, 446, 446-7

Etymologising 1, 4-5, 6, 73, 115, 162, 211, 216, 285, 292, 345-6, 444-5; in Call. 93, in Catull. 340f., in *HyAphr* 96, in Ovid 1-5

Exclamatory οἷα (δέ) 381 (?); infin. 375-6 (?)

'Formulae,' presumed Argonautic 2, 13, 58, (88), 169, 194, 240, 357, 390; formulaic veneer 230, 231, 232, 410, 411, 412; 'neoformulaic' elements in *Arg*. e.g. 24, 178 & 196, 299, 301, 423; 'formulaic doublets' 174. Cf. s. repetition

Gemination 37, 74, 109-10, 111, 149, 150, 181, 300, 301, 396, 456

Genitive ambiguous 33; of object grasped 146-7, source 136, 225-7; gen. participle after οἱ 371; with ἀγέραστος 65, θελκτήριος 33, ἀθερίζω 80, ἐπικύρω 342, πείθομαι 307-8, ἀνά 198; allegedly with ἐπισχερώ 170; function misunderstood by schol. 114

Hiatus, genuine and mistaken cases of, 26, 154, 170, 201, 207f., 262, 263, 323, 327, 354-5

Humour 7-166, 11, 14-5, 21, 25, 27, 32, 34, 45-7/50, 46-7, 56, 81-2, 82, 91f., 91-2, 106, 108f., 130, 154-5, 176f., 225-7

Illogicality 103, 377/379

Imperative pres./aor. 1, 85

Indicative, pres. with εἰ 80; pres. indic. with κεν to be rejected 401; cf. s. conditional clauses, optative, tenses

Infinitive, fut. + ἄν 28-9; fut. with μέμονα 351; ? exclamatory 375-6

Intensification 148, 192, 336-9 & 337-8, 376, 427

Irony of various kinds 51f., 52, 62, 89, 134, 135-41, 152, 168f., 171, 176, 191, 192, 243, 266, 288-9, 290, 306, 309-13, 326-7, 328, 336, 382-5, 405-6, 419, 429, 437

Koine see popular speech

Lament, atmosphere of formal lament-scene evoked 253-6, 259

Lengthening, metrical before *lambda* 300, 444-5, before *mu* 36, 457-8; 'Wernicke's Law' 185

COMPOSITION, LANGUAGE AND STYLE, METRE AND PROSODY 415

Literary allusion in general 7-166; mélange of literary reminiscences in heavy concentration 1-5

Lyric, influence of, see e.g. 1-5, 1, 4-5, 114, 288-9, 290, 367, and under individual authors

Middle, various uses of, 45, 46-7, 62, 97, 128, 136, 146-7, 205, 263-4, 283, 300, 413; medio-passive 66, 95

'Mimetic' element in Olympian scene 7-166

Muse(s), poet travels with Muses 1-5, 2 (Muse-chariot 1), as transmitter 1-5, 6, uses ἄγε in appeals 1, invocation-pattern involving 'how...' 2, parodies Muse-address 11, fires questions 12; have to do with 'anxieties' sim. and practise bewitchment 4-5; differentiation of functions 5; Muse(s) named 1-5, 1, 5, as Erato 1-5, form and import of name 1, 5, transfunctional nature 3, 3-4, 4-5, has to do with dancing and marriage 4-5; Muse(s) in *Arg.*, Call. *Aetia*, Ovid 1-5, in *Il.*, Emped. 1, in Pindar 1-5, 1; Muse-substitute in Call. 1, in Colluth. 6; their presence implied 2 *bis*

Narrator/narrative (cf. also under *aporia*, brevity, irony, Muses) Ap. in first person 1; Jason as summary narrator 4-5, poet's resumé of Orpheus' song in i 134; Call. as narrator in *Hymn to Artemis* 1, 2; aspects of technique, narrative compression, economy, haziness, speed 6-7, 64-5, 191, 196f., 265-6, 270-4, 309-13, 333f., 336-9; 'focalisation,' perspective 159-63 ('zooming-in' technique), 166, 199, 200-9, 210-4, 215f., 215, 219, 220f., 225, 228-9; foreshadowing 215f., 230f., 245-6, 276-7, 291f., 291, 297, 384; interweaving of scenes and simultaneity of action 167-8, 275; resumption of narrative unexpectedly suspended 228-9, 235; retardation 215f.; veracity, narrator's attitude to 225-7, 225

Negative in ἠὲ καὶ οὔ sim. 181; 'not *x* but *y*' in *ethnographica* 200-9

Nomenclature, validation of by appeal to professional usage 277; cf. s. etymologising

Nominative for vocative 1; alleged example of exclamatory nominative 375-6

Obligation, poetic 12

Optative (cf. s. conditional clauses) in imprecation 79; (+ κεν) in polite request 34-5; in negat. potential clause 14-5, aor. optat. + κεν as past potential 265-7; in protasis, not easily definable 99; expressing readiness 355; in relative clause 12-3 (+ κεν), 195; alternation of pres. and aor. optat. 398, of optat. and fut. indic. 435-6

Orthography, possible cases of authorial variation in 162, 195, 224; points of modern orthography 296-7, 453

Oxymoron 290

Participles in series 148-50; partic. with article 406; coincident aor. partic. 412

Passive see s. middle

Path of song 2

Pictorialism/links with fine art 7-166, 41f., 45-7/50, 51f., 117f., 119-21, 123-4, 157, 159-63, 278f., 281

Place-name, both 'mythical' and present-day version employed 233-4

Poet cf. s. narrator

Polar expression 464-6

Popular speech/koine, alleged/possible borrowings from 10, 50, 118, 123, 192; coarseness of diction 464-6

Prepositions (cf. s. accusative, dative, genitive), prep. expressed only in second of two coordinated clauses 60; prepositional phrase dependent on noun 345; different preps in series 198

Preverb in 'open form' 120; applied to achieve parallelism 174; otiose 327, 332; dispensed with 48, 205, 222-3; force of ἐπιπρο- 123-4, 379; status of προπρο(-) 453. Cf. s. tmesis

Pronouns, personal pronoun in lieu of proper name 464-6; κεῖνος as emphatic 3rd pers. pronoun 28-9; ὅγε, ὅδε see Index I; relative, unHomeric use of 408

Repetition, repeated elements in *Arg.* see esp. 145; cf. s. 'formulae'
Rhyme see s. alliteration

Scene-transference 168f., 172
Self-variation *passim*, e.g. 7a, 8-9, 28-9, 119, 192, 202, 239, 257, ?261, 290, 304
Sigma, intervocalic 1
Sigmatism 353
'Significant object' 196f., 444-5
Similes, distribution/frequency 276-7, 291f.; lead-in to 276, 291; foreshadowing and other aspects 291f.; simile by-passed 367-8, 371
Singular verb by attraction to adjacent clause 193; with closely paired subjects 343, 457-8
Speeches, direct: number in poem 17, clusters 10f., monologues 464-70, tonal variety 7-166; spare style/generalisations in Jason's speeches 188-90, 386-95, 409f., their mild undemonstrative tone 189-90, 385, 396, 427-31, possible Euripidean influence in eulogy of 'spoken word' 188-90; erratic syntax etc. in Aeetes' utterances see Index IV s. Aeetes; high-flown style etc. of Argos' speech to Aeetes 320-66 and successive notes; modes of introducing direct speech 10, 17, 24, 31, 51f., 51, 55, 78, 90, 101, 107, 169, 259, 303, 369-71 (extended sequence), 382/385, 385, 400, 426, 432-3, 463, identification of speaker in run-up 10; modes of speech closure 17, 22, 30, 76, 83, 111, 145, 317, 367, 382/385, 396, 432-3, 471; unreported speech 148-50; no speaking part for Eros 129f., 148
Spondee see clausula
'Stage-action' 247
Subjunctive with εἰ καί περ 61; with ἤν κε 404; with ὅτε in generalisation 345
Superlative for comparative, real and supposed exx. 91-2; in neut. sing. in type 'if <there is> anything ...' 347
Syntax, strained, broken, see Index IV s. Aeetes and cf. s. illogicality

Tags, Παλλὰς 'Ἀθήνη avoided by Ap. (contrast at 340); αὐτὰρ ἔπειτα 159; aetiological 200-9, 203
Tenses: (1) present, ἀκούω English 'have heard' 362-3; (2) imperfective, in verb of naming 246, of ordering 264-5, replying (interchanged with aor.) 385, speaking (id.) 83; (3) frequentative 383; function of ἔσκ- 195; (4) aorist, various uses 1, 3-4, 63, 65, 76f., 83, 85, 175, 189-90, 264-5, 369-70, 385, 444-5; aor. partic., 'coincident' 412; (5) pluperfect expressing instantaneous past action 270-1; (6) future (cf. s. conditional clauses; infinitive) in gloomy forecast 429-31; οὐ + fut. in urgent command 372; switch to fut. indic. to express certainty 181; (7) alternation of pres./perf. 200-9; of frequent./imperf. 223
Tmesis 261, 343-4, 424; bifunctional preverb 378-9; rejected/doubtful exx. 73, 385; anastrophic 46
Tragedy, influence of, see e.g. 1-5, 378-9, 392, also under individual authors and Index IV s. Aeetes *ad fin.*

Vocative represented by nominative 1
Voyage ~ song 2

Word order: delayed γάρ 386, postpositive οὕνεκα 370, subst. after possessive οἱ 470, wide hyperbaton (cf. s. epithet) 154-5, conveying natural rhythms of speech 98-9, 265-7; dislocation in 13, 153, cf. Index IV s. Aeetes; emphatic *incipit*, normally followed by strong pause, adverb 97, postpositive epithet 15, 82, 118, 202-3, 259, 292, 378-9, 412, main verb 10, participle 189-90, 405, substantive/proper name 2-3, 166, 200, 209, 222-3, 252, 254, 263-4, 281, 318, 352, 369-70; emphatic subst. before main caesura 333; prepositive possessive gen. for emphasis 27
Word-play see s. alliteration

INDEX IIIB
THE *ARGONAUTICA*,
TEXT, TESTIMONIA, SCHOLIA

Accentuation see Index IIIA s.v.
Aratus, corruption stemming from? 159-63
Assimilation see s. *Echoschreibung*
Asyndeton, preposterous example left unquestioned
Atticising variant 450

Callimachea foisted on Ap. 93, 277

Division of words see s. Misdivision
Dual imported by conjecture 360, 410

Echoschreibung 287-8, ?419; involving assimilated terminations 100-1, 119-20, 165, 166, 250-1, 239/241
Emendations (1) Medieval see under Manuscripts, esp. E; (2) Modern, obligatory or desirable cases in iii: 48, 76, 101, 146-7, 159-63, 209, 210-4, 263-4, 294, 363; recommended in i-ii, iv: 42-3 (i.729), 45 (iv.604), 46-7 (iv.27), 120 (iv.1562), 154 (iv.24), 170 (iv.451), 432-3 (ii.1218); normalising, simplifying, Homerising emendations in iii rejected 10, 14-5, 44, 46-7, 93, 97, 99, 109-10, 148-50, 165, 202, 225-6, 263, 294-5, 309-13 & 310-11, 321, 355, 371, 386, 413-5, 419 (?), 429-31, 442; cf. ad 199 (ii.823), 370 (iv.1410)

Gemination, variations in MSS 37, 149, 150, 396, 456
Gloss infiltrates text 290; marginal gloss corrupted? 195

Hiatus, cases mistakenly eliminated 170, 207f.; wrongly acquiesced in 262
Homerising errors, certain or likely 1, 84, 158, 185, 222-3 (pap. at i.374), 292, 323, 467

Lacuna, inevitable 248-9, minor specimen 254; inplausible 375, 386, 413-5
Lower-case *eros* 296-7, ctr. 452

Manuscripts, individual/families:
A 292, 450
D 81, 119-20, 201, 264-5, 275, 276, 278, 379, 404, 444-5, 454, 457-8
E 12, 14-5, 21, 36, 42-3, 48, 70, 82, 84, 115, 121-2, 165, 179, 181, 190f., 198, 224, 248-9, 293, 323, 331, 346, 349, 360, 375-6, 375, 396-7, 398, 413-5, 418, 450, 454
G 195, 290, 331
L 9, 170, 292, 369
O 346
S 14-5, 81, 156, 239-41, 262, 300, 444-5, 467
d 293, 457-8
m 293
w 68, 75, 398, 450
Method, textual interesting variants and emendations 14-5, 26-8, 32 (Fränkel *Einleitung*), 100-1, 146-7, 158, 159-63, 162, 190f., 198, 210-4, 216, 224, 225, 248-9, 261, 262, 263-4, 290, 294, 321, 346, 375-6, 386, 401, 404, 413-5, 418, 419, 426, 429-31, 442, 454
Misdivision 48, 76, 190; uncertainties about word-division 393, 453

Papyri, remarks on readings presented by 5, 14-5, 17, 26-8, 34, 158, 216, 222-3 (f.v.l. at i.374), 263-4, 264-5, 268-70, 270, 404
Punctuation 2 (alleged break after *incipit*), 102, 189-90, 202, 306, 334, 362-3, 375, 381, 386

Scholia (cf. s. Theon), on Hellas 13
i.320 (con. L): 215
i.734: 291

i.1129: 133-4
ii.399-401a: 200
ii.955-61d: 17
ii.1010-14, al.: 200-9
iii.1-5: 4-5
iii.17: 17; 52: 52
iii.107: 107
iii.114-7a: 114
iii.114-7b: 158f.
iii.129: 129
iii.134: 133-4
iii.225-7a: 225-6
iii.233-4a: 223-4
iii.237-8: 237
iii.240: 242-3
iii.242-4: 242-3
iii.257: 221
iii.275: 275
iii.281b: 281
iii.368b: 367-8
iii.375f. Brunck: 375
iii.375-6b: 376
iii.388: 388
iii.408b: 408
iii.414: 413-5
iv.1217-9a: 245-6

Testimonia
Athenaeus 1-5
Choeroboscus 1
EtG^{A/B} 199, 200, 201, 217-8, 232, 278, 283
EtM 71, 199, 200, 217-8

Hesychius (corrupt) 76
schol. T *Il.* ~ Eust. 8-10
Theon 1-5, 107, 133-4, 134

Variants adverted to in i-ii, iv: 101 (iv.1260), 116, 134 (iv.1131), 156 (i.1194), 216 (i.786), 224 (i.1146), 273 (i.734), 276 (ii.662), 358f. (ii.1160)
Systematic:
ἀλωή ἀλ- 158
ἀπαμείρ- ἀπομείρ- 186
δέρος -ας 88
ἐγ- ἐνι- 282
ἐνί ἐπί 396-7
ἐπετέλλετ' -ετείλατ' 264-5
ἐπήνησαν -νεσ(σ)αν 194
ἔρξ- ἔρξ- 109
ἐώλπει ἐόλπ- 370
ἧμιν ἄμμιν *et sim.* 314
ἵκω ἥκω 275
μῦθος θυμός 34
νίσσομαι νίσομαι 210
ὅγε ὅδε 14-5, 81, 326
πασσυδίῃ πανσ- 195
περί πυρί 291
προμολή -βολή 215
σφε σφι 370
τε κε 209
τέλλω στέλλω 277
τοι οἱ 5
φθείσ- φθίσ- 459
χέρες χεῖρες *et sim.* 50
χεύετο -ατο *et sim.* 291
ὦλλοι ὦλλ- 176

INDEX IV
MYTHOLOGY, RELIGION, GEOGRAPHY, ETHNOGRAPHY, AETIOLOGY

Achilles, evoked for various reasons, 14-5, 53, 65, 73, 74-5, 81-2, 94, 109-10, 122, 124, 135-41, 171-95, 179, 187, 216, 243, 283, 337-8, 371, 382-5, 396-400, 429, 437-8, 441, 470
Acontius 27
Adamant, associated with gods 230f., 232, 233
Adresteia 133-4
Aea, location of/links with Helios 159-63, 244, 309-13; indefiniteness of name 306; 'Colchian' 313; Aeaean Island/Mainland 311-2, 313
Aeacus 363, 364
Aeetes, parentage/family connexions 215f., 242-3, 243, 309-13, 320-66, 337-8; κρείων 240, as 'infernal ruler' 216; his palace 215f. and successive notes, his bulls 230f., 230, 408, 409f., 410, his spear 416, and Helios' chariot 159-63, 233-4, 245-6, 309-13, 309; his flashing eyes 371, 372; agitated, strained, abnormal patterns of speech 369-70, 370, 375-6, 375, 377/379, 381, 404, 413-5, 418; wrath 337-8, 449, and general traits/attitude to strangers 14-5, 15, 171-95, 176f., 181, 191, 304f., 386-95, 390; lives under a shadow 307, 315, 328, 333f., 333, 335, 361; aspects of reception of Jason and co. 268-70, 270-4, 271-2, 299-303, 303, 304f., 306, 307-8, 309-13, 314, 326, 332, 342, 363-3, 365-6, 372-81, 374, 375-6, 375, 377f., 378-9, 381, 386-95, 386, 398, 399, 401, 402-3, 402, 403, 405, 405-6, 406, 419, 420-1, 422f., 434f., 434, 437, 441, 470; in *Naupactia* 8, ? tragic influence in portrayal 304f., 367-8, 371, 378-9, 401-21, 409f., 411, 413, 418
Cf. s. Amycus, Eiduia, Hera, Jason, Pelias
Aegisthus 207

Aeolids 335, 360, 361, 364
Aeolus 306 (in *Od.*; Philetas); (~ Aeolids) 364
Aethalides 196f., 197-8
Aetia, language/style 200-9, 203, 225-7, 233-4; tags adopted by personages in poem 312-3, 314
Agamemnon 179, 437-8
Agos 203, 336-9
Aisa 261, 328
Ajax 423, 424
Alcimede 259, 461-2
Alcinous' palace, Odysseus at 215f. and successive notes; cf. also 270-1
Amazons 200-9
Amphidamas 324
Amycus, character, flouts laws of hospitality 171-95, 181, label in Theoc. 428; mirrored by Aeetes 407, 408, 437-8; his challenge 422f., Polydeuces defies him 196f.
Anauros 66-74, 67, 385
Ancaeus 6-7, 15, 171-95, 423
Andromache 253-6
Aphrodite see Cypris
Apollo, behind expedition 66-74, 389-90; Iliadic A. evoked 27-8, 284, 285
Apsyrtus, family background/age 242-3, 245-6, 246; ~ Phaethon 242-3, 245-6; in Val Flacc. 309; entrapment and murder 117/124, 192, 384, burial 200-9
Ares, 'reaper' 416; his island 322, 324, birds on 325; his plain 326, 409, 422f., ploughed field 411, 412; Cf. s. Cypris, Eros
Argo, etymology 345-6; building involved Athena/Argos 8, 320-1, 340f., 340, Jason 340, and Pelias 340f.; build-quality 340f., 343, low-lying 6-7, how propelled 345-6; ~ Pagasae/Iolcus 2; importance to Jason and crew 171-95, 176

Argonauts, parentage/demigods 365-6; age-span 194; Panhellenes 13, 347, 391-2; ἀριστῆες 6-7, 7a, ἥρωες 167, νέοι 194, στόλος 175, oarsmen 170; nature of task 194f., 194, 'catabatic' 61-3, 216; involved in collective decision-making 171-95, 194f.; importance of their 'return home' 175; 'non-combatants' 6-7, 7b, 168, 171-95, 184; ἀμηχανίη/dejection 422f., 432-3, 446-7

Argos the Phrixid and A. Arestorides 340f., 341, 343-4, 345-6; oldest and dominant Phrixid 178, 317, 319; dealings with Jason/Argonauts 6-7, 168, 171-95, 176f., 188, 190f., 215f., 318, 320-66, 333f., 354f., 362-3; with Aeetes 176f., 193, 318, 320-66, 320-1, 321, 323, 327, 328, 331, 332, 333f., 333, 336, 336-9, 340f., 341, 342, 346, 347, 348, 349, 350, 352-3, 354f., 354-5, 355, 361, 362-3, 422f., in aftermath of interview 441

Cf. s. Chalciope, Jason, Phrixids

Ariadne 286bf., 287-8, 464
Artemis in Call.'s *Hymn* 1
Asterodeia 242-3, 245-6
Astyanax 245-6
Atabyrius, Mt, bronze bulls on 228-9
Atalanta 464-6
Athamas 336-9, 360
Athena, called Ἀθηναίη Παλλάς by the grandiloquent Argos 340; role in *Arg.* 8 and *passim*, fades out 111; involved with Argo see s.v., had dealings with Aeetes 340f.; assoc. with Hera/Iliadic backdrop esp. 7-166, also e.g. 25, 107, 113-5, 275 (and Trojan Horse 340); parentage 30, 32; martial 16, 25, 33, meek 25, 26, 27, 31; (supposedly) resourceful 11, 12, 21, 24, 30, 33, 210, yet (incontrovertibly) clueless 13, 18, 19-20, 21, 22-4 (cf. s. Hera, as manipulator ...); and bedrooms/sex 8-10, 10, 11, 14-5, 16, 25, 27, 32, 33, 39
Atlas 159-63, 161
Augeias 196f., 197, 362-3

Ball of Zeus see s. Zeus
Beauty Competition on Ida 45-7/50, 46, 51f.

Bellerophon 230f., 333, 353, 409, 422f.
Boreads 309-13
Bronze Race, Hesiodic 230f.
Bulls see s. Aeetes
Burial/Cremation, Hellenic mode of 205; cf. s. Colchians

Calypso 46, 89, 108f., 151, 220f., 222, 388-9
Caucasus 159-63
Chalciope, mother of Phrixids 248; importance for plot 248, 449; in relation to her sons 253-6, 260, 441, 'lament' over them 259; 'domesticated' 255
Chalybes 200-9
Charis 36f., 82
Cheiron and Jason 66-74, 73, 385
Chimaera 230f., 231
Circe, parentage/family connexions 243, 309-13, ~ Medea cf. s.v.; at Colchis 200, her plain there 200-9, 200, Aeaean Island in east 311-2; C. in the west 309-13, 311-2, 313, an 'exile' 309-13; Homeric Circe evoked 47-50, 200, 201, 215; as witch in Ovid 467-8
Cleinis 309
Colchians, numerical superiority 171-95, 212; ships 341, 342; 'civilised' habits 176f.; religion/treatment of corpses 200-9, 207f.
Colchis, terrain 6; Colchian Aea 313
Crete 133-4
Cyclops, Polyphemus-episode evoked 176f., see also notably 172, 193, 239, 325-6, 422f., 426
Cypris, never called 'Aphrodite' by Ap. 3-4 (*cypris* metonymically 5), 'Cytherea' 108; sea-born 276; wife of Hephaestus 37, 41f., 136, enthroned 43-4, 47-50, 51f., solitary 39, 41f., not 'domesticated' 43-4; mother of Eros by ... 136, (not) differentiated from him 8, 91f., her dealings with him 105, 128, 129f., 129, 131f., 131, 148-50; involved with Aeneas 96 and with Ares (Hephaestus-escapade) 41f., 62, 89, 102, 136, 145; her allotted functions 4-5, 'tamer' 4-5, 288-9, inflicts anxieties 4-5, ἀμηχανίη 126, bewitches 4-5, 33; provocatively attractive 41f., 45, hair 45-7/50, 46, 50, 51f., skin-tone 45; de-

ceitful/tricky 12, 51, 89, 97, 130, 133, 150, 152 ('oath of Aphr.'), 154-5; catty/sarcastic 51f., 52, 53, 54; laughter-loving sim. 51f., 51, 100-1, 107, 130, 150; ill-humoured 109-10, an avenger 64-5; powerful 81-2, delicate/feeble 61-3, 81-2, 84, 106, 144; dislikes publicity 103; role in *Arg.* esp. 3-4, 7-166, 8, 12 (*Naupactia*), 262, Iliadic backdrop 7-166, 81-2, 100-1, 101, 106, 107 and *passim*; disguised as old woman 72, cf. s. Phaon; in Empedocles 1
Cf. s. Eros, Hephaestus, Hera
Cyta etc. 228-9
Cytherea see Cypris

Daimon 389-90
Deo 413
Dicte ~ Ida 133-4
Dionysus 220f.
Dipsacus 191
Doublets in myth-cycles 66-74

Eagle of Zeus 116, 158f., 158, 162
Earth as Colchian deity 200-9, 207f.
Earthborn 230f., 416
Echetus 378-9
Egypt, Ptolemaic 220f., 225-7, 291f.; Egyptians 227, 308
Eiduia (Iduia) 242-3, 243, 244, 269
Elements 200-9 (sacred); 207f.
Enyalius 322
Epeius 340
Equality in sphere of cosmological forces 207f.
Eros, Eros ~ eros 275, 281, 285, 291f., 296-7, 297, Eros ~ Erotes 117/124, 136, 452; parentage 136; (not) differentiated from Cypris 8, a problem-child, threatens mother 85, 91f., 91-2, 95-6; 'little'/a baby 281, no speaking-part 148, καγχαλόων 124, 286a, ruddy complexion 114, 121-2, 163, winged 285, naked 119-21; assoc. with knucklebones 114, 117/124, 119-21, 123-4, ball 114, 135-41, garden/flowers 114; a *daimon* 7-166, 389-90, a vital force 165, his power and influence 115-7, 135-41, 158, 159-63, 288-9; deceitful/tricky 12, 114, 130 (~ ἀδικίη), shameless, impudent 92-3, 93; dispels shame 287-8, a κακόν/πῆμα 129, assoc. with ἀμηχανίη 126 (cf. on 284), bewitchment 27, 27-8, 131f., liquefaction 290, μαργοσύνη 114, 120, 150, a 'sting' 276, destructive violent wind 288-9; a destroyer 291f., 296-7, 297, stirs up strife (ἔρως ~ ἔρις), madness etc. 91f., 136, 276, Eros ~ Ares 91f., 136, 287, 297, like warrior on battlefield esp. 280, 281, an archer with weapons 8, 27-8, 91f., 95, 96, 120, 131f., 135-41, 141, 276-7, 276, 278f., 278, 279, 282, 284, 285, 286bf., 286b-7, 287, 287-8; attributes detectable in victims 92, 120, 126, conversely 276; role in *Arg.* esp. 8; descent from Olympus screened by mist/invisible operator 158f., 158, 159-63, 163, 165, 166, 275, 278f., 280, 281, 296; 're-appearance' in iv.276-7, 279, 286bf., 296-7, 297, 384, 389-90; depiction in art 117f., 119-21, 123-4, 135-41, 157, 278f., 280, 281
Ethnographica (cf. Index of Greek Authors esp. s. Herodotus, Nymphodorus) 200-9, 209; Hellenistic colouring 207f.; inverted values of foreigners 205
Cf. s. *agos*, Amazons and others, burial, Earth, Egypt, Elements, Equality, Heaven, willows
Eurystheus 390, 420-1

Fleece, terminology assoc. with 2, 12-3, 13, 58, 88, 163, 186, 375-6, 375, 404; problem posed by 6-7, 171-95, 188; stored in Aeetes' palace 419; Argos on 6-7, to Aeetes 320-66, 333, 336-9; Medea and Fleece 468; ? 'mummifies' Phrixus 200-9
Folktale atmosphere 66-74

Ganymede 113-5, 114, 115-7, 115, 116, 158f.
Ge see Earth
Gigantomachy 233-4 cf. s. Phlegra
Gods, 'some god' as saviour (shipwreck) 323; ~ δαίμων 389-90; apportionment of spheres of influence 3, 3-4, 207f.; attitude to mortals 66-74, callousness 64-5, μῆνις 337-8, pity 66-74, 328, re-

ciprocity-principle 78, 82, 233-4, *themis* prescribed by them 193, 203, test humans (disguised) 66-74, 68; mocking tone of Iliadic gods 51f., 'omniscience' 7b/can they be said to 'search'? 113-5, 113, speed of movement 36, 111-2; their golden possessions 118, 156; comic/serious tone in relation to gods *passim*, e.g. 120, 154-5; (almost) no divine brawls in *Arg.* 7-166, and no persecution of Args 8-10; Olympian scene transferred to terrestrial plane 168f., 172

Hades, Ixion punished there, voyage to, ? by Args 61-3, 61; gates of, *catabasis*-motif, Aeetes in relation to 216; ~ Zeus Chthonios, ἀμείλικτος 337
Halitherses 307-8
Heaven as Colchian deity 200-9, 207f.
Hecate in Hes. *Theog.*, transfunctional 3, 3-4; her temple 252; and Circe/ Medea (cf. s.v.) 309-13; Perseis 467
Hector 181, 235f., 253-6, 371, 407, 422-6, 437-8
Helios, family connexions 242-3, father of Augeias cf. s.v.; eyes of his descendants 371; his cattle 326-7, chariot (cf. s. Aeetes) 159-63, 230f., 233-4, 245-6, cup 230f., palace 215f., 230f., rays at Aea 244, springs 225-7; rises at Aea 159-63, 159, 163, 244, heads for 'Hesperian Land' 311; in Gigantomachy (cf. s. Hephaestus) 233-4
Hellas 13, 306, 347, 375-6
Hephaestus, husband of Cypris (q.v.) 37, 41f., 136, of Charis 36f., 82; physically abnormal 37, 82, 197, ?? 233-4; a workaholic 41f., 41, 42-3, his place of work 42, craftsman/builder in Aeetes' palace etc. 37, 41f., 42-3, 44, 46, 118, 131f., 135-41, 136, 137, 215f., 222-3, 228-9, 229 (epithets; marvel-worker), 230f. (animate figures), 231f. (id.), 235f., 237; assoc. with Helios 230f., 233-4 (Gigantomachy)
Hera, 'Thessalian'/'Pelasgian' 8, 64-5; role as unseen helper in *Arg.* esp. 7-166, 8, 210, 250-2, Iliadic backdrop *passim*, e.g. 7-166, 100-1, 107; slighted by Pelias 7-166, 8, 66-74, 68, 86-9, 390, her egocentricity and callousness in that connexion 36f., 64-5, 66-74; disguised, tested 'men' but esp. Jason 66-74, 72; as deceiver/trickster 12, 107, manipulates Athena and Cypris 7-166, Athena 10, 11, 25, 34-5, Cypris 56f., 61-3, 63, 64-5, 74-5, 81-2, 83, 89, 100-1, 106, 109-10; acts much like Odysseus' Athena (but impersonally) 210, 211, 443; in iv helps out/interferes with meteorological phenomena 111, 210-4, 211, cf. Ἥρη ~ ἠήρ, ἀήρ 210-4, 211, 214, 275; Hera and Zeus (q.v.) 8-10, 211; as Cypris' senior 52; and Ixion 61-3; and Thetis cf. s.v.; her bedroom 8-10; her βουλή 7-166, 10, 33; in bondage 62
Heracles, tutored by Linus 117/124; labours/Eurystheus 390, 420-1, *daimon*/labours 389-90, motivation for labours 336-9, wanderer 261, 'mercenary' 352-3, hero ambushes Hippolyte 6-7, as 'Hellenic' expedition-leader 347; in *Arg.*, H. and loss of Hylas 276, 'atrabilious' 422f., spoken of by Telamon 347, described by Aegle 192; in heaven 116
Hermes, and Calypso 108f., 388-9, Homeric descent to earth 159-63; and Aethalides, heraldic function 196f., 197-8; and Aeetes 196f., 200-9; in Eratosthenes 135-41, 159-63
Hesperian Land 311
Hiera Hephaestou 42
Horse, Trojan 340
Hunter-hero 66-74
Hylas 2-3, 121-2, 163, 276, 444-5
Hyperboreans 309
Hypsipyle 216

Ida 133-4, 134
Idas 422f.
Idmon 199, 205
Iduia see Eiduia
Ilioneus 215f., 319, 386, 391-2
Ino (aka ...) 190, 191
Io 276, 277
Iolcus 2, 265-6
Iphias 252
Isis/Anti 66-74
Ixion 61-3, 62, 63

MYTHOLOGY, RELIGION, GEOGRAPHY, ETHNOLOGY, AETIOLOGY

Jason, 'son of Aeson/Aesonides'/parentage 169, 357, 365-6; physical attractiveness 443f., 443, 444-5; favourite of Hera 8, 56f., 64-5, 66-74, 66, 74, hunter-hero 66-74 tested by her (cf. s. Hera); J. and the Fleece 2-3, 121-2, 176f.; a reluctant Argonaut 348-9, 349, 386-95, 386-8, 388-9, prone in desperate situations to ἀμηχανίη (cf. s. Argonauts) 176f., 336, 422f., 423, 432-3, advocate of 'softly softly'/flattering approach in appropriate circumstances 189-90, 190, 195, 196f., 385, 396, 457-8, with a spare, non-confrontational style of speaking 188-90, 386-95, 409f., conscious of his responsibilities to crew 171-95, 333f.; sometimes naively branded an 'anti-hero' or worse 73, 388-9, but essentially (and increasingly) a tactician constantly striving against the odds 6-7, 168f., 171-95, 171, 173-4, 175, 176f., 178, 179, 181, 182, 183-4, 183, 184, 188, 189-90, 190, 194f.; aspects of his dealings with the Phrixids/Argos 320-66, 336-9, 340f., 352-3, 354f., 358f., and with Aeetes 171-95, 352-3, 375-6, 385, 386-95, 386, 386-8, 389-90, 391, 392, 393, 396, 422f., 423, 425, 426, 427-31, 428, 429, 429-31, 429-30; miscellaneous: loses sandal 66-74; issue of reinstatement at Iolcus 333; part in building of Argo 340; his πεῖρα in ii 107; conduct in iv 192
Cf. also notably s. Aeetes, Argos, Cheiron, Hera, Medea, Odysseus, Pelias, Phrixus
Juno in Virgil 211

Lycus 314

Medea, first mentioned in iii 2-3, in proems of iii/iv 1-5; 'daughter of Aeetes' 27, 247, M. and Circe 27, 89, 309-13, priestess of/attitude to Hecate 252, 309-13, 467-8, 467, and chariot of Helios 309; age 276, significant name 288-9, complexion 297-8, mantilla 444-5, bedroom 215f., 216, 235-6, 247, 248, 451; her φάρμακα/cleverness/guile 27, 89, 288-9, hence tool of Hera 8, 86-9; assailed by Erotes as well as by Eros 452; in relation to Jason, her 'hero-worship' 453f., 'dream experiences' 446-7, 453f., 457-8, sensations of acute anxiety 446, 452, 453f., of pity 461-2, indecisiveness and lack of comprehension 464-70, 464, pessimism 468-9; qua witch, her helplessness, in Ap. and in Ovid 467-8; her monologues, in Ap. and in Val. Flacc. 464-70; marriage to Jason 290, 291f., her children 291f.; M. in [Theog.] 27, in tragedy 290
Mene 286bf., 288-9, 467-8
Menelaus 437-8
Minyas/-ans 265-6
'Mist,' divinely applied; see s. Hera; Eros
Monte Circeo 311-2
Mossynoeci 200-9, 209

Nausicaa 4-5, 444-5
Nestor 171-95, 314
Night, gates of in west 159-63, 159; chariot 233-4

Oceanus/-ids 242-3, 243, 244, 245-6
Odysseus, evoked in connexion with Jason and for other reasons 56f., 74-5, 87, 89, 100-1, 109-10, 113-5, 164, 175, 176f., 178, 183-4, 185, 188-90, 195, 198, 261, 270-4, 280, 281, 283, 291, 306, 320f., 320-1, 321, 322, 326-7, 343-4, 348-9, 374, 389-90, 391-2, 394, 405, 407, 422f., 423, 426, 444-5, 453f., 454, 468
Cf. also s. Alcinous, Athena, Calypso, Circe, Cyclops, Hera, Penelope, suitors
Old woman, divine disguise 66-74, 72
Olympus 166; its πτύχες 113, 114; gates of, ~ οὐρανός, downward path hence 159-63, 159, 160-1, 162; Zeus' garden there see s. Zeus
Orchomenos 265-6, 266
Orpheus 4-5, 134, 165
Ouranos see Heaven

Pagasae 2
Pallene 233-4

Panachaea 347
Pandarus 96, 105, 113-5, 123-4, 131f., 276-7, 278f., 278
Panhellenes 347
Paris 340
Parnassus (Indian Caucasus) 159-63
Patroclus 117/124, 216, 253-6
Peisidice 470
Peleus 6-7, 171-95, 180, 184, 185, 195, 196f., 434
Pelias, an Aeolid 335; character 65, 66-74, 68, 190, 390, 428, P. and Aeetes 14-5, 171-95, 189-90, 333f., 336, 401, 405-6, 427-31, 429-31; dealings with Jason 66-74, 189-90, 190, 261, 333f., 333, 390, 422f., 427-31, 429-30, reception accorded to Jason and co. in Pindar 268-70; tries to 'fix' Argo 340f.; his eventual death 64, 429
Cf. s. Hera
Penelope 259, 444-5, 453f., 454
Perse/-eis 243 cf. s. Hecate
Phaedra 290
Phaethon 230f., 242-3, 245-6, 309, 310; see Apsyrtus
Phaon 66-74
Phasis 6, 244
Phineus, esp. his forecasts and reflections in ii, 7-166, 12, 74-5, 183-4, 185, 200-9, 200, 228-9, 314, 335, 350, 361, 422f., 446-7
Phlegra/-aean 215f., 230f., 233-4
Phrixids, 'sons of Phrixus' 178; leave Colchis, shipwrecked, encounter Argonauts 178, 194f., 264-5, 265-6, 266, 306, 315-6, 320f., 320-1, 321, 327, 329, 341, 343-4, 375-6
Cf. s. Argos, Chalciope
Phrixus, character 190, Phrixus ~ Jason 190; and stepmother/Athamas 191, 336-9; taken in by Dipsacus 191 and Aeetes 171-95, 176f., 190, 304-5; a mummy? 200-9
Plancte Nesos 42
Polydamas 171-95
Polydeuces see Tyndaridae; Amycus
Polyphemus, Argonaut 200-9; cf. s. Cyclops

Pontus 159-63
Presbon, a Phrixid 319
Priam 65, 100-1, 262, 448, 468-9; his palace 235f., 237
Prometheus 159-63

Rivers of earth, numinous, 165

Sauromatae 352-3
Scamander 225-7, 227
Sidero 64-5
Sirens 4-5
Suitors of *Odyssey* evoked 68, 74-5, 276, 378-9

Talos 230f.
Telamon 196f., 382f., 382-5, 422f., 429
Theseus 286bf., 287-8, 408
Thetis 7-166, 64-5, 66-74
Tibareni 200-9
Tiphys 107
Trojan War, Panhellenic 347
Tyche 250-2, 323, 328
Tyndaridae 196f., see Polydeuces
Typhonomachy 233-4
Tyro 64-5
'Tyrsenian' 311-2

Willows, funereal 201

Zeus, birthplace, infancy on Crete/eagle 116, 133-4, 134, his ball, an infant's toy 135-41, 150, his garden on Olympus 113, 114, 158f.; husband of Hera 8-10, 69, father of Muse 1-5, Aeacus 196f., 363, 364, Aeolus 364, Tyndaridae 196f.; sky-god 211, 'great Zeus' 158, Zeus Chthonios 337, Zeus Xenios 171-95, 176f., 179, 190, 192, 193, 196f., 328; his βουλή 10, his νόος 10, 328, feels pity 328; remote figure in *Arg.* 8-10, 364; angry over Phrixus 336-9, 337, 337-8, 364, involved in salvation of Phrixids 328, 342, 343, at Colchis 200-9; in Typhonomachy 233-4; the Aratean Zeus 192
Cf. s. Adresteia, Athena (parentage), eagle, Ganymede

SUPPLEMENTS TO MNEMOSYNE

EDITED BY J.M. BREMER, L.F. JANSSEN, H. PINKSTER, H.W. PLEKET, C.J. RUIJGH AND P.H. SCHRIJVERS

86. VERDENIUS, W.J. *A Commentary on Hesiod: Works and Days*, vv. 1-382. 1985. ISBN 90 04 07465 1
87. HARDER, A. *Euripides' 'Kresphontes' and 'Archelaos'*. Introduction, Text and Commentary. 1985. ISBN 90 04 07511 9
88. WILLIAMS, H.J. *The 'Eclogues' and 'Cynegetica' of Nemesianus*. Edited with an Introduction and Commentary. 1986. ISBN 90 04 07486 4
89. McGING, B.C. *The Foreign Policy of Mithridates VI Eupator, King of Pontus*. 1986. ISBN 90 04 07591 7
91. SIDEBOTHAM, S.E. *Roman Economic Policy in the Erythra Thalassa 30 B.C.-A.D. 217*. 1986. ISBN 90 04 07644 1
92. VOGEL, C.J. DE. *Rethinking Plato and Platonism*. 2nd impr. of the first (1986) ed. 1988. ISBN 90 04 08755 9
93. MILLER, A.M. *From Delos to Delphi*. A Literary Study of the Homeric Hymn to Apollo. 1986. ISBN 90 04 07674 3
94. BOYLE, A.J. *The Chaonian Dove*. Studies in the Eclogues, Georgics and Aeneid of Virgil. 1986. ISBN 90 04 07672 7
95. KYLE, D.G. *Athletics in Ancient Athens*. 2nd impr. of the first (1987) ed. 1993. ISBN 90 04 09759 7
97. VERDENIUS, W.J. *Commentaries on Pindar. Vol. I. Olympian Odes 3, 7, 12, 14*. 1987. ISBN 90 04 08126 7
98. PROIETTI, G. *Xenophon's Sparta*. An introduction. 1987. ISBN 90 04 08338 3
99. BREMER, J.M., A.M. VAN ERP TAALMAN KIP & S.R. SLINGS. *Some Recently Found Greek Poems*. Text and Commentary. 1987. ISBN 90 04 08319 7
100. OPHUIJSEN, J.M. VAN. *Hephaistion on Metre*. Translation and Commentary. 1987. ISBN 90 04 08452 5
101. VERDENIUS, W.J. *Commentaries on Pindar. Vol. II*. Olympian Odes 1, 10, 11, Nemean 11, Isthmian 2. 1988. ISBN 90 04 08535 1
102. LUSCHNIG, C.A.E. *Time holds the Mirror*. A Study of Knowledge in Euripides' 'Hippolytus'. 1988. ISBN 90 04 08601 3
103. MARCOVICH, M. *Alcestis Barcinonensis*. Text and Commentary. 1988. ISBN 90 04 08600 5
104. HOLT, F.L. *Alexander the Great and Bactria*. The Formation of a Greek Frontier in Central Asia. Repr. 1993. ISBN 90 04 08612 9
105. BILLERBECK, M. *Seneca's Tragödien; sprachliche und stilistische Untersuchungen*. Mit Anhängen zur Sprache des Hercules Oetaeus und der Octavia. 1988. ISBN 90 04 08631 5
106. ARENDS, J.F.M. *Die Einheit der Polis*. Eine Studie über Platons Staat. 1988. ISBN 90 04 08785 0
107. BOTER, G.J. *The Textual Tradition of Plato's Republic*. 1988. ISBN 90 04 08787 7
108. WHEELER, E.L. *Stratagem and the Vocabulary of Military Trickery*. 1988. ISBN 90 04 08831 8
109. BUCKLER, J. *Philip II and the Sacred War*. 1989. ISBN 90 04 09095 9
110. FULLERTON, M.D. *The Archaistic Style in Roman Statuary*. 1990. ISBN 90 04 09146 7
111. ROTHWELL, K.S. *Politics and Persuasion in Aristophanes' 'Ecclesiazusae'*. 1990. ISBN 90 04 09185 8
112. CALDER, W.M. & A. DEMANDT. *Eduard Meyer*. Leben und Leistung eines Universalhistorikers. 1990. ISBN 90 04 09131 9
113. CHAMBERS, M.H. *Georg Busolt. His Career in His Letters*. 1990. ISBN 90 04 09225 0
114. CASWELL, C.P. *A Study of 'Thumos' in Early Greek Epic*. 1990. ISBN 90 04 09260 9

115. EINGARTNER, J. *Isis und ihre Dienerinnen in der Kunst der Römischen Kaiserzeit.* 1991. ISBN 90 04 09312 5
116. JONG, I. DE. *Narrative in Drama.* The Art of the Euripidean Messenger-Speech. 1991. ISBN 90 04 09406 7
117. BOYCE, B.T. *The Language of the Freedmen in Petronius'* Cena Trimalchionis. 1991. ISBN 90 04 09431 8
118. RÜTTEN, Th. *Demokrit — lachender Philosoph und sanguinischer Melancholiker.* 1992. ISBN 90 04 09523 3
119. KARAVITES, P. (with the collaboration of Th. Wren). *Promise-Giving and Treaty-Making.* Homer and the Near East. 1992. ISBN 90 04 09567 5
120. SANTORO L'HOIR, F. *The Rhetoric of Gender Terms.* 'Man', 'Woman' and the portrayal of character in Latin prose. 1992. ISBN 90 04 09512 8
121. WALLINGA, H.T. *Ships and Sea-Power before the Great Persian War.* The Ancestry of the Ancient Trireme. 1993. ISBN 90 04 09650 7
122. FARRON, S. *Vergil's Æneid: A Poem of Grief and Love.* 1993. ISBN 90 04 09661 2
123. LÉTOUBLON, F. *Les lieux communs du roman.* Stéréotypes grecs d'aventure et d'amour. 1993. ISBN 90 04 09724 4
124. KUNTZ, M. *Narrative Setting and Dramatic Poetry.* 1993. ISBN 90 04 09784 8
125. THEOPHRASTUS. *Metaphysics.* With an Introduction, Translation and Commentary by Marlein van Raalte. 1993. ISBN 90 04 09786 4
126. THIERMANN, P. *Die* Orationes Homeri *des Leonardo Bruni Aretino.* Kritische Edition der lateinischen und kastilianischen Übersetzung mit Prolegomena und Kommentar. 1993. ISBN 90 04 09719 8
127. LEVENE, D.S. *Religion in Livy.* 1993. ISBN 90 04 09617 5
128. PORTER, J.R. *Studies in Euripides'* Orestes. 1993. ISBN 90 04 09662 0
129. SICKING, C.M.J. & J.M. VAN OPHUIJSEN. *Two Studies in Attic Particle Usage.* Lysias and Plato. 1993. ISBN 90 04 09867 4
130. JONG, I.J.F. DE, & J.P. SULLIVAN (eds.). *Modern Critical Theory and Classical Literature.* 1994. ISBN 90 04 09571 3
131. YAMAGATA, N. *Homeric Morality.* 1994. ISBN 90 04 09872 0
132. KOVACS, D. *Euripidea.* 1994. ISBN 90 04 09926 3
133. SUSSMAN, L.A. *The Declamations of Calpurnius Flaccus.* Text, Translation, and Commentary. 1994. ISBN 90 04 09983 2
134. SMOLENAARS, J.J.L. *Statius*: Thebaid VII. A Commentary. 1994. ISBN 90 04 10029 6
135. SMALL, D.B. (ed.). *Methods in the Mediterranean.* Historical and Archaeological Views on Texts and Archaeology. In preparation. ISBN 90 04 09581 0
136. DOMINIK, W.J. *The Mythic Voice of Statius.* Power and Politics in the Thebaid. In preparation. ISBN 90 04 09972 7
137. SLINGS, S.R. *Plato's Apology of Socrates.* A Literary and Philosophical Study with a Running Commentary. Edited and Completed from the Papers of the Late E. DE STRYCKER, S.J. In preparation. ISBN 90 04 10103 9
138. FRANK, M. *Seneca's* Phoenissae. Introduction and Commentary. In preparation. ISBN 90 04 09776 7
139. MALKIN, I. & Z.W. RUBINSOHN (eds.). *Leaders and Masses in the Roman World.* Studies in Honor of ZVI YAVETZ. In preparation. ISBN 90 04 09917 4
140. SEGAL, A. *Theatres in Roman Palestine and Provincia Arabica.* In preparation. ISBN 90 04 10145 4
141. CAMPBELL, M. *A Commentary on Apollonius Rhodius* Argonautica III 1-471. 1994. ISBN 90 04 10158 6
142. DeFOREST, M.M. *Apollonius'* Argonautica: A Callimachean Epic. 1994. ISBN 90 04 10017 2
143. WATSON, P.A. *Ancient Stepmothers.* Myth, Mysogyny and Reality. In preparation. ISBN 90 04 10176 4
144. SULLIVAN, S.D. *Psychological and Ethical Ideas.* What Early Greeks Say. In preparation. ISBN 90 04 10185 3